Microstructure: The Organization of Trading and Short Term Price Behavior
Volume II

The International Library of Critical Writings in Financial Economics

Series Editor: Richard Roll

Allstate Professor of Economics
The Anderson School at UCLA, USA

This major series presents by field outstanding selections of the most important articles across the entire spectrum of financial economics – one of the fastest growing areas in business schools and economics departments. Each collection has been prepared by a leading specialist who has written an authoritative introduction to the literature. Wherever possible, the articles in these volumes have been reproduced as originally published using facsimile reproduction, inclusive of footnotes and pagination to facilitate ease of reference.

1. The Theory of Corporate Finance (Volumes I and II)
   Michael J. Brennan
2. Futures Markets (Volumes I, II and III)
   A.G. Malliaris
3. Market Efficiency: Stock Market Behaviour in Theory and Practice (Volumes I and II)
   Andrew W. Lo
4. Microstructure: The Organization of Trading and Short Term Price Behavior (Volumes I and II)
   Hans R. Stoll

Future titles will include:

The Debt Market
Stephen A. Ross

Empirical Corporate Finance
Michael J. Brennan

Options Markets
G.M. Constantinides and A.G. Malliaris

Continuous Time Finance
Stephen M. Schaefer

Emerging Markets

International Securities

Financial Markets

Asset Pricing Theory and Tests

Wherever possible, the articles in these volumes have been reproduced as originally published using facsimile reproduction, inclusive of footnotes and pagination to facilitate ease of reference.

For a list of all Edward Elgar published titles visit our site on the World Wide Web at
http://www.e-elgar.co.uk

Microstructure: The Organization of Trading and Short Term Price Behavior Volume II

Edited by

Hans R. Stoll

The Anne Marie and Thomas B. Walker Professor of Finance and Director of the Financial Markets Research Center, Owen Graduate School of Management, Vanderbilt University, USA

THE INTERNATIONAL LIBRARY OF CRITICAL WRITINGS IN FINANCIAL ECONOMICS

An Elgar Reference Collection
Cheltenham, UK • Northampton, MA, USA

© Hans R. Stoll 1999. For copyright of individual articles, please refer to the Acknowledgements.

All rights reserved. No part of this publication may be reproduced, stored in a retrieval system or transmitted in any form or by any means, electronic, mechanical, photocopying, recording, or otherwise without the prior permission of the publisher.

Published by
Edward Elgar Publishing Limited
Glensanda House
Montpellier Parade
Cheltenham
Glos GL50 1UA
UK

Edward Elgar Publishing, Inc.
6 Market Street
Northampton
Massachusetts 01060
USA

A catalogue record for this book is available from the British Library.

Library of Congress Cataloguing in Publication Data

Microstructure: the organization of trading and short term price behavior / edited by Hans R. Stoll.
 (The international library of critical writings in financial economics : 4)
  Includes bibliographical references and index.
  1. Capital market—Mathematical models. 2. Securities—Prices—Mathematical models. I. Stoll, Hans R., 1939– . II. Series.
III. Series: An Elgar reference collection.
HG4523.M53   1999
332.63'2—dc21   98–46610
                                                            CIP

ISBN 1 85898 749 0 (2 volume set)
Printed and bound in Great Britain by
MPG Books Ltd, Bodmin, Cornwall

Contents

Acknowledgements ix
An Introduction by the editor to both volumes appears in volume I

PART I   **PRICE IMPACTS OF TRADING**

1. Alan Kraus and Hans R. Stoll (1972), 'Price Impacts of Block Trading on the New York Stock Exchange', *Journal of Finance*, **XXVII** (3), June, 569–88   3
2. André F. Perold (1988), 'The Implementation Shortfall: Paper Versus Reality', *Journal of Portfolio Management*, **14** (3), Spring, 4–9   23
3. Louis K.C. Chan and Josef Lakonishok (1995), 'The Behavior of Stock Prices Around Institutional Trades', *Journal of Finance*, **L** (4), September, 1147–74   29

PART II   **THEORY OF MARKET DESIGN**

4. Kenneth D. Garbade and William L. Silber (1979), 'Structural Organization of Secondary Markets: Clearing Frequency, Dealer Activity and Liquidity Risk', *Journal of Finance*, **XXXIV** (3), June, 577–93   59
5. Kalman J. Cohen, Steven F. Maier, Robert A. Schwartz and David K. Whitcomb (1981), 'Transaction Costs, Order Placement Strategy, and Existence of the Bid–Ask Spread', *Journal of Political Economy*, **89** (2), April, 287–305   76
6. Thomas S.Y. Ho and Hans R. Stoll (1983), 'The Dynamics of Dealer Markets Under Competition', *Journal of Finance*, **XXXVIII** (4), September, 1053–74   95
7. Ananth Madhavan (1992), 'Trading Mechanisms in Securities Markets', *Journal of Finance*, **XLVII** (2), June, 607–41   117
8. Lawrence R. Glosten (1994), 'Is the Electronic Open Limit Order Book Inevitable?' *Journal of Finance*, **XLIX** (4), September, 1127–61   152

PART III   **EVIDENCE ON MARKET DESIGN AND TRADING COSTS**

     A   **Opening Call Markets**

9. Yakov Amihud and Haim Mendelson (1987), 'Trading Mechanisms and Stock Returns: An Empirical Investigation', *Journal of Finance*, **XLII** (3), July, 533–53   191

B Dealer Versus Auction Markets

10. Seha M. Tinic and Richard R. West (1974), 'Marketability of Common Stocks in Canada and the U.S.A.: A Comparison of Agent Versus Dealer Dominated Markets', *Journal of Finance*, **XXIX** (3), June, 729–46 — 215
11. William G. Christie and Paul H. Schultz (1994), 'Why do NASDAQ Market Makers Avoid Odd-Eighth Quotes?' *Journal of Finance*, **XLIX** (5), December, 1813–40 — 233

C Competition Across Markets

12. William G. Christie and Roger D. Huang (1994), 'Market Structures and Liquidity: A Transactions Data Study of Exchange Listings', *Journal of Financial Intermediation*, **3**, 300–326 — 263
13. Charles M.C. Lee (1993), 'Market Integration and Price Execution for NYSE-Listed Securities', *Journal of Finance*, **XLVIII** (3), July, 1009–38 — 290

PART IV OTHER MARKETS

A Options Markets

14. Anand M. Vijh (1990), 'Liquidity of the CBOE Equity Options', *Journal of Finance*, **XLV** (3), July, 1157–79 — 325

B Futures Markets

15. Lester G. Telser and Harlow N. Higinbotham (1977), 'Organized Futures Markets: Costs and Benefits', *Journal of Political Economy*, **85** (5), 969–1000 — 351
16. Steven Manaster and Steven C. Mann (1996), 'Life in the Pits: Competitive Market Making and Inventory Control', *Review of Financial Studies*, **9** (3), Fall, 953–75 — 383

C Currency Markets

17. Richard K. Lyons (1995), 'Tests of Microstructural Hypotheses in the Foreign Exchange Market', *Journal of Financial Economics*, **39**, 321–51 — 409

D Treasury Auction

18. Narasimhan Jegadeesh (1993), 'Treasury Auction Bids and the Salomon Squeeze', *Journal of Finance*, **XLVIII** (4), September, 1403–19 — 443

PART V MARKET MICROSTRUCTURE AND ASSET PRICING

19. Yakov Amihud and Haim Mendelson (1986), 'Asset Pricing and the Bid–Ask Spread', *Journal of Financial Economics*, **17** (1), September, 223–49 — 463
20. Michael J. Brennan and Avanidhar Subrahmanyam (1996), 'Market Microstructure and Asset Pricing: On the Compensation for Illiquidity in Stock Returns', *Journal of Financial Economics*, **41**, 441–64 — 490

Name Index — 515

Acknowledgements

The editor and publishers wish to thank the authors and the following publishers who have kindly given permission for the use of copyright material.

Academic Press, Inc. for article: William G. Christie and Roger D. Huang (1994), 'Market Structures and Liquidity: A Transactions Data Study of Exchange Listings', *Journal of Financial Intermediation*, **3**, 300–326.

American Finance Association for articles: Alan Kraus and Hans R. Stoll (1972), 'Price Impacts of Block Trading on the New York Stock Exchange', *Journal of Finance*, **XXVII** (3), June, 569–88; Seha M. Tinic and Richard R. West (1974), 'Marketability of Common Stocks in Canada and the U.S.A.: A Comparison of Agent Versus Dealer Dominated Markets', *Journal of Finance*, **XXIX** (3), June, 729–46; Kenneth D. Garbade and William L. Silber (1979), 'Structural Organization of Secondary Markets: Clearing Frequency, Dealer Activity and Liquidity Risk', *Journal of Finance*, **XXXIV** (3), June, 577–93; Thomas S.Y. Ho and Hans R. Stoll (1983), 'The Dynamics of Dealer Markets Under Competition', *Journal of Finance*, **XXXVIII** (4), September, 1053–74; Yakov Amihud and Haim Mendelson (1987), 'Trading Mechanisms and Stock Returns: An Empirical Investigation', *Journal of Finance*, **XLII** (3), July, 533–53; Ananth Madhavan (1992), 'Trading Mechanisms in Securities Markets', *Journal of Finance*, **XLVII** (2), June, 607–41; Charles M.C. Lee (1993), 'Market Integration and Price Execution for NYSE-Listed Securities', *Journal of Finance*, **XLVIII** (3), July, 1009–38; Narasimhan Jegadeesh (1993), 'Treasury Auction Bids and the Salomon Squeeze', *Journal of Finance*, **XLVIII** (4), September, 1403–19; Lawrence R. Glosten (1994), 'Is the Electronic Open Limit Order Book Inevitable?' *Journal of Finance*, **XLIX** (4), September, 1127–61; William G. Christie and Paul H. Schultz (1994), 'Why do NASDAQ Market Makers Avoid Odd-Eighth Quotes?' *Journal of Finance*, **XLIX** (5), December, 1813–40.

Blackwell Publishers, Inc. for articles: Anand M. Vijh (1990), 'Liquidity of the CBOE Equity Options', *Journal of Finance*, **XLV** (3), July, 1157–79; Louis K.C. Chan and Josef Lakonishok (1995), 'The Behavior of Stock Prices Around Institutional Trades', *Journal of Finance*, **L** (4), September, 1147–74.

Elsevier Science Ltd for articles: Yakov Amihud and Haim Mendelson (1986), 'Asset Pricing and the Bid–Ask Spread', *Journal of Financial Economics*, **17** (1), September, 223–49; Richard K. Lyons (1995), 'Tests of Microstructural Hypotheses in the Foreign Exchange Market', *Journal of Financial Economics*, **39**, 321–51; Michael J. Brennan and Avanidhar Subrahmanyam (1996), 'Market Microstructure and Asset Pricing: On the Compensation for Illiquidity in Stock Returns', *Journal of Financial Economics*, **41**, 441–64.

Institutional Investor, Inc. for article: André F. Perold (1988), 'The Implementation Shortfall: Paper Versus Reality', *Journal of Portfolio Management*, **14** (3), Spring, 4–9.

Oxford University Press for article: Steven Manaster and Steven C. Mann (1996), 'Life in the Pits: Competitive Market Making and Inventory Control', *Review of Financial Studies*, **9** (3), Fall, 953–75.

University of Chicago Press for articles: Lester G. Telser and Harlow N. Higinbotham (1977), 'Organized Futures Markets: Costs and Benefits', *Journal of Political Economy*, **85** (5), 969–1000; Kalman J. Cohen, Steven F. Maier, Robert A. Schwartz and David K. Whitcomb (1981), 'Transaction Costs, Order Placement Strategy, and Existence of the Bid–Ask Spread', *Journal of Political Economy*, **89** (2), April, 287–305.

Every effort has been made to trace all the copyright holders but if any have been inadvertently overlooked the publishers will be pleased to make the necessary arrangement at the first opportunity.

In addition the publishers wish to thank the Library of the London School of Economics and Political Science and Marshall Library of Economics, Cambridge University for their assistance in obtaining these articles.

Part I
Price Impacts of Trading

[1]

PRICE IMPACTS OF BLOCK TRADING ON THE NEW YORK STOCK EXCHANGE

ALAN KRAUS AND HANS R. STOLL*

I. INTRODUCTION

IN AN EFFICIENT market, prices reflect underlying values. This insures the proper allocation of new funds to the most productive areas of the economy. Additionally, individual investors benefit by knowing that prices at which they trade are not subject to forces which have little or nothing to do with the underlying value of the company.

Extensive empirical tests which tend to support the efficiency of the stock market have been carried out in the past.[1] Until recently, however, no tests have been carried out to assess directly the impact of institutional investors on the efficiency of the stock market.[2] The purpose of this paper is to examine the extent to which block trading by institutional investors contributes to or detracts from efficient markets. A block trade can be defined as a transaction involving a larger number of shares than can readily be handled in the normal course of the auction market.

II. REASONS FOR PRICE MOVEMENTS IN INDIVIDUAL SECURITIES

A. *Information*

In a perfectly efficient market where there are many small buyers and sellers each having equal access to information and where there are no transaction costs, prices of securities change (at any moment of time) only in response to new information[3] about the expected return of the security or about its riskiness or because of a widespread change in investors' risk-return preferences. A new piece of information establishes a new price level for the stock, which tends to be maintained until additional information warrants another

---

* Assistant Professor of Finance, Stanford University and Associate Professor of Finance, University of Pennsylvania.

The research on which this paper is based was conducted by the authors as members of the Staff of the Institutional Investor Study, Securities and Exchange Commission. Research for the Study was a cooperative effort; members of the Staff who contributed to this paper are too numerous to list completely. However, particular credit is due Eric Scheuer, who was involved in all stages of the research and did almost all of the programming, and Seymour Smidt and Donald Farrar, who made many valuable suggestions. Robert Litzenberger read an earlier draft of this paper and his comments materially improved the exposition. The authors alone are responsible for errors that remain.

1. See [3] for a review of theory and empirical work.

2. See [4] and [7]. The latter work is an important precursor to the present paper, in terms of both underlying issues and analytical techniques.

3. The term "information" has a broad meaning in this context and refers to all news which might affect a particular stock. This includes general economic news as well as specific news such as an earnings report.

price change.[4] In and of themselves, transactions have no discernable effect on market prices since there are many other investors willing to buy or sell small amounts of the security at very close to the prevailing price.

B. Distribution Effect Due to Different Investor Preferences for a Given Security

In a less ideal market made up of relatively few investors in a particular security, trading may produce a discernable price change if the expectations or preferences of the marginal seller of the security are different from those of the marginal buyer.[5] For example, a large seller may find it difficult to distribute his shares because there is no one willing to hold the number of shares he did at the same price.[6] Stated differently, the equilibrium price of a security may be changed by the actions of large investors.

Empirically, the price change due to this type of distribution effect is distinguished from the price change due to new information by the effect on rate of return. Under the information effect, the expected rate of return after the transaction is different from that before the transaction only if the new information concerns a change in the riskiness of the stock. Under the distribution effect, the expected rate of return must increase in the case of sales to convince less willing buyers to hold the security and must fall in the case of purchases to convince less willing sellers to part with the security.

The distribution effect due to different investor preferences depends not only on the number of investors in a single security but also on the substitutability of one security for another. Willing buyers come not only from investors with new capital but also from investors holding other securities. The existence of a distribution effect of this type implies securities are less than perfect substitutes.[7]

In any short run analysis, distribution effects due to different preferences for a given security are likely to be difficult to observe. The higher rate of return that one would expect to observe in the long run to compensate a buyer for accepting the stock is unlikely to be large. It will be difficult to distinguish price changes due to new information from those due to changes in preference of the marginal holder solely on the basis of observed rates of return before and after the transaction.

C. Distribution Effect Due to Short Run Liquidity Costs

In the short run, trading in a less than perfectly efficient market may have a temporary effect on price even if willing buyers or sellers exist. This can occur because of the difficulty (*i.e.*, cost) of finding the willing investors. To

---

4. The new equilibrium level may be a moving one. For example, a no-dividend stock should show price increases or decreases over time in order to reflect retention of earnings.

5. It is not necessary to assume different access to information, only that different investors interpret given information differently or have preferences for risk-return combinations which differ.

6. For exposition of this theory of a downward sloping demand curve for shares, see [5] and [6].

7. Because of the cost, legal restrictions and general reluctance to sell short, this service is much less common for block purchases than for block sales.

the party initiating the trade, liquidity costs can take the form of an explicit commission or a price away from the equilibrium price (lower in the case of sales; higher in the case of purchases).

The commission or price movement compensates intermediaries for their services: (1) Communicating among investors the desire to buy or sell. (finding the "other side.") (2) Inventorying securities when the other side cannot be found immediately. (3) Clearing trades and keeping records.[8]

If transaction costs are not levied separately (as in the case of principal trades in the over-the-counter market), the market price of the security may deviate from its equilibrium value to compensate the dealer, or the party providing the services of the dealer.[9] On a sale by an investor, the security may be sold to the dealer at a price below what the dealer believes to be the equilibrium price. The dealer receives a gain by reselling the security at its equilibrium price, or at some price between what he paid and the equilibrium price. On a purchase, the price behavior is reversed: the dealer sells at a price above equilibrium so that he may receive a gain by repurchasing at a lower price.

Conceptually, the price impact described here is of a different nature from that produced by differences in investor preferences. The latter involves a change in equilibrium price associated with a change in expected rate of return and is not inherently a temporary effect. By contrast, the price impact produced by short run liquidity effects involves a transaction away from the equilibrium price (for small transactions) rather than a change in the equilibrium price. Expected rate of return is altered only temporarily, since the price is expected to return to equilibrium fairly quickly.

If the full costs of transacting are levied separately, one need not observe a market price movement as the result of transaction costs.[10] In a free market the dealer that positions stock (or finds another party to position for him) can choose to charge for his services either through a commission or by buying the stock at a different price from that at which it is sold. If commissions are fixed, he can raise/lower effective commissions by buying in at less/more than he sells out.

III. THE DATA

The New York Stock Exchange (NYSE) collects information on all block trades over 10,000 shares carried out on the Exchange. This information is made public by Vickers and data for a subsample of NYSE stocks covering the period July 1, 1968 to September 30, 1969 are utilized in this study.[11] This

---

8. Commission rates on exchanges also cover the costs of research and other services, but it is not clear that, at present, these services are directly related to the carrying out of transactions.

9. An investor might be willing to accept a security if the price discount is great enough and he would collect the "fee" for positioning the stock rather than the dealer.

10. However, prices could deviate from their equilibrium by as much as the transaction cost before an investor found it profitable to trade the security.

11. The data supplied are the date, the price of the block, price of immediately preceding trade, number of shares, whether block was crossed (*i.e.*, whether same broker acted for both sides). The price information used in the analyses was taken from the Standard and Poor's ISL daily price tapes.

subsample contains 225 stocks selected randomly[12] and 177 stocks selected because they have certain characteristics such as being involved in mergers, experiencing large price changes, and the like. The sample of blocks consists of 7,009 blocks in the 402 stocks.[13]

The total sample of blocks is classified in Table 1 by sign of difference

TABLE 1

NUMBER OF BLOCKS IN SAMPLE CLASSIFIED BY DIRECTION OF PRICE CHANGE FROM PRIOR TRADE (TICK) AND VALUE OF BLOCK

Value of Block	Tick		
	Minus	Zero	Plus
Less than $1 million	1830	1626	1354
$1-2 million	603	425	247
$2-5 million	421	171	99
Over $5 million	175	38	20
Subtotal over $1 million	1199	634	366

between block price and price of trade prior to block (tick) and by dollar value.[14] Blocks less than $1 million in value are not used in the analyses described in this study.[15] This reduces the underrepresentation of high priced stocks in the sample, which occurs because the NYSE definition of a block trade uses a cutoff based on number of shares (10,000 and over) rather than dollar value. By eliminating blocks less than $1 million, only stocks selling for $100 and over are underrepresented relative to the others.

IV. BLOCK TRADES CLASSIFIED BY TICK

Whether a block is purchased or sold is an ambiguous concept—there is a buyer and seller in every trade. For this study, blocks are classified into three groups: those that traded below the price prior to the block (minus tick), those that traded at a price equal to the price prior to the block (zero tick) and those that traded at a price above the price prior to the block (plus tick). Detailed analysis of trading by both buying and selling parties in the case of a small sample of blocks indicates that these tick classifications identify quite

---

12. The random sample consists of an exhaustive sampling of the largest 27 publicly held NYSE stocks (about 35% of the total market value of all NYSE stocks) and a random sample of 198 from the remaining stocks. For a detailed description of the sample, see [8], especially Vol. 4, Chap. X, Appendix A.

13. About 600 blocks are excluded because the data contain errors or are incomplete.

14. When blocks occur, they tend to be an important fraction of total exchange volume on that day. For each block, the ratio of the number of shares in the block to total NYSE volume in that stock on that day was calculated. The average value of this ratio by size category of block is:

Less than $1 million	33.6%
$1-2 million	45.9
$2-5 million	60.0
Over $5 million	69.3

15. As noted in the following section, the analysis also excludes blocks on zero ticks.

closely the active and passive sides of a trade.[16] Discussions with market-makers and institutional traders also tend to support this classification scheme. It is, therefore, convenient and reasonably accurate to think of blocks on minus ticks as being initiated by sellers and blocks on plus ticks as being initiated by buyers.[17] The fact that 1,199 blocks traded on minus ticks and only 366 traded on plus ticks substantiates the comment by market professionals that "blocks are sold, not bought."

Due to the mechanics of block trading there is a tendency for some blocks initiated by sellers and some blocks initiated by buyers to fall into the zero tick category rather than the minus tick or plus tick categories, respectively. The price negotiated for the block trade is frequently below the specialist's current bid in the case of a block initiated by a seller and frequently above the specialist's current ask in the case of a block initiated by a buyer. In such cases the floor broker handling the block may have to make transactions with the specialist's book before he is able to execute the block trade at the price agreed upon. That is, all orders in the book at prices between the current quote and the block price must be executed before the block. The last such trade prior to the block may be at the same price as that at which the block is to be executed; in such a case the block would fall in the zero tick category. Since the mechanics of block trading typically involves taking the specialist's book to the price agreed upon for the block, it is highly unlikely that a block initiated by a seller will fall in the plus tick category or that one initiated by a buyer will fall in the minus tick category.

There are several reasons for separating minus tick and plus tick blocks in the analyses. To the degree that these categories correspond to trades initiated by a seller and trades initiated by a buyer, respectively, both the information and distribution hypotheses suggest that the price effects associated with these categories ought to be in opposite directions, on the average. Combining these categories would obscure the price effect of interest. Furthermore, blocks initiated by a buyer may differ from those initiated by a seller in other respects. For example, blocks are sometimes actively solicited in the course of a merger or takeover situation. In this connection, it should be noted that the sample of stocks used in this study contain more than the normal number of stocks involved in transfers of control.

Perhaps of even more importance is the point that a distribution effect due to liquidity costs may be of much less significance in the case of blocks initiated by a buyer than those initiated by a seller. The reason for this is that, while block positioning firms will frequently buy for their own account a portion of a block initiated by a seller, market makers rarely go short to

---

16. The active side is the side of the block trade with fewer parties. When the active side is buying, the tick tends to be positive; when the active side is selling, the tick tends to be negative. See [8, Vol. 4 p. 1588].

17. It would have been desirable to select randomly a "control group" of other than block trades, classify them in the same way as block trades, and carry out the same analyses as for block trades. However, resource and data limitations prevented this.

facilitate a block purchase actively sought by a buyer.[18] On blocks in which a market maker takes no position, there is little incentive for him to attempt to negotiate a price away from equilibrium.

V. Price Effects Within the Day of the Block Trade

Under the distribution hypothesis, prices tend to return (relative to the market) toward their prior levels following a block trade. Thus, prices of minus tick blocks should rise after the block and prices of plus tick blocks should fall after the block. The speed with which prices return distinguishes the liquidity cost version of this hypothesis from the distribution effect due to differences in marginal preferences. The price movement associated with the former version should be of short duration, whereas the latter version should produce a gradual return of prices. Under the information hypothesis, no particular price movement (relative to the market) is expected, on the average, after the block.

For convenience in all the analyses, trading days are numbered with reference to the day of the block trade, which is considered day zero. For example, mean price movement on day $+1$ for a sample of blocks refers to the average price movement on the first trading day following each block, irrespective of the calendar dates on which the blocks occurred.

The data available for the within-day analyses are the closing price on day -1, the closing price on day zero, the price of the last trade before the block, the price of the block trade, and Standard and Poors' Composite Index. Using these data, Figures 1 and 2 present mean price changes for minus tick blocks and plus tick blocks greater than $1 million. For each block, the price changes are calculated as follows:

$$E_1 = \frac{PB + D_0 - P_{-1}}{P_{-1}}$$

$$E_2 = \frac{P_0 - PB}{P_0}$$

$$E_3 = \frac{PB - PPB}{PPB}$$

$$M = \frac{I_0 - I_{-1}}{I_{-1}}$$

where

PB = price of block
PPB = price of last trade before block
P_t = closing price on day t
D_t = dividend (if any) paid on day t
I_t = market index at close of day t.

---

18. Interviews and detailed examination of a smaller sample of blocks emphatically support this point.

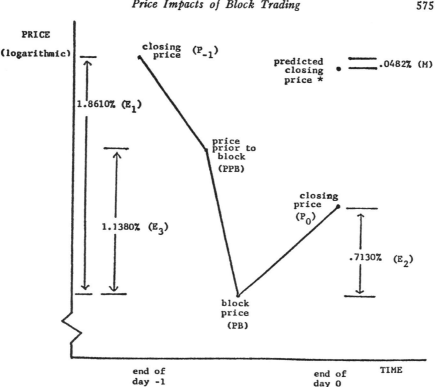

FIGURE 1
Minus Tick Blocks

Average Percentage Price Differences between Selected Prices in the Period from the Close of Trading on Day −1 to the Close of Trading on Day 0.
* Closing price if stock's price had changed by same percentage as market index.

For minus tick blocks (Figure 1), the mean price decline between the closing price on day −1 and the block price (E_1) is 1.86 per cent.[19] (The median decline is 1.64 per cent.) The major component of the 1.86 per cent decline is the 1.14 per cent average size of the minus tick (E_3). Subsequent to the block, the average price movement (E_2) is a rise of .71 per cent.[20] (The median rise is .55 per cent). If the stock's price had changed by the mean percentage change in the market index (M), price on day zero would have fallen about .05 per cent. The important point in these numbers is that price,

---

19. The standard error of the mean of E_1 is .068 per cent. By standard statistical techniques, this implies that the mean of E_1 is significantly different from zero. However, Fama [1] and others have pointed out that a stable Paretian distribution of price changes, with characteristic value below 2.0, may lead to upward bias in standard tests of significance (which assume normality). No adjustment for this bias is made in the current study.

20. The standard error of the mean is .047 per cent. Since some blocks occur at the close, the mean of E_1 understates the average price recovery over transactions following the block.

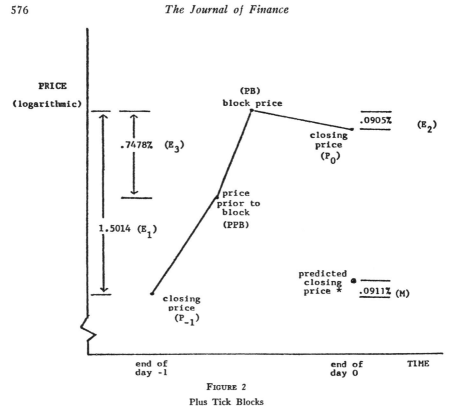

FIGURE 2
Plus Tick Blocks

Average Percentage Price Differences between Selected Prices in the Period from the Close of Trading on Day −1 to the Close of Trading on Day 0.
* Closing price if stock's price had changed by same percentage as market index.

on the average, tends to rise relative to the market following a minus tick block. This pattern supports the distribution hypothesis. The mean price rise is slightly more than one commission.[21] On the average, the buyers of these blocks saved one commission and the sellers (the side initiating the transactions) paid an extra commission. The price return (about 142% on an annual basis) is too large and too swift to reflect a permanent higher rate of return accruing to new and less willing holders. Instead, it appears to reflect payment for providing short run liquidity. The results, therefore, tend to support the liquidity cost version of the distribution hypothesis.

The existence of a price recovery, on the average, from the block trade to the day's close indicates that knowledge of a minus tick block is of potential value. The mean price recovery is not large enough to provide a trading profit to a nonmember of the NYSE. An arbitrage transaction would require the purchase of the block at the block price and its sale at the close. Such

---

21. The commission on 10,000 shares of a $40 stock was .62 per cent of the total value of the transaction after the volume discount instituted on December 5, 1968.

a transaction would involve two commissions. In addition, there are the interest costs of tying up funds. Members of the NYSE, and particularly specialists, could profitably act on such a price recovery, however. Specialists would incur clearing charges on two trades, amounting only to about .14 per cent of the value. Other members might be required to pay floor brokerage as well as clearing charges, the total for two trades amounting to about .37 per cent.[22] The immediate profit (usually unrealized) of purchasers of blocks is protected, therefore, from arbitrage by non-members. However, it may be shared with the specialist.[23]

There is uncertainty about the sign and size of the price change after the block trade. Of the sample of minus tick blocks analyzed, 64% experienced a price rise, 22% experienced a price decline and 14% experienced no price change subsequent to the block trade. While the average subsequent movement is a recovery of .71%, the standard deviation is 1.62%. However, there is a weak correlation between the price movement following the block (E_2) and the price change from day -1 to the block (E_1), which explains some of the variation in the price recovery.[24] In addition, the block trading firm and the specialist frequently possess information on the identity of the seller(s) and buyer(s), on whether they positioned some of the block, and on other factors not publicly available that may explain much of the variation. By permitting others to have access to the relevant information and to arbitrage the price recovery at less cost, one might reduce the liquidity costs of block trading. This goal could be reached, at least to some extent, by eliminating fixed minimum commissions and by permitting competing market makers.[25]

It was noted earlier that market makers or other investors rarely act as dealers by taking a short position in blocks initiated by a buyer. Therefore, there is much less reason to expect a distribution effect based on liquidity costs for plus tick blocks than for minus tick blocks since one must deal directly with the permanent holders of the stock. The results shown in Figure 2 seem to confirm this. For plus tick blocks, the mean initial price rise (E_1) is 1.50 per cent and is of the same order of magnitude as the mean initial price fall of minus tick blocks.[26] However, there is no marked price decline

---

22. Floor brokerage on 100 shares of a $40 stock is $3.60. Clearing charges are $2.75.

23. The Institutional Investor Study [8] reports that block trading firms have difficulty in keeping specialists from "breaking up" a block. Typically an arrangement allowing the specialist to participate or benefit in some way from the block trade is reached. See pp. 1598-1601.

24. The relation is negative as expected. For 1199 minus tick blocks, the simple regression results are as follows (t value in parentheses):

$$E_2 = .449 - .142 E_1 \quad R^2 = .042$$
$$(7.25)$$

The reason for using E_1 as the explanatory variable, rather than E_3, is that the process of taking the specialist's book to the price agreed upon for the block may result in some of the price effect of the block occurring prior to the transaction at PPB.

25. As we indicate below, we do not intend to imply that block trading has introduced inefficiencies into the market place. To the contrary; block trading is more efficient than the use of secondary distributions. We only suggest that market efficiency could be greater.

26. The standard error of the mean is .127 per cent.

subsequent to the block trade (E_2).[27] Furthermore, the relation across blocks between the price movements before and after the block is not significant.[28] For plus tick blocks, the price movements within the day of the block trade are consistent with the information hypothesis.

VI. Price Effects in Closing Prices

A. *Measurement Technique*[29]

The effect of a block trade on closing market prices is measured by comparing actual closing prices of the stock with closing prices one would have expected had the stock's price changed by the same percentage amount as a market index (Standard and Poor's Composite Index). Thus, if the market drops by one per cent on the day of a block trade, but the stock itself falls by three per cent, the effect of the block trade on that day is measured as a two per cent drop. More precisely, the *current impact* on day t for a particular stock is given by

$$U_t = \ln\left(\frac{P_t + D_t}{P_{t-1}}\right) - A - B \ln\left(\frac{I_t}{I_{t-1}}\right)$$

where P_t, D_t, and I_t are defined in the previous section. A and B are parameters peculiar to each stock and reflect the "normal" relation between that stock and the market.[30] Estimates of A and B were calculated for every stock, but sample runs showed that the findings were unchanged under the assumption that $A = 0$, $B = 1$ for each stock. All analyses presented below incorporate this assumption.

It is also desirable to present the cumulative effect of current impacts over a period around the block trade. If day m is the first day of this period, the *impact index* on day t for a particular stock is given by

$$S_t = e^{\sum_{j=m}^{t} U_j}$$

where U_j is the current impact for this stock. The impact index is approximately equal to the value of one dollar invested at the succession of rates

---

27. The slight average decline shown (.0905 per cent) is not statistically significant. The standard error is .099 per cent.

28. For 366 plus tick blocks, the simple regression results are as follows (t value in parentheses):

$$E_2 = .026 - .775\, E_1 \qquad R^2 = .010$$
$$(1.90)$$

29. The general technique described in this section was first employed in [2].

30. Estimates of A and B are generally obtained by fitting the following regression to time series data for the particular stock and for the market:

$$\ln R = A + B \ln M + u$$

where: R = investment relative for that stock
M = investment relative for a market index
u = disturbance

For example, see [2], p. 4.

represented by the current impacts for days m, m + 1, ... , t. This can be seen by using the fact that ln $(1 + r) \cong r$, for small r. Thus,

$$\ln S_t = \Sigma_{j=m}^t U_j$$
$$\cong \Sigma_{j=m}^t \ln(1 + U_j)$$
$$\cong \ln [\Pi_{j=m}^t (1 + U_j)].$$

B. *Price Effects of Minus Tick and Plus Tick Blocks*

Tables 2 and 3 present means and standard deviations, across blocks, of the current impact (U_t) and the impact index (S_t). The tables also give the

TABLE 2
CROSS SECTIONAL RESULTS FOR 1121 BLOCKS ON MINUS TICKS

	Current impact (U_t)			Impact index (S_t)	
Day (t)	Mean	Proportion negative	Standard deviation	Mean	Standard deviation
−20	−0.0006	0.5424	0.0201	0.9995	0.0227
−15	0.0001	0.5397	0.0205	0.9989	0.0517
−10	−0.0005	0.5219	0.0194	0.9963	0.0674
− 5	0.0002	0.5165	0.0192	0.9976	0.0858
− 4	0.0002	0.5245	0.0200	0.9980	0.0877
− 3	−0.0021	0.5807	0.0194	0.9961	0.0897
− 2	−0.0029	0.5879	0.0205	0.9935	0.0929
− 1	−0.0033	0.5789	0.0218	0.9905	0.0949
0	−0.0115	0.7386	0.0248	0.9798	0.1002
1	−0.0001	0.5022	0.0214	0.9797	0.1014
2	−0.0007	0.5174	0.0227	0.9792	0.1024
3	0.0010	0.4960	0.0211	0.9803	0.1043
4	0.0004	0.5040	0.0209	0.9808	0.1055
5	0.0004	0.5067	0.0205	0.9813	0.1060
10	0.0002	0.5183	0.0204	0.9833	0.1103
15	−0.0001	0.5370	0.0210	0.9848	0.1216
20	0.0002	0.5022	0.0189	0.9844	0.1278

proportion of negative values of U_t. The mean of S_t over time from Tables 2 and 3 is shown graphically in Figures 3 and 4, respectively. Table 2 and Figure 3 are based on data for 1121 blocks on minus ticks; Table 3 and Figure 4 are based on data for 345 blocks on plus ticks.[31] Only blocks over $1 million are considered. The period of analysis is 41 consecutive trading days around the day of each block (day zero).

By definition, minus tick blocks would be expected to have, and do have, a negative average impact on day zero and plus tick blocks a positive average impact. For stocks in which blocks traded on minus ticks (Table 2 and

---

31. Daily price data were available only through September 30, 1969. In order to have price data for 20 days after the block, it was necessary to exclude 78 minus tick blocks and 21 plus tick blocks that occurred within 20 trading days of September 30, 1969.

TABLE 3
CROSS SECTIONAL RESULTS FOR 345 BLOCKS ON PLUS TICKS

Day (t)	Current impact (U_t)			Impact index (S_t)	
	Mean	Proportion negative	Standard deviation	Mean	Standard deviation
−20	0.0005	0.5362	0.0240	1.0007	0.0251
−15	0.0026	0.4696	0.0212	1.0072	0.0539
−10	0.0009	0.4899	0.0191	1.0121	0.0698
− 5	0.0045	0.4725	0.0296	1.0203	0.0894
− 4	0.0007	0.4696	0.0227	1.0212	0.0909
− 3	0.0030	0.4986	0.0250	1.0246	0.0958
− 2	0.0036	0.4783	0.0277	1.0288	0.1015
− 1	0.0072	0.4029	0.0279	1.0371	0.1113
0	0.0129	0.3072	0.0274	1.0514	0.1213
1	0.0023	0.4783	0.0264	1.0545	0.1268
2	−0.0003	0.5362	0.0195	1.0545	0.1299
3	0.0002	0.5333	0.0192	1.0549	0.1312
4	0.0010	0.5043	0.0211	1.0557	0.1299
5	−0.0007	0.5565	0.0233	1.0550	0.1304
10	−0.0012	0.5391	0.0201	1.0552	0.1397
15	0.0015	0.4638	0.0212	1.0578	0.1519
20	−0.0010	0.5246	0.0187	1.0552	0.1578

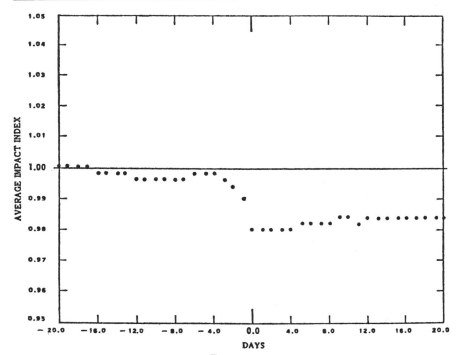

FIGURE 3
Cross Sectional Results for 1121 Blocks on Minus Ticks

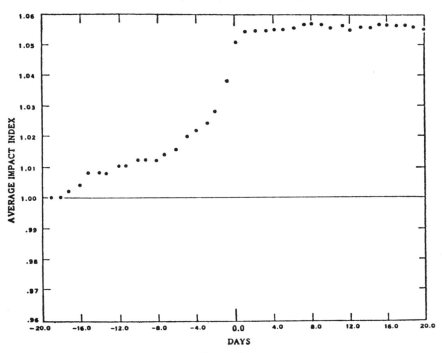

FIGURE 4
Cross Sectional Results for 345 Blocks on Plus Ticks

Figure 3), closing price on day zero relative to closing price 20 days earlier shows an average drop of 2.02 per cent relative to the market.[32] Much of this average decline (1.15 per cent) occurs on the day of the block. Closing price on day zero for stocks having blocks on plus ticks (Table 3 and Figure 4) is, on average, 5.14 per cent (relative to the market) above closing price 20 days before the block. The average impact on the day of the block is a rise of 1.29 per cent. On day zero, 74 per cent of the blocks on minus ticks have a negative impact and 69 per cent of the blocks on plus ticks have a positive impact.

Because the price impacts on day zero are, to a large extent, predetermined by the classification of blocks by tick,[33] the analysis is concerned not only with price change on day zero, but also with the pattern of prices before and after the block trade. Table 2 and Figure 3 show that a new (lower) level of prices tends to be established for minus tick blocks after the block trade. Prices recover slightly 10 days after the block (about .25 per cent) but are still below the original level of prices by more than 1.50 per cent. Conversely,

---

32. That is, the average impact index is set at 100.00 per cent on day −21. By day zero, it has fallen to 97.98 per cent.

33. Compare the average sizes of the ticks (E_2) in Figures 1 and 2 with the average current impacts on day zero in Tables 2 and 3.

plus tick blocks tend to establish a new higher level of stock prices, as shown in Table 3 and Figure 4. In both cases, the new level is established rather quickly, and there is little drift after day 10. These results do not show evidence of a change in rate of return subsequent to the block, reflected in a subsequent rise or fall of prices, that would support the existence of a distribution effect. Prices seem to experience a once-and-for-all rise or fall depending on whether the block was purchased or sold. Such a pattern is consistent with the information hypothesis. However, further tests tend to support the liquidity cost version of the distribution hypothesis.

C. *Relation of Price Effect to Dollar Value of Block*

An implication of the distribution hypothesis is that the size of the price impact should be correlated with the size of the block. If different securities are imperfect substitutes, the larger the block the greater the price change required to induce other investors to hold this quantity of the stock. In addition, the value of the block affects liquidity costs in terms of the costs of locating the other side and in terms of the potential inventory costs that market makers might be requested to bear. Under the information hypothesis, on the other hand, block trades are associated with price changes only because they happen to accompany the disclosure of new information, which changes the equilibrium price of the stock. If the significance of new information about companies is not correlated with the dollar value of blocks, one would under this hypothesis not expect a systematic relation between the size of the price adjustment and the value of the block.

To test the relation between size of block and size of price effect, current impact on day zero (U_0) is regressed on block value (V). Separate regressions are run for minus tick blocks over \$1 million and plus tick blocks over \$1 million. In the results shown below, U_0 is in per cent, V is in millions of dollars, and the numbers in parentheses are t values.

Minus tick blocks (1199 observations):

$$U_0 = -.767 - .129 \, V \qquad R^2 = .042$$
$$(7.26)$$

Plus tick blocks (366 observations):

$$U_0 = .951 + .131 \, V \qquad R^2 = .020$$
$$(2.72)$$

The regression results tend to support the distribution hypothesis, particularly in the case of minus tick blocks where the relation between price impact and block size is more significant. The regression coefficient is of the proper sign in both cases.[34] The fact that a less significant relation is observed for plus tick blocks, in which market makers take a position much less frequently, is consistent with the findings described in Section V above. The results indicate that an increase of \$1 million in block size results, on the average, in

---

34. Including non-block dollar trading volume on the same day or alternatively monthly dollar trading volume as an additional independent variable does not materially alter the size or significance of the coefficient.

an increase in price effect of about .13 percentage points. Put in dollar terms, this means that if the size of a block of $50 stock were to go from 20,000 shares to 100,000 shares, for example, the price effect would be increased by about $0.25 per share.

If information is the result of analysis rather than of the release of data by corporations, one may argue that the above regression results are not support for the distribution hypothesis. Institutions with greater resources than the general public would be expected to carry out more research and block trading may occur as a result of information gathered in this way. Furthermore, the size of the block may reflect the importance of the research results. Such reasoning does not account for trading that occurs because of cash needs or cash surpluses. In addition, as noted below, the absence of a significant relation between the price effects and sizes of secondary distributions has been cited by Scholes [7] as strong evidence in favor of the information hypothesis and against the distribution hypothesis. Therefore, one must either regard the current study's findings as supporting the opposite choice between the competing hypotheses or dismiss the test (in both cases) as having no power to distinguish between these hypotheses.

D. Price Effects of Trailing and Leading Blocks

A second test of the distribution hypothesis involves a classification of blocks by the pattern of blocks before and after the block trade being analyzed. If the distribution hypothesis is correct, prices would tend to return to their original level after a block trade. Blocks may, however, be followed by additional blocks that may put additional pressure on prices and prevent them from returning to their prior level. As a result, the flat pattern of post-block prices in Figures 3 and 4 is consistent with either the information hypothesis or the distribution hypothesis.

In order to distinguish further these hypotheses, interday price behavior is examined for subsamples of blocks for which no additional blocks over $1 million occurred in the stock during days 1-10. Blocks meeting this criterion are termed "trailing" blocks. There are 591 trailing minus tick and 150 trailing plus tick blocks.

On the average, the price of trailing minus tick blocks recovers by .62% within 10 days and 1.1% within 20 days.[35] This evidence supports the distribution hypothesis. As is the case with other analyses, plus tick blocks exhibit a different pattern. The price maintains its new level as in Figure 4.[36]

The findings for trailing minus tick blocks are subject to the same criticism as the test based on the relation between size of block and price effect; namely,

---

35. On day −1 the average impact index is .9881. On day zero it falls to .9772 and recovers to .9834 and .9879 on days 10 and 20, respectively.

The amount of the recovery depends on the definition of blocks. If blocks with subsequent blocks of any size over 10,000 shares are excluded (rather than only those with subsequent blocks over $1 million), the recovery is larger and more swift. The sample size in this case is 320. The impact index values for days −1, 0, 10 and 20 are .9924, .9819, .9921 and .9956, respectively.

36. On day −1 the average impact index is 1.0337. On day zero it rises to 1.0469. On day 10 it is 1.0468 and on day 20 it is 1.0452.

that blocks may signal the existence of information. The majority of blocks are minus tick blocks and under the information hypothesis are associated with unfavorable information. Therefore, choosing blocks for which no subsequent blocks occurred amounts to choosing blocks followed by less bad news than usual. Therefore, the price recovers.[37]

There are several counterarguments. First, although the number of blocks is heavily weighted in favor of minus ticks, the average price effect for all blocks includes the greater average absolute price effect of plus tick blocks. The average U_0 for all blocks over \$1 million is $-.34\%$, and the average number of such blocks following minus tick blocks within 10 trading days is .96. Under the information hypothesis, a typical minus tick block should discount subsequent bad news in the amount of $(.96)(-.34\%) = -.32\%$. As shown above, the average price recovery of trailing minus tick blocks is considerably greater than this. Second, if the analysis of trailing blocks excludes more bad news than usual, the average price of trailing plus tick blocks should rise also. This does not happen.

Third, there is a possibility that minus tick blocks cluster so that more than the average amount of bad news follows a typical minus tick block. Therefore, in the absence of subsequent blocks, the price recovery would be greater than the average price effect of all blocks. There appears, however, to be no tendency for minus tick blocks to cluster. The frequency of minus ticks among blocks that follow a minus tick block within 10 days is slightly less than the frequency of minus tick blocks in the population as a whole (.52 versus .55; recall that the total population includes zero tick blocks). On the other hand, there is a tendency for plus tick blocks to cluster. First, the frequency of following blocks is greater. On the average, 1.33 blocks follow a plus tick block within 10 days. Second, the following blocks are plus ticks with a greater frequency than blocks in general (.33 versus .17). The fact that trailing plus tick blocks show no price return in spite of this apparent clustering indicates that during the period analyzed the market did not anticipate additional blocks.

As a further test of the possibility that minus tick blocks may cluster, "leading" minus tick blocks are analyzed separately. A leading block is (arbitrarily) defined as one for which no blocks over \$1 million occur in that stock during the previous three trading days. If the same information gives rise to a cluster of blocks, for whatever reason, and there is no distribution effect, one would expect leading blocks to exhibit substantially larger current impact on the day of the trade than other blocks that follow. This behavior is not apparent in the data; the average day zero current impacts of leading and nonleading blocks are almost identical (-1.16% and -1.11%, respectively).

Thus, when a sample of blocks unaffected by subsequent blocks is chosen, the pattern of price movement subsequent to the block tends to support the

---

37. The authors are grateful to William Beaver for his suggestions on this point. It should be noted that there can be no counterarguments if the information hypothesis is made tautologically true. It is easy to argue, for example, that block trades *are* news.

distribution hypothesis in the case of minus tick blocks. As before, this hypothesis is not supported in the case of plus tick blocks, which indicates that the distribution effect for minus tick blocks reflects liquidity costs.

E. *Serial Independence of Price Changes*

There are indications of price trend in the mean current impacts previous to the block trade. Mean U_t tends to turn negative for minus tick blocks (Table 2) and positive for plus tick blocks (Table 3) about three days before day zero. This pattern may be due to serial correlation in the price of each stock or simply to the averaging process if some blocks have an impact before day zero. To distinguish between these alternatives, current impact on day zero is regressed on current impact on day -1. The results, with t values in parentheses, follow.

Minus tick blocks:

$$U_0 = -.011 + .113\ U_{-1} \qquad R^2 = .011$$
$$(3.59)$$

Plus tick blocks:

$$U_0 = .012 + .132\ U_{-1} \qquad R^2 = .021$$
$$(2.79)$$

The tendency toward positive serial dependence indicated by these results is clearly not strong. The serial dependence (if any) which does exist need not imply market irrationality or be inconsistent with the random walk hypothesis. The prices used in the regressions are conditioned on the subsequent occurrence of a block. Unless market participants are aware of the impending block, serial dependence of price changes before the block trade is not exploitable in trading.

The regression results imply that the major cause of mean price drift before day zero is due to different timing of impacts for different blocks. Such differences are probably due to some blocks being "shopped" (described to potential buyers or sellers on the other side) less expertly than others. If the news is out that a large block is for sale, price may drop prior to the day of the block transaction.

Subsequent to day zero, there is no marked trend in the mean current impact. (See Figures 3 and 4.) The mean price recovery noted in the case of trailing blocks on minus ticks depends on considering only blocks for which no subsequent blocks occurred. If an investor could predict the subsequent occurrence of blocks, he could make profits by buying immediately after a trailing block on a minus tick. Since the subsequent occurrence of blocks is not known, however, the investor can only expect the level post-block pattern shown in Figure 3.

VII. COMPARISON OF PRICE EFFECTS OF BLOCK TRADES AND SECONDARY DISTRIBUTIONS

A secondary distribution is similar to a minus tick block trade in the sense that both involve sales of a large quantity of stock. Secondaries are handled much like new issues and cannot be carried out as quickly as block trades. Secondaries are useful when a block of stock is to be distributed widely (perhaps because no institutional buyer is available). It is interesting to compare Scholes' [7] principal findings concerning price effects of secondaries with those described here for blocks, since Scholes employs many of the same techniques used in the present study. Unlike the present study, however, Scholes finds no evidence of a distribution effect.

Scholes calculated essentially what this study has termed current impact (U_t) and impact index (S_t) for 272 nonregistered NYSE secondaries in 1961-65.[38] His results on the behavior of mean S_t for 25 days before and 14 days after the secondary are roughly similar to the pattern in Table 2 and Figure 3 except that the prices of secondaries tended to fall further for a few days after the offering. For the secondaries, mean S_t on day -1 is .995. On day zero it falls to .989. For the next few days mean S_t falls further, reaching .975 on day five and has the same value on day 10. In Table 2, in comparison, mean S_t is .991 (rounded) on day -1, falls to .980 on day zero, and is .983 on day 10. In neither case is there a pattern of price recovery following day zero. In regressing size of current impact on day zero (U_0) on size of secondary, Scholes does not find a significant relation.[39] As noted earlier, the evidence for minus tick block trades, on the other hand, shows a significant relation between U_0 and size of block.

The difference in these empirical results appears to be due to differences in institutional arrangements for handling large sales through secondary distributions and through block trades. In a secondary, the underwriter usually takes the entire issue at risk and is not constrained in the commission he charges. Contrary to Scholes' assumption, commissions on secondary distributions are significantly higher than normal NYSE commissions.[40]

In a block trade the entire issue is rarely positioned and a single commission

---

38. This is the sample from [7] that is most comparable to the block trade sample. Registered secondaries are not comparable since the advance announcement presumably leads to discounting of any price effect before the offering date.

39. For example, Scholes's regression for 345 registered and unregistered secondaries of U_0 (his E_{10}) against the logarithm of the dollar value of the secondary (V) gave the following results, where the number in parentheses is a t value. (No regression was run for the unregistered issues taken separately.)

$$U_0 = -.0022 - .0042 \ln V \quad R^2 = .0009$$
$$(0.53)$$

Scholes, however, was able to group secondaries by type of institution selling. His analysis of price effects by type of seller produced results consistent with the information hypothesis. Similar data were not available for the block trades analyzed in the present study.

40. Scholes in [7] assumes 2 commissions to be the typical charge to the seller. (The buyer pays no commission.) During the period studied this would be about 2%. The NYSE, in its booklet *Marketing Methods For Your Block of Stock*, reports that during the period 1942-1959 (1140 observations) the cost of using a secondary distribution was on the average 4.84 times as large as the minimum commission. An analysis by one of the authors of 56 NYSE secondaries offered in the period July 1967 to June 1970 finds the average cost to be 4.47% of the value of the offering. Since the minimum commission was about 1%, this corroborates the figures of the NYSE.

is charged the buyer and the seller.[41] As a result, a price recovery is necessary to convince buyers to take over some of the underwriting function, at the very least to offset the commission they are compelled to pay under the NYSE rules. A liquidity cost therefore exists in secondary distributions, but appears in the form of higher commissions, whereas in the case of block trades it appears in the form of a price recovery.

VIII. Summary and Conclusions

The purpose of the preceding analyses was to investigate whether the price effects accompanying block trades can be ascribed to a change in the underlying value of the stock (information effect) or to a temporary deviation of prices (distribution effect). Separate analyses were conducted for blocks over $1 million trading on minus ticks and on plus ticks.

For plus tick blocks, the evidence indicates that price effects reflect changes in the underlying value of the stock. It was noted that a number of stocks in the sample were involved in mergers or takeovers. More fundamentally, there is little reason to expect a distribution effect based on liquidity costs for blocks that are actively purchased, since market makers in blocks and other investors rarely go short.

The majority of blocks, however, trade on a minus tick. These blocks produce evidence, although not uniformly strong, of some form of distribution effect. Within the day, closing price showed a significant average reversal from the block trade price. This price recovery, approximately equal to one commission, is consistent with a temporary discount necessary to bring in willing buyers quickly. The analysis of inter-day price effects, which found that price impacts are associated with the size of the block and that prices of trailing blocks tend to recover also supports the distribution hypothesis. These findings imply that the pressure of institutional trading is a significant factor in the observed price effects of block trades.

The evidence tends to support the liquidity cost version of the distribution hypothesis, and there is little evidence on whether differences in marginal preference are operative. This conclusion is based on a number of pieces of evidence the most important of which is the rapid price recovery of minus tick blocks on the day of the block. The price recovery of trailing blocks, the effect of the size of the block, and the difference in the effect for plus tick blocks, however, all point to the same effect. The short period covered makes it difficult to determine whether differences in marginal preferences are important. The market may be perfect in this latter sense and still be subject to the costs found in this paper of bringing willing buyers and sellers together quickly.

There are several practical implications of the findings. First, they suggest that, under the present structure of markets, the actions of institutions do indeed affect market prices, at least temporarily. Second, they imply that

---

41. On the portion positioned, the block trader usually collects two commissions since he charges a commission when he sells the stock out of inventory. However he often benefits even when he does not position because he acts as broker for both sides.

the efficiency with which large blocks are sold is worthy of examination. There appears to be a cost to the seller over and above the commission charge, which is particularly evident in the within-day price return. This cost may be reduced if more investors are given the opportunity and the incentive to participate in blocks. Elimination of the fixed minimum commission and permitting and encouraging competing specialists would be steps in the right direction.

Third, the effect on market price is at a cost to the institution itself. The institution typically sells at the low price during the 41 day period analyzed. The judgment by the institution that the stock should be sold is not vindicated by the price behavior of the blocks analyzed, since the price does not on the average fall below the closing price on the day of the block. There is, in fact, a price recovery on the day of the block trade averaging more than .70 per cent. This amount, which can be considered an inducement to bring in buyers, plus the commission charge of about .60 per cent makes the transaction costs to the seller quite high. Such costs can be justified if alternative investments can be identified that will prove to outperform the stock sold. Available evidence on the investment skill of mutual funds lends little credence to this being the typical situation.[42] Absent the ability to identify superior alternatives, high portfolio turnover, even when effected through block trades, can be costly to the beneficiaries of the portfolio.

REFERENCES

1. E. Fama. "The Behavior of Stock Market Prices," *Journal of Business,* Vol. 37 (January, 1965), pp. 34-105.
2. E. Fama, L. Fisher, M. Jensen and R. Roll. "The Adjustment of Stock Prices to New Information," *International Economic Review,* Vol. 10 (February, 1969), pp. 1-21.
3. E. Fama. "Efficient Capital Markets: A Review of Theory and Empirical Work," *Journal of Finance,* Vol. 25 (May, 1970), pp. 383-417.
4. I. Friend, M. Blume and J. Crockett. *Mutual Funds and Other Institutional Investors: A New Perspective.* New York: McGraw-Hill, 1970.
5. M. Gordon. *The Investment, Financing and Valuation of the Corporation.* Homewood, Illinois: Richard D. Irwin, 1962.
6. J. Lintner. "Dividends, Earnings, Leverage, Stock Prices and the Supply of Capital to Corporations," *Review of Economics and Statistics,* Vol. 44 (August, 1962), pp. 243-269.
7. M. Scholes. "A Test of the Competitive Market Hypothesis: The Market for New Issues and Secondary Offerings," unpublished Ph.D. dissertation, University of Chicago, 1969. A paper based on this dissertation, entitled "The Market for Securities: Substitution Versus Price Pressure and the Effects of Information on Share Prices," is forthcoming in the *Journal of Business.*
8. Securities and Exchange Commission. *Institutional Investor Study Report of the Securities and Exchange Commission* (92nd Congress, 1st Session, House Document No. 92-64). Washington: U.S. Government Printing Office, 1971.

42 For recent findings on the investment performance of mutual funds, see [4].

[2]
The implementation shortfall: Paper versus reality

Reality involves the cost of trading and *the cost of not trading.*

André F. Perold

After selecting which stocks to buy and which to sell, "all" you have to do is implement your decisions. If you had the luxury of transacting on paper, your job would already be done. On paper, transactions occur by mere stroke of the pen. You can transact at all times in unlimited quantities with no price impact and free of all commissions. There are no doubts as to whether and at what price your order will be filled. If you could transact on paper, you would always be invested in your ideal portfolio.

There are crucial differences between transacting on paper and transacting in real markets. You do not know the prices at which you will be able to execute, when you will be able to execute, or even whether you will ever be able to execute. You do not know whether you will be "front-run" by others. And you do not know whether having your limit order filled is a blessing or a curse — a blessing if you have just extracted a premium for supplying liquidity, a curse if you have just been bagged by someone who knows more than you do. Because you are so much in the dark, you proceed carefully, and strategically.

In the end, your actual portfolio looks different from your ideal portfolio. It also performs differently. If the differences in performance were small, the problems of implementation would be minor. The evidence, however, says the difference in performance can be very big. And implementation can be a major problem.

If you are looking for evidence that paper portfolios consistently outperform real portfolios, you probably need go no further than to your own investment shop. How often have you tested an investment strategy on paper, found it to perform superbly, only to discover mediocre performance when it goes live? How often have directors of research been able to show that paper portfolios based on their analysts' recommendations outperform the firm's actual portfolios?

Perhaps the best known example of this phenomenon, and the one with the longest publicly available record, is the Value Line ranking system. The Value Line funds that make use of the system have excellent long-term track records, but none has done as well as the paper portfolios based upon the Value Line rankings. For example, over the period 1965-1986, the Value Line Fund has outperformed the market by 2.5% a year, while the paper portfolio based upon the Value Line rankings with weekly rebalancing has outperformed the market by almost 20% a year.[1,2]

THE BASIC APPROACH

This article proposes a way to assess the drag on performance caused by the problems of implementation. The proposal is for you to run a paper portfolio alongside your real portfolio. The paper portfolio should capture your "wish list" of decisions just before you try to implement them. You should manage this paper portfolio within the same restrictions and guidelines as the real portfolio with respect to diversification and riskiness. The performance of

---

ANDRÉ F. PEROLD is Associate Professor of Business Administration at the Harvard Graduate School of Business Administration in Boston (MA 02163). He wishes to thank Jay Light and Robert Salomon for thought-provoking discussions on the subject, and Fischer Black, Paul Samuelson, Evan Schulman, and Wayne Wagner for their comments.

this paper portfolio will tell you a lot about your skill at selecting stocks that outperform. The difference between your performance on paper and in reality is what we call the *implementation shortfall* (or just "shortfall"). The implementation shortfall measures the degree to which you are unable to exploit your stock selection skill.

We shall see that the shortfall measures not only what are traditionally thought of as "execution costs," but also the opportunity costs of not transacting. Measuring the shortfall in conjunction with execution costs therefore allows you to separate out opportunity costs. To reduce the shortfall, you have to improve how you manage the trade-off between execution costs and opportunity costs. Minimizing execution costs alone may be no good if it results in unacceptably high opportunity costs. Minimizing opportunity costs will not be worthwhile if it leads to execution costs that are too high.

While they can measure certain types of execution cost, outsiders generally cannot reconstruct the shortfall after the fact by working with only transaction data. The paper portfolio must be managed internally and in real time. Depending on the investment process, its management may require great care and diligence.

We should note also that a large implementation shortfall is not bad per se. If your overall performance is good, a large shortfall may be a necessary cost of doing business. On the other hand, a small shortfall is not necessarily good — it is no help if your overall performance is bad.

The point of this article is that monitoring the shortfall will enable you to measure and better understand the sources of drag on your investment performance. You will be able to separate bad research from poor implementation. If you can improve your understanding of performance drag, you can better control it.

HOW TO CALCULATE THE IMPLEMENTATION SHORTFALL

To calculate the shortfall, you must calculate the performance of both your real and paper portfolios. The performance of your real portfolio will obviously be net of brokerage commissions, transfer taxes, and any other charges incremental to your investment decisions. The result should not include management fees, whether fixed or incentive in nature.

To calculate the performance of the paper portfolio, you use the principle that on paper you transact instantly, costlessly, and in unlimited quantities. For example, if you would like to buy 50,000 shares at current prices, simply look at the current bid and ask, and consider the deal done at the average of the two. The same applies if you want to sell.

Using the average of the prevailing bid and ask means that you get the same price whether you are buying or selling. If you bought at the ask and sold at the bid, you would be incurring transaction costs. These occur only in real world implementations, not on paper.

WHAT IS THE SHORTFALL MEASURING?

The shortfall measures the degree to which you have been unable to exploit your stock selection skills. Just how it measures this will depend on your implementation strategy. In some situations — such as trading on the basis of an impending earnings announcement — you may want to execute quickly by means of a block trade and may be quite willing to move the market to do so. In other situations, your only concern may be to transact at the "right price," and you may be willing to wait "forever" if necessary. Here, you may wish to place a limit order, either explicitly, or implicitly by indicating interest at your chosen price. If the order does not execute, you may later be willing to pay a higher price to get the execution. Generally, your implementation strategy will involve combinations of these and other approaches.[3]

The implementation shortfall has two basic components. The first, *execution cost*, relates to the transactions you actually execute. The second, *opportunity cost*, relates to the transactions you fail to execute. The shortfall is the sum of these two. The derivation of this relationship is given in Appendix B.

Execution cost measures all the obvious costs such as brokerage commissions and transfer taxes. This follows directly from the way the implementation shortfall is calculated. Opportunity cost (the cost of not transacting) simply measures the paper performance of the buys and sells you did not execute.

Execution cost also measures price impact. For the purposes of this discussion, let us define price impact to be the difference between the price you could have transacted at on paper (the average of the bid and ask at the time of the decision to trade) and the price you actually transacted at, whether immediately following the decision to trade or later. For example, if you buy at the ask (or sell at the bid) prevailing at the time of the decision to trade, your price impact will be half the bid–ask spread.

Price impact may occur because you have to move the market temporarily away from its current price in order to induce someone to supply the liquidity you are seeking. From time to time, there may be negative price impact, because you are able to take advantage of someone on the other side who needs the liquidity more than you do. When the price impact is purely a liquidity effect, the price of the stock will usually return to the level it was at before you traded.

Price impact may occur also because the market suspects you know something. Think of the block trader who has to find the other side of the trade for you. If you often show up with "soiled merchandise," he is going to go out of business if he always accommodates you at current prices and bags his clients on your behalf. More likely, he will adjust the price somewhat. The smarter he thinks you are, the bigger the adjustment. Once you have traded, the price may not return to its previous level because the cat is now out of the bag. In that case, part of the price impact will be permanent.

Included in the shortfall is something called the cost of *adverse selection*.[4] Typically, some of the transactions that execute on paper but not in the real portfolio do not execute because you choose not to incur the price impact; some, particularly limit orders, do not execute because the market chooses not to execute them. When you place a limit order to buy, you are giving the market a free put option, and when you place a limit order to sell, you are giving the market a free call option.[5]

The market will often exercise these options strategically. If the order executes, it is because you are offering the best price — your price is better than "fair value." Thus, to some extent, your real portfolio tends to get stuck with stocks you are paying top dollar for, even though you are executing at your limit price. You will tend not to own the stocks the market decides it likes better than your limit price. Meanwhile, your paper portfolio owns both the ones the market likes and the ones it does not like.

Thus, the shortfall measures the cost of adverse selection through the opportunity cost represented by the trades the market chooses not to execute. To the extent that you later transact at a less advantageous price after your limit order has expired unexecuted, this is still a cost that can be attributed to adverse selection, but it will show up under execution cost under the general heading of price impact.

You could not begin to measure opportunity costs without the paper portfolio. Execution costs, on the other hand, are regularly measured in practice. The methods employed are usually different from the component of the shortfall that we have labeled execution cost. In part, this is because of the lack of access to prices prevailing at the time of the decision to trade. The methods used in practice can give you information that is valuable, particularly when you use them in conjunction with the implementation shortfall. Accordingly, Appendix A discusses how these methods fit within the framework of this paper.

PACE OF TRADING AS THE KEY DETERMINANT OF EXECUTION AND OPPORTUNITY COSTS

What determines the amount of your execution costs and opportunity costs? In general, there will be many factors, including how smart a trader you are or how well you manage your relationships with the Street. The chief factor, however, is how quickly you trade.

If you trade quickly and aggressively, you will tend to pay a bigger price to transact. It is much harder to find the other side over the next hour than over the next week. When you are in a hurry, you also indicate your need to get in or out, which in turn may signal valuable information to others. Hence, the faster you trade, the larger your execution costs will be. On the other hand, you will have more of your ideal portfolio in place, and your opportunity costs consequently will be lower.

If you trade slowly and patiently, your execution costs will tend to be lower. For example, if you execute a large order in deliberate piecemeal fashion, you will not disturb the market very much. Alternatively, if you do not break up the order but bide your time until the other side shows up in size, then you may even reap a premium to market. Nevertheless, although your execution costs will be lower, your opportunity costs will be higher. For the more slowly you trade, the more you will be forgoing the fruits of your research, and the more you will become prone to adverse selection (which shows up mostly in opportunity cost). The longer you are out there, the more time others have to act strategically against you.

USING THE SHORTFALL TO FOCUS MANAGEMENT EFFORT

Once you know what the shortfall in performance is relative to your ideal paper portfolio, how might you use this knowledge to focus your management concerns and effort? Is your time best spent on improving the investment process? Or should you pay greater attention to implementation?

The easy case occurs when the shortfall is small. Implementation is not a significant problem, and the greatest payoff will be derived from directing your efforts toward improving the investment process.

If the shortfall is large, then implementation is obviously significant. To say more, you need to separate how much of the shortfall is due to execution cost and how much to opportunity cost.[6] If the bulk of the shortfall is execution cost, then you are being hurt chiefly by price impact. Your efforts should go toward trading less aggressively. To the extent that this strategy lowers price impact by more than it increases opportunity cost, you will have been successful in reducing the shortfall.

If the shortfall is mostly opportunity cost, then you are being hurt by trading too slowly. You should focus on speeding up execution. Your shortfall will be lower to the extent that you can constrain the resulting increase in price impact to be less than the reduction you achieve in opportunity cost (and adverse selection).

IMPLEMENTATION SHORTFALL AND ASSET MANAGEMENT CAPACITY

An important problem for asset managers is how to assess the capacity of their investment operations. Managers with good performance usually have little difficulty attracting new business. All too often, as they grow, their investment performance deteriorates, even though larger firms have greater resources that should provide a competitive advantage over smaller firms.

The reasons for a slowdown in performance are many, including the increased focus of investment "stars" on business rather than investment matters. The key reason is that increased size brings increased inefficiency in implementation. It is harder to execute an investment decision swiftly when you need to seek peer approval and persuade committees. It is harder to execute million-share purchases than 50,000-share purchases.

Faced with these realities, large firms try to adapt their investment operations. They offer alternative investment products, sometimes managed in decentralized fashion. At some point they may curtail asset growth within a particular discipline. If firms fail to take this step themselves, clients will eventually take it for them.

How do you know when you have grown too big? One indicator is the performance of your paper portfolio relative to that of your real portfolio. If your paper portfolio continues to do well as assets grow, but your real portfolio does not, you may be growing too large. That is, good performance on paper coupled with a growing implementation shortfall reflects increased inefficiencies in executing investment decisions. These inefficiencies may be due either to organizational inefficiencies or to increased frictions arising from trying to execute larger transactions, or both.[7]

On the other hand, if your shortfall is not growing but your performance on paper is deteriorating, then probably it is not asset growth that is causing the implementation problem. Rather, your problem lies with the investment process.

Managing a paper portfolio along with your real portfolio is the best way to separate the effect on performance of operational inefficiencies from a weakening of your investment process.

SUMMARY AND CONCLUSIONS

Implementing investment decisions can be costly. The costs arise both in executing decisions (execution cost) and in failing to execute decisons (opportunity cost). These costs lead to a shortfall in performance. You can measure the shortfall by managing a paper portfolio that reflects the output of your investment process, then comparing the performance of this portfolio with that of your real portfolio. The amount of the shortfall will depend on the type of decisions you are trying to implement and how good you are at implementing them.

Execution costs and opportunity costs are at opposite ends of a seesaw. Lowering one generally will increase the other. To reduce the shortfall, you must lower one by more than you increase the other.

Through ongoing monitoring of the shortfall, you can assess how much of your research effort is being diluted in the process of implementation. You can also separate research-related problems from implementation-related problems, with implications on how to best focus your management concerns and efforts. These distinctions are particularly important to large managers who have to cope with greater organizational complexity as well as the increased frictions that flow from transacting in large amounts.

APPENDIX A: A COMPARISON OF APPROACHES TO MEASURING EXECUTION COSTS

Most services that measure execution costs do so with the use of transaction data. They compare the prices at which you transacted to various measures of "fair value." One measure of fair value is tonight's closing price. Another might be tomorrow night's closing price, or next week's closing price, or some price prevailing after you have finished trading in the stock. Yet another measure of fair value may be the average of the high and the low for the day, or some (weighted) average of all prices at which market participants transacted during the day, and so on. These measures of fair value usually are adjusted to reflect overall market moves, industry moves, and other kinds of moves. In the end, if on average you buy at prices higher than "fair value," and sell at prices lower than "fair value," you will record positive execution costs.

Just how execution costs should be measured is a controversial subject. The debate usually concerns at least the following:

1. Should fair value be based on prices that existed prior to any market disturbance caused by you? Or should it be

based on prices that fully reflect whatever impact your trading may have had? Or, might it suffice to use prices prevailing while you were still in the market?
2. If traders know they are being measured under a particular method, can they game the system so as to look good under that method?
3. What are you not measuring when you restrict yourself to using only transaction data?

The discussion can be made most concrete by considering the commonly used "after trade" execution cost measure (see Beebower and Priest, 1980, and Beebower and Surz, 1980). This measure of execution cost is the difference between the price at which you actually transact and some price prevailing after you have finished transacting. Also add in the easy-to-measure costs of transacting such as commissions.

Now compare this after-trade measure with the execution cost we discussed earlier. Ours is a "before trade" measure, as the paper portfolio involves comparing the actual transaction price to the paper price, that is, the price prevailing at the time of the decision to trade.[6]

First, and most important, execution costs are calculated only with actual transaction data, so neither the before-trade nor the after-trade measure tells us anything about the opportunity cost of not transacting.

Second, the after-trade execution cost measures only temporary price impacts, because it is measuring how much the price rebounds after you transact. To the extent that your attempts to transact signal the value of your research to the market, and thereby adjust prices permanently (before you can put your position in place), this will not be measured by an after-trade execution cost measure. The extreme case is that of the smart manager whom the block traders have come to know well. Whenever she tries to trade, they move the price against her — permanently — to reflect the full value of her research. Her research effort is thus completely wasted. This manager will measure a zero execution cost after the fact because she trades at fair prices. Fair, that is, taking into account her research. Of course, she will register a big before-trade execution cost, because she can trade on paper without communicating with others.

Third, the after-trade execution cost does measure the cost of adverse selection. To the extent the market chooses to transact with you because yours is the best price given what it knows about where the stock is going, then you are transacting at "unfair" prices. This is by definition an after-trade execution cost.

The before-trade execution cost does not measure the full cost of adverse selection, because you find out only after the fact whether you were selected against or not. As we discussed in the body of the article, the before-trade execution cost measures only that portion of adverse selection cost that shows up when, having failed to get your preferred price, you "chase the market" to execute anyway. The balance of the adverse selection cost is captured in the implementation shortfall through the opportunity cost.

The way in which the implementation shortfall measures adverse selection cost is the mirror image of the way in which the after-trade execution cost measures adverse selection. The latter does so by looking at the trades the market chooses to execute, while the former does so by looking at the trades the market chooses *not* to execute. Statistically, and over many transactions, the differences between these two approaches to measuring adverse selection will be small.

Fourth, if we ask whether execution cost measures can be gamed against, the answer surely is yes for all of them. All you need to do is execute nothing but the obviously "easy" trades. Then your execution cost will be negligible, no matter how it is measured. Short of executing only the easy trades, however, the after-trade execution cost basically cannot be gamed even though the before-trade execution cost can. If you know you are being measured on a before-trade basis, you simply wait a while. Then you buy the stocks on your order list whose prices have fallen (since receipt of the order), and sell the stocks whose prices have risen. You dismiss the other orders as being "too expensive" to execute.

If you are being measured by the implementation shortfall, on the other hand, there is no way to game it. By definition, your yardstick of performance is the paper portfolio — one that reflects perfect implementation. If you try to get an artificially low execution cost by executing only the "easy" trades, you will measure a high shortfall because of the opportunity cost. If you minimize your opportunity cost by trading aggressively, you may still measure a high shortfall because of a large execution cost. The only way to obtain a low implementation shortfall is to have both a low execution cost and a low opportunity cost.[9]

Taken all together, we can say that the implementation shortfall, made up of the opportunity cost plus the before-trade execution cost, measures what after-trade execution costs measure plus two things: the opportunity cost incurred when you choose not to transact, and the cost that arises when your attempt to trade signals valuable information to the market. For most managers, the opportunity cost will represent the great bulk of the difference.

---

[1] Sources: *The Value Line Investment Survey* and *Barron's*.

[2] These numbers should be interpreted with some caution. The Value Line Fund on occasion has had fairly substantial holdings in debt securities. And mutual funds generally maintain cash balances to facilitate transactions. This causes a drag on performance in up markets. Value Line's fund managers also have had to compete for trades with subscribers to the *Value Line Investment Survey*. These likely explain at least part of the shortfall in performance. If the need to hold cash balances and competition for trades are sources of performance drag, however, they represent some of the very problems of implementation that concern us here.

[3] See Cuneo and Wagner (1975) and Treynor (1981) for discussions of implementation strategy.

[4] Treynor (1981) theorizes that nearly all of the shortfall is due to adverse selection.

[5] For a further discussion, see Copeland and Galai (1983).

[6] You can do this using the formulas given in Appendix B.

[7] In certain circumstances, transactions in the real portfolio may subsidize the performance of the paper portfolio, and so may overstate the "true" amount of the shortfall. For example, you can look good on paper merely by selling immediately after having forced prices up with a large real buy order. This is something you can and should monitor,

and, if necessary, you should make allowance for it when interpreting the performance of the paper portfolio.

[8] It is harder to be as explicit about just what you are measuring when the calculation of fair value is based on prices prevailing during the period of trading (e.g., the average of the high and low of the day, or the volume-weighted price as described in Berkowitz and Logue, 1986). Absent gaming considerations, these methods should be roughly equivalent to averaging the before-trade and after-trade measures.

[9] As footnote 7 notes, playing games with the paper portfolio can make it possible to overstate the shortfall but not to understate it artificially.

APPENDIX B: DERIVATION OF THE BREAKDOWN OF IMPLEMENTATION SHORTFALL

This appendix shows formally how the shortfall breaks down into its execution cost and opportunity cost components. The breakdown is helpful if you wish to calculate the components separately.

We will measure the shortfall over periods of no trading in the paper portfolio. For example, if changes are made in the paper portfolio on a weekly basis, then we will measure the shortfall weekly. The length of the measurement period is unimportant. It need not be regular. The only requirement is that the period lie between transactions in the paper portfolio.

At the beginning of a measurement period, the paper portfolio will be assumed to have the same value of assets as the real portfolio. At the end of the period, they will differ in value by the shortfall.

Trading in the real portfolio can occur at any time.

Suppose there are N securities in total, and that one of these is a cash account.

Let n_i denote the number of shares of security i in the paper portfolio (held throughout the measurement period).

Let m_i^b be the number of shares of security i held in the real portfolio at the beginning of the period, and m_i^e the number of shares held at the end of the period. m_i^e will differ from m_i^b by the net shares traded in security i during the period.

Denote by $j = 1, \ldots, K$ the times (during the period) at which trades occur in the real portfolio. Denote by t_{ij} the number of shares you trade of security i at time j. t_{ij} is positive if you are buying and negative if you are selling. If you do not trade in security i at time j, then t_{ij} is zero. The end-of-period shareholding in security i is given by

$$m_i^e = m_i^b + \Sigma t_{ij},$$

where the summation is over $j = 1$ to K.

Denote by p_{ij} the prices at which transactions take place. The p_{ij} are assumed net of incremental costs such as commissions and transfer taxes.

Let the paper price of security i at the beginning of the period be p_i^b, and at the end of the period be p_i^e.

For simplicity, we will assume there are no net cash flows into or out of the real portfolio. Hence, all transactions in the real portfolio are financed with proceeds of other transactions. That is, at each time j, $\Sigma t_{ij} p_{ij}$ is zero when summed over $i = 1$ to N. We can do this because one of the securities is a cash account.

Let the value of the paper and real portfolios at the beginning of the period be V_b:

$$V_b = \Sigma n_i p_i^b = \Sigma m_i^b p_i^b.$$

Let the end-of-period values of the real and paper portfolios be V, and V_p, respectively:

$$V_p = \Sigma n_i p_i^e, \text{ and } V_r = \Sigma m_i^e p_i^e.$$

The performance of the paper portfolio is $V_p - V_b$, and the performance of the real portfolio is $V_r - V_b$. The implementation shortfall is the difference between the two.

The performance of the real portfolio can be expanded as

$$\Sigma(m_i^e p_i^e - m_i^b p_i^b),$$

which may be rewritten as

$$\Sigma m_i^e (p_i^e - p_i^b) - \Sigma p_i^b (m_i^e - m_i^b).$$

In turn, this can be shown to be equal to

$$\Sigma m_i^e (p_i^e - p_i^b) - \Sigma\Sigma(p_{ij} - p_i^b)t_{ij}.$$

The performance of the paper portfolio can be expanded as

$$\Sigma n_i (p_i^e - p_i^b).$$

Subtracting real performance from paper performance gives the desired result:

Implementation Shortfall = $\Sigma\Sigma(p_{ij} - p_i^b)t_{ij} + \Sigma(p_i^e - p_i^b)(n_i - m_i^e)$

= Execution cost + Opportunity cost.

This can be interpreted as follows: The term $(p_{ij} - p_i^b)$ is the cost of transacting at p_{ij} instead of at p_i^b. t_{ij} is the number of shares with respect to which you incur this cost. The product of the two, summed over j, is the before-trade execution cost incurred in achieving a position of m_i^e shares in security i. The term $(p_i^e - p_i^b)$ is the paper return on security i over the period. The term $(n_i - m_i^e)$ is the position in security i that remains unexecuted by the end of the period. The product of the two is the opportunity cost of the unexecuted position in security i.

REFERENCES

Beebower, Gilbert L., and William Priest. "The Tricks of the Trade." *Journal of Portfolio Management*, Winter 1980, pp. 36-42.

Beebower, Gilbert L., and Ronald J. Surz. "Analysis of Equity Trading Execution Costs." Center for Research in Security Prices Seminar, November 1980, pp. 149-163.

Berkowitz, Stephen A., and Dennis Logue. "Study of the Investment Performance of ERISA Plans." Prepared for U.S. Department of Labor, Office of Pension and Welfare Benefits, by Berkowitz, Logue & Associates, Inc., July 1986.

Copeland, Thomas E., and Dan Galai. "Information Effects on the Bid-Ask Spread." *Journal of Finance*, Vol. 38, No. 5, December 1983, pp. 1457-1469.

Cuneo, Larry L., and Wayne H. Wagner. "Reducing the Cost of Stock Trading." *Financial Analysts Journal*, November-December 1975, pp. 35-44.

Treynor, Jack L. "What Does It Take to Win the Trading Game?" *Financial Analysts Journal*, January-February 1981, pp. 55-60.

The Behavior of Stock Prices Around Institutional Trades

LOUIS K. C. CHAN and JOSEF LAKONISHOK*

ABSTRACT

All trades executed by 37 large investment management firms from July 1986 to December 1988 are used to study the price impact and execution cost of the entire sequence ("package") of trades that we interpret as an order. We find that market impact and trading cost are related to firm capitalization, relative package size, and, most importantly, to the identity of the management firm behind the trade. Money managers with high demands for immediacy tend to be associated with larger market impact.

FINANCIAL ECONOMISTS HAVE LONG studied the equity trading process and its impact on stock prices. Much prior empirical research isolates individual trades and analyzes the behavior of the stock price around each trade. See, for example, Kraus and Stoll (1972a), Holthausen, Leftwich, and Mayers (1987, 1990), Keim and Madhavan (1991), Petersen and Umlauf (1991), Hausman, Lo, and MacKinlay (1992) and Chan and Lakonishok (1993). Evaluating the behavior of stock prices around trades provides a means of discriminating among various hypotheses as to the elasticity of the demand for stocks; yields an estimate of the cost of executing trades and a measure of the liquidity of a market; and permits tests of different models of the determination of quotes and transaction prices.

For many institutional investors, however, even a moderately-sized position in a stock may represent a large fraction of the stock's trading volume. Accordingly, an investment manager's order is often broken up into several trades. It is often misleading, therefore, to consider an individual trade as the basic unit of analysis in the study of trading activity and its effects on prices. This paper uses the record of trades executed by 37 large investment manage-

---

* College of Commerce, University of Illinois at Urbana-Champaign, Champaign, Illinois. We thank Gil Beebower and Vasant Kamath from SEI for providing us with the data and for sharing their insights on various aspects of trading. This article has been presented at the 1994 AFA Meetings, the Amsterdam Institute of Finance, the Berkeley Program in Finance (Squaw Valley), Columbia University, the CRSP seminar at the University of Chicago, INSEAD, the 1992 NBER Summer Conference on Behavioral Finance, the University of Illinois, the 1994 USC/UCLA/NYSE Conference on Market Micro-Structure, and the 1994 WFA Meetings. We thank David Mayers (the editor), Bill Bryan, Peter Colwell, Dick Dietrich, Eugene Fama, Gene Finn, William Goetzmann, George Gross, Joel Hasbrouck, Eric Hughson, Jayendu Patel, Jay Ritter, Andrei Shleifer, an anonymous referee, and seminar participants for their comments. Rohit Gupta and Peng Tu provided outstanding research assistance. Computing support was provided by the National Center for Supercomputing Applications, University of Illinois at Urbana-Champaign.

ment firms to identify cases in which the same investment manager is in the market for a stock (buying or selling) over the course of several trades. The innovation of this article is to treat the entire sequence ("package") of trades as the basic unit of analysis in our examination of the price impact and execution cost of institutional trading. We also examine the behavior of stock prices immediately before and after trade packages.

Using our definition of a trade package, we find that multi-day trades are a very substantial portion of institutional trading—more than half of the dollar value traded in our sample takes four or more days for execution. Such order-splitting behavior by a group of large, sophisticated investors provides strong evidence that the short-term demand curve for stocks is not perfectly elastic, and that large excess demand for a stock can only be accommodated by a price concession. Indeed, the price impact associated with trade packages is quite sizeable: the average price change (weighted by the dollar size of the trade) from the open on the package's first day to the close on the last day is almost 1 percent for buys, and -0.35 percent for sells. Not only is the price impact larger for buys, but the subsequent reversal is also much smaller than for sells; thus there is an asymmetry in the overall impact of buys and sells.

We also provide evidence on the controversial issue of the execution cost of institutional trading. The dollar-weighted round-trip cost relative to the first opening price of a package is 1.32 percent (or forty-nine cents per share for the average-priced stock in our sample); relative to the closing price five days after the package's completion, the dollar-weighted round-trip cost is 0.08 percent (three cents per share). Commission costs are 0.19 percent each way (seven cents per share).

The price impact and execution cost of packages are related to the capitalization of the stock traded and to relative trade size (package size in relation to normal daily volume). However, the dominant influence is the identity of the money management firm undertaking the package. Some preliminary evidence suggests that differences across money managers stem mainly from their demands for immediacy in execution. We find that managers following a growth-oriented strategy, or with higher turnover rates (who would in general be perceived as being less patient in trade execution) incur larger price impact and execution costs.

The remainder of the article is organized as follows. After a discussion of the characteristics of our sample in Section I, the behavior of stock prices around institutional trade packages is analyzed in Section II. Section III provides several measures of the market impact cost of trade packages. In the subsequent sections we investigate the importance of various determinants of price impact and execution cost—firm size and relative trade size (Section IV), and the identity of the money management firm undertaking the trade (Section V). Regression results are presented in Section VI, together with some preliminary evidence on the cost of immediacy. Conclusions are contained in Section VII.

The Behavior of Stock Prices Around Institutional Trades

I. Preliminaries

A. Data

Our data set records the transactions of 37 large investment management firms from July 1986 until the end of 1988. These data are collected by SEI Corp., a large consulting organization in the area of financial services for institutional investors. We supplement the SEI data with transaction data from the Francis Emory Fitch Company, and also with data from the Center for Research in Security Prices (CRSP). The recorded trades involve issues listed on the New York and American Stock Exchanges. In total, there are roughly 1.2 million trades, representing about 5 percent of the total value of trading on the two exchanges over this period. For each transaction, the stock's CUSIP (Committee on Uniform Security Identification Procedures) number, the trade date, trade price, number of shares, and dollar commissions (before soft dollar rebates) are recorded. In addition, each trade is identified as a purchase or sale by the investment manager, who in turn is also identified by a numeric code (the name of the manager is not disclosed to us).

The sample is larger than in many previous studies. Since each trade is explicitly identified as a purchase or sale, it is not necessary to infer trade direction from the prior behavior of prices (as under the "tick test" used in previous studies, and described by Lee and Ready (1991)). We are also able to examine trades according to the identity of the manager. The investment managers in the sample represent all the major investment styles (growth, value, small cap, and large cap) and trading strategies.

B. Trade Packages

We use each manager's trading history to reconstruct the manager's trading packages in each stock. In particular, we define a "buy package" to include the manager's successive purchases of the stock; the package ends when the manager stays out of the market for the stock for a specified period of time. We choose a five-day break to end a package; we have, however, replicated the results with packages defined by shorter gaps in trading. "Sell packages" are defined similarly. To illustrate, suppose a manager buys a stock for three days in succession and then, after a one-day gap, engages in another buy transaction in the same stock. Suppose also that there are no further trades in this stock by this manager. Under a one-day gap definition, the first three days' purchases would constitute a buy package, while the last day's trades would make up another buy package. Under a five-day gap definition, all of these trades would be considered as part of one buy package.

Ideally, our measure of a trade package corresponds to a money manager's ex ante order. Conceptually, however, our measure might be problematic in some situations—for example, price movements subsequent to a trade may beget further trades, creating a proximate sequence of trades. The issue, therefore, is how well our definition of a package approximates an ex ante order. We provide the following reasons to think that the approximation is close.

In the first place, several studies with access to investors' ex ante orders (Keim and Madhavan (1993), Perold and Sirri (1993)) find that the proportion of orders not completely executed is small (generally less than six percent), and that the opportunity cost of unexecuted orders is not the dominant component of execution costs. Secondly, active money managers transact in stocks that they believe are substantially mispriced. A small movement in price is not likely to lead them to revise their buying or selling decisions (otherwise, portfolio turnover levels would be far higher than the observed average of 50 percent for institutional investors—see Lakonishok, Shleifer, and Vishny (1992)). Thirdly, the idea of trade packages has been widely used in the investment industry for the last ten years. The widespread acceptance in the industry of the concept of a package provides some assurance that, in practice, the correspondence between a package and an ex ante order is close. Fourthly, on an operational level, we experimented with alternative definitions, using windows of different lengths to end a package. The results are basically unchanged. We have therefore maintained the definition with a five-day trading gap, to allow for the possibility that in the smaller stocks a manager may strategically choose to stay out of the market for long periods of time.

It would, on the face of it, be desirable to know a manager's order, or more generally, his trading intentions. Upon further reflection, however, it is not clear how an investor's original intent can be quantified in any objective manner. Some issues, raised in our discussions with professional traders, include the following. A manager may submit an order with a limit price that is far removed from the market (and hence is not likely to be executed); one may question whether this should be counted as a legitimate unexecuted order, compared to other noncontingent orders. A manager may also provide to the trading desk a number of different substitute stocks, leaving the actual discretion of which stock to buy up to the desk. As another possibility, a manager may submit an order and give the desk time for its execution; before it is executed, however, the manager may cancel the order. This limited set of examples highlights the difficulty in correctly capturing the ex ante order (even if such data were readily available). On this account, the widespread adoption of a comparatively straightforward procedure based on executed orders and observed packages can be more easily understood.

C. Summary Statistics for Packages

Applying the five-day gap definition of a package to our sample yields 155,789 packages with a total trade principal value of roughly 187 billion dollars. Table I reports the frequency distribution of trade packages by package length (the number of days within the package on which trades occurred). Panels A and B describe the results for purchases and sales, respectively. In each panel, we report the frequency distribution for all trades and also for each of five size groups classified by the market value of the outstanding equity at

Table I
Frequency Distribution of Trade Packages, by Package Length

Each number in this table represents the percent of packages completed in the indicated number of trading days. Numbers in parentheses report percent of total dollar principal. Results are presented for all packages, and also classified by the capitalization of the stock at the end of the prior quarter. The size classification is based on the quintiles of the size distribution of all New York Stock Exchange (NYSE) and American Stock Exchange (AMEX) stocks. A buy (sell) package in a stock is a case where the same money management firm executed successive purchases (sales) of the same stock, with a break of less than 5 days between successive trades. The sample comprises all trades of NYSE and AMEX stocks by 37 institutional money management firms from July 1, 1986 to December 30, 1988 (excluding October 1987).

Packages in Size Group	1 Day	2–3 Days	4–6 Days	>6 Days
Panel A: Buys (74,581 Packages; $87.0 Billion Principal)				
All Buys	58.5 (20.1)	26.6 (26.7)	9.7 (21.7)	5.3 (31.5)
1 (small) 3.1% of packages 0.2% of principal	48.6 (28.9)	31.2 (27.9)	13.7 (19.4)	6.5 (23.8)
2 7.4% of packages 1.0% of principal	48.2 (29.5)	31.1 (26.0)	14.0 (20.4)	6.7 (24.1)
3 13.2% of packages 4.2% of principal	52.7 (24.3)	29.8 (28.4)	11.3 (20.3)	6.2 (27.0)
4 24.3.% of packages 17.3% of principal	58.6 (21.4)	26.2 (27.0)	9.9 (23.0)	5.3 (28.6)
5 (large) 52.0% of packages 77.4% of principal	61.9 (19.4)	25.0 (26.5)	8.3 (21.5)	4.8 (32.6)
Panel B: Sells (81,208 Packages; $99.7 Billion Principal)				
All Sells	62.7 (22.1)	24.1 (27.2)	8.4 (20.5)	4.9 (30.2)
1 (small) 1.3% of packages 0.1% of principal	57.6 (30.1)	24.1 (25.6)	10.9 (24.8)	7.4 (19.5)
2 4.1% of packages 0.7% of principal	54.7 (24.7)	26.2 (25.1)	11.4 (19.8)	7.7 (30.5)
3 11.2% of packages 4.2% of principal	57.0 (28.7)	25.7 (27.3)	10.6 (20.7)	6.7 (23.3)
4 24.3% of packages 16.5% of principal	62.6 (25.3)	23.5 (28.0)	8.8 (21.2)	5.1 (25.5)
5 (large) 59.1% of packages 78.5% of principal	64.5 (21.0)	23.8 (27.1)	7.5 (20.3)	4.2 (31.6)

the end of each quarter. The size classification is based on the quintiles of the size distribution of all New York Stock Exchange (NYSE) and American Stock Exchange (AMEX) stocks.

Previous studies have treated each trade in isolation. However, only about 20 percent of the value of institutional purchases is completed within a day, while as much as 53.2 percent takes four or more days of trading to be completed. Note that, under our definitions, while the length of a package may be, say, five days (meaning that the manager traded on five days from the start to the finish of a package), the number of days elapsed from the package's beginning to its end could be much longer. This is because each day of trading in the package could be followed by a pause of up to four days. About 22 percent of the value of sells is completed in one day; on the other hand, programs taking four or more days account for about half of the value of institutional sales.

The bulk of institutional purchases and sales is concentrated in the largest quintile of stocks. This group makes up approximately 52 percent (59 percent) of the number of buy (sell) packages, or about 77 percent (78 percent) by dollar value. The smallest 40 percent of firms, in contrast, make up only 10 percent (5 percent) of the number of buys (sells), and only about 1 percent of the dollar value of either buys or sells. While one might expect that institutional trades in smaller firms take longer to complete, Table I suggests otherwise for both buys and sells—if anything, packages in the smaller companies take fewer days than packages in the larger companies. This finding, however, may be due to differences in managers' investment styles and trading strategies across size groups.[1]

Table II describes other characteristics of packages. Panel A provides statistics on the number of shares per package. Packages are larger than individual trades—the median number of shares traded is 6,800 and 6,500 shares for buy and sell packages, respectively. In contrast, the median number of shares in a single institutional transaction is less than 3,000 shares (Chan and Lakonishok (1993)). The distribution for packages is highly skewed to the right, and in the extreme, the largest 1 percent of packages exceed 450,000 shares.

Panel B presents the distribution of the dollar value of packages. The mean value of a package is approximately $1.2 million. However, there are some very large packages (the top 1 percent of packages are in excess of $16 million). The largest 25 percent of packages by dollar principal account for approximately 75 percent of the total dollar value. In Panel C, package size is measured relative

---

[1] There is some weak evidence in Table I that buy packages take longer to complete than sell packages—53.2 percent of the value of buy packages take four days or longer, compared to 50.7 percent for sell packages. This evidence suggests that sales may be easier for the market to accommodate than purchases. We also replicated Table I for the frequency distribution of packages under a one-day gap definition of a package. Under this definition, about a quarter of the principal value of packages runs four days or longer, compared to about half when a five-day gap definition is used. It is thus quite common for institutional trading in a stock to be interrupted by pauses, even in the midst of a package.

The Behavior of Stock Prices Around Institutional Trades

TABLE II

Mean and Fractiles of Distribution of Trade Packages by Institutional Money Managers

This table reports summary statistics for institutional trade packages. A buy (sell) package in a stock is a case where the same money management firm executed successive purchases (sales) of the same stock, with a break of less than 5 days between successive trades. Results are presented for all packages, and also classified by the capitalization of the stock at the end of the prior quarter. The size classification is based on the quintiles of the size distribution of all New York Stock Exchange (NYSE) and American Stock Exchange (AMEX) stocks. The sample comprises all trades of NYSE and AMEX stocks by 37 institutional money management firms from July 1, 1986 to December 30, 1988 (excluding October 1987).

	All Buys	(Small) 1	2	3	4	(Large) 5	All Sells	(Small) 1	2	3	4	(Large) 5
Panel A: Shares Traded (Thousands)												
Mean	35.3	8.9	15.6	22.8	36.6	42.3	36.2	18.4	25.5	29.6	35.3	38.9
Median	6.8	3.2	6.0	8.0	8.7	6.3	6.5	5.0	8.0	10.0	8.2	5.4
25%	1.7	1.3	2.0	2.5	2.0	1.4	1.5	2.0	2.3	2.5	1.7	1.1
75%	26.9	7.5	15.5	21.6	30.0	31.2	28.0	17.6	23.1	30.0	30.0	27.0
99%	450.0	92.6	144.0	242.8	407.1	545.0	463.8	204.2	247.2	300.0	400.0	535.1
Panel B: Dollar Value of Package (Thousand $)												
Mean	1167	68	159	379	850	1723	1228	124	242	487	846	1619
Median	175	23	66	138	202	270	197	32	78	162	201	239
25%	44	10	24	45	47	58	44	12	25	44	42	50
75%	801	51	150	350	779	1371	854	111	231	482	763	1166
99%	16038	780	1622	3948	9042	21568	16402	1484	2552	4925	9137	20960
Panel C: Package Size Relative to Normal Trading Volume[a]												
Mean	0.66	2.19	1.75	1.19	0.72	0.25	0.61	3.24	2.25	1.57	0.69	0.22
Median	0.11	0.89	0.68	0.42	0.18	0.03	0.07	0.92	0.70	0.46	0.15	0.03
25%	0.02	0.39	0.25	0.14	0.04	0.01	0.01	0.33	0.23	0.12	0.03	0.01
75%	0.53	2.09	1.71	1.15	0.66	0.17	0.39	2.97	2.13	1.49	0.59	0.14
99%	7.98	23.38	17.48	12.21	7.70	3.31	8.17	31.54	21.90	16.31	7.76	3.11
Panel D: Package Size Relative to 95th Percentile of Trading Volume[b]												
Mean	0.38	4.86	0.66	0.44	0.28	0.11	0.26	1.41	0.83	0.74	0.29	0.10
Median	0.04	0.35	0.24	0.15	0.07	0.01	0.03	0.36	0.27	0.18	0.06	0.01
25%	0.01	0.15	0.08	0.05	0.01	0.00	0.00	0.12	0.09	0.05	0.01	0.00
75%	0.20	0.84	0.67	0.42	0.25	0.07	0.15	1.12	0.79	0.54	0.22	0.06
99%	3.08	10.27	6.30	4.72	3.10	1.36	3.07	16.28	8.14	6.71	2.95	1.35

[a] Normal trading volume is computed as the average daily trading volume over a prior 40-day interval.
[b] Package size is divided by the 95th percentile of the distribution of trading volume over a prior 40-day interval.

to normal daily trading volume, which is computed as the average daily volume over a prior 40-day interval. An institutional package generally represents a substantial portion of normal daily volume—the averages are 0.66 and 0.61 for buys and sells respectively. Even in the largest firms, an average package takes up 25 percent of normal daily volume, while an average package in the smallest firms is two or three times daily volume. In the extreme, the largest packages are many times larger than normal daily volume in the stock. A typical package, however, is quite small—the medians are 0.11 and 0.07 for all buys and all sells, respectively. Given the variability in daily trading volume, a package may be large relative to average volume and yet may not be problematic when it comes to execution. To account for this possibility, Panel D of Table II provides summary statistics for package size relative to the 95th percentile of the distribution of daily volume over a prior 40-day interval. The 95th percentile of the distribution of volume captures the upper range of normal daily volume, without being affected by occasional spikes in trading activity. The results with this alternative measure are generally similar to those obtained with average daily volume—the largest packages are still in general several multiples of the 95th percent heaviest prior trading volume.

II. The Price Impact of Trade Packages

This section provides evidence on the behavior of stock prices around institutional packages. Our measures adjust for market-wide stock price movements, as reflected by the returns on similarly-sized firms. The size-adjustment procedure is as follows. We rank and divide all NYSE and AMEX stocks into deciles, based on market capitalization at the beginning of each quarter. A control portfolio is formed from all stocks in the same size decile. The return for a package in a particular stock is measured in excess of the return from buying the control portfolio on the package's first day and holding the portfolio for as long as it takes to execute the package. Our buy-and-hold procedure for the control portfolio avoids the bias discussed by Blume and Stambaugh (1983) that would arise with daily rebalancing.

Figure 1 graphically summarizes the behavior of stock prices around trade packages, for both buy and sell programs. Our focus is on excess returns averaged across all packages, using the dollar value of the package as weights (hereafter denoted the principal-weighted average). Additional summary statistics are provided in Table III.

A. Buys

On a principal-weighted average basis, money managers tend to buy stocks that have risen in price (relative to the market). In the twenty-day period preceding buy packages, there is a sizeable return of 0.86 percent. Much of this increase occurs before the five-day period preceding purchases. This price appreciation could be indicative of short-term positive feedback trading behavior ("trend-chasing"), in the sense that increases in the stock price trigger trading. Alternatively, money managers could be herding and responding in common to news events such as earnings announcements. There is evidence,

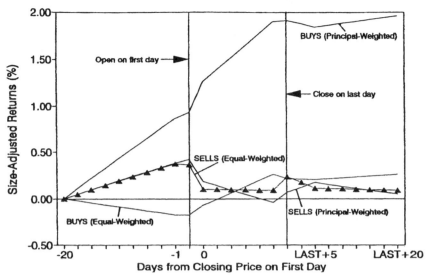

Figure 1. **Cumulative size-adjusted returns around institutional trade packages.** Returns are calculated for various time intervals around institutional trade packages, beginning from the closing price twenty days before the first day of the package and ending with the closing price twenty days after the last day of the package. Returns are adjusted for the return on a size control portfolio over the corresponding interval. Cumulative average returns are depicted separately for buy packages and for sell packages, where the averaging uses the package's dollar value as weights (principal-weighted) or uses equal weights. A buy (sell) package is a case where the same money management firm executed successive purchases (sales) of the same stock, with a break of less than five days between successive trades. The sample comprises all trades on NYSE and AMEX stocks by 37 institutional money management firms from July 1, 1986 to December 30, 1988 (excluding October 1987).

however, that the price increase beforehand is mainly associated with the larger packages. The simple mean return (i.e., the average return giving equal weight to all packages) in the twenty-day period prior to buys is −0.18 percent. It may be the case that a manager requires a stronger confirmation (higher return) before initiating large buys, or that larger trades are undertaken by managers who follow a price momentum strategy.

On a principal-weighted average basis, the first day's trade price is 0.33 percent above the opening price. The rise on the first day amounts to roughly twelve cents (one tick), given the average stock price of $36.50 in our sample. By the close on the last day of the package, the price is 0.98 percent higher than the opening price on the first day of the package. The simple mean returns, however, are much smaller. The return from the opening price to the first day's trade price is 0.11 percent, while the return from the first open to the last close is 0.39 percent.

Table III
Summary Statistics for Returns Before, During, and After Institutional Buy Packages and Institutional Sell Packages

Returns (in percent) are reported for selected intervals before, during, and after institutional buy packages and institutional sell packages. All returns are in excess of the buy-and-hold returns on a matching size decile portfolio over a holding period corresponding to the selected interval. A buy (sell) package in a stock is a case where the same money management firm executed successive purchases (sales) of the same stock with a break of less than 5 days between successive trades. Sample comprises all trades of New York Stock Exchange (NYSE) and American Stock Exchange (AMEX) stocks by 37 institutional money management firms from July 1, 1986 to December 30, 1988 (excluding October 1987).

	Panel A: Returns Before Trade Packages		
	Performance 20 Days Before Package	From 5 Days Before to Close Before Package	From Close Before Package to Open on First Day
Buys			
Principal-weighted average	0.86	0.23	0.07
Mean	−0.18	−0.08	0.00
Median	−0.55	−0.26	−0.01
Standard deviation	7.83	4.01	1.18
Sells			
Principal-weighted average	0.38	0.21	0.04
Mean	0.37	0.20	−0.01
Median	−0.20	−0.08	−0.03
Standard deviation	8.24	4.18	1.26

	Panel B: Returns During Trade Packages			
	From Open on First Day to Average Price on First Day	From Average Price on First Day to Average Price on Last Day of Package	From Open on First Day to Close on Last Day of Package	From Average Price on Last Day to Close on Last Day
Buys				
Principal-weighted average	0.33	0.64	0.98	0.01
Mean	0.11	0.33	0.39	−0.05
Median	0.06	0.08	0.11	−0.08
Standard deviation	1.79	1.91	3.26	1.72
Sells				
Principal-weight average	−0.24	−0.22	−0.35	0.11
Mean	−0.26	−0.01	−0.13	0.14
Median	−0.20	−0.30	−0.02	0.07
Standard deviation	1.79	1.86	3.20	1.59

Table III—Continued

Panel C: Returns After Trade Packages

	From Close on Last Day to Open on Day After Package	From Close on Last Day to Close on Day After Package	From Close on Last Day to Close Five Days After Package	Performance 20 Days After Package
Buys				
Principal-weighted average	−0.02	0.03	−0.07	0.05
Mean	−0.02	0.05	−0.01	0.05
Median	−0.03	−0.08	−0.18	−0.30
Standard deviation	1.06	2.10	3.81	7.67
Sells				
Principal-weighted average	0.03	0.12	0.10	−0.02
Mean	−0.01	0.02	−0.12	−0.14
Median	−0.02	−0.08	−0.25	−0.47
Standard deviation	1.02	2.03	3.72	7.44

The price increase over the course of a buy package is consistent with various explanations. As in the preceding discussion, managers could be acting in a positive-feedback manner or they may be "herding." Alternatively, they could be trading on favorable private information, which is gradually revealed over the course of the package. Short-term liquidity effects, and perhaps imperfect substitution between stocks in the long run, could also account for the price pressure from buy packages. It may also be the case that the price changes while a package is underway may lead to a revision in the manager's original intention. More trades may be submitted if the price movement confirms the manager's original beliefs, or trades may be cut short if the price moves against the manager. These possibilities have been raised in the literature on herding (Kraus and Stoll (1972b), Scharfstein and Stein (1990)) and trend-chasing (De Long et al. (1990)). If managers are responding to price changes before or during their trades, therefore, their original ex ante orders may not coincide with the observed packages that are executed.

If short-term liquidity effects are at work, then there should be a reversal in the stock price after the package ends. However, there is only limited evidence of a price reversal. On the contrary, for buy packages the principal-weighted average return from the close on the last day to the close one day afterwards is slightly positive (0.03 percent).[2] Extending the returns out to five days after

---

[2] To provide some indication as to the standard errors of our estimates, consider the excess return from the closing price on the package's last day to the closing price a day later. The standard deviation of this return is 2.10 percent for buys (calculated across all 74,581 buy packages) and 2.03 percent for sells (across all 81,208 sell packages). The standard error of the mean is thus about 0.008 for buys and 0.007 for sells. These calculations assume that the observations are mutually uncorrelated, so the true standard errors may be much larger.

the completion of a package yields a modest reversal of only −0.07 percent (or about three cents for the average-priced stock in our sample). Accordingly, the price stays at the new higher level so that the price change appears to be permanent.

Our sample of investment managers does not appear to have predictive ability with respect to short-term price movements. The stocks that they purchase experience average abnormal returns of only 0.05 percent in the twenty-day period following the completion of the package. This finding is consistent with related evidence (discussed in Fama (1991) and Lakonishok, Shleifer, and Vishny (1992)) that use longer horizons and sample periods and generally find that professional investors do not display superior performance.

B. Sells

Prices also tend to rise in advance of sells (Panel A of Table III), although the principal-weighted average return of 0.38 percent in this case is less than that for buys. The positive return prior to sell packages is consistent with evidence that volume (and hence both buying and selling activity) tends to rise after increases in the stock price (Lakonishok and Smidt (1986)). On the first day of a sell package, the price drops by 0.24 percent from the open, and there is a further decline from the first to the last day of 0.22 percent. The same factors as in the case of buy packages could account for the price movement over the course of a sell package. After the completion of a sell package, however, the price partially recovers. The reversal occurs as early as the last day of the package: the return from the average price of the last day's trades to the closing price that day is 0.11 percent, with a further reversal of 0.12 percent one day after the package ends. Our sample of money managers appears to be as unsuccessful in predicting price changes following sales as they are in predicting returns after purchases.

C. Overview

In sum, when institutional trades are analyzed in terms of packages instead of individually, purchases are associated with a price change of almost 1 percent from the open on the package's first day to the close on its last day. The corresponding price change of −0.35 percent for sell packages is less dramatic. Chan and Lakonishok (1993) measure price changes around each institutional transaction. They find a much smaller return from the open on the trade date to the same day's close (0.34 percent in the case of buys and −0.04 percent for sells). The use of benchmark prices from around the time of the trade, however, fails to recognize that in most cases an institutional investor is in the market for a stock several days at a time.

The behavior of prices after purchases and after sales displays an intriguing asymmetry, as noted earlier by Kraus and Stoll (1972a), Holthausen, Leftwich, and Mayers (1987, 1990), Keim and Madhavan (1991), Chan and Lakonishok (1993). The magnitude of the overall price impact for buys and sells is very different, reflecting in part the stronger reversal after sells than after buys.

Chan and Lakonishok (1993) review various conjectures as to the sources of the asymmetry.

III. The Execution Cost of Institutional Trade Packages

The cost of equity trading is a controversial issue. Many studies find that portfolio managers are unable to match the performance of various passive benchmarks (Brinson, Hood, and Beebower (1986), Berkowitz, Finney, and Logue (1988), Lakonishok, Shleifer, and Vishny (1992) and under-perform by about one or two percent. The existing literature on the price impact of block trades suggests that market impact costs are nonnegligible and hence may account, at least in part, for managers' poor performance. Table IV provides several different measures of the market impact and commission cost of institutional trades. Each measure of market impact cost compares the execution price to a particular benchmark price, so that a positive cost indicates that purchases (sales) are carried out at prices above (below) the benchmark. Our earlier caveats about the possible endogeneity of trade packages are worth reiterating. In particular, the observed package may not in all cases correspond to the ex ante order.

A. Same-Day Benchmark

Following one commonly-used cost measure, we compare each transaction in a package to the volume-weighted average price calculated over all transactions in the stock on the trade date. Note that trades belonging to a given package but executed on different days have different benchmarks. The cost for a package is the weighted average (using trade principal as weights) across all trades in the package. Under this cost measure, institutional purchases and sales are accommodated at virtually no cost: the cost is 0.03 percent and 0.05 percent for buys and sells, respectively. Based on this benchmark, market impact costs are dwarfed by the average commission cost in our sample of 0.19 percent.

However, the manager may be incurring substantial execution cost if his trade prices were compared to a fixed benchmark price taken from a period disjoint from the package. Suppose, for example, that an investment manager trades on several days and is able to capture the day's volume-weighted average price on every trade. Then, under the above procedure, the manager would have zero execution cost, even though the manager's buying pressure could be pushing up the price of the stock over the course of the package. In order to address this shortcoming, we also use three other cost measures based on benchmarks from disjoint trading periods.

B. Pre-Execution Benchmark

An alternative cost measure uses the opening price on the first day of a package as the fixed benchmark. If the portfolio manager's trading intentions were known at the beginning of the first trading day, the price at the opening

Table IV
Summary Statistics for Percentage Price Impact Cost and Commission Rate for Institutional Buy and Sell Packages
(A Positive Number Denotes a Cost; a Negative Number Denotes a Benefit)

This table reports summary statistics on price impact cost and commission cost for buy packages (Panel A) and sell packages (Panel B). A buy (sell) package in a stock is a case where the same money management firm executed successive purchases (sales) of the same stock, with a break of less than 5 days between successive trades. Impact cost from the open on first day to package is measured as follows. We measure the returns from the opening price on a package's first day to each trade in the package; the cost for the package is then the principal-weighted average of these returns in excess of the buy-and-hold returns on a matching size decile control portfolio over the corresponding interval. Impact costs from the package to the closing price one (five) days after the package's last day are similarly defined, using the principal-weighted average of the excess returns from each trade in the package to the closing price one (five) days after the package's last day. Cost using the same-day volume-weighted price is the return from the volume-weighted average of all transaction prices in the stock on the trade date to the trade price; the cost for a package is the principal-weighted average of the costs for all trades in the package. Sample comprises all trades of New York Stock Exchange (NYSE) and American Stock Exchange (AMEX) stock by 37 institutional money management firms from July 1, 1986 to December 30, 1988 (excluding October 1987).

	Open on First Day to Package (%)	Package to Close One Day After Last Day (%)	Package to Close Five Days After Last Day (%)	Using Same-Day Volume-Weighted Price (%)	Commission Rate (%)
		Panel A: Buys			
Principal-weighted average	0.88	−0.21	−0.13	0.03	0.19
Mean	0.29	−0.14	−0.10	0.06	0.31
Median	0.00	0.03	0.10	0.04	0.20
Standard deviation	2.32	2.77	4.14	0.80	0.32
		Panel B: Sells			
Principal-weighted average	0.44	0.22	0.22	0.05	0.19
Mean	0.30	0.18	0.05	0.14	0.29
Median	0.17	0.06	−0.09	−0.10	0.21
Standard deviation	2.33	2.65	4.01	0.79	0.57

auction could have been captured (at least for small trades). We calculate the return from the benchmark to each trade in the package (adjusting for the holding period return on the size control portfolio), and average these excess returns across all trades in the package, using trade principal values as weights. This is equivalent to calculating the principal-weighted average price of all trades in the package, and then measuring the return from the benchmark to this average price; this return is then adjusted for price movements in similarly-sized firms.

When measured relative to the opening price on the package's first day, the market impact cost is fairly large (see Table IV): combining the cost of 0.88 percent for buys with the cost of 0.44 percent for sells yields a round-trip cost of 1.32 percent, or 49 cents per share for the average-priced stock in our sample. This echoes the evidence in Table III that packages are accompanied by sizeable price changes. However, the cost is heavily influenced by large trades—the simple mean round-trip cost of 0.59 percent is much lower than the principal-weighted average, and the median costs are also lower.

C. Post-Execution Benchmarks

Instead of using a price from before the package, a price can also be taken as a benchmark from the period after a package ends, once the short-term price pressure from the package has eased.[3] Beebower and Priest (1980) adopt this approach. There is a natural interpretation to costs measured relative to a post-execution benchmark. If purchases (sales) are accomplished at prices below (above) their values after the trading pressure has waned, the package has added value to the portfolio (generated an abnormal return) and the manager does not regret executing the transaction.

We use the closing prices one and five days after a package ends for post-execution benchmarks. The excess return from each trade in the package to the post-execution benchmark price is calculated and then averaged across all the component trades, using trade principal as weights, to yield the cost of a package.

Since prices stay high after buying activity, the manager generally does not regret buying when the benchmark is the closing price one day after the package: there is actually a benefit of 0.21 percent for buys. However, sales tend to be followed by a partial recovery in the price, so that there is a cost of 0.22 percent. If more time is allowed for the effects of trading to clear, the round-trip cost relative to the closing price five days after the package is 0.08 percent on a principal-weighted average basis, or three cents a share.[4] Stoll (1993) uses data on the securities industry's aggregate trading profits on equities and estimates an average impact cost of about 0.09 percent on exchange-listed securities over 1986 to 1988.

---

[3] Since the post-execution benchmark is not established until after a package has ended, it has the added virtue that it cannot be easily "gamed." If, on the other hand, traders are being evaluated against a benchmark that is known before they trade, they can "game" the cost-measurement system and appear to trade favorably. In particular, a trader who cannot do better than the known benchmark can defer trades indefinitely.

[4] The standard deviation for the cost relative to the closing price five days after the package is 4.14 percent for purchases (based on 74,581 packages) and 4.01 percent for sales (based on 81,208 packages). The standard error of the mean is thus less than 0.02 percent (assuming that the observations are uncorrelated).

D. Overview

Previous research has documented that large block trades have a substantial price impact relative to the prior day's closing price in excess of 1 percent (Kraus and Stoll (1972a), Holthausen, Leftwich, and Mayers (1987)). It is difficult to make any exact comparison with the findings in Tables III and IV, given the differences in methodologies and samples. In general, our evidence suggests weaker price impacts, even in the context of trade packages, than have been documented in earlier research based on individual trades. Specifically, our highest estimate of round-trip impact cost is 1.32 percent (based on our pre-execution benchmark). Assuming an average turnover rate of 50 percent (Lakonishok, Shleifer, and Vishny (1992)), our results on execution cost can account for up to half of the performance shortfall documented in the literature. Lakonishok, Shleifer, and Vishny (1992) discuss other possible reasons for the underperformance of money managers.

IV. The Role of Firm Size and Trade Complexity

We have also followed the lead of prior research and analyzed the relation between firm size, trade size, and the behavior of stock prices around institutional trade packages. These results are available upon request. It is also important to see how market impact costs vary with these factors, as a prerequisite to evaluating the success of any proposed investment strategy. Other things equal, a larger trade is more likely to be associated with larger liquidity effects, or with more severe adverse selection problems (Kyle (1985), Easley and O'Hara (1987)). In practice, larger trades would be considered by traders to be more difficult to execute without high impact costs. While in general the difficulty of a trade is a multi-dimensional attribute, we follow the spirit of industry practice and interpret complexity in terms of package size relative to normal volume.

Table V provides statistics on market impact cost, classified by firm size and trade complexity, for a round-trip transaction (a buy package and a sell package). Within each classification of firm size, we rank and categorize packages by our measure of trade complexity—package size relative to normal daily volume, where normal daily volume is measured over a forty-day period prior to the package. The bottom panel of the table aggregates across all complexity groups (using the proportion of dollar principal as weights) and thus reports results as firm size varies. Similarly, the last column in the table gives results for each complexity classification. In order to simplify the presentation, we report only the principal-weighted means, and only for a subset of our complexity classifications. Note that positive values in the table denote costs while negative values denote benefits. Similar results (available upon request) have also been obtained using an alternative measure of trade complexity (package size relative to the 95th percentile of daily volume over a prior 40-day period).

The polar cases in Table V illustrate the variation in impact costs. At one extreme of Table V, the easiest packages in the largest firms incur a round-trip

Table V
Principal-weighted Average Round-Trip Impact Costs (in Percent) Classified by Firm Size and Relative Package Size
(A Positive Number Denotes a Cost; a Negative Number Denotes a Benefit)

This table reports summary statistics on price impact cost under different benchmarks. A buy (sell) package in a stock is a case where the same money management firm executed successive purchases (sales) of the same stock, with a break of less than 5 days between successive trades. Impact cost from the open on first day to package is measured as follows. We measure the returns from the opening price on a package's first day to each trade in the package; the cost for the package is then the principal-weighted average of these returns in excess of the buy-and-hold returns on a matching size decile control portfolio over the corresponding interval. Impact costs from the package to the closing price one (five) days after the package's last day are similarly defined, using the principal-weighted average of the excess returns from each trade in the package to the closing price one (five) days after the package's last day. Cost using the same-day volume-weighted price is the return from the volume-weighted average of all transaction prices in the stock on the trade date to the trade price; the cost for a package is the principal-weighted average of the costs for all trades in the package. Round-trip costs are the costs for buy packages plus the costs for sell packages. Sample comprises all trades of New York Stock Exchange (NYSE) and American Stock Exchange (AMEX) stocks by 37 institutional money management firms from July 1, 1986 to December 30, 1988 (excluding October 1987). Packages are classified by market value of outstanding equity at end of prior quarter, and by package principal value relative to average daily volume over a prior 40-day period.

Cost Relative to	Smallest Firms	2	3	4	Largest Firms	All Firms
Panel A: 25th Percentile of Relative Package Size Distribution						
Opening price on first day of package	1.98	0.69	0.57	0.43	0.18	0.25
Closing price 1 day after last day of package	0.25	−0.25	0.19	0.36	0.11	0.15
Closing price 5 days after last day of package	0.84	−0.17	−0.22	0.01	0.07	0.05
Same-day volume weighted average price	0.06	0.03	0.24	0.42	0.18	0.22
Panel B: 50th–75th Percentiles of Relative Package Size Distribution						
Opening price on first day of package	1.55	1.17	1.05	0.90	0.52	0.62
Closing price 1 day after last day of package	0.39	−0.47	0.02	−0.05	−0.06	−0.06
Closing price 5 days after last day of package	−0.43	−0.55	−0.11	−0.06	−0.23	−0.19
Same-day volume weighted average price	0.09	0.12	0.05	0.13	0.16	0.16
Panel C: 90th–95th Percentiles of Relative Package Size Distribution						
Opening price on first day of package	3.32	1.68	2.42	1.09	1.29	1.32
Closing price 1 day after last day of package	0.16	−1.47	0.07	−0.22	−0.09	−0.12
Closing price 5 days after last day of package	−0.42	−0.11	0.51	0.04	−0.06	−0.02
Same-day volume weighted average price	−0.09	−0.17	0.01	0.07	0.07	0.06
Panel D: Top 1% of Relative Package Size Distribution						
Opening price on first day of package	−1.81	2.90	2.74	1.79	2.45	2.35
Closing price 1 day after last day of package	−4.94	−0.10	1.45	−0.85	0.58	0.65
Closing price 5 days after last day of package	−2.40	1.96	1.72	1.53	0.90	1.04
Same-day volume weighted average price	−2.12	−0.01	−0.07	0.01	0.03	0.02
Panel E: All Trades						
Opening price on first day of package	1.83	1.72	1.78	1.31	1.28	
Closing price 1 day after last day of package	−0.21	−0.25	0.14	0.12	−0.01	
Closing price 5 days after last day of package	0.21	0.67	0.27	0.35	0.02	
Same-day volume weighted average price	−0.19	0.02	0.03	0.08	0.08	

cost of 0.18 percent when measured relative to the first opening price of a package. The corresponding round-trip cost relative to the closing price five days after the end of a package is 0.07 percent. There is very little trading activity at the other extreme of the table (the largest trades in the smallest stocks), so it is necessary to aggregate some of the cells in order to provide a meaningful comparison. The three smallest quintiles of stocks in the most complicated packages (which together account for a similar fraction of principal as the easiest trades in the largest stocks) are associated with a round-trip cost relative to the first opening price of 1.48 percent. These packages incur a round-trip cost of 0.71 percent relative to the closing price five days after the end of the package. If the impact cost is measured by comparing each trade with the same-day volume-weighted average price, the relation between round-trip costs, firm size, and trade complexity in many cases runs counter to intuition: for instance, the round-trip cost for the easiest packages in the largest firms is 0.18 percent, while the three smallest quintiles in the hardest packages incur a round-trip benefit of 0.11 percent.

A voluminous amount of research focuses on investing in low-capitalization stocks. In Table V, the impact cost is not systematically related to firm size. Managers investing in smaller stocks, however, are not likely to be trading with the same degree of urgency as when they invest in large companies nor would they take similarly sized positions. Instead, strategic breaking up of orders and opportunistic trading may be more commonplace for smaller stocks—in Table II, the average size of a package is lower for small stocks than for large stocks.

V. Price Impact and Execution Cost by Money Manager

The average impact costs presented in Table IV are in general not strikingly large. This does not imply, however, that investors should be unconcerned with execution costs. In particular, what is of concern to any single institutional investor is not so much the average cost of trading but rather its own cost of trading. Our data set allows us to examine costs at the level of the individual money management organization.

The execution performance of a money management firm depends upon both the money manager and the trading desk.[5] Our various measures of price

---

[5] Numerous intangible factors also affect the outcome of the trade execution process. Typically, a large investment management firm has a trading desk, responsible for order execution. An order submitted to the desk may also be accompanied by more or less detailed instructions from the investment manager as to how the order is to be filled. Depending upon the manager's investment style, for example, there may be a higher or lower degree of urgency to trade. The instructions to the trading desk will, to a greater or lesser degree, constrain the desk's ability to trade strategically in such a way as to reduce execution cost. Within these constraints, the desk has flexibility in choosing which and how many brokers to employ; the time frame within which the order is to be executed; and how the trade is to be brought to the floor—as a market order, limit order, or whether a floor broker is to work the order, for example. In general, all these aspects of the trading process will affect the price impact or execution cost of the trade. Our results in Tables III and IV for price impact and execution cost are therefore best interpreted as averages across a large number of trades made by managers with many different investment styles and many different trading strategies.

impact and execution cost provide a set of benchmarks to evaluate a money management organization's performance along several different dimensions. In the context of trading, a "successful" money management organization would be regarded as one that is able to buy below and sell above the open or one that is able to buy at prices below (sell at prices above) the closing price after the end of the package. A firm that trades a stock in a timely fashion and hence does not miss too many opportunities (or one that does not tip its hand before trading) would be characterized by a relatively low price movement in the stock before the initiation of a package. The behavior of the stock price in the five-day period after the completion of a package can be suggestive of the firm's skill in avoiding transitory price disruptions, while the stock return over the twenty-day period after the package provides an indication of the quality of the manager's stock-picking skills in the short-run.

Table VI confirms that there is substantial dispersion across managers in their principal-weighted average round-trip returns. If execution performance is measured relative to the opening price, then the difference between the top and bottom 10 percent of managers is about four percent. The corresponding difference in costs relative to the closing price five days after the package is smaller but still very substantial (1.25 percent). Such large variation across managers' average returns (which are based upon several thousand observations) suggests that the identity of the money management firm may have an impact on execution performance. The other variables reported in Table VI display similar ranges across managers.

Since there are so many aspects to successful execution performance, no single measure can completely capture an individual organization's overall performance. To take a specific case, manager number 37 trades at prices that are on average 1.81 percent better than the pre-execution benchmark; nonetheless, the firm's trades lose money because the closing price five days after the package is on average 0.22 percent worse than the execution price. As another example, manager 21 incurs a substantial round-trip cost of 1.47 percent relative to the first open, but its trades add value to the portfolio (by 0.49 percent). These examples indicate that no single measure suffices for evaluating execution cost; instead a comprehensive analysis is necessary.

VI. The Determinants of Price Impact and Execution Cost

The variables influencing price impact and cost are, of course, correlated. In this section, we use a regression model to disentangle the separate effects of firm size, relative package size and the money manager's identity. The focus in the previous sections is on principal-weighted means; the regression model, however, uses no such weighting scheme. We also provide some direct evidence on the cost of immediacy.

Table VI
Mean, Standard Deviation, and Fractiles of Distribution of Principal-Weighted Average Round-Trip Price Impact Costs and Returns (in Percent) Across 37 Money Management Firms

Price impact costs and returns are calculated for each package, and a principal-weighted average cost or return is calculated over all packages executed by each money management firm. This table summarizes the distribution of these average costs and returns across the 37 money management firms in the sample. A buy (sell) package in a stock is a case where the same money management firm executed successive purchases (sales) of the same stock, with a break of less than 5 days between successive trades. Round-trip costs (returns) are the costs (returns) for buys plus (minus) the costs (returns) for sells. The sample comprises all trades of New York Stock Exchange (NYSE) and American Stock Exchange (AMEX) stocks by 37 institutional money management firms from July 1, 1986 to December 30, 1988 (excluding October 1988).

	Cost (%) Relative to (+ is Cost, − is Benefit)			Return (%)^c	
	Opening Price on First Day of Package^a	Closing Price 5 Days After Last Day of Package^b	5 Days Before First Day	From Close on Last Day to Close 5 Days After Package	From Close on Last Day to Close 20 Days After Package
Mean	0.50	0.14	0.19	−0.11	0.11
Std. deviation	1.33	0.47	1.10	0.50	0.78
Median	0.70	0.16	0.22	−0.08	0.26
10-percentile	−1.84	−0.47	−1.46	−0.71	−0.95
25-percentile	0.09	−0.27	−0.47	−0.43	−0.49
75-percentile	1.38	0.38	0.98	0.23	0.59
90-percentile	2.13	0.78	1.81	0.58	1.40
Difference between 90- and 10-percentiles	3.97	1.25	3.27	1.29	2.35

^{a} Returns are computed from the opening price on a package's first day to each trade in the package; the return for a package is the principal-weighted average of these returns across all trades in the package. Returns are in excess of the buy-and-hold returns on a matching size decile control portfolio over the corresponding interval.

^{b} Returns are computed from each trade in a package to the closing price five days after the package's last day; the return for a package is the principal-weighted average of these returns across all trades in the package. Returns are in excess of the buy-and-hold returns on a matching size decile control portfolio over the corresponding interval.

^{c} Returns are in excess of the buy-and-hold returns on a matching size decile control portfolio over the corresponding interval.

A. Regression Analysis

We use the following regression model:

$$r_i = \alpha + \beta c_i + \sum_{j=2}^{5} \delta_j S_{ij} + \sum_{j=2}^{7} \gamma_j D_{ij} + \sum_{j=2}^{37} \phi_j M_{ij} + \varepsilon_i. \tag{1}$$

For each package i, we use as the dependent variable r_i two measures of price impact and two measures of execution cost. The price impact measures are: the excess return from the first opening price to the closing price on the package's last day, and from the last close to the closing price five days after the end of the package. The cost measures are: from the first opening price to the package, and from the package to the closing price five days after the end of the package. The explanatory variables include the commission cost for the package in dollars per share, c_i, and dummy variables to capture the effects of market capitalization, S_{ij}, package complexity, D_{ij}, and managerial strategy, M_{ij}.[6] For example, M_{ij} takes the value of one if the ith package is traded by the jth manager and is zero otherwise. The coefficients for S_{ij}, D_{ij}, and M_{ij} are normalized relative to the first category of each effect (the smallest firms, the easiest trades, and the first manager in the data set, respectively). Separate regressions are fit for buy packages and for sell packages.

Panel A of Table VII assesses the relative importance of each set of dummy explanatory variables. It reports the adjusted R^2 for variants of equation (1) when each set of dummy variables is excluded, one at a time, from the full model. Most of the explanatory power of the model comes from the identity of the money manager behind the trade. For example, in the equation for the return from the first open to the last close for buys, the R^2 of the model drops markedly from 4.69 percent to 1.39 percent when the dummy variables for the money managers are excluded, but is only slightly altered when the dummy variables for firm size and package complexity are dropped.

Panel B of Table VII reports the estimated coefficients of the full model for buys, along with the significance levels of their t-statistics (results for the equation for sells are in parentheses). Since the observations are not independent, the statistical significance levels should be interpreted with caution, and we therefore focus on the economic significance of the coefficients.

The coefficient for commission cost reflects any trade-off between commission expenses and market impact cost.[7] It might be argued that a higher commission cost is associated with better execution. On the whole, however, the coefficient for commission expense is not large (even when it has the hypothesized sign). The largest coefficient with the hypothesized sign is -0.87, suggesting that an increase in the commission cost of one cent per share lowers the impact cost by 0.0087 percent, equivalent to a dollar savings of 0.32 cents on an average-priced stock. The weak association between price impact or cost and commission expenses may, however, be due to various unobserved com-

---

[6] We use dummy variables as explanatory variables in the regression in order to mitigate the effects of outlier observations.

[7] The commission cost for institutional investors (at least for trading in U.S. equities) is customarily set on a cents per share basis, irrespective of the stock price level. For a given package, the less expensive broker is thus the one charging fewer cents per share. Nonetheless, the cheaper broker, if given packages in lower-priced stocks for execution, will appear to have a high percentage commission rate. In assessing the relation between commission cost and market impact cost across packages with different price levels, therefore, it is necessary to express the commission cost on a dollar, rather than on a percentage, basis.

Table VII
Regression Results

Regression estimates of the model,

$$r_i = \alpha + \beta C_i + \sum_{j=2}^{5} \delta_j S_{ij} + \sum_{j=2}^{7} \gamma_j D_{ij} + \sum_{j=2}^{37} \phi_j M_{ij} + \varepsilon_i$$

where r_i is the return from the opening price on the package's first day to the closing price on the package's last day; the return from the closing price on the package's last day to the closing price five days after; the impact cost relative to the opening price on the package's first day; the impact cost relative to the closing price five days after the package's last day. All returns and costs are in excess of the buy-and-hold return on a matching size decile control portfolio over the corresponding interval. C_i is the dollar commission cost; S_{ij} is a dummy variable for the package's classification by market capitalization; D_{ij} is a dummy variable for the package's classification by relative package size; M_{ij} is a dummy variable for the money manager. The equation is estimated separately for buys and for sells. A buy (sell) package in a stock is a case where the same money management firm executed successive purchases (sales) of the same stock, with a break of less than 5 days between successive trades. There are five classifications by market capitalization, corresponding to the quintiles of the distribution of value of outstanding equity at the end of the prior quarter for all New York Stock Exchange (NYSE) and American Stock Exchange (AMEX) stocks. There are seven classifications by relative package size corresponding to the 25th, 50th, 75th, 90th, 95th and 99th percentiles of the distribution within each size category of package principal value in relation to average daily volume over a prior 40-day period. The sample comprises all trades of NYSE and AMEX stocks by 37 institutional money management firms from July 1, 1986 to December 30, 1988 (excluding October 1987).

Panel A: Adjusted R^2 (in Percent) for Full Model, and Models With Each Set of Dummy Variables Excluded One Set at a Time. Results from the Equation for Sells are in Parentheses

	Price Impact		Execution Costs	
	Dependent Variable: Return (%) From		Dependent Variable: Cost (%) Relative to	
	Opening Price on First Day to Closing Price on Last Day	Closing Price on Last Day to Closing Price Five Days After Package	Opening Price on First Day	Closing Price Five Days After Package
Full model	4.69 (2.42)	0.54 (0.42)	7.01 (3.53)	0.40 (0.48)
Excluding manager effects	1.39 (0.84)	0.11 (0.13)	1.77 (0.96)	0.04 (0.19)
Excluding size effects	4.59 (2.30)	0.53 (0.38)	6.89 (3.25)	0.39 (0.43)
Excluding complexity effects	4.14 (2.37)	0.48 (0.37)	6.59 (3.49)	0.38 (0.38)

Panel B: Estimated Coefficients for Full Model for Buys and for Sells (in Parentheses)

Intercept	1.14* (−0.59)*	−0.29 (−0.64)*	0.83* (1.01)*	−0.01 (−0.24)
Commission	0.09 (−0.69)*	0.39 (−0.26)	0.09 (0.09)	−0.40 (−0.87)
Size				
2	−0.26* (0.29)*	0.29* (0.53)*	−0.27* (−0.30)*	−0.30* (0.53)*
3	−0.36* (0.57)*	0.23* (0.55)*	−0.29* (−0.51)*	−0.16 (0.62)*
4	−0.49* (0.68)*	0.30* (0.65)*	−0.36* (−0.65)*	−0.18* (0.70)*
(Largest) 5	−0.65* (0.66)*	0.32* (0.69)*	−0.48* (−0.75)*	−0.16 (0.62)*
Relative package size				
2	−0.02 (0.07)*	0.06 (−0.12)*	−0.01 (−0.11)*	−0.05 (−0.15)*
3	0.20* (−0.08)	0.04 (−0.05)	0.13* (−0.03)	−0.11* (−0.16)*
4	0.36* (−0.26)*	−0.12* (−0.00)	0.27* (0.08)*	0.03 (−0.18)*
5	0.74* (−0.28)*	−0.28* (0.15)*	0.55* (0.10)*	0.09 (−0.03)
6	1.18* (−0.32)*	−0.20* (0.34)*	0.86* (0.20)*	−0.12 (0.22)*
(Biggest) 7	1.47* (0.10)	−0.32* (0.39)*	1.05* (0.08)	−0.10 (0.57)*
Manager				
Difference between 90- and 10-percentiles[a]	1.48 (1.70)	0.68 (0.86)	1.34 (1.45)	0.67 (0.87)
Number of manager coefficients significant at 5% level	24 20	7 11	24 24	9 15

[a] The estimated regression coefficients for the dummy variables representing manager effects are ranked and the percentiles are calculated. The summary statistic reported in the table is the difference between the ninetieth and tenth percentiles of the set of 36 estimated coefficients.

* Denotes significance at the 5 percent level or better.

ponents of commissions. Commissions include payments for services unrelated to trade execution such as research services, and some brokers may also rebate part of the commission expenses in the form of "soft-dollar" services.

The results for the influence of firm size and package complexity in Panel B of Table VII generally parallel the findings from the previous section of this article, and from other work as well. Controlling for firm size and package complexity, considerable variation still exists across managers with respect to their impact costs. When the cost is measured relative to the opening price on the first day of a package, the difference between the top and bottom ten percent of managers for buys is 1.34 percent; the dispersion for sales is similar at 1.45 percent. The spread between the top and bottom ten percent of managers by costs relative to the post-execution benchmarks is lower.[8]

B. The Cost of Immediacy

We conjecture that the differences across money managers observed in Table VII stem mainly from differences in their patience or demand for immediacy in trading. Other things equal, a less patient trader will tend to incur larger impact costs, perhaps because he perceives his information to be highly perishable. A manager's degree of patience is difficult to quantify.[9] Nevertheless, a money manager's demand for immediacy is very likely to be related to observable characteristics such as the manager's investment style and portfolio turnover rate. Data on investment style (value versus growth) and on portfolio turnover are available for 16 of our 37 money management organizations. Other things equal, a portfolio manager with a longer investment horizon (low turnover) is considered a patient investor and will tend to have a lower demand for liquidity. An investor for whom immediacy is more important (such as a growth-oriented manager) would tend to have higher impact cost.

We classify managers either by their style (Panel A, Table VIII), or into two equally-sized groups on the basis of average portfolio turnover rate (Panel B), and compare the average round-trip principal-weighted returns achieved by the two groups. In Panel A, the differences between the two groups are striking: growth-oriented managers incur a round-trip cost relative to the first open of 0.70 percent, while value-oriented managers experience a benefit of 0.40 percent, so that the difference amounts to a full 1.10 percent. Similar differences also exist between growth-oriented and value-oriented managers in terms of their price impact from the first day's open to the last day's close. If

---

[8] Since the opening price on the first day of a package is known if and when a manager begins to trade, managers might differ in several respects: their skill in seeking out liquidity, ability to trade in advance of information, as well as how they react to price changes after the opening price. If, on the other hand, the benchmark price is not established until after a manager has finished trading, the dispersion across managers would be expected to be smaller.

[9] Other influences on price impact or execution cost such as the competence of the portfolio manager and trading desk, as well as the management firm's investment in trading facilities, are not observable by us.

Table VIII
Average Round-Trip Principal-Weighted Price Impact Costs and Returns (in Percent; Standard Deviation in Parentheses) of Money Management Firms, Classified by Investment Style (Panel A), by Portfolio Turnover Rate (Panel B), and by Package Length (Panel C)

Price impact costs and returns are calculated for each package, and a principal-weighted average cost or return is calculated over all packages executed by each money management firm. In Panels A and B, 16 money management firms with available data on investment style and portfolio turnover rate are classified into two groups: by investment style in Panel A (9 growth and 7 value), or by whether portfolio turnover rate is higher or lower than the median turnover rate, in Panel B. This table reports the average costs or returns in each category of money management firms. For Panel C, in each size-complexity classification of Table V, all active money managers (out of a total of 37) are divided into two equally sized groups based on the average length of their packages. The mean reported in Panel C for each category is the weighted average across all the size-complexity classifications (using the relative dollar value traded in each classification as weights). Standard deviations across all the observations within each category of money managers are reported in parentheses. A buy (sell) package in a stock is a case where the same money management firm executed successive purchases (sales) of the same stock, with a break of less than 5 days between successive trades. Round-trip costs (returns) are the costs (returns) for buy packages plus (minus) the costs (returns) on sell packages. The sample comprises all trades of New York Stock Exchange (NYSE) and American Stock Exchange (AMEX) stocks by 16 institutional money management firms from July 1, 1986 to 6 December 30, 1988 (excluding October 1987).

	Cost (%) Relative to: (+ is cost, − is benefit)		Return (%) From[c]		
	Opening Price on First Day of Package[a]	Closing Price 5 Days After Last Day of Package[b]	From Open on First Day to Close on Last Day of Package	From Close on Last Day to Close 5 Days After Package	From Close on Last Day to Close 20 Days After Package
Panel A: Classified by Investment Style					
Growth	0.70 (1.86)	−0.05 (0.26)	0.88 (1.89)	−0.09 (0.35)	−0.20 (0.67)
Value	−0.40 (1.42)	0.04 (0.61)	−0.71 (1.63)	0.20 (0.65)	0.34 (0.37)
Panel B: Classified by Portfolio Turnover Rate					
High turnover	0.87 (1.33)	0.07 (0.46)	0.78 (1.52)	−0.11 (0.47)	0.30 (0.44)
Low turnover	−0.49 (2.09)	−0.13 (0.43)	−0.45 (2.22)	0.19 (0.56)	0.20 (0.55)
Panel C: Classified by Package Length					
Short packages	1.44 (0.92)	0.13 (0.18)	1.56 (0.85)	−0.23 (0.21)	0.17 (0.28)
Long packages	0.79 (0.65)	0.02 (0.23)	0.83 (0.86)	−0.02 (0.27)	0.47 (0.21)

[a] Returns are computed from the opening price on a package's first day to each trade in the package; the return for a package is the principal-weighted average of these returns across all trades in the package. Returns are in excess of the buy-and-hold returns on a matching size decile control portfolio over the corresponding interval.

[b] Returns are computed from each trade in a package to the closing price five days after the package's last day; the return for a package is the principal-weighted average of these returns across all trades in the package. Returns are in excess of the buy-and-hold returns on a matching size decile control portfolio over the corresponding interval.

[c] Returns are in excess of the buy-and-hold returns on a matching size decile control portfolio over the corresponding interval.

[d] Package length is the number of days in the package on which trading occurred.

growth managers trade with greater impatience and give up a temporary price concession for greater immediacy, while value managers trade more patiently and supply immediacy to other investors, then the price reversals should be larger following the packages of growth-oriented managers. There is indeed a relatively large difference between the 0.09 percent reversal following the packages executed by growth-oriented managers, compared to the 0.20 percent continuation subsequent to value-oriented managers' packages. The larger market impact incurred by growth-oriented managers might be justified if their trades subsequently experience higher returns. In fact, the short-term performance in the twenty-day period following the package is actually somewhat lower for growth-oriented managers than for value-oriented managers.

Dramatic differences also arise when managers are classified into high- and low-turnover groups (Panel B): managers with high turnover rates experience higher costs and larger price impact across-the-board than do managers with low turnover rates. In particular, there is a difference of 0.30 percent between the price reversal following packages executed by high-turnover managers and the price continuation following packages executed by low-turnover managers. These findings are consistent with the notion that growth-oriented managers and managers with high turnover pay a price concession for greater immediacy.

Since the analysis in Panels A and B of Table VIII is based on a relatively small subset of our managers, the results are only suggestive of the cost of immediacy in trading. Moreover, the results do not control for differences across managers in the size of their trades, or the capitalization of the traded stocks. Panel C of Table VIII provides an additional clue as to the cost of immediacy. Within each of the 35 categories of firm size and trade complexity as described in Table V, we calculate the principal-weighted average impact cost and length across all the packages of each money manager. Package length is defined as the number of trading days on which trades are executed over the course of a package. All the managers in a size-complexity classification are then divided into two equally-sized groups on the basis of the average package length. We then average the cost measures associated with each group of managers across all the size-complexity classifications, using the number of dollars traded in each classification as weights. The results thus signify the average market impact cost for short packages (denoting high demand for immediacy) and long packages (denoting low demand for immediacy) for similarly-sized trades in similarly-sized firms.

The results in Panel C strongly confirm the cost differences between the packages executed by relatively impatient managers versus relatively patient managers. Impact costs are lower for lengthier packages: the cost relative to the pre-execution benchmark for long packages is 0.79 percent, compared to the cost for short packages of 1.44 percent; the cost relative to the post-execution benchmark is also lower for long packages. In addition, the price pressure from the first open to the last close is lower for lengthier packages, as is the post-package price reversal. All in all, Table VIII provides evidence suggesting that price impact and execution costs are heavily influenced by the trader's demand for immediacy in trading, as proxied by investment style, turnover rate and package length. Further research to spell out the precise nature of these linkages is clearly called for.

VII. Conclusions

Multi-day trade packages make up a common and sizeable portion of institutional equity trading. Only twenty percent of the dollar value traded in our sample is completed within a day, while more than half of the dollar value traded requires four or more trading days for execution. This finding suggests that the price impact and execution cost of institutional trades is best analyzed at the level of trade packages. Our results are based on an analysis of institutions' actual trading behavior on a very large sample of transactions. Some caution in interpreting our results for packages is warranted, however, since our measure of a package is based on observed trades rather than the ex ante order.

As it turns out, the estimates of the price impact of institutional trades are substantially higher when trades are evaluated not individually but in the broader context of a package. Buy packages are associated with a principal-weighted average price change of almost 1 percent from the open on the package's first day to the close on the last day. The corresponding price change of -0.3 percent for sell packages is less dramatic, but still sizeable. By way of comparison, if the analysis is conducted at the level of individual transactions (Chan and Lakonishok (1993)), the principal-weighted price change from the open to the close on the trade date is 0.34 percent for buys and -0.04 percent for sells. The overall price impact of purchases and sales is not symmetric, echoing earlier evidence based on individual transactions (Kraus and Stoll (1972a), Holthausen, Leftwich, and Mayers (1987, 1990), Keim and Madhavan (1991), Chan and Lakonishok (1993)).

Our results on market impact cost, when measured for packages, are also substantially higher than comparable results for individual trades, including both block and nonblock trades in Chan and Lakonishok (1993). The round-trip impact cost for packages reaches 1.32 percent when the opening price of the first day is the benchmark and the packages are principal weighted. Giving the same weight to each package would lower the price impact to 0.59 percent. When post-execution benchmarks are used, the average round-trip impact costs are less than 0.10 percent.

There is, of course, no single unambiguous definition of market impact cost. Our various measures differ with respect to the choice of a benchmark price, and each benchmark has some merit and some problems. For example, the opening price as a benchmark can be "gamed" with relative ease; only trades for less than the open will be executed. We have money managers in our sample who are making money on execution, based on the opening price: they buy below the open and sell above the open. However, based on a post-execution benchmark, some of these money managers perform poorly and several days after the package are sorry for having done the trade (in the sense that they buy above or sell below the post-execution benchmark). Clearly, buying below the open is not good enough if one day later the price is lower than the price at which the trades were executed. Accordingly, the execution performance of a money manager cannot be summarized by one single cost measure; instead it is necessary to conduct a comprehensive examination at the level of packages.

Regardless of the specific cost measure, we find that market impact differs greatly across money managers. Indeed, our regression analysis suggests that the importance of firm size and trade complexity as determinants of price impact and execution cost pales beside the importance of the identity of the money manager behind the trade. Some preliminary evidence suggests that the differences across money managers are, in turn, related to their different degrees of urgency to trade, as indicated by such variables as investment style and portfolio turnover. Costs tend to be generally higher for growth-oriented managers than for value-oriented managers, and are higher for managers with high turnover rates.

The idea that a higher demand for immediacy in trade execution tends to be associated with a larger price impact or execution cost is not new. For example, Loeb (1983) measures trading cost as the spreads quoted for immediate execution of orders of varying size. It would be naive, of course, to think that an institutional investor would bring its entire order to market at once and bear the cost of immediate execution. Instead, as we have documented in this article, an institutional order is likely to be worked over a period of several days. Only by tracking the behavior of the stock price around and during the entire sequence of trades can any reliable measure of price impact or execution cost be obtained.

REFERENCES

Beebower, Gilbert, and William Priest, 1980, The tricks of the trade, *Journal of Portfolio Management* 6, 36–42.

Berkowitz, Stephen, Louis Finney, and Dennis Logue, 1988, *The investment performance of corporate pension plans* (Quorum Books, New York, NY).

Blume, Marshall E., and Robert F. Stambaugh, 1983, Biases in computed returns: An application to the size effect, *Journal of Financial Economics* 12, 387–404.

Brinson, Gary L., Randolph Hood, and Gilbert Beebower, 1986, Determinants of portfolio performance, *Financial Analysts Journal* 42, 39–44.

Chan, Louis K. C., and Josef Lakonishok, 1993, Institutional trades and intra-day stock price behavior, *Journal of Financial Economics* 33, 173–199.

De Long, J. Bradford, Andrei Shleifer, Lawrence H. Summers, and Robert J. Waldmann, 1990, Positive feedback investment strategies and destabilizing rational speculation, *Journal of Finance* 45, 379–395.

Easley, David, and Maureen O'Hara, 1987, Price, trade size, and information in securities markets, *Journal of Financial Economics* 19, 69–90.

Fama, Eugene, 1991, Efficient capital markets: II, *Journal of Finance* 46, 1575–1617.

Hausman, Jerry, Andrew Lo, and Craig MacKinlay, 1992, An ordered probit analysis of transaction stock prices, *Journal of Financial Economics* 31, 319–379.

Holthausen, Robert, Richard Leftwich, and David Mayers, 1987, The effect of large block transactions on security prices: A cross-sectional analysis, *Journal of Financial Economics* 19, 237–268.

Holthausen, Robert, Richard Leftwich, and David Mayers, 1990, Large-block transactions, the speed of response, and temporary and permanent stock-price effects, *Journal of Financial Economics* 26, 71–95.

Keim, Donald, and Ananth Madhavan, 1991, The upstairs market for large-block transactions: Analysis and measurement of price effects, Working paper, University of Pennsylvania.

Keim, Donald, and Ananth Madhavan, 1993, Anatomy of the trading process: Empirical evidence on the motivation, execution and performance of institutional equity trades, Working paper, University of Pennsylvania.

Kraus, Alan, and Hans Stoll, 1972a, Price impacts of block trading on the New York Stock Exchange, *Journal of Finance* 27, 569–588.

Kraus, Alan, and Hans Stoll, 1972b, Parallel trading by institutional investors, *Journal of Financial and Quantitative Analysis* 7, 2107–2138.

Kyle, Albert, 1985, Continuous auctions and insider trading, *Econometrica* 53, 1315–1335.

Lakonishok, Josef, Andrei Shleifer, and Robert Vishny, 1992, The structure and performance of the money management industry, *Brookings Papers on Economic Activity: Microeconomics*, 339–391.

Lakonishok, Josef, and Seymour Smidt, 1986, Volume for winners and losers: Taxation and other motives for stock trading, *Journal of Finance* 41, 951–976.

Lee, Charles, and Mark Ready, 1991, Inferring trade direction from intraday data, *Journal of Finance* 46, 733–746.

Loeb, Thomas, 1983, Trading cost: The critical link between investment information and results, *Financial Analysts Journal* 39, 39–44.

Perold, André, and Erik Sirri, 1993, The cost of international equity trading, working paper, Harvard Business School.

Petersen, Mitchell, and Steven Umlauf, 1991, An empirical examination of the intraday behavior of the NYSE specialist, Working paper, University of Chicago.

Scharfstein, David S., and Jeremy C. Stein, 1990, Herd behavior and investment, *American Economic Review* 80, 465–479.

Stoll, Hans, 1993, *Equity trading costs*, Institute of Chartered Financial Analysts, Charlottesville, VA.

Part II
Theory of Market Design

Structural Organization of Secondary Markets: Clearing Frequency, Dealer Activity and Liquidity Risk

KENNETH D. GARBADE and WILLIAM L. SILBER*

1. Introduction

A FINANCIAL INSTRUMENT IS commonly considered liquid if it has at least one of two attributes. First, the instrument may be traded in a market with a sufficient number of participants to make feasible purchases and sales on short notice at prices near the contemporaneous equilibrium value of the instrument. Thus, common stocks actively traded on the New York Stock Exchange are considered more liquid than most municipal bonds. There exists an almost purely competitive market for the former securities, whereas secondary market sales of municipals often require substantial price discounts if they are to be completed quickly. Second, an asset is regarded as liquid if its equilibrium value is unlikely to change substantially over a given interval of time. Even though short-term municipals do not trade in an active secondary market, their values are not as volatile as those of common stock issues. A seller of a short-term municipal can therefore spend time searching for a favorable trading partner without bearing excessive price risk during the search process.

In this paper we show that the two aspects of liquidity just noted, the number of market participants and equilibrium price volatility, are important determinants of the structural characteristics of secondary markets. The key structural characteristics are the frequency of market clearing and the level and effect of dealer participation. The relationships between these characteristics and their determinants are derived using a concept of market performance which focuses on liquidity risk. This measure of risk is defined as the variance of the difference between the equilibrium value of an asset at the time a market participant decides to trade and the transaction price ultimately realized. We also show that this measure of liquidity risk encompasses both aspects of liquidity noted above.

Clearing Frequency of a Market

Secondary markets differ with respect to clearing frequency. For example, the New York Stock Exchange operated as a twice-daily call auction before the Civil

---

* The authors are Associate Professor and Professor, respectively, of Economics and Finance at the Graduate School of Business Administration, New York University. We are indebted to William J. Baumol whose comments sparked the development of this paper. Financial Support from NSF Grant #RDA75-17953 is gratefully acknowledged.

War. Modern examples of periodic call markets include the Paris Bourse, Eiteman and Eiteman, [3] and the Tel Aviv Stock Exchange, Silber, [15]. At the other extreme, since the Civil War clearings on the New York Stock Exchange can be considered continuous. The liquidity risk of trading a particular financial asset depends on the frequency of market clearings. To see this effect, consider that our price variance measure may be separated conceptually into two components. First is the variance of the change in the equilibrium value of an asset between the time an investor decides to trade and the time the trade is completed. This component of risk is clearly an increasing function of the time taken to complete a trade. Its presence creates a demand for prompt order execution, i.e., frequent or continuous clearing.

The second part of liquidity risk is the variance of the difference between contemporaneous transactions prices and equilibrium values. Transactions prices, i.e., market clearing prices, can differ from equilibrium prices when potential participants in a market do not enter orders. Except for the timeless and spatially integrated world of a Walrasian auction, market clearing prices are always determined by subsets of transactors. Thus, market clearing prices will, in general, differ from the equilibrium price derived from a Walrasian auction as a consequence of the temporal fragmentation of potential market participants. Ceteris paribus, the longer the time between clearings, the greater the number of participants in a given clearing. Thus, transactions prices in markets with frequent or continuous clearings are more likely to exhibit transient random deviations from current equilibrium values than are prices in markets with less frequent and more consolidated clearings.[1] To reduce the deviations of transactions prices from equilibrium values one would prefer to execute orders in consolidated markets with infrequent clearings.

The optimal clearing frequency of a market is that time interval which minimizes total liquidity risk, i.e., the sum of the variance of equilibrium price changes (an increasing function of the time interval) and the variance of transient random differences between transactions prices and equilibrium values (a decreasing function of the time interval). We expect that observed market structures reflect the optimal clearing frequencies of different securities. This follows from the assumption that investors will trade in those markets organized to minimize their exposure to liquidity risk.

In section 3 we develop a model of the behavior of securities prices in a public market, and then consider the implications of that model for market organization. In particular, we show that the optimal frequency of market clearings is an increasing function of the equilibrium price volatility of a security and an increasing function of the number of market participants. The role of technological innovations in expanding the size of a market is also considered.

---

[1] The Walrasian auction assumes that all potential transactors have instantaneous access to the market whenever the market clears, i.e., whenever transactions are executed. In this paper we consider the consequences of clearings with incomplete investor participation. The New York Stock Exchange noted [13, p. 1] that, "Dispersion of orders over time can result in temporary imbalances of supply and demand unrelated to real changes in values." In a companion paper we expect to demonstrate that dispersion of orders over multiple trading centers, i.e., spatial fragmentation, can be analyzed in a fashion similar to that presented here.

Dealer Participation

Another important characteristic of a market is the presence of professional securities dealers who trade against transient imbalances in public purchase and sale orders. We show that dealer participation in a market increases the optimal frequency of clearing or, looked at another way, reduces the length of time typically required to complete a transaction. We also show that dealer participation reduces the liquidity risk born by public transactors. Thus, investors may be expected to prefer to trade in dealer markets rather than what may be defined as purely public markets.[2] We suggest that dealers are more active the larger the size of the market and the lower the volatility of equilibrium prices. Thus, these two aspects of a financial instrument affect the frequency of market clearings and the level of liquidity risk both directly and indirectly through dealer activity.

In section 4 we develop a model of how dealers might behave in the market introduced in section 3, and we then present the implications of their behavior for optimal clearing frequencies (increased) and for the magnitude of the liquidity risk borne by public transactors (decreased). Before proceeding with the formal analysis, the next section discusses a number of historical and contemporaneous examples of alternative forms of market organization. These illustrations should motivate the broad conclusions which flow from the analysis of sections 3 and 4.

II. Comparative Market Organization

The analytical results derived below suggest that as a market becomes larger, or as securities prices become more volatile, investors will be led to prefer exchange mechanisms which provide for faster execution of their orders. In our terms this means more frequent market clearings, approximating, in the limit, continuous trading. The institutional evolution of the New York Stock Exchange (NYSE) illustrates clearly these principles.

The Exchange traces its ancestry to a meeting of securities brokers held in May, 1792 to formalize trading practices in the securities markets of New York City. The brokers organized their market as a periodic auction, usually with a morning session and an afternoon session. Securities were called for trading sequentially, and buyers and sellers competed collectively to get the best price on their orders. The basic structure of periodic auctions on the New York Stock and Exchange Board (as the market was known after March, 1817) lasted until the Civil War.

With the advent of the Civil War, securities prices became measurably more volatile as a consequence of the flow of war-related information. As our model suggests, this increased volatility led to a demand for opportunities for more frequent trading, Sobel, [16]. When the governors of the New York Board refused to introduce a continuous market during the war, trading largely moved onto off-board markets. Sobel [16] notes that, "there were literally dozens of separate trading groups in operation by 1865...." The most important of these was the Open Board of Stock Brokers, organized in 1864, with continuous trading between the hours of 8:30 AM and 5:00 PM. By the middle of 1865 the volume of

---

[2] It is interesting to observe that the the Securities and Exchange Commission considered, in the 1930s, the feasibility of prohibiting dealer activity on the New York Stock Exchange. See Sobel [17, pp. 22-23]. Our analysis suggests the initiative was misguided.

transactions on the NYSE (renamed in 1863) was only a tenth the volume on the Open Board, Sobel, [16]. The demand for trading facilities during the Civil War was so great that there even existed an Evening Exchange, so that purchases and sales of securities could be completed in New York City at any time of the day or night, Sobel, [16].

Following the Civil War the Open Board and the NYSE continued with their respective trading practices. However, in 1868 and 1869 the governors of the two markets negotiated a merger which was ultimately concluded on May 8, 1869. The consolidated NYSE employed both discrete call auctions and continuous trading, but by 1870 the call auctions had become relatively unimportant (they were formally eliminated for stocks in 1882).

Securities prices became relatively stable with the end of the Civil War, yet continuous trading survived and in fact flourished as the main form of secondary market organization. The explanation is found in a series of technological innovations which expanded the number of participants with ready access to the market. The first innovation was the stock ticker, invented in 1867 by E. A. Calahan and put into operation at the end of that year by the Gold and Stock Telegraph Company, Hotchkiss, [9]. The ticker was important because it permitted market participants located away from the Exchange floor to follow even a continuous market with virtually no time delay. The ticker fostered continuous trading because it created a larger number of fully informed market participants.

Although tickers provided price information quickly to participants located away from the floor of the NYSE, the devices had no capability for transmitting orders back to the floor. Orders continued to be sent via general telegraph companies, and suffered the attending delays between origination and execution. These delays were largely eliminated with the introduction of private brokers wires. The first such wire opened in 1873 between the uptown head office of a New York securities firm and its downtown office in the financial district, Meeker, [11]. This private wire (actually, a telegraph line leased for private use from a general telegraph company and operated by the leasee) facilitated the transmission of orders to the floor of the Exchange by eliminating the necessity to deliver a telegraph message to an uptown office and to redeliver the message from a downtown receiving office. In subsequent years brokers wires were extended to firms with offices outside New York City.

The introduction of the stock ticker and brokers wires expanded the size of the market for NYSE-listed issues in the sense of increasing the number of participants with rapid access to the floor. Meeker [11] noted the expanded scope of the New York markets made possible by technology when he observed that, "..... the Stock Exchange system [including wire houses and tickers] has practically annihilated the considerations of time and space in the operation of America's principal securities market".[3] Our model suggests that the increased size of the NYSE markets was a factor contributing to the dominance of continuous trading even in the relatively stable post-Civil War environment.

The organization of the municipal debt markets provides a contemporary example of the effect of equilibrium price volatility and market size on the

---

[3] Garbade and Silber [7] provide a more detailed evaluation of the impact of telegraphic communication on financial market integration. Garbade [4] evaluates similar developments in the government securities market during the 1970s.

Organization of Secondary Markets

organizational structure of a market. As debt instruments bearing (outside of exceptional cases) little credit risk, municipals exhibit relatively low equilibrium price volatility over intervals of time up to a few days. There are, however, an enormous number of municipal issues outstanding, many in issue sizes no greater than a few million dollars. The number of market participants actively seeking to buy or sell a given issue at a particular point in time is quite small. The low price volatility and limited market size characteristic of municipals leads us to expect that the time required to complete a favorable transaction is relatively long or, in our terms, that the municipal market clears relatively infrequently. This is in fact the case. Institutional traders of municipal bonds (bank trust departments) rely on bond brokers to locate potentially compatible trading partners. The traders call their purchase and sale interests into as many as forty bond brokers in the morning and then wait until they receive replies in the afternoon before they choose the best bids and offerings. Their behavior appears very much like a process of once-daily market clearings.

III. A Model of a Public Market

The historical experience reported in the preceeding section supports the intuitive analysis of liquidity risk and market organization discussed in section 1. We now present a formal model that can be used to derive more precise relationships between liquidity risk and market organization. Our model assumes an exchange structure characterized by periodic clearings, such as the New York Stock Exchange before 1869 or the contemporary gold fixings market in London, Jarecki, [10]. The time between clearings is an unspecified variable whose optimal value is to be determined. Markets in which securities transactions are completed quickly, such as the present day NYSE, can be considered a limiting case where the time between clearings becomes small, approximating continuous trading in the limit. To focus attention on the issues of immediate interest, we consider here a market in which there are only public transactors. The analysis of a market in which dealers also participate is more complex and is deferred to section 4.

The process by which public orders enter the market is simply specified. Suppose there are K public transactors participating in a given clearing, each with an endowment of E of the security. Each transactor tenders his full endowment to the market. This behavior is justified by the assumption that the market is perfectly competitive, so that no transactor perceives his activities as affecting the market clearing price. The gross demand schedule of the ith transactor as a function of the market clearing price p is given by:

$$D_i(p) = E + a(r_i - p) \qquad a > 0 \qquad (1)$$

r_i is the reservation price of the ith participant. If the market clears at a price greater than r_i that transactor will be a net seller of securities, so that $D_i < E$. If it clears at a price below r_i he will be a buyer. For simplicity we assume the values of the endowment E and the slope a of the demand schedule are common to all transactors.

Since there are only public transactors in the present model the market will clear at the price which equates aggregate public supply with aggregate demand, or when:

$$KE = \sum_{i=1}^{K} [E + a(r_i - p)] \tag{2}$$

The market clearing price thus equals the mean reservation price of the public participants. Let r denote that market clearing price:

$$r = K^{-1} \sum_{i=1}^{K} r_i \tag{3}$$

The model is completed by specifying how investor reservation prices are related to each other in the same market meeting, and through time in different meetings. We assume there exists, at time t, an unobservable equilibrium value m_t for the security, which is not necessarily equal to the market clearing price. The reservation price of a given transactor at time t is a normally distributed random variable with mean m_t and variance σ^2. The difference between m_t and the reservation prices of different investors are uncorrelated. Let r_t denote the mean reservation price at time t which, according to the discussion preceeding equation (3), means that r_t is the market-clearing or transactions price at that time. Equation (3) implies the distribution of r_t is:

$$r_t = m_t + f_t \tag{4a}$$

$$f_t \sim N(0, \sigma^2/K) \tag{4b}$$

For simplicity we assume f_t is a serially uncorrelated process.

As K grows large the distribution of r_t collapses towards a singular distribution at m_t. It is therefore natural to speak of m_t as the equilibrium value of the asset, since the market clearing price r_t approaches m_t in probability as the number of participants in the market at time t grows large. Our definition of equilibrium value agrees with its usual definition as the market clearing price when the number of participants active in the market is large.

The equilibrium value of the asset is assumed to evolve continuously through time in a random walk. The change in equilibrium value from one market clearing to the next therefore follows the process:

$$m_t = m_{t-1} + e_t \tag{5a}$$

$$e_t \sim N(0, \tau\psi^2) \tag{5b}$$

ψ^2 is the variance of the change in equilibrium value per unit time. τ is the time between market clearings. e_t is a serially uncorrelated process and is uncorrelated with the random process f_t in equation (4a). One could make other assumptions on the dynamics of equilibrium value, including secular drift, without altering the results of interest in this paper.

We assume that over an interval of time of length τ there will be $w\tau$ transactors entering the market. w is the time rate of exposure of transactors to the market. In general, w will vary across securities as a function of the extent of trading interest in those securities. It will also depend on the sophistication of communication technologies.[4] We pointed out above that the innovations of stock tickers

---

[4] The extent of trading in a security should be determined, in part, endogenously, as in Garbade and Silber [6]. For our purposes, this is an unnecessary complication since we are interested primarily in the impact of exogenous changes in market size such as those due to technological innovations.

Organization of Secondary Markets

and private brokers wires expanded significantly the number of investors with ready access to the NYSE. This expansion is represented in the present model by a larger value of w.

If the time between market clearings is τ, there will be $K = w\tau$ participants in each clearing. Smaller values of τ imply smaller markets in each clearing. Although the foregoing model was formally developed for discrete values of K, the equations remain valid for the continuum case as well if we interpret K as a scale parameter characterizing the size of a clearing. From equation (4) we have that the transient difference between the clearing price r_t and the contemporaneous equilibrium value m_t is:

$$r_t = m_t + f_t \tag{6a}$$

$$f_t \sim N(0, \sigma^2/w\tau) \tag{6b}$$

The change in equilibrium value between clearings is given by equation (5).

Liquidity Risk and the Optimal Clearing Frequency of a Public Market

Using the model of equations (5) and (6) we can now derive an expression for liquidity risk as a function of the price volatility of the asset being traded and the size of its market. We then determine the market structure which minimizes this liquidity risk.

Liquidity risk is defined as the variance of the difference between the equilibrium value (m) of an asset at the time an investor decides to trade and the transaction price (r) ultimately realized on that trade. The present model assumes that the typical investor makes the decision to trade at time $t - \frac{1}{2}$ for execution at time t. His liquidity risk is then:

$$\text{Var}[r_t - m_{t-1/2}] = \text{Var}[(r_t - m_t) + (m_t - m_{t-1/2})] \tag{7}$$

We can treat the random term $e_t = m_t - m_{t-1}$ in equation (5a) as the sum of two independent random terms, $m_t - m_{t-1/2}$ and $m_{t-1/2} - m_{t-1}$, each written with variance $\frac{1}{2} \tau \psi^2$. Neither of these terms is correlated with $r_t - m_t = f_t$. From equations (5) and (6), the liquidity risk V_p of an investor trading in a public market is then:

$$V_p = \sigma^2/w\tau + \frac{1}{2} \tau \psi^2 \tag{8}$$

As shown in Figure 1, liquidity risk is a function of the time τ between clearings for two reasons. First, a larger value of τ leads to more participants in a given metting and, based on equation (6), this reduces the transient deviation of the clearing price from the contemporaneous equilibrium value. The induced reduction in liquidity risk is shown in the first term of equation (8). It is this effect which leads transactors to prefer to trade in infrequently clearing, consolidated, markets (or to spend time waiting for the arrival of compatible trading partners). They bear less risk of getting a transiently unfavorable price in such markets. However, larger values of τ, according to equation (5), increase the exposure of a transactor to the market risk of changes in equilibrium values. This is represented by the second term of equation (8).

From equation (8) it is easy to show that the time between clearings which

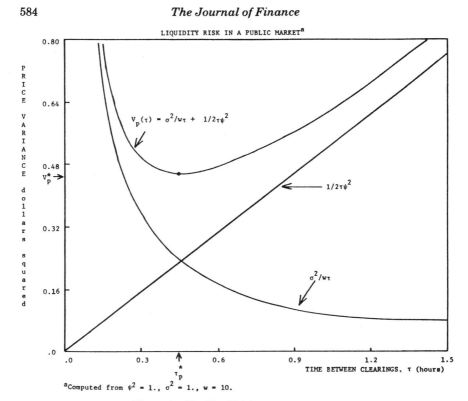

Figure 1. Liquidity Risk in a Public Market[a]

minimizes total liquidity risk is:

$$\tau_p^* = (2/w)^{1/2}\sigma/\psi \qquad (9)$$

Equation (9) shows that the optimal time between clearings is a decreasing function of the size of the market, represented by w, and a decreasing function of the equilibrium price volatility of the security, represented by ψ. A shorter time between clearings means more frequent clearings. In the limit, equation (9) indicates that clearings become almost continuous as market size increases and as equilibrium price volatility increases.

These results yield conjectures regarding real world observations once we assume that investors prefer to trade in markets which minimize their exposure to liquidity risk. The dominant exchange structure for a security will reflect the risk-minimizing clearing frequency for that security. In terms of our previous illustrations, the demand during the Civil War for trading in markets which cleared more than twice a day can be explained as a response to the increased volatility of securities prices (larger ψ). The survival of continuous markets after the Civil War can be attributed to the effect of stock tickers and brokers wires in enlarging the geographic scope of those markets (larger w). The same analysis also provides an explanation for the observation that most transactions in actively traded common stock issues are today completed quickly (their high price volatility implies a small optimal time to clear the order), while favorable transactions in thinly traded municipals with stable equilibrium values may take up to several days to complete.

The minimum liquidity risk borne in trading an asset is the value of V_p in equation (8) evaluated at $\tau = \tau_p^*$. That minimum risk is:

$$V_p^* = \sigma\psi(2/w)^{1/2} \qquad (10)$$

Recall, from section 1, that an asset is commonly considered liquid if it trades in a large-sized market or if it has a relatively stable equilibrium value. These two dimensions of liquidity are captured in the expression for V_p^*. In particular, V_p^* is a decreasing function of market size, represented by w, and an increasing function of price volatility, represented by ψ. This shows why actively traded volatile stocks and inactively traded short-term debt instruments with stable prices can both be considered liquid assets. Note, however, that the optimal times taken to execute transactions in the two instruments will be quite different, and that the organization of their respective exchange markets will consequently differ.

IV. Dealer Activity in a Public Market

If participation in a market is restricted to the public transactors identified in the model of section 3, the market clearing price r_t will evolve through time as a random walk with additive and serially uncorrelated transient deviations in each clearing (see equations (5) and (6)). It can be shown, Garbade and Lieber, [5] that clearing prices in such a market will exhibit a reversal structure, so that a price increase, $r_t > r_{t-1}$, would be expected to follow a decline, $r_{t-1} < r_{t-2}$, and conversely. Such reversals imply the existence of profit opportunities. We first consider how market participants can exploit these opportunities in their trading and then turn to the effect of their actions on liquidity risk and market organization.

From equation (6) we have that the clearing price in a public market will sometimes be greater and sometimes smaller than the contemporaneous equilibrium value of the asset, but that the former is an unbiased estimator of the latter. There exists, however, an estimator of m_t with a variance smaller than that of r_t. This creates an incentive for transactors to use this estimator and to enter the market as buyers when r_t is smaller than their estimate of the current equilibrium value and as sellers when it is larger. We first describe the estimation algorithm. For expositional convenience we refer to those who trade on the basis of the algorithm as dealers. There is, however, no reason why any public transactor could not function as a dealer in addition to entering his own orders according to the demand schedule of equation (1). After describing the algorithm we develop the characteristics of a market which includes both dealer and public transactors.

Recursive Estimation of Equilibrium Value

As an estimator of m_t, r_t uses only the most current observation on the market clearing price. However, because successive clearing prices have a temporal dependence, one can estimate m_t more efficiently using the entire past sequence of observations on r_t. The resulting estimation algorithm is known as Kalman filtering, Athans, [1]; Sage and Melsa, [14].

Let $\hat{m}_t$ denote the estimate of m_t based on the observations $(r_t, r_{t-1}, r_{t-2}, \cdots)$, i.e., based on observations of the mean reservation prices up to and including time t. It is shown in an appendix that this estimator follows the recursive process:

$$\hat{m}_t = \hat{m}_{t-1} + G[r_t - \hat{m}_{t-1}] \tag{11a}$$

where:

$$G = 2\tau\psi^2/[\tau\psi^2 + (\tau^2\psi^4 + 4\psi^2\sigma^2/w)^{1/2}] \tag{11b}$$

$\hat{m}_t$ is an unbiased estimator of m_t with estimation variance S where:

$$S = [(\tau^2\psi^4 + 4\psi^2\sigma^2/w)^{1/2} - \tau\psi^2]/2 \tag{11c}$$

The Kalman gain parameter G is bounded from above by unity and is an increasing function of τ, the time between market clearings, and w, the time rate of exposure of public transactors to the market. The estimation variance S is strictly less than $\sigma^2/w\tau$ and approaches that value as either w or τ increase. This shows that $\hat{m}_t$ is more efficient than r_t as an estimator of the equilibrium value m_t at time t.

The Effect of Dealer Activity on Market Clearing Prices

We now show the consequences of dealer trading based on the above algorithm for estimating the equilibrium value of a security. To avoid complications to the analysis we assume the mean reservation price r_t of public investors is observable, even when dealer activity forces a divergence between r_t and the market clearing price.[5] We also assume that dealers as well as public transactors perceive the market as perfectly competitive.

Let $\hat{m}_t$ be the estimate of the equilibrium value of the asset at time t from equation (11a) and let p_t be the market clearing price at time t. All trades at time t are executed at the clearing price. The aggregate gross dealer demand for securities is assumed to be:

$$Q_t = c(\hat{m}_t - p_t) \qquad c > 0 \tag{12}$$

This demand schedule may be a summation of the demand schedules of many dealers. For the present analysis we take c, the magnitude of the dealers' response to discrepancies between their estimate of equilibrium and the market clearing price, as given. In fact, c would be determined competitively by the risk-adjusted rate of return on dealer capital. We expect c to be larger for securities with a large number of active public transactors (w) and for securities with low price volatility (ψ), since both conditions would imply smaller risk exposure of dealer capital.[6]

---

[5] For dealers (or stock exchange specialists) this might be quite reasonable given the flow of public orders seen directly.

[6] The Special Study of the Securities Markets [18] reports that specialists (p. 86–87) and floor traders (p. 205–207, 220–221) are more active in heavily traded issues than in thinly traded issues. This concurs with our conjecture that c is an increasing function of w.

Organization of Secondary Markets

At time t the securities brought by dealers to the market are their positions Q_{t-1} from the preceeding market meeting. Since the market is competitive, no dealer perceives the potential liquidation of his holdings as affecting the clearing price. This allows us to treat the net change in dealer inventories, $Q_t - Q_{t-1}$, in the auction at time t as a liquidation of their existing inventories Q_{t-1} and the acquisition of a new position Q_t.

The market clears at the price where aggregate supply equals aggregate demand. To the earlier supply/demand balance of equation (2) we now have to add the participation of the dealers. If there are K public transactors the market equilibrium condition is:

$$KE + Q_{t-1} + \sum_{i=1}^{K} [E + a(r_i - p_t)] + c(\hat{m}_t - p_t) \qquad (13)$$

The market clearing price is then:

$$p_t = \alpha r_t + (1 - \alpha)\hat{m}_t - \gamma Q_{t-1} \qquad (14)$$

where:

$$\alpha = aK/(aK + c)$$

$$\gamma = 1/(aK + c)$$

Substituting p_t into equation (12) we have the quantity of securities absorbed by dealers:

$$Q_t = (1 - \alpha)Q_{t-1} + aKc\gamma(\hat{m}_t - r_t) \qquad (15)$$

As above we can pass to the continuum case by replacing the discrete number K of public transactors in equations (14) and (15) with $w\tau$.

Several features of equations (14) and (15) are worth noting. If dealers are carrying no net inventories from time $t - 1$, so that $Q_{t-1} = 0$, the market will clear at a price which is a convex combination of r_t (the price it would have cleared at were there no dealers) and $\hat{m}_t$ (the dealers' estimate of m_t). The weights on r_t and $\hat{m}_t$ depend on the relative slopes of the aggregate demand schedules of the public participants, $aK = aw\tau$, and of the dealers, c. The larger the slope c of the dealers demand schedule, the closer will p_t be to $\hat{m}_t$.[7] From the discussion above $\hat{m}_t$ is a more efficient estimator of m_t than r_t. Thus dealers will eliminate more transient price fluctuations the larger the value of c.

If the dealers are carrying over positive inventories into the market meeting at time t, $Q_{t-1} > 0$, the clearing price p_t will be lower than if $Q_{t-1} = 0$, and conversely if they are carrying over short positions. The existence of dealer inventories moderates the contribution of dealers to the stabilization of the clearing price around the equilibrium value. However, Q_{t-1} will be positive only if the market would have otherwise cleared below $\hat{m}_{t-1}$ at time $t - 1$, i.e., only if $r_{t-1} < \hat{m}_{t-1}$. By buying securities at time $t - 1$ the dealers gave a "fairer" price to market

---

[7] As the slope c of the dealers' demand schedule increases and α decreases the steady-state variance of Q_t will increase, see equation (15). When c goes to infinity Q_t follows a random walk because the innovation $r_t - \hat{m}_t$ in a serially uncorrelated process (Mehra, [12]). It follows that the dealers can "peg" the market to their estimate of the equilibrium value only by accepting a loss of control over their inventory. This result has also been derived by Garman [8] in a quite different model of dealer behavior.

participants in that meeting, and carried over what they perceived as an excess supply of securities into the meeting at time t. Public participants at time t have the opportunity to participate in part of the excess supply from time $t-1$ through the purchase of dealers inventories.

It should also be noted that the distribution of p_t collapses to a singular distribution at the contemporaneous equilibrium value m_t with increasing w.[8] As was the case with a public market, the clearing price in a dealer market approaches the concurrent equilibrium value of the asset as the size of the market increases.

Liquidity Risk and the Optimal Clearing Frequency of Dealer Markets

We can now compare the liquidity risk and optimal clearing frequency of dealer markets with that of pure public markets. When only public participants transact in the market, the difference between the market clearing price (which then equals r_t) and the contemporaneous equilibrium value m_t is, by equation (6), a serially uncorrelated process with mean zero and variance $\sigma^2/w\tau$. When dealers enter the market the dynamics of the market clearing price are more complex and are developed in detail in an appendix.

As before, liquidity risk is measured by the variance of the difference between equilibrium prices and subsequent transactions prices. For an investor who decides to trade at time $t - \frac{1}{2}$, for execution at time t, the variance is:

$$\mathrm{Var}[p_t - m_{t-1/2}] = \mathrm{Var}[(p_t - m_t) + (m_t - m_{t-1/2})]$$
$$= \mathrm{Var}[p_t - m_t] + \mathrm{Var}[m_t - m_{t-1/2}]$$
$$+ 2\,\mathrm{Cov}[p_t - m_t, m_t - m_{t-1/2}] \qquad (16)$$

The covariance term in equation (16) is zero when only public investors are active in the market, but will be non-zero when dealers are present. The reason is that p_t depends on $\hat{m}_t$, and $\hat{m}_t$ is not statistically independent of the equilibrium price change $m_t - m_{t-1/2}$.

The liquidity risk measure for a dealer market given in equation (16) can be compared to that of equation (7) for the case of a public market. Let $\theta(\tau)$ denote the steady-state value of $\mathrm{Var}[p_t - m_t]$. If dealers are inactive, so that $c = 0$, $\theta(\tau)$ will equal $\sigma^2/w\tau$. For values of c greater than zero $\theta(\tau)$ will be less than $\sigma^2/w\tau$ because of the price stabilizing effect of dealer intervention (See Figure 2). It is shown in an appendix that the covariance term in (16) is equal to $\frac{1}{2}(1 - \alpha)(G - 1)\tau\psi^2$. The total liquidity risk of trading in a dealer market is therefore:

$$V_d = \theta(\tau) + \frac{1}{2}\tau\psi^2 + (1 - \alpha)(G - 1)\tau\psi^2 \qquad (17)$$

Comparing equations (8) and (17) we have that, for any value of τ, the liquidity risk of trading in a dealer market is less than that of trading in a market open only to public transactors, i.e., $V_d < V_p$. This follows because $\theta(\tau) < \sigma^2/w\tau$ and

---

[8] This occurs because in equation (14) γ goes to zero, $\hat{m}_t$ goes to r_t and, from equation (6), the distribution of r_t collapses to a singular distribution at m_t with increasing w. Hence the distribution of p_t collapses to a singular distribution at m_t with increasing w. $\hat{m}_t$ converged to r_t with increasing w because the Kalman gain coefficient G converged to unity with increasing w, see equations (11a) and (11b).

Organization of Secondary Markets

because $G < 1$ and $\alpha < 1$ for all values of τ. Figure 2 compares the behavior of the liquidity risk measures V_d and V_d as functions of τ, and also shows the behavior of the determinants of V_d from equation (16). Because $V_d < V_p$ for all τ, we anticipate that public investors will prefer to trade in dealer markets. In particular, if there were two competing markets, alike in all respects except one permits and one prohibits dealers, we expect that the former market would gain public participants at the expense of the latter.

We can show also that dealer participation in a market reduces the optimal time between clearings, or increases the optimal frequency of clearing. Thus, liquidity risk in dealer markets is lower than that for public markets for all values of τ and, in addition, the value of τ which minimizes liquidity risk in a dealer market is smaller than that which minimizes liquidity risk in a purely public market. The latter assertion may be verified by noting that the derivative of V_d with respect to τ, denoted V'_d, is positive at τ_p^* taken from equation (9), the value of τ which minimizes liquidity risk in a public market.[9] This behavior of V_d is noted in Figure 2.

If the slope c of the dealers demand schedule is large, it may be that the minimum value of V_d occurs at $\tau = 0$. In this case the market literally clears continuously, so that all public orders are executed immediately upon their arrival in the market. For smaller values of c market participants will find waiting for the arrival of compatible trading partners in their self-interest.

We have shown thus far that dealers improve the liquidity of markets in two ways. First, for any given time interval between clearings they reduce the liquidity risk borne by public transactions. Second, they also reduce the optimal time between clearings (or increase the optimal frequency of clearing) and in so doing reduce liquidity risk even further. The magnitude of these effects depends upon how much dealers buy when the market price would otherwise clear below their estimate of equilibrium and how much dealers sell when it would otherwise clear above. In other words, the slope c of the dealer demand schedule in equation (12) determines the magnitude of dealer impact on market structure and on the liquidity characteristics of the asset being traded.

We suggested above that the extent of dealer participation, c, would be determined in a general equilibrium model by the risk-adjusted competitive rate of return on dealer capital. While such a treatment is beyond the scope of this paper, one point may be noted. Technological devices which allow dealers to expand their contacts with potential transactors should increase the level of

---

[9] From equation (17) we have:

$$V'_d = \theta' + \frac{1}{2}\psi^2 + (1-\alpha)(G-1)\psi^2 - \alpha'(G-1)\tau\psi^2 + G'(1-\alpha)\tau\psi^2$$

$$= [\theta' + \frac{1}{2}\psi^2] + [1 - \alpha - \tau\alpha'](G-1)\psi^2 + [G'](1-\alpha)\tau\psi^2$$

V'_d will be positive if each of the bracketed terms in the above equation are positive. Since the Kalman gain parameter is a monotonically increasing function of τ we have $G' > 0$. From the definition of $\alpha = aw\tau/(aw\tau + c)$ it follows that $1 - \alpha - \tau\alpha' = c^2/(aw\tau + c)^2 > 0$. As noted in the text, $\theta < \sigma^2/w\tau$ for all $\tau > 0$ because of the stabilizing effect of dealer intervention in the market. As τ increases, however, the importance of public participation relative to dealer participation increases, so that $d(\sigma^2/w\tau)/d\tau < \theta' < 0$ (see Figure 2) or $-\sigma^2/w\tau^2 < \theta'$. At $\tau = \tau_p^*$ we have $\frac{1}{2}\psi^2 = \sigma^2/w\tau^2$ (see equation (9)) so that $\theta' + \frac{1}{2}\psi^2 > 0$ at $\tau = \tau_p^*$. It follows that $V'_d > 0$ at $\tau = \tau_p^*$.

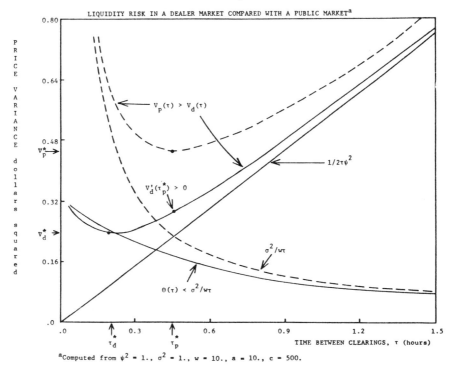

Figure 2. Liquidity Risk in a Dealer Market Compared with a Public Market[a]

[a] Computed from $\psi^2 = 1.$, $\sigma^2 = 1.$, $w = 10.$, $a = 10.$, $c = 500.$

dealer participation. Communications and information storage technologies which reduce the riskiness of dealer positions will increase the value of c and therefore improve further the liquidity characteristics of dealer markets.

The development of on-line data bases disclosing the portfolio holdings of institutional investors and permitting the recall of the purchase and sale interests of those investors is an area of major interest among securities firms active in the corporate bond markets. In addition, the "blue list" of purchase and sale interests in municipal bonds, published by Standard and Poors, is currently being converted from a daily printed listing to a computer listing disclosed through CRT devices with a capability for instantaneous updating. These devices are likely to lead to improved liquidity in these markets.

V. Concluding Remarks

This paper departs from the standard analysis of secondary markets by treating the structural organization of exchange endogenously. We hypothesized that, through competition between markets with different organizational characteristics, a surviving market will be organized to minimize trader exposure to liquidity risk. The optimal frequency of market clearing was shown to depend upon the volatility of securities prices and the number of market participants. Dealer participation in market trading reduces liquidity risk and increases the optimal frequency of clearing. Advances in communications and information technology have similar effects. The empirical relevance of these results was illustrated by a number of historical and contemporary examples of the structure of secondary markets.

Appendix A: Recursive Estimation of Equilibrium Values

The structure of equation (11) is a direct application of Kalman filtering, Athans, [1]; Sage and Melsa, [14]. From equations (5) and (6) we have:

$$m_t = m_{t-1} + e_t \qquad e_t \sim N(0, \tau\psi^2) \qquad \text{(A1a)}$$

$$r_t = m_t + f_t \qquad f_t \sim N(0, \sigma^2/w\tau) \qquad \text{(A1b)}$$

The problem is to estimate m_t using the concurrent and past values of r_t.

Let $\hat{m}_t$ be the estimate of m_t based on $(r_t, r_{t-1}, r_{t-2}, \cdots)$ and let $\bar{m}_t$ be the estimate of m_t based on $(r_{t-1}, r_{t-2}, \cdots)$. Then from (A1) we have:

$$\bar{m}_t = \hat{m}_{t-1} \qquad \text{(A2a)}$$

$$\hat{m}_t = \bar{m}_t + G_t[r_t - \bar{m}_t] \qquad \text{(A2b)}$$

where:

$$G_t = R_t/(R_t + \sigma^2/w\tau) \qquad \text{(A3a)}$$

$$R_t = S_{t-1} + \tau\psi^2 \qquad \text{(A3b)}$$

$$S_t = R_t - G_t R_t \qquad \text{(A3c)}$$

It can be shown that the estimators are distributed as:

$$\bar{m}_t \sim N(m_t, R_t) \qquad \text{(A4a)}$$

$$\hat{m}_t \sim N(m_t, S_t) \qquad \text{(A4b)}$$

As t increases G_t, R_t and S_t will converge to steady-state values denoted by G, R and S. These values may be computed by solving the set of simultaneous equations:

$$G = R/(R + \sigma^2/w\tau) \qquad \text{(A5a)}$$

$$R = S + \tau\psi^2 \qquad \text{(A5b)}$$

$$S = R - GR \qquad \text{(A5c)}$$

Thus we have:

$$R = S + \tau\psi^2$$
$$= [R - GR] + \tau\psi^2$$
$$= R - [R/(R + \sigma^2/w\tau)]R + \tau\psi^2$$

or:

$$R^2 - \tau\psi^2 R - \psi^2\sigma^2/w = 0$$

Solving the quadratic gives:

$$R = \tfrac{1}{2}[\tau\psi^2 + (\tau^2\psi^4 + 4\psi^2\sigma^2/w)^{1/2}] \quad (A6)$$

since the other root is negative. The value of S follows immediately as $S = R - \tau\psi^2$. The value of G follows from: $GR = R - S = \tau\psi^2$ or $G = \tau\psi^2/R$.

Appendix B: Dynamics of Clearing Prices in a Dealer Market

Four equations summarize the dynamic behavior of clearing prices relative to equilibrium values in a dealer market. From equation (4a) we have:

$$r_t - m_t = f_t \quad (B1)$$

From equation (6a) we have:

$$\hat{m}_t - m_t = (1 - G)\hat{m}_{t-1} + Gr_t - m_{t-1}$$
$$= (1 - G)(\hat{m}_{t-1} - m_t) + G(r_t - m_t)$$

Noting that $m_t = m_{t-1} + e_t$ from equation (5a) this becomes:

$$\hat{m}_t - m_t = (1 - G)(\hat{m}_{t-1} - m_{t-1}) + G(r_t - m_t) - (1 - G)e_t \quad (B2)$$

Equation (14a) may be written in terms of deviations from m_t:

$$p_t - m_t = \alpha(r_t - m_t) + (1 - \alpha)(\hat{m}_t - m_t) - \gamma Q_{t-1} \quad (B3)$$

and equation (15) similarly:

$$Q_t = (1 - \alpha)Q_{t-1} + aKc\gamma(\hat{m}_t - m_t) - aKc\gamma(r_t - m_t) \quad (B4)$$

Equations (B1, B2, B3, B4) provide a system of simultaneous recursive stochastic equations for the price differences $r_t - m_t$, $\hat{m}_t - m_t$ and $p_t - m_t$, and for the quantity Q_t of securities held by positioning agents. These equations describe the transient characteristics of the market. The equations may be summarized in a multi-variate linear dynamic model:

$$A_0 x_t = A_1 x_{t-1} + B_1 \epsilon_t \quad (B5a)$$

$$\epsilon_t \sim N(0, \Sigma) \quad (B5b)$$

with:

$$x_t = \begin{bmatrix} r_t - m_t \\ \hat{m}_t - m_t \\ p_t - m_t \\ Q_t \end{bmatrix} \quad A_0 = \begin{bmatrix} 1 & 0 & 0 & 0 \\ 0 & 1 & 0 & 0 \\ -\alpha & \alpha - 1 & 1 & 0 \\ aKc\gamma & -aKc\gamma & 0 & 1 \end{bmatrix}$$

$$A_1 = \begin{bmatrix} 0 & 0 & 0 & 0 \\ 0 & 1-G & 0 & 0 \\ 0 & 0 & 0 & -\gamma \\ 0 & 0 & 0 & 1-\alpha \end{bmatrix} \quad B_1 = \begin{bmatrix} 1 & 0 \\ G & G-1 \\ 0 & 0 \\ 0 & 0 \end{bmatrix}$$

$$\epsilon_t = \begin{bmatrix} f_t \\ e_t \end{bmatrix} \quad \Sigma = \begin{bmatrix} \sigma^2/w\tau & 0 \\ 0 & \tau\psi^2 \end{bmatrix}$$

Note that the random process ϵ_t is serially uncorrelated.

The reduced-form version of (B5a) is:

$$x_t = A_0^{-1} A_1 x_{t-1} + A_0^{-1} B_1 \epsilon_t \tag{B6}$$

Stationary stochastic models of this type have been studied by Chow, [2], who shows that the steady-state covariance matrix of x_t is the matrix U which satisfies the equation:

$$U = A_0^{-1} A_1 U (A_0^{-1} A_1)' + A_0^{-1} B_1 \sum (A_0^{-1} B_1)' \tag{B7}$$

The steady-state value of the variance of $p_t - m_t$, which is denoted $\theta(\tau)$ in the text, is equal to $U_{3,3}$. The steady-state value of the covariance of $p_t - m_t$ with $m_t - m_{t-1/2}$ is $\frac{1}{2}[A_0^{-1} B_1 \sum]_{3,2} = [A_0^{-1} B_1]_{3,2} (\frac{1}{2}\tau\psi^2)$. It may be verified directly that:

$$A_0^{-1} = \begin{bmatrix} 1 & 0 & 0 & 0 \\ 0 & 1 & 0 & 0 \\ \alpha & 1-\alpha & 1 & 0 \\ -aK c\gamma & aKc\gamma & 0 & 1 \end{bmatrix}$$

so $[A_0^{-1} B_1]_{3,2} = (1 - \alpha)(G - 1)$.

References

1. Michael Athans. "The Importance of Kalman Filtering Methods for Economic Systems." *Annals of Economic and Social Measurement*, 3 (January, 1974).
2. Gregory Chow. "The Acceleration Principle and the Nature of Business Cycles." *Quarterly Journal of Economics*, 82 (August, 1968).
3. David Eiteman and Wilfod Eiteman. *Leading World Stock Exchanges: Trading Practices and Organization*. Michigan International Business Studies, No. 2, (1964).
4. Kenneth Garbade. "The Effect of Inter-Dealer Brokerage on the Transactional Characteristics of a Dealer Market." *Journal of Business*, 51 (July, 1978).
5. _____ and Zvi Lieber. "On the Independence of Transactions on the New York Stock Exchange." *Journal of Banking and Finance*, 1 (September, 1977).
6. _____ and William Silber. "Price Dispersion in the Government Securities Market." *Journal of Political Economy*, 84 (August, 1976).
7. _____. "Technology, Communication and the Performance of Financial Markets, 1840–1975." *Journal of Finance*, 33 (June, 1978).
8. M. B. Garman. "Market Microstructure." *Journal of Financial Economics*, 3 (June, 1976).
9. Horace Hotchkiss. "The Stock Ticker." in *The New York Stock Exchange*, Edmund Stedman, ed. (New York: Greenwood Press Publishers, 1905).
10. Henry G. Jarecki. "Bullion Dealing, Commodity Exchange Trading and the London Gold Fixing: Three Forms of Commodity Auctions." in *Bidding and Auctioning for Procurement and Allocation*, Yakov Amihud, ed. (New York: New York University Press, 1976).
11. J. E. Meeker. *The Work of the Stock Exchange*, rev. ed. (New York: The Ronald Press Company, 1930).
12. Raman Mehra. "On the Identification of Variances and Adaptive Kalman Filtering." *IEEE Transactions on Automatic Control*, 15 (April, 1970).
13. New York Stock Exchange. *Report of the Committee to Study the Stock Allocation System* (New York: New York Stock Exchange, 1976).
14. Andrew Sage and James Melsa. *Estimation Theory with Applications to Communications and Control* (New York: McGraw-Hill, 1971).
15. William L. Silber. "Thinness in Capital Markets: The Case of the Tel Aviv Stock Exchange." *Journal of Financial and Quantitative Analysis*, 10 (March, 1975).
16. Robert Sobel. *The Big Board, A History of the New York Stock Exchange* (New York: The Free Press, 1965).
17. _____. *N.Y.S.E.* (New York: Weybright and Talley, 1975).
18. U.S. Securities and Exchange Commission. *Report of Special Study of Securities Markets*, Part 2, House Document No. 95, pt. 2, 88th Congress, 1st Session (Washington, D.C.: U.S.G.P.O., 1963).

[5]

Transaction Costs, Order Placement Strategy, and Existence of the Bid-Ask Spread

Kalman J. Cohen and Steven F. Maier
Duke University

Robert A. Schwartz
New York University

David K. Whitcomb
Rutgers University

By considering investor order placement strategy, this paper demonstrates that transaction costs cause bid-ask spreads to be an equilibrium property of asset markets. With transaction costs, the probability of a limit order executing does not go to unity as the order is placed infinitesimally close to a counterpart market quote; thus, with certainty of execution at the counterpart market quote, a "gravitational pull" is generated that keeps counterpart quotes from being placed infinitesimally close to each other. An equilibrium spread is defined and its size linked to market thinness; implications are noted for the design of a trading system.

I. Introduction

This paper establishes that transaction costs in secondary asset markets cause individual investors to use order placement strategies that result in a nontrivial market bid-ask spread.[1] We define an *equilibrium market spread* and demonstrate that it will be greater for thinner securities.

The analysis fits into a growing body of literature which increasingly is being referred to as the microstructure of security markets. Stigler (1964), Demsetz (1968), West and Tinic (1971), Tinic (1972), and Tinic and West (1972, 1974), along with Farrar, Smidt, Stoll, and others involved in the institutional investor study (see U.S. Securities and Exchange Commission 1971), were among the first to focus rigorous analytical attention on the operations of security markets. More recently, microstructure theory has been explicitly considered by, among others, Garman, who coined the term (1976), Beja and Hakansson (1977), and Cohen, Maier, Schwartz, and Whitcomb (hereinafter CMSW) (1978). The analytical issues addressed involve the interplay among market participants, trading mechanisms, and the dynamic behavior of security prices. In the present paper, we study the formulation of optimal investor trading strategies and how these interact with one aspect of the dynamic behavior of security prices, the bid-ask spread. Spreads are of concern to investors because they are a variable cost of trading by market order and because they cause an inflation of transaction-to-transaction returns variance.

The pioneering analysis of bid-ask spreads was provided by Demsetz (1968). Further studies include: Tinic (1972), Tinic and West (1972, 1974), Benston and Hagerman (1974), Garman (1976), Hamilton (1976, 1978), Branch and Freed (1977), Stoll (1978a, 1978b), Ho and Stoll (1979, 1980), Newton and Quandt (1979), Schleef and Mildenstein (1979), Smidt (1979), and Amihud and Mendelson (1980). In CMSW (1979) we discuss this literature and contrast it with the formulation presented here. Except for Ho and Stoll (1980), there has been no explicit consideration of the transition from individual spreads to the market spread. It will be clear from our analysis that this transition is not a simple aggregation process and that the market spread is the product of a dynamic interaction involving many market participants. Also, previous theoretical models have generally assumed that investors can be dichotomized into two groups—immediacy demanders and immediacy suppliers. Our model of investor order placement strategy suggests that such a dichotomy will not be observed in the marketplace.

For the market, the spread is the difference between the lowest ask and the highest bid of all participants. In markets composed of many

---

[1] We have elsewhere (Cohen et al. 1980) considered how the impact of transaction costs on stock price movements introduces serial correlation in returns data and causes estimates of the market model beta coefficient to be biased.

traders with heterogeneous beliefs and trading propensities, one might expect to have orders at virtually every permissible price in the neighborhood of equilibrium and hence to find no significant market spread.[2] However, we show that even when expectations and trading propensities are heterogeneous, the spread is a property of asset markets that have temporarily cleared.[3] The analysis yields an existence proof of a noninfinitesimal spread with continuous pricing; a fortiori this proves for discrete prices the existence of a positive spread for nontrivial reasons.[4]

The essence of our argument is as follows. At any point in time, any investor might alternatively seek to trade via a limit order (be an immediacy supplier), trade with certainty via a market order (be an immediacy demander), or not seek to trade at all. Limit orders create the book, and market orders clear out limit orders. Because execution via market order is certain, while execution via limit order is not, it never pays for any investor to place a limit order (e.g., a bid) at a price too close to that of a counterpart limit order (e.g., an ask). Intuitively stated, as a trader contemplates placing a bid closer and closer to an ask already established on the market, he is increasingly attracted by this counterpart offer; at some point, the "gravitational pull" exerted by the established ask will dominate. The trader will "jump" his price and execute with certainty via a market order.

Section II establishes the scenario for our analysis. Section III focuses on the probability of a limit order executing and shows that, with transaction costs, this probability does not go to unity as the price at which a limit order is placed becomes infinitesimally close to a counterpart market quote. This demonstration underscores an investor's need for an order placement strategy and provides the foundation for our gravitational pull model. Section IV models the investor's order placement decision and develops conditions under which he will transmit limit or, alternatively, market orders to the market, or do nothing. The analysis is developed in a dynamic programming framework, although we are interested in the descriptive modeling of

---

[2] When an asset market has cleared, there is neither excess demand nor excess supply in the sense that at that moment no market participant is willing to buy the asset at a price equal to or greater than the ask, and no one is willing to sell at a price equal to or less than the bid. Hence we must have a market spread that is at least equal to the minimum allowable price change for the asset in question (on the major U.S. stock exchanges, this is 1/8 of a dollar for most common stocks). However, it is not obvious why spreads greater than minimum allowable price changes are commonly observed.

[3] While the analysis presented here is applicable to any asset market, our formal model treats the secondary market for financial securities. Security markets have two convenient properties: All units of an asset are identical, and such markets are impersonal (which means that bargaining, as distinct from trading, strategies need not be considered).

[4] See n. 2 above.

an investor's decision process rather than in actually generating a normative solution. Section V demonstrates that implementation of the strategic order placement decision (which implies the gravitational pull effect) causes a noninfinitesimal bid-ask spread to exist. This section also defines an equilibrium bid-ask spread, discusses conditions under which it will exist, and shows that it is positively related to market thinness. Section VI considers implications for the design of a security market trading system and summarizes our analysis.

II. The Scenario

Consider an investor who maximizes the expected utility of terminal wealth and, for simplicity, let him allocate funds between only two assets: a risk asset and cash (which we take to be the numeraire asset). In the absence of transaction costs, the market would be monitored continuously and appropriate transactions would be made with each change in the market price and the investor's demand propensities. Then, if price were continuous, there would be no spread and the market price would be determined by a straightforward aggregation of individual demand propensities.

However, a variety of transaction costs impact on the investor's trading decisions. The fixed (with respect to number of shares traded) costs of assessing information, monitoring the market, and conveying orders to the market imply that the investor will make trading decisions only periodically. Further, when decisions are made, he will not convey his full set of demand propensities to the market. For one thing, trades that involve sufficiently small portfolio adjustments would not justify the transaction costs incurred.[5] Also, attempts to transmit several limit orders simultaneously would be likely to overload our current system. Furthermore, a continuous auction which does not generate a Walrasian solution cannot readily handle multiple buy-sell orders that, ex ante, are intended to be alternatives.[6]

In light of transaction costs (and also taking account of the timing and magnitude of exogenous cash flows), the investor will establish a discrete set of decision points. In the analysis presented in Section IV, we take the frequency of these points as predetermined. Upon reaching a decision point, an investor can do nothing, or hit an

[5] It can be readily demonstrated that variable as well as fixed transaction costs make sufficiently small portfolio adjustments prohibitively expensive.

[6] That is, if any array of buy and sell orders from one investor is executed sequentially, the desired quantities at each price should be dependent on the exact sequence of purchases and sales followed. However, the investor does not know ex ante which specific sequence will occur. This problem could, of course, be handled (at a cost) by conditioning orders on the sequence of prior transactions (i.e., if the limit order to buy 200 at $50 executes, then sell 100 at $56).

existing limit order with his own market order, or place his own limit order at a "better" price and run the risk of its not executing. A concurrent strategy issue also exists when the investor finds it prohibitively expensive to convey his entire set of demand propensities to the market; for all intents and purposes, he must select the single best alternative to transmit.

III. The Probability of a Limit Order Executing

In this section, we establish the conditions under which the probability of execution does not approach a limit of unity as the price at which the limit order is placed is taken to be infinitesimally close to the counterpart market quote. Under these conditions we obtain a probability jump (at the counterpart market quote) that underlies the gravitational pull effect developed in Section V. By showing that the probability jump can be attributed to the existence of transaction costs, we establish the basic linkage between spreads and transaction costs.

Consider the case where an investor contemplates submitting a limit bid at the price P_t^{LB} at time t, and let price be a continuous variable. A similar argument can be constructed for the case of a limit ask. Assume that if the limit order is unfilled by the next decision point at time $t + 1$ the order will be canceled. Let L be the length of time between decision points t and $t + 1$.

Let P_t^{MA} be the market ask price at time t. Consistent with the random walk version of the efficient markets hypothesis, we make the Markov assumption that each subsequent market ask depends only on the last previous market ask. If we also assume that each change in the natural log of the market ask, Z_i, is a random variable that is independently and identically distributed over time with mean zero and variance var (Z_i), then we can model the market ask price generation process as a compound Poisson stochastic process:[7]

---

[7] For expositional simplicity we assume that the stochastic processes considered in this section have no drift (that is, their expected value is zero). It should be noted that even though ln P_t^{MA} is assumed to have no drift, the price series itself, P_t^{MA}, may have drift. For example, when ln (P_{t+1}^{MA}/P_t^{MA}) is normal, with mean zero and standard deviation σ, then P_{t+1}^{MA}/P_t^{MA} is log normal with mean exp $(\frac{1}{2} \sigma^2)$.

There will be a realization of the random variable Z_i at each point of time when any one of the following events occurs to affect the specific limit order which sets the market ask: (a) it is withdrawn; (b) it executes against a crossing buy order; or (c) it remains on the book but is no longer the market ask since a lower limit sell has been submitted. Note that events of types a and b necessarily result in a change in the market ask when price is continuous and utility functions are heterogeneous (which implies a zero probability of having two or more orders at a specific price). Also note that only events of type b are associated with transactions; hence the number of Z_i which materialize during any interval will usually exceed the number of transactions in that interval.

$$\ln P_t^{MA}(\Delta) = \ln P_t^{MA} + \sum_{i=1}^{N(\Delta)} Z_i, \qquad (1)$$

where Δ is the time from the last decision point. When Δ equals L, we have $P_t^{MA}(\Delta) = P_{t+1}^{MA}$; when Δ equals $2L$, we have $P_t^{MA}(\Delta) = P_{t+2}^{MA}$, etc. The number of changes in the market ask that take place in the time interval Δ is $N(\Delta)$. We assume $N(\Delta)$ follows a Poisson process with arrival rate ν.

The next step is to determine the probability of execution (during a time interval of length L) of a limit bid which is submitted at a price P_t^{LB} greater than the current market bid (P_t^{MB}) but less than the current market ask (P_t^{MA}). Clearly, as the limit bid price approaches (from below) the market ask, the probability of execution increases. One might suppose that this probability approaches unity as the limit bid approaches the market ask; however, this need not be the case. In the Appendix we restate formally and prove:

PROPOSITION 1: *If P_t^{MA} is generated by the compound Poisson process of equation (1), then no matter how close the limit bid approaches (from below) the market ask, the probability of the limit order executing is less than unity in any time interval of finite length.*

Since a market order will always execute with probability one, proposition 1 gives a probability jump at the market ask.

Transaction costs are crucial to the existence of the probability jump. In the absence of transaction costs, one might expect that, following the work of Merton (1973), the logarithm of the market ask would best be described by a Wiener process with zero drift:

$$d \ln P_t^{MA}(\Delta) = \sigma dZ(\Delta), \qquad (2)$$

where σ is the instantaneous variance of the process and $dZ(\Delta)$ is a standardized Wiener process. In this case, the price $P_t^{MA}(\Delta)$ would experience an infinite number of adjustments in the interval $0 \leq \Delta \leq L$. In the Appendix we restate formally and prove:

PROPOSITION 2: *If $P_t^{MA}(\Delta)$ is generated by the Wiener process of equation (2), then as the limit bid approaches (from below) the market ask, the probability of the limit order executing approaches unity for all time intervals of the finite length.*

Proposition 2 implies that for the Wiener process there will be no probability jump at the market ask.

We next consider whether there is a relationship between the compound Poisson process of equation (1) and the Wiener process of equation (2). In the Appendix we restate formally and prove:

EXISTENCE OF THE BID-ASK SPREAD

PROPOSITION 3: If the random variable Z_i in the compound Poisson process of equation (1) has two equally likely possible values, $+\alpha$ and $-\alpha$, and if the arrival rate ν of this compound Poisson process increases without bound while α simultaneously decreases in such a way that $\nu\alpha^2$ is constant, then the compound Poisson process approaches the Wiener process described by equation (2) with the variance of the Wiener process, σ^2, equaling $\nu\alpha^2$.

Proposition 3 states that the compound Poisson process can be expected to approach the Wiener process under appropriate assumptions.[8] Thus the probability jump of proposition 1 would disappear as ν increased and var (Z_i) decreased. In the Appendix we restate formally and prove:

PROPOSITION 4: As the arrival rate ν in the compound Poisson process of equation (1) increases, the probability of a limit order executing increases for all $P_t^{LB} < P_t^{MA}$.

Hence the probability of a limit order executing increases at all $P_t^{LB} < P_t^{MA}$ as the activity proxy ν increases. Stated conversely, the "thinner" a security, that is, the less active are investors in submitting orders to trade in the security, the lower will be the probability of execution at each $P_t^{LB} < P_t^{MA}$, and therefore the greater will be the probability jump at P_t^{MA}.

The four propositions stated in this section (and proved in the Appendix) have important implications for the analysis of the impact of transaction costs on bid-ask spreads. Without transaction costs, the market price could be expected to behave as a Wiener process; that is, there would be an infinite number of infinitesimally small price adjustments. The investor who was considering placing a limit order could reduce the probability of his order not executing to as close to zero as desired simply by placing his order close enough to the counterpart market quotation.

On the other hand, with transaction costs and a finite number of investors, the market price would generally not behave as a Wiener process. Investors would find continuous adjustments in their portfolios too expensive, and market prices would behave as a stochastic jump process (proposition 3 shows that this process could generally be expected to approach a Wiener process as the order arrival rate is increased). One such jump process is the compound Poisson, and it also is consistent with a (martingale) efficient market.

---

[8] The particular distribution chosen for Z_i in proposition 3 is not critical. Other appropriately chosen discrete or continuous distributions can also be shown in the limit to go to the Wiener process.

Proposition 1 demonstrates that for such a stochastic jump process a probability jump exists. Proposition 4 has shown that the probability jump will be greater for thinner securities. In Section V we will show that the larger probability jump for thinner issues leads to equilibrium market spreads which are larger for thinner issues.

IV. A Model of Investor Order Placement Strategy

We now consider the question of when an investor will choose to trade via a market order or limit order, or not seek to trade at all. The problem is structured as follows. Because of the costs of monitoring the market, let the investor consider rebalancing his portfolio only at preselected points in time, $t = 1, 2, \ldots, T - 1$, where T is the investment horizon.[9] In order to simplify the analysis, we now consider the placement of only purchase orders for the risk asset (omitting the symmetric case of sell orders without loss of generality).

At any of the $T - 1$ decision points, the investor is faced with three possible courses of action:

   a) Submit a market order to buy shares at the current market ask price of P_t^{MA}.

   b) Submit a limit order to buy shares at a limit bid price of $P_t^{LB} < P_t^{MA}$.

   c) Do nothing.

In modeling the investor's choice among these three alternatives, we find it convenient to make the following assumptions that simplify the analysis without materially affecting the nature of the conclusions. We assume that all orders are for a fixed number of shares ΔN and that when any market or limit order is executed, it is satisfied fully at the stated price; this avoids the tedium of writing (average) transaction price and transaction costs as functions of the number of shares exchanged and of defining probabilities of partial execution. We assume that unfilled limit orders are canceled prior to the next decision point; this avoids both the need to include additional state variables (the price and quantity of any limit order outstanding) and the need to analyze additional courses of action (submit a market order and leave the old limit order outstanding, or submit a market order and remove the limit order, etc.). Finally, we assume no lags in the transmission of information and orders; this avoids the complexity of dealing with changes in the current market quotes during the time the investor formulates and implements his decision.

---

[9] Note that the rebalancing points need not be the same for all investors, so that trades can occur at any time when the market is open even if specific traders are not continually in the market.

EXISTENCE OF THE BID-ASK SPREAD

If option a is chosen, the market order will be executed, and the investor's holdings at time $t + 1$ become $N_{t+1} = N_t + \Delta N$, for which the investor pays a total cost of $\Delta N \cdot P_t^{MA} + C^M$ where C^M is the total cost of transmitting and executing the market order.

If option b is chosen, then one of two events can take place: ($b1$) The limit order is executed. The investor's share holdings then become $N_{t+1} = N_t + \Delta N$, for which the investor pays a total cost of $\Delta N \cdot P_t^{LB} + C^{L1} + C^{L2}$ where C^{L1} is the cost of transmitting a limit order to the market and C^{L2} is the cost of executing a limit order. ($b2$) The limit order does not execute and is canceled prior to the next decision point. The investor's share holdings then remain unchanged ($N_{t+1} = N_t$) and his cash is decreased by the cost of transmitting the limit order, C^{L1}. Option b will be chosen over a if the gain associated with the possibility of trading at a more favorable price outweighs the loss associated with the probability of not trading at all.

The investor must consider four subjective probability distributions in order to make an optimal decision. These are: (1) the joint probability distribution of market bid and ask prices at time $t + 1$, conditional upon the quotes at time t; (2) the probability of a limit bid order submitted at time t executing before time $t + 1$; (3) and (4) the joint probability distribution of market bid and ask prices at time $t + 1$, conditional upon the quotes at time t and further conditional on whether a limit bid submitted at time t either did or else did not execute prior to time $t + 1$. In the Appendix we discuss in more detail these four subjective probability distributions (only three of which are independent).

A dynamic programming model of the investor's choice among options a, b, and c is formulated in the Appendix. The investor is assumed to maximize his expected utility of terminal wealth, max (U_1, U_2, U_3), where U_1 is the expected terminal utility of choosing option a, trading via a market order; U_2 is the expected terminal utility of choosing option b, seeking to trade via a limit order; and U_3 is the expected terminal utility of choosing option c, doing nothing. It is convenient to focus on the utility gain, ΔU_1 or ΔU_2, which results from choosing option a or b rather than option c: $\Delta U_1 = U_1 - U_3$; $\Delta U_2(P_t^{LB}) = U_2(P_t^{LB}) - U_3$ (note that U_2 and ΔU_2 are functions of the limit bid price). Clearly $\Delta U_2(P_t^{LB} = P_t^{MA}) = \Delta U_1$, since, at this price, the market order and limit order strategies are effectively the same (the probability is unity of the limit order executing at a price of P_t^{MA}).

Let us now consider the conditions under which $U_1 > \max (U_2, U_3)$, in which case the investor will submit a market order, or $U_2 > \max (U_1, U_3)$, in which case the investor will submit a limit order. Suppose that at the current market quotes the do-nothing strategy is dominated (i.e., max $[U_1, U_2] > U_3$). Given our utility gains ΔU_1 and

$\Delta U_2(P_t^{LB})$ and the probability function for limit order execution developed in Section III above, we know the utility gain from placing a market order and can readily obtain an expected utility gain function for the limit order strategy. These are depicted in figure 1; the shape of the function is explained as follows:

1. While the utility of a consummated trade decreases monotonically with P_t^{LB}, the probability of execution increases with P_t^{LB}, with two probability jumps (at the market bid and the market ask). The jump at P_t^{MB} simply reflects the institutional reality that orders placed at prices less than or equal to P_t^{MB} would not have priority over the current market bid, whereas an order placed at a price above P_t^{MB} would be at the top of the limit order book. The jump at P_t^{MA} follows from proposition 1.

2. Since the probability of execution is constant to the right of P_t^{MA}, the expected utility gain has a peak at P_t^{MA}, corresponding to the utility gain of transacting by a market order.

3. The probability of execution increases between P_t^{MB} and P_t^{MA}, with the greatest relative increase just to the right of P_t^{MB}. We expect this large probability increase in this neighborhood because the strategy considerations of other investors might lead them to place limit orders just to the right of P_t^{MB} in order to capture the largest price advantage. Hence the second peak in the expected utility gain function will occur at some point P'', between P_t^{MB} and P_t^{MA}.

4. The probability of execution decreases rapidly in a neighborhood just to the left of P_t^{MB} because of existing limit orders on the book. However, since there would be a clustering of limit orders near

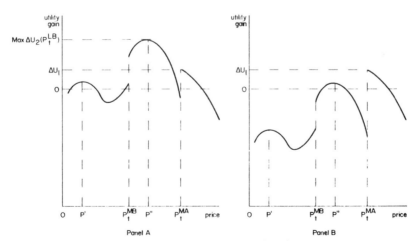

FIG 1.—Illustrative utility gain functions

EXISTENCE OF THE BID-ASK SPREAD

P_t^{MB}, we would expect the probability of execution to decrease more slowly as the limit price, P_t^{LB}, moves further from P_t^{MB}. Hence, we might find a third peak in the expected utility gain function to occur at some point P' to the left of P_t^{MB}.

Which of the three peaks in $\Delta U_2(P_t^{LB})$ will dominate depends on the particular form of the probability function for limit order execution as well as the expected utility function. In the particular diagram presented in figure 1A, $\Delta U_2(P_t^{LB})$ has positive values (hence a do-nothing strategy is dominated), has values greater than ΔU_1 (hence the market order strategy is dominated), and gives a global maximum at P''. Assuming only one limit order per investor, the optimal strategy is to place a limit bid at P'', and hence P'' will become the new market bid. The setting of such a bid quotation can be considered a Stigler (1961)-type search activity.[10]

Clearly the limit order strategy need not always be superior; in selecting this strategy, the investor also accepts the chance that the limit order may fail to execute, in which case the investor would be worse off than had he done nothing since he would have also lost the cost of placing the limit order, C^{L1}. If the probability of failing to execute is high enough and $\Delta U_1 > 0$, the investor will prefer the market order strategy as illustrated in figure 1B.[11]

V. The Market Spread

It is clear from the preceding analysis (Sec. IV) that, with a continuous auction market, each investor's order placement decision is made with reference to prices already established on the market—the bid and ask quotations which define the market spread. In turn, each investor's order may affect the market spread to which subsequent traders react. Hence, the market spread is the product of a dynamic interactive process. In this section we show that a nonzero market spread must exist, define the equilibrium market spread, and relate a security's equilibrium spread to its thinness.

The limit order book comprises the limit orders transmitted to the market by a subset of the many traders in a security, and the spread is essentially a gap in the limit order book. Therefore, having estab-

---

[10] By the placement of such a limit order, a seller or buyer announces his propensity to trade with the hope of getting the attention of a counterpart market participant who would also be willing to trade.

[11] There are two other versions of fig. 1. One would be analogous to panel A, but with the global maximum at P' rather than at P''; in this case, the investor would submit a limit bid at P' (below the market bid). The second version would be where the zero point on the utility gain axis is higher than both max $\Delta U_2(P_t^{LB})$ and ΔU_1; in this case, the investor would do nothing.

lished that individual investors will sometimes seek to trade via limit orders, we must show why a noninfinitesimal gap in the array of such orders exists between the market quotes. We do so by considering the impact that the jump in the probability of a limit order executing (Sec. III) has on the investor's optimal order placement strategy (Sec. IV).

We have established the conditions under which a limit order will be placed; we can now consider whether or not limit orders will necessarily be placed so as always to preserve a nonzero bid-ask spread. By continuity of the utility function, and because of the discontinuous drop in the probability of execution that must occur at the market ask as we move to lower prices, we must have a discontinuous drop in $\Delta U_2(P_t^{LB})$ as we move past the market ask to lower prices. Then, because of continuity of the probability function until we get to the market bid (at which point another discontinuous drop occurs), it necessarily follows that $\Delta U_2(P_t^{LB})$ cannot exceed ΔU_1 within a nonzero neighborhood to the left of P_t^{MA}. Hence, no limit bid will be placed infinitesimally close to the market ask, and therefore we must have a nonzero bid-ask spread.

Intuitively viewed, consider an investor who is thinking about whether or not to place a limit bid at some price below the market ask. As the potential limit price rises toward the market ask, it becomes relatively more attractive to transact at the market ask with certainty. At some point, the investor will prefer buying at a discretely higher, unitary probability of execution. In other words, certainty of execution at the market ask creates a kind of gravitational pull which causes investors to jump their price once their potential limit bid gets close enough to the market ask. This clears out limit bids when they get too close to the market ask, thereby leaving a nonzero spread between the market bid and ask.

We next consider the issue of an equilibrium market spread.

DEFINITION: In a dynamic trading process we define the equilibrium market spread as the bid-ask spread at which, for the next instant of time, the probability of the spread increasing is equal to the probability of the spread decreasing.[12]

This definition does not imply that if away from equilibrium the

---

[12] Note that the probability is not conditioned on the current status of individual investors, recent prices, or other market conditions.
Note that we use the term "equilibrium market spread" to refer to one particular point in the probability distribution of the market spread, rather than to refer to a statistic for the central tendency of the entire distribution. We do not adopt a central tendency definition (such as expected value, mode, or median) of the equilibrium spread because it does not provide a ready link to the market forces that generate the spread and to thinness. For empirical research, the average market spread is likely to be a reasonable proxy for our definition of the equilibrium market spread.

EXISTENCE OF THE BID-ASK SPREAD

spread will necessarily move toward it on the next order, but only that it is more likely to do so than not.

We assume that a unique equilibrium exists. To examine the reasonableness of this assumption, first consider an arbitrarily small spread. Because the probability of a limit order being placed has a discrete jump at P_t^{MA}, we have already argued that there will be no limit orders placed in some nonzero neighborhood below P_t^{MA} by *all* investors seeking to buy the security. (The generalization from a single investor to all investors takes place simply by choosing the smallest neighborhood found among all investors.) Therefore, for a sufficiently small bid-ask spread, the unconditional probability of the spread increasing must exceed the unconditional probability of the spread decreasing as analyzed from the standpoint of the buyer. A similar argument holds for the seller.

Now consider what occurs when the spread widens. The larger the spread is, the greater the potential utility gain from an optimally priced limit order, while the utility gain from a market order will remain unchanged or fall. The gain in utility occurs because the shares can be bought (sold) at a lower (higher) price via limit order than by market order.[13] With the rise in utility $U_2(P_t^{LB})$, investors will begin to shift their preferences from market orders to limit orders. As more and more investors shift to limit orders, the probability of the spread increasing falls, while the probability of it decreasing rises.

One of two situations must occur. Either the spread would tend to reach a point at which the two probabilities would be equal, in which case it would be the equilibrium market spread, or the limit order book would be empty on one or both sides.[14] Since when the order book is empty market orders cannot transact, we would be at a point where the probability of a limit order is greater than that of a market order. Although such a point might be achieved without the equilibrium market spread ever being attained, we believe it would be atypical.[15]

---

[13] We assume that the spread does not impart any information to the investor on the direction of future price movements.

[14] No other possibility exists. So long as there is a greater probability that the spread will increase than that it will decrease, the spread will on expectation grow—limited only by the collapse of the limit order book on one side or the other.

[15] With regard to the assumption of uniqueness, investors might have utility functions which could lead to more than one equilibrium market spread. Consider the case where an investor views a very wide spread as signaling the advent of new information which may cause a price adjustment of unknown direction. The investor sensing greater risk might now choose a do-nothing strategy over placing either a limit or market order. This could support a very wide spread as a new market equilibrium spread. Of course, investors would eventually conclude that the new information was not forthcoming, and trading would resume at its former frequency with the old equilibrium spread reestablished.

Our definition of the equilibrium market spread provides a direct link between the market spread and thinness. Recall that proposition 4 showed that the probability of a limit order executing decreases, for all values of P_t^{LB}, as a security's order arrival rate decreases. Thus, ceteris paribus, thin issues have a lower probability of limit orders executing than do thick issues. This lower probability in turn decreases the proportion of investors choosing limit orders over market orders at any given size of the spread; this implies that, for a thinner issue, a wider spread would be required for the forces that increase and decrease the spread to be in equilibrium. Hence we have:

PROPOSITION 5: Thinner securities will, ceteris paribus, have larger equilibrium market spreads.

VI. Conclusion

We have presented a proof of the existence of market spreads in markets with many traders. The formulation treats continuous prices and allows for heterogeneous trading propensities. The proof is not dependent on the demand of traders for immediacy or on the cost to market makers of providing immediacy.

The literature on bid-ask spreads does not appear to have recognized that aggregation from individual to market spreads is a considerably more complex process than the standard aggregation from individual to market demand and supply functions. Neither has it been established that ordinary investors may sometimes seek to trade via limit orders (and at other times via market orders), hence that these investors will sometimes supply (and at other times demand) immediacy, and that in choosing between market and limit orders investors implement an order placement strategy. In addressing these issues, we have sought to establish the links between transaction costs, individual investor order placement strategy, market thinness, and market spreads.

We have first established that, with transaction costs, the probability of a limit order executing does not rise to unity as the price at which the order is placed gets infinitesimally close to a counterpart market quote. We have next shown that the resulting investor trading strategies generate what we have referred to as a gravitational pull effect. Essentially, in the neighborhood of the current market bid and ask quotations, what might otherwise have been limit orders are instead submitted as market orders (at slightly less desirable prices) so as to achieve certainty of execution. These market orders trigger trades which clear limit orders off the book, widening the market spread. The gravitational pull effect explains why market spreads may be substantial even in markets composed of many traders. Finally, we have defined an equilibrium market spread (where the forces that tend to widen and to narrow the spread are in balance) and have shown it to be positively related to a security's thinness (measured inversely by the order arrival rate).

Our formulation has several implications for the design of a market system. A primary objective of system design should be to expand the extent and frequency with which investors interact with the market by minimizing various transaction costs. Decreasing variable transaction costs will decrease individual spreads and generate a greater order flow; decreasing the costs of monitoring and communicating with the market will also increase the frequency with which investors rebalance their portfolios; and consolidating the currently fragmented system (by, e.g., instituting a consolidated limit order book) will reduce search costs and further shrink spreads by increasing the effective thickness of the market. These costs are all a function of market structure and hence should be amenable to reduction by appropriate system design. However, a major cost of interacting with the market is the cost of decision making, and this might not be subject to significant reduction by exchange organization. For this reason, it is possible that, especially for thinner issues, spreads will remain sizable in a restructured national market system.

Appendix

In this Appendix, we restate formally and prove propositions 1–4 of Section III above and develop the more technical aspects of the arguments presented in Section IV.

Section III

Equation (1) of Section III presents a compound Poisson process as the stochastic process which generates a sequence of market ask prices over time. This can be used to determine the probability that a limit bid order will execute during a particular time period.

Suppose that the price of the limit order to be submitted is greater than the current market bid but less than the current market ask, that is, that $P_t^{MB} < P_t^{LB} < P_t^{MA}$. To determine the probability that the potential limit bid will execute in a time interval of length L, we must find the probability that $P_t^{MA}(\Delta)$ will decrease to a price equal to or less than P_t^{LB}.[16] Therefore, let $Y(L, P_t^{MA}, P_t^{LB})$ be the probability that the minimum value that $P_t^{MA}(\Delta)$ achieves in the interval $0 \leq \Delta \leq L$ is equal to or less than P_t^{LB}. As P_t^{LB} approaches P_t^{MA}, we would expect the probability of the potential limit bid executing to increase, since the amount that $P_t^{MA}(\Delta)$ would have to decline would be reduced. However, in the

[16] For P_t^{MA} discretely greater than P_t^{LB}, the possibility of another investor submitting a limit order with a price greater than P_t^{LB} will only tend to decrease the probability of execution of the original limit order. Thus our proof of existence of the probability jump at P_t^{MA} is conservative.

limit as P_t^{LB} approaches P_t^{MA} from below, without further analysis it is unclear how far the probability will rise. Therefore, let

$$\phi(L, P_t^{MA}) = 1 - \lim_{P_t^{LB} \to P_t^{MA}} Y(L, P_t^{MA}, P_t^{LB}),$$

where the limit is understood to be from below. We now prove:

PROPOSITION 1: If $P_t^{MA}(\Delta)$ is generated by the compound Poisson process of equation (1), then $\phi(L, P_t^{MA}) > 0$ for all intervals of length $L < \infty$.[17]

PROOF: Since Z_i is stochastic with mean zero, $P(Z_i \geq 0) > 0$. Furthermore, the value of the Poisson random variable $N(L)$ will be finite in any interval of length L less than infinity. Therefore, the probability of $N(L)$ consecutive Z_i observations that are greater than or equal to zero is given by $[P(Z_i \geq 0)]^{N(L)}$, which, since $N(L)$ is finite, must be strictly greater than zero. Notice that if all the Z_i observations are greater than or equal to zero, the value of $P_t^{MA}(\Delta)$ must be greater than or equal to P_t^{MA} throughout the interval $0 \leq \Delta \leq L$; thus the limit order P_t^{LB} would not have executed. This is sufficient to demonstrate the probability jump. Clearly, there are other sample paths that $P_t^{MA}(\Delta)$ could have followed which also would have failed to execute the limit order.

PROPOSITION 2: If $P_t^{MA}(\Delta)$ is generated by the Wiener process of equation (2), then $\phi(L, P_t^{MA}) = 0$ for all intervals of length $L < \infty$.

PROOF: By the reflection principle for a continuous Wiener process (see Karlin 1968, pp. 276–77) and since $\ln P_t^{MA}(\Delta)$ is driftless,

$$Y(L, P_t^{MA}, P_t^{LB}) = \Pr\{\min_{0 \leq \Delta \leq L} P_t^{MA}(\Delta) \leq P_t^{LB}\} = \Pr\{\min_{0 \leq \Delta \leq L} \ln P_t^{MA}(\Delta) \leq \ln P_t^{LB}\}$$

$$= 2 \Pr\{\ln P_{t+1}^{MA} < \ln P_t^{LB}\} = 2 \Pr\{P_{t+1}^{MA} < P_t^{LB}\}$$

$$= \frac{2}{\sigma\sqrt{2\pi L}} \int_{-\infty}^{P_t^{LB}} \exp\left\{-\frac{1}{2L}\left(\frac{x - P_t^{MA}}{\sigma}\right)^2\right\} dx,$$

where the latter probability distribution follows from the definition of the Wiener process. Now

$$\lim_{P_t^{LB} \to P_t^{MA}} Y(L, P_t^{MA}, P_t^{LB}) = \frac{2}{\sigma\sqrt{2\pi L}} \int_{-\infty}^{P_t^{MA}} \exp\left\{-\frac{1}{2L}\left(\frac{x - P_t^{MA}}{\sigma}\right)^2\right\} dx.$$

Substituting the variable $y = (x - P_t^{MA})/(\sigma\sqrt{L})$, the preceding limit equals $(2/\sqrt{2\pi}) \int_{-\infty}^{0} \exp\{-\frac{1}{2} y^2\} dy = 2(\frac{1}{2}) = 1$.

PROPOSITION 3: If the random variable Z_i is expressed as a Bernoulli random variable, with $Pr(Z_i = \alpha) = Pr(Z_i = -\alpha) = 1/2$, and if the arrival rate ν of the Poisson process $N(\Delta)$ goes to infinity, while simultaneously reducing the size of α in such a way that $\nu\alpha^2$ remains constant, the compound Poisson process approaches the Wiener process described by equation (2) with $\sigma^2 = \nu\alpha^2$.

PROOF: This follows from the theorem that the characteristic function for the compound Poisson approaches that of the Wiener process (see Parzen 1962, p. 99).

PROPOSITION 4: $[\partial Y(L, P_t^{MA}, P_t^{LB})]/\partial \nu > 0$ for all $P_t^{LB} < P_t^{MA}$ and $L < \infty$.

PROOF: By the Markov property of the compound Poisson process, increasing (decreasing) the order arrival rate by some factor λ is identical to

---

[17] This proposition would also hold for other stochastic jump processes where the number of price changes is finite in any finite interval.

EXISTENCE OF THE BID-ASK SPREAD

increasing (decreasing) the length of time L between decision points by λ. When λ is increased, those sample paths of the process which initially satisfied

$$\min_{0 \leq \Delta \leq L} P_t^{MA}(\Delta) \leq P_t^{LB}$$

will still continue to do so. On the other hand, some sample paths where

$$\min_{0 \leq \Delta \leq L} P_t^{MA}(\Delta) > P_t^{LB}$$

will now satisfy the inequality

$$\min_{0 \leq \Delta \leq \lambda L} P_t^{MA}(\Delta) \leq P_t^{LB}.$$

Therefore, $Y(L, P_t^{MA}, P_t^{LB})$ would increase for $\lambda > 1$ for all values of $P_t^{LB} < P_t^{MA}$. Similarly, $Y(L, P_t^{MA}, P_t^{LB})$ would decrease if the order arrival rate λ is decreased.

Section IV

We now present the more technical aspects of the model of an investor's order placement strategy discussed in Section IV. The subjectively determined probability distributions are specified as follows. First, the probability distribution of future market bid and ask prices is given by $h(P_{t+1}^{MA}, P_{t+1}^{MB} | P_t^{MA}, P_t^{MB})$, where h is a joint density function for market asks and bids $(P_{t+1}^{MA}, P_{t+1}^{MB})$ at time $t + 1$, given the prices at t. Consistent with random walk models of security price behavior, we condition future prices only on current prices. Consistent with Section III, we let the investor's subjective probability of a limit order executing before $t + 1$ be given by $p(P_t^{LB}, P_t^{MA}, P_t^{MB})$, where P_t^{LB} is the limit bid price. (Again, this is consistent with random walk theory, since we need know only current market quotes to predict whether or not the limit order will be executed.) Last, we assume the investor determines conditional probability distributions of future prices in the event of either a successful or unsuccessful limit order. That is, for a limit bid at price P_t^{LB} submitted at time t, let $k(P_{t+1}^{MA}, P_{t+1}^{MB} | P_t^{MA}, P_t^{MB}, P_t^{LB})$ be the joint density function of market bid and ask prices at time $t + 1$ if the limit bid executes prior to $t + 1$, and let $l(P_{t+1}^{MA}, P_{t+1}^{MB} | P_t^{MA}, P_t^{MB}, P_t^{LB})$ be the joint density function at time $t + 1$ if the limit bid fails to execute prior to $t + 1$. Note that only three of the four subjective probability distributions h, p, k, and l can be independently determined, since by Bayes's theorem we must have

$$h(x, y | P_t^{MA}, P_t^{MB}) = p(P_t^{LB}, P_t^{MA}, P_t^{MB}) k(x, y | P_t^{MA}, P_t^{MB}, P_t^{LB})$$
$$+ [1 - p(P_t^{LB}, P_t^{MA}, P_t^{MB})] l(x, y | P_t^{MA}, P_t^{MB}, P_t^{LB})$$

for all possible values of P_t^{MA}, P_t^{MB}, and P_t^{LB}.

We can now give a formal statement of the model. Given observed market quotes of P_t^{MA} and P_t^{MB} and holdings by the investor of N_t shares of the security and S_t dollars in cash, at time t the investor's expected utility of terminal wealth can be written as $\psi_t = f_t(P_t^{MA}, P_t^{MB}, N_t, S_t)$.[18]

---
[18] Note that the investor's underlying utility function measures the utility of the wealth he will possess at some horizon T, where $T > t$. The investor will choose those decisions at times $t, t + 1, \ldots, T - 1$ which maximize the expected utility of his terminal wealth. As of time t (the investor's current decision point), viewing the expectations operator as ranging over relevant random variables pertaining to times between t and T, we define ψ_t to be the expected utility of the investor's terminal wealth. Clearly this depends upon the assets the investor has at time t (N_t and S_t) and the current market prices at which the investor can buy or sell shares (P_t^{MA} and P_t^{MB}).

We now derive an expression for ψ_t in terms of the various probability assessments and costs. Write $\psi_t = \max(U_1, U_2, U_3)$, where $U_1 =$ expected terminal utility if a market order is placed at time t, $U_2 =$ expected terminal utility if a limit order is placed at time t, and $U_3 =$ expected terminal utility of doing nothing at time t. More precisely, letting x and y be values for the ask and bid prices at time $t + 1$, respectively, we have

$$U_1 = \int_0^\infty \int_0^\infty f_{t+1}(x, y, N_t + \Delta N, S_t - C^M - N \cdot P_t^{MA}) \cdot h(x, y \mid P_t^{MA}, P_t^{MB}) dx dy.$$

As stated in Section IV, we assume that the number of shares to be purchased, ΔN, is fixed. Define the function

$$U_2(P_t^{LB}) = p(P_t^{LB}, P_t^{MA}, P_t^{MB}) \int_0^\infty \int_0^\infty f_{t+1}(x, y, N_t + \Delta N,$$

$$S_t - C^{L1} - C^{L2} - \Delta N \cdot P_t^{LB}) \cdot k(x, y \mid P_t^{MA}, P_t^{MB}, P_t^{LB}) dx dy$$

$$+ [1 - p(P_t^{LB}, P_t^{MA}, P_t^{MB})] \int_0^\infty \int_0^\infty f_{t+1}(x, y, N_t, S_t - C^{L1})$$

$$\cdot l(x, y \mid P_t^{MA}, P_t^{MB}, P_t^{LB}) dx dy$$

for all possible prices of the limit order. Then we have

$$U_2 = \max_{P_t^{LB}} U_2(P_t^{LB}).$$

Finally, for the do-nothing option we have

$$U_3 = \int_0^\infty \int_0^\infty f_{t+1}(x, y, N_t, S_t) \cdot h(x, y \mid P_t^{MA}, P_t^{MB}) dx dy.$$

The dynamic programming recursion permits us to obtain a solution for f_t in the order $T - 1, T - 2, \ldots, 2, 1$. This is possible since we assume the utility value for f_T is known for all values of the parameter P_T^{MA}, P_T^{MB}, N_T, and S_T. We have defined this recursion in terms of the four state variables P_t^{MA}, P_t^{MB}, N_t, and S_t. We also have two decision variables, P_t^{LB} and the decision as to which of the three courses of action to take.

References

Amihud, Yakov, and Mendelson, Haim. "Dealership Market: Market-making with Inventory." *J. Financial Econ.* 8 (March 1980): 31–53.
Beja, Avraham, and Hakansson, Nils H. "Dynamic Market Processes and the Rewards to Up-to-Date Information." *J. Finance* 32 (May 1977): 291–304.
Benston, George J., and Hagerman, Robert L. "Determinants of Bid-Asked Spreads in the Over-the-Counter Market." *J. Financial Econ.* 1 (December 1974): 353–64.
Branch, Ben, and Freed, Walter. "Bid-Asked Spreads on the Amex and the Big Board." *J. Finance* 32 (March 1977): 159–63.
Cohen, Kalman J.; Hawawini, Gabriel A.; Maier, Steven F.; Schwartz, Robert A.; and Whitcomb, David K. "Implications of Microstructure Theory for Empirical Research on Stock Price Behavior." *J. Finance* 35 (May 1980): 249–57.
Cohen, Kalman J.; Maier, Steven F.; Schwartz, Robert A.; and Whitcomb,

David K. "The Returns Generation Process, Returns Variance, and the Effect of Thinness in Securities Markets." *J. Finance* 33 (March 1978): 149–67.

———. "Market Makers and the Market Spread: A Review of Recent Literature." *J. Financial and Quantitative Analysis* 14 (November 1979): 813–35.

Demsetz, Harold. "The Cost of Transacting." *Q.J.E.* 82 (February 1968): 33–53.

Garman, Mark B. "Market Microstructure." *J. Financial Econ.* 3 (June 1976): 257–75.

Hamilton, James L. "Competition, Scale Economies, and Transaction Cost in the Stock Market." *J. Financial and Quantitative Analysis* 11 (December 1976): 779–802.

———. "Marketplace Organization and Marketability: NASDAQ, the Stock Exchange, and the National Market System." *J. Finance* 33 (May 1978): 487–503.

Ho, Thomas, and Stoll, Hans R. "Optimal Dealer Pricing under Transactions and Return Uncertainty." Working Paper, New York Univ., Graduate School Bus. Admin., 1979.

———. "On Dealer Markets under Competition." *J. Finance* 35 (May 1980): 259–67.

Karlin, Samuel. *A First Course in Stochastic Processes.* 2d ed., enl. New York: Academic Press, 1968.

Merton, Robert C. "An Intertemporal Capital Asset Pricing Model." *Econometrica* 41 (September 1973): 867–87.

Newton, William, and Quandt, Richard E. "An Empirical Study of Spreads." Working Paper, Princeton Univ., Dept. Econ., 1979.

Parzen, Emanuel. *Stochastic Processes.* San Francisco: Holden-Day, 1962.

Schleef, Harald J., and Mildenstein, Eckhard. "A Dynamic Model of the Security Dealer's Bid and Ask Prices." Paper presented at meetings of the Western Economic Association, Las Vegas, 1979.

Smidt, Seymour. "Continuous vs. Intermittent Trading on Auction Markets." Working Paper, Cornell Univ., Graduate School Bus. and Public Admin., 1979.

Stigler, George J. "The Economics of Information." *J.P.E.* 69, no. 3 (June 1961): 213–25.

———. "Public Regulation of the Securities Markets." *J. Bus.* 37 (April 1964): 117–42.

Stoll, Hans R. "The Supply of Dealer Services in Securities Markets." *J. Finance* 33 (September 1978): 1133–51. (*a*)

———. "The Pricing of Security Dealer Services: An Empirical Study of NASDAQ Stocks." *J. Finance* 33 (September 1978): 1153–72. (*b*)

Tinic, Seha M. "The Economics of Liquidity Services." *Q.J.E.* 86 (February 1972): 79–93.

Tinic, Seha M., and West, Richard R. "Competition and the Pricing of Dealer Service in the Over-the-Counter Stock Market." *J. Financial and Quantitative Analysis* 7 (June 1972): 1707–27.

———. "Marketability of Common Stocks in Canada and the U.S.A.: A Comparison of Agent versus Dealer Dominated Markets." *J. Finance* 29 (June 1974): 729–46.

U.S. Securities and Exchange Commission. *Institutional Investor Study Report.* 92d Cong., 1st sess. House Document no. 92-64, 1971.

West, Richard R., and Tinic, Seha M. *The Economics of the Stock Market.* New York: Praeger, 1971.

The Dynamics of Dealer Markets Under Competition

THOMAS S. Y. HO and HANS R. STOLL*

ABSTRACT

The behavior of competing dealers in securities markets is analyzed. Securities are characterized by stochastic returns and stochastic transactions. Reservation bid and ask prices of dealers are derived under alternative assumptions about the degree to which transactions are correlated across stocks at a given time and over time in a given stock. The conditions for interdealer trading are specified, and the equilibrium distribution of dealer inventories and the equilibrium market spread are derived. Implications for the structure of securities markets are examined.

IN THIS PAPER the behavior of competing dealers in security markets is examined. Much of the theoretical work on dealers (Demsetz [6], Tinic [18], Garman [8], Stoll [16], Amihud and Mendelson [1], Ho and Stoll [11], Copeland and Galai [3], Mildenstein and Schleef [13]) has recognized that dealers may face competition from other dealers or investors placing limit orders, but nonetheless has analyzed only a single (representative) dealer. This approach is quite reasonable for the New York Stock Exchange specialist who has a quasi-monopoly position, but it is less applicable when considering other markets such as the over-the-counter market where there are several dealers with equal access to the market. Similarly the empirical studies of dealer bid-ask spreads (Demsetz [6], Tinic [18], Tinic and West [19], Benston and Hagerman [2], Stoll [17], Smidt [15]) have either been based on models of a single dealer or have lacked a theoretical foundation based on the microeconomics of the dealer.

This paper develops a theoretical model of equilibrium in a market with competing dealers and provides a basis for empirical work that would distinguish competing and monopolistic dealer markets. The paper is concerned with the behavior and interaction of individual competing dealers and with the determination of the market bid-ask spread. Markets with several dealers, several stocks and several periods are considered. Dealers bear risk arising not only from uncertainty about the returns on their inventories but also from uncertainty about the arrival of transactions. Each dealer also recognizes that his welfare depends on the actions of other dealers and each sets bid and ask prices to maximize his own expected utility of terminal wealth. A recent paper by Cohen, Maier, Schwartz and Whitcomb [5] examines similar issues in the context of an auction market in which the market spread is determined by limit orders. However, unlike the model of this paper, their analysis is not based as clearly on a model of individual traders' maximizing behaviors nor are the costs of placing

* Financial support of the Dean's Fund for Faculty Research at the Owen Graduate School of Management is gratefully acknowledged.

limit orders explicitly derived. In an interesting paper, Garbade and Silber [7] examine some of the broader issues of structuring a securities market in terms of the effect of dealers on the frequency with which markets clear. However, they do not examine the transaction-by-transaction dynamics of a market, something with which we deal.

Our approach is to apply a model of an individual dealer operating under return and transactions uncertainty (Ho and Stoll [11]) to the case of more than one dealer and the problem of determining the equilibrium market bid-ask spread.[1] The paper is organized as follows. The dynamics of the individual dealer and the dynamic programming problem of the dealer in the presence of a competitor are specified in Section I. In Section II dealer reservation buying and selling fees under a one period horizon are derived. The interaction of dealers and of incoming orders is examined in Section III, and the equilibrium distribution of inventories across dealers and the equilibrium market spread are derived under the assumption of homogeneous risk preferences. In Section IV we show that the equilibrium market spread is not affected by the introduction of heterogeneous opinions about the true price of the stock. The effect on dealer fees of extending the time horizon and of permitting serial correlation in transactions is examined in Section V. The paper concludes with an examination of the implications of the model for the structure of securities markets and with a section summarizing the major conclusions of the paper.

I. The Individual Dealer

As a simplifying assumption, the formal analysis in this paper is restricted to two dealers, A and B, each making a market in two stocks. Unless specified otherwise, the dealers have homogeneous opinions about the true value of each stock. At various points, the analysis is extended to many stocks, to many dealers, and to heterogeneous opinions. In this section the return dynamics and transaction dynamics affecting each component of dealer A's wealth are presented, and the dealer's maximization problem is specified. The dynamics for dealer B are the same except for a change of notation. Our notational convention is to denote variables of dealer B by the superscript "0".

A. Dynamics of a Dealer

Each dealer's wealth consists of three components: inventory of each of the stocks, cash and base wealth.

1. Inventory. The dollar values of the dealer's inventories of his two stocks are given by

$$M_{t-1} = (1 + r_M)[M_t + q_M(Q, -Q)] + [M_t + q_M(Q, -Q)]Z_M \qquad (1)$$

and

$$N_{t-1} = (1 + r_N)[N_t + q_N(Q, -Q)] + [N_t + q_N(Q, -Q)]Z_N \qquad (2)$$

---

[1] The formal model is changed slightly in that we use discrete time stochastic processes in this paper rather than the continuous time stochastic processes in Ho and Stoll [11]. Some preliminary results under competition—particularly the idea of second best pricing and a preliminary formulation of the condition for interdealer trading are in Ho and Stoll [10].

where

M, N Dollar value of dealer's inventory of stock M or N. As a subscript also serves as an identifier of the stock.

t Subscript giving the number of periods remaining to the horizon date.

$r_i, i = M, N$ Dealer's expected per period rate of return in stock i in the absence of bid or ask fees.

$Z_i \sim N(0, \sigma_i^2), i = M, N$ Stochastic component in the return of stock i.

Q Dollar transaction size in each stock.[2]

$q_i(Q, -Q)$ Realization of the stochastic transaction process in stock i, defined as follows:

$$q_i(Q, -Q) \begin{cases} \dfrac{\lambda_i}{} \; Q & \text{if } b_i < b_i^0, \; 0 \text{ otherwise} \\ \dfrac{\lambda_i}{} \; -Q & \text{if } a_i < a_i^0, \; 0 \text{ otherwise} \\ 1 - 2\lambda_i \; \; 0 & \end{cases} \quad (3)$$

$\lambda_i, i = M, N$ Probability of a public sale (dealer purchase) of Q dollars or of a public purchase (dealer sale) of $-Q$ dollars in each period. Unless indicated otherwise we assume that transactions in a given stock or in different stocks are independent and therefore that the probability of two transactions in a period—λ^2—is small enough to be ignored.

$a_i, b_i, i = M, N$ Dealer's proportional reservation selling fee and proportional reservation buying fee, respectively. (The superscript "0" indicates the fee of dealer B.) The reservation fee is the minimum fee such that the dealer's expected utility of terminal wealth would not be lowered were he to buy at a bid price, $p(1 - b_i)$ or sell at an asking price, $p(1 + a_i)$, where p is the dealer's opinion of the true price of the stock. Inventories (M, N) and transactions (Q) are valued by the dealer at his true price; and the return, $r_i, i = M, N$, is calculated on the basis of his opinion of the true price. For simplicity this price is the same for each stock, something that can be accomplished by appropriate stock splits.

The transaction process (3), facing dealer A, depends on his reservation fee relative to the fee of his competitor, B. (However, the fee which dealer A will set is not generally equal to his reservation fee. This issue is discussed below.) Although the probability of a public sale (dealer purchase) in stock i is λ_i, the

---

[2] Contrary to actual practice, we assume a fixed transaction value rather than a fixed number of shares per transaction. This is because the transaction value is the relevant variable in determining dealer fees. Since one can pick any value of Q, the assumption does not constrain our conclusions in any way.

probability that dealer A makes the transaction is λ_i only if $b_i < b_i^0$. In words, (3) says that, conditional on having the lower reservation fee, the process $q_i(Q, -Q)$ for dealer A takes on the value Q with probability λ_i and $-Q$ with the same probability, λ_i; and no transaction occurs with probability $1 - 2\lambda_i$. The probability of a transaction is zero if B has the lower reservation fee.

The interpretation of (1) or (2) is now as follows. The dealer enters period t with an inventory M_t, N_t that is changed according to the stochastic transaction process, $q_i(Q, -Q)$. The new inventory is then subject to return dynamics consisting of two components: a deterministic return, r_i, and a stochastic return, Z_i. Thus both transaction uncertainty and return uncertainty affect the position of the dealer as he moves from period t to period $t - 1$.

2. Cash. Cash is accumulated when the dealer sells securities (short selling is permitted) and paid out when the dealer buys securities. Any balance in the cash account earns (or pays) the risk-free rate, r. Then the value of the cash account is

$$F_{t-1} = (1 + r)[F_t + q_M(-Q + b_M Q, Q + a_M Q)$$
$$+ q_N(-Q + b_N Q, Q + a_N Q)] \quad (4)$$

where the transaction arrival process, q_M or q_N is the same as (3) with q taking on the values $-Q + bQ$, $Q + aQ$ or 0; i.e., the dollar cash flows are opposite in sign from the value of shares traded and different by the amount of the dealer's fee.

3. Base wealth. Base wealth is an efficient portfolio of the dealer's assets other than cash and share inventory generated by his dealership activity. Base wealth is used as collateral for the borrowing of money or shares. The dollar value of the dealer's base wealth, Y, follows the following return dynamics:

$$Y_{t-1} = (1 + r_Y)Y_t + Y_t Z_Y \quad (5)$$

where r_Y = expected return on base wealth and $Z_Y \sim N(0, \sigma_Y^2)$.

B. Competitive Equilibrium and the Dealer's Problem

Analogous to a progressive auction, investors are assumed to interrogate dealers to elicit the maximum buying price and minimum selling price each dealer is willing to post at each point in time. Trading is assumed to take place only at the bid or ask prices posted by the dealers.

The dealer determines his buying and selling fee so as to maximize expected utility of terminal wealth for every state of the world in which the dealer may find himself. The dealer must set bid and ask prices not only in anticipation of random transaction arrivals and returns, but also in anticipation of what his competitor may do. Indeed only if the dealer believes he can make transactions at fees in excess of his reservation fees, is it worthwhile to continue as a dealer; and he must determine if his competitor's position will allow him this freedom.

Dealer A's elementary utility function over terminal wealth (at $t = 0$) is $U(W_0)$ where

$$W_0 = F_0 + Y_0 + M_0 + N_0 \quad (6)$$

Viewed from earlier periods ($t > 0$), terminal wealth is uncertain and dependent on dealer actions in the intervening periods. At each earlier period, dealer A acts on the basis of a derived utility function $J(\ )$ defined as

$$J(t, F, M, N, Y, F^0, M^0, N^0, Y^0)$$
$$= \max_{\substack{a_M, b_M \\ a_N, b_N}} EU(W_0 | t, F, M, N, Y, F^0, M^0, N^0, Y^0) \quad (7)$$

The function $J(\ )$ is the solution to the maximization problem. It is the derived utility when the dealer follows the optimal strategy for setting a_i, b_i at each point in time; and it depends on the state of the world described by the variables in the function; namely, time remaining and the portfolio characteristics of both dealers.[3]

We have elsewhere solved an analogous function $J(\ )$ in a continuous time framework for the case of a single monopoly dealer (Ho and Stoll [11]). The procedure for two dealers trading two stocks is the same except that the optimal strategies of the two dealers must be simultaneously determined. Many insights may be achieved, however, without solving this complicated dynamic programming problem. We consider first the determinates of dealer reservation fees in a simple one period environment.

II. Dealer Reservation Fees Under a One Period Horizon

Only when there is one period remaining does the reservation fee of each dealer not depend on the inventory position of the other dealer. This is because all positions are assumed to be liquidated in the next period at next period's true price. As a result, the probability of trading next period and the price to be received are independent of the other dealer's actions.

Proposition 1: With independent transactions in M and N and with one period left to the horizon date, a dealer with inventories of M and N has reservation buying and selling fees for stock M that are approximately given by

$$b_M = \frac{1}{2} \sigma_M^2 R(Q + 2I_M) \quad (8a)$$

$$a_M = \frac{1}{2} \sigma_M^2 R(Q - 2I_M) \quad (8b)$$

where

$I_M = M + \beta_{NM} N$
$\beta_{NM} = \sigma_{NM}/\sigma_M^2$
σ_M^2 = per period variance of return of stock M.
σ_{NM} = per period covariance of return between stock M and N.
$R = \dfrac{-U''(W)}{(1+r)U'(W)}$, a discounted coefficient of absolute risk aversion.

[3] It may not be necessary to know the portfolio characteristics of the other dealer directly since they may be inferred from pricing actions.

The same result, with appropriate changes in notation, holds for stock N.

Proof: When the return dynamics are given as in (5), the expected utility, using the Pratt-Arrow approximation, is given by

$$EU(Y_0) = U(Y_1) + r_Y Y_1 U'(Y_1) + \frac{1}{2} U''(Y_1) \sigma_Y^2 Y_1^2 \tag{9}$$

where $U'(\ )$ and $U''(\ )$ are the first and second derivatives of the elementary utility function. In an analogous fashion, for the return dynamics of the dealer's total portfolio (which is $W_1 = M_1 + N_1 + F_1 + Y_1$), the expected utility without any transaction is given by

$$EU(W_0) = U(W) + (r_Y Y + r_M M + r_N N + rF)U'(W)$$
$$+ \frac{1}{2} U''(W)(Y^2 \sigma_Y^2 + M^2 \sigma_M^2 + N^2 \sigma_N^2 + 2MN\sigma_{MN} + 2MY\sigma_{MY} + 2NY\sigma_{NY}) \tag{10}$$

where the time subscripts on the right hand side of (10) are omitted, and it is understood that one period remains. Immediately after a sale of stock M (such that, in (10), M becomes $M - Q$ and F becomes $F + Q + \pi Q$, π being the dealer's proportional fee) the dealer's expected utility of his new uncertain terminal wealth position, W_0^s is

$$EU(W_0^s) = EU(W_0) + U'(W)(1 + r)\pi Q \tag{11}$$
$$+ \frac{1}{2} U''(W)(\sigma_M^2 Q^2 - 2\sigma_M^2 MQ - 2\sigma_{MN} NQ)$$

where we assume stock M is in the efficient portfolio Y and, therefore, meets the standard first order condition:

$$r_M - r = \frac{-U''(W)}{U'(W)} Y\sigma_{MY}. \tag{12}$$

If expected utility is not to be lowered after the transaction, we require that $EU(W_0^s) \geq EU(W_0)$. By the definition of the reservation selling fee a_M being the minimum of the selling fees π meeting this condition, Equation (8b) follows directly from (11) and the condition that $EU(W_0^s) = EU(W_0)$. The reservation buying fee for stock M and the reservation fees for stock N can be calculated by the same procedure. Q.E.D.

Inspection of (8) shows that the dealer's fee depends on the stock's risk as measured by the variance of return, on his attitude toward risk, R, on the transaction size, Q, and on the current inventory of the dealer in his stocks, M and N. The appropriate measure of risk is σ_M^2, not σ_{MY}. The optimal holding of stock M, which is part of Y, has a risk measured by σ_{MY}, but this "systematic" risk is offset by the excess return of the stock, $r_M - r$, and therefore does not appear in (8). Because any holding of the stock in the dealer's inventory is non-optimal, σ_M^2 is the relevant measure of risk with respect to that amount by which inventory exceeds the optimal.

The impact of a transaction, Q, depends on the dealer's initial inventory. For example, a purchase by a dealer with a short position would be risk reducing and would result in a negative buying fee. In measuring the initial inventory for the purpose of evaluating the impact of a transaction in stock i, all stocks, j, correlated with stock i are aggregated, using $\beta_{ji} = \sigma_{ji}/\sigma_i^2$ as a weight. In other words, the size of the dealer's initial inventory is measured in terms of equivalent risk units of stock i, where equivalence is determined from the covariance of returns between other stocks and stock i. An implication of this result is that a change in the holding of any stock changes the bid and ask fees of every other stock with which it is correlated, the fee change depending on the size of the change in holdings and the degree of equivalence between the two stocks as measured by β_{ji}.

Corollary: From the definition of the spread as $s = a + b$, it follows immediately from (8) that the reservation spread in stock i is given by

$$s_i = \sigma_i^2 RQ \qquad (13)$$

In a one period world, while the dealer's inventory affects a or b alone, the reservation spread is independent of inventory. A positive inventory raises the reservation buying fee but reduces the reservation selling fee by a corresponding amount. Thus, in adjusting to changes in inventory, the dealer raises or lowers both the reservation bid and ask price relative to the true price without changing the distance between them.

It is often suggested that diversification of the dealer's inventory beyond one or two stocks would reduce return risk and thereby reduce the reservation spread. However, since inventory does not appear in (13), it follows that the degree of diversification of the dealer's inventory has no effect on his reservation spread. This is because bid and ask prices are adjusted to the dealer's inventory with the result that the spread reflects only the risk of the incremental transaction.[4] Thus under the assumption of independent transactions processes for stocks, the spread is independent of the number of stocks in which the dealer makes a market. Furthermore the dealer is indifferent as to whether the next transaction is a purchase or sale because bid and ask fees are prices of contingent services determined such that dealer welfare is unaffected by the outcome of the transaction process.

When transaction processes in different stocks are not independent, dealer reservation fees and the reservation spread are affected by the degree to which transactions in the dealer's stocks are correlated. Intuitively, if returns are positively correlated, positively correlated transactions in two stocks have the same effect as increasing the transaction size in a single stock; and we know dealer fees increase with Q. Conversely offsetting transactions in two stocks with positively correlated returns have the same effect as reducing the transaction size and the fee in a single stock. The dealer is thus concerned to diversify his set of stocks against transaction uncertainty (rather than return uncertainty), and he will attempt to choose stocks in which transactions are offsetting or independent. The reservation fee in the case of correlated transactions is derived in the appendix.

[4] Base wealth of the dealer is optimally diversified and the issue is whether there is any benefit to diversification of that portion of total wealth which is the dealer's trading account. Since R is a function of wealth, the spread depends on dealer wealth.

We now turn to the process by which the market bid-ask spread is determined, and we shall assume in the following section that transactions are uncorrelated. If transactions are correlated the results would be modified in a straight forward way along the lines discussed in the appendix.

III. The Market Bid-Ask Spread Under a One Period Horizon

A. Dealer Pricing Strategy and Conditions on the Market Spread

While reservation bid and ask prices may differ across dealers, there is at each moment only one market bid price and one market ask price. The competitive market equilibrium we assume reduces the profits that would accrue to a single dealer (as in Ho and Stoll [11]), but it does not necessarily cause each dealer to quote his reservation price. Indeed, if that were the case, no incentive to be a dealer would exist. A dealer is able to quote a fee above his reservation fee because he is in a temporarily advantageous position (in terms of inventory and/ or attitude toward risk) with respect to his competitor, and thereby earns a temporary producer surplus. Thus, which dealer makes the next transaction and what market fee above the reservation fee can be charged depends on the relative positions of the dealers.

Consider a market with any number of competing dealers. Rank dealers in ascending order of their reservation buying fees and their reservation selling fees. The first dealer is the dealer with the lowest reservation fee. The second dealer is the dealer with the next lowest reservation fee, which may be the same fee. Reservation fees of different dealers are identified by different superscripts as follows:

First seller	a	b
Second seller	a^0	b^0
Second buyer	a'	b'
First buyer	a^*	b^*

where

$$a \leq a^0 \leq a' \leq a^* \quad \text{and} \quad b^* \leq b' \leq b^0 \leq b$$

Then the market bid-ask spread, s, is

$$s = \frac{p(1 + a^0) - p(1 - b')}{p} = a^0 + b'. \quad (14)$$

The dealer with the lowest reservation fee has no incentive to quote that fee. He will instead quote his nearest competitor's reservation fee (less a small amount). In other words the second best dealers set the market spread. This result requires knowledge of competing dealers' inventory positions, which might be inferred from observed transactions, and knowledge of competing dealers' risk attitudes.[5]

---

[5] Alternatively, one can view the process of setting public bid-ask quotes as a progressive auction in which all dealers (except one) raise bid prices and lower ask prices to their reservation prices and thereby reveal their reservation prices. The theory of such auctions is discussed in Vickrey [20].

The first seller and the first buyer are determined by their risk attitudes and inventories. Given identical inventories for all dealers, the dealer with the lowest value of R is both first buyer and first seller. However, as he acquires (disposes of) inventory, he changes his fee so that he loses his position as first buyer (seller). Thus the least risk averse dealer does not have a natural monopoly.

Given identical R, the dealer with most inventory of a stock (measured in equivalent risk units of all his stocks) is the first seller. If a dealer trades two stocks, M and N, the inventory of the first seller in equivalent risk units of stock M is said to exceed that of the second seller if

$$I_M = M + \beta_{NM}N > I_M^0 = M^0 + \beta_{NM}N^0,$$

a condition that can be satisfied even if $M < M^0$. The dealer with the least inventory of a stock (measured in equivalent risk units of all stocks) is the first buyer.

B. Inter-dealer Trading and the Equilibrium Distribution of Inventories Under Homogeneous Risk Preferences

Since inventory differences are responsible for differences in reservation fees, one is immediately led to ask whether inter-dealer trading would eliminate such differences and thereby would eliminate the producer surplus dealers periodically earn. Inter-dealer trading arises if a dealer prefers to trade immediately with another dealer rather than wait to trade with the next incoming order with probability λ. We modify the model to allow an instant of time for inter-dealer trading prior to the public order flow and the period of price uncertainty. Consider a market with two dealers trading two stocks and examine the problem from the point of view of dealer A and stock M.

Proposition 2: Assume dealer A is the first seller and has a larger inventory of stock M than does dealer B the second seller; and assume the dealers have the same R. Then A will choose option 1—wait to sell Q of stock M to the next incoming market order if

$$\pi_M > R\sigma_M^2[I_M - \tfrac{1}{2}Q - Q(\lambda_M + \lambda_N\beta_{NM})]. \tag{15}$$

Otherwise A will choose option 2—sell Q of stock M immediately, and pay a fee of π_M.

Proof: Under option 1 (to wait), A's expected utility of terminal wealth can be shown to be

$$EU(W_0) + (1 + r)U'(W_1)Q[\lambda_M(a_M^0 - a_M) + \lambda_N(a_N^0 - a_N)] \tag{16}$$

where $EU(W_0)$ is given by (10) and a_M and a_N are given by (8). Equation (16) says that the expected increment to A's expected utility of waiting for an incoming market order depends on the difference between the market fees (a_M^0, a_N^0) and A's reservation fees (a_M, a_N) weighted by the probabilities (λ_M, λ_N) of receiving the differences. Note that marginal utility is being evaluated just prior to a transaction. Thus, the probability of each transaction enters. There is no possibility that A will make the next buy transaction in either stock, and buying fees do not therefore appear. Under option 2 (to trade now and pay a fee of π_M), A's expected utility of terminal wealth is

$$EU(W_0^\#) + (1 + r)U'(W)Q[\lambda_M(a_M^0 - a_{M\#}) + \lambda_N(a_N^0 - a_{N\#})]$$

where $EU(W_0^\#)$ is given by (11) and represents the dealer's expected utility after a transaction of size Q, and $a_{M\#}$ and $a_{N\#}$ represent the reservation ask fees of dealer A immediately after the inter-dealer transaction in stocks M and N and before realization of the random transactions and return processes. (We assume A continues to be the first seller.) For option 1 to exceed option 2 requires:

$$U'(W)(1 + r)\pi_M Q - \tfrac{1}{2}U''(W)(\sigma_M^2 Q^2 - 2\sigma_M^2 MQ - 2\sigma_{MN}NQ)$$
$$+ U'(W)Q[\lambda_M(a_{M\#} - a_M) + \lambda_N(a_{N\#} - a_N)] > 0$$

Using (8) and simplifying yields the desired result, (15). Q.E.D.

Thus, whenever the fee, π_M, that A must pay B to trade immediately meets condition (15), A would prefer to set an ask fee and bear the uncertainties of waiting to trade with an incoming market order. The decision of dealer A is thus like the decision of any investor coming to the market considering placing a limit order. The investor will place a limit order and trade with the next market order if the fee charged in the market satisfies (15). Otherwise the investor will trade at the market quote.

From (14) we know that dealer A pays the market bid price set by the second buyer. In the case of two dealers, A himself is the second buyer; and therefore $\pi_M = b_M$. Substituting the expression for b_M (Equation 8) for π_M in (15) shows that (15) is always satisfied under the reasonable assumption that $(1 + \lambda_M + \lambda_N\beta_{NM}) > 0$.[6] The reason is simple. Even if λ, the probability of selling to a market order, were zero, A would not sell to B and pay b_M to reduce inventory he is willing to add to at b_M. If $\lambda > 0$, A has the additional possibility of selling to a market order and earning a fee.

Proposition 2 holds for a market with any number of dealers since B can be chosen to be any dealer other than A. However, when there are more than two dealers, the market buying fee may be set by a dealer other than A. In this case, inter-dealer trading may arise. As noted above let a prime (') refer to the second dealer on the buy side who sets the market buying fee. Then $\tau_M = b'_M$ in (15). Applying (8) and simplifying yields the condition for A to wait for an incoming order rather than to sell at b'_M:

$$I_M - I'_M < Q[1 + \lambda_M + \lambda_N\beta_{NM}] \tag{17}$$

Since inter-dealer trading will not occur if condition (17) is met, (17) imposes a limit on the divergence of inventories. We examine this first in the single stock case. Reference to Table 1 is helpful in understanding our notation and the allowable inventory divergence. In the case of one stock (17) becomes

$$M - M' < Q(1 + \lambda_M) \tag{17.a}$$

---

[6] The substitution yields

$$R\sigma_M^2 Q > -R\sigma_M^2 Q(\lambda_M + \lambda_N\beta_{NM})$$

which is always satisfied when $(1 + \lambda_M + \lambda_N\beta_{NM}) > 0$.

Since $0 < \lambda_M < 1$, the largest divergence between the first seller (dealer A) and the second buyer (dealer E) is $M - M' = Q$. Similarly, the largest divergence between the first buyer (dealer F) and the second seller (dealer B) is $M^0 - M^* = Q$. This implies that the largest divergence of inventories between first seller and first buyer is $M - M^* = 2Q$. In Table 1 inventory patterns one and two are not equlibria. In each case there is an incentive for interdealer trading because market bid and ask prices determined by the inventories of the second dealers on each side of the market are "cheap" relative to the inventory holding costs of some of the dealers.

In inventory patterns three and four, all pairs of dealers meet the conditions for no interdealer trading, (17.a). In pattern three, there are no ties of inventory positions at the margin so that the second dealers have no probability of trading with an incoming order. As a result (17.a) applied to second dealers yields $M^0 - M' < Q$, which implies that all dealers other than first dealers have identical inventories. If only three dealers make a market, two will be first dealers; and there can only be one second dealer. In that case it is necessarily true that $M^0 - M' < 0$ since the second seller and second buyer are the same dealer.

In pattern four, a first and a second dealer have the same inventory and would therefore quote the same price. We assume that the second dealer as well as the first has a non-zero probability of trading with the next incoming order. In that case λ_M in (17.a) is not zero when applied to second dealers, and $M^0 - M' = Q$. To the extent that dealers differ on dimensions other than those considered in this paper—such as clerical efficiency—the likelihood of ties at the margin is reduced and with it the likelihood that second dealers have different inventories.

If one makes the reasonable assumption that $0 < \lambda_M + \lambda_N \beta_{NM} < 1$, everything that has been said about the individual stock also applies to the dealer's inventory stated in risk units of stock M, I_M. The difference in inventories of first dealers is $I_M - I_M^* < 2Q$. The difference in inventories of any other pairs of dealers is Q, or less, directly from (17). If no second dealer has the same inventory as a first dealer, the difference in inventories of second dealers is 0 from (17); and, in this case, the probability of trading is zero for a second dealer.

In the case of two stocks, the allowable divergence of inventories in stock M is dependent on the divergence in stock N:

$$M - M' < -\beta_{NM}(N - N') + Q(1 + \lambda_M + \lambda_N) \tag{18}$$

This follows directly from (17) by writing I_M and I'_M in terms of individual stocks as in proposition 1. When returns are correlated, the inventory divergence in M is dependent on the divergence in N. Assuming $\beta_{NM} > 0$, a divergence in excess of Q in M can be offset by an opposite divergence in N.

Corollary: Interdealer trading will not be observed if all transactions of a stock are of a fixed size, Q.

Proof: Once an equilibrium distribution of inventories is established that satisfies (17) for all pairs of dealers, an incoming order cannot disturb inventories in a way that induces interdealer trading. If dealers have identical inventories, an incoming transaction can only produce an inventory difference of Q, which is insufficient to induce interdealer trading. If dealer inventories differ, an incoming transaction is carried out by the dealer whose inventory is most divergent, and

Table 1

Example of Alternative Inventory Patterns in a Market for One Stock Made by Six Dealers

Dealers Ranked on Inventory	Dealer Description	Reservation Fee	Disequilibria			Equilibrium, No Ties at Margin		Equilibrium With Ties at Margin	
			Prob. of a Trade	Pattern One	Pattern Two	Prob. of a Trade	Pattern Three	Prob. of a Trade	Pattern Four
A	First Seller	a	λ	$M = 3Q$	$M = 2Q$	λ	$M = Q$	½λ	$M = Q$
B	Second Seller	a^0	0	$M^0 = 2Q$	$M^0 = Q$	0	$M^0 = 0$	½λ	$M^0 = Q$
C		0	0	0	0	0	0	0	
D		0	0	0	0	0	0	0	
E	Second Buyer	b'	0	$M' = -Q$	$M' = -Q$	0	$M' = 0$	½λ	$M' = 0$
F	First Buyer	b^*	λ	$M^* = -2Q$	$M^* = -Q$	λ	$M^* = -Q$	½λ	$M^* = 0$

who is therefore able to offer the lowest fee. As a result the transaction can only narrow inventory differences. Q.E.D.

C. Equilibrium Market Spread

The "second best" pricing rule specified above and the conditions for inter-dealer trading given in proposition 2, along with the resulting equilibrium distribution of inventories implied by (17) yield limits on the value of the equilibrium market spread when dealers have identical coefficients of absolute risk aversion and identical opinions of the true price of the stock. The limits on the spread depend on the number of dealers making a market in the stock.

Proposition 3: Under homogeneous preferences and opinions, the equilibrium market bid ask spread in a stock satisfies the following conditions, depending on the number of dealers making a market in the stock.

Two dealers:	$s \geq R\sigma^2 Q$	(19.a)
Three dealers:	$s = R\sigma^2 Q$	(19.b)
More than three dealers	$0 \leq s \leq R\sigma^2 Q$	(19.c)

where $R\sigma^2 Q$ is the reservation spread of any dealer.

Proof: From (14), the market bid-ask spread is $s = a^0 + b'$. From (8) and the assumption of identical R, $s = R\sigma^2[Q - (I^0 - I')]$. Thus the equilibrium market spread depends on the equilibrium inventory difference between the second seller and the second buyer which is specified by proposition 2 and by (17). For two dealers, the nearest competitor to the first (and only) seller is the first (and only) buyer. Thus I^0 is to be interpreted as the first buyer's inventory and I' is to be interpreted as the first seller's inventory. By definition of first buyer and first seller, $I^0 \leq I'$ which is sufficient to prove (19.a).[7] For three dealers, we have shown $I^0 - I' = 0$, which is sufficient to prove (19.b). For four or more dealers, we have shown $0 \leq I^0 - I' \leq Q$, which is sufficient to prove (19.c). Q.E.D.

While the market spread may be less than $R\sigma^2 Q$ when there are more than three dealers, this would be relatively rare since it depends on the existence of ties on each side of the market and for an inventory difference between second dealers of Q. In the absence of ties, second dealers would have the same inventory and the market spread would be $R\sigma^2 Q$.[8] Furthermore, should $s = 0$, there is a tendency for inflowing orders to cause this spread to jump to its upper bound of $R\sigma^2 Q$. A public sell order will be traded by the first buyer who will then lower his bid price. Correspondingly a public buy order will be traded by the first seller who will then raise his ask price.

With two dealers there is a corresponding tendency of inflowing orders to push

---

[7] In the case of one dealer, which we have considered in Ho and Stoll [11], there is no limit on the spread from the supply side. There is a limit determined by the demand for dealer services, which is modeled in the cited paper. With only two competing dealers, demand conditions could affect the desirability of setting a price permitted by the competitor's inventory position. However, the flow of incoming orders keeps inventories from diverging by an amount that would make this an important consideration.

[8] This could, for example, be broken by slight differences in risk aversion or clerical costs.

the spread to its lower bound of $R\sigma^2 Q$. A public sell order will be purchased by the dealer with the smaller inventory. This process narrows inventory differences and narrows the market spread. Under homogeneous preferences there is thus a tendency for the equilibrium market spread to be the reservation spread of any dealer.

IV. Equilibrium Market Spread Under Heterogeneous Opinions

In this section the effect of disagreement about the true price of the stock on the pattern of dealer inventories and on the equilibrium market spread is analyzed. We assume there are more than three dealers each with the same R, and that all dealers initially agree and have $I = 0$. Now suppose new information generates disagreement about the true current price of the stock without changing opinions of σ^2 or the underlying market clearing price. Disagreement induces trading until the inventory risk of the shares acquired by optimistic dealers tends to offset the optimists' more favorable opinion, and conversely such that the inventory risk of the short position of pessimistic dealers tend to offset the pessimists' unfavorable opinion.

Under heterogeneous expectations, (14) may be written as

$$s = \frac{p^0(1 + a^0) - p'(1 - b')}{1}$$

where subscripts for the stock are suppressed and where

1   underlying market clearing price in the absence of any dealer trading costs— an average of dealer's opinions of the true price. The price is scaled to one for convenience.[9]

$p^0 = (1 + \varepsilon^0)$ opinion of stock's true price of second seller who sets ask price; $\varepsilon^0 < 0$ is the deviation of his opinion from the average.

$p' = (1 + \varepsilon')$ opinion of true price of second buyer who sets bid price; $\varepsilon' > 0$ is the deviation of his opinion from the average.

We can write the market spread as

$$s = (a^0 + b') - (\varepsilon' - \varepsilon^0) \tag{20}$$

(where we have assumed $a^0 \varepsilon^0 = -b' \varepsilon'$), and using (8) this becomes

$$s = \tfrac{1}{2} R\sigma^2 (Q^0 + Q') - R\sigma^2 (I^0 - I') - (\varepsilon' - \varepsilon^0) \tag{21}$$

where Q^0 and Q' are the transaction values at the personal valuations of each of the dealers.

Under homogeneous opinions, $Q^0 = Q' = Q$, $\varepsilon^0 = \varepsilon' = 0$, and $I' - I^0 \leq Q$ in equilibrium. Under heterogeneous opinions, differences of opinion generate inventory differences such that the last two terms of (21) tend to be offsetting.

---

[9] When dealers disagree it is not clear how one should define the proportional market spread. We have simply chosen to divide by the average "true" price. In fact, otherwise identical dealers will, simply because they have different opinions of the true price, define different proportional spreads. This causes some unnecessary complexities that do not invalidate the basic points. Thus we have simply assumed that proportional spreads are the same for different dealers.

However the effect may not be exact just as in the case of homogeneous expectations $(I' - I^0)$ is not necessarily zero. Define the net unwanted inventory as

$$\Omega^0 = I^0 - \varepsilon^0/R\sigma^2 \qquad (22.\text{a})$$

$$\Omega' = I' - \varepsilon'/R\sigma^2 \qquad (22.\text{b})$$

Suppose, for example, that the second seller is a pessimist so that $\varepsilon^0 < 0$. He will sell shares to acquire a short inventory position. To the extent his short position exceeds or falls short of his desired inventory determined by ε^0 and $R\sigma^2$, he has unwanted inventory of Ω^0, The market spread can now be written as

$$s = R\sigma^2 Q - R\sigma^2(\Omega^0 - \Omega') \qquad (23)$$

where we let $Q = \frac{1}{2}Q^0 + \frac{1}{2}Q'$, which is the transaction value at the average price. It can be shown that the propositions about the equilibrium distribution of inventories under homogeneous opinions also apply to the net unwanted inventories, Ω. And since the market equilibrium spread depends directly on Ω^0 and Ω', it can be shown that proposition 3 specifying the equilibrium market spread holds under heterogeneous opinions.

The key concept, as before, is that if the unwanted inventory difference between second dealers exceeds Q, interdealer trading is induced. In equilibrium, pessimistic dealers have acquired a (desired) short position and attendant inventory risk which is reflected in a high bid and ask price relative to their opinion of the true price. Optimistic dealers have acquired a (desired) long position and attendant inventory risk which is reflected in a low bid and ask price relative to their opinion of the true price. In equilibrium, the reservation bid and ask prices of all dealers are in the neighborhood of the market clearing price. Under proposition 3, reservation bid or ask prices may differ at most by the fee on a transaction of size Q.

The reservation spread of each dealer is independent of his inventory. Therefore, under the assumption of identical R, all dealers have the same reservation spread under heterogeneous as well as homogeneous opinions. Furthermore, as in the case of homogeneous opinions, there is a tendency for the observed market spread to be the reservation spread of any dealer. This should be of some comfort to those undertaking empirical studies of the spread.

V. Effect on Dealers' Reservation Fees of Extending Horizon to Two Periods

The dynamic programming character of a dealer's problem and the dependence of a dealer's fee on the position of his competitors can be shown in a two period case. In this context the effect of serially correlated transactions can also be examined.

In this section a dealer—A—operating in a market with several other competing dealers is analyzed. For simplicity the analysis is restricted to one stock—stock M—and all dealers are assumed to have identical absolute risk aversion and to start with zero inventory of the stock. The problem is considered from the perspective of what selling fee to set with two periods remaining. In the dynamic programming framework discussed earlier that selling fee is set such that expected derived utility of wealth (the J function) next period, under optimal pricing strategy in later periods, is maximized.

Proposition 4. Assume that two periods remain ($t = 2$) and initial inventory of each dealer of the one stock being traded is $M = 0$. Since dealers are assumed to have identical R, this implies that no dealer earns a producer surplus at $t = 2$. Assume that, given a purchase at $t = 2$ by A, the following conditional probabilities apply with respect to transactions in the next period ($t = 1$):

Event at $t = 1$ Given a sale by A at $t = 2$	Market's Conditional Probability	Dealer A's Conditional Probability
No trade	θ	$\theta + \gamma$
Purchase	μ	μ
Sale	γ	0

Then A's reservation selling fee at $t = 2$ is

$$a_2 = \frac{1}{2(1 + r)} \sigma_M^2 RQ(1 - 2\mu) \qquad (24)$$

Proof: When one period remains, dealer A's derived utility, given a sale at $t = 2$ is

$$J(1) = E_1 U(W_0^+) + (1 + r)U'(W_1)Q\mu(b_1^0 - b_1) \qquad (25)$$

where $E_1 U(W_0^+)$ is given by (10) letting $N = 0$ and $M = -Q$, and the subscript on the expectation operator indicates the point in time at which the expectation is taken. The last term in (25) represents the marginal utility of the expected producer surplus earned by A at $t = 1$. Since A is assumed to be the seller at $t = 2$, he will be the first buyer at $t = 1$ earning $b_1^0 - b_1$, where b^0 is the reservation buying fee of the second buyer. From the principle of dynamic programming we know that $J(2) = E_2 J(1)$; for if a change in derived utility were expected, the dealer would choose some other strategy for selecting buying and selling fees.

At $t = 2$, A set a selling fee, a_2, such that the derived utility conditional on a sale, $J(2 | \text{sale})$, equals the derived utility conditional on no transaction in the remaining two periods. The derived utility when there is no trading for two periods is the two period analog of (10) where we have made the additional assumption that $M = N = F = 0$:

$$J(2 | \text{no trade}) = E_2 E_1 U(W_0)$$

The derived utility if A sells Q shares at $t = 2$ is

$$J(2 | \text{sale}) = J(2, F_2 + Q, M_2 - Q, Y_2, \bullet) + J_F(2, F_2 + Q, M_2 - Q, Y_2, \bullet)aQ$$

$$= E_2 J(1) + U'(W_0)aQ$$

$$= E_2 E_1 U(W_0^+) + E_2(1 + r)U'(W_1)Q\mu(b_1^0 - b_1) + U'(W_0)aQ$$

Setting $J(2 \mid \text{no trade}) = J(2 \mid \text{sale})$, noting that

$$E_2 E_1 U(W_0^+) - E_2 E_1 U(W_0)$$
$$= E_2[(-r_M Q + rQ)U'(W_1) + \tfrac{1}{2} U''(W_1)(Q^2 \sigma_M^2 - 2QY\sigma_{MY})],$$

and dropping certain small cross product terms gives

$$a = \frac{1}{1+r}\left[\frac{1}{2} \sigma_M^2 RQ - \mu(b_1^0 - b_1)\right]$$

Using (8) and noting the assumption that M_1^0 0, $M_1 = -Q$ and $N_1^0 = N_1 = 0$, yields the desired result. Q.E.D.

The implications of (24) are quite straight forward. The greater the probability of a reverse transaction in the next trading interval the lower the reservation fee today. Indeed, the fee will be lower than if the dealer were able to cover his short position in the next trading interval at the true price (as in the one period case). This is due to the fact that he is able to collect a producer surplus next period by buying at a price below the true price. Since we have assumed that all dealers start from identical positions, each would have a lower reservation fee; and as a result the market spread is lower in a two period framework. Since actively traded stocks have a larger μ, it also follows directly that actively traded stocks have a lower spread than infrequently traded stocks.

It should be noted that even though purchases and sales have the same probability of arrival, dealer competition introduces negative serial correlation in transactions as far as the inventory of a single dealer is concerned. Dealer A, having sold, is unlikely to sell again. He dominates the bid side of the market in the second period and his probability of a purchase next period is the probability of a public sale, as reflected in (24).

Were the assumption of a single transaction of size Q to be modified, A would no longer dominate the bid side in the second period. If several dealers each purchase Q at $t = 2$, competition would deny them a producer surplus in period 2 and the fee at $t = 2$ would be the same as in the one period case. This is immediately evident from (25).

VI. Implications: Exchange Markets Versus Dealer Markets

This paper has implications for two strands of research that have been subsumed under the heading of "the microstructure of securities markets." First, it provides a basis for analyzing the transaction-by-transaction price behavior of individual stocks and specifies the role of dealers in causing the observed transaction price to deviate from the underlying true price. Research in this area is frequently concerned with statistical modeling of the time series of security returns. For a review of this strand of research see Cohen, Hawawini, Maier, Schwartz and Whitcomb [4]. Second, the paper provides a framework for analyzing alternative structures of securities markets. First we show that the model is applicable to the analysis of auction markets in which investors place limit orders; and, second, we consider the relationship between spreads in a dealer market and an auction market such as the NYSE.

A. Limit Orders

In an auction market, investors (represented by brokers) trade directly with each other either by meeting at the same time or, more likely, by trading against a previously entered limit order. In a dealer market, investors (represented by brokers) trade at the quoted bid or ask price of dealers. While our analysis has been framed in terms of a dealer market, the framework is equally applicable to an auction market.[10] The decision of an investor in an auction market to leave a limit order or to trade immediately with an existing limit order is exactly analogous to the decision of a dealer to post his price and wait or to trade immediately with another dealer.

In an auction market the depth and liquidity of the market is sometimes measured by the thickness of the book of limit orders (i.e., the number of orders at each price). However, under the assumption of our model one would expect a relatively thin book regardless of the activity in the stock. We have shown that second dealers (or investors), who have no chance of trading with the next incoming order, would rather trade immediately than place an order and wait to trade. Anyone with a reservation bid price below the market bid price would sell stock at the market bid or place a limit order to sell inside the market ask rather than placing a buy order at a price which has no probability of being executed against the next incoming order. Analogously, anyone with a reservation ask price above the market ask would buy at the market ask or place a limit order to buy slightly inside the market bid rather than placing a limit sell order which has no probability of being met in the next trading interval. Since all orders except the one at the margin in each side of the market (and those tied with it at the same price) will be executed, a thin book results.

If monitoring costs are high for investors or if investors face short sales constraints, they may choose to place limit orders outside the market spread in anticipation of a hoped-for change in the market price. In the absence of continuous monitoring such limit orders offer an option to traders continuously in the market to trade at known prices should new information justify a change in the underlying market price. On the New York Stock Exchange the option is particularly valuable to the specialist because he has knowledge of the book of limit orders.[11]

B. Bid-ask Spread on the New York Stock Exchange (NYSE) and on the Over-the-Counter (OTC) Market

The NYSE combines aspects of auction and dealer markets in that there is a single dealer—the specialist—who is responsible for quoting bid and ask prices while there is also a book of limit orders, maintained by the specialist. In the OTC markets in stocks or bonds, several dealers compete by simultaneously

---

[10] Cohen, Maier, Schwartz & Whitcomb [5] analyze an auction market.

[11] Copeland and Galai [3] have treated the deviation of the bid or ask price from the true market price as reflecting the premium on an option to trade at a known price. This assumes that even the dealer cannot monitor the market continuously and is unable to change bid and ask prices rapidly in response to new information. While we are not willing to accept this assumption, we are willing to assume their model applies to investors who face monitoring costs.

quoting bid and ask prices. An important issue in the development of securities markets is whether an evolving national market should be structured along the lines of the NYSE or of the OTC.

It has been argued elsewhere, both on theoretical and empirical grounds, that the specialist system is a monopoly franchise and as such sets a monopoly spread.[12] Furthermore, markets in certain stocks may be poor simply because of excessive risk aversion or inadequate wealth of the particular specialist making a market in the stock. From this perspective, a market of competing dealers is generally judged to be preferable. However, empirical work by Newton and Quandt [12] indicates that the OTC market spread appears to be higher than the specialist's spread on the NYSE when similar stocks are compared.[13] The analysis of this paper provides a framework for examining this result and for comparing the two types of markets.

An important characteristic of the specialist system is that each order is funneled through the single specialist, thereby enforcing the transaction size limit, Q, for which the specialist's quote applies. The specialist then has the opportunity to reset his quotes prior to the next transaction. On the OTC it is possible for an investor simultaneously to make several transactions each of size Q with the different dealers. In effect the dealer market offers greater liquidity at each spread and, therefore, could be expected to have a larger spread.

To see the effect more precisely, imagine two ways of organizing trading in a single stock. One in which there is a single specialist with wealth of W and one—an OTC market—in which there are 10 dealers each with wealth $W/10$. Now suppose a sell order of $10Q$ is to be traded. On the OTC market that order could be split into 10 orders and sold at posted bid prices. On the exchange only Q could automatically be traded at the posted bid, and successive sales would take place at lower bid prices. Because the coefficient of absolute risk aversion declines with wealth, each of 10 small dealers sets a higher spread for a transaction of size Q than a large dealer with the same total wealth. Assume the coefficient of relative risk aversion $Z = RW$ is constant. Then, from (13), the reservation spread of the specialist is $\sigma_i^2 ZQ/W$; and the reservation spread of each of the 10 dealers is $\sigma_i^2 10ZQ/W$. We have shown that the market spread tends to the reservation spread of any dealer. Thus the market spread can be expected to be higher in the OTC market than on the NYSE.

VII. Summary and Conclusions

The behavior of competing dealers in securities markets is analyzed in this paper. Securities are characterized by stochastic returns and stochastic transactions of a fixed size, Q. Reservation bid and ask fees of dealers are derived under alternative assumptions about the degree to which transactions are correlated across stocks at a given time and over time in a given stock. In a multi-period

---

[12] See for example Smidt [14], Stoll [16] and Ho and Stoll [11].

[13] Newton and Quandt calculate the market spread for OTC stocks traded on NASDAQ (an automated quotation system) by taking the difference between the lowest ask price of any dealer and the higher bid price of any dealer—the inside quote.

framework, reservation fees of a dealer depend on the anticipated actions of other dealers. The dynamic programming formulation of this problem is presented for the case of two dealers in two stocks; but, except for a two period case, solutions are not attempted.

The interaction of any number of dealers and the determination of the market spread are examined under the assumption that dealers have a one-period horizon. The market spread is shown to be determined by the second best dealers. An equilibrium market spread is defined to exist when the distribution of inventories across dealers is such that no dealer wishes (at that moment) to trade with any other dealer. The conditions under which the dealer would trade immediately with another dealer rather than wait for an incoming order is specified. We show that the equilibrium market spread must be non-negative. Under homogeneous risk preferences and with at least four competing dealers, the equilibrium market spread may be zero; but such a spread is not stable over time and would tend to be driven to the reservation spread of an individual dealer by the flow of incoming orders. That the equilibrium market spread tends to the reservation spread of any dealer holds true under heterogeneous as well as homogeneous opinions about the true price of the stock (so long as dealers have homogeneous risk preferences and agree on the variance of the stock's return).

The model is shown to be applicable to the placement of limit orders by investors as well as the placement of bid and ask prices by dealers, and it can therefore be used in comparing spreads between dealer markets such as the OTC and exchange markets such as the NYSE. We show that spreads on comparable stocks may be expected to be higher in an OTC market with many dealers than in an exchange market with a single specialist because a market with many dealers stands ready to trade more shares at quoted prices.

The model potentially has a much wider applicability than to the securities markets. Any sequential bidding problem under uncertainty in which a bidder's price depends on his position relative to that of his competitors may be analyzed in our framework. The problem of bidding on securities is perhaps simpler than others since the stochastic processes for returns and transactions can be specified in a realistic way.

Appendix: Dealer Reservation Fee When Trading in Two Stocks is Correlated

When the two stocks arrive together, the dealer can only determine fees for buying or selling the combination. The fee for each stock is indeterminate without some additional assumptions. To investigate the effect of correlated transaction arrivals in stock M and N, we assume the stocks have the same risk—$\sigma_M^2 = \sigma_N^2 = \sigma^2$—and the inventory of the stocks is $M = N = 0$. Under independent transactions arrival this implies $b_M = b_N = a_N$ by proposition 1. We assume the fees are equal under correlated transactions arrival and investigate the level of the common fee as compared with independent arrival.

Proposition A: Assume that one period remains to the horizon date, that $\sigma_M^2 = \sigma_N^2 = \sigma^2$, that $M = N = 0$, that the joint probability of transactions in stock

Dynamics of Dealer Markets Under Competition

M and N is symmetric as given in Table A. Then the common bid or ask fee, π_i, in each stock, i, is given by

$$\pi_i = \frac{1}{2} R\sigma^2 Q\left(1 + 2\beta_{ji} \frac{\mu - \gamma}{\lambda_i + \mu + \gamma}\right), \quad i = M, N \tag{A.1}$$

where $\beta_{ji} = \sigma_{ji}/\sigma^2$.

Proof: We sketch the proof from the perspective of a dealer setting the bid price in stock M but because of our assumptions any other perspective would give a corresponding result. Define the change in the dealer's expected utility of terminal wealth, ϕ_k, for each possible event, k, under which M may be purchased:

Buy M, no trade in N $\phi_1 = EU(W^t_{01}) - EU(W_0)$

Buy M, Buy N $\phi_2 = EU(W^t_{02}) - EU(W_0)$

Buy M, Sell N $\phi_3 = EU(W^t_{03}) - EU(W_0)$

The values of $EU(W^t_{0k})$ are calculated in the manner of (11) for the alternative uncertain terminal wealth positions implied by each event. We place the dealer just an instant before the transaction and assume one period of return uncertainty remains after the realization of the event. Then the expected change in expected utility of terminal wealth conditional on a purchase of stock i, ψ_i, is

$$\psi_i = \frac{\theta}{\lambda_i} \phi_1 + \frac{\mu}{\lambda_i} \phi_2 \frac{\gamma}{\lambda_i} \phi_3$$

Substituting for ϕ_k in the above equation and requiring $\psi_i = 0$ then yields (A.1) Q.E.D.

We see from a comparison of (A.1) and (8) (under the assumption of $M = N = 0$) that the effect of correlated transactions is to modify the transaction size, Q. The condition under which (A.1) becomes (8) are (a) $\beta_{ji} = 0$. If returns are not correlated, correlated transactions do not increase return risk. (b) $\mu = \gamma$. If the probability of parallel transactions equals the probability of offsetting transactions, there is no increase in expected return risk (c) If $\mu = \gamma = 0$, we have the assumption leading to (8). Since the spread is the sum of the bid and ask fees, the spread is changed in proportion to the change in the effective transaction size.

Table A
Probabilities of Transactions in Stocks M and N

Transaction Amount in Stock M	Transaction Amount in Stock N			Marginal Probabilities of Transactions in Stock M
	Q	$-Q$	0	
Q	μ	γ	θ	λ_M
$-Q$	γ	μ	θ	λ_M
0	θ	θ		$1 - 2\lambda_M$
Marginal Probabilities of Transactions in Stock N	λ_N	λ_N	$1 - 2\lambda_N$	

The practical effect of proposition A is that the dealer is concerned about the stocks in which he makes a market when transactions are correlated. One can imagine two sets of stocks for which return variances of all stocks are the same. Yet the dealer handling the set of stocks for which transactions arrive in parallel would set a higher spread for each stock than the dealer for which transactions are offsetting or independent.

REFERENCES

1. Y. Amihud and Y. Mendelson. "Dealership Market: Market Making with Inventory." *Journal of Financial Economics* 8 (March 1980), 31-53.
2. G. Benston and R. Hagerman. "Determinants of Bid-Asked Spreads in the Over-the-Counter Market." *Journal of Financial Economics* 1 (March 1974), 353-364.
3. T. Copeland and D. Galai. "Information Effects on the Bid-Ask Spread" UCLA Working Paper, (October, 1982).
4. K. Cohen, G. Hawawini, S. Maier, R. Schwartz and D. Whitcomb. "Implications of Microstructure Theory for Empirical Research on Stock Price Behavior." *Journal of Finance*, 35 (May, 1980), 249-257.
5. K. Cohen, S. Maier, R. Schwartz and D. Whitcomb. "Transaction Costs, Order Placement Strategy, and the Existence of the Bid-Ask Spread." *Journal of Political Economy* 89 (April, 1981), 287-305.
6. Harold Demsetz. "The Cost of Transacting." *Quarterly Journal of Economics* 82 (February, 1968), 33-53.
7. K. Garbade and W. Silber. "Structural Organization of Secondary Markets Clearing Frequency, Dealer Activity and Liquidity Risk," *Journal of Finance* 34 (June 1979), 577-593.
8. M. Garman. "Market Microstructure," *Journal of Financial Economics* 3 (June, 1976), 257-275.
9. J. Hamilton. "Marketplace Fragmentation, Competition and the Effieciency of the Stock Market." *Journal of Finance* 34 (March, 1979), 171-187.
10. T. Ho and H. Stoll. "On Dealers Markets Under Competition," *Journal of Finance*, 35 (May, 1980), 259-267.
11. T. Ho and H. Stoll. "Optimal Dealer Pricing Under Transactions and Return Uncertainty." *Journal of Financial Economics*, 9 (March, 1981), 47-73.
12. W. Newton and R. Quandt. "An Empiricial Study of Spreads," Research Memorandum No. 30, Financial Research Center, Princeton University (January, 1979).
13. E. Mildenstein and H. Schleef. "The Optimal Pricing Policy of Monopolistic Marketmaker in the Equity Market." Working Paper, University of Oregon, Eugene, Oregon (1980).
14. S. Smidt. "Which Road to an Efficient Market: Free Competition vs. Regulated Monopoly." *Financial Analysts Journal* 27 (September-October 1971), 18ff.
15. S. Smidt. "Continuous Versus Intermittent Trading on Auction Markets." *Journal of Financial and Quantitative Analysis* 14 (November, 1979), 837-866.
16. H. Stoll. "The Supply of Dealer Services in Securities Markets," *Journal of Finance*, 33 (September, 1978), 1133-1151.
17. H. Stoll. "Pricing of Security Dealer Services: An Empirical Study of NASDAQ Stocks." *Journal of Finance* 33 (September, 1978), 1153-1172.
18. S. Tinic. "The Economics of Liquidty Services," *Quarterly Journal of Economics* 86 (February, 1972), 79-83.
19. S. Tinic and R. West. "Competition and the Pricing of Dealer Services in the Over-the-Counter Market," *Journal of Financial and Quantitative Analysis*, 7 (June, 1971), 1707-1727.
20. W. Vickrey. "Counterspeculation, Auctions, and Competitive Sealed Tenders," *Journal of Finance*, 16 (March, 1961), 8-37.

Trading Mechanisms in Securities Markets

ANANTH MADHAVAN*

ABSTRACT

This paper analyzes price formation under two trading mechanisms: a continuous *quote-driven* system where dealers post prices before order submission and an *order-driven* system where traders submit orders before prices are determined. The order-driven system operates either as a *continuous auction*, with immediate order execution, or as a *periodic auction*, where orders are stored for simultaneous execution. With free entry into market making, the continuous systems are equivalent. While a periodic auction offers greater price efficiency and can function where continuous mechanisms fail, traders must sacrifice continuity and bear higher information costs.

THERE IS A REMARKABLE diversity in the method by which trading is accomplished around the world and across assets. For example, a trader on the International Stock Exchange (London) can obtain price quotations before trading, and order execution at those prices is generally assured. By contrast, some stocks on smaller European exchanges can be traded only once a day and orders must be irrevocably submitted before prices are determined. Yet, we know little about how differences in trading designs affect price formation. This paper examines and contrasts the process of price formation under different forms of market organization when information is imperfect and traders act strategically.

Understanding the relationship between trading structures and price behavior is important for theoretical and applied reasons. From a theoretical viewpoint, the extensive literature on rational expectations suggests that prices efficiently aggregate information when trading is organized as an auction with large numbers of traders. Yet, most securities markets in the

---

* From the University of Pennsylvania. This paper is based on Chapter II of my dissertation from Cornell University. I thank Franklin Allen, Marshall Blume, David Easley, Margaret Forster, Thomas George, Lawrence Glosten, Mark Grinblatt, Robert Jarrow, Nicholas Kiefer, Robert Masson, Maureen O'Hara, Seymour Smidt, René Stulz (editor), and the anonymous referee for their valuable suggestions. Seminar participants at Carnegie-Mellon University, Cornell University, New York University, the University of California Santa Barbara, the University of North Carolina, the University of Pennsylvania, the University of Pittsburgh, the University of Southern California, Vanderbilt University, the Econometric Society Meetings, and the Berkeley Program in Finance provided many helpful comments. Support from the Geewax-Terker Research Fund is gratefully acknowledged.

United States are not organized as auction markets, but rely instead upon market makers to provide liquidity by buying or selling on demand. This is the case even for active securities where it is feasible to maintain a high degree of continuity by conducting auctions at frequent intervals. Models of the trading process that incorporate institutional detail and strategic behavior may exhibit equilibria quite distinct from that of a frictionless Walrasian market, the traditional economic benchmark. Furthermore, recent empirical research suggests that market structure has important effects on properties of asset prices.[1] Finally, the securities industry is in the process of rapid structural changes generated by intermarket competition, innovations in communications technology, and the proliferation of new financial instruments. Understanding the relationship between market structure and price formation is necessary to evaluate the impact of these changes and to guide public policy.

The crucial function of a trading mechanism is to transform the latent demands of investors into realized transactions. The key to this transformation is *price discovery*, the process of finding market clearing prices. No two trading mechanisms are alike in the performance of price discovery; they differ in the types of orders permitted, the times at which trading can occur, the quantity and quality of market information made available to investors at the time of order submission, and the reliance upon market makers to provide liquidity.[2]

An important distinction is often made between *continuous* and *periodic* mechanisms. In a continuous market an investor's order is executed immediately upon submission. A continuous trading system is characterized by a sequence of bilateral transactions at (possibly) different prices. In a periodic system, however, investors' orders are accumulated for simultaneous execution at a pre-determined time. The periodic system (commonly referred to as a *call auction* or *batch market*) is characterized by a set of multilateral transactions at one price.

Another useful distinction is between *quote-driven* and *order-driven* trading mechanisms. In a quote-driven system such as NASDAQ or the International Stock Exchange (London), investors can obtain firm price quotations from market makers prior to order submission.[3] This mechanism is also known as a *continuous dealer market* because an investor need not wait for order execution, but instead trades immediately with a market maker.

---

[1] See for example, Amihud and Mendelson (1987), Stoll and Whaley (1990), Amihud, Mendelson, and Murgia (1990), and Amihud and Mendelson (1991).

[2] A number of excellent papers analyze this diversity. Cohen, Maier, Schwartz, and Whitcomb (1986) provide a comprehensive survey of international trading structures and their relative merits. Stoll (1990) discusses the principles underlying various trading arrangements. Harris (1990) examines a number of policy issues in the design of trading protocols.

[3] Market makers' bid and ask quotations typically depend on the size of the order. In London, for example, dealers quote price schedules. Other examples include the market for foreign exchange and the secondary market for U.S. Treasury bills.

By contrast, in an order-driven system, investors submit their orders for execution through an auction process. Order-driven mechanisms can operate either as continuous systems or as periodic systems. In the first type, known as a *continuous auction*, investors submit orders for immediate execution by dealers on an exchange floor or against existing limit orders submitted by public investors or dealers. The system is continuous, since orders are executed upon arrival, but operates as an auction because the price is determined multilaterally.[4] The second type of order-driven system is known as a *periodic auction*, where the orders of investors are stored for execution at a single market clearing price.[5]

Most trading mechanisms are complex hybrids of these three systems. For example, the NYSE opens with an auction or batch market, and then switches to a dealer market. For some thickly traded stocks, the market has been described as a *continuous double auction*. These compound mechanisms can be understood only through the analysis of their simpler component structures.

Previous studies of market mechanisms have examined the differences between continuous and periodic trading when traders have fixed reservation prices.[6] This paper differs from this line of research by modeling trading as a game between strategic traders with rational expectations. We compare and contrast a quote-driven system with an order-driven system that can operate as a continuous auction or as a batch market. These mechanisms differ in many respects, most importantly in the sequence of order submission and the amount of market information made available to traders.

We show that equilibrium may not exist in continuous mechanisms (i.e., the quote-driven system and the continuous auction) unless there is a minimum amount of noninformation trading. With free entry into market making, the quote-driven system is equivalent to the continuous auction mechanism. By contrast, the periodic auction aggregates information efficiently and is more robust to problems of information asymmetry in that it can operate where continuous markets fail. The trade-off comes in the form of

---

[4] Examples of continuous auction systems include the à la criée or open-outcry system for active stocks on the Paris Bourse, the Swiss Option and Financial Futures Exchange (SOFFEX), the Frankfurt Stock Exchange, the Toronto Stock Exchange's Computer Assisted Trading System (CATS), the Tokyo Stock Exchange's Computer Assisted Routing and Execution System (CORES), and 'crowd trading' in U.S. futures markets. Many continuous auction systems are proprietary automated systems, where order submission is electronic. See Domowitz (1990) for a description of the mechanics of automated trading.

[5] Periodic systems are used to open many continuous markets such as the New York Stock Exchange (NYSE) and Tokyo Stock Exchange. In addition, many European stock exchanges operate batch markets, although these systems are being supplanted by continuous trading systems. In the U.S., by contrast, new proprietary periodic systems such as the *Wunsch auction* are complementing the operation of continuous markets.

[6] See, for example, Garbade and Silber (1979), Ho, Schwartz, and Whitcomb (1985), Pithyachariyakul (1986), Mendelson (1987), and Gammill (1990).

loss of continuity of trading and the costs of gathering market information that would otherwise be revealed through price quotations. The Bayes-Nash equilibrium for the auction game is shown to have a close analogy in the classical notion of a Walrasian auction, but the two equilibria are quite distinct. Finally, we derive several testable hypotheses regarding the time-series properties of prices and the cross-sectional determinants of bid-ask spreads and price volatility.

The rest of the paper proceeds as follows. In Section II, we set up the basic framework, and in Section III we analyze a continuous market where dealers post prices before trading occurs. In Section IV we model an order-driven mechanism that can operate as a continuous auction or as a periodic mechanism. We derive a number of comparative statics results that yield testable implications. Section V compares the operation of these mechanisms, and relates our game-theoretic market model to classical ideas of equilibrium. Section VI summarizes the paper. All proofs are in the appendix.

I. The Model

The model is based on a framework familiar in the rational expectations literature. There are two assets, cash and a single risky asset with a stochastic liquidation value, denoted by $\tilde{v}$, which is realized after time 1. There are two types of agents in this model. The first type, termed 'traders' (indexed by i) enter the market according to an exogenous stochastic process at calendar times $\{t_i\}_{i=1}^{\infty}$ in the interval (0, 1). Thus, trader i is the trader who trades at time t_i. The second type of agent, termed 'dealers' or 'market makers' provide liquidity by trading with the first group of traders. We will examine two different forms of market organization: a quote-driven system and an order-driven system that operates either as a continuous auction system or a periodic auction mechanism.

We first describe the objectives and information of the agents in the model and then discuss the specifics of the trading arrangements. Let q_i represent the order quantity of trader i who arrives at time t_i with the convention that $q > 0$ denotes a trader purchase and $q < 0$ a trader sale. Denote by p_i the security's price. For simplicity, we assume that each trader trades only once.[7] In a dynamic model, each trader's strategy would depend on the probability of repeat trading not only for herself, but for all other traders as well, greatly complicating the analysis.[8]

---

[7] This assumption could be motivated by the Prisoner's Dilemma nature of competition among traders with private information. Since all traders possess private information, a trader who fails to fully exploit his information when he gets a chance to trade runs the risk that his information will already be impounded in prices when he next obtains an opportunity to trade.

[8] See, for example, Seppi (1990) and Leach and Madhavan (1990) who provide dynamic models where agents act strategically.

Traders maximize the expected utility of final period wealth. Each trader is assumed to have a negative exponential utility function:

$$u(W_{1i}) = -e^{-\rho W_{1i}}$$

where W_{1i} is the final period wealth of trader i, and $\rho > 0$ is the coefficient of absolute risk aversion. Trader i's initial endowment is described by the vector (x_i, c_{0i}), where x_i is the initial inventory of risky securities and c_{0i} represents cash holdings. Endowments of the risky asset are distributed normally across traders with mean 0 and precision (the reciprocal of the variance) ψ.[9] Since traders are risk averse, variation in asset endowments generates portfolio hedging trade which is not information motivated. The amount of this 'liquidity' trading is inversely related to the value of ψ.

For trader i, final period wealth, $\tilde{W}_{1i}$, is a random variable given by:

$$\tilde{W}_{1i} = (q_i + x_i)\tilde{v} + c_{0i} - p_i q_i. \tag{1}$$

Let Φ_i represent the information set of trader i at time t_i.[10] If $\tilde{W}_{1i}$ is normally distributed conditional upon Φ_i, then maximizing expected utility is equivalent to maximizing:

$$E[\tilde{W}_{1i} | \Phi_i] - \left(\frac{\rho}{2}\right) \text{Var}[\tilde{W}_{1i} | \Phi_i] \tag{2}$$

where $E[\cdot | \Phi_i]$ and $\text{Var}[\cdot | \Phi_i]$ represent the conditional expectation and variance operators relative to Φ_i.

We turn now to the determinants of traders' information sets. At time 0, the risky security is known to be distributed normally with mean μ and precision τ. This is public information and is known to both dealers and traders. In addition to public information, trader i ($i = 1, \cdots, N$) observes the realization of a random variable, $\tilde{y}_i = v + \tilde{\epsilon}_i$ where $\tilde{\epsilon}_i$ is white noise and v is the time 1 value of the risky asset. We assume that $\tilde{\epsilon}_i$ is independently normally distributed with mean 0 and precision θ. The realized value of the random variable $\tilde{y}_i$ is denoted y_i. The private information of trader i is the pair (x_i, y_i). Then, trader i's *prior* distribution of $\tilde{v}$ is normal with mean y_i and precision θ. Of course, the trader's order strategy depends on his or her *posterior* beliefs, which take into account the information contained in prices. We discuss this in more detail later. The distributional assumptions concerning the information structure are common in models of this type, but unfortunately permit prices to be negative.[11] A possible source for diverse prior

---

[9] The assumption of a zero mean is without loss of generality. We also assume the security is 'widely' held so that information on x_i does not convey information about x_j, for $i \neq j$.

[10] Formally, the information set is the σ-algebra generated by public and private information.

[11] The probability of this occurrence could be made arbitrarily small by assuming the variance of the risky asset is small relative to its mean.

beliefs may be differences in access to market information as described by Working (1958):

> The amount of pertinent information potentially available to traders in most modern markets is far beyond what any one trader can both acquire and use to good effect. Circumstance and inclination lead different traders to seek out and use different sorts of information. In short, traders are forced to engage in a sort of informal division of labor in their use of available information. Using different information, different traders must find themselves often of different opinions, one buying at the same time that another sells, even though all may stand at an equal level of intelligence, steadiness in judgement, and quantity of information at their command (pp. 188–199).

The assumption of independent signals can be relaxed to allow correlation among conditional expectations, but at considerable notational cost.

Turning now to the dealers, we assume that there are $M > 2$ competitive dealers. These dealers are assumed to be risk-neutral and their objective is to maximize expected profits, subject to competitive constraints. Unlike traders, dealers do not receive private information signals; they know the prior distribution of $\tilde{v}$, which is public information, and, over time, make inferences about the security's value from the order flow. Since the signals dealers receive from order flow will depend on the way in which trading is accomplished, we must first discuss the specifics of the trading arrangements. Before doing so, however, it is useful to define a measure of information quality at the start of the trading day. Define Υ as:

$$\Upsilon \equiv \frac{(\theta + \tau)\theta}{\tau}. \tag{3}$$

The measure Υ has an important role in our analysis; it can be thought of as a proxy for the initial degree of information asymmetry. A security with pronounced information asymmetries has (relatively) large values of θ and low values of τ, implying Υ is large. Conversely, for securities where information asymmetries are inconsequential, τ is large and θ is small, implying Υ is small. We now address the specifics of market organization, and then discuss the various performance measures used to assess these regimes.

A. *The Quote-Driven Mechanism*

We consider first the quote-driven mechanism. The model of the quote-driven system is based on the single-period model of Glosten (1989), who contrasts a monopolistic market maker system with a competitive market maker system. Trading is accomplished through M competitive, risk-neutral market makers who take the opposite side of all transactions. The critical feature of this mechanism is that it is quote-driven; market makers provide bid-ask quotations to traders on demand, and can revise their quotes only after a transaction is complete. Strict price priority prevails, so that the market maker with the lowest ask price or the highest bid price is matched with the trader.

We model the dealer mechanism as a two-stage game. In the first stage, the dealers determine their quoted prices and in the second stage the trader chooses his or her order given the quoted prices. Price competition forces the expected profits of market makers on each trade to zero. Rational dealers set prices so that the price for a given order size is an unbiased estimate of the asset's value given initial beliefs, the trading history, and the information provided by the size of the order, i.e., quoted prices are 'regret-free' or ex post rational.[12] Since order size is variable, this discussion implies that the quoted prices are contingent on order size. Formally, at time t_i, market makers determine a quotation schedule $p_i(\cdot)$, then observe q_i, the order placed by trader i, after which market makers can revise their quotation schedules for trader $i + 1$, i.e., choose $p_{i+1}(\cdot)$. In setting $p_i(\cdot)$, market makers use the information contained in the trading history, $h_i = \{(p_1, q_1), \cdots, (p_{i-1}, q_{i-1})\}$, and their prior information (μ, τ). Let Φ_d^i represent the pre-trade information set of market makers at time t_i.[13] The quote-driven (continuous dealer) mechanism in each period is described as a game $\Gamma_c = (\{p_i(\cdot), q_i(y_i, x_i)\})$ characterized by the players and their strategies.

Definition 1: At time t_i, equilibrium for the quote-driven mechanism Γ_c is a differentiable price quotation function, $p_i : \Re \to \Re_+$, and a corresponding demand, q_i, such that:

(a) Each market maker ($j = 1, \cdots, M$) quotes a price schedule that ensures non-negative expected profits on each transaction

$$(E[\tilde{v} \mid q_i, \Phi_d^i] - p_i(q_i))(-q_i) \geq 0.$$

(b) Strict price priority prevails, i.e., there does not exist another function, p_i^o, satisfying condition (a) such that:

$$qp_i^o(q) \leq qp_i(q) \text{ for all } q \in \mathcal{R}$$

and

$$qp_i^o(q) < qp_i(q) \text{ for some } q \in \mathcal{R}$$

(c) Trader i maximizes expected utility given $p_i(\cdot)$:

$$q_i \in \text{argmax}_{\{q_i\}} \{ E[u(\tilde{W}_{1i}(q_i)) \mid \Phi_i, p_i] \}.$$

---

[12] Glosten and Milgrom (1985) use this condition to demonstrate the existence of an information-based bid-ask spread. In their model, order size is fixed.

[13] Formally, this set is the σ-algebra generated by the history h_i and public information.

Condition (a) is the requirement that market makers earn nonnegative expected profits given post-trade information, while condition (b) requires that the quotation function p_i not be dominated by another function, p_i^o, with lower ask prices and/or higher bid prices. Together, these conditions imply that market makers earn zero expected profits on every trade. Finally, condition (c) states that each trader maximizes the expected utility of final period wealth given the price schedule posted by dealers. Definition 1 implies that equilibrium is a fixed point in the space continuous functions.

B. The Order-Driven Mechanism

An alternative to the quote-driven continuous dealer system is an order-driven system where traders submit orders to an exchange for execution by floor traders or dealers. This type of system includes continuous auctions, where orders are executed immediately, as well as periodic auctions where orders are accumulated for simultaneous execution at a single market clearing price.[14]

Unlike a posted-price system, the transaction price in an auction mechanism is not known at the time of order submission. We argue, however, that traders can effectively condition their beliefs on the price. Rational investors know that the equilibrium price reveals information, so that the demand schedule they submit is the set of price-quantity combinations such that the quantity demanded at each price is the desired order quantity conditional upon that particular price clearing the market.[15] In this respect, the equilibrium corresponds to the rational expectations model of Kyle (1989), with the difference that liquidity trading is endogenous in our model.[16] Consider an auction with N traders and M dealers. We denote the vector of trader demand functions by $\vec{q} = (q_1(\cdot), \cdots, q_N(\cdot))$, and the vector of dealer demands by $\vec{d} = (d_1(\cdot), \cdots, d_M(\cdot))$, with the usual sign convention. Let $\vec{q}_{-1} = (q_1, \cdots, q_{i-1}, q_{i+1}, \cdots, q_N)$, and similarly define $\vec{d}_{-j}$. We model the order-driven process as a game $\Gamma_a = (\{q_i\}_{i=1}^N, \{d_j\}_{j=1}^M)$ indexed by the players and their strategy functions.

Definition 2: A Bayes-Nash equilibrium for the order-driven mechanism Γ_a consists of a vector of strategy functions, $\vec{d}$, for dealers $j = 1, \cdots, M$, a vector of strategy functions, $\vec{q}$, for traders $i = 1, \cdots, N$, and a price, p^*, such that:

---

[14] Batch markets have been examined by Ho, Schwartz, and Whitcomb (1985), Mendelson (1982), and Mendelson (1987). In these models traders do not condition on prices or act strategically.

[15] This is analogous to our construction of the dealer quotation schedule using a sequential rationality argument.

[16] In Kyle's model (1989), there is exogenous noise trading in addition to trading by investors and speculators. In our paper, liquidity trading takes the form of portfolio adjustment for hedging purposes. The endogeneity of liquidity trading is critical to our argument about the viability of trading systems.

(a) $\sum_j^M d_j(p^*) + \sum_i^N q_i(p^*, y_i, x_i) = 0$,
(b) $q_i(p^*, y_i, x_i) \in \text{argmax } E_i[u(\tilde{W}_{1i} | p^*, (\vec{q}_{-i}, \vec{d}))]$,
(c) $d_j(\cdot) \in \text{argmax}_{\{d_j\}}\{E_j[(\tilde{v} - p)d_j(p) | p^*, (\vec{q}, \vec{d}_{-j})]\}$, subject to non-negativity.

Condition (a) requires that the market clear in equilibrium, while condition (b) requires that the strategy of trader i maximize expected utility given the equilibrium price and the strategy functions of other agents. Finally, condition (c) requires that the strategy (demand schedule submitted) of a dealer be a best-response to the strategies of other dealers and traders. The differences in the two systems lie in the sequence of trading, which leads to differences in the information provided to players and the strategic nature of the game. In the order-driven system, traders do not know the price until after the market clears, whereas in the quote-driven system, traders know the execution price for their order. In the order-driven system, competition among dealers takes the form of competition in demand schedules rather than pure price competition, as in a quote-driven system. Before turning to the analysis of the different systems, we first discuss a number of performance measures used to evaluate trading systems.

C. Performance Measures

To compare the different trading mechanisms considered here we will examine a number of objective measures of 'market quality' that have been the focus of recent policy debates. Of course, there are innumerable potentially reasonable 'yardsticks,' but we will focus on those measures that are well known and readily quantified. Our objective is to provide criteria that can be used to empirically validate our hypotheses as well as guide policy discussions without making value judgements as to which attributes are preferred. The performance measures we consider are the following.

C.1. The Bid-Ask Spread Measures the Costs of Trading

The bid-ask spread is explicitly defined in a quote-driven system, since it is just the difference between the price for a buy order and the price for a sell order. However, even in an auction system with one price, an analogous measure or *effective* bid-ask spread can be constructed because buy orders raise prices while sell orders lower prices. Let $p(q)$ represent the price in a particular mechanism as a function of order quantity, q, where we assume $p(\cdot)$ is continuous. For an order quantity, q, the ask price is defined as $p(|q|)$ and bid price is $p(-|q|)$. Then, the *effective bid-ask spread* for an order q is a function $s_i(q) = p_i(|q|) - p_i(-|q|)$. In intraday transactions data, bid-ask quotations are typically good only for certain order sizes. Accordingly, it is important to distinguish between the effective spread and the quoted spread. In the case of a quote-driven system, we define a *bid-ask quotation* for one round lot by the pair $(p_i^a, p_i^b) \equiv (p_i(1), p_i(-1))$.

C.2. *Closely Related to the Definition of the Quoted Bid-Ask Spread is the Notion of Market Depth, Which Measures the Sensitivity of Prices to Order Flow*

Kyle (1985) defined market depth as the volume required to generate a unit price change. Following Kyle, the *market depth* at volume q is $\nabla = [p'(q)]^{-1}$, assuming that the price functional is differentiable. Market depth is a measure of liquidity, with higher depth implying more liquidity, i.e., greater ability to absorb order flow without large changes in price.

C.3. *Price Efficiency Measures the Extent to Which Prices Reflect Public Information About the Asset's Value*

A mechanism is *semi-strong form efficient* if $p_i = E[\tilde{v} \mid p_i]$. If prices reflect all available information, including private information, they are *strong-form efficient*. Strong-form efficiency corresponds to a fully revealing rational expectations equilibrium.

C.4. *Price Variance, i.e., $\mathrm{Var}[\tilde{p}_i]$, Measures the Volatility of Prices*

A related issue concerns how closely prices reflect the underlying asset value, which can be measured by the predictive or forecast error $e_i \equiv (v - p_i)$.

C.5. *A Trading System Is Robust if It Can Function under a Variety of Economic Conditions*

We show in this paper that differences in trading arrangements imply differences in the robustness to asymmetric information, in a sense that is formally defined below.

II. Equilibrium in the Quote-Driven Mechanism

Our first objective is to characterize equilibrium in the quote-driven (continuous dealer) system. Proposition 1 shows that a sufficient condition for the existence of a unique equilibrium is that the information parameter Υ be bounded above.

Proposition 1 (The Quote-Driven System): *If* $\Upsilon < \dfrac{\rho^2}{\psi}$, *equilibrium exists at time* $t_i (i = 1, 2, \cdots)$. *At time* t_i *equilibrium is linear*:

(a) *The demand function is:*

$$q_i = \frac{E[\tilde{v} \mid \Phi_i] - p_{i-1} - \alpha_i x_i}{\alpha_i + 2\lambda_i}.$$

(b) *The price quotation schedule is:*

$$p_i(q_i) = p_{i-1} + \lambda_i q_i$$

where λ_i *and* α_i *are constants defined in the appendix and* $p_0 = \mu$.

The sequence of the game, where dealers 'move first,' means that dealers cannot offer a single price to traders in equilibrium. Rather, they offer a price schedule such that each price on this schedule is the expected value of the asset given the size of the order. In turn, the trader selects a particular point on this schedule taking into account the effect of order quantity at the margin on the price of the entire trade. In addition, the trader conditions on any information revealed by the quotation schedule posted by the dealer. As a result, the dealer is at an informational disadvantage relative to traders. Intuition suggests that if the degree of information asymmetry is sufficiently great, this disadvantage may be so severe that dealers cannot make non-negative expected profits.

Proposition 1 shows that this is indeed the case. Equilibrium exists in every period if the information asymmetry parameter Υ (where $\Upsilon = (\theta^2/\tau) + \theta$) is less than a critical bound which is related to the noninformation motives for trade. We denote this upper bound by $\Upsilon^c \equiv \rho^2/\psi$. The higher the coefficient of risk aversion, ρ, the greater the upper bound Υ^c. Similarly, Υ^c is an increasing function of the variance of initial endowments of the risky asset, ψ^{-1}. Clearly, if there is insufficient liquidity trading, because ρ is low or ψ is high, dealers may be unable to open markets without suffering expected losses. If markets cannot open in the first period they cannot open in any subsequent periods and there is no way for information to be aggregated over time. We refer to this phenomenon as market failure. Proposition 1 shows that a continuous system may not be viable in periods of severe information asymmetry (i.e., Υ is high because τ is low relative to θ) or when there is little liquidity trading and Υ^c is low. Possible violations may be at the start of the trading day or immediately preceding the public revelation of new information. We will show below that these problems can be overcome by a switch to an alternative trading system.

A. Price Dynamics

Recall that the predictive (forecast) error $e_i = (v - p_i)$. Proposition 2 shows that prices are efficient with respect to public information, but that this result is consistent with autocorrelation in the predictive errors.

Proposition 2 (Price Dynamics): *If equilibrium exists:*

(a) *Transaction prices follow a martingale, i.e., $E[\tilde{p}_{i+1} | p_i] = p_i$, and prices are semi-strong form efficient, i.e., $E[v | \Phi_d^{i+1}] = p_i$.*

(b) *The predictive errors are positively correlated:*

$$E[\tilde{e}_{i+1} | e_i] = \eta_i e_i$$

where $0 < \eta_i < 1$ for all i

(c) *The effective spread is an increasing function of order size, $s(q_i) = 2\lambda_i | q_i |$. Further, the quoted bid-ask spread decreases over the day:*

$$(p_i^a - p_i^b) < (p_{i-1}^a - p_{i-1}^b).$$

The martingale property of prices is present in models of competitive dealer markets such as Glosten and Milgrom (1985) and Easley and O'Hara (1987). Part (b) shows that although prices follow a martingale (relative to post-trade public information Φ_d^{i+1}), the predictive errors are still positively correlated, so that any initial mispricing is partly carried forward. This is quite consistent with part (a), which says that prices follow a martingale with respect to post-trade public information. The parameter η_i measures the informational efficiency of the market, i.e., the rate of convergence of transaction prices to the full-information price. High values of η_i are associated with less rapid convergence, since errors persist longer. Since $\eta_i < 1$ for all i, any mispricing at time t_i exerts a diminishing influence on future prices. Prices converge in the limit to the full information value.

The model provides some insights into the nature of the bid-ask spread implicit in the price-quotation schedule. First, observe that the size and placement of the spread are informative, and form a sufficient statistic for the entire history of trading. Since the $E[\tilde{v} | \Phi_d^i] = (p_i^a + p_i^b)/2$, the mid-quote provides a point estimate of the asset's value given pre-trade public information. The precision of this estimate can be inferred from the spread since τ_i is a monotonically decreasing in $(p_i^a - p_i^b)$. The size of the bid-ask quotation, therefore, is linked to the variability of observed transaction prices.

Second, the linearity of the quotation schedule implies the entire quotation schedule can be inferred from a single bid-ask quotation. For a given order, the effective bid-ask spread, $s_i(q)$, is strictly increasing in q, and the quoted bid-ask spread, $(p_i^a - p_i^b)$ is strictly decreasing with the number of trades.[17] The result suggests that the components of volume (order size and the frequency of trading) have opposite effects on the bid-ask spread. A security whose trading volume is composed of a few large trades will have a wider effective spread than a security with identical volume composed of many small-sized trades. This point has been ignored in previous empirical studies of the cross-sectional determinants of bid-ask spreads which use total transaction or dollar volume as an independent variable. In these studies, transaction volume and bid-ask spreads are inversely related. Proposition 2 implies that in a cross-sectional regression of bid-ask spreads on average order size (relative to daily volume) and trading frequency (per unit time), the coefficient of trading frequency will have a negative sign and the coefficient of order size will have a positive sign.

Third, spreads narrow over the day because each trade reduces the information asymmetry between dealers and traders. Evidence for a decline in spreads over the day is provided by McInish and Wood (1988) who analyze intraday bid-ask spreads for NYSE stocks for five months of 1987. McInish and Wood group the sample into quintiles by trading frequency and find that

---

[17] A similar prediction for order quantity arises from the model of Ho and Stoll (1983) because of the dynamic inventory control policies pursued by market makers. Easley and O'Hara (1987) consider a model with two order sizes and show that the spread is strictly higher for the larger order size.

bid-ask spreads decline rapidly after opening within each quintile. The decline is most evident in the first 15 minutes of trading, after which spreads remain stable, possibly because the discreteness of prices generates a minimum spread.

The model makes other time-series predictions. From the proposition, we can write $p_i = p_{i-1} + \lambda_i q_i$. Given data on transaction prices and signed order flow, this equation can be estimated directly. Glosten and Harris (1988) estimate a similar model (correcting price discreteness) using time-series data for a sample NYSE stocks. In the estimation, they assume λ_i is a constant. Glosten and Harris then use three-stage least squares to examine the cross-sectional determinants of the estimated parameters. They find that λ is a decreasing function of trading frequency and an increasing function of the percentage of shares held by insiders (a proxy for information asymmetry), findings consistent with our predictions. Similarly, Madhavan and Smidt (1991) estimate a model of intraday price formation using inventory data obtained from a NYSE specialist and find that λ is significantly positive. They show that this reflects the effects of perceived information asymmetries, not transaction or inventory carrying costs. Proposition 2, however, implies that if an intraday pricing equation such as the Glosten-Harris of Madhavan-Smidt model is estimated by trading hour, the estimated hourly coefficients λ should decrease over the course of the day. This procedure could be carried out on a daily basis in order to isolate any 'day-of-the-week' effects, providing an alternative test for the model of Foster and Vishwanathan (1990).

III. Equilibrium in the Order-Driven Mechanism

Having established the equilibrium for the quote-driven system we now consider the order-driven mechanism that takes two forms: a continuous auction and a batch market.

A. The Continuous Auction Mechanism

Consider a continuous auction, where an order is executed upon arrival by the 'trading crowd' of dealers who are present on the exchange floor.[18] The continuous auction is a special case of the order-driven mechanism Γ_a, with $N = 1$. Let d_j^i be the demand of dealer j in time t_i. We represent this mechanism by the game Γ_{ca}.

Proposition 3 (The Continuous Auction): *If* $\Upsilon < \Upsilon^a \equiv \left(1 - \dfrac{2}{M}\right)\dfrac{\rho^2}{\psi}$, *there exists an equilibrium for the continuous auction mechanism* Γ_{ca} *at time* t_i *where:*

---

[18] It is convenient to think of orders being price-contingent, but whether traders submit limit orders or market orders has no effect on the equilibrium outcome, as shown in the appendix.

(a) Dealer j's ($j = 1, \cdots, M$) strategy function is linear:

$$d_j^i(p_i) = \gamma_i(p_{i-1} - p_i) - \gamma_i \zeta_{i-1} q_{i-1}.$$

(b) The trader's demand function is:

$$q_i(p_i) = \frac{E[\tilde{v} | \Phi_i] - p_i - \alpha_i x_i}{\alpha_i + \zeta_i}.$$

(c) The equilibrium price is:

$$p_i^* = \frac{[M\gamma_i(\alpha_i + \zeta_i) + (1 - \delta_i)](p_{i-1} - \zeta_{i-1} q_{i-1}) + \delta_i y_i - \alpha_i x_i}{M\gamma_i(\alpha_i + \zeta_i) + 1}.$$

where α_i, γ_i, δ_i, and ζ_i are constants described in the appendix and $p_0 = \mu$. Otherwise, if $\Upsilon > \Upsilon^a$, there does not exist a symmetric linear equilibrium.

Proposition 3 demonstrates the existence of equilibrium under general conditions. We require $M > 2$ for a linear equilibrium.[19] As before, equilibrium is linear, but there are significant differences from the equilibrium for the quote-driven mechanism Γ_c. We discuss these differences next, but note in passing that the proposition has an important empirical implication for studies of market making. From part (a) of Proposition 3, dealers sell when prices rise and buy when prices fall (i.e., $\gamma > 0$), so that a time series regression of dealer activity against price changes would suggest that dealers 'stabilize' the market. However, this behavior arises from profit maximization, not from a desire to create a societal benefit.

Proposition 4 (Continuous Markets): *If the number of dealers M is finite, then*:

(a) *If an equilibrium exists for the quote-driven mechanism Γ_c, then it exists for the continuous auction mechanism Γ_{ca}.*
(b) *Prices in the continuous auction system do not follow a martingale (i.e., $E[\tilde{p}_{i+1} | p_i] \neq p_i$, a.s.), and prices are not semi-strong form efficient (i.e., $E[\tilde{v} | p_i, \Phi_d^i] \neq p_i$, a.s.).*
(c) *The unconditional variability of prices in the continuous auction system is higher than in the continuous dealer system. However, the trading history is equally informative, i.e., $E[\tilde{v} | h_i]$ is the same in both mechanisms.*

Proposition 4 demonstrates that continuous trading is more robust to problems of asymmetric information if organized as a dealer system. If both mechanisms are viable, prices in the auction system are not efficient and are more volatile than in the dealer system. Intuitively, in the dealer system,

---

[19] It is possible that other equilibria exist (e.g., mixed strategy equilibria) but throughout the paper we will focus on linear equilibria to facilitate the comparisons across different mechanisms. One may also argue that the linear equilibrium is the most 'natural' equilibrium given the computational burden facing agents in the economy.

price competition between dealers to quote bid and ask prices eliminates the 'wedge' between the transaction price and the expected value of the asset that is the source of dealers' expected profits. In the auction system, the price is determined simultaneously so that each player has some influence on price. Strategic behavior distorts prices, inducing inefficiency and making the system more sensitive to the problems of information asymmetry. However, the trading history in both cases is equally informative since rational traders can 'undo' the distortion due to strategic behavior in the continuous auction system when making inferences about the security's value.

When are the two mechanisms equivalent? Proposition 5 shows that with free entry into market making, the equilibria for the two mechanisms coincide.

Proposition 5 (Equivalence): *For any time period t_i, as $M \to \infty$, the equilibrium price-quantity pair (p_i, q_i) for the continuous auction Γ_{ca} converges to the equilibrium price-quantity pair of the quote-driven mechanism Γ_c.*

With this limiting proposition, we can derive a number of interesting comparative statics results for both markets, assuming free entry into market making.

Proposition 6 (Comparative Statics): *If there is free entry into market making and if $\Upsilon < \Upsilon^c$ then:*

(a) *The quoted bid-ask spread ($p_i^a - p_i^b$) increases in θ and ψ and decreases in ρ and τ. Further, as $\Upsilon \to \Upsilon^c$, bid-ask spreads become arbitrarily large. Market depth ∇ decreases in θ and ψ and increases in ρ and τ.*

(b) *In any period, price variability is decreasing in θ, τ, and ψ and is increasing in ρ. Over the course of the day, price variability and the conditional variance of $\tilde{v}$ given public information is monotonically decreasing.*

The comparative statics results of Proposition 6 shows that the quality of market maker and trader signals are critical determinants of market depth and the size of the bid-ask spread. The greater the precision of the trader's signal, θ, the wider the spread, since traders have better information than before and a greater revision in prices is needed for any order size. Similarly, the greater the precision of the market maker's signal, τ, the smaller are spreads, since this reduces information asymmetry. A decrease in the precision of risky asset endowments, ψ, implies more liquidity trading so that order quantity conveys less information and requires a smaller revision in beliefs, decreasing spreads. Finally, spreads decline monotonically as the coefficient of risk aversion, ρ, increases, as this implies more liquidity trade.

When we consider the efficiency of pricing, however, the results are altered. Higher precision information signals always reduce price variance whether they are public or private. The higher the precision of asset endowments, the lower the amount of noninformation trading, and the more accurate the pricing. The discussion above suggests that price efficiency and the size of the bid-ask spread are related in a complex manner. A security with high price volatility may have narrower bid-ask spreads than a security whose volatility is low because the quantity of available information is poor in the first case, while in the second, despite high quality signals, the ratio of public to private information is low. The results imply that price volatility and spreads decline with the number of traders, a prediction which is testable by regressing price volatility on the average number of trades per unit time in a cross-section of assets. Having examined the nature of quote-driven and order-driven continuous systems, we turn our attention to periodic systems.

B. The Periodic Auction

We now consider the general case for the order-driven mechanism Γ_a, where the market only clears after $N > 1$ traders have submitted their orders. The next proposition shows that if the number of traders in the auction system Γ_a is sufficiently large, the periodic mechanism provides less variable prices and is more robust than the continuous system.

Proposition 7 (The Periodic Auction): *There exists N such that*:

(a) *The auction mechanism Γ_a is viable in economies where continuous mechanisms fail. The equilibrium strategy functions of traders and dealers are linear in price.*

(b) *In a particular periodic auction, the price p_N^a, is semi-strong form efficient and over a sequence of periodic auctions, the auction prices follow a martingale.*

(c) *The price in the auction mechanism Γ_a is less variable than each of the corresponding sequence of N prices in the continuous mechanism Γ_c.*

Corollary 1: *As the number of traders participating in a given auction grows large, prices converge to the strong form efficient price, i.e., $\lim_{N \to \infty} p_N^a = v$.*

Proposition 7 shows that a large enough auction can provide more efficient prices than a continuous market. In a periodic system, all traders observe a noisy estimate of their aggregate information, in addition to public and private information signals. The more traders participating in the auction, the more efficient the price is as a signal of asset value. Further, the system can function in economies where continuous systems fail. The disadvantage of the periodic system is that it does not provide for continuous trading. Rather, investors must wait until pre-specified times for order execution.[20]

Corollary 1 shows that prices are strong form efficient in the limit, i.e., the prices are fully revealing. Another interesting case of Proposition 7 concerns the limiting equilibrium as the quality of public information becomes extremely poor, i.e., as $\tau \to 0$. Since $\lim_{\tau \to 0} \Upsilon = \infty$ our previous analysis of continuous systems (both the quote-driven system Γ_c and the continuous

---

[20] See Garbade and Silber (1979) who provide a model where there exists an optimal time between market clearings that minimizes investors' liquidity risk.

auction system Γ_{ca}) implies that there does not exist an equilibrium for τ sufficiently small. Intuitively, for any $\theta > 0$, the degree of information asymmetry is increasing as τ grows small, so dealers condition more and more on order flow. This implies the volume of liquidity trading goes to zero, so that dealers cannot make nonnegative expected profits, and M goes to zero. Intuition suggests that a periodic auction can function without the presence of intermediaries with the N traders sharing risk among themselves. The following proposition establishes that this intuition is correct, provided the quality of private information signals, θ, is bounded above.

The next proposition establishes a link between the strategic rational expectations equilibrium of this paper and the classical description of an auction market. In the classical Walrasian auction, traders act competitively and have fixed reservation prices. The equilibrium price is found by computing the zero of the aggregate excess demand function. Proposition 8 establishes that the price in the periodic auction game Γ^a is the *same* price that would prevail in the classical framework, but that the two equilibria are quite distinct.

Proposition 8 (Market Clearing without Dealers): *If* $\theta < \left(1 - \dfrac{2}{N}\right)\dfrac{\rho^2}{\psi}$, *there exists a linear equilibrium for the auction mechanism* Γ_a *with* $\tau = 0$ *where:*

(a) *The equilibrium strategy functions of traders are linear in price and dealers do not trade. The price is efficient and price volatility is a decreasing function of the number of traders N, the precision of signals θ, and is increasing in the amount of liquidity trading, as measured by endowment variation, ψ^{-1}.*

(b) *The Walrasian equilibrium is defined for all $\theta > 0$. The price in the auction mechanism Γ_a is equal to the price that would prevail in a Walrasian auction. However, the volume of trade in the auction mechanism Γ_a is strictly lower than in the Walrasian auction.*

Note that in Proposition 8, existence requires that the precision of signals, θ, be bounded above. The bound is $\left(1 - \dfrac{2}{N}\right)\dfrac{\rho^2}{\psi}$, which, for large N, converges to the bound Υ^c. So market failure may occur even if the number of traders is large. This is directly attributable to the fact that traders in the game are strategic; the Walrasian equilibrium exists for all $\theta > 0$, even if we extend the model to allow traders to have rational expectations. From a policy viewpoint, Proposition 8 implies that an auction system can function even in a situation where public information is so poor that dealers choose to withdraw from market making activities.

Part (b) shows the Walrasian price equals the periodic auction price. Intuitively, a trader's *reservation price*, at which demand equals zero, is the same in both mechanisms because traders view the auction price as distributed symmetrically about their prior mean. Since an auction mechanism operates by averaging traders' reservation prices, both mechanisms yield the same price. However, the equilibria are distinct because strategic traders in the periodic system trade less to reduce their price impact, implying a smaller trading volume.

IV. Continuous versus Periodic Trading

In this section, we consider the relative merits of continuous versus periodic trading systems and the implications for public policy. We also discuss the effect of explicitly introducing trading costs into the model.

A. Circuit Breakers and Trading Halts

Propositions 1 and 5 shows that market failure can occur in a continuous market with free entry into market making if the degree of information asymmetry Υ, exceeds the bound, $\Upsilon^c = \dfrac{\rho^2}{\psi}$. In this case, dealers cannot make non-negative expected profits on the first trade and on all subsequent trades. The upper bound Υ^c measures the noninformation motives for trading; it increases with risk aversion, ρ, and the variance of initial endowments of the risky asset, ψ^{-1}. For some securities there may be periods when θ is high relative to τ, so that Υ exceeds the critical bound and a continuous system may not be viable. Possible violations may be at the start of the trading day or immediately preceding the public revelation of new information.

Our analysis of the continuous system implies that trading could be restarted by increasing the ratio of public to private information. Casual observation suggests many devices and procedures to supply dealers with information on current market conditions when market failure is likely. For example, many continuous markets open (or re-open following a trading halt) with a call auction to allow the assimilation of new information.

However, our results show that continuous trading cannot always be restarted with a public information signal. To see this, note that as $\tau \to \infty$, $\Upsilon \downarrow \theta$, so that when $\Upsilon^c < \theta$, a continuous market is not viable even if the quality of public information is very high. The results suggest that proposals to reduce the market stress in continuous systems with 'circuit breakers' (trading halts triggered by large price movements) can exacerbate the original problem. Once trading is halted, it may be difficult or impossible to restart the process. Proposition 7 suggests a possible solution is to switch to a periodic trading mechanism in times of market stress, since this system can operate even if dealers choose not to make markets.

A related issue concerns the timing of the switch. In most markets, trading halts are triggered by large price movements. However, if these movements are warranted by changes in fundamentals, a trading halt will reduce market efficiency. Proposition 6 suggests a superior trigger. The proposition establishes that the quoted bid-ask spread becomes arbitrarily large as the measure of degree of information asymmetry Υ approaches from below the level at which the market fails. This suggests initiating a halt or a mechanism switch when the quoted bid-ask spread exceeds a critical level based on trading volume and historical spreads.

Empirical validation of these hypotheses is hampered by the difficulty in comparing trading structures across different markets and securities. Amihud and Mendelson (1987) examine NYSE stock returns from open-to-open, where trading is organized as an auction market, and close-to-close, where prices are determined in a continuous dealer market. They find significant differences in the two returns distribution, noting that the open-to-open returns variance is generally higher than the close-to-close returns variance. Stoll and Whaley (1990) confirm these findings, attributing them to NYSE opening practices. However, it is not clear whether these results reflect differences in the trading mechanism or the effect of the preceding overnight trading halt. Two recent papers attempt to resolve this issue using evidence from what comes close to controlled experiments.

Amihud and Mendelson (1991) use data for 50 stocks traded on Tokyo Stock Exchange, where a periodic auction, the *Itayose*, is used to open the two trading sessions of the day, during which trading is accomplished through a continuous mechanism, the *Zaraba*. Although the daily returns from the opening auction transaction are more volatile than the returns from the continuous market, this is not the case for the returns from the auction mechanism used to open the afternoon session. This suggests that the higher volatility at the opening found in studies of the U.S. market primarily reflects the preceding non-trading interval rather than the auction mechanism itself. Amihud and Mendelson, (1991) find that the mid-day auction "may well exhibit the least volatility and most efficient value discovery process" consistent with Proposition 7. They also establish that "a sequence of recent transaction prices facilitates value discovery and eases traders' inference on the current value of the security," as predicted by Proposition 6(b). In a similar study of 12 stocks traded on the Milan Stock Exchange, Amihud, Mendelson, and Murgia (1990) conclude that a call auction mechanism "provides a more efficient value discovery process for opening the trading day" than a continuous system. Further, they find that over the course of the day, "...investors correct perceived errors or noise in the prices set at the [opening] call," as predicted by Proposition 2(b).

B. Trading Costs and the Choice of Market Design

Although our discussion has emphasized the importance of asymmetric information, the choice of market design may be affected by other factors, especially the costs of operating the system. In this section, we consider the impact of introducing a fixed cost of providing market making services into the model. We focus on fixed costs since variable (order execution) costs appear to be relatively small in comparison.[21] Certainly, in models that exhibit linear equilibria (as is the case here) it is straightforward to incorpo-

---

[21] Glosten and Harris (1988) and Stoll (1989) decompose the bid-ask spread into its component parts and find that variable costs are a small portion of the spread.

rate a constant per share variable cost, without altering our qualitative results. Suppose now that there are a large number of potential dealers who can enter the market if they choose to do so. Each dealer must bear a fixed cost $F > 0$ at time 0 in order to trade.

The cost F may include the opportunity costs of capital, the costs of exchange membership, as well as fixed costs associated with order routing, processing, and settlement. Formally, we modify the model to incorporate a pre-game round where market makers enter the market until further entry would lead to negative expected profits. Thus, M is determined endogenously.

Proposition 9 (Trading Costs): *If there are fixed costs to providing continuous market making services, the quote-driven system Γ^c can function only with a monopolistic market maker. However, the continuous auction mechanism Γ^{ca} can support multiple market makers provided the fixed costs of dealers are sufficiently small.*

Proposition 9 demonstrates that a monopolistic market maker system is the only form of a quote-driven system that is viable when there are fixed costs to market making. Intuitively, pure price competition implies prices are set on the basis of marginal costs, which are below average costs. Without regulations to ensure a minimum bid-ask spread, the equilibrium number of dealers, if any, is one. The continuous auction Γ^{ca} does not suffer from such problems since expected trading profits are positive if the number of dealers is finite; in fact, the fixed costs determine the equilibrium number of market makers. The result provides some insight into the nature of exchange mandated price discreteness, as well as the persistence of quasi-monopolistic market making regimes. The periodic system Γ^a, of course, can function without dealers, but can impose high submission costs on traders, requiring either the physical presence of traders on the exchange floor or the costly submission of written demand schedules.

A related issue concerns the trading costs borne by investors. Without empirical evidence, it is difficult to assess the relative magnitudes of these costs, but the model provides some theoretical guidance. Traders' information costs in a dealer market are lower because traders need only solicit the dealer's bid-ask quotes. These quotes are sufficient statistics for the entire trading history. By contrast, in an auction market, investors must collect past trading information, which imposes private costs directly and social costs through duplication. Thus, there is no unambiguous ranking of mechanisms by their operating costs. The determination of which system has lower operating costs must be resolved empirically.

V. Conclusions

This paper models the process of price discovery under two alternative forms of market organization: a quote-driven system and an order-driven system. The quote-driven system relies on competitive dealers to post prices before orders are submitted while the order-driven system requires all participants to submit their orders before prices are determined. The quote-driven system is a continuous system since orders are executed upon submission. The order-driven system can operate either as a continuous system, with immediate execution on the exchange floor, or as a periodic system, where orders are stored for simultaneous execution. Trading is modeled as a game where order quantities and beliefs are determined endogenously and players act strategically. We showed that a quote-driven system provides greater price efficiency than a continuous auction system. However, with free entry into market making, the equilibria of the two mechanisms coincide.

We demonstrated that a periodic trading mechanism can function where a continuous market fails. This occurs because pooling orders for simultaneous execution can overcome the problems of information asymmetry that cause failure in a mechanism where trading takes place sequentially. However, a periodic system cannot provide immediate order execution. Further, a periodic system imposes higher costs for traders who must collect market information instead of observing price quotations. If a continuous market fails, it cannot re-open unless the degree of information asymmetry is lowered. Consequently, proposals to halt trading in times of market stress may actually exacerbate the original problem, possibly leading to market failure. Our results suggest a better alternative to a trading halt would be a switch to an auction market since this system can operate when dealers refuse to make markets. Such a switch would allow the public to observe a common information signal (the auction price) that may allow continuous trading to re-open at a future date. Casual observation suggests that thickly traded securities are generally traded in continuous markets, whereas thinly traded securities are traded in periodic auction systems. To the extent that information asymmetry is inversely related to the market value and trading activity, the model is consistent with the observation. Our results provide a partial explanation for differences in trading structures across markets and assets.

Appendix

Proof of Proposition 1: The proposition is a straightforward extension of Glosten's single-period model. We provide a detailed proof here for the sake of completeness. The price at time t_i is a function of the order quantity of the traders, and we write $p_i = p_i(q)$. Using (1), we see:

$$E[\tilde{W}_{1i} | \Phi_i] = (q_i + x_i) E[\tilde{v} | \Phi_i] + c_{0i} - p(q_i) q_i \qquad (A1)$$

and

$$\text{Var}[\tilde{W}_{1i} | \Phi_i] = \text{Var}[\tilde{v} | \Phi_i] (q_i + x_i)^2. \qquad (A2)$$

To simplify the notation, define $r_i \equiv E[\tilde{v} | \Phi_i]$ and $\alpha_i \equiv \rho \text{Var}[\tilde{v} | \Phi_i]$. Expected utility maximization in equation (2) implies that q_i, solves:

$$r_i - p_i(q_i) - p_i'(q_i) q_i - \alpha_i q_i - \alpha_i x_i = 0. \qquad (A3)$$

The second order condition is:

$$-p_i''(q_i)q_i - 2p_i'(q_i) - \alpha_i < 0. \tag{A4}$$

Suppose at time t_i, trader i places an order for q_i securities, given $p_i(q)$, the market maker's quotation function. Define $\hat{r}_i$ as follows:

$$\hat{r}_i(q_i) \equiv p_i(q_i) + p_i'(q_i)q_i + \alpha_i q_i. \tag{A5}$$

At time t_i, suppose the prior distribution of $\tilde{v}$ given public information (including any information revealed through the quotation schedule itself) is a normal distribution with mean μ_i and precision τ_i. Applying a basic proposition from statistical decision theory (see, e.g., DeGroot (1970)), the trader's posterior mean of $\tilde{v}$ given the signal, y_i, is:

$$r_i = \frac{\theta y_i + \tau_i \mu_i}{(\theta + \tau_i)}. \tag{A6}$$

The posterior precision of this estimate is $(\theta + \tau_i)$ so, by definition, $\alpha_i = \dfrac{\rho}{(\theta + \tau_i)}$. Define $z_i(q_i)$ by:

$$z_i(q_i) = \frac{\hat{r}_i(q_i)(\tau_i + \theta) - \mu_i \tau_i}{\theta}. \tag{A7}$$

Using the definition of $\hat{r}(q)$, we see that $\hat{r}_i(q_i) = r_i - \alpha_i x_i$. Substituting this and equation (A6) into equation (A7), we obtain

$$z_i(q_i) = \frac{\theta y_i - \alpha_i x_i (\tau_i + \theta)}{\theta}. \tag{A8}$$

Using the definition of α_i, $z_i = y_i - (\rho/\theta)x_i$. Recall $y_i = v + \epsilon_i$ so we can write:

$$z_i = v + \epsilon_i - \dot{x}_i\left(\frac{\rho}{\theta}\right). \tag{A9}$$

Using equation (A9), we see that, from a market maker's perspective, z_i is drawn from a normal distribution with mean v and precision ω, where:

$$\omega \equiv \frac{\theta^2}{\left(\theta + \dfrac{\rho^2}{\psi}\right)}. \tag{A10}$$

The parameter ω is a critical constant, reappearing in our analysis of the order-driven mechanism. Note that ω is time-independent. As $\text{Cov}(z_i, \mu_i) = 0$, we see that the market maker's posterior distribution of $\tilde{v}$ has mean:

$$E[\tilde{v} \mid q_i, \Phi_d^i] = \frac{\omega z_i + \tau_i \mu_i}{(\omega + \tau_i)} \tag{A11}$$

and precision $(\omega + \tau_i)$. To solve for the equilibrium quotation schedule, we express z_i in terms of q_i by substituting equation (A5) into (A7):

$$z_i = \frac{(\tau_i + \theta)(p_i(q) + p_i'(q)q + \alpha_i q) - \mu_i \tau_i}{\theta}. \tag{A12}$$

Substituting (A12) into equation (A11) and using the zero expected profits condition $p_i(q) = E[\tilde{v} \mid q_i, \Phi_d^i]$, we obtain:

$$p_i(q) = \frac{\omega}{(\omega + \tau_i)}\left[\frac{(\tau_i + \theta)}{\theta}(p_i(q) + p_i'(q)q + \alpha_i q) - \frac{\tau_i \mu_i}{\theta}\right] + \frac{\tau_i \mu_i}{(\omega + \tau_i)}.$$

Some algebraic manipulation yields the following expression:

$$q p_i'(q) = \kappa_i (p_i(q) - \mu_i) - \alpha_i q \tag{A13}$$

a first-order differential equation in q, where $\kappa_i \equiv \dfrac{\tau_i(\theta - \omega)}{\omega(\theta + \tau_i)}$ is a constant.

The solution to (A13) is given by

$$p_i(q) = \mu_i + \left[\frac{\alpha_i}{\kappa_i - 1}\right]q + K\,\text{sign}(q)\,|q|^{\kappa_i} \tag{A14}$$

for $\kappa_i \neq 1$, where K is an arbitrary constant of integration. If $\kappa_i = 1$, the solution to (A13) is:

$$p_i(q) = \mu + Kq - \alpha_i q \ln(|q|).$$

We have derived the general functional form of the quotation function. The next step in the proof is to show that the linear function is the unique function satisfying the conditions of Definition 1.

Consider first the general case, where $\kappa_i \neq 1$. It is conventional to define $\lambda_i \equiv \alpha_i/(\kappa_i - 1)$. Suppose $\kappa_i < 1$ (i.e., $\lambda_i < 0$) and K < 0. Then, $p(q) < p(-q)$ for all $q > 0$, an arbitrage opportunity that will be eliminated by interdealer trading. Now suppose K > 0. Using (A14), the second order condition (A4) is:

$$\kappa_i(\kappa_i - 1)K|q|^{\kappa_i - 1} + 2\lambda_i + 2\kappa_i K|q|^{\kappa_i - 1} > -\alpha_i.$$

Inspection of the second order condition shows there exist some q^* and q_*, where $q^* > 0 > q_*$, such that the second order condition (A4) is violated if q does not lie in the interval (q^*, q_*), so that this cannot be an equilibrium.

Now assume $\kappa_i > 1$ (equivalently $\lambda_i > 0$) and K < 0. The previous argument applies directly, so that K ≥ 0. If K > 0, then the second order condition (A4) is always satisfied. However, the family of curves defined by equation (A14) is bounded from below (above) in the positive (negative) orthant by the linear equilibrium, and using condition (b) of Definition 1, K $= 0$. Hence, if $\kappa_i \neq 1$, then K $= 0$ in equilibrium, and the equilibrium is unique and linear in every period. Finally, the analysis of the case where $\kappa_i = 1$ is treated exactly like the case of $\kappa_i < 1$. The linear equilibrium is the unique equilibrium if $\kappa_i > 1$.

At time t_{i+1}, market makers' posterior distribution of v, given q_i, is normal if the initial prior is normal, because the normal distribution is closed under sampling (a conjugate family). This distribution becomes the prior distribution in determining $p_{i+1}(q)$. At time t_{i+1}, the dealer's prior distribution of $\tilde{v}$ is normal with mean μ_{i+1}. By definition, $p_i(q_i)$ is the posterior mean of $\tilde{v}$ given q_i:

$$\mu_{i+1} = p_i(q_i). \tag{A15}$$

and the posterior precision is:

$$\tau_{i+1} = \tau_i + \omega \tag{A16}$$

where ω is defined in (A10). In the first period, market makers have a normal prior distribution with mean μ and precision τ. Hence, by induction, the proposition holds, if equilibrium exists in every period. It remains to show that if the equilibrium condition is met in the first period, it will be satisfied in all subsequent periods.

For $\kappa_i > 1$ (equivalently, when $\lambda_i > 0$), we see that $\tau_i(\rho^2/\psi - \theta) > \theta^2$. From (A16), τ_i is increasing in i, so that if $\tau\rho^2/\psi > \theta(\theta + \tau)$ at time 1 then equilibrium exists in all subsequent periods. So, from equations (A14), (A15), and the definition of λ_i, the unique equilibrium at time t_i is linear. Then

$$p_i(q_i) = p_{i-1}(q_{i-1}) + \lambda_i q_i \tag{A17}$$

where $p_0 = \mu$ and λ_i is given by:

$$\lambda_i = \frac{\rho\theta}{\dfrac{\tau_i \rho^2}{\psi} - \theta(\theta + \tau_i)}. \tag{A18}$$

Let $\Upsilon^c = \dfrac{\rho^2}{\psi}$. Clearly, if $\Upsilon < \Upsilon^c$, the unique equilibrium is given by (A17) and (A18).

Proof of Proposition 2: (a) Note from proposition 1 that:

$$p_{i+1} = p_i + \lambda_{i+1} q_{i+1}$$

so that it is sufficient to show:

$$E[\tilde{q}_{i+1} | p_i] = 0.$$

From (A3), q_{i+1} is:

$$q_{i+1} = \frac{(r_{i+1} - p_i) - \alpha_{i+1} x_{i+1}}{(\alpha_{i+1} + 2\lambda_{i+1})}. \tag{A19}$$

Now

$$E[\tilde{r}_{i+1} - p_i | p_i] = E\left[\frac{\tilde{y}_{i+1}\theta + p_i\tau_{i+1}}{\theta + \tau_{i+1}} - p_i \Big| p_i\right]$$

$$= \frac{\theta}{\theta + \tau_{i+1}}(E[\tilde{v} + \tilde{\epsilon}_{i+1} | p_i] - p_i).$$

Since $p_i = E[\tilde{v} | p_i]$ and $E[\tilde{\epsilon}_{i+1} | p_i] = E[\tilde{x} | p_i] = 0$, the result follows immediately.

(b) Since $e_{i+1} = v - p_{i+1}$, we obtain using (A17):

$$E[\tilde{e}_{i+1} | e_i] = -\lambda_{i+1}E[\tilde{q}_{i+1} | e_i] + e_i.$$

From the definition of q_i, we obtain:

$$E[\tilde{e}_{i+1} | e_i] = \eta_i e_i$$

where

$$\eta_i = 1 - \frac{\lambda_{i+1}}{(\alpha_{i+1} + 2\lambda_{i+1})} \cdot \frac{\theta}{(\theta + \tau_{i+1})}.$$

Clearly, $0 < \eta_i < 1$. Thus the predictive errors are positively correlated.

(c) The parameter λ_i depends on i through τ_i. Comparative statics shows that λ_i is a decreasing function of τ_i. Since τ_i is strictly increasing in i, it follows from (A18) that $\lambda_i < \lambda_{i-1}$, hence $s_i(1) < s_{i-1}(1)$.

Proof of Proposition 3: The proof constructs the Bayes-Nash equilibrium for the continuous auction mechanism Γ_{ca} by solving for a trader's best response to the conjectured strategies adopted by other traders and then shows the conjectures are consistent. Suppose at time t_i, the prior distribution of $\tilde{v}$, based on public information, is normal with mean μ_i and precision τ_i, where $\mu_1 = \mu$ and $\tau_1 = \tau$. Suppose trader i, who arrives at time t_i, conjectures that dealers (indexed by $j = 1, \cdots, M$) adopt strategy functions of the form:

$$d_j^i(p_i) = \gamma_i(\mu_i - p_i). \tag{A20}$$

We will show this conjecture is correct in equilibrium, and that the conjectured demand function satisfies all the conditions of the Definition 2. Using part (a) of Definition 2, we see that in equilibrium:

$$M\gamma_i(\mu_i - p_i) + q_i = 0. \tag{A21}$$

Using (A21) the price can be written as a function of q_i:

$$p_i = \mu_i + \zeta_i q_i \tag{A22}$$

where $\zeta_i \equiv \dfrac{1}{M\gamma_i}$. We turn now to the functional form of the demand schedule submitted by trader i. From equation (A6), it follows that:

$$E[\tilde{v} | \Phi_i] = \delta_i y_i + (1 - \delta_i)\mu_i \tag{A23}$$

where $\delta_i = \theta/(\tau_i + \theta)$ is a constant. From the utility maximization condition (A3), the demand schedule $q_i(p)$ given the price functional (A22) is:

$$q_i(p) = \frac{E[\tilde{v}|\Phi_i] - p_i - \alpha_i x_i}{(\alpha_i + \zeta_i)}. \quad (A24)$$

where we define $\alpha_i = \rho/(\tau_i + \theta)$.

Substituting (A23) and equation (A22) into equation (A24) and simplifying, we can express the optimal demand of trader i as:

$$q_i = \frac{\delta(y_i - \mu_i) - \alpha_i x_i}{\alpha_i + 2\zeta_i}. \quad (A25)$$

This equation shows that if the trader has rational expectations and correctly conjectures the price functional, he can submit a market order that is equivalent to the limit order, so that order form is irrelevant.

Consider now the strategic decision of a dealer, say dealer m. From (A21) and the market clearing condition, we obtain:

$$(M-1)\gamma_i(\mu_i - p_i) + q_i + d_m^i(p_i) = 0. \quad (A26)$$

It follows that for dealer m the price functional is given by:

$$p_i = (\mu_i + \beta_i q_i) + \beta_i d_m \quad (A27)$$

where we define $\beta_i \equiv \dfrac{1}{(M-1)\gamma_i}$. The expected profits of dealer m at time t_i are given by:

$$\pi_i = (E[\tilde{v}|p_i] - p_i)d_m^i(p_i) \quad (A28)$$

where the conditional expectation reflects rational expectations on the part of the dealer. Substituting (A27) into (A28), and solving for the optimal demand, we obtain:

$$d_m^i(p) = \frac{E[\tilde{v}|p_i] - \mu_i - \beta_i q_i}{2\beta_i}. \quad (A29)$$

Now consider the conditional expectation of the dealer. The dealer has rational expectations, and learns from the market clearing price and order submitted. Noted that a dealer who knows his own order quantity and the price knows q_i since $q_i = -Md_m$; under the conjectured strategies the trader's order is absorbed equally by the M dealers. From equation (A25), observing q_i is equivalent to observing:

$$\hat{y}(q_i) = \mu_i + \frac{\alpha_i + 2\zeta_i}{\delta_i} q_i. \quad (A30)$$

From equation (A25), we can express the signal as:

$$\hat{y}(q_i) = y_i - \left(\frac{\alpha_i}{\delta_i}\right) x_i. \tag{A31}$$

So, $\hat{y}$ is the minimum variance unbiased estimator of the private information of trader i a dealer can make given the order quantity q_i. Since $\alpha_i/\delta_i = \rho/\theta$, the signal is distributed normally with mean v and precision ω, where ω is given by (A10). Using Bayes' rule, we obtain:

$$E[\tilde{v}\mid p_i] = \chi_i \hat{y}(q_i) + (1 - \chi_i)\mu_i \tag{A32}$$

where $\chi_i = \dfrac{\omega}{\omega + \tau_i}$. Substituting (A27) into (A29), we can write the desired order quantity of dealer m as:

$$d_m^i(p) = \frac{E[\tilde{v}\mid p] - p}{\beta_i}. \tag{A33}$$

Using (A32) and (A30), (A33) can be written as:

$$d_m^i(p) = \frac{\mu_i - p + C_i q_i}{\beta_i} \tag{A34}$$

where $C_i \equiv \dfrac{\chi_i(\alpha_i + 2\zeta_i)}{\delta_i}$ is a constant. Since $q_i = -Md_m^i$, we obtain:

$$d_m^i(p) = \frac{\mu_i - p}{MC_i + \beta_i} \tag{A35}$$

which has the conjectured form, with $\gamma_i = (MC_i + \beta_i)^{-1}$. Since both β_i and C_i depend on γ_i, we must verify that γ_i is well-defined and satisfies the second order conditions for a maximum. This requires that $\gamma_i > 0$. Only then are the proposed strategies an equilibrium. Substituting in the definitions of C_i and β_i, we see that γ_i satisfies:

$$\frac{1}{\gamma_i} = M\chi_i\left(\frac{\rho}{\theta} + \frac{2}{M\delta_i\gamma_i}\right) + \frac{1}{\gamma_i(M-1)}. \tag{A36}$$

The solution is:

$$\gamma_i = \frac{\theta(\omega + \tau_i)}{M\omega\rho}\left[1 - \frac{2\omega(\theta + \tau_i)}{\theta(\omega + \tau_i)} - \frac{1}{M-1}\right]. \tag{A37}$$

Given that $M > 2$, for $\gamma_i > 0$ we require (using equation (A37)) that:

$$\frac{\theta(\theta + \tau)}{\tau} < \left(1 - \frac{2}{M}\right)\frac{\rho^2}{\psi}. \tag{A38}$$

If the inequality in (A38) is satisfied, $\gamma_i > 0$ and equilibrium is well-defined. Note that if γ_1 exists, then equilibrium exists in all subsequent periods since $\tau_i = \tau + (i - 1)\omega$. The conjugate property of the normal distribution ensures that the prior distribution is in fact normal. The prior is given by $\mu_i = p_{i-1} - \zeta_{i-1} q_{i-1}$, so the strategies and price functional can be easily expressed in the form stated in the proposition.

Proof of Proposition 4: (a) From equation (A38), equilibrium for the continuous auction system exists only if γ_1 exists. Define by Υ^a the right-hand side of (A38), so that $\Upsilon^a < \Upsilon^c$, implying the quote-driven system is viable in economies where the order-driven mechanism does not possess an equilibrium.

(b) To show that prices are not efficient (in a semi-strong form sense), suppose to the contrary that $p_i = E[\tilde{v} \mid p_i]$. Using (A33), this implies that $d_j^i = 0$ for all $j = 1, \cdots, M$. This implies that $q_i = 0$ for all $i = 1, \cdots, N$, or equivalently that:

$$\delta_i(\tilde{y}_i - \tilde{\mu}_i) - \alpha_i \tilde{x}_i = 0.$$

Since the probability of this event is (almost surely) zero, we obtain a contradiction. From equation (A33) we obtain:

$$p_i = E[\tilde{v} \mid \Phi_d^i, q_i] + \zeta_i q_i \qquad (A39)$$

which shows that prices are not efficient.

(c) To distinguish the prices in the two mechanisms, at time t_i, let p_i^{ca} denote the price in the continuous auction Γ_{ca} and denote by p_i^c the price in the quote-driven system Γ_c. Now, using equation (A32) and the definition of χ, we see that the first term in equation (A39) is the price that prevails in time t_i in the continuous dealer mechanism, i.e., $E[\tilde{v} \mid \Phi_d^i, q_i] = p_i^c$. Accordingly, we can write the continuous auction price as:

$$p_i^{ca} = p_i^c + \zeta_i q_i \qquad (A40)$$

Note that the quantity q_i differs from the quantity traded in the continuous dealer market because of differences in market liquidity as measured by ζ_i. Equation (A40) shows that the trading history under a continuous auction contains the information necessary to recover the unbiased dealer market prices; both histories are equally informative. Taking the unconditional variance of p_i^{ca} in (A40), we obtain:

$$\mathrm{Var}[\tilde{p}_i] = \mathrm{Var}[\tilde{p}_i^c] + 2\zeta_i \mathrm{Cov}(\tilde{p}_i^c, \tilde{q}_i) + \zeta_i^2 \mathrm{Var}[\tilde{q}_i].$$

Since the covariance term is positive, the variance of price at times $\{t_i\}$ in the continuous auction is higher than the price in the continuous dealer market.

Proof of Proposition 5: By definition, $\zeta = \dfrac{1}{\gamma M}$, and taking limits we obtain:

$$\lim_{M \to \infty} \frac{1}{\gamma M} = \frac{\rho \theta}{\dfrac{\tau_i \rho^2}{\psi} - \theta(\theta + \tau_i)}. \qquad (A41)$$

From (A18), this limit is the parameter λ_i, showing that with an infinite number of traders, the existence condition (A38) for the game Γ_{ca} coincides with the condition for the game Γ_c. The equilibria of the two mechanisms coincide only in the limit. Note that as $M \to \infty$, $\gamma \to 0$, so that $d_m(p) \to 0$, i.e., each dealer's trade size becomes arbitrarily small, so the allocation of q_i across dealers differs from the market maker system.

Proof of Proposition 6: (a) A change in the parameters ρ, τ, ψ, and θ affects the quoted bid-ask spread through λ_i, and we consider each of these in turn. Since market depth is $\nabla = \lambda^{-1}$, spreads and liquidity are inversely related.

1. The effect of a change in ρ on λ_i is given by:

$$\frac{\partial \lambda_i}{\partial \rho} = \lambda_i \left[\frac{1}{\rho} - \frac{2\tau_i \lambda_i}{\psi \theta} \right] \tag{A42}$$

which is always negative in equilibrium. To demonstrate this, assume to the contrary that an increase in ρ increases λ_i. Then, it follows that $(1/\rho) > 2\lambda_i \tau_i /(\theta \psi)$, or $\psi/(\rho \tau_i) > 2(\lambda_i /\theta)$. Substituting the expression for λ_i in equation (A18), we obtain $1 > \dfrac{2\rho^2 \tau_i}{\tau_i \rho^2 - \psi \theta (\theta + \tau_i)}$, which is a contradiction.

2. The effect of a change in τ_i on λ_i is given by:

$$\frac{\partial \lambda_i}{\partial \tau_i} = \lambda_i \left[\frac{\theta - \dfrac{\rho^2}{\psi}}{\rho \theta} \right] \tag{A43}$$

which is always negative since if equilibrium exists, $\rho^2 > \psi \theta$. Similarly, it is straightforward to show that λ_i is increasing in θ and in ψ.

(b) Zero ex post expected profits implies that the transaction price at time t_i is the posterior mean of $\tilde{v}$ given public information, i.e., that $p_i = \mu_{i+1}$. Now the prior distribution of $\tilde{v}$ at time t_{i+1} has mean μ_{i+1}, where μ_{i+1} is normally distributed with mean v and precision τ_{i+1}. Since traders have rational expectations, this distribution is correct. This implies that price volatility, conditional on public information at time t_{i-1} is:

$$\text{Var}[\tilde{p}_i] = \tau_{i+1}^{-1} = (\tau + i\omega)^{-1}.$$

Clearly, the variance of price is decreasing in τ. Since ω is an increasing function of θ, it follows that higher private information quality implies more accurate pricing. Similarly, since ω is increasing in ψ, more noise trading means greater price variability. The opposite is true with the coefficient of risk aversion ρ, since intuitively greater risk aversion is associated with relatively less liquidity trading and hence more accurate pricing. Since $\text{Var}[e_i] = \text{Var}[v - p_i]$, these results also hold for the pricing error.

Proof of Proposition 7: (a) Consider an auction N traders. If $\tau > 0$, open entry for dealers implies the equilibrium price is the conditional expectation of $\tilde{v}$ given public information and the price itself, although the finite number of traders will act strategically. Formally, the market is efficient in that:

$$p = E[\tilde{v} \mid p]. \tag{A44}$$

The proof constructs the Bayes-Nash equilibrium by solving for a trader's best response to the conjectured strategies adopted by other traders and then shows the conjectures are consistent. Suppose trader i, $(i = 1, \cdots, N)$ conjectures that all other traders (indexed by $h = 1, \cdots, i-1, i+1, \cdots, N$.) adopt strategy functions of the form:

$$q_h(p) = a_0 \mu + a_1 y_h - a_2 x_h - bp \tag{A45}$$

for $h \neq i$, where p is the batch market price and $b > 0$ is a constant. Note that (y_h, x_h) is the private information of trader h and is not known to trader i. In this mechanism, the orders are submitted directly to dealers, so that each dealer observes the net order flow $Q \equiv \Sigma_i q_i$. Then, a dealer can form a statistic $\hat{y}^N(Q)$ defined as:

$$\hat{y}^N(Q) = \frac{Q + Nbp - Na_0\mu}{Na_1}. \tag{A46}$$

From (A45), the statistic $\hat{y}$ is simply:

$$\hat{y}^N(Q) = \frac{\Sigma_i y_i - \left(\dfrac{a_2}{a_1}\right)\Sigma_i x_i}{N} \tag{A47}$$

This statistic is distributed normally with mean v and with precision denoted by $N\pi$, where π is the precision of $\tilde{y} - \dfrac{a_2}{a_1}\tilde{x}$. Accordingly, using (A44), the equilibrium price can be written as:

$$p = \xi\mu + (1 - \xi)\hat{y}^N \tag{A48}$$

where we define $\xi \equiv \tau/(\tau + N\pi)$. Rearranging, we obtain:

$$p = \frac{a_1\xi - a_0(1 - \xi)}{a_1 - (1 - \xi)b}\mu + \frac{1 - \xi}{N(a_1 - (1 - \xi)b)}Q. \tag{A49}$$

We turn now to the construction of the demand function of trader i, where $i = 1, \cdots, N$. From (A49), the price functional faced by trader i takes the form:

$$p = \left(\phi_1\mu + \phi_2 \sum_{h \neq i} q_h\right) + \phi_2 q_i \tag{A50}$$

where $\phi_1 \equiv \dfrac{a_1\xi - a_0(1-\xi)}{a_1 - (1-\xi)b}$ and $\phi_2 \equiv \dfrac{1-\xi}{N(a_1 - (1-\xi)b)}$. Utility maximization implies that:

$$q_i(p) = \frac{E[\tilde{v}\mid y_i, p] - p - \alpha' x_i}{\alpha' + \phi_2} \qquad (A51)$$

where $\alpha' \equiv \rho \operatorname{Var}[\tilde{v}\mid y_i, p]$. The conditional expectation depends on price, so to ensure the conjectures are correct and equilibrium exists, we must write this out in full. Given the market clearing price, trader i can compute:

$$\sum_{h \neq i} q_h = \frac{p - \phi_1 \mu}{\phi_2} - q_i$$

Now, when $N \geq 2$, trader i can form the statistic:

$$\tilde{v}_i \equiv \frac{\phi_2^{-1}(p - \phi_1 \mu) - q_i - (N-1)\mu a_0 + (N-1)bp}{(N-1)a_1}. \qquad (A52)$$

Note that $\hat{v}_i = (N-1)^{-1}[\sum_{h \neq 1} y_h - (a_2/a_1)\sum_{h \neq i} x_h]$ is a sufficient statistic for the information content of the market clearing price. By construction, $\hat{v}_i$ is distributed normally with mean v and precision $(N-1)\pi$, independently of y_i and x_i. Now define:

$$\delta_0 = \frac{\tau}{\tau + \theta + (N-1)\pi}$$

$$\delta_1 = \frac{\theta}{\tau + \theta + (N-1)\pi}$$

$$\delta_2 = \frac{(N-1)\pi}{\tau + \theta + (N-1)\pi}.$$

Then, using Bayes' rule, we can write the conditional expectation of trader i as follows:

$$E[\tilde{v}\mid \Phi_i, p] = \delta_0 \mu + \delta_1 y_i + \delta_2 \hat{v}_i. \qquad (A53)$$

Substituting (A53) into (A51), and rearranging, we see that q_i has the conjectured form where the coefficients solve:

$$a_0 = \frac{\delta_0 - \delta_2\left[(N-1)a_1\phi_1\phi_2\right]^{-1} - \delta_2 a_0 a_1^{-1}}{\alpha' + \phi_2 + \delta_2\left[(N-1)a_1\right]^{-1}} \qquad (A54)$$

$$a_1 = \frac{\delta_1}{\alpha' + \phi_2 + \delta_2\left[(N-1)a_1\right]^{-1}} \qquad (A55)$$

$$a_2 = \frac{\alpha'}{\alpha' + \phi_2 + \delta_2[(N-1)a_1]^{-1}} \tag{A56}$$

$$b = \frac{-\delta_2[(N-1)a_1\phi_2]^{-1} - \delta_2 a_1^{-1} b + 1}{\alpha' + \phi_2 + \delta_2[(N-1)a_1]^{-1}}. \tag{A57}$$

The system consists of four equations in nine unknowns, $a_0, a_1, a_2, b, \phi_1, \phi_2, \delta_0, \delta_1$, and δ_2. The parameters ϕ_1 and ϕ_2 are functions of the a's and b while the δ's depend on π which in turn depends on $\frac{a_2}{a_1}$. To ensure a closed-form solution, we must express the ratio a_2/a_1 in terms of the original parameters of the model, ρ, ψ, θ, τ, and N.

From the definition of a_1 and a_2, we have:

$$\frac{a_2}{a_1} = \frac{\alpha'}{\delta_1} = \left(\frac{\rho}{\tau + \theta + (N-1)\pi}\right) \bigg/ \left(\frac{\theta}{\tau + \theta + (N-1)\pi}\right) = \frac{\rho}{\theta}.$$

Hence, $\pi = \omega$, where ω was defined in equation (A10). Using this result, we can directly determine the values of δ_0, δ_1, and δ_2. Now consider, ϕ_1. If the market clears without dealer participation ($Q = 0$), by symmetry, the base price should be μ, which implies that $\phi_1 = 1$. Alternatively, since ϕ_1 does not depend on N, setting $N = 1$ should correspond to the limiting equilibrium of the continuous auction game Γ_{ca} as shown by Proposition 5, which implies that $\phi_1 = 1$. This implies that in equation (A49) $b = a_0 + a_1$. Substituting in the equation for ϕ_2, the solution can be obtained from the system (A54)–(A57) by first solving simultaneously for a_1 and b and then computing the remaining parameters. A sufficient condition for these coefficients to be well-defined is $\theta < \frac{(N-2)\rho^2}{N\psi}$. In the proof of Proposition 8 we construct an example where continuous markets fail but an auction market is viable.

(b) Using (A44), we see the auction mechanism Γ_a is semi-strong form efficient. This condition implies that in a sequence of periodic auctions, indexed by t, with N_t traders in each auction, the auction prices follow a martingale. To show this, note that

$$E[\tilde{p}_{t+1} | p_t] = E[E[\tilde{v} | p_{t+1}] | p_t] = E[\tilde{v} | p_t] = p_t.$$

(c) From equation (A48), the unconditional price variability is:

$$\operatorname{Var}[\tilde{p}_i] = \xi^2 \tau^{-1} + (1-\xi)^2 \operatorname{Var}[y^N(\tilde{Q})] \tag{A58}$$

which is simply $(\tau + N\omega)^{-1}$. Now consider a sequence of N transactions in the quote-driven mechanism Γ_c. Using Proposition 1, the variance of these prices is monotonically decreasing over time as market makers learn. Consequently, of this sequence, p_N has the lowest variance which is $(\tau + N\omega)^{-1}$. It follows that the unconditional variance of the auction price is (weakly) less than the unconditional variance of the entire sequence of corresponding prices $p_1, \cdots, p_N$ in the dealer market.

The corollary follows from substituting equation (A47) into (A48), and noting that as $N \to \infty$, $\xi \to 0$ and $\hat{y}_N \to v$.

Proof of Proposition 8: (a) Consider the limiting case where $\tau = 0$, i.e., there is no public information.

In this case, $M = 0$, since dealers cannot make expected profits if they absorb any net order flow. The proof is a straightforward repetition of the proof technique from Proposition 7 where equation (A44) is replaced with the market clearing condition $Q(p) = 0$, and we set $a_0 = 0$. We now summarize the results of this exercise: The demand function of trader i is linear of the form:

$$q_i = a_1(y_i - p) - a_2 x_i \tag{A59}$$

where

$$a_1 = \frac{\bar{a}\theta}{(N-1)\omega + \theta}$$

$$a_2 = \frac{\bar{a}\rho}{(N-1)\omega + \theta}$$

and $\bar{a}$ is a constant given by:

$$\bar{a} = \frac{((N-1)\omega + \theta)[(N-2)\theta - 2(N-1)\omega]}{(N-1)\rho\theta}$$

and ω was defined in (A10). From this, the equilibrium price is:

$$p^* = \frac{1}{N} \sum_i^N \left[y_i - \left(\frac{\rho}{\theta}\right) x_i \right]. \tag{A60}$$

Equilibrium exists if $\theta < \frac{\rho^2(N-2)}{\phi N}$. This argument demonstrates the auction system can function in markets where a continuous system is not defined. Since $E[\tilde{v}] = p$, the price is efficient. The variance of the price is $\text{Var}[\tilde{p}^*] = \frac{1}{N\theta} + \left(\frac{\rho}{\theta}\right)^2 \frac{1}{N\psi}$, and the comparative statics results follow immediately.

(b) In the classical model, traders ignore their effect on price and correspondingly ignore the information contained in price. Utility maximization yields the trader's demand function:

$$q_i(p) = \frac{\theta(y_i - p)}{\rho} - x_i$$

where we have used the fact that the trader i's unconditional beliefs regarding the asset's value have mean y_i and precision θ. Setting $\Sigma_i q_i(p) = 0$, the equilibrium price is given by equation (A60), the same price when traders have rational expectations and act strategically. The equilibria are distinct, however, in that the quantities traded differ. The quantities demanded coincide only if $a_1 = \theta/\rho$ and $a_2 = 1$, but this is not the case. Write the demand function (A59) as:

$$q_i = a_2 \left[\frac{\theta}{\rho}(y_i - p) - x_i \right].$$

Since the term in brackets is the demand in the classical Walrasian auction and $a_2 < 1$, the volume of trade is smaller in the auction system Γ_a than in the Walrasian auction.

Proof of Proposition 9: In the quote-driven system, if $M \geq 2$, pure price competition implies that $p_i = E[\tilde{v} \mid q_i, \Phi_d^i]$. This implies that expected trading profits are zero, and any positive fixed costs are not recoverable. Only if $M = 1$ can a dealer hope to cover his fixed costs, and the equilibrium corresponds to that of Glosten (1989). In the continuous auction system expected dealer profits are given by (A28), and we define by $\pi(M)$ the expected profits of a dealer as a function of M. It is readily verified that for finite M, $\pi(M) > 0$, provided equilibrium exists. Further, it can be shown that $\pi'(M) < 0$. So, if F is sufficiently small, there exists a $M^* > 1$ such that $\pi(M^*) \geq F$ and $\pi(M^* + 1) < F$.

REFERENCES

Amihud, Yakov and Haim Mendelson, 1987, Trading mechanisms and stock returns: An empirical investigation, *Journal of Finance*, 42, 533–553.

────── and Haim Mendelson, 1991, Volatility, efficiency and trading: Evidence from the Japanese stock market, *Journal of Finance*, 46, 1765–1790.

──────, Haim Mendelson, and M. Murgia, 1990, Stock market microstructure and return volatility: Evidence from Italy, *Journal of Banking and Finance*, 14, 423–440.

Cohen, Kalman, Steven Maier, Robert Schwartz, and David Whitcomb, 1986, *The Microstructure of Securities Markets* (Prentice-Hall, Englewood Cliffs, N.J.).

DeGroot, Morris H., 1970, *Optimal Statistical Decisions* (McGraw-Hill Book Company, New York).

Domowitz, Ian, 1990, The mechanics of automated trade execution systems, *Journal of Financial Intermediation*, 1, 167–194.

Easley, David and Maureen O'Hara, 1987, Price, quantity, and information in securities markets, *Journal of Financial Economics*, 19, 69–90.

Foster, Douglas and S. Vishwanathan, 1990, A theory of intraday variations in volume, variance, and trading costs in securities markets, *Review of Financial Studies*, 3, 593–624.

Gammill, James, 1990, The organization of financial markets: Competitive versus cooperative market mechanisms, Working paper, Harvard Business School.

Garbade, Kenneth and William Silber, 1979, Structural organization of secondary markets: Clearing frequency, dealer activity and liquidity risk, *Journal of Finance*, 34, 577–593.

Glosten, Lawrence, 1989, Insider trading, liquidity, and the role of the monopolist specialist, *Journal of Business*, 62, 211–235.

────── and Lawrence Harris, 1988, Estimating the components of the bid-ask spread, *Journal of Financial Economics*, 21, 123–142.

────── and Paul Milgrom, 1985, Bid, ask, and transaction prices in a specialist market with heterogeneously informed agents, *Journal of Financial Economics*, 14, 71–100.

Harris, Lawrence, 1990, Liquidity, trading rules, and electronic trading systems, Working paper, University of Southern California.

Ho, Thomas and Hans Stoll, 1983, The dynamics of dealer markets under competition, *Journal of Finance*, 38, 1053–1074.

——, Robert Schwartz, and David Whitcomb, 1985, The trading decision and market clearing under transaction price uncertainty, *Journal of Finance*, 40, 21–42.

Kyle, Albert, 1985, Continuous auctions and insider trading, *Econometrica*, 53, 1315–1335.

——, 1989, Informed speculation with imperfect competition, *Review of Economic Studies*, 56, 317–356.

Leach, J. Chris and Ananth Madhavan, 1990, Price experimental and security market structure, Working paper, Wharton School, University of Pennsylvania.

Madhavan, Ananth and Seymour Smidt, 1991, A bayesian model of intraday specialist pricing, *Journal of Financial Economics*, 30, 99–134.

McInish, T. and R. Wood, 1988, An analysis of intraday patterns in bid/ask spreads for NYSE stocks, Working paper, University of Texas.

Mendelson, Haim, 1982, Market behavior in a clearing house, *Econometrica*, 50, 1505–1524.

——, 1987, Consolidation, fragmentation, and market performance, *Journal of Financial and Quantitative Analysis*, 22, 189–207.

Pithyachariyakul, Pipit, 1986, Exchange markets: a welfare comparison of market maker and walrasian systems, *Quarterly Journal of Economics*, 101, 69–84.

Seppi, Duane, 1990, Equilibrium block trading and asymmetric information, *Journal of Finance*, 45, 73–94.

Stoll, Hans, 1989, Inferring the components of the bid-ask spread: Theory and empirical tests, *Journal of Finance*, 44, 115–134.

——, 1990, Principles of trading market structure, Working paper 90-31, Vanderbilt University.

—— and Robert Whaley, 1990, Stock market structure and volatility, *Review of Financial Studies*, 3, 37–71.

Working, H., 1958, A theory of anticipatory prices, *American Economic Review*, 188–199, May.

Is the Electronic Open Limit Order Book Inevitable?

LAWRENCE R. GLOSTEN*

ABSTRACT

Under fairly general conditions, the article derives the equilibrium price schedule determined by the bids and offers in an open limit order book. The analysis shows: (1) the order book has a small-trade positive bid-ask spread, and limit orders profit from small trades; (2) the electronic exchange provides as much liquidity as possible in extreme situations; (3) the limit order book does not invite competition from third market dealers, while other trading institutions do; (4) If an entering exchange earns nonnegative trading profits, the consolidated price schedule matches the limit order book price schedule.

THIS ARTICLE PROVIDES AN analysis of an idealized electronic open limit order book. The focus of the article is the nature of equilibrium in such a market and how an open limit order book fares against competition from other methods of exchanging securities. The analysis suggests that an electronic open limit order book mimics competition among anonymous exchanges. As a result, there is no incentive to set up a competing anonymous dealer market. On the other hand, any other anonymous exchange will invite "third market" competition. These conclusions suggest that an electronic open limit order book of the sort considered here has a chance of being a center of significant trading volume. The analysis does not imply that an electronic limit order book will be, or should be the only trading institution. It does suggest some of the characteristics that an alternative institution should have in order to successfully compete with an electronic exchange. The results are obtained in a fairly general environment, and hence would appear to be robust.

The motivation for the article lies in recent developments in information processing technology, the interest in institutional innovation in the securities industry, and the uncertainty about future developments in trading

---

* Columbia University. Former versions of this article were immodestly titled "The Inevitability and Resilience of an Electronic Open Limit Order Book" and then too modestly titled "Equilibrium in an Electronic Open Limit Order Book." I have benefitted from the insights of Fischer Black, Puneet Handa, Pete Kyle, Bruce Lehmann, Matt Spiegel, Subra Subramanyam, and the comments of seminar participants at Baruch, Rutgers, New York University, the Atlanta Fed, University of Michigan, Northwestern University, University of Chicago, and Ohio State. Part of this research was done as a Visiting Economist at the New York Stock Exchange. The comments, opinions, and errors are those of the author only. In particular, the views expressed here do not necessarily reflect those of the directors, members or officers of the New York Stock Exchange, Inc.

institutions. Such systems as INSTINET, the "Wunsch Auction," and electronic trading on the regional exchanges represent different approaches to the use of information processing technology. The results in this article are indicative of the direction such developments might take. The analysis suggests that the open limit order book is a stable institution and, within the set of economic environments and trading structures considered, the only stable institution.

The model assumes away a number of frictions and costs that may well be important. The model deals with the architecture of the open limit order book only in general terms and does not address a host of potentially important technological issues—computing capacity, trade execution speed, display technology and clearing to name a few.[1] Certain other limitations will be discussed below in the concluding remarks.

There are a number of important antecedents to this work. Trading on private information is an important aspect of the analysis—without it, all of the propositions become trivial. As in Kyle (1985), investors may submit orders of any quantity, but, in contrast, orders arrive one at a time as in Glosten and Milgrom (1985). This combination of features recalls Easley and O'Hara (1987) and Glosten (1989). The design of the trading mechanism is, however, different from both of these models, and the environment is more general.

The model of the open limit order book and the specification of equilibrium are very similar to the limit order book analysis in Rock (1989). The most important difference is that the model here does not allow a specialist or market maker to disrupt trading against the book. A key feature of the Rock (1989) model is that a market maker can foist a second adverse selection problem onto those providing bids and offers—the book is only hit if the market maker decides to back away (because of order size) from a trade. A second difference is that the quantities traded in the Rock model are exogenous, whereas they are determined endogenously in this article. This allows an analysis of market breakdown and is very important for the analysis of competing exchanges.

The equilibrium of the model in this article is similar to the one of the model in Gale (1991). In that article, informed "hedgers" have the opportunity to trade more than once. In the equilibrium, large traders with extreme news trade twice, while small traders with less extreme news trade once. The two prices at which a large buyer buys are precisely the first and second lowest offers that would prevail in the open limit order book considered here.

The discussion in Black (1992) and its predecessors was a major inspiration for this analysis. In an earlier version (Black (1991)) an institution was developed that used taxes and subsidies to break the equivalence of the net price paid or received and revised expectations in response to a trade. This

---

[1] Harris (1990) provides an analysis of some of these and other issues. Also, see Domowitz (1991).

article shows that a similar structure of implicit taxes and subsidies can arise in the equilibrium considered here. In all versions, the "Black Market" requires an exchange official to set the terms of trade. In the market considered here, competing individuals determine the terms of trade.

The electronic open limit order book is modelled as a publicly visible screen providing bids and offers, each of which specify a price and a quantity. Transactions against the book pick off the limit orders at their limit prices. These market orders are presumed to be the result of rational optimization on the part of risk-averse and possibly informed investors, while bids and offers are assumed to reflect this. The source of bids and offers is a large population of (essentially) risk-neutral "patient traders." The large population and risk neutrality imply that equilibrium is characterized by a zero expected profit condition.

After setting up the economic environment, and analyzing the trades of investors who trade against the book of limit orders, the article presents an analysis of the bids and offers that will be provided. In an environment with discrete prices, the bids and offers submitted are seen to be related to, respectively, "lower tail" and "upper tail" conditional expectations. This is due to the "discriminatory" nature of the book—limit orders are picked off in succession. The possibility of information-motivated trade, as formulated here, implies that the schedule of offers is generally upward sloping—it costs more per share to purchase a large number of shares than to purchase a small number of shares. Furthermore, there is a positive small-trade bid-ask spread.

The open limit order book does as well as can be hoped at handling extreme adverse selection problems—if no liquidity is supplied by the open limit order book, then every other anonymous exchange would expect to lose money by staying open for trade. The reason for this is that the architecture of the open limit order book leads to an averaging of profits across trades—a feature shared with a monopolist specialist architecture.

The next propositions show that the open limit order book is uniquely immune to competing exchange "cream skimming" of orders when the only way to ascertain "cream" is with trade size—i.e. competing exchanges are anonymous. The key assumption here is that investors can costlessly split their orders among competing exchanges. The discriminatory design of the open limit order book implies that the book breaks up a trade into many smaller transactions (each at the lowest (highest) offers (bids)), and furthermore, the profits from such a breakup are competed away. Thus, a competing exchange cannot profitably allow investors to break up their order further. That is, the discriminatory limit order book mimics the competition among exchanges.

The subsequent sections defend the above assertions with a more rigorous analysis. Section I analyzes the equilibrium at a point in time by first examining the behavior of market order users (Section I.A), and then the behavior of limit order users (Section I.B). Section II explores some implications of the equilibrium, and Section III examines intermarket competition. Section IV discusses dynamic issues. Section V identifies and discusses limitations of the results and points to further analysis. Section VI concludes. All proofs are contained in the Appendix.

I. Equilibrium in the Electronic Market

It is assumed that all potential participants in the market have access to an electronic screen that provides an anonymous list of all limit orders, buy and sell, that have been entered. If an individual wishes to add a bid or offer to the market, this can be done costlessly. Furthermore, any bid or offer may be costlessly retracted at any time, except in the middle of the execution of a trade. Execution of a trade against the book occurs in a "discriminatory" fashion. That is, if a trade is large enough to execute against several limit orders at different prices, each limit order transacts at its limit price. For example, if there were two offers at 50 for 1,000 shares of each, and two offers at 51, each for 1,000 shares, a 4,000-share purchase would in effect lead to four transactions—two at 50 and two at 51. The marginal price for this 4,000-share trade would be 51, while the average price would be 50.5.[2]

Four assumptions are made to restrict the behavior of participants: 1) investors who trade against the book are rational and risk averse in that they choose their trade to maximize a quasi-concave function of their cash and share position; 2) there is the possibility of informed trade in that an investor's marginal valuation is affiliated with the future payoff of the security; 3) there are a large number of risk-neutral limit order submitters; 4) in the presence of more than one exchange, investors can costlessly and simultaneously split their orders among the exchanges.

The analysis takes place at a point in time. Though some expectations and probabilities are written as unconditional, they should be understood to be conditional on all past public information. Similarly, conditional probabilities and expectations should be understood to be conditional on the specific argument, as well as on all past information. The analysis thus looks at (i) the terms of trade provided conditional on all past public information; (ii) the trade made in response to these terms, conditional on all past information and possibly some private information; and (iii) subsequent revisions in expectations in response to this trade. After the trade, a new public information set is determined—the original public information, new public information, plus the trade that occurred. At that point, new terms of trade are determined in the same manner.

---

[2] One could also imagine a nondiscriminatory electronic limit order book. Analogous to a nondiscriminatory auction, a nondiscriminatory order book would transact all limit orders at the same price. There are reasons for considering the nondiscriminatory book, and these will be discussed below.

A. Investor Behavior

Bids and offers are submitted without knowing what the next arriving order will be. The next trader to come to market chooses the trade based on his or her privately known but generally unobservable characteristics—preferences, information, portfolio position, etc. The analysis uses the notation, ω, to indicate this vector of unobservable characteristics.

The terms of trade are determined by the list of bids and offers available. The schedule of bids and offers is denoted by the function $R'(q)$. For q positive (an investor purchase), $R'(q)$ is the ask price paid for the last share in a purchase of q shares. For q negative (an investor sale), $R'(q)$ is the bid price received for the last share in a sale of $-q$ shares. The "prime" notation is used to remind the reader that $R'(q)$ is a *marginal* price. For any q, $R(q)$ is defined to be the (Lebesgue) integral of $R'(\cdot)$ from zero to q. Thus (if all prices are positive), if q is positive, $R(q)$ is positive and represents the total amount paid for a purchase of q shares. If q is negative, $R(q)$ is negative and $-R(q)$ is the amount received for a sale of $-q$ shares.[3]

With this notation, the following assumption regarding investor behavior is offered.

ASSUMPTION 1: *An arriving investor with a vector of characteristics, ω, facing a schedule of bids and offers described by the function $R'(\cdot)$, chooses a quantity to trade, q, to maximize $W(-R(q), q; \omega)$. The function $W(c, q; \omega)$ is strictly quasi-concave in (c, q) and strictly increasing in c for all ω.*[4]

The first argument of W represents the change in the investor's cash position as a result of a trade, while the second argument represents the change in the investor's position in the security as a result of a trade. That W is strictly increasing in the first argument means that more cash is preferred to less. Quasi-concavity of W in (c, q) means that in the (c, q) plane, indifference curves are convex to the origin. As the following examples show, it is related to an assumption of risk aversion.

Formulation of examples, and the subsequent analysis of the equilibrium limit orders requires a specification of the probabilistic structure of the payoff from a position in the security in question. At time LD (a possibly random stopping time), the security will have a liquidation value of X_{LD}^*. Let F_t denote all the information, public and private, available at time t, and define X_t by $X_t = E[\exp(-r(LD - t))X_{LD}^*|F_t]$, where r is the appropriate continuously compounded discount rate. Finally, let H_t denote the public information available at time t, and define x_t by $x_t = E[\exp(-r(LD - t))X_{LD}^*|H_t] = E[X_t|H_t]$. If the private information is of an "unsystematic sort" (i.e., the

---

[3] It should be noted that $R'(q)$ may have discontinuities. Thus, while $R(q)$ must be continuous in q, it need not be differentiable, and hence while $R(q)$ is the integral of $R'(q)$, $R'(q)$ is not necessarily the derivative of $R(q)$.

[4] If W_i indicates the first partial derivative of W with respect to the ith argument and W_{ij} indicates the second partial derivative with respect to arguments i and j, then we require $W_1 > 0$, $W_2^2 W_{11} + W_1^2 W_{22} - 2W_1 W_2 W_{12} < 0$.

information does not change the discount rate), X_t is the "full information" value of the security while x_t is the value of the security given all public information.

Example: Myopic portfolio adjustment and consumption. Define $W(c, q; \omega)$ by:

$$W(c, q; \omega) = U_0(c^*(c, q, \omega)) + E[U(Y_T + (\nu + q)x_T - TC(\nu + q)$$
$$+ (\phi + c - c^*(c, q, \omega))(1 + r_T); Y_T, x_T)|S].$$

In this case, the next arriving investor chooses q to maximize the expected (possibly state-dependent) utility of consumption now and at time T in the future. The security in question will have a value at time T of x_T, the investor has other sources of wealth represented by Y_T, has an initial position, ν, in the security in question, an initial cash position of ϕ, and chooses optimal consumption $c^*(c, q, \omega)$ now. Unwinding the position leads to transactions costs of $TC(\nu + q)$. The investor earns a risk-free return r_T over the T periods. Furthermore, the investor has a (possibly null) signal about the future random variables. The vector of unobservable characteristics consists of a specification of the utility function, the time horizon, the joint distribution of Y_T, S and x_T, the initial cash and security positions, the risk-free rate, and the nature of and realization of the signal S. Quasi-concavity of W is implied by concavity of U and convexity of the transaction cost function $TC(\cdot)$, while $W_1 > 0$ is implied by positive marginal utility of wealth. The formulation is myopic in the sense that the investor ignores future opportunities to trade. An informational motive for trade results from non-null S, while a "liquidity" motive for trade arises from suboptimal ν and ϕ given the random variables Y_T and x_T and/or a particular desire for or aversion to current consumption relative to future consumption.

Example: Dynamic portfolio adjustment. Define $W(c, q; \omega)$ by:

$$W(c, q; \omega) = E[U(Y_T + \phi + c - R_2(q_2) - \cdots - R_{T-1}(q_{T-1})$$
$$+ (\nu + q + q_2 + \cdots + q_{T-1})x_T|S],$$

where q_i are the future optimal trades in the security, and R_i are the future terms of trade. In this case, the maximum depends upon the individual's expectations of the future terms of trade. Whether $W(\cdot, \cdot; \omega)$ is quasi-concave or not will depend upon how the investor believes future R_is will depend upon a current trade. For example, if the investor believes that future terms of trade will be unaffected by a current trade, then concavity of U will imply quasi-concavity of W. Such beliefs will also typically involve the investor planning on trading more than once. If this independence of a current trade and future bids and offers does not hold, then $W(\cdot, \cdot; \omega)$ may not be quasi-concave. For example, some expectations over future terms of trade and some utility functions may invite "destabilizing trade" (a sequence of small buys followed by a large sale, for example). In this case, quasi-concavity is unlikely to hold for all ω. This and other dynamic issues will be discussed further below.

Assumption 1 does rule out one specification that enjoys frequent academic consideration. That the marginal "utility" of cash is positive precludes the pure noise trader" specification in much of the "Rational Expectations Equilibrium" literature (for example, Hellwig (1980)), as well as the specification in Kyle (1985). While the general model admits a reasonably wide range of motives for trade, it still requires that investors care about the amount they pay for purchases or receive for sales.

The quasi-concavity assumption means that characterization of an investor's decision is conveniently derived. Essentially, the investor chooses a trade so that his or her "marginal valuation" equals the marginal price. The marginal valuation is given by:

$$M(q, R(q); \omega) = W_2(-R(q), q; \omega)/W_1(-R(q), q; \omega).$$

Quasi-concavity implies that in the neighborhood of any solution, the marginal valuation is decreasing in q. Since the institution requires that the marginal price function be nondecreasing, there can only be one solution to the marginal condition.

LEMMA 1: *Suppose that W is strictly quasi-concave, and that $R'(q)$ is any arbitrary nondecreasing marginal price function defined for q in the interval $[q_0, q_1]$ (q_0 may be negative infinity, and q_1 may be positive infinity). Define the marginal valuation of an investor with characteristics vector ω at a trade q and transfer $R(q)$, $M(q, R(q); \omega)$, by:*

$$M(q, R(q); \omega) = W_2(-R(q), q; \omega)/W_1(-R(q), q; \omega).$$

Then one of the following mutually independent and collectively exhaustive conditions holds:

(i) $M(q, R(q); \omega) > R'(q)$ *for all q in $[q_0, q_1)$;*
(ii) $M(q, R(q); \omega) < R'(q)$ *for all q in $(q_0, q_1]$;*
(iii) *There exists exactly one $q^*(\omega) \in [q_0, q_1]$ such that:*

$$q < q^*(\omega) \text{ implies } M(q, R(q); \omega) > R'(q)$$
$$q > q^*(\omega) \text{ implies } M(q, R(q); \omega) < R'(q).$$

The examples above the lemma illustrate some of the investor fundamentals that will imply quasiconcavity. The lemma illustrates the force of this assumption. The optimal trade of an investor can be characterized as the solution to a first-order condition. Strict quasi-concavity will make this solution unique. The characterization is provided in the following proposition.

PROPOSITION 1: *Suppose that W is strictly quasi-concave for all ω, and $R'(\cdot)$ is nondecreasing and defined for $q \in [q_0, q_1]$. Then an investor with a vector of* characteristics ω will choose $D_R(\omega)$ as the trade where $D_R(\omega)$ is the unique solution to the following:

(i) *if a solution to* $M(q, R(q); \omega) = R'(q)$ *exists, then* $D_R(\omega)$ *is this unique solution;*
(ii) *if the solution to the equation in (i) does not exist, but there is a point of discontinuity in* R' *at* q^* *and* $M(q^*, R(q^*); \omega)$ *lies between the limit from below* q^* *and the limit from above* q^*, *of* $R'(\cdot)$, *then* $D_R(\omega)$ *is* q^*.
(iii) *if neither (i) nor (ii) hold, then* $D_R(\omega) = q_1$ *if* $M(q, R(q); \omega) > R'(q)$ *for all q and* $D_R(\omega) = q_0$ *if*

$$M(q, R(q); \omega) < R'(q) \quad \text{for all } q.$$

Before leaving the analysis of the individual investor, a corollary is provided that will be useful in the subsequent subsection. To the extent that investors have private information, limit order submitters may care about how individual investors value a share of the security. The following corollary shows the link between how investors value the security and the decisions that they make. The proof is immediate from Lemma 1 and Proposition 1.

COROLLARY 1: *If W is strictly quasi-concave, and* $R'(\cdot)$ *is any nondecreasing marginal price function that is left continuous for* $q > 0$ *and right continuous for* $q < 0$, *then the following two identities hold*:

(A) for $q > 0$, $\{\omega: D_R(\omega) \geq q\} = \{\omega: M(q, R(q); \omega) \geq R'(q)\}$;
(B) for $q < 0$, $\{\omega: D_R(\omega) \leq q\} = \{\omega: M(q, R(q); \omega) \leq R'(q)\}$;

Where $D_R(\omega)$ is defined in Proposition 1 above.

There may be marginal price functions decreasing in some interval that also satisfy the conclusions of the corollary. Any marginal price function that does satisfy the conclusions of the corollary shall be said to have the "single crossing" property. This will be important in the analysis of competing exchanges and market breakdown. What the property does is unambiguously link marginal valuations and trades.

B. Equilibrium Bids and Offers

The subsection above characterizes the behavior of investors taking the schedule of bids and offers as given. It is assumed that suppliers of liquidity—those who provide limit orders—recognize this behavior and take account of it in the provision of bids and offers. As stated in the introduction, this analysis focuses on the effects of asymmetric information. Rather than taking a particular parametric specification of information and division of information among potential investors, the assumption that defines the presence of private information encompasses a number of specific models.

The trading behavior of market order users is determined by their marginal valuation functions and the terms of trade offered. The anonymity of the electronic market implies that liquidity suppliers observe only an arriving investor's marginal valuation at the trade chosen. This suggests that, if there is private information that is of concern to liquidity suppliers, observing this point on the marginal valuation function must be, in general, informative. To avoid making assumptions about endogenous objects, it is assumed that any point on the marginal valuation function provides information about X, the current "full information value" of the security.[5] It will be assumed that all private information is "unsystematic," and hence a condition on conditional expected values is all that is needed.

ASSUMPTION 2: *For each q and R and m, define the "upper tail expectation" function, $V(m, q, R)$ to be the expectation of X conditional on the next arrival's marginal valuation at q and R being greater than or equal to m, and the "lower tail expectation" function, $v(m, q, R)$, to be the expectation of X conditional on the next arrival's marginal valuation at q and R being less than or equal to m:*

$$V(m, q, R) = E[\,X \mid M(q, R; \omega) \geq m\,];$$
$$v(m, q, R) = E[\,X \mid M(q, R; \omega) \leq m\,].$$

The functions $V(\cdot, \cdot, \cdot)$ and $v(\cdot, \cdot, \cdot)$ satisfy:

$$V(m, q, R) \geq E[\,X \mid M(q, R; \omega) = m\,] \geq v(m, q, R).$$

The economy exhibits strict adverse selection if the inequalities above are strict.[6]

A high marginal valuation (given R and q) could be due to the investor being short in the security; it could be due to a relative aversion to current consumption; or it could be due to the investor having another source of income negatively correlated with the security's return. Assumption 2 states that a possible explanation for a high marginal valuation is information indicating that X, the current full information value, is more likely to be large. It should be noted that the inequality must hold for each q and R, and hence it is not an assumption about endogenous objects.

The assumption is implied by the condition that the "point" conditional expectation, $E[\,X \mid M(q, R; \omega) = m\,]$, be increasing in m. The assumption is equivalent to the assumption that the functions $V(m, \cdot, \cdot)$ and $v(m, \cdot, \cdot)$ are both increasing in m. This, and another useful property of these functions, is proven in the following Lemma.

LEMMA 2: *Assuming strict concavity of the investors' objective functions, and given Assumption 2, the expectation of X conditional on the next arrival's marginal valuation at q and R being greater than or equal to m, $V(m, q, R) = E[\,X \mid M(q, R; \omega) \geq m\,]$ and the expectation of X conditional on the next*

---

[5] The random variable X_t was defined above as the discounted expected liquidation value conditional on all public and private information at time t. The analysis now focuses on a particular point in time and the subscript t is dropped.

[6] This assumption is in the spirit of the affiliation assumption in the auction literature (see for example Milgrom and Weber (1982)). In the case at hand, however, any quantity may be chosen, and hence the simple and elegant affiliation assumption of Milgrom and Weber is insufficient.

arrival's marginal valuation at q and R being less than or equal to m, $v(m, q, R) = E[X \mid M(q, R; \omega) \leq m]$ are increasing in m, while the expectation, $V(m, q, R + qm)$ is increasing in q for $q > 0$, and the expectation, $v(m, q, R + qm)$, is increasing in q for $q < 0$, for all R and m.

The first result follows immediately from the observation that the expectation conditional on the marginal valuation being greater than or equal to m is an average of expectations conditional on the marginal valuation being equal to m' for $m' \geq m$. In an environment with a single ask price m, $V(m, q, R + qm)$ is the expectation of X conditional on an investor choosing q or larger. By the strict concavity of the investors' objective functions, an investor who chooses q or larger must have a marginal valuation at q that is m or larger. Thus, the expectation conditional on an investor choosing q or larger exceeds the expectation conditional on an investor choosing q. The result follows.

The following examples illustrate Assumption 2, and are used throughout this article to illustrate the propositions.

Example: Consider the environment of Glosten (1989). The next arrival has an endowment w, which, from the point of view of limit order submitters, is normally distributed with mean zero. The full information value of the security, X, is normally distributed. The next arrival has seen a signal $S = X + \varepsilon$, with ε normally distributed with mean zero, independent of X. Finally, the next arrival maximizes the expected utility of future wealth, and the utility function is exponential with risk-aversion parameter r. Let σ be the standard deviation of X conditional on S. Standard calculations show that the marginal valuation is given by:

$$M(q, R; \omega) = E[X \mid S] - rw\sigma^2 - rq\sigma^2.$$

This example will be referred to below (call it the exponential-normal example), and it is convenient to choose some normalizations to minimize the number of parameters. If we interpret all conditional expectations and prices as deviations from the ex ante mean, we can choose the mean of X to be zero. Normalize the quantity units by setting $r\sigma^2 = 1$. Finally, let the variance of w be $\alpha < 1$ and set the variance of $E[X \mid S]$ equal to $1 - \alpha$. Roughly speaking, α is the proportion of the variance of trade explained by the liquidity motive. Then,

$$M(q, R; \omega) = \omega - q,$$

where $\omega = E[X \mid S] - r\sigma^2 w$, and, under the above assumptions, ω is a standard normal random variable. Furthermore, X and ω are correlated and $E[X \mid \omega] = (1 - \alpha)\omega$. Thus the following holds:

$$E[X \mid M(q, R, \omega) = m] = (1 - \alpha)(m + q).$$

If $\alpha < 1$, this is strictly increasing in m, and hence the assumption is satisfied.

Example: This example shows that Assumption 2 is not innocuous and can fail in a reasonable model of informed trade. The assumption can fail when extreme marginal valuations could only come from uninformed investors.

Suppose that there are informed agents and uninformed agents. Let U be a (zero, one) random variable that takes the value one if the next arrival is uninformed, and put $E[U] = \alpha$. Suppose that the uninformed have a marginal valuation given by $(\varepsilon - q)$. Informed have seen the realization of a signal, S, correlated with X, and they are risk neutral. Assume that U, ε, $E[X|S]$ are mutually independent, and $E[X] = 0$. Let $f(\cdot)$ denote the density of $E[X|S]$ and let $g(\cdot)$ be the density of ε. Then,

$$M(q, R; \omega) = (1 - U)E[X|S] + U(\varepsilon - q), \text{ and } \omega = (U, S, \varepsilon).$$

Furthermore:

$$E[X|M(q, R; \omega) = m] = (1 - \alpha)f(m)m/[(1 - \alpha)f(m) + \alpha g(m + q)].$$

While increasing for m near zero, this conditional expectation need not be increasing for all m and q. For example, suppose that f and g are both uniform densities, but the support of f is strictly contained in the support of g. Then, for extreme m, and small (in absolute value) q, the conditional expectation above will be zero, and the assumption will not hold for all m and q. With f and g uniform, this will be referred to as the uniform example.

Note that the above two examples entail marginal valuations that are independent of the amount paid or received for a trade of q. This was, of course, due to the constant absolute risk aversion and the absence of wealth effects in the marginal valuation. Examples using other utility functions that exhibit wealth effects can be constructed, although they tend to be difficult to manipulate.

To derive the equilibrium among competing suppliers of liquidity (limit order submitters), the following assumption is made.

ASSUMPTION 3: *Let N be the number of potential limit order submitters. Private information is unsystematic in that each limit order submitter maximizes expected trading profit given only publicly available information. That is, a liquidity supplier provides bids and offers to maximize $E[P - XQ]$ where P represents the liquidity supplier's (signed) proceeds from the next arrival, and Q is the (signed) quantity provided by the liquidity supplier to the next arrival. Each liquidity supplier can submit any number of bids and offers. A limit order can be for any positive quantity. Competing limit orders at one price are executed in a pro rata fashion. Equilibria will considered for the limit as N goes to infinity.*

We can think of these liquidity suppliers as "patient" or "value" traders in that their only interest in trading is expected profit. It might be reasonable to think of this population as consisting of managers of reasonably large portfolios, both institutional and individual. Since the portfolios are large, even participation in a sizeable trade does not make a substantial difference in the diversification of the portfolios. Such an interpretation calls into question the consideration of a large population, but one should think of this analysis as a base case. More will be said on this issue below.

While most of the analysis in this article considers the case in which the set of allowable prices is the continuum, understanding the equilibrium is facilitated by first considering the more realistic case in which prices are restricted to a discrete set. The continuous price equilibrium is then the limiting equilibrium as the discreteness in prices goes to zero. The details of the derivation of the discrete price equilibrium are provided in the Appendix; the following provides an outline of the logic.

Let the set of allowable prices be $P = \{\ldots p_{-1}, p_0, p_1, \ldots\}$ where this set is arranged in increasing order. Let p_0 be the allowable price closest to the ex ante mean of X That is, $p_{-1} < E[X] < p_1$. It seems reasonable, and will be proven below, that no liquidity supplier offers quantities at p_{-1} or below or bids for quantities at p_1 or higher. Given this set up, the strategy for each liquidity supplier consists of a specification of $\{q_i^A, q_i^B\} \geq 0$ where q_i^A is the quantity offered at price i and q_i^B is the quantity bid at price i. Quantities of zero are to be interpreted as no bid or offer provided. The analysis seeks the Nash equilibrium of the game in which liquidity suppliers expect investors to behave as derived in the subsection above. Each liquidity supplier observes the bids and offers of all other liquidity suppliers and chooses his or her profit-maximizing response.

The Appendix shows that with an infinite number of limit order providers, the Nash equilibrium is characterized by the following zero-profit condition for prices at which positive quantities are offered:

$$\int_{AQ_{i-1}}^{AQ_i} (p_i - V(p_i, d, R_{i-1} + p_i(d - AQ_{i-1})))$$
$$\times P\{M(d, R_{i-1} + p_i(d - AQ_{i-1})) \geq p_i\} = 0 \quad (1)$$

where AQ_{i-1} is the quantity offered at prices lower than p_i, and R_{i-1} is the total cost of these shares. That is, a positive quantity is offered at p_i as long as p_i is, on average, at least the "upper tail expectation" of X conditional on a market order trading at the price p_i. On the other hand, by Lemma 2, if p_i is less than the upper tail expectation conditional on the arrival of an order large enough to pick off the first share offered at p_i, $p_i < V(p_i, AQ_{i-1}, R_{i-1})$, then $p_i < V(p_i, AQ_{i-1} + q, R_{i-1} + qp_i)$ for all positive q. If this holds, no shares will be offered at p_i. Proposition 2 summarizes the equilibrium derived from these two observations.

PROPOSITION 2: *Given the maintained assumptions, the following describes the equilibrium*:

(i) *If $p < V(p, 0, 0)$ for all $p \in P$, then no offers are provided. If $p > v(p, 0, 0)$ for all $p \in P$, then no bids are provided.*
(ii) *If there exists a $p \in P$ satisfying $p > V(p, 0, 0)$, then the lowest ask, A_1 is the smallest such p. If there exists a $p \in P$ satisfying $p < v(p, 0, 0)$, then the highest bid, B_1 is the largest such p.*

(iii) If the expression for the ask side first-order condition, equation (1), with $p_i = A_1$, $R_{i-1} = 0$ is positive for all q, then an infinite quantity will be offered at A_1. Otherwise, the quantity offered at A_1 will be the solution to the zero-profit condition. If the expression for the bid side first-order condition with $p_i = B_1$ is positive for all q, then an infinite quantity will be bid at B_1. Otherwise the quantity offered at B_1 will be the solution to the first-order condition.

(iv) If positive quantities are offered at k different ask prices, and letting AQ_k^* equal the aggregate quantity offered at the k ask prices and letting R_k equal the amount paid for the quantity AQ_k^* then:

(a) If $\{p \in P: p > V(p, AQ_k^*, R_k)\}$ is empty, then there are no higher offers.
(b) Otherwise, A_{k+1} is $\min\{p \in P: p > V(p, AQ_k^*, R_k)\}$
(c) If the integral in (1) with $p_i = A_{k+1}$ is nonnegative for all q, then an infinite quantity is offered at A_{k+1}.
(d) Otherwise, Q_{k+1}^* is the solution to the first-order condition.

If positive quantities are bid at k different bid prices, and letting BQ_k^* equal the aggregate quantity bid at the k bid prices and setting R_k equal to the amount received for the quantity BQ_k^* then:

(a) If $\{p \in P: p < v(p, -BQ_k^*, -R_k)\}$ is empty, then there are no lower bids.
(b) Otherwise, B_{k+1} is $\max\{p \in P; p < v(p, -BQ_k^*, -R_k)\}$.
(c) If the first-order condition with $p_i = B_{k+1}$ is nonnegative for all q, then an infinite quantity is bid at B_{k+1}.
(d) Otherwise, Q_{k+1}^* is the solution to the bid side first-order condition.

Some fairly general characteristics of the equilibrium fall out of the above derivation, and these are provided in Proposition 3. Consideration of these general characteristics gives some insight into the driving forces of the equilibrium.

PROPOSITION 3: *Assume that $V(m, q, R)$ is strictly increasing in m, while $E[X \mid M(q, pq; \omega) = p]$ is continuous in q.*

(i) *If the market is open, then for ε small but positive,*

$$A_1 > V(A_1, 0, 0) > v(B_1, 0, 0) > B_1; \text{ and}$$
$$A_1 > E[X \mid M(\varepsilon, \varepsilon A_1; \omega) = A_1];$$
$$B_1 < E[X \mid M(-\varepsilon, -\varepsilon B_1; \omega) = B_1].$$

(ii) *If there are offers at k different ask prices, and bids at k different bid prices, then for ε positive but small:*

$$E[X \mid D = AQ_{k-1}^* + \varepsilon] < E[X \mid D \geq AQ_{k-1}^*] < A_k < E[X \mid D \geq AQ_k^*];$$
$$E[X \mid D = -BQ_{k-1}^* - \varepsilon] > E[X \mid D \leq -BQ_{k-1}^*] > B_k > E[X \mid D \leq BQ_k^*];$$

Part (i) of Proposition 3 shows that if the economy exhibits strict adverse selection, then the limit order book will have a positive bid-ask spread no matter what the set of allowable prices is; the set of prices can be made arbitrarily fine, and the small-trade bid-ask spread will persist. The reason for this is the possible trading on private information. An individual that provides an offer at the smallest ask price, will transact on every trade. Not only will he or she get a portion of small trades, but on all large trades, the total quantity offered will be taken. This means that in order to place an offer at the smallest ask, the individual has to be concerned with the informational implications of all investor purchases. Similarly, an individual placing a limit order at the largest bid needs to be concerned with the informational implications of all investor sales.

The first part of the proposition also shows that limit order submitters profit from small investor purchases and sales. The second part of the proposition stresses the importance of the "upper tail" expectations for the determination of offers, and the "lower tail" expectations for the determination of bids. The proposition also shows that if the realized trade is just greater than AQ_{k-1}, then an offer at A_k will be profitable.

Part (i) of Proposition 3 has a further implication. If the equilibrium does not provide an infinite quantity at any ask price, then every offer has a zero expected profit. But if each limit order breaks even, the book in aggregate expects to break even. That is, in expectation, the average price received by the book, $R(q)/q$ equals the revised expectation. Since small trade are profitable, some larger trades must be unprofitable. That is, for small trades the average price paid by a buying investor exceeds the revised expectation, while for some larger trades the revised expectation is greater than the average price paid by a buying investor.

Part (ii) of Proposition 3 points out an interesting feature of the market. Suppose an order for $AQ_{k-1} + \varepsilon$ arrives. This will clear out all the offers at A_1 through A_{k-1}, and part of the orders at A_k. The revised expectation in response to this realized trade lies strictly between B_1 and the now lowest ask price at A_k. Thus, there are no offers lying exposed below the revised expectation, and no bids lying exposed above the revised expectation. It is not necessarily the case that offers need to be canceled after this trade. Even though the model assumes constant vigilance on the part of limit order submitters, constant monitoring need not be necessary to avoid unfavorable trades.[7]

Examples: Before proceeding to a further analysis of the electronic open limit order book, it is perhaps informative to examine some examples of the above general analysis. First consider the normal-exponential example introduced above. Recall that $E[X \mid M(q, R; \omega) = m] = (1 - \alpha)(m + q)$. Thus, if f

---

[7] Limit orders are still exposed to movements due to public information arrivals. Perhaps as Black (1992) suggests limit orders could be "marked to market" by moving all limit orders up or down in response to a, respectively, positive or negative public announcement.

is the standard normal density and F is the standard normal distribution function, $V(m, q, R)$ is given by:

$$V(m, q, R) = (1 - \alpha) f(m + q) / (1 - F(m + q)).$$

As long as α is positive, there exists a solution to $p = V(p, q, R)$ for all q. Thus, the order book will, in principle, provide terms of trade for arbitrarily large orders. In fact, if the set of prices is coarse enough, and α is large enough, an infinite quantity will be offered at A_1.

It can be seen that the lowest offer is nonincreasing in α. That is, the small-trade spread tends to increase in the severity of the adverse selection problem.[8]

Figures 1 and 2 illustrate, respectively, the derivation and description of the equilibrium when $\alpha = 0.8$. There are three distinct offer prices—0.25, 0.375 and 0.5. Finite quantities are offered at the first two prices, while, in principle, an infinite quantity is offered at 0.5.[9]

The second example provides a somewhat different equilibrium. Recall the uniform example discussed above:

$$M(q, R; \omega) = (1 - U) E[X|S] + U(\varepsilon - q),$$

where U, $E[X|S]$, and ε are mutually independent, $E[U] = \alpha$, and suppose that $E[X|S]$ and ε are both uniformly distributed on $[-L, L]$. In this case, for $L > m > 0$, $q \geq 0$:

$$V(m, q, R) = (1 - \alpha)(L^2 - m^2) /$$
$$\left[2(1 - \alpha)(L - m) + 2\alpha(L - m - q) I_{\{q \leq L - m\}} \right],$$

where I_E is the indicator function of the set E. In particular, $V(m, 0, 0) = (1 - \alpha)(L + m)/2$. As long as the set of prices is not too coarse and/or α is large enough, some quantity will be offered. All that is required is that there be an allowable price in the interval $((1 - \alpha)L/(1 + \alpha), L)$. However, arbitrarily large trades are not possible in this environment. At any ask an infinite quantity is not offered, and if q exceeds $L(1 - (1 - \alpha^2)^{0.5})/\alpha$, the function $V(m, q, R)$ lies above m for all m. Thus, after the book has provided a quantity up to the above limit or higher, no subsequent offers will arrive. The exact quantity provided depends upon the allowable price set and the other parameters. That the quantity offered is finite is true regardless of the allowable price set.

In this example, α measures the importance of liquidity trade, just as in the previous example. As in the previous example, the lowest ask price is decreasing in α, while the maximum quantity offered is increasing in this parameter.

---

[8] Some care is needed in interpreting this result. Recall that a particular normalization was used in this example to minimize the number of parameters. Thus, a change in α represents a simultaneous change in the variance of the arrival's endowment, the variance of the value of the security and the precision of the information.

[9] The offering of an infinite quantity at some price seems to be a feature of the normal-exponential model with discrete prices.

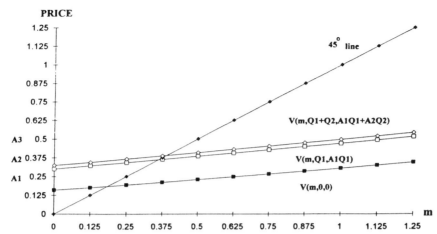

Figure 1. Determination of the equilibrium offers for the exponential-normal model.
The function $V(m, q, R(q))$ is the expectation of the terminal payoff, X, conditional on an arriving investor who pays $R(q)$ for q shares having a marginal valuation greater than or equal to m. The marginal valuation, $M(q, R(q); \omega)$ is the amount that an investor paying $R(q)$ for q shares would be willing to pay for an additional share. It is given by $M(q, R(q); \omega) = \omega - q$, where ω is a standard normal random variable, and $E[X \mid \omega] = (1 - \alpha)\omega$. Thus, $V(m, q, R(q))$ is given by:

$$V(m, q, R(q)) = E[X \mid M(q, R(q); \omega) \geq m] = (1 - \alpha)f(m + q)/(1 - F(m + q)),$$

where $f(\cdot)$ and $F(\cdot)$ are, respectively, the standard normal density and distribution function. The adverse selection parameter, α, is set at 0.8 (i.e., 20% of trade is motivated by private information) and the set of allowable prices is 1/8's. Approximately one unit is offered at 0.25, a small amount is offered at 0.375 and an arbitrarily large amount is offered at 0.5. The details of the calculations are provided at the end of the Appendix.

Finally, the above example can be modified to show that there are situations in which the market will not open; i.e., no bids or offers will be provided. Suppose that ε is uniformly distributed on $[-L_u, L_u]$, while $E[X \mid S]$ is uniformly distributed on $[-L, L]$, and $L > L_u$. Then it can be verified that $V(p, 0, 0)$ exceeds p for all p if $\alpha < 2(L - L_u)/(2L - L_u)$. That is, if the adverse selection problem is severe enough (α is small), and the liquidity motive for trade is relatively limited (L_u is small), the market will close down.

For the remainder of the analysis, it will be convenient to drop the assumption that only a discrete set of prices is allowed. While admittedly unrealistic, the mathematics is simplified tremendously. It should be noted that relatively few of the characteristics derived above in the general analysis and the specific examples relied on the particular set of allowable prices. The passage to continuous prices will be accomplished by taking limits of the discrete analysis above as the set of prices becomes finer. Thus, one may think of the continuous price case as a mathematically convenient approximation to the more realistic step function marginal price schedule.

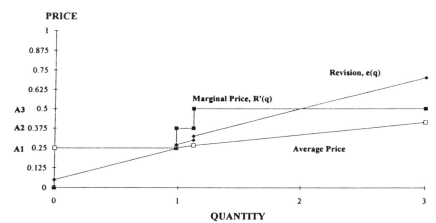

Figure 2. **Illustration of the exponential-normal model equilibrium with discrete prices.** The marginal price, $R'(q)$ is calculated in Figure 1: 0.98 units are offered at 0.25, 0.14 units are offered at 0.375, and an arbitrarily large amount is offered at 0.5. The average price is $R(q)/q$, and the revision in expectations, $e(q)$, is given by $e(q) = (1 - \alpha)(q + R'(q))$. Note that $e(q)$ lies below the average price for $q < 0.98$ and hence small buys are profitable for the limit order submitters. Since the investor's marginal valuation, $M(q, R(q); \omega) = \omega - q$, and ω is a standard normal random variable, roughly 73%, $(F(0.98 + 0.25) - F(0.25))/(1 - F(0.25))$, of market order purchases are less than 0.98. For $q > 2$, the revision in expectations exceeds the marginal offer of 0.5 (which exceeds the average price). Roughly 1.5% of the market order purchases will exceed 2 units.

The Appendix provides the details of the limiting argument. In the discrete case, offers are approximately "upper tail" expectations and bids are approximately "lower tail" expectations. In the continuous price case, marginal offers equal "upper tail" expectations, while marginal bids equal "lower tail" expectations. The remaining conditions in Proposition 4 insure that the equilibrium picks out the lowest offers and highest bids satisfying the expectation condition.

PROPOSITION 4: *For $Q > 0$, the marginal price function $R'(Q)$ must satisfy:*

$$R'(Q) = V(R'(Q), Q, R(Q)) = E[X| M(Q, R(Q); \omega) \geq R'(Q)]$$
$$V_1(R'(Q), Q, R(Q)) \leq 1; \; R'_+(0) = \inf\{p: p > V(p, 0, 0)\},$$

where $R'_+(0)$ is the limit of $R'(q)$ as q goes to zero from above.
For $Q < 0$, the marginal price function must satisfy:

$$R'(Q) = v(R'(Q), Q, R(Q)) = E[X| M(Q, R(Q); \omega) \leq R'(Q)]$$
$$v_1(R'(Q), Q, R(Q)) \leq 1; \; R'_-(0) = \sup\{p: p < v(p, 0, 0)\},$$

where $R'_-(0)$ is the limit of $R'(q)$ as q goes to zero from below.

A finite solution to this system will exist for some interval of quantities, if $m > V(m, 0, 0)$ for some interval of m's and $m < v(m, 0, 0)$ for some interval of m's. Furthermore, $R'_+(0) > R'_-(0)$, and for $\epsilon > 0$ but small,

$$E[X \mid D = -\varepsilon] > R(-\varepsilon)/(-\varepsilon) \text{ and } E[X \mid D = \varepsilon] < R(\varepsilon)/\varepsilon.$$

Examples: In the exponential-normal example, we have

$$R'(q) = (1 - \alpha)f(R'(q) + q)/(1 - F(R'(q) + q)) \quad \text{for } q > 0$$
$$R'(q) = -(1 - \alpha)f(R'(q) + q)/F(R'(q) + q) \quad \text{for } q < 0.$$

The equilibrium can be illustrated in a neater form by deriving the equilibrium trade by an individual of type z. Denote by $q(z)$ the solution to $z - q(z) = R'(q(z))$. Then, for $q(z) > 0$:

$$z - q(z) = (1 - \alpha)f(z)/(1 - F(z)).$$

The solution will be positive as long as z exceeds z^*, the solution to $z^* - (1 - \alpha)f(z^*)/(1 - F(z^*)) = 0$. For $z < -z^*$, the solution is given by:

$$q(z) = z + (1 - \alpha)f(z)/F(z) < 0.$$

Note that z^* is the limit of $R'(q)$ as $q > 0$ goes to zero. Note also that $q(z)$ is increasing in α. That is, as the severity of the adverse selection declines, the marginal price function declines and, in equilibrium, investors make larger trades. The marginal price function, $R'(q)$ and the revision in expectations, $e(q)$, can be found numerically by graphing (respectively) $(q(z), z - q(z))$ and $(q(z), (1 - \alpha)z)$ for various z's. This is done in Figure 3 for the case $\alpha = 0.8$.

For the uniform distribution example, $R'(q)$ is the solution to a quadratic equation. Depending upon q, the quadratic equation has two roots, one root, or no roots. If two roots are available, the partial derivative condition $V_1 \leq 1$ requires taking the smaller root. The lack of a root indicates that a marginal price is not offered for that quantity. Using the expression for V developed above in the previous discussion of the example (with $L_u = L$), $R'(q)$ for $q > 0$ is:

$$R'(q) = \left\{L - \alpha q - (\alpha^2 q^2 - 2\alpha q L + \alpha^2 L^2)^{0.5}\right\}/(1 + \alpha)$$

for $q < L(1 - (1 - \alpha^2)^{0.5})/\alpha$. Note that the total quantity offered is increasing in α, while the marginal price schedule is decreasing in α. As noted above, if $L_u < L$, and α is small enough, there will be no offers less than L and the market will close down.

II. Further Characteristics of The Electronic Market

One characteristic of a trading mechanism that may be important is its ability to consistently provide some liquidity. The ability of the monopolist specialist system to provide liquidity is the focus of Glosten (1989). The key

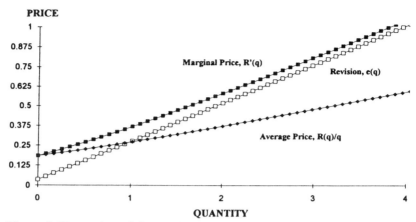

Figure 3. Illustration of the continuous price exponential-normal model equilibrium. $R'(q)$ is the marginal price schedule, $e(q)$ is the revision in expectations due to a trade of q, $e(q) = e[X \mid M(q, R(q); \omega) = R'(q)]$, and $R(q)/q$ is the average price schedule for $q > 0$. The picture for $q < 0$ (bids) is symmetric. The calculations are for the exponential-normal model with $\alpha = 0.8$: the investor's marginal valuation is given by $M(q, R(q); \omega) = \omega - q$, ω is a standard normal random variable and $E[X \mid \omega] = (1 - a)\omega$,. $R'(q)$ is the solution to $R'(q) = (1 - a)f(q + R'(q))/(1 - F(q + R'(q))$ where $f(\cdot)$ and $F(\cdot)$ are, respectively, the standard normal density and distribution function. Note that the lowest offer is strictly positive, as is the smallest revision in expectations, and for large q, the revision in expectations exceeds the average price. The functions $R'(q)$, $R(q)/q$, and $e(q)$ are convex, but approximately linear for large q.

property that allows a specialist to keep the market open when the competitive mechanism closes down is the ability of the specialist to average profits across trades. Notice, that this is a feature that the electronic market considered here shares with the specialist system. A reasonable question is whether this electronic market does it as well. The answer to this question is a restricted yes. If the electronic market provides no liquidity (formally there is no finite solution for $R'(q)$, or the only solution precludes trade with probability one), then any other market mechanism that has a "nice" marginal price function will expect to lose money. Thus, a large set of markets will be open in an environment only if the electronic exchange would be open in that environment.

PROPOSITION 5: *Suppose that there is no finite fixed point, m, $m = V(m, 0, 0)$ so that the electronic market will not open, and assume an economy in which marginal valuations are independent of cash positions so that $V(m, q, R)$ is independent of R. Then any other price schedule that has the single crossing property (see the discussion following Corollary 1) will expect to lose money.*

For the electronic market to open, all that is required is that liquidity suppliers be willing to make a small trade. Any other exchange, if open, would have to make this small trade, plus trades that are worse from an informational perspective. Thus, if the liquidity suppliers are unwilling to provide quotes in the electronic market, any other market would be unlikely to provide terms of trade.

One can measure liquidity in a variety of ways. Based on the size of the small-trade spread, one might be tempted to say the electronic market is not liquid. Indeed, it is possible to specify an economic environment in which a nondiscriminating (or single price) electronic market has no small-trade spread. This is the example of competitive pricing in Glosten (1989). However, such a market might close down too quickly. The above proposition states that if the measure of liquidity is resilience in the face of severe adverse selection problems, then the electronic market as conceived here is as good as one can do.

If the electronic market is open for some quantity, then a monopolist specialist would keep the market open for some quantity as well. Thus, in the normal-exponential example, both the monopolist specialist and the electronic open limit order book would be open for all quantities and in all environments (as long as α exceeds 0). In the modified uniform example (presented following Proposition 3), both the electronic open limit order book and a myopic monopolist specialist will close if the adverse selection is too severe.[10] The proposition raises the possibility that an electronic market may be able to reap the benefits of competition, while at the same time preserving the monopolist specialist liquidity in the face of severe adverse selection problems. The normal-exponential example that has been considered above indicates that, in at least one environment, this statement is true. Proposition 6 provides the details.

PROPOSITION 6: *Consider the normal-exponential example. No trader is worse off, and many are strictly better off with the open limit order book when compared to a monopolist specialist.*

III. Competition Among Exchanges

This section of the article considers competition among exchanges, and asks how susceptible the electronic exchange and other conceivable exchanges are to entry of competitors. For this analysis, the article considers a wide open regulatory environment in which anyone can offer to make a market in the security. Furthermore, setting up such a "market" is costless. On the investor side, market orders can be costlessly split up among "exchanges." It turns out that this assumption is a very powerful one and is a driving force behind the results. This is put formally as Assumption 4.

ASSUMPTION 4: *In the presence of more than one exchange, an investor can costlessly and simultaneously send separate orders to each exchange. A com-*

---

[10] A monopolist specialist may not close if what is learned from trade reduces the subsequent adverse selection problem. See the discussion in the conclusion of Glosten and Milgrom (1985). This issue is also addressed in Leach and Madhavan (1993).

peting exchange can be costlessly established and supplies a marginal price schedule that satisfies the single crossing property (see the discussion following Corollary 1).[11]

The first question to be asked is whether, given the existence of the electronic exchange, any potential entrant would be willing to enter. The standard Nash assumption is made—the entrant takes the marginal price function of the electronic market as given. It might appear that, since small trades are profitable for the electronic market, there will be an incentive to offer a price schedule to capture these small trades and skim the cream. This will not work because if small orders find it profitable to go to the competing exchange, then all investors will find it profitable to send some part of their order to the competing exchange. Even if the quantity accepted by the competing market is limited, it would still get a portion of all trades. The structure of the proof is as follows: since investors optimally split their orders, the marginal price received will be the marginal price in the electronic exchange. This marginal price is the upper tail expectation if there were only the electronic market. However, this artificial upper tail expectation is less than the actual upper tail expectation if the quantity traded in the competing market is positive, since upper tail expectations are increasing in quantity (in a world with no wealth effects). Thus, the competing market will consistently receive marginal prices that are less than the upper tail conditional expectations. However, expected profit is a weighted average of the marginal price, less the upper tail conditional expectation.

PROPOSITION 7: *Assume an economy in which marginal valuations are unaffected by cash positions so that $V(m, q, R)$ is independent of R. Suppose $R'_e(q)$ satisfying $R'_e(q) = V(R'_e(q), q, R_e(q))$ is the marginal price schedule in the electronic exchange. Assuming this price schedule fixed, an entrant with a marginal price schedule satisfying the single crossing property will expect to make nonpositive trading profits.*

The proposition asserts that, in a sense, the electronic market is competition proof. One Nash equilibrium is that there will be no entrance. The proposition is almost, but not quite, trivial. After all, an entrant supplying a competing nondecreasing schedule could as easily provide this schedule by participating in the limit order book. The assertion of equilibrium in the limit order book implies that there are no profit opportunities, and that any such effort would lead to negative profits. The slight addition is the allowance of marginal price schedules with a downward sloping portion, as long as the single crossing property is satisfied. What the proposition provides is the first hint that the competition in the discriminatory limit order book mimics the competition among exchanges. This point will, it is hoped, become clearer with subsequent results.

Reference to the proof above suggests that should an entrant come in, unless the limit orders change, limit order submitters will lose money as well.

---

[11] That the exchange must post a price schedule rules out "quote matching" type competition. See Glosten (1991).

Thus one equilibrium is no entrance. In fact, there will be other equilibria. For example, two competing open limit order books, each offering half the liquidity provided by a single limit order book, will be an equilibrium. The result will be terms of trade identical to those provided by a single order book. The next proposition shows that this is more generally true: if the entrant makes nonnegative profits, the composite price schedule provided by the two markets replicates the price schedule that would be determined if there were only the electronic exchange. The proof uses the same approach as above. If there are two exchanges, the marginal price received in the competing exchange will be driven by the marginal price in the open limit order book. But this is determined to be an upper tail conditional expectation taking into account the existence of the other exchange. Thus, in every case, as long as the competing exchange does not undercut for small trades, the marginal price equals the upper tail expectation. But this is precisely the equilibrium when there is only one order book. The non-negative profit assumption rules out undercutting at small trades.

PROPOSITION 8: *Suppose that there is an equilibrium in which a competing market enters and supplies a marginal price schedule $R'_c(q)$, satisfying the single crossing property. Then there is an equilibrium in which the total revenue function defined by,*

$$R_T(q) = R_e(q_e) + R_c(q_c) \quad \text{and} \quad q_c + q_e = q$$

is equal to $R(q)$ the schedule determined when there is only the electronic market.

The above two propositions state that if there is a great deal of competition in the provision of limit orders, any additional competition is either unprofitable or redundant. The question that remains to be answered, however, is whether this result is due merely to the great deal of competition that has been assumed, or does the actual architecture of the discriminatory limit order book play a role? The next proposition shows that the architecture is important. It is the particular zero-profit condition determined by the architecture of the discriminating limit order book that discourages further competition. Specifically, any other exchange that expects non-negative profits, but does not replicate the electronic exchange, will invite entrants.

PROPOSITION 9: *Consider an exchange with marginal price functin $R'(q)$, and suppose that for some interval of q's it does not equal the electronic exchange marginal price schedule. Suppose further that this schedule has nonnegative expected trading profits, and satisfies the single crossing property. Then, holding this schedule constant, there exists a competing schedule that will earn positive profits.*

The idea of the proof is that, if an entrant offers a small quantity, every investor with marginal valuation greater than or equal to the price offered will be interested in trading with the entrant. Thus, the cost of supplying the offer is the conditional upper tail expectation. By hypothesis, the price is greater than the upper tail expectation, and the entrant expects to make money. The proof of this proposition shows that while the electronic exchange is not open to cream skimming, any other exchange is.

The proposition implies that the particular design of the electronic market is important; it is not just the competition among a large number of liquidity suppliers that leads to the resilience of the electronic exchange. For example, an alternative design of an electronic market would be a "nondiscriminating" exchange. Liquidity suppliers submit limit bids and offers for quantities of the security. If a market order to purchase q units arrives, then the first limit orders totaling q all transact at the price of the highest offer to transact. Equilibrium among the large number of liquidity suppliers dictates that the price for an order of size q, $P(q)$, satisfy $P(q) = E[X \mid Q = q]$. Since $R(q)$ is given by $P(q)q$, we have $R(q)/q = E[X \mid M(q, R(q); \omega) = R'(q)]$.

In the event that there is no private information, both designs will yield the same result—all bids and offers will stack up at $E[X]$. If there is private information, however, the two designs will lead to different marginal price functions. Recall that with private information, the original specification of the electronic market had $R'_+(0) > E[X]$. Taking limits of the above expression for the alternative design "nondiscriminating" exchange, $R'(0) = E[X \mid M(0,0) = R'(0)]$. In some environments (for example, the normal-exponential example) the solution to this is $R'(0) = E[X]$. Thus, the alternative design will have $R'(q) < E[X \mid Q \geq q]$ for q small. Since the exchange earns zero profits on average, for larger q the opposite inequality must hold. The above proposition demonstrates that such an exchange will invite competition.

It should be added that the analysis in Glosten (1989) shows that the nondiscriminatory exchange will break down if the adverse selection problem is too severe. Thus, the analysis has suggested two reasons for preferring a discriminating design: it is less likely to break down, and it does not invite competitive reaction. The comparison is not unambiguous, however, since the nondiscriminating form will tend to offer lower spreads for small quantities.

IV. Dynamic Issues

The analysis of the order book concerns the development of the book at a point in time. However, as Black (1992) has argued, characterizations of equilibrium may be flawed if dynamic issues are ignored. This section provides no general answers to the Black critique, but some examples are suggestive.

The simplest destabilizing (or bluffing) strategy to consider is the following: buy using a market order and then reverse the trade using limit orders. If one could be assured of there being a buy order following the initial purchase, then this would clearly be a profitable strategy. The initial buy would push up the market's expectations and the average price received would exceed the average price paid. The problem, of course, is that one cannot be assured that the next trade will be an investor buy. Furthermore, one would expect informed investors' expectations to be less influenced by the bluff than the remainder of the market. Consequently, the probability of an informed sell as assessed by the bluffer will be larger than the probability assessment of the uninformed market. That is, the bluffer will find it relatively unlikely that the next trade will be a purchase and, consequently, the expected average price received from using limit orders may be less than the average price paid using the market order.

The above logic can be illustrated more rigorously using an example. Suppose the environment is as follows: there are essentially risk-neutral informed traders who know the future payoff of the security, and this payoff is either zero or one. The proportion of such traders is $1 - \alpha$. There are extremely risk-averse uninformed traders, half of whom are long one unit of the security and half of whom are short one unit. The extreme risk aversion implies that the "shorts" are willing to pay almost any price to buy one unit, and the "longs" are willing to receive almost any price to sell one unit. This environment is like the example in Glosten and Milgrom (1985). The equilibrium will involve market orders for one unit only. One unit will be offered at the expected value of the payoff conditional on a market buy order, while the expected value of the payoff conditional on a market sell will be bid for one unit.

Define N to be the time (in number of transactions) of the first market buy. Denote by A_n the ask price for the nth transaction. To evaluate the profitability of the bluff described above we need to calculate the expected value of $-A_0 + A_N$ conditional on knowing that the time-zero transaction is an uninformed buy. First note that since A_N is a revised expectation (it is the ask at the time of a market buy), the expected value of A_N conditional on an initial buy is A_0. The expectation conditional on an initial buy is an average of the expectation conditional on an uninformed buy (the expectation when A_0 was set) and the expectation conditional on an informed buy (one). The former of these two is smaller and hence the expected profit from the strategy is negative.

Consider, now, the exponential-normal example. A feature of this example is that the revision in expectations function, $e(q)$, is positive and not infinitesimal for infinitesimal q (see Figure 3). This might suggest that the equilibrium would elicit the following bluff: make a very large number of very small buys and then reverse using a single market sell order. Absent any other trades or public announcements, the large number of buys would push the market's expectations up substantially. However, the bluffer should expect that both information, and the arrival of other traders will tend to reverse the effects of the bluff. This is because the bluffer knows that the market's expectations have been artificially pushed up, and, hence, public announcements will, on average, provide correcting information. Furthermore, other informed traders should be less sensitive to the bluff than liquidity suppliers, and will, on average, provide correcting trades. Whether or not this completely erases the expected profitability of the bluff is an open question.

The next set of questions concerns the strict dichotomy between those who supply limit orders and those who use market orders. An informed trader may have two reasons for using a market order: (1) public announcements will tend to "depreciate" the value of the information and hence "patience" is costly; (2) competing informed traders, using market orders will tend to be on the same side of the market as the informed limit order user—they will tend to move the price against the informed limit order user, and he or she will assess a relatively smaller probability of execution. In the example above, one can show that if α is small enough (there are enough informed market order users), or the depreciation rate of private information is large enough, then informed traders will prefer to use market orders.

In a similar vein, if market order users use market orders gradually, they might just as well use limit orders. Note that in the exponential-normal example, a trader who chooses a trade to equate marginal price and marginal valuation will not wish to trade again immediately if the new schedule is merely translated by the change in expectations. Even though expectations will not move all the way to the marginal price, the posttrade marginal valuation at a zero new trade will lie within the new bid-ask spread (see Figure 3). This is because the distance between the revision in expectations function, $e(q)$, and the marginal price schedule, $R'(q)$, is greatest at q equal to zero. Thus, it does not appear that market order traders will wish to trade gradually.

It is probably true that some "liquidity" traders would use limit orders. This is particularly true if access to the book were very inexpensive. If the model were to allow this, it is possible to make rough predictions about the results. Consider the discrete price analysis. There is now no longer any reason to expect a zero-profit condition to hold at every price where there is a positive quantity. A liquidity trader may be willing to experience negative expected trading profits in return for a more optimally balanced portfolio and consumption. However, if there are positive profits at some price, one would expect the patient traders to step in to remove those profits. This would suggest that the resulting marginal price function would offer larger aggregate quantities at each price than the schedule considered here. However, the arguments of Cohen, Maier, Schwartz, and Whitcomb (1981) would suggest that the positive small-trade spread would not disappear. If there is value to immediacy, certain execution with small transaction costs will dominate the uncertain execution and losses to informed traders resulting from a limit order strategy.

V. Extensions and Speculations

The assumption of a large number of "patient traders" providing limit orders is unlikely to be met in reality. After all, providing limit orders is, in fact, not costless since it requires some monitoring to insure that orders are not left exposed after, for example, a public information release. As the discussion of the discrete price case suggests, the quantity competition that results in this sort of environment does not lead to the "Bertrand" conclusion that $N = 2$ is large. Of course, if there are a small number of liquidity suppliers, then there is an incentive for others to provide quotes. It is probably cheapest, however, for such liquidity suppliers to merely join the book by providing limit orders, and compete directly with the "patient traders," rather than establish a new exchange.

The analysis here describes the equilibrium in a "full" electronic limit order book. Note, however, that the profitability of low offers is unaffected by the existence or lack of higher offers. Thus, the lowest equilibrium offer is independent of the terms of higher offers.[12]

As the uniform example illustrates, it is not difficult to come up with reasonable examples that do not conform to the "affiliation" Assumption 2. If this assumption fails to hold, it may mean that the resulting pattern of bids and offers is roughly upward sloping but involves many "flat" spots—prices at which a large quantity is bid or offered.

The restriction of the analysis to anonymous exchanges is important. It is possible, and perhaps likely, that exchange floors provide the sort of information that allows either (1) some further determination of who does and does not have information, or (2) the possibility of disciplining via future penalties those who make information-based trades. Indeed, Admati and Pfleiderer (1991) argue that (1) can occur via "sunshine trading." Benveniste and Wilhelm (1992) argue that (2) is an important role of the specialist and floor traders. Specialists insist that these other sources of information are important for the smooth running of the New York Stock Exchange. Perhaps this floor information is important for some trades, unimportant for others. An important area of research is first, to determine the importance of this other information and second, to determine if the securities industry can simultaneously enjoy the benefits of competition and liquidity that an open limit order book appears to provide with the information benefits that a floor may provide.[13]

VI. Conclusion

After setting up a reasonably general model of investor behavior, the article develops some characteristics of the equilibrium in an electronic market when there are a large number of limit order submitters. It is shown that the equilibrium involves an "upper (lower) tail" conditional expectation

---

[12] Note that this is not a feature of a nondiscriminating limit order book, and hence limit order submitters in a nondiscriminating book face the risk that the profitability of their orders may be harmed by changes in other orders. Thus, the discriminating order book may attract more orders than a nondiscriminating order book in the realistic case in which the book may not have time to fill up.

[13] Junius W. Peake of Peake/Ryerson has suggested in private conversation that "floor information" could be represented in an electronic market.

in the determination of offers (bids). While exhibiting a small-trade spread, the open limit order book provides as much liquidity as can be expected in extreme adverse selection environments. The article suggests that if there is a large population of potential liquidity suppliers, and if the actual costs of running an exchange are small, then among exchanges that operate continuously and anonymously, and supply nice marginal price schedules, the electronic exchange is the only one that does not tend to engender additional competing exchanges.

Simultaneous trading of equities on the London Stock Exchange (a dealer market) and the Paris Bourse (an electronic open limit order book) would seem to refute the immunity characteristics derived in this analysis. However, the structure of the London Stock Exchange provides something outside the analysis in this article. Specifically, trading on the London Stock Exchange need not be anonymous. More generally then, the results regarding competing exchanges might usefully be interpreted in the following way: with an electronic open limit order book a competing exchange may well survive, but to survive it must provide something outside of the analysis in this article.

Appendix

Proof of Lemma 1: Suppose that (i) and (ii) do not hold, and suppose there exists $q(\omega)$ such that:

$$M(q(\omega), R(q(\omega)); \omega) = R'(q(\omega)).$$

The derivative of $M(q, R(q); \omega)$ evaluated at $q(\omega)$ is:

$$(W_1^2 W_{22} + W_2^2 W_{11} - 2W_1 W_2 W_{12})/W_1^3 < 0, \quad \text{by strict quasi-concavity.}$$

Thus, since $R'(\cdot)$ is nondecreasing, if $M(q, R(q); \omega)$ and $R'(q)$ ever cross, M crosses from above (i.e., if $q < q(\omega)$, $M(q, R(q); \omega) > R'(q)$). If there is no solution, $q(\omega)$, then either condition (i) or (ii) is satisfied, or there is a discontinuity in $R'(q)$ at q_0 and M passes through this discontinuity. Since $R'(q)$ is nondecreasing, any discontinuity must involve a jump up. If M goes through this discontinuity it must do so from above. If whenever M crosses R' it does so from above, then the two functions can cross at most once and conclusion (iii) holds. Q.E.D.

Proof of Proposition 1: The derivative of $W(-R(q), q; \omega)$ with respect to q is:

$$-W_1(-R(q), q; \omega)R'(q) + W_2(-R(q), q; \omega)$$
$$= W_1(-R(q), q; \omega)[M(q, R(q); \omega) - R'(q)].$$

After observing that W_1 is strictly positive by assumption, and applying the uniqueness results of Lemma 1, the result is immediate. Q.E.D.

Proof of Lemma 2: First note that if Y is a random variable with density f and distribution function F:

$$E[X | Y \geq y](1 - F(y)) = \int_y^\infty E[X | Y = t] f(t) \, dt$$

$$E[X | Y \leq y] F(y) = \int_{-\infty}^y E[X | Y = t] f(t) \, dt$$

Taking the derivatives of the above with respect to y shows that:

$$(d/dy) E[X | Y \geq y] = f(y)\{E[X | Y \geq y] - E[X | Y = y]\}/(1 - F(y)),$$
$$(d/dy) E[X | Y \leq y] = f(y)\{E[X | Y = y] - E[X | Y \leq y]\}/F(y).$$

Given Assumption 2 with $Y = M(q, R; \omega)$ shows that $V(m, q, R)$ and $v(m, q, R)$ are increasing in m. For the second part of the proposition, define $Q_{Rm}(\omega)$ as the optimal trade of an investor with characteristic vector ω but with cash position reduced by R facing a fixed price m for any quantity. Such a "schedule" is nondecreasing, and hence by Corollary 1 above:

$$E[X | Q_{Rm}(\omega) \geq q] = E[X | M(q, R + qm; \omega) \geq m] = V(m, q, R + qm)$$
$$E[X | Q_{Rm}(\omega) \leq q] = E[X | M(q, R + qm; \omega) \leq m] = v(m, q, R + qm).$$

Also, $E[X | Q_{Rm}(\omega) = q] = E[X | M(q, R + qm; \omega) = m]$. Thus, we have by Assumption 2:

$$E[X | Q_{Rm}(\omega) \geq q] \geq E[X | Q_{Rm}(\omega) = q] \geq E[X | Q_{Rm}(\omega) \leq q].$$

By the demonstration above, both $E[X | Q_{Rm}(\omega) \geq q]$ and $E[X | Q_{Rm}(\omega) \leq q]$ are increasing in q. That is, both $V(m, q, R + qm)$ and $v(m, q, R + qm)$ are increasing in q. Q.E.D.

Proof of Proposition 2: The analysis will deal with the derivation of the equilibrium on the offer side. The analysis for the bid side can be easily derived from this analysis. Let q_i be the quantity offered at the ith price by a typical liquidity supplier. Let Q_i be the total quantity offered by all N liquidity suppliers at the ith price, and let AQ_i be the total quantity offered by all N liquidity suppliers at the ith price and lower. Finally, define R_i by $R_i = p_0 Q_0 + \cdots + p_i Q_i$, the amount paid for a purchase of AQ_i. Since the set of allowable prices is discrete, the marginal price function will be a step function. Thus, even if cross-sectionally the marginal valuation functions are continuously distributed, the probability that D, the quantity traded at the next arrival, is equal to AQ_i may be positive. In particular:

$$P\{D = AQ_i\} = P\{p_i \leq M(AQ_i, R_i; \omega) < p_{i+1}\}.$$

Denote the density of D, for $AQ_{i-1} < d < AQ_i$ by $f_i(d)$. Note that the above probabilities and densities are functions of the actual bids and offers provided. If a trade arrives strictly between AQ_{i-1} and AQ_i, then the excess over AQ_{i-1} needs to be allocated among those supplying offers. It is assumed that the allocation is pro rata according to the size of the offer provided. With this specification, the expected profit to the liquidity supplier who offers $\{q_i\}$ while others offer $\{Q_i - q_i\}$ is:

$$\sum_{i=0}^{\infty} q_i(p_i - E[X \mid D \geq AQ_i])P\{D \geq AQ_i\}$$

$$+ \sum_{i=0}^{\infty} \left[\frac{q_i}{Q_i}\right] \int_{AQ_{i-1}}^{AQ_i} (d - AQ_{i-1})(p_i - E[X \mid D = d])f_i(d) \quad \text{(A1)}$$

If a liquidity supplier offers q_i, then all of this quantity will be transacted at price p_i if a trade comes in for AQ_i or greater. If this happens, the revised value of the share is $E[X \mid D \geq AQ_i]$, and this happens with probability $P\{D \geq AQ_i\}$. If a trade comes in for an amount strictly between AQ_{i-1} and AQ_i, say d, then $d - AQ_{i-1}$ will be allocated in a pro rata fashion. The revised expectation will be $E[X \mid D = d]$. Integrating over all such d's weighted by the density provides the expected profit in this event. Sum over all possible prices to obtain the expected profit from the choice of q's. To obtain the first-order condition that Q_i must satisfy, take the derivative of the above expression with respect to q_i. This yields:

$$(p_i - E[X \mid D \geq AQ_i])P\{D \geq AQ_i\} + \frac{Q_i - q_i}{Q_i^2}$$

$$\times \int_{AQ_{i-1}}^{AQ_i} (d - AQ_{i-1})(p_i - E[X \mid D = d])f_i(d)$$

$$+ \sum_{j=1}^{\infty} \left\{ q_j \frac{d}{dq_i}(p_j - E[X \mid D \geq AQ_j])P\{D \geq AQ_j\} \right.$$

$$\left. + \frac{q_j}{Q_j} \frac{d}{dq_i} \int_{AQ_{j-1}}^{AQ_j} (d - AQ_{j-1})(p_j - E[X \mid D = d])f_i(d) \right\} = 0 \quad \text{(A2)}$$

This condition must hold for all liquidity suppliers, so sum this derivative over all liquidity suppliers and divide by N.
If $Q_i > 0$ but finite:

$$(p_i - E[X \mid D \geq AQ_i])P\{D \geq AW_i\}$$

$$+ \frac{N-1}{N} \frac{1}{Q_i} \int_{AQ_{i-1}}^{AQ_i} \times (p_i - E[X \mid D = d])(d - AQ_{i-1})f_i(d) + \frac{K}{N} = 0$$

(A3)

The term K/N indicates a number of individual terms reflecting the effect of adding a unit of quantity more at p_i on the probability and profitability of trades larger than AQ_{i-1}. As N gets large, this term vanishes. After integrating the second term in equation (3) by parts, substituting $V(p_i, d, R_{i-1}$

$+ p_i(d - AQ_{i-1}))$ for $E[X \mid D \geq d]$ and ignoring terms of order $1/N$, it is found that if $Q_i > 0$, but finite:

$$\int_{AQ_{i-1}}^{AQ_i} (p_i - V(p_i, d, R_{i-1} + p_i(d - AQ_{i-1}))$$

$$\times P\{M(d, R_{i-1} + p_i(d - AQ_{i-1}) \geq p_i\} = 0 \quad (A4)$$

By Lemma 2, if $p_k < V(p_k, 0, 0)$, then $p_k < V(p_k, q, qp_k)$ for all positive q, and the first-order condition can never be satisfied at p_k. The second-order condition at a price p_i with a positive quantity is found by taking the derivative of the initial first-order condition, equation (A2), summing across all liquidity suppliers, dividing by N and ignoring terms of order $1/N$. This yields: $P\{D_j \geq AQ_j\}(p_j - V(p_j, AQ_j, R_j))/Q_j < 0$. The results of Lemma 2 imply that a point that satisfies the first-order condition also satisfies the second-order condition.

Proof of Proposition 3: The first inequality in (i) follows immediately from the definition of A_1. The second inequality follows from Assumption 2, and the third inequality follows from the analogous definition of B_1. The second set of inequalities follow from Assumption 2 and continuity. The same arguments apply for part (ii). Q.E.D.

Proof of Proposition 4: The analysis will deal with the ask side; the analysis for the bid side is completely analogous. The limit as q goes to zero from above of $R'(q)$ is:

$$R'_+(0) = \inf\{p: p > V(p, 0, 0)\} \quad \text{if the set is nonempty.} \quad (A5)$$

If the set is empty, there are no offers provided. Now suppose that offers totaling Q are available. The following limiting argument will indicate the conditions that $R'(Q)$ and $R(Q)$ must satisfy. Suppose that $R'(Q) + \varepsilon$ is the next allowable price, and further that a positive quantity will be offered at $R'(Q) + \varepsilon$. Following the development above, this implies that:

$$R'(Q) + \varepsilon > V(R'(Q) + \varepsilon, Q, R(Q)). \quad (A6)$$

Let the quantity offered at $R'((Q) + \varepsilon$ be εq. Then the first-order condition must be equal to 0:

$$\frac{\int_Q^{Q+\varepsilon q} (R'(Q) + \varepsilon - V(R'(Q) + \varepsilon, t, R(Q) + (t - Q)(R'(Q) + \varepsilon)))}{\varepsilon q} \times G(Q, t, R'(Q) + \varepsilon) \, dt$$

Where $G(Q, t, R'(Q) + \varepsilon) = P\{M(t, R(Q) + (t - Q)(R'(Q) + \varepsilon); \omega) > R'(Q) + \varepsilon\}$. Taking the limit as ε goes to zero yields:

$$R'(Q) = V(R'(Q), Q, R(Q)).$$

It is also required that $1 > [V(R'(Q) + \varepsilon, Q, R(Q)) - R'(Q)]/\varepsilon$ (from equation (A6). Taking limits yields the additional condition that $(\partial/\partial p)V(p, Q, R(Q))|_{p=R'(Q)} \leq 1$. There may still be more than one solution. The solution is pinned down by condition (A5).

Proof of Proposition 5: For any $R(\cdot)$ the expected profit is:

$$\int_{-\infty}^{\infty} dP\{Q_R \leq q\}(R(q) - qE[X|Q_R = q])$$

Integrate by parts to get:

$$\int_0^{\infty} P\{Q_R \geq q\}(R'(q) - E[X|Q_R \geq q])\, dq$$

$$+ \int_{-\infty}^0 P\{Q_R \leq q\}(E[X|Q_R \leq q] - R'(q))\, dq$$

This follows since:

$$(d/dq)P\{Q_R \geq q\}E[X|Q_R \geq q] = -E[X|Q_R = q](d/dq)P\{Q_R \leq q\}, \text{ and}$$
$$(d/dq)P\{Q_R \leq q\}E[X|Q_R \leq q] = E[X|Q_R = q](d/dq)P\{Q_R \leq q\}$$

(see the proof of Lemma 2). Under the hypothesis of the proposition,

$$m < V(m, 0, 0) \leq V(m, q, R(q)) \text{ for all } m.$$

The second inequality follows from Lemma 2 and the absence of wealth effects. Then in particular, for the $R'(q)$ considered here:

$$R'(q) < V(R'(q), q, R(q)) = E[X|M(q, R(q); \omega) \geq R'(q)] = E[X|Q_R \geq q],$$

where the last equality follows from the single crossing property. Thus, this R leads to negative expected profits. Q.E.D.

Proof of Proposition 6: Under the normalization chosen above, the certainty equivalent of a trader of type ω, making optimal trade $q(\omega)$ is given by: $CE(\omega) = \omega q(\omega) - 0.5q(\omega)^2 - R(q(\omega))$. The derivative of this is given by:

$$CE'(\omega) = q(\omega) + q'(\omega)(\omega - q(\omega) - R'(q(\omega))) = q(\omega)$$

since $q(\omega)$ satisfies the first-order condition for optimality. Since the certainty equivalent is zero when the optimal quantity traded is zero, the certainty equivalent evaluated at ω is the integral from 0 to ω of $q(t)$. A monopolist will set a marginal price schedule so that the quantity traded by a investor of type ω is given by:

$$q_m(\omega) = \alpha\omega - (1 - F(\omega))/f(\omega), \omega > \omega_m$$
$$= \alpha\omega + F(\omega)/f(\omega), \omega < -\omega_m$$
$$= 0 \quad \text{otherwise};$$

where $\alpha\omega_m - (1 - F(\omega_m))0/f(\omega_m) = 0$. The full details of this derivation are in Glosten (1989); a sketch is provided below. In contrast, the electronic market determines $q_e(\omega)$ as:

$$q_e(\omega) = \omega - (1 - \alpha)f(\omega)/(1 - F(\omega)), \quad \omega > \omega^*$$
$$\omega + (1 - \alpha)f(\omega)/F(\omega), \quad \omega < -\omega^*$$
$$0, \quad \text{otherwise.}$$

It can be shown that $0 < f(t)[(f(t)/(1 - F(t))) - t]/(1 - F(t)) < 1$. Hence, $\omega^* < \omega_m$ and for $\omega > \omega^*$, $q_e(\omega) > q_m(\omega)$ and for $\omega < -\omega^*$, $q_e(\omega) < q_m(\omega)$. Thus, for ω outside of $[-\omega^*, \omega^*]$ the certainty equivalent is strictly larger with the electronic market.

Derivation of Monopolist Solution in Proposition 6

If the monopolist chooses a marginal price schedule $R'(\cdot)$, then the choice of a trader, $Q(z)$, is determined by $R'(Q(z)) = z - Q(z)$. The monopolist's problem on the offer side is to maximize:

$$\int_{t_m}^{\infty} [R(Q(z)) - (1 - \alpha)zQ(z)]f(z)\,dz$$

Integrate the first term by parts, noting that $R(Q(t_m)) = 0$, and $R'(Q(z)) = z - Q(z)$ to get:

$$\int_{t_m}^{\infty} (1 - F(z))Q'(z)(z - Q(z)) - (1 - \alpha)zQ(z)f(z)\,dz$$

Integrate the first term by parts again to get:

$$\int_{t_m}^{\infty} f(z)\left[\alpha zQ(z) - \frac{1 - F(z)}{f(z)}Q(z) - 0.5Q(z)^2\right]dz$$

The maximizing $Q(z)$ is as claimed.

Proof of Proposition 7: Call $R'_c(q)$ the marginal price schedule in the competing market, and Q_c, a random variable, the next trade at the competing exchange. After integrating by parts, the expected profit to the entrant is:

$$\int_0^{\infty} P\{Q_c \geq q\}(R'_c(q) - E[X|Q_c \geq q])\,dq$$
$$+ \int_{-\infty}^{0} P\{Q_c \leq q\}(E[X|Q_c \leq q] - R'_c(q))\,dq$$

Where Q_c is the quantity chosen in the entering market. Consider only the offer side. If $R'_c(0) > R'_e(0)$ then if $Q_c > 0$, $Q_e > 0$, where Q_e is the quantity chosen in the electronic market. Furthermore, $R'_c(Q_c) = R'_e(Q_e)$ and hence $Q_e = R'^{-1}_e(R'_c(Q_c))$. To simplify the notation, define $q_e = R'^{-1}_e(R'_c(q))$, $q_T = q_e + q$ and $R_T = R_c(q) + R_e(q_e)$. That is, q_e is the trade made in the electronic market when q is traded in the competitive market, q_T is the total trade, while R_T is the total amount paid for a purchase of q_T shares. By the single crossing property, the events $\{Q_c \geq q\} = \{Q_e \geq q_e\}$, and furthermore:

$$E[X \mid Q_c \geq q] = E[X \mid Q_e \geq q_e]$$
$$= E[X \mid M(q_T, R_T; \omega) \geq R'_c(q)]$$
$$= V(R'_c(q), q_T, R_T) = V(R'_e(q_e), q_T, R_T)$$
$$\geq V(R'_e(q_e), q_e, R_e(q_e)) = R'_e(q_e) = R'_c(q).$$

The last inequality follows from the fact that $q_T > q_e$ and the use of Lemma 2 in the case of no wealth effects. For any q such that $R'_c(q) \geq R'_e(0)$, the term in the integral is nonpositive. Suppose that $R'_c(q) < R'_e(0)$. Then, for some q:

$$R'_c(q) - E[X \mid Q \geq q] = R'_c(q) - E[X \mid M(q, R_c(q); \omega) \geq R'_c(q)]$$
$$= R'_c(q) - V(R'_c(q), q, R_c(q)).$$

Since $R'_c(q) < R'_e(0)$ and $V(R'_c(q), q, R_c(q)) \geq V(R'_c(q), 0, 0))$ this term is not positive since $R'_e(0)$ is the smallest m with $m \geq V(m, 0, 0)$. Q.E.D.

Proof of Proposition 8: If both q_c and q_e are positive for some q, then they are determined by: $q_c + q_e = q$ and $R'_c(q_c) = R'_e(q_e)$. Thus, $R'_T(q)$ equals $R'_e(q_e)$, and:

$$R'_T(q) = R'_e(q_e) = E[X \mid M(q, R_T(q); \omega) \geq R'_e(q_e)]$$
$$= V(R'_e(q_e), q_T, R_T(q)) = V(R'_T(q), q, R_T(q)).$$

That is, $R_T(q)$ is a solution to $R'_T(q) = V(R'_T(q), q, R_T(q))$. One such solution is the electronic open limit order book solution, $R(q)$. The entrant cannot set $R'_c(0) < R'_e(0)$ and expect to make nonnegative profits, for if he or she did, some marginal prices would be below upper tail expectations while other marginal prices would equal upper tail expectations. Q.E.D.

Proof of Proposition 9: Suppose, without loss of generality, that the schedule diverges from the electronic exchange schedule on the offer side. If

$$\int_0^\infty P\{Q \geq q\}(R'(q) - E[X \mid Q \geq q]) \geq 0$$

but $R'(q)$ is not the electronic exchange marginal price schedule, then there exists q^* with $R'(q^*) > E[X \mid Q \geq q^*]$. Consider the following strategy of an entrant. Set $P = R'(q^*)$ and announce that up to Q units will be sold at price P. The expected profit from this strategy is:

$$QP\{Q_c = Q\}(P - E[X \mid Q_c = Q] + \int_0^Q dP\{Q_c < q\}q(P - E[X \mid Q_c = q])$$

where Q_c is the random quantity picked in the competing market. From the investors maximization problem $\{\omega \mid Q_c = Q\} = \{\omega \mid M(Q + q^*, R(q^*) + PQ; \omega) \geq P\}$, and hence $E[X \mid Q_c = Q] = V(P, Q + q^*, R(q^*) + PQ)$. Divide the expression for profits by Q and let Q go to zero. The first term vanishes, the second becomes $(P - V(P, q^*, R(q^*))P\{M(q^*, R(q^*); \omega) \geq P\} = (R'(q^*) - V(R'(q^*), q^*, R(q^*))P\{M(q^*, R(q^*); \omega) \geq R'(q^*)\} > 0$. Thus, for some $Q > 0$ expected trading profits will be positive. Q.E.D.

Determination of the Equilibrium in Figure 1

The function $V(m, q, R(q)) = (1 - \alpha)f(m + q)/(1 - F(m + q))$ where $f(\cdot)$ and $F(\cdot)$ are, respectively, the standard normal density and distribution. A1 is the solution to $A1 = \min\{p: p > (1 - \alpha)f(p)/(1 - F(p))\}$ and is found to be 0.25. The first-order condition to determine Q_i is:

$$\int_{AQ_{i-1}+p_i}^{AQ_{i-1}+Q_i+p_i} p_i(1 - F(t)) - (1 - \alpha)f(t)\, dt = 0$$

The integral can be evaluated as:

$$\{(1 - F(p_i + AQ_{i-1} + Q_i))(1 - \alpha + p_i(p_i + AQ_{i-1} + Q_i$$
$$- f(p_i + AQ_{i-1} + Q_i)/(1 - F(p_i + AQ_{i-1} + Q_i)))\}$$
$$- \{(1 - F(p_i + AQ_{i-1}))(1 - \alpha + p_i(p_i + AQ_{i-1} - f(p_i + AQ_{i-1})/$$
$$(1 - F(p_i + AQ_{i-1})))\} = 0.$$

Letting $\alpha = 0.8$, $AQ_{i-1} = 0$, and $p_i = 0.25$, the above can be solved numerically to get Q1 = 0.98. The next highest offer, A2 is the solution to $A2 = \min\{p: p > (1 - \alpha)f(p + 0.98)/(1 - F(p + 0.98))\}$ and is found to be 0.375. Letting $AQ_{i-1} = 0.98$ and $p_i = 0.375$ and solving numerically, leads to Q2 = 0.14. The next highest offer is the solution to $A3 = \min\{p: p > (1 - \alpha)f(p + 1.12)/(1 - F(p + 1.12))\}$ and is found to be 0.5. Letting $AQ_{i-1} = 1.12$ and $p_i = 0.5$, it can be verified that the left side of the first-order condition is positive for all Q_i, that is $-(1 - F(1.62))(0.2 + 0.5(1.62 - f(1.62)/(1 - F(1.62)) > 0$, and hence the equilibrium involves an infinite amount offered at 0.5.

REFERENCES

Admati, A., and P. Pfleiderer, 1991, Sunshine trading and financial market equilibrium, *Review of Financial Studies* 4, 443–481.

Benveniste, Lawrence M., Alan J. Marcus, and William J. Wilhelm, 1992, What's special about the specialist? *Journal of Financial Economics* 32, 61–86.

Black, Fischer, 1991, Trading in equilibrium with bluffing, credits and debits, Working paper, Goldman Sachs, New York, NY.

———, 1992, Equilibrium exchanges, working paper, Golman Sachs, New York, NY.

Cohen, K., S. Maier, R. Schwartz, and D. Whitcomb, 1981. Transactions costs, order placement strategy and the existence of the bid-ask spread, *Journal of Political Economy* 89, 287–305.

Domowitz, Ian (1991). Automating continuous double auctions in practice: automated trade execution in financial markets, Working paper, Northwestern University.

Easley, David, and M. O'Hara, 1987, Price, trade size and information in securities markets, *Journal of Financial Economics* 19, 69–90.

Gale, Ian, 1991. Sequential trade and information revelation, Working paper, University of Wisconsin.

Glosten, L. R., and P. R. Milgrom, 1985. Bid, ask and transaction prices in a specialist market with heterogeneously informed traders, *Journal of Financial Economics* 14, 71–100.

Glosten, Lawrence R., 1989, Insider trading, liquidity, and the role of the monopolist specialist, *Journal of Business* 62, 211–235.

———, 1991, Asymmetric information, the third market and investor welfare, Working paper, Columbia University.

Harris, Lawrence, 1990, Liquidity, trading rules and electronic trading systems, Monograph Series in Finance and Economics, New York University Salomon Center, New York.

Hellwig, Martin, 1980, On the aggregation of information in competitive markets, *Journal of Economic Theory* 22, 477–498.

Kyle, Albert S., 1985, Continuous auctions and insider trading, *Econometrica* 53, 1315–1335.

Leach, J. C., and A. N. Madhavan, 1993, Price experimentation and security market structure, *Review of Financial Studies* 6, 375–404.

Milgrom, Paul R., and Robert Weber, 1982. A theory of auctions and competitive bidding, *Econometrica* 50, 1089–1122.

Rock, Kevin, 1989. The specialist's order book, Working paper, Harvard University.

Part III
Evidence on Market Design and Trading Costs

A
Opening Call Markets

Trading Mechanisms and Stock Returns: An Empirical Investigation

YAKOV AMIHUD and HAIM MENDELSON*

ABSTRACT

This paper examines the effects of the mechanism by which securities are traded on their price behavior. We compare the behavior of open-to-open and close-to-close returns on NYSE stocks, given the differences in execution methods applied in the opening and closing transactions. Opening returns are found to exhibit greater dispersion, greater deviations from normality and a more negative and significant autocorrelation pattern than closing returns. We study the effects of the bid-ask spread and the price-adjustment process on the estimated return variances and covariances and discuss the associated biases. We conclude that the trading mechanism has a significant effect on stock price behavior.

I. Introduction

WHILE SECURITIES exchanges in the United States typically operate as continuous trading markets where specialists and dealers act as market-makers, the operation of many exchanges around the world resembles a periodic call market, where buy and sell orders accumulate during some time interval and are then executed simultaneously at a price which equates the quantity supplied to the quantity demanded.[1]

Recent developments in securities markets induce policy makers to critically evaluate existing trading procedures. The plans to establish a national market system, the increase in trading volumes, the fierce competition between exchanges and over-the-counter markets and the expansion of electronic trading, all made the securities industry ready for a change. All major U.S. exchanges are continuously evaluating new (mostly automated) trading procedures, and European capital markets are already allowing forms of continuous trading together with their ordinary call market procedures.[2] Thus, it is of interest to examine the effects that these alternative trading methods may have on stock price behavior.

---

* Amihud is from Tel Aviv University and New York University, Mendelson from the University of Rochester. We acknowledge partial financial support by the Managerial Economics Research Center of the University of Rochester and the Salomon Brothers Center at New York University, as well as helpful comments by Robert Schwartz.

[1] For a recent survey of trading methods in the main world exchange markets, see Whitcomb (1985), Cohen, Maier, Schwartz and Whitcomb (1986, Ch. 2) and Ho, Schwartz and Whitcomb (1981).

[2] For example, the *Borsa di Milano*, where orders are batched and executed periodically applying the call method, is moving to continuous trading in some active stocks. On the other hand, Ho, Schwartz and Whitcomb (1981) proposed to adopt a batched trading system for some NYSE stocks. Amihud and Mendelson (1985) proposed an integrated computerized trading system which will allow the two trading mechanisms to operate simultaneously. A system that applies some of their principles is to be implemented, on an experimental basis, in the Tel Aviv Stock Exchange.

The dealership market regime has been studied quite extensively, both theoretically and empirically (see a review by Stoll (1985)). The periodic call trading procedure received less attention, and was recently studied by Mendelson (1982, 1985, 1986, 1987a) and by Ho, Schwartz and Whitcomb (1985). Theoretical comparisons of the two market mechanisms are scarce (Garbade and Silber (1979), Mendelson (1985, 1987a)), and empirical comparisons of price behavior under these mechanisms are virtually non-existent. The difficulty with the empirical comparison is that different markets trade different assets and these assets are traded in different environments, hence it would be hard to discern differences resulting from the trading mechanism itself from differences due to dissimilarities of securities and environments.[3]

This paper offers to resolve this difficulty by comparing the price behavior of New York Stock Exchange stocks in the opening transactions with the price behavior of the same stocks traded at the same exchange during the same period in the closing transactions. The opening transactions represent the outcome of a call trading procedure, whereas trading at the close is carried out at prices which are set or affected by the exchange's market-makers.

Our analysis of the opening and closing transaction prices distinguishes between the intrinsic *value* of a security and its observed *price*; the difference between the two may be attributed to *noise* (Black (1986)). We propose that this noise is due in part to the process by which prices are set in the market, i.e., to the trading mechanism. Studying the effect of the trading mechanism on observed prices will enable us to account for this part of the noise, and will improve our understanding of the price discovery process.[4]

This study examines the characteristics of stock returns, as reflected by their time-series behavior, under different trading mechanisms. We compare the dispersion of the observed return distributions, the nature of convergence of prices to values, the return serial correlation patterns and their implications for market efficiency, and the effects of the bid-ask spread.

In what follows, Section II discusses the differences between the two trading mechanisms and Section III presents a simple model of price adjustment. Section IV outlines the nature of the opening and closing transactions on the NYSE, which constitute the data analyzed in this study. Our empirical analysis starts in Section V by comparing the dispersion of stock returns. In Section VI we examine the deviations of the return distribution from normality, Section VII tests the random-walk form of market efficiency under the two trading mechanisms, and Section VIII studies the effect of the bid-ask spread. Our concluding remarks are offered in Section IX. Our findings show that the trading mechanism has distinct implications on stock price behavior.

---

[3] For example, a comparison of price behavior in the *Bourse de Paris* (which operates as a periodic call market) with the price behavior on a U.S. exchange may reflect differences which are due to factors other than the trading mechanism, such as differences in the securities themselves, differences in the regulatory and economic environment, etc.

[4] Price discovery is the process by which transaction prices adjust to asset values (see Schreiber and Schwartz (1986)).

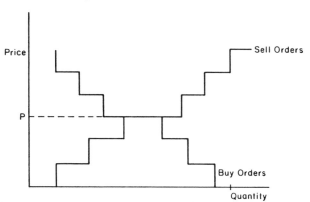

Figure 1. Price setting in a clearing house. The schedules depict the orders submitted to the market at limit prices in steps of $1/8.

II. The Dealership Market and the Clearing House

Two trading mechanisms which model many of the securities exchanges around the world are the dealership market and the clearing house. In the dealership market, trading is carried out continuously through market-makers who quote bid and ask prices at which they are willing to buy or sell (respectively). In the New York Stock Exchange, a designated specialist makes the market in a security and has an affirmative obligation to provide continuous quotes. In other markets, such as the OTC market or the New York Futures Exchange, the trading process is carried out by multiple traders making a market in the security.

An alternative trading mechanism is the clearing house (cf. Mendelson (1982))—a periodic market clearing procedure under which traders submit two types of orders to buy or sell specified quantities of the traded security: limit orders, which state the order quantity and the minimum sale price or the maximum purchase price at which the order is to be executed; and market orders, which specify only the quantity to be sold or bought with no price limits.[5] Orders accumulate and remain sealed until clearing time. Then, all sell orders are sorted according to the type of order (market or limit; market orders are sorted first) and limit orders are further sorted by increasing price sequence. Buy orders are sorted by type of order (market orders first) and by decreasing price sequence. This gives rise to supply and demand schedules constructed from the orders submitted to the market (see Figure 1). These schedules are then intersected at a single price which clears the market and applies to all executed orders. The clearing house procedure is employed extensively by European stock exchanges, where the market is cleared periodically (see references in footnote 1), and is also applied in some commodities exchanges (Jarecki (1976)). This form of exchange is closely related to the classical concept of competitive market clearing; it was

---

[5] A market order may be construed as a limit order whose limit buy or sell price is arbitrarily high or low, respectively.

the subject of a number of empirical laboratory experiments (e.g., Smith (1976)), and was studied theoretically by Mendelson (1982, 1986, 1987a) and by Ho, Schwartz and Whitcomb (1985).

The interest in comparing the two trading mechanisms is related to the reevaluation of prevailing trading procedures under the plans to establish a national market system in the U.S., to forthcoming changes in European securities markets, and to the expected expansion in the role of electronic trading (Amihud and Mendelson (1985)). These factors may lead to the establishment of one of the competing forms of exchange or both, and it is important to study the effects that each trading mechanism is expected to have on securities price behavior and on the liquidity of the market.[6]

III. A Simple Model of Price Adjustment

In this section we outline a simple model of price behavior which will guide our empirical tests. The model distinguishes between the intrinsic *value* of a security at time t, V_t, and its observed *price*, P_t. The difference between value and price is attributable to noise (Black (1986)). These two effects are formally captured by a partial-adjustment model with noise,[7]

$$P_t - P_{t-1} = g \cdot [V_t - P_{t-1}] + u_t, \qquad (3.1)$$

where V_t and P_t are in logarithms and the adjustment coefficient g satisfies $0 < g < 2$. As usual, $\{u_t\}$ is a "white noise" sequence of i.i.d. random variables with zero mean and finite variance σ^2. This noise, which pushes the observed price of the security away from its value, comes from two main sources: First, it is the result of noise trading (Black (1986)) induced, e.g., by transitory liquidity needs of traders and investors and by errors in the analysis and interpretation of information. Second, it reflects the impact of the trading mechanism by which prices are set in the market. The latter includes, for example, the random arrival of buy and sell orders to the market (Mendelson (1982, 1985, 1986, 1987a)), the transitory state of dealers' inventory positions (cf. Amihud and Mendelson (1980)), the discreteness of stock prices (Gottlieb and Kalay (1985)), delayed price discovery (Cohen, Maier, Schwartz and Whitcomb (1986)) and price fluctuations between the bid and the ask. The bid-ask effect is obviously pronounced in the dealership market.

The coefficient g reflects the adjustment of transaction prices towards the security's value. In particular, $g = 0$ represents the extreme case of no price reaction to changes in value, and $0 < g < 1$ represents partial price adjustment. A unit adjustment coefficient ($g = 1$) represents full (though noisy) price adjustment, since then (3.1) reads

$$P_t = V_t + u_t,$$

i.e., (log) price is given by (log) value plus noise. When $g > 1$, we have *overshooting* or *over-reaction* of traders to new information.

---

[6] The trading mechanism has a paramount effect on the liquidity of the market, which in turn affects securities returns. Amihud and Mendelson (1986a, 1986b) have shown that increased liquidity has a significant positive effect on stock prices.

[7] Cf. Goldman and Beja (1979), Garbade and Silber (1979).

We follow the convention that the logarithms of security values $\{V_t\}$ follow a random walk process with drift, i.e.,

$$V_t = V_{t-1} + e_t + m, \qquad (3.2)$$

where m represents the expected daily value return and $\{e_t\}$ are i.i.d. random variables, independent of u_t, with zero mean and finite variance ν^2. We shall call the differences $(V_t - V_{t-1})$ the *value returns* of the security.

It is easy to demonstrate that (3.1) and (3.2) imply (by induction)

$$P_t = g \cdot \sum_{i=0}^{\infty} (1-g)^i V_{t-i} + \sum_{i=0}^{\infty} (1-g)^i u_{t-i}. \qquad (3.3)$$

The *observed* returns, defined by $R_t = P_t - P_{t-1}$, are then

$$R_t = m + g \sum_{i=0}^{\infty} (1-g)^i (e_{t-i} - u_{t-i-1}) + u_t. \qquad (3.4)$$

Using (3.4), we can now study the properties of the returns resulting from the price-adjustment equations. First, the observed return variance is given by

$$\text{Var}(R_t) = g^2 \sum_{i=0}^{\infty} (1-g)^{2i} (\nu^2 + \sigma^2) + \sigma^2$$

which, after rearrangement, yields

$$\text{Var}(R_t) = \frac{g}{2-g} \nu^2 + \frac{2}{2-g} \sigma^2. \qquad (3.5)$$

The first term on the right-hand-side of (3.5) represents the contribution of the value return variance, ν^2, to the observed return variance, and the second—the contribution of the noise. When $0 < g < 1$, only a fraction of the value return variance ν^2 is transmitted over to the observed returns due to the "smoothing" effect of the partial adjustment process. When $g = 1$, the full extent of the value return fluctuations is passed on to the observed returns. When $g > 1$ (the over-reaction case), the first term of (3.5) (and hence certainly the overall observed return variances) becomes greater than the value return variance, since then value fluctuations are amplified by traders' over-reaction.[8]

The second term in (3.5) represents the contribution of the noise to the observed return variance. This term is an increasing function of the noise variance σ^2 and of the adjustment coefficient g. Intuitively, since the price disturbance in one period is transmitted by the partial adjustment process to the following period's price, the larger the adjustment coefficient—the larger the transmission of the noise to the observed return variance (see (3.1)). In sum, both a high adjustment coefficient g and a high noise variance σ^2 contribute to increase the observed return variance for any given level of the value return variance ν^2.

Equation (3.5) suggests that the measured return variance $\text{Var}(R_t)$ is a biased estimator of the value return variance, ν^2. In the case $g = 1$, where there is full (though noisy) price adjustment, $\text{Var}(R_t) = \nu^2 + 2\sigma^2$, i.e., the observed return

---

[8] French and Roll (1986) show that the assumption of price over-reaction is consistent with their findings on the relationship between stock return variances over trading and non-trading periods. Our formulation of the variance, (3.5), is also consistent with their findings that the variance of two-day holiday returns is less than twice the variance of a normal trading day. While the value return variance ν^2 should increase linearly with time, the noise variance, σ^2, remains unchanged, hence the observed return variance increases less than proportionately in time.

variance is the sum of the value return variance and the contribution of the noise variance. This corresponds to Black's (1986) suggestion that the volatility of price is greater than the volatility of value.

More generally, by (3.5), $\text{Var}(R_t) \geq (\leq) \nu^2$ when $\sigma^2 \geq (\leq) \nu^2(1-g)$, respectively. Partial adjustment, i.e., $0 < g < 1$, induces a *downward* bias in the measurement of ν^2 whereas the noise variance biases it upwards. Thus, in general, the observed return variance may either over-estimate or under-estimate the value return variance, and the relationship between the two is an empirical question.

Next, we consider the first order *autocovariance* of the observed returns,

$$\text{Cov}(R_t, R_{t-1}) = \frac{g}{2-g}[(1-g)\nu^2 - \sigma^2], \tag{3.6}$$

and the first-order autocorrelation coefficient

$$\text{Corr}(R_t, R_{t-1}) = \frac{g(1-g)\nu^2 - g\sigma^2}{g\nu^2 + 2\sigma^2}. \tag{3.7}$$

The sign of the first order autocorrelation coefficient is determined by two factors: The adjustment process and the noise. The contribution of the noise to the first-order autocorrelation is always negative, whereas the contribution of the adjustment process is positive when $0 < g < 1$ (the case of partial price adjustment) and negative when $g > 1$ (the over-reaction case). By (3.7), the sign of the first-order autocorrelation is determined by the magnitude of the adjustment coefficient g and by the relationship between the variances σ^2 and ν^2. In the special case $g = 1$, the correlation is negative and equals the relative weight of the noise variance in the total return variance.

IV. The Opening and Closing Transactions on the NYSE

Our empirical comparison of price behavior under the two trading mechanisms uses the daily opening and closing prices of the 30 New York Stock Exchange stocks which constituted the Dow Jones Industrial list during the period February 8, 1982–February 18, 1983.[9] The active opening in these stocks closely resembles the clearing house trading procedure, whereas the closing transaction represents the dealership market regime. This comparison enables us to focus on the effects of the trading mechanism *per se*, holding almost all "other things equal": We are comparing the same securities traded on the same exchange during the same time period.

The opening prices on the NYSE are determined in the following manner. Before the opening, there is a flow of orders to buy or to sell a specified quantity of the stock at a limit price or at the market price. Trading is performed at a *single* price which clears the market, and which applies to all orders executed at the opening. Clearly, there is no difference between the buying and selling price, i.e., prices do not fluctuate between the bid and the ask, as is the case during the day. This mechanism closely resembles the clearing house model of trade. The

---

[9] The composition of the list was slightly different until August 30, 1982, when John Manville was replaced by American Express.

closing prices on the NYSE (like other transaction prices over the trading day) are determined by trading with market-makers and thus pertain to the dealership market mechanism.

The importance of the opening transaction is demonstrated by its share of the daily trading volume (see Table 1). The volume on the opening transaction constituted on average 5.6% of the total NYSE daily volume in the sampled stocks, and was on average 8.4 times greater than the volume on the closing transaction.

Our empirical study considers the open-to-open returns,

$$R_{o,t} = \log(P_{o,t} + D_t) - \log(P_{o,t-1})$$

where $P_{o,t}$ is the day-t opening price, adjusted for splits and stock dividends, and D_t is the cash dividend (if t is an ex-dividend day). Similarly, the close-to-close

Table 1

Opening Trading Volume vs. the Trading Volume at the Close, and Total Daily Volume

	Stock Symbol	Mean Opening Volume/ Mean Closing Volume	Mean Opening Volume/ Mean Daily Volume
1	AA	5.9	.041
2	AC	2.9	.066
3	ALD	5.2	.025
4	AMB	3.0	.069
5	AXP	11.2	.070
6	BS	1.6	.051
7	DD	6.9	.077
8	EK	10.4	.054
9	GE	15.9	.073
10	GF	3.8	.040
11	GM	13.6	.053
12	GT	6.0	.049
13	HR	9.9	.076
14	IBM	19.4	.025
15	IP	4.6	.052
16	MMM	9.5	.083
17	MRK	6.5	.081
18	N	4.5	.073
19	OI	1.4	.056
20	PG	3.9	.064
21	S	13.2	.046
22	SD	6.1	.067
23	T	22.1	.025
24	TX	11.5	.018
25	UK	5.4	.068
26	UTX	7.2	.061
27	WX	10.7	.084
28	X	10.4	.036
29	XON	12.4	.021
30	Z	5.9	.083
Mean		8.4	.056

returns are defined by

$$R_{c,t} = \log(P_{c,t} + D_t) - \log(P_{c,t-1})$$

where $P_{c,t}$ is the day-t closing price (similarly adjusted). Thus, we obtain a sequence of open-to-open returns $\{R_{o,t}\}$ and a sequence of close-to-close returns $\{R_{c,t}\}$ which cover the very same period of time. Clearly, information which changes the values of the examined stocks is equally reflected in both $R_{o,t}$ and $R_{c,t}$.[10] Thus, observed differences in the distributions of $R_{o,t}$ and $R_{c,t}$ may be attributed to the different trading procedures. These differences may also reflect investors' different order-placement strategies under the two trading regimes.

V. The Dispersion of Stock Returns

The stochastic nature of stock returns is affected by two major factors: (1) the arrival of new information, which induces shifts in stock values, and (2) noise transactions and the trading process which perturb the value returns and generate the observed returns. In terms of the price adjustment model of Section 3, the first factor is captured by the random variable e, and the second—by the adjustment coefficient g and by the random variable u. Studies of market microstructure suggest that the trading mechanism should affect the probability distribution—in particular, the dispersion—of observed returns. In this section we discuss the resulting hypotheses and test them empirically.

Theoretical studies and institutional knowledge suggest that market-makers stabilize prices and reduce the observed return variances.[11] The price stabilizing effect of the specialist in the context of his inventory-based pricing policy was suggested by Amihud and Mendelson (1980, 1982). When a change in the relative arrival intensity of buy or sell orders is not immediately perceived by the specialist, he absorbs part of the resulting imbalance into his stock inventory while partially inhibiting the market price change. Consequently, the bid-ask prices change gradually until the specialist, having perceived the change in value, shifts his whole inventory-based price vector, restoring his inventory position to its preferred level. As a result, a change in the stock's value is partially absorbed by the specialist's inventory, but this is only transitory in nature.[12]

Garbade and Silber (1979) and Goldman and Beja (1979) suggest that market-makers, observing the market buy and sell orders, try to estimate the stock value and set prices accordingly. They would attribute observed excess demand or supply partly to a change in value and partly to noise. They thus mitigate shifts in value by inducing partially offsetting changes in the transaction prices, resulting in reduced return variance.[13]

Institutional rules of conduct also induce price stabilization since NYSE

---

[10] Except for the small differences due to the first and last day, which should be negligible when the covered period is sufficiently long.

[11] The stabilizing role of the specialist was studied by West and Tinic (1971), Barnea (1974), Cohen, Maier, Schwartz and Whitcomb (1977), Schwartz and Whitcomb (1977a, 1977b) and Mendelson (1987a), and was surveyed by Stoll (1985).

[12] A similar pattern can be inferred from Ho and Stoll (1981).

[13] Garbade and Silber (1979) show that the optimal estimator of the equilibrium value from transaction prices, obtained by the Kalman Filtering algorithm, implies a partial-adjustment model.

specialists are explicitly required to act as "price stabilizers" and provide "price continuity". The specialist is expected to sell from his own account when prices go up and to buy into his own account when prices decline, so as to reduce price variations.[14] In fact, the surveillance systems of the NYSE continuously monitor compliance with these rules by the specialists. These price continuity requirements should induce a reduction in price dispersion.

Finally, in the daily transactions, traders can monitor prices continuously and infer from these prices on the impact of new information as soon as it arrives to the market. The market-maker's quotes signal current price information to all public traders (Mendelson (1987a)) and reduce errors of interpretation since traders have at their disposal the most recently available information set. In contrast, at the opening, there is likely to be a greater amount of information which has accumulated since the last transaction and has not yet been reflected in market prices. Although not necessarily so, there may be a relationship between the size of the error in determining the price and the amount of accumulated information, leading to greater price dispersion in the opening.

While the above arguments suggest that the return variance is higher in a clearing house compared to the dealership market, there are a few factors which operate in the opposite direction. In a dealership market, transactions fluctuate between the bid and ask prices—an effect which introduces noise in stock returns, and does not exist in the clearing house. In terms of our model, the greater the bid-ask spread, the greater the noise-induced variance σ^2 (see (3.5); this is further discussed in Section VIII). In addition, the batching of orders in the clearing house tends to reduce the resulting price variance (cf. Mendelson (1982, 1985, 1986, 1987a)). If these effects dominate, the return variance in a dealership market will be greater than in a clearing house. The comparison between the two mechanisms is thus an empirical question.

The results in Table 2 suggest that the trading mechanism has a distinct effect on the dispersion of stock returns: $\text{Var}(R_{o,t})$ exceeds $\text{Var}(R_{c,t})$. For 29 out of 30 stocks (Table 2, column 3) and, on average, the variance of the open-to-open returns is 20% greater than that of the close-to-close returns.[15] This suggests that traders who choose to transact at the opening are usually exposed to a higher variance than those who trade at the closing. Put differently, the return volatility is greater in the clearing house than in the dealership market.

Another measure of dispersion is the range of the return distribution. Comparing the extreme values of the observed returns in the opening and the closing, we found (Table 2, columns 4 and 5) that on average, the minimum of $R_{o,t}$ is 17% smaller than the minimum of $R_{c,t}$ and the maximum of $R_{o,t}$ is 14% greater than the maximum of $R_{c,t}$. This further shows that open-to-open returns have greater dispersion than close-to-close returns.[16]

Despite its greater return volatility, we observe that trading is heavy at the

---

[14] See *Report of the Committee to Study the Stock Allocation System*, The New York Stock Exchange, January 27, 1976, Exhibit A-5.

[15] We also ran a similar test on a much smaller sample, using mid-day to mid-day returns (at 12:00 and at 14:00 hours) instead of close-to-close returns, and obtained similar results.

[16] It can also be shown that for most stocks in our sample, the empirical distribution of opening returns is a median-preserving spread (Mendelson (1987b)) of the closing return distribution.

Table 2

Comparison of the Dispersion and Deviations from Normality for the Open-To-Open Returns, R_o, and Close-To-Close Returns, R_c

Stock (1)	Stock Symbol (2)	$Var(R_o)/Var(R_c)$ (3)	$Min(R_o)/Min(R_c)$ (4)	$Max(R_o)/Max(R_c)$ (5)	$CRT(R_o)/CRT(R_c)$ (6)	$SR(R_o)/SR(R_c)$ (7)
1	AA	1.25	1.85	1.05	2.80	1.24
2	AC	1.11	.94	.97	1.01	.91
3	ALD	1.23	1.20	1.31	1.61	1.12
4	AMB	1.43	1.26	1.71	3.57	1.25
5	AXP	1.20	1.02	1.29	1.28	1.08
6	BS	1.07	1.30	.82	1.06	1.00
7	DD	1.33	1.08	.99	.56	.89
8	EK	1.18	1.14	.96	.71	.94
9	GE	1.23	1.42	.99	.95	1.02
10	GF	1.30	1.07	1.40	2.45	1.10
11	GM	1.16	1.06	.90	.61	.89
12	GT	1.09	1.10	1.01	1.19	1.02
13	HR	0.80	.88	1.14	1.12	1.01
14	IBM	1.30	1.83	1.14	2.51	1.25
15	IP	1.32	1.08	1.02	1.19	.91
16	MMM	1.21	1.42	.99	1.12	1.04
17	MRK	1.21	1.31	1.20	1.39	1.13
18	N	1.16	1.23	1.09	1.32	1.07
19	OI	1.27	1.23	.93	.67	.94
20	PG	1.12	1.07	1.09	1.34	1.02
21	S	1.32	.90	1.26	1.26	.97
22	SD	1.10	1.06	1.11	.64	1.04
23	T	1.15	1.53	.93	.98	1.08
24	TX	1.22	.76	1.13	.60	.84
25	UK	1.15	1.34	1.05	1.43	1.09
26	UTX	1.22	1.04	1.44	9.63	1.12
27	WX	1.23	1.04	1.19	.75	1.19
28	X	1.00	.80	.93	.78	.93
29	XON	1.48	1.08	1.51	1.13	1.51
30	Z	1.13	.99	1.73	4.56	1.73
Mean		1.20	1.17	1.14	1.67	1.04
Std. Error		.02	.05	.04	.32	.07
Number of cases where ratio > 1		29	24	20	20	21

Notes: Var(R) is the variance of the returns; Min and Max are the minimum (always negative) and maximum (always positive) values of the returns in the sample.
CRT is the estimated curtosis; SR is the estimated studentized range of the distribution.

opening, implying that the latter has some advantages. A trader placing a limit order in the opening can expect an execution price which is *better* than his limit price, generating an expected surplus (cf. Mendelson (1982, 1985)), whereas daytime limit orders are executed at their limit price with no such surplus. Also, daytime traders may face a greater adverse selection problem due to the risk of their limit orders being executed by better-informed traders. This problem is mitigated at the opening by the batching of orders, which reduces the likelihood that an uninformed trader's order will determine the execution price. Finally, market traders in the opening can avoid the cost of the bid-ask spread, which may be viewed in part as the cost traders pay to reduce uncertainty. As a result, there are those who prefer to trade at the opening, whereas others opt for continuous daytime execution.

VI. Deviations from the Normal Distribution

The normality of stock returns is a widely applied hypothesis in the theory of investment finance. In his well-known study, Fama (1965, 1976) found that the distribution of daily stock returns deviates from normality. In Fama's study, returns were computed from closing prices and are similar to our $R_{c,t}$. Here, we shall compare the deviations of $R_{o,t}$ and $R_{c,t}$ from normality. If not for the effect of the trading mechanism, we should hardly expect differences in this respect.

Under the normality hypothesis, the third central moment of the return distribution, measured by the skewness coefficient, should be equal to zero. In our sample (as in Fama) the skewness was positive in most cases, both for R_o (29 out of 30 cases) and for R_c (27 out of 30 cases), and there was no appreciable difference in the magnitudes of the skewness coefficients between the open-to-open and close-to-close returns.

The coefficient of curtosis is also expected to be zero under the hypothesis of normal return distribution, whereas, in reality, daily stock returns have positive curtosis, indicating greater peakedness than under normality. While this was also the case for all the stocks in our sample, the curtosis of the open-to-open returns R_o was greater than that of the close-to-close returns R_c for 20 out of the 30 stocks in our sample, and on average the curtosis of R_o was 67% greater than the curtosis of R_c (Table 2, column 6).[17]

Finally, we compared the studentized range (SR, the sample range divided by the sample standard deviation) of the two distributions. As in Fama (1976), most cases exhibited statistically significant deviations from normality: The average studentized range of R_o was 7.27 and it deviated from normality (at the .9 fractile) in 29 out of 30 cases; the average studentized range of R_c was 7.02 and it deviated from normality in 24 out of 30 cases. In comparison, the studentized range of the opening returns is usually greater than the studentized range of the closing returns (21 out of 30 cases; see Table 2, column 7).

Looking at the evidence as a whole, the distribution of open-to-open returns has greater dispersion, fatter tails and more peakedness than the distribution of close-to-close returns. We thus find that trading at the opening is associated

---

[17] If we omit the extreme ratio of stock 26, we obtain that the average curtosis of R_o is 40% greater than that of R_c.

with greater deviations from normality than at the closing, suggesting that the method of trading affects the probability distribution of stock returns.

VII. Market Efficiency: Tests of Serial Correlation

Market efficiency implies that security prices fully reflect all available information at any point in time. Fama (1976) suggested that "if the market is efficient, there is no way to use any information available at time $t - 1$ as the basis for a correct assessment of an expected value of R_t which is different from the assumed constant equilibrium expected return, $E(R)$. Since part of the information available at $t - 1$ is the time series of past returns, there is no way to use the past returns as the basis for a correct assessment of the expected return from $t - 1$ to t which is other than $E(R)$" (p. 44). This gives rise to Fama's random walk form of the market efficiency hypothesis,

$$E[R_t | R_{t-1}] = E[R], \qquad (7.1)$$

that is, the expected conditional return is equal to the unconditional mean. Then, if past returns have no information content, the return autocorrelations should be zero. Testing this hypothesis using close-to-close returns, Fama (1965) found that the first-order autocorrelation coefficient was positive for most stocks in his sample, averaging 0.026, and that in eleven cases out of 30 the correlation coefficients were significantly different from zero (10 out of these 11 coefficients were positive).

The market efficiency hypothesis may be applied to market prices observed at any point in time under any trading mechanism. This calls for examining whether the opening price contains all the information available in the sequence of opening prices which preceded it, and whether the closing price reflects all the information contained in the sequence of preceding closing prices. The above form of the market efficiency hypothesis implies that the serial correlations of both open-to-open and close-to-close returns should be equal to zero.[18] On the other hand, if different trading mechanisms give rise to different price adjustment processes, we may observe a different serial autocorrelation pattern for the open-to-open and close-to-close returns.

To test the above hypothesis, we first replicated Fama's tests of first-order autocorrelation using both close-to-close and open-to-open returns. The closing return series (see Table 3) exhibit the same pattern as in Fama (1965). Most correlation coefficients are positive (24 out of 30), their average is .0464 (compared with Fama's .026), and a few are significantly different from zero. The open-to-open returns, however, exhibit an opposite pattern altogether: most of the autocorrelation coefficients of open-to-open returns are negative (23 out of 30), and their mean is $-.0635$; the few significant coefficients are all negative. By

---

[18] One may argue that there is more information available to traders at the closing than at the opening, since the former is preceded by a sequence of transactions whereas the latter follows a period of no trade. However, the returns utilized in our tests, R_o and R_c, are both computed over 24-hour periods. Hence, in both cases we test efficiency not with respect to information contained in the immediately preceding stock price, but with respect to information contained in the stock price observed 24 hours earlier.

Table 3
First-order Autocorrelation Coefficients for the Open-To-Open and Close-To-Close Returns

Stock	Open	Close
1	−.1078	.0403
2	.0104	.0672
3	−.0647	.0458
4	−.1448*	−.0066
5	−.0804	.0280
6	.0561	.0776
7	−.1924**	.0019
8	−.1924**	−.0921
9	−.1420*	−.0186
10	−.0072	.1423*
11	−.1172	.0070
12	−.0101	.0420
13	.0687	−.0006
14	−.1738**	−.0412
15	−.0670	.1381
16	−.0795	.0449
17	−.0819	.0500
18	−.0427	.0938
19	−.0415	.0827
20	−.0898	.0036
21	−.1055	.0497
22	.0180	.1121
23	−.0863	−.0086
24	−.0695	.0464
25	.1026	.1933**
26	−.0900	.0042
27	−.1112	.0085
28	.0878	.1992**
29	−.1588*	.0010
30	.0084	.0788
Mean	−.0635	.0464
Standard Error	.0146	.0119
No. of Negative	23	6

* = Significant at the 0.05 level.
** = Significant at the 0.01 level.

expression (3.7) for the autocorrelation coefficient, these results suggest that in the opening, $\sigma^2 > (1 - g)\nu^2$, whereas in the close the inequality is reversed. This is consistent with larger values of the noise variance σ^2 and of the adjustment coefficient g in the opening. Note that this implies that an overshooting effect (i.e., $g > 1$) is unlikely at the close but possible in the opening.[19]

As a further test of the random-walk form of the market efficiency hypothesis, we estimated the standard autoregressive moving-average process of the form

$$R_t = \alpha + \beta R_{t-1} + \epsilon_t + \theta \epsilon_{t-1}, \qquad (7.2)$$

[19] Hasbrouck and Schwartz (1986) suggested to estimate a T-period Market Efficiency Coefficient given by $\text{MEC}_T = \text{Var}(\sum R_t)/T \cdot \text{Var}(R_t)$, similar to French and Roll (1986). MEC_T deviates from unity when the return autocorrelation is nonzero. We estimated MEC_T for $T = 1, 2, 3, 4$, and obtained that they were greater than 1 for R_c and smaller than 1 for R_o, consistent with our other findings.

where $\{\epsilon_t\}$ are i.i.d. random variables with zero mean. This ARMA (1, 1) model was estimated for our opening and closing return series. By (7.1), we should obtain $\beta = \theta = 0$.

The results in Table 4 show significant violations of the hypothesis $\beta = \theta = 0$ for the open-to-open returns, whereas the results for the close-to-close return series were mostly insignificant.[20] Twenty-five of the open-to-open return series were invertible, and 12 of them had autoregressive *and* moving average coefficients that were significantly different from zero (three additional ones were marginal). The dominant pattern was a negative autoregressive coefficient β and a positive moving average coefficient θ (in 11 out of the 12 significant series and 18 out of the 25 series estimated). On average, $\beta = -.400$ and $\theta = .330$.

As for the close-to-close return series, five produced significant estimates and one was marginal. Out of these six, four followed the same pattern as the open-to-open series; but in general, the pattern of the estimated coefficients was mixed.

Our results suggest that simple autocorrelation tests may be insufficient to detect market inefficiencies, since they disguise the pattern given by equation (7.2). For opening returns, the results of the ARMA (1, 1) model imply more significant deviations from the random-walk form of the market efficiency hypothesis than those obtained under serial correlation tests. The autocorrelation of the ARMA (1, 1) process (7.2) is given by

$$\text{Corr}(R_t, R_{t-1}) = \frac{(1 + \beta\theta)(\beta + \theta)}{1 + \theta^2 + 2\beta\theta}$$

(see Judge et al. (1980), p. 172). When $\beta \approx -\theta$, as for most stocks in our sample (the mean value of β in the opening is $-.4$, and that of θ is .33), the correlation coefficients will be small even though $|\beta|$ and $|\theta|$ themselves are relatively high. Thus, simple autocorrelation tests may not detect a pattern rejecting the random-walk hypothesis when one exists.

Finally, we still observed that the residual noise in R_o was greater than that of R_c, even after having accounted for the variance explained by past returns, and despite the better fit of the open-to-open return series (see last three columns of Table 4). It should be noted that unlike the comparison of the raw return variances in Table 2, here we are comparing only the variances of the unexpected residual disturbances. These differences between the residual variances represent more forcefully the difference in the return volatility associated with the clearing house as compared to the dealership market.

In sum, Table 4 reveals a number of results:

1. There are numerous violations of the random-walk form of the market efficiency hypothesis, primarily at the opening, with many of the open-to-open return series being well-explained by the ARMA (1, 1) model.
2. The pattern of first-order serial correlation is generally negative in the opening and positive in the closing.

---

[20] Smidt (1979) tested market efficiency using intraday data and accounting explicitly for the spread. His results reject the weak-form market efficiency hypothesis. An autoregressive-moving-average test using intraday data was carried out by Hasbrouck and Ho (1986). Their results reject the hypothesis that price behaves as a random walk plus bid/ask spread and affirm the existence of a lagged adjustment effect.

3. The residual variance of the open-to-open returns is greater than that of the close-to-close returns, reflecting less noise in the dealership market than in the clearing house.

The trading mechanism thus has a distinct impact on the stochastic process governing the behavior of observed returns.

VIII. The Effect of the Bid-Ask Spread

Our analysis provides an insight into the effect of the bid-ask spread on the variance and covariance of closing stock returns. Assume that the noise in the closing price is due to the fluctuations between the bid and the ask, with a partial-adjustment equation of the form

$$P_t^* = P_{t-1} + g \cdot (V_t - P_{t-1}), \tag{8.1}$$

where P_t^* denotes the (log) price as estimated by market participants and P_t is the actually observed (log) price. Denote the relative (percentage) spread by $2s$, and assume that the observed price satisfies

$$P_t = P_t^* + \epsilon_t, \tag{8.2}$$

where

$$\epsilon_t = \begin{cases} \log(1+s) & \text{w.p. } \tfrac{1}{2} \\ \log(1-s) & \text{w.p. } \tfrac{1}{2} \end{cases}$$

(see Roll (1984)). Using a first-order approximation (as in Roll (1984)), we obtain (3.1) with[21]

$$u = \begin{cases} +s & \text{w.p. } \tfrac{1}{2} \\ -s & \text{w.p. } \tfrac{1}{2} \end{cases}$$

and $\sigma^2 = s^2$. By equation (3.6) we obtain

$$s = \sqrt{(1 - 2/g)\text{Cov}(R_t, R_{t-1}) + (1 - g)\nu^2} \tag{8.4}$$

which, for $g = 1$ (i.e., full price adjustment) gives Roll's (1984) result[22]

$$s = \sqrt{-\text{Cov}(R_t, R_{t-1})}. \tag{8.5}$$

Roll's (1984) analysis implies that $\text{Cov}(R_t, R_{t-1})$ must be *negative* for all stocks. However, his findings (as well as our own results) cast doubt on the validity of the assumption that $g = 1$. Contrary to (8.5), the first-order autocorrelations between closing returns are predominantly positive in our sample, suggesting that $0 < g < 1$ for close-to-close returns. Further, Roll (1984) pointed out that
  (i) the magnitudes of the spreads implied by the estimated covariances are less than reasonable values of the spread;
  (ii) the spreads implied from weekly covariances are higher and more reasonable than those estimated from daily covariances.

Both of these observations are consistent with the hypothesis that in model

---
[21] As pointed out earlier, there may be additional sources of noise which can simply be added to u.
[22] See also Hawawini (1978), Cohen, Maier, Schwartz and Whitcomb (1980).

Table 4
Results of ARMA (1, 1) Estimation for Open-To-Open and Close-To-Close Returns
(t-values are in parentheses)
— Indicates that the Process is non-invertible

Stock Number (1)	Open AR(1) (2)	Open MA(1) (3)	Close AR(1) (4)	Close MA(1) (5)	Residual Variance (×10000) Open (6)	Residual Variance (×10000) Close (7)	Variance Ratio (6)/(7) (8)
1	-.682 (2.56)	.586 (1.97)	.391 (.48)	-.349 (.42)	6.716	5.439	1.235
2	—	—	.881 (32.39)	-.959 (45.28)		2.834	
3	-.857 (6.91)	.802 (5.49)	.445 (.76)	-.375 (.62)	5.239	4.285	1.223
4	.405 (1.36)	-.553 (2.04)	—	—	2.993		
5	-.660 (2.45)	.570 (1.94)	.462 (.56)	-.418 (.50)	5.937	4.991	1.190
6	.200 (.57)	-.134 (.37)	.690 (2.87)	-.585 (2.17)	5.034	4.726	1.065
7	-.864 (9.95)	.742 (6.39)	—	—	4.254		
8	-.388 (1.45)	.198 (.70)	-.192 (.45)	.096 (.22)	3.381	2.936	1.152
9	-.761 (4.98)	.630 (3.45)	-.684 (3.42)	.634 (2.94)	2.697	2.231	1.209
10	—	—	.259 (.64)	-.117 (.28)		2.306	
11	-.460 (1.47)	.340 (1.01)	—	—	4.248		
12	—	—	-.833 (2.57)	.820 (2.42)		5.019	
13	.280 (.43)	-.200 (.30)	-.166 (.049)	.164 (.048)	27.087	34.006	0.800
14	-.147 (.46)	-.028 (.09)	—	—	2.890		

Trading Mechanisms and Stock Returns

15	-.477 (1.26)	.404 (1.02)	.019 (.044)	.123 (.283)	4.795	3.599	1.332
16	-.713 (3.13)	.620 (2.44)	—	—	3.381	—	1.198
17	-.570 (1.72)	.483 (1.37)	.155 (.14)	-.100 (.09)	2.883	2.406	1.142
18	-.875 (9.50)	.805 (7.05)	.485 (1.05)	-.391 (0.81)	8.227	7.201	1.273
19	-.496 (.60)	.458 (.54)	.056 (.08)	.027 (.038)	3.623	2.847	1.106
20	-.636 (2.68)	.546 (2.10)	-.915 (9.98)	.876 (7.97)	2.144	1.938	1.286
21	-.860 (9.17)	.770 (6.51)	-.032 (.027)	0.082 (.069)	5.510	4.284	1.125
22	.800 (5.52)	-.837 (6.16)	-.395 (1.46)	.510 (1.99)	6.711	5.965	
23	-.945 (17.4)	.905 (12.68)	—	—	1.874		
24	—	—	.105 (.14)	-.060 (.08)		2.080	1.150
25	.065 (.20)	.038 (.12)	.257 (.83)	-.066 (.21)	3.086	2.684	1.211
26	-.350 (.65)	.260 (.47)	.427 (.20)	-.407 (.18)	4.805	3.968	
27	-.675 (4.17)	.573 (3.13)	—	—	5.545		1.028
28	.043 (.13)	.047 (.14)	-.140 (.57)	.374 (1.62)	4.921	4.789	
29	-.372 (1.13)	.220 (.64)	—	—	2.443		
30	—	—	.222 (.31)	-.143 (.20)	—	5.212	
Mean	-.400	.330	.068	-.012	4.306*	3.892*	1.183
Standard Error	.092	.087	.100	.097			.020
No. of Obs.	25	25	22	22	25*	22*	16*
No. Positive	6	20	14	10			

* Excluding stock 13 (HR), which is an outlier.

(8.1), $0 < g < 1$ for close-to-close returns. Then, Roll's finding (i) is consistent with the fact that (8.4) implies $-\text{Cov}(R_t, R_{t-1}) < s^2$, and hence use of the return covariances in (8.5) underestimates the spread. The second finding is consistent with the fact that the effective value of the adjustment coefficient g should tend to unity as the return-measurement interval increases. This implies that the five-day return covariance (and hence also the resulting spread estimate) should be greater (in absolute value) than the corresponding single-day estimate.

The bid-ask spread effect should also be considered when estimating the return variance. Under (8.3), equation (3.5) reads

$$\text{Var}(R_t) = \frac{g}{2-g} \nu^2 + \frac{2}{2-g} s^2, \qquad (8.6)$$

implying that the larger the spread, the larger the measured return variance for any given level of the value return variance ν^2. This suggests a positive cross-sectional relationship between the measured closing return variance and the spread. We thus estimated the regression equation

$$\text{Var}(R_{c,j}) = 0.000279 + 0.000986 \, s_j,$$
$$(t=) \qquad\qquad\qquad (4.01)$$

where $\text{Var}(R_{c,j})$ is the close-to-close return variance for stock j and s_j is the average spread of stock j over our sample period (relative to its price). The result supports the hypothesis that the greater the spread, the greater the close-to-close return variance. Further, since the opening price has no spread, we should also expect a negative relationship between the spread and the ratio of the open-to-open return variance to the close-to-close return variance. Indeed, we obtained the following relationship

$$\frac{\text{Var}(R_{o,j})}{\text{Var}(R_{c,j})} = 1.29 - 13.62 \, s_j,$$

$$(t=) \qquad\qquad (3.68)$$

thus supporting our hypothesis.

Equation (8.6) suggests a spread effect whereby the measured return variance $\text{Var}(R_t)$ is a biased estimator of the value return variance, ν^2. This bias is an increasing function of the spread, and its overall impact also depends on the adjustment coefficient g (see Section 3). Given the empirical regularity of a negative relation between the bid-ask spread and both firm size and stock price (cf. Stoll and Whaley (1983)), the upward bias in the computed return variance due to the spread is more severe for small firms and for low-priced stocks. This relationship between the bid-ask spread and the bias in the estimate of the value return variance complements the analysis of Blume and Stambaugh (1983) on biases in computed mean returns due to the spread, which are more severe in small firms.

The above analysis can be applied to the use of estimated return variances in the pricing of options. The standard Black-Scholes option pricing model assumes that stock prices evolve as a continuous diffusion process (or a discrete random walk), where the (value) return variance increases linearly with time. In practical applications, the measured return variance of the underlying stock is often used as an estimator of the value return variance to calculate the option price. However, by (8.6) (or (3.5)) it is clear that this practice may be erroneous. This may explain the systematic difference found between measured return variances and the variances implied from option prices.[23]

The positive effect of the bid-ask spread on the observed return variance may explain part of the increase in the measured return variance following stock splits, documented by Ohlson and Penman (1985), if the percentage bid-ask spread increases when the stock price decreases. This is also consistent with Ohlson and Penman's (1985) finding that it is the actual split rather than the split announcement which affects volatility.

We also suggest that caution is called for when observed return variances are used in empirical studies in finance. For example, in "event studies", the objective is to examine the value effects of an event, i.e., the changes in V_t. While the appropriate variance for testing the related hypotheses is the value return variance ν^2, the variance actually used is $\text{Var}(R_t)$, which is quite different.

IX. Conclusion

This paper examines the effects of two prevalent trading mechanisms—the periodic clearing house and the continuous dealership market—on the behavior of stock returns. The empirical investigation employed price data from the opening and closing transactions in active NYSE stocks, utilizing the fact that each of these transaction series is generated by a different trading mechanism. The clearing house mechanism was represented by the opening transaction, whereas the closing transaction represented the dealership market. This enabled us to compare the effects of the trading mechanism on the behavior of the returns on the same stocks in the same market during the same time period. We interpreted the results using a model where prices follow a lagged partial-adjustment process with noise.

Our results show that the trading mechanism has a significant effect on a number of characteristics of stock returns. First, the distribution of open-to-open returns has greater variance than that of close-to-close returns. And while both show deviations from normality, the opening return distribution exhibits greater peakedness and fatter tails than that of the closing returns. Second, the serial correlation pattern is quite different in the two return series. Further, employing an ARMA (1, 1) model we find that in the opening, returns exhibit higher residual noise and stronger dependence on past returns, reflecting stronger deviations

---

[23] A possible test of our hypothesis is to relate the difference between the measured return variance and the variance implied from the option price with the underlying stock's bid-ask spread and its estimated adjustment coefficient. Note that since the percentage spread usually decreases when stock prices increase, the noise may be decreasing in the stock price. This was observed by Black (1976) and in more recent studies of option pricing.

from the random-walk form of the market efficiency hypothesis.[24] Finally, we analyze the effects of the bid-ask spread and the adjustment process on the estimated serial covariance and variance of stock returns. We show that the practice of estimating the parameters of the value return distribution using observed returns can produce misleading results.

Taken as a whole, the evidence suggests that trading at the opening exposes traders to a greater variance than in the close, reflecting the differences between the trading mechanisms. Both the nature of lagged price adjustment and the level of transitory noise are different. Thus, when considering the implications of changing the method of trading in a market, the effects on return behavior should not be overlooked.

[24] It is interesting to entertain the thought of how Finance textbooks would have treated the issue of market efficiency had the first empirical studies been carried out using open-to-open rather than close-to-close returns.

REFERENCES

Amihud, Yakov and Haim Mendelson, "Dealership Market: Market-Making with Inventory." *Journal of Financial Economics* 8 (March 1980), 31–53.

———, "Asset Price Behavior in a Dealership Market." *Financial Analysts Journal* 38 (May/June 1982), 50–59.

———, "An Integrated Computerized Trading System." In Y. Amihud, T. Ho and R. Schwartz (eds.), *Market Making and the Changing Structure of the Securities Industry.* Lexington: 1985, 217–236.

———, "Asset Pricing and the Bid-Ask Spread." *Journal of Financial Economics* 17 (1986), 223–249.

———, "Liquidity and Stock Returns." *Financial Analysts Journal* 42 (May/June 1986), 43–48.

Barnea, Amir, "Performance Evaluation of New York Stock Exchange Specialists." *Journal of Financial and Quantitative Analysis* (September 1974), 511–535.

Black, Fischer, "Studies of Stock Price Volatility Changes." *Proceedings of the 1976 Meetings of The American Statistical Association,* Business and Economics Statistics Section. Washington, DC: American Statistical Association, 1976, 177–181.

Black, Fischer, "Noise." *Journal of Finance* 41 (July 1986), 529–543.

Blume, Marshall E. and Robert F. Stambaugh, "Biases in Computing Returns: An Application to the Size Effect." *Journal of Financial Economics* 12 (1983), 387–404.

Cohen, Kalman, Steven Maier, Robert Schwartz and David Whitcomb, "On the Existence of Serial Correlation in an Efficient Securities Market." *TIMS Studies in the Management Science* 11 (1979), 151–168.

———, "The Impact of Designated Market Makers on Security Prices." *Journal of Banking and Finance* 1 (1977), 219–247.

———, *The Microstructure of Securities Markets.* Englewood Cliffs, NJ: Prentice Hall, 1986.

Cohen, Kalman, Gabriel Hawawini, Steven Maier, Robert Schwartz and David Whitcomb, "Implications of Microstructure Theory for Empirical Research on Stock Price Behavior." *Journal of Finance* 35 (May 1980), 249–257.

Fama, Eugene F., "The Behavior of Stock Market Prices." *Journal of Business* 38 (January 1965), 34–105.

———, *Foundations in Finance.* New York: Basic Books, 1976.

French, Kenneth R. and Richard Roll, "Stock Return Variances: The Arrival of Information and the Reaction of Traders." *Journal of Financial Economics* 17 (1986), 5–26.

Garbade, Kenneth D. and Zvi Lieber, "On the Independence of Transactions on the New York Stock Exchange." *Journal of Banking and Finance* 1 (1977), 151–172.

Garbade, Kenneth D. and William Silber, "Structural Organization of Secondary Markets: Clearing Frequency, Dealer Activity and Liquidity Risk." *Journal of Finance* 34 (June 1979), 577–593.

Goldman, Barry M. and Avraham Beja, "Market Prices vs. Equilibrium Prices: Returns' Variance, Serial Correlation and the Role of the Specialist." *Journal of Finance* 34 (June 1979), 595–607.

Hasbrouck, Joel and Thomas S. Y. Ho, "Intraday Stock Returns: Empirical Evidence of Lagged Adjustment." Mimeograph, 1986.
Hasbrouck, Joel and Robert A. Schwartz, "The Efficiency of Stock Exchange and Over-the-Counter Markets." Mimeograph, 1986.
Hawawini, Gabriel, "A Note on Temporal Aggregation and Serial Correlation." *Economics Letters 1* (1978), 237–242.
Ho, Thomas, Robert A. Schwartz and David K. Whitcomb, *A Comparative Analysis of Alternative Security Market Trading Arrangements.* (Volumes I and II), New York Stock Exchange, 1981.
———, "The Trading Decision and Market Clearing under Transaction Price Uncertainty." *Journal of Finance* 40 (March 1985), 21–42.
Ho, Thomas and Hans Stoll, "Optimal Dealer Pricing Under Transaction and Return Uncertainty." *Journal of Financial Economics* 9 (1981), 47–73.
Jarecki, H. G., "Bullion Dealing, Commodity Exchange Trading and the London Gold Fixing: Three Forms of Commodity Auctions:" In Y. Amihud (ed.), *Bidding and Auctioning for Procurement and Allocation.* New York: New York University Press, 1976.
Judge, George G., William E. Griffiths, R. Carter Hill and Tsoung-Chao Lee, *The Theory and Practice of Econometrics.* New York: John Wiley and Sons, 1980.
Mendelson, Haim, "Market Behavior in a Clearing House." *Econometrica* 50 (November 1982), 1505–1524.
———, "Random Competitive Exchange: Price Distributions and Gains from Trade." *Journal of Economic Theory* 37 (1985), 254–280.
———, "Exchange with Random Quantities and Discrete Feasible Prices." Working Paper, Graduate School of Management, University of Rochester, 1986.
———, "Consolidation, Fragmentation and Market Performance." *Journal of Financial and Quantitative Analysis* (forthcoming), 1987a.
———, "Quantile-Preserving Spread." *Journal of Economic Theory* (forthcoming), 1987b.
Ohlson, James and Stephen H. Penman, "Volatility Increases Subsequent to Stock Splits, An Empirical Aberration." *Journal of Financial Economics* 14 (1985), 251–266.
Roll, Richard, "A Simple Implicit Measure of the Bid/Ask Spread in an Efficient Market." *Journal of Finance* 39 (September 1984), 1127–1139.
Schwartz, Robert A. and David K. Whitcomb, "Evidence on the Presence and Causes of Serial Correlation in Market Model Residuals." *Journal of Financial and Quantitative Analysis* (June 1977a), 291–313.
———, "The Time-Variance Relationship: Evidence on Autocorrelation in Common Stock Returns." *Journal of Finance* (March 1977b), 41–55.
Schreiber, Paul S. and Robert A. Schwartz, "Price Discovery in Securities Markets." *Journal of Portfolio Management* (Summer 1986), 43–48.
Smidt, Symour, "Continuous vs. Intermittent Trading on Auction Markets." *Journal of Financial and Quantitative Analysis* (November 1979), 837–866.
Smith, Vernon L., "Bidding and Auctioning Institutions: Experimental Results." In Y. Amihud (ed.), *Bidding and Auctioning for Procurement and Allocation.* New York: New York University Press, 1976.
Spray, D. E., *The Principal Stock Exchanges of the World: Their Operation, Structure and Development.* Washington, D.C.: International Economic Publishers, Inc., 1964.
Stoll, Hans R., "Alternative Views of Market Making." In Y. Amihud, T. Ho and R. Schwartz (eds.), *Market Making and the Changing Structure of the Securities Industry.* (Lexington-Heath), 1985.
Stoll, Hans R. and Robert E. Whaley, "Transaction Costs and the Small Firm Effect." *Journal of Financial Economics* 12 (1983), 57–59.
West, Richard and Seha Tinic, *The Economics of the Stock Market.* (New York: Praeger Publishers), 1971.
Whitcomb, David K., "An International Comparison of Stock Exchange Trading Structures." In Y. Amihud, T. Ho and R. Schwartz (ed.), *Market Making and the Changing Structure of the Securities Industry.* (Lexington-Heath), 1985, 237–255.

B
Dealer Versus Auction Markets

The Journal of FINANCE

MARKETABILITY OF COMMON STOCKS IN CANADA AND THE U.S.A.: A COMPARISON OF AGENT VERSUS DEALER DOMINATED MARKETS

SEHA M. TINIC AND RICHARD R. WEST*

I. INTRODUCTION

THIS PAPER presents the results of an analysis of the price of marketability services on the Toronto Stock Exchange (TSE) and compares them with previously published findings concerning the price of marketability on the New York Stock Exchange (NYSE) and the U.S. over-the-counter market (OTC). More specifically, the paper examines the determinants of bid-ask spreads on the TSE and their behavior relative to spreads in the NYSE and OTC markets.

In the next section, we present some background concerning the methods of market making employed in the TSE, NYSE and OTC and discuss several tentative, working hypotheses concerning the determinants of bid-ask spreads. In Section III, the discussion turns to the empirical analysis of spreads on the TSE. This is followed in Section IV by a comparison of previously published results from the NYSE and OTC markets. Finally, in Section V some implications of the analysis are discussed.

In brief, we will argue that the comparative results support the conclusion that the price of marketability services is higher in the TSE than in either the NYSE or OTC market. In this context, the word "higher" does not simply imply that spreads on the TSE are absolutely wider, but rather that they are wider holding factors that influence spreads constant from market to market.

The question of the relative merits of various methods of organizing trading in common stocks is receiving considerable attention in the U.S. at the present time and promises to be a topic of debate for some time to come.[1] Unfortunately, however, much of the discussion lacks rigor because of the paucity of "hard" empirical finding concerning the relative merits of various possible methods of organizing trading. Comparative analysis of the type provided in

---

* Professor of Managerial Economics and Management Science, University of Alberta and Dean and Professor of Finance, University of Oregon, respectively. The authors would like to acknowledge their gratitude to Seymour Smidt who read an earlier draft of this paper and made a number of valuable suggestions.

1. See Martin (1971).

this paper would appear to represent a stem in the direction of redressing this deficiency. Moreover, when it involves stock markets in more than one nation, such analysis would also seem to be relevant to the recently stimulated discussion of the benefits of international diversification of portfolios.[2] Thus far, this discussion has taken place within a zero transactions cost context. In point of fact, however, transactions costs are positive in any stock market. Furthermore, they often differ from market to market and country to country. If we are to go beyond the point of simply applying standard portfolio theory to the analysis of investment possibilities from several nations, the nature of these differences must be understood.

From a slightly narrower perspective, the comparative analysis of the TSE, NYSE, and OTC seems particularly relevant at this time. In Canada there is a growing concern over the degree of foreign investment in the economy and the extent to which Canadians invest in securities outside the country.[3] In discussions of these two issues one of the most widely cited reasons for Canadian purchases of U.S. securities is the superior marketability of stocks traded in the New York market.[4] To some extent, of course, this argument boils down to little more than an assertion that it is easier to take or change positions in securities which are traded in a larger marketplace. The question remains, however, whether given its relative size, the Canadian market, as reflected in the TSE, provides marketability services on terms as efficient as those provided in the United States.

II. Background and Theory

In this section, we present some background materials concerning the structural characteristics of the TSE, NYSE, and OTC and discuss the basic theory of the determinants of the price of marketability services.

A. Structural Characteristics of the Markets Studied

Although the basic purposes and functions of the TSE, NYSE, and OTC are similar, the detailed practices and procedures of these three markets vary greatly. For the purposes at hand, the most important differences relate to the way in which the dealership function is (or is not) organized. It is the dealer, after all, who is the primary supplier of marketability services to traders who want to buy or sell without delay; hence, the way the dealership function is organized (or not organized) has much to do with the determination of the price of marketability services.

In the preceding paragraph, we used the parenthetical phrase "or not organized" because trading on the TSE is structured in such a way that dealer services are not encouraged to be provided by exchange members, except as they are needed to meet the trading needs of buyers and sellers who submit odd-lot orders. Put somewhat differently, the TSE discourages its members from being active participants in the market for their own accounts, preferring instead to have them make an agency market. Members other than those who

---

2. See Grubel (1968) and Levy and Sarnat (1970).
3. Baxter (1972), pp. 13-15.
4. *Ibid.*

are designated "registered traders" are explicitly prohibited from trading for their own accounts except through the channels provided for non-members, i.e., except by entering orders in the same way as members of the trading public. Registered traders (RTs), in contrast, have the privilege of trading on the floor for firm accounts in which they participate in the profits. Moreover, according to some interpretations, RTs have an obligation to "make a market" in the stocks in which they are registered. The by-laws on trading note, for example, that "the RT category was established in order to restrict active trading for non-client accounts by members or persons employed on the floor to a limited number of supervised, experienced and well financed persons who in return would accept certain responsibilities which would increase liquidity, add stability and generally improve the market for listed stocks in Toronto."[5] The *Canadian Securities Course* is even more explicit concerning the nature of the RT's "responsibilities." It states unequivocally that "if there is a lack of either bids or offers for board (round) lots by the public, he is expected to provide a bid or an offer, whichever is needed, at a price reasonably related to the last trade."[6] The TSE's floor trader's manual, on the other hand, states only that "in order to have a reasonable board lot market quoted in each security, the Floor Procedure Committee *may from time to time* prescribe obligations in that regard of each RT."[7] Recent communications with the TSE concerning the precise meaning of this statement have revealed that the Floor Procedure Committee's activities deal primarily with establishing rules for the responsibilities of RTs at the opening of each day's trading session. Beyond this, the RT's only major, well defined responsibility appears to be that of providing odd-lot bids and offers at premiums or discounts no greater than those outlined by the Board of Governors and the Floor Procedure Committee. In short, the TSE's method of market making focuses primarily on the development of an agency marketplace in which, for the most part, public buyers and sellers trade with each other and RTs act as odd-lot dealers.

In contrast to the RTs, the dealers on the NYSE, commonly referred to as specialists, are expressly charged with performing a continuing market-making function for round lot trades.[8] In return for a virtual monopoly in the trading done on the exchange in a given stock, the specialists are expected to play a fairly active role in the trading process. It is their function to keep trading orderly and to prevent "undue" fluctuations in price, i.e., to maintain price continuity. The notion of an agency market, in which ultimate buyers and sellers trade primarily with each other and the intermediary acts largely in the role of a central broker, is contrary to the organizational design of the NYSE. To be sure, the specialist does act as a central broker; but his more important function is that of acting as a dealer.

Recently, there has been a good deal of attention devoted to the question of whether NYSE specialists do an adequate job of meeting their responsi-

---

5. TSE (1972), p. 9.
6. The Canadian Securities Course (1969), pp. 242-3.
7. TSE (1972), p. 10.
8. For a more full blown discussion of the specialist's function see SEC (1962), Part 2, especially Chapters 5 and 6.

bilities.[9] In addition, there has been some talk about whether they should even be expected to meet these responsibilities as the market becomes more oriented to the trading done by institutional investors.[10] The fact remains, however, that the NYSE's basic approach to market making has been and continues to be more "activist" and dealer oriented than the TSE's.

Whereas in the TSE many members are prohibited from taking an active part in the market making process and in the NYSE certain members are required to take an active part, the degree of dealer participation in the OTC market is determined largely on the basis of individual choice.[11] It is not necessary for those who desire to perform the dealership function in the OTC market to purchase a seat or in some analogous way obtain formal entry to the trading process.[12]

Because of the comparative absence of formal constraints, the strength of the market in a particular stock is subject to considerable variation over time. If a large number of firms are actively making a two-way market in a stock, i.e., are providing firm bid and ask quotations for "reasonable" sized orders, buyers and sellers have little difficulty in taking or disposing of their positions. On the other hand, if firms are backing away from the market, either by widening their bid and ask spreads or reducing their willingness to take positions, or both, investors find it difficult to do business on reasonable terms. Indeed, when firms back completely away, as is sometimes the case if the market is characterized by extreme uncertainty, investors are faced with a situation in which orders either are refused outright or are accepted only on the basis that they will be transacted if and when offsetting orders appear.

The freedom to enter the market and compete does, however, encourage firms to "stand on their markets" and to provide a reasonable amount of dealer services. Dealers that habitually back away from the market or take a haphazard approach to making markets discover that they cannot receive the flow of inquiries necessary to sustain a profitable OTC business.

B. *The Theory of Pricing Liquidity Services: A Summary*

Earlier studies of the pricing of marketability services by Demsetz (1968), NYSE (1968), Tinic (1972), and Tinic and West (1972) have utilized the spread between a dealer's bid and ask prices as an operational measure of the price of dealer services in a stock market—that is, as an estimate of an issue's marketability.[13] In the absence of a highly organized market-making

---

9. See Smidt (1971).
10. West and Tinic (1971), especially Chapter 9.
11. For more on the OTC market see Tinic and West (1972).
12. To some degree the development of NASDAQ is leading to an increase in the obligations assumed by OTC dealers. It is still too early, however, to know precisely how NASDAQ will influence dealer behavior in the long run.
13. For other criteria see Smidt (1971). In some secondary markets, the publication of a bid or offer is not intended to indicate the price at which transactions are likely to take place but only to advertise the existence of a potential buyer or seller. Publication of a bid or offer in those markets allows persons who are interested in completing an immediate transaction to contact the person who has published the bid or offer and to begin a process of negotiation that leads to a final transaction. In such cases, the spread between the best bid and the best offer at any particular moment in time may significantly overestimate the actual price of immediacy. To avoid this bias,

function in the TSE, however, bid and ask prices are not necessarily those quoted by a dealer: the reported prices in the TSE simply represent the highest bid and the lowest ask prices that are available at any point in time; it is quite possible that at any given moment, neither will have originated from the floor of the Exchange. Frequently, perhaps even typically, these quotations represent the best outstanding limit buy and sell tenders submitted by non-member traders. Hence, unlike the bid-ask spreads that are quoted in the NYSE or OTC, spreads in TSE need not measure the gross margin earned by market-makers. Nevertheless, they do provide an estimate of the value of "immediacy" to traders who want to execute transactions without delay, and therefore, constitute a measure of the marketability of various TSE listed stocks.

In his seminal article on the determinants of the price of marketability, Demsetz argued that the time rate of transactions is the most important factor influencing the width of the bid-ask spread. According to Demsetz, the level of the limit orders submitted by traders reflects their anticipations concerning the expected waiting time associated with having an order executed. But waiting time is itself a function of the time rate of transactions: as the time rate of transactions increases, waiting time decreases. Thus, as Demsetz stated, "the greater the frequency of transacting, the lower will be the cost of waiting in a trading queue of specified length and therefore the lower will be the spreads that traders are willing to submit to pre-empt positions in the trading queue."[14]

The level of trading activity in a stock can be measured in a variety of ways. We believe, however, that it is necessary to develop measures which take account of both the average volume of transactions over some relevant trading interval and the continuity of trading from interval to interval. Measures of the average volume serve as an excellent surrogate for the speed with which an intra-interval trading queue of a given length can be serviced; measures of continuity provide an estimate of the frequency with which these queues are organized. Particularly in the case of "speculative" issues which, on the average, experience active markets, a measure of trading continuity can help explain the effects of relatively clustered trading patterns on the bid-ask spread. Moreover, for traders who may submit limit orders on both sides of the market and act as dealers, the effect of trading continuity on bid-ask spreads reflects the costs of carrying positions for prolonged periods of time.

Next to the time rate of transactions, the single most important factor influencing the width of bid-ask spreads is the price level of the stock in question. Spreads tend to increase with the level of stock prices so that the cost of transacting, per dollar exchanged, is equalized. If this were not the case, those who submit limit orders would find it "profitable to narrow spreads on those securities for which spread per dollar exchanged is larger."[15]

---

the actual price of immediacy would have to be estimated on the basis of a record of price changes between consecutive transactions. This issue is especially relevant for the bid-ask spreads that are quoted in the over-the-counter market which are referred to later in this paper. Unfortunately, however, transaction-to-transaction price series are not available in the TSE and the OTC.

14. Demsetz (1968), p. 40.
15. *Ibid.*, p. 45.

In recent years, a good bit of empirical support for the relationship between spreads and the level of stock prices has been assembled. In contrast, the empirical evidence on the relationship between spreads and the volatility of stock prices is somewhat ambiguous and, yet, there is some reason to expect that such a relationship might exist. Particularly without a dealer, it seems reasonable to hypothesize that the probability of large deviations between the highest bid and the lowest ask prices might increase as the dispersion of the distribution of stock prices becomes more diffuse.

Thus far, we have focused entirely on variables which reflect the trading conditions in an individual stock. It must be recognized, however, that the multiple listing of a security might also have an effect on the width of the bid-ask spread in a particular marketplace. This point seems especially important in the context of the analysis of the TSE. As of November, 1971, there were 1166 issues listed on TSE, 112 of which were also listed on either or both NYSE/ASE and Montreal/Canadian Stock Exchange(s).[16] Understandably, one might expect the marketability of these issues to be affected by the bid and ask quotations of the specialists on the NYSE and ASE. In particular, to the extent dealers are able to narrow bid-ask spreads due to economies of specialization in the market-making function, we would expect multiple-listed TSE stocks to experience narrow spreads. Multiple listing also enables traders to select the exchange on which their transactions are consummated. Even if rank and file traders are not in a position to select an exchange independently, dealers who may have acquired positions on one exchange may be able to offset them by transactions on another exchange(s).

Finally, multiple listing is likely to be a proxy for the total volume of trading in a particular security and the bid-ask spread in any market may be a function not only of the volume of transactions in that security in that market, but also of the volume of trading in that security in all markets combined.

III. THE MODEL AND THE FINDINGS

The hypotheses outlined in the preceding section may be stated more formally in the following linear multiple regression equation:

$$S = \beta_0 + \beta_1 P + \beta_2 \ln V + \beta_3 \Delta P + \beta_4 C + \beta_5 N + u, \qquad (1)$$

where,

S = average bid-ask spread,
V = average number of shares traded per day,
P = average price of the stock,
ΔP = price volatility = $(P_{high} - P_{low})/P$,
C = trading continuity $\left[\dfrac{\text{no. of days the stock is traded}}{\text{no. of days in the sample}} \right]$ and
N = the number of markets in which the security is traded.[17]

---

16. Toronto Stock Exchange Review (Nov., 1971), pp. 60-61. The TSE sample contains 28 of these multiple-listings.

17. The average bid-ask spread, S, is calculated by using the closing bid-ask spread for each day and averaging over nine trading days. Price volatility, ΔP is the difference between the high and low price over the nine day period for which data were collected, and is expressed as a per cent

According to the logic outlined above, the following relationships are to be expected:

$$\frac{\partial S}{\partial P} = \beta_1 > 0,$$

$$\frac{\partial S}{\partial V} = \frac{\beta_2}{V} < 0 \text{ (where } V > 0\text{)},$$

$$\frac{\partial S}{\partial \Delta P} = \beta_3 > 0,$$

$$\frac{\partial S}{\partial C} = \beta_4 < 0, \text{ and}$$

$$\frac{\partial S}{\partial N} = \beta_5 < 0.$$

To estimate the coefficients of this model for the TSE, 200 common stocks were selected at random. Because data on trading volume and/or bid-ask spreads were not available for 23 of these issues, however, we were forced to reduce our sample to 177 stocks. Daily trading volume, bid-ask spreads and prices were gathered for these issues and averaged over the nine trading days December 1-13, 1971.[18]

The estimated coefficients of equation (1) are presented in Table 1. All of the coefficients carry the hypothesized signs and, with the exception of trading continuity, C, and the number of listing, N, they are statistically significant. The model itself is statistically significant at $\alpha = 0.0005$ level. The results imply that marketability of TSE-listed common stocks improves with increased trading volume but deteriorates with greater price volatility.

TABLE 1
ESTIMATED COEFFICIENTS OF EQUATION (1)

Regressors	Coefficients	$S_{\hat{\beta}_i}$	t-ratio	r^2
$\hat{\beta}_0$	2.2304	0.22463	9.9293*	—
P	0.04106	0.00485	8.4635*	0.2952
ln V	−0.25999	0.04645	−5.5975*	0.1549
ΔP	0.42016	0.15251	2.7549**	0.0425
C	−0.31894	0.31739	−1.0049	0.0059
N	−0.13568	0.09964	−1.3617	0.0107
$R^2 = 0.5127$		R^2 (adjusted) = 0.4985		$F(5,171) = 35,986*$

* Significant beyond $\alpha = 0.0005$ level.
** Significant beyond $\alpha = 0.005$ level.

---

of the average price during the period. This volatility measure may be expected to be sensitive to the length of the time period over which volatility is measured. Indeed, one would expect it to be larger for longer intervals. Any bias that may result from differences in the length of the time periods in the NYSE, TSE and the OTC samples, however, does not appear to be significant. The nine day period for the TSE sample is longer than that of the OTC sample (5 days) but shorter than the NYSE sample (19 days).

18. TSE, *Daily Record* (December 1-13, 1971).

The low t-ratios for β_4 and β_5, however, fail to provide support for hypotheses regarding the effects of trading continuity, C, and multimarket trading, N, on the bid-ask spreads. One fairly common cause of low t-ratios is the reduction in the efficiency of estimates due to multicollinearity; when equation (1) is tested for multicollinearity, however, the null hypothesis that $|r_{ij}| = 0$ is rejected at a lower level than $\alpha = 0.0001$ ($\chi^2(10) \cong 84.203$), indicating that the intercorrelation among the exogenous variables is not very severe. In other words, sample data do not indicate that trading continuity and multiple-listing exert any systematic influence on the bid-ask spreads of the TSE-listed issues when the hypothesized relationship among these variables is expressed in the linear model in equation (1). Indeed, when these two regressors are omitted from the model, the explanatory power of the regression equation is not significantly reduced. Haitovsky's heuristic test for multicollinearity[19] reflects the reduction in inter-correlation when these two regressors are omitted ($\chi^2(3) \cong 299.393$). The estimated coefficients of this revised model, without C and N, are presented in Table 2.

TABLE 2
COEFFICIENTS OF EQUATION (1) AFTER OMITTING TRADING CONTINUITY, C, AND NUMBER OF LISTINGS, N

Regressors	Coefficients	S_{β_1}	t-ratio	r^2
β_0	2.15596	0.21765	9.9056*	—
P	0.03890	0.00464	8.3917*	0.28930
ln V	−0.30457	0.02804	−10.8610*	0.40543
ΔP	0.41563	0.15270	2.7219**	0.04106
$R^2 = 0.5052$		R^2(adjusted) $= 0.4966$		$F(3,173) = 58.870*$

* Significant beyond $\alpha = 0.0005$ level.
** Significant beyond $\alpha = 0.005$ level.

An alternative functional form of the general relationship under investigation is given by the following equation:

$$\frac{S}{P} = \beta_0 + \beta_1 \ln V + \beta_2 \Delta P + \beta_3 C + \beta_4 N + v. \qquad (2)$$

In this form, spreads are expressed as a percentage of the price of the stock, $\frac{S}{P}$; the remaining variables are the same as in equation (1). The estimated coefficients of this equation (Table 3) all carry the anticipated signs and, with the exception of the number of listing, N, are statistically significant. In contrast to equation (1), trading continuity, C, exhibits a systematic influence on the spreads per dollar of stocks being traded. Given the relatively good "fit" of the model ($R^2 = 0.8035$) and $\chi^2(6) \cong 107.467$, we are reasonably assured of the efficiency of the estimated coefficients, and of the partitioning of the explanatory power of trading volume, V, and the continuity index, C, on the bid-ask spreads. In this form, the model implies that the bid-ask spread per

19. Haitovsky (1969), pp. 486–489.

dollar of stocks exchanged decreases with larger trading volume and more continuous trading pattern. It also reflects the fact that, ceteris paribus, traders dealing in issues having relatively high price volatility incur higher costs for "immediacy" per dollar of securities traded.

TABLE 3
ESTIMATED COEFFICIENTS OF EQUATION (2)

Regressors	Coefficients	$S_{\hat{\beta}_i}$	t-ratio	r^2
$\hat{\beta}_0$	0.19944	0.01345	14.8300*	—
ln V	−0.01057	0.00279	−3.7947*	0.7725
ΔP	0.20475	0.00907	22.5610*	0.7474
C	−0.09721	0.01901	−5.1127*	0.1319
N	−0.00812	0.00571	−1.5424	0.0136

$R^2 = 0.8079$ $R^2(\text{adjusted}) = 0.8035$ $F(4,172) = 180.91*$

* Significant beyond $\alpha = 0.0005$ level.

Generally speaking, the results in Tables 2 and 3 are quite similar in their implications. Both indicate that the marketability of the TSE-listed stocks is primarily influenced by the level of trading activity and the variability of the stock prices. In addition, both indicate a statistically insignificant relationship between the bid-ask spreads and the number of markets in which a stock is traded, leading us to the tentative conclusion that, other things being the same, the marketability of TSE issues is not materially influenced by the bid-ask quotations of specialists in the NYSE or the ASE. This finding, incidentally, could have very important implications about the costs of arbitraging and the efficiency of the registered arbitrage traders in TSE, especially if these jointly-listed issues experience narrower spreads on the NYSE or ASE.

IV. BID-ASK SPREADS IN THE TSE, NYSE AND OTC: A COMPARISON

As noted in Section II, the structure of the market-making function in the TSE is substantially different from that of the NYSE and the OTC market in the U.S.A. This, of course, raises the question of whether this difference affects the marketability of stocks traded in these three markets, and if so, in what ways. To investigate this question, we compared the TSE results with the findings of earlier studies of NYSE-listed stocks and unlisted issues traded in the over-the-counter markets.[20]

To permit direct comparisons, however, the NYSE and the OTC equations had to be re-estimated with precisely the same independent variables as those in the TSE equation (1).[21] The resulting coefficients of these models and the associated regression statistics are presented in Tables 4 and 5.[22] A comparison

---

20. Tinic (1972) and Tinic and West (1972).

21. The NYSE data in Tinic (1972) pertained to March 1969 while the OTC data in Tinic and West (1972) was gathered for the first five trading days in November 1971. For the length of period over which observations were collected from the NYSE and the OTC see *supra* note 17.

22. In addition to these variables, Tinic (1972) also studied the effects of trading continuity, the extent of institutional holdings, intermarket competition, size of the specialty portfolios and dealer capitalization on the bid-ask spreads of NYSE-listed common stocks. Since, the TSE and

of these results with Table 2 reveals that the overall explanatory power of the OTC-equation is roughly comparable to that of the TSE model, while the NYSE equation accounts for a substantially larger portion of the variation in the bid-ask spreads ($R^2 = 0.7278$). All three equations indicate, as expected, that bid-ask spreads vary inversely with trading activity and directly with price. Only the TSE equation, however, establishes a statistically significant, positive relationship between spreads and short run price volatility. We will have more to say about this finding below.

TABLE 4
ESTIMATED COEFFICIENTS OF THE NYSE-EQUATION
$$S = \beta_0 + \beta_1 P + \beta_2 \ln V + \beta_3 \Delta P + w$$

Regressors	Coefficients	$S_{\hat{\beta}_i}$	t-ratio	r^2
$\hat{\beta}_0$	0.77261	0.06493	11.9000*	—
P	0.00431	0.00043	10.1340*	0.5747
ln V	−0.06863	0.00699	−9.8211*	0.5593
ΔP	0.13579	0.15869	0.8557	0.0095
$R^2 = 0.7381$		R^2(adjusted) $= 0.7278$		$F(3, 76) = 71.40*$

* Significant beyond $\alpha = 0.0005$ level.

TABLE 5
ESTIMATED COEFFICIENTS OF THE OTC-EQUATION
$$S = \beta_0 + \beta_1 P + \beta_2 \ln V + \beta_3 \Delta P + u$$

Regressors	Coefficients	$S_{\hat{\beta}_i}$	t-ratio	r^2
$\hat{\beta}_0$	1.39717	0.12800	10.9150*	—
P	0.01340	0.00087	15.3860*	0.4444
ln V	−0.13346	0.01608	−8.2994*	0.18877
ΔP	0.00686	0.01234	0.5559	0.00104
$R^2 = 0.4767$		R^2(adjusted) $= 0.4713$		$F(3,296) = 89.880*$

* Significant beyond $\alpha = 0.0005$ level.

For now, however, let us turn to the question of whether or not the average levels of spreads in the three markets differ, after taking account of the effects of price level, trading volume and price variability. If we could be certain that the coefficients of the variables included in the three equations were not significantly different, this question could be answered simply by adding a dummy variable to a pooled regression to take account of any significant variations in intercept terms. Lacking such assurance, however, we must begin by testing the null hypothesis that $\beta_{1i} = \beta_{2i} = \beta_{3i}$; where, the first subscript refers to the TSE, NYSE and the OTC equations respectively, and i = 0, 1, 2, 3 designates the intercept and the three slope coefficients in the model. Fisher has suggested a test based on the calculation of the following statistic:[23]

OTC data on these variables were not available at the time of this study, the re-estimated NYSE equation did not include these variables.

23. Fisher (1959), p. 232.

Agent Versus Dealer Dominated Markets

$$\Omega = \sum_{j=1}^{n} \frac{(\hat{\beta}_{ji} - \hat{\beta}^*_i)^2}{S_{ji}^2}, \text{ where} \quad (3)$$

$$\hat{\beta}^*_i = \frac{\sum\limits_{j=1}^{n} \hat{\beta}_{ji}/S_{ji}^2}{\sum\limits_{j=1}^{n} 1/S_{ji}^2}.$$

This statistic is approximately distributed as χ^2, with n-1 degrees of freedom. Unusually large values for Ω result in the rejection of the null hypothesis.

The results obtained from applying this test to the coefficients of the TSE, NYSE and OTC regressions are presented in Table 6. As the reader can see, the extremely large values of Ω require us to reject the null hypothesis for all four coefficients. In other words, the results require us to conclude that the various β_j. do not represent observations drawn from a common population. It should be noted, however, that the power of this test is rather low for all $j > 2$. More importantly, the mere rejection of the null hypothesis does not necessarily imply that all three of the coefficients differ from each other. Indeed, it is quite possible that we can reject the null hypothesis even though, say, $\beta_{1i} \neq \beta_{2i} = \beta_{3i}$. However, since the TSE-listed stocks would presumably be more nearly comparable to the unlisted issues in the OTC, a comparison of the coefficients of these two equations is also presented in Table 6.

TABLE 6
THE RESULTS OF THE χ^2-TEST ON THE REGRESSION COEFFICIENTS OF THE TSE, NYSE AND OTC EQUATIONS

	TSE, NYSE and OTC			TSE and OTC	
Coeff.	$\Omega(2)$	α-level	Coeff.	$\Omega(1)$	α-level
β_0	50.0125	<0.0001	β_0	9.0308	<0.005
β_1	137.3783	<0.0001	β_1	29.1769	<0.0001
β_2	75.2083	<0.0001	β_2	28.0230	<0.0001
β_3	7.7489	<0.025	β_3	7.1195	<0.01

Based on the results of the "Fisher test," in Table 6, we must not only add an intercept shifter variable to a pooled regression equation, but slope shifter variables as well. That is, we must estimate

$$S = \beta_0 + \beta_1 P + \beta_2 \ln V + \beta_3 \Delta P + \beta_4 D_1 + \beta_5 D_2 + \beta_6 \lambda_{v1} \quad (4)$$
$$+ \beta_7 \lambda_{v2} + \beta_8 \phi_{v1} + \beta_9 \phi_{v2} + \beta_{10} \delta_{\Delta 1} + \beta_{11} \delta_{\Delta 2} + u,$$

where,

S = average bid-ask spread,

P = average price of the stock,

ΔP = price volatility,

$$D_1 = \begin{cases} 1 & \text{if the stock is listed on TSE} \\ 0 & \text{otherwise,} \end{cases}$$

$$D_2 = \begin{cases} 1 & \text{if the stock is traded in OTC} \\ 0 & \text{otherwise,} \end{cases}$$

$^\lambda P1 = D_1 P; \quad ^\lambda P2 = D_2 P,$

$^\phi V1 = D_1 \ln V; \quad ^\phi V2 = D_2 \ln V$

$^\delta \Delta 1 = D_1 \Delta P; \quad ^\delta \Delta 2 = D_2 \Delta P$ and

u = random error.

If the coefficients of this model are directly estimated by the method of ordinary least squares, however, the standard errors of the coefficients are quite large because of serious heteroscedasticity in the error distributions: although the distributions of the random errors are reasonably well behaved in each equation, pooling the three samples with diverse regression variances violates the condition of constant error variance. For the NYSE, TSE, and OTC observations in the sample, the respective error variances can be expressed by the following proportional relationships:

$$E(e^2_{NYSE}) = \hat{\sigma}_u^2,$$
$$E(e^2_{TSE}) = 80.7 \hat{\sigma}_u^2, \text{ and} \qquad (5)$$
$$E(e^2_{OTC}) = 25.3 \hat{\sigma}_u^2.$$

To improve the efficiency of the estimates, the observations in the TSE and the OTC sub-groups are weighted by $\dfrac{1}{\sqrt{80.7}}$ and $\dfrac{1}{\sqrt{25.3}}$, respectively, and the classical least squares estimator, $[\hat{\beta}]$, is computed on the transformed data.

The resulting estimates and the associated statistics are reported in Table 7. The general findings of this model indicate that with the exception of the price volatility variable, the absolute values of the estimated coefficients of the TSE equation are significantly larger than the values of the estimates for the NYSE model. In terms of the specific regressors, this implies that, ceteris paribus, a dollar increase in the average price of a share in the TSE would cause bid-ask spreads to increase by roughly four cents, while a similar increase in the price of a NYSE stock would result in a change in the spread of only slightly more than one tenth of this amount. The larger coefficient of price, P, reflects, no doubt, the absence of specialized economies in financing the market-making function in the TSE in contrast to the NYSE. Lacking a well organized and somewhat privileged dealership function, the TSE issues cannot obtain the benefits of the lower margin requirements and larger leverage capacities enjoyed by NYSE specialists. Of course, traders who submit contemporaneous limit buy and sell tenders in the TSE behave very much like specialists, but they have to incur two-way brokerage commissions, which must be reflected in the coefficient of the price variable; to the extent the brokerage commissions increase roughly as a step function of the price per share, the bid-ask spreads of the higher priced TSE stock would incorporate this differential cost.[24]

TABLE 7
ESTIMATED COEFFICIENTS OF POOLED-VARIANCE REGRESSION EQUATION (4)[25]

Regressors	Coefficient	$S_{\hat{\beta}_i}$	t-ratio	r^2
$\hat{\beta}_0$	0.77317	0.29846	2.5905*†	—
P	0.00431	0.00196	2.2046††	0.0319
ln V	−0.06869	0.03212	−2.1383††	0.0301
ΔP	0.13570	0.72922	0.1861	0.0002
D_1	1.38279	0.44765	3.0890**	0.0607
D_2	0.62400	0.39749	1.5698	0.0164
λ_{P1}	0.03459	0.00737	4.6931*	0.1299
λ_{P2}	0.00909	0.00265	3.4308*	0.0739
ϕ_{V1}	−0.23589	0.05366	−4.3958*	0.1158
ϕ_{V2}	−0.06477	0.04604	−1.4069	0.0132
$\phi_{\Delta 1}$	0.27993	0.76587	0.3655	0.0009
$\delta_{\Delta 2}$	−0.12884	0.72966	−0.2994	0.0002

$R^2 = 0.5365$ $R^2(\text{adjusted}) = 0.5020**$

* Significant beyond $\alpha = 0.0005$ level.
** Significant beyond $\alpha = 0.005$ level.
*† Significant beyond $\alpha = 0.01$ level.
†† Significant beyond $\alpha = 0.025$ level.

As far as the OTC equation is concerned, the coefficient of the price variable is slightly larger than the NYSE, but considerably smaller than the TSE estimate. The difference between the OTC and the NYSE values for β_1 implies that the bid-ask spreads in OTC increase by about one cent more than they would in the NYSE per dollar increase in the equilibrium level of a stock. This difference may be interpreted as one per cent higher borrowing cost for the dealers in the over-the-counter markets. The coefficients of the remaining slope and intercept shifters for the OTC stocks, ϕ_{V2}, $\delta_{\Delta 2}$, and D_2, are not statistically significant, implying that the coefficients of trading volume and price

---

24. The Toronto Stock Exchange discourages members other than registered traders from submitting two-sided tenders for non-client accounts. See, TSE, *Floor Trader's Manual*, pp. 9 and 30-31.

25. The mean and standard deviation of the variables, S, P, V, ΔP, C and N are presented below:

	TSE	NYSE	OTC
S	0.384	0.360	0.632
s_S	0.977	0.148	0.532
P	11.088	41.822	22.046
s_P	11.414	20.584	26.153
V	4427.314	12736.180	7197.903
s_V	5675.784	14057.840	12436.630
ΔP	0.132	0.089	0.069
$s_{\Delta P}$	0.345	0.056	0.182
C	0.837	0.988	0.958
s_C	0.270	0.040	0.119
N	1.198	2.725	n.a.
s_N	0.564	1.387	n.a.

volatility for the OTC issues are not significantly different from their counterparts in the NYSE model.

The difference in the coefficients of trading volume in the NYSE and the TSE equations, on the other hand, almost certainly reflects the differences in the listing requirements of the two stock exchanges. A large number of the TSE-listed stocks would be considered extremely "inactive" by NYSE standards. Moreover, the TSE sample does not include any issues which have trading volumes as large as those of the more active NYSE stocks.

Practically speaking, nevertheless, the difference in the effect of changes in trading volume on the bid-ask spreads in the two markets are negligible for stocks experiencing reasonably active trading. For a given level and volatility of price per share, the rate of change in the bid-ask spreads with respect to trading volume is a function of V, i.e., $\frac{\partial S}{\partial V} = \frac{\beta_2}{V}$ and $\frac{\partial^2 S}{\partial V^2} = \frac{-\beta_2}{V^2}$. As such, even for moderately active issues, the difference in the estimated values of β_2 is dominated by the trading volume, V, and differences in the effect of marginal volume changes on the bid-ask spreads in the two markets are negligible.[26]

In the pooled-variance regression equation, the coefficients of the slope shifters for price volatility, $\delta_{\Delta 1}$ and $\delta_{\Delta 2}$, are not significantly different from zero, which implies that the effects of price volatility in the TSE, NYSE and OTC are roughly comparable. This result, which contradicts the earlier findings obtained by the Fisher's χ^2-test, no doubt reflects the fact that the use of several dummy variables as slope and intercept shifters in equation 4 introduces serious multicollinearity and makes the partitioning of explanatory power of individual regressors rather difficult. Indeed, as evidenced by relatively low t-ratios, the efficiency of the estimated coefficients in the pooled-variance regression equation is substantially reduced. It should be recalled; however, that the coefficient of the price volatility variable is not statistically different from zero in the NYSE or OTC models, while in the TSE model it exhibits a statistically significant positive relationship with the bid-ask spreads. This being the case, we are inclined to place our confidence in the results of the χ^2-test for this regressor.

Finally, when we examine the coefficients of the intercept shifters, D_1 and D_2, we observe that only β_4 is significantly different from zero. This, of course, implies a significant difference between the intercept estimates of the TSE and the NYSE regressions. In other words, a significant part of the variance in the bid-ask spreads in the pooled-variance regression model is accounted for by the difference between the average level of spreads in the TSE and the NYSE samples. We regard this result as extremely important, since it implies that the average bid-ask spread in the TSE is larger than its counterpart in the NYSE, even after adjustments are made for the differential effects of price per share, trading activity and price volatility. Put somewhat differently, this result indicates that the marketability of a TSE security, having the same

---

26. Although the TSE equation (2) has a much better fit, equation (1) is used for purposes of comparative analysis because the model in (2) possesses very little explanatory power when it is estimated with the NYSE and especially the OTC data.

price as a NYSE listed stock and experiencing a comparable level of trading activity, is inferior irrespective of its price volatility.

V. Further Analysis and Some Implications

As we have noted on several occasions, some of the observed marketability differences are probably caused by the substantial differences in the structures of the TSE, NYSE and OTC. For example, in terms of listing requirements, the TSE would have to be placed somewhere between the NYSE and the over-the-counter markets in the United States.[27] The TSE lists a large number of speculative oil and mining issues as well as relatively seasoned industrial stocks. Some of the TSE-listed stocks are also listed on other exchanges in Canada and the United States, but in contrast to the U.S. there is not a substantial OTC market in Canada which can divert trading volume from the TSE. Hence, all of the TSE-listed issues are traded on one or more auction-type market(s). In this context, market-splitting does not seem to have a systematic effect on the marketability of the TSE stocks.

In addition, the TSE tends to favor an "agency" type of market which mitigates against the development of well-defined, effective dealership function. Unlike the NYSE specialists or the OTC dealers, the registered traders of the TSE do not appear to have an important influence on the depth and cost of marketability. Rather than making continuous markets, their principal responsibilities seem to be confined to a role as odd-lot dealers; their market-making function in the board-lot (unit of trading similar to the round lot in the NYSE, but not necessarily 100 shares for all stocks) market is largely comprised of assembling or "looking out" for positions that were acquired in odd-lot trading and occasionally participating in delayed openings. They are not subject to minimum capital requirements by the exchange; in their somewhat ambiguous role in enhancing the "orderliness" of the market, one cannot consider them as an effective and continuous market-making institution.

We would be inclined to interpret the findings of the statistical analyses as reflecting in large part the basic differences in the marketability of securities under structurally distinct market organizations. In both the NYSE and the OTC, the price continuity and orderliness of the market depends upon the presence of dealers. In the OTC, competition among dealers seems to be the force governing and assuring reasonable marketability. In the NYSE, on the other hand, self-regulation has displaced the natural forces of competition in governing the depth and continuity of supply of marketability. The relative effectiveness of self-regulation and competition is itself a valid subject for discussion and analysis.[28] Notwithstanding the differences in the economic organization of the market-making function in the NYSE and the over-the-counter markets, however, the results of our statistical analyses indicate that both provide marketability at lower cost, on the average, than the Toronto Stock Exchange. The TSE, it would appear, has neither adequate competition nor

---

27. Walter and Williamson (1960), p. 319.
28. West and Tinic (1972).

adequate regulation. If anything, it has regulations that, in effect, work against the development of marketability.

Another noteworthy point closely associated with the presence or absence of dealers in the market is the short-run stability of stock prices. Theoretically, dealers might be expected to reduce the amplitude and the frequency of short-run price fluctuations, leading to generally more stable prices. Indeed, the recently completed *Institutional Investor Study* contains direct empirical evidence supporting this proposition.[29] In this context, lacking effective dealer participation and inventory activity that can stabilize market imbalances, the price volatility of the TSE stocks might be expected to be substantially greater than what they would otherwise be in the presence of dealers in the market. The statistically significant coefficient obtained for the price volatility variable in the TSE model may reflect in part the "double-barrelled" effect of the absence of a reasonably continuous market-making function which would tend to temper day-to-day fluctuations in stock prices. To be sure, some of the oil and mining stocks that are listed on the TSE are extremely speculative and experience substantial price instability which could not be totally avoided even if dealers were active in this market. Nevertheless, it seems inappropriate to attribute the effects of price variability on the bid-ask spreads in the TSE solely to the speculative characteristics of the issues involved. After all, there are a large number of highly speculative issues being traded in the over-the-counter markets in the United States, and the effects of their price volatility on spreads seem to have been tempered by dealers who can position in these issues and yet diversify the risks associated with their varying equilibrium prices.[30] The presence of dealers who are willing to position in relatively riskier stocks, in turn, helps to reduce short-term price variability. Furthermore to the extent that the risks of these stocks are diversifiable, lower expected returns on positioning may become acceptable, thus leading to narrower bid-ask spreads.[31]

As we see things, the relatively higher bid-ask spreads of the TSE stocks have two important policy implications. The first relates to the marketability needs of investors and emigration of Canadian savings to the stock markets in the United States; the second concerns the cost of equity capital of Canadian corporations. Even with a well established specialist system, the virtues of the auction method of market-making have come under increasing attack, particularly in regard to its weaknesses in supplying liquidity to large institutional portfolios. The TSE, however, lacking the market making facilities of the NYSE, would be hard put even to supply marketability to small investors, let alone block traders. Being unable to execute large block transactions at reasonable prices in the TSE, member brokers tend to divide them into smaller lots and channel them to two or more stock exchanges whenever it is possible

29. SEC (1971), pp. 1885-1891.

30. See *supra* note 25 for a comparison of the mean values of the price volatility variable in the TSE, NYSE and OTC.

31. To the extent price volatility is hypothesized to be a cause of wide spreads and a result of ineffective dealer activity, the single equation model used in this study may contain a specification error and possibly yield a biased estimate of the coefficient of this variable. The causal importance of the price volatility variable, however, is not sufficiently large to justify a simultaneous equation model.

to do so.³² In light of this experience, it is not difficult to understand why institutional investors in Canada have tended to displace TSE-listed stocks in their portfolios in favor of the NYSE listed issues with comparable risk-return characteristics. In other words, in addition to the risk-return framework that was developed by Grubel (1968) and Levy and Sarnat (1970), liquidity must be recognized as a third parameter in the international flow of capital, at least as far as the flow between Canada and the United States is concerned.

All other things being the same, of course, the emigration of Canadian savings to stock markets which provide better marketability tends to reduce demand for TSE-listed stocks and, thereby, depress their prices. Lower stock prices in the TSE in turn imply a higher cost of equity capital for Canadian corporations. What is worse, this higher cost is in excess of the prevailing price of equity which already incorporates a very high cost of inventorying and waiting.³³

In summary, the analysis presented in this paper indicates that, on the average, the price of liquidity on the TSE is higher than on the NYSE and OTC, even after taking such factors as lighter trading volume and lower average prices into account. While the reasons for this finding are not completely clear, the evidence suggests to us that the higher price is attributable, at least in part, to the lack of a well established dealer market in the TSE. Considering the substantial negative effects of the higher price of liquidity, whether measured in terms of international capital flows or the cost of equity to Canadian corporations, it seems reasonable to suggest that a careful re-examination of the current market organization in the TSE is in order.

REFERENCES

C. Baxter. "Where the Money Goes," *The Financial Post* (December 4th, 1971), pp. 13-15.

H. Demsetz. "The Cost of Transacting," *The Quarterly Journal of Economics*, 82 (February 1968), pp. 33-53.

L. Fisher. "Determinants of Risk Premiums on Corporate Bonds," *Journal of Political Economy*, 67 (June 1959), pp. 217-237.

Y. Haitovsky. "Multicollinearity in Regression Analysis: Comment," *The Review of Economics and Statistics*, LI (November 1969), pp. 486-489.

H. G. Grubel. "Internationally Diversified Portfolios: Welfare Gains and Capital Flows," *American Economic Review*, 58 (December 1968), pp. 1299-1314.

H. Levy and M. Sarnat. "International Diversification of Investment and Capital Flows," *American Economic Review*, 60 (September 1970), pp. 668-675.

W. M. Martin. "The Securities Markets: A Report with Recommendations" (submitted to the Board of Governors of the New York Stock Exchange, August 1971).

New York Stock Exchange, "Economic Effects of Negotiated Commission Rates on the Brokerage Industry's Practices and the Market for Corporate Securities" (unpublished report, August 1968).

SEC, *Report of the Special Study of the Securities Markets of the Securities and Exchange Commission*, U.S., 88th Congress, 1st sess. House of Representatives Document 95, Washington, D.C., Government Printing Office, 1965.

SEC, *Institutional Investor Study Report of the Securities and Exchange Commission*, U.S., 92nd Congress, 1st sess. House of Representatives Document 92-64, Washington, D.C., Government Printing Office, 1971.

---

32. Walter and Williamson (1960), p. 312.

33. The bid-ask spread of a hypothetical stock with a price of $30.00, average daily trading volume of 1000 shares and a price volatility of 0.026 can be estimated from the revised version of Model (1). On the basis of the coefficients reported in Tables 2 and 4, the estimated cost of waiting for this security would be approximately $1.23 in the TSE, in contrast to $0.43 in the NYSE.

S. Smidt. "Which Road to an Efficient Stock Market: Free Competition or Regulated Monopoly," *Financial Analysts Journal* (September-October 1971), pp. 18ff.

S. M. Tinic. "The Economics of Liquidity Services," *The Quarterly Journal of Economics*, 86 (February 1972), pp. 79-93.

S. M. Tinic and R. R. West. "Competition and the Pricing of Dealer Service in the Over-the-Counter Stock Market," *Journal of Financial and Quantitative Analysis*, VII, No. 3 (June 1972).

Toronto Stock Exchange, *Daily Record* (December 1-13, 1971).

Toronto Stock Exchange, *Floor Trader's Manual*, January 1972.

Toronto Stock Exchange, *Toronto Stock Exchange Review* (November 1971).

J. E. Walter and J. P. Williamson. "Organized Securities Exchanges in Canada," *The Journal of Finance*, XV (September 1960), pp. 307-324.

R. R. West and S. M. Tinic. "Crisis in the Stock Market: The Martin Report and the Public Interest," *Public Policy* (Winter 1972), pp. 103-131.

R. R. West and S. M. Tinic. *The Economics of the Stock Market*, Praeger Publishers, New York, 1971.

Why do NASDAQ Market Makers Avoid Odd-Eighth Quotes?

WILLIAM G. CHRISTIE and PAUL H. SCHULTZ*

ABSTRACT

The NASDAQ multiple dealer market is designed to produce narrow bid-ask spreads through the competition for order flow among individual dealers. However, we find that odd-eighth quotes are virtually nonexistent for 70 of 100 actively traded NASDAQ securities, including Apple Computer and Lotus Development. The lack of odd-eighth quotes cannot be explained by the negotiation hypothesis of Harris (1991), trading activity, or other variables thought to impact spreads. This result implies that the inside spread for a large number of NASDAQ stocks is at least $0.25 and raises the question of whether NASDAQ dealers implicitly collude to maintain wide spreads.

THIS ARTICLE PROVIDES EMPIRICAL evidence on the degree of competition among dealers who make markets in the National Association of Securities Dealers Automated Quotation system (NASDAQ). Several hundred firms currently act as dealers in NASDAQ stocks, with the number of market makers per stock ranging from 2 to over 50. Individual dealers enjoy relatively free entry and exit, subject to a one-day delay before quotes can be posted. In a market where the inside spread is determined by the actions of multiple dealers, competitive spreads might be considered a natural outcome. However, our results suggest otherwise.

Unlike previous studies that compute summary measures of bid-ask spreads, we examine the entire distribution of dollar spreads using an extensive sample of inside bid and inside ask quotes for 100 of the most active

---

*Christie is from the Owen Graduate School of Management, Vanderbilt University, and Schultz is from the Max Fisher College of Business, the Ohio State University. The article has benefitted from the comments and suggestions of Utpal Bhattacharya, Bernard Dumas, Thomas George, Lawrence Harris, Charles Lee, Craig Lewis, Kelly McNamara, Junius Peake, James Shapiro, Erik Serri, René Stulz (the editor), Hans Stoll, Ralph Walkling, Robert Wood, an anonymous referee, and seminar participants at Northwestern University, the Ohio State University, the University of Pennsylvania, Vanderbilt University, and the University of Southern California/University of California Los Angeles/NYSE 1994 Conference on Market Microstructure. Christie acknowledges the financial support of the Dean's Fund for Faculty Research at the Owen Graduate School of Management and the Financial Markets Research Center at Vanderbilt University. Schultz acknowledges the financial support from the Dice Center for Financial Research at the Ohio State University. All errors are the joint property of the authors.

NASDAQ stocks in 1991. We find that spreads of one-eighth are virtually nonexistent for a majority of this sample. The lack of one-eighth spreads can be traced to an absence of either inside bid or inside ask quotes ending in odd-eighths (1/8, 3/8, 5/8, and 7/8) for 70 of the 100 stocks. In contrast, a sample of 100 New York Stock Exchange (NYSE) and American Stock Exchange (AMEX) firms of similar price and market value to our NASDAQ sample consistently use the full spectrum of eighths. The absence of odd-eighth quotes for the majority of the NASDAQ sample, including such active issues as Apple Computer, Intel, and Lotus Development, implies an inside spread of at least $0.25. We believe that this surprising result reflects an implicit agreement among market makers to avoid using odd-eighths in quoting bid and ask prices and that a large number of market makers per stock is not necessarily synonymous with competition.

The finding that market makers enforce a minimum spread of $0.25 by not posting odd-eighth quotes for a majority of large NASDAQ stocks may partially explain the higher trading costs for firms listed on NASDAQ documented in previous research. For example, Goldstein (1993) examines closing bid-ask spreads for both NYSE and NASDAQ stocks during 1990. He first adjusts NASDAQ spreads to reflect the fact that institutional traders do not always pay commissions on NASDAQ trades but must pay them on NYSE transactions. He then estimates a cross-sectional regression of adjusted spreads on price, market capitalization, volume, volatility, and a dummy variable for exchange listing and finds that spreads for stocks that meet NYSE listing requirements but trade on NASDAQ are $0.15 to $0.18 wider than similar NYSE-listed stocks.

Christie and Huang (1994) use all intraday quote changes and trades for the 60 days surrounding exchange listing to study a sample of stocks that moved from NASDAQ to either the NYSE or the AMEX during 1990. They find that quoted spreads decline by an average of $0.31 per share when stocks move to the AMEX and by $0.06 per share when stocks are listed on the NYSE. The average liquidity premium, measured as the difference between trade prices and the midpoint of the prevailing bid and ask quotes, declines by about $0.05 per share when stocks are listed on either exchange.[1]

Affleck-Graves, Hegde, and Miller (1994) present evidence that order-processing costs, the component of the spread that is unrelated to information asymmetry or dealer inventory positions, is larger for NASDAQ stocks than comparable NYSE firms. They claim that exchanges facilitate the matching of buy and sell orders by increasing competition between market participants and by reducing the need for direct dealer intervention. Similarly, Vijh (1990) compares the market depth and bid-ask spreads for NYSE stocks and Chicago

---

[1] Christie and Huang (1994) report that the source of the reduction in liquidity premiums for firms that move from the NASDAQ to the NYSE is shared equally by the improvement in quotes that originate from the NYSE rather than NASDAQ and the ability to trade inside the spread more frequently when the trades are executed on the NYSE.

Board Options Exchange (CBOE) options, which trade in a multiple-dealer market, and finds that, although the CBOE offers greater depth, the relative bid-ask spreads are appreciably wider than for NYSE stocks. He further shows that the wider spreads on the CBOE do not arise from differences in information asymmetries since the adverse selection component of the spread is similar across market structures.

The lack of odd-eighth quotes for the majority of NASDAQ stocks in our sample suggests that the organizational structures utilized by NASDAQ and the NYSE/AMEX differ in their effectiveness in promoting competitive spreads.[2] The NYSE or AMEX specialist is awarded an exclusive franchise to act as a dealer and auctioneer in each stock. In return, specialists are closely regulated and are bound by an affirmative obligation to maintain a "fair and orderly market." Although specialists have an exclusive franchise in their stocks, they face competition for order flow from floor traders on the exchange, from other exchanges, and from public limit orders. Limit order prices are part of the spread displayed to the market and take precedence over specialists' trades for their own account.[3]

In contrast to exchange specialists, NASDAQ dealers do not have an exclusive franchise to make a market in a stock and are not as closely regulated. The NASDAQ firms studied in this article trade on the National Market System (NMS). One of the few affirmative obligations imposed on dealers is that they must provide firm quotes on both sides of the spread with a depth of at least 1,000 shares per dealer. However, Chan, Christie, and Schultz (1995) find that market makers rarely post quotes that place them at both the inside bid and inside ask.

The fundamental premise of the NASDAQ system is that competition for order flow among dealers will produce narrow spreads. In contrast to the organized exchanges, NASDAQ limit orders are not exposed to the public and are executed if and only if the inside spread reaches the limit price. Thus, the public cannot use limit orders to compete directly with NASDAQ market makers, and inside quotes do not reflect the presence of limit orders. The

---

[2] Differences in the institutional organization of the dealer and specialist markets may also translate into intraday differences in the width of bid-ask spreads. For example, McInish and Wood (1992), Brock and Kleidon (1992) and Kleidon and Werner (1993) show that bid-ask spreads of listed stocks narrow steadily until early afternoon and then widen at the close. Similarly, Chan, Fong, and Stulz (1994) find that bid-ask spreads of NYSE stocks follow a U-shaped pattern over the day. However, they also find that the spreads of European stocks listed on the NYSE decline steadily over the day. Foster and Viswanathan (1993) examine the intraday behavior of the adverse selection component of the spread for NYSE stocks and find that it displays a U-shaped pattern over the day. In contrast, Chan, Christie, and Schultz (1995) show that bid-ask spreads of NASDAQ stocks decline throughout the day and are narrowest at the close of trading. Kleidon and Werner (1993) also find a similar pattern of declining spreads for London Stock Exchange stocks, which operates as a multiple dealer market.

[3] Harris and Hasbrouck (1992) analyze the types of NYSE orders handled by the automated SuperDot system for a sample of 144 stocks from November 1990 through January 1991. They find that 45 percent of day orders are limit orders and that limit orders are more common than market orders for trades of 500 shares or more.

competitive structure of the dealer market is summarized by Schwartz (1991, p. 58):

> Dealers compete with each other, and have been reluctant to accept additional competition from the public order flow. The NASD depends on this interdealer competition to keep markets fair, orderly and liquid. ... Competing dealers face fewer regulatory restrictions than NYSE specialists because the NASD relies more on the constraints of a competitive environment to discipline dealer firms.

While our evidence suggests that the structure of the NASDAQ market may permit tacit collusion among its dealers, we also consider alternative explanations. The first is provided by the negotiation hypothesis of Harris (1991), who suggests that the use of coarse price increments to minimize negotiation costs may explain the (far less severe) price clustering of NYSE/AMEX stocks. Since most small trades on NASDAQ are executed automatically, while large trades are negotiated, this hypothesis predicts that a smaller percentage of large than small trades should be transacted on odd eighths. However, we find that among NASDAQ stocks where odd-eighth quotes are rare, negotiated trades in excess of 1,000 shares are far more likely to be transacted on the odd eighths than trades of 1,000 shares or less.

We also provide evidence that the lack of odd eighths is unrelated to trading activity, equity value, and the number of market makers. While prices and return volatility have some ability to predict the firms that are quoted in odd eighths, the greatest predictive power lies in the historical use of odd eighths. Thus, our results suggest that the important factor in predicting the use of odd-eighth quotes is not the economic costs and risks of market making, but whether a practice of avoiding odd-eighth quotes is already established.

The rest of the article is organized as follows. Section I describes our samples of NASDAQ and NYSE/AMEX firms. Section II reports the differences in dollar spreads between the NASDAQ and the NYSE/AMEX samples. Section III traces the differences in spreads across exchanges to the frequency of odd-eighth quotes and examines whether these results can be reconciled by a negotiation explanation, the risks of market making, or tacit collusion among dealers. Section IV concludes the article and summarizes our findings.

I. Data and Sampling Procedures

The data consist of all trades and quote revisions in 1991 for 100 large, actively traded NASDAQ stocks and 100 NYSE/AMEX stocks of comparable price and end-of-year equity value. NASDAQ stocks are selected by first calculating the end-of-year capitalized market value of equity computed using prices and the number of outstanding shares from the Center for Research in Securities Prices (CRSP) for all NASDAQ stocks in 1991. The 50 largest stocks are intentionally included in our sample, with the remaining 50 firms selected randomly from those with an equity value of at least $100 million. The final sample includes such actively traded firms as Apple Computer, MCI Communications, Lotus Development, Intel, St. Jude Medical, and Food Lion. NYSE/AMEX stocks that traded throughout 1991 are then matched with NASDAQ stocks using the average daily closing prices during 1991 and then the end-of-year capitalized value of equity.[4] NYSE and AMEX stocks include Caesers World, Kerr-McGee, Morton International, and Amdahl.

Table I provides the distribution of closing prices and end-of-year equity capitalizations for the two samples. Panel A provides the mean, minimum, maximum, and quartiles of the distribution of average closing prices across stocks. The average prices of NASDAQ stocks correspond closely to the average prices of the listed (i.e., NYSE/AMEX) stocks. Panel B describes the distribution of end-of-year equity capitalizations across stocks. While the two samples are very similar, NASDAQ stocks have slightly larger capitalizations, perhaps as a result of intentionally including the 50 largest NASDAQ stocks in the sample.

All trade and quote data are obtained from the Institute for the Study of Securities Markets (ISSM). Trade data contain both the transaction price and the number of shares, while quote data include all intraday inside quote revisions. Quotes that originate from the NASDAQ market reflect the inside bid and inside ask computed from the best individual dealer quotes, while NYSE/AMEX quotes are updated electronically by the specialist and can reflect either their own quotes or those of the limit order book. A series of filters are then applied to the intraday trades and quotes. Since ISSM assigns a negative value to suspicious trade prices, volumes and bid-ask quotes prior to releasing the data, we exclude all negative trades and quotes. In addition, we eliminate all locked or crossed-quotes (where the bid either equalled or exceeded the ask) since they are not sustainable. We also discard all quotes that originate in markets other than the exchange where the stock is listed. Thus, the quotes for firms that are listed on the NASDAQ originate from the dealer market, while the quotes for firms listed on the NYSE or AMEX emerge from their respective exchanges. An additional filter eliminates quote revisions that reflect a change in the depth (i.e., the number of shares for which the quote is valid) without affecting the inside bid or inside ask. We

---

[4] The matching procedures do not consider volume due to reporting differences on the NASDAQ versus the NYSE/AMEX. The batching procedure used at the open on the organized exchanges combines a number of trades that would have been observed separately on the NASDAQ/NMS. In addition, buy and sell orders involve separate transactions on the NASDAQ/NMS whereas the orders may cross in specialist markets. Imposing additional matching criteria beyond price and size is of limited importance in the present context since firm-by-firm comparisons are not made across trading structures. Indeed, our emphasis is not on the direct comparison of trading costs but, rather, the way stocks are quoted on NASDAQ versus the organized exchanges. In addition, our empirical results for the sample of NYSE/AMEX stocks are consistent with prior studies of dollar spreads, suggesting that our sample is representative of the population of exchange-listed stocks.

Table I
The Distribution of Average Daily Closing Prices and End-of-Year Market Capitalizations for the Samples of 100 NASDAQ and 100 NYSE/AMEX Firms in 1991

The samples are first matched using average prices, and then paired using market capitalizations.

	NASDAQ Stocks ($)	NYSE/AMEX Stocks ($)
Panel A: The Distribution of Average Prices		
Maximum	106.41	116.99
75th percentile	43.46	43.43
Median	30.08	30.21
25th percentile	17.92	17.94
Minimum	4.82	4.89
Mean	32.39	32.55
Panel B: The Distribution of End-of-Year Equity Capitalizations (in 000s)		
Maximum	19,724,624	15,781,525
75th percentile	2,299,012	2,187,686
Median	1,391,891	960,784
25th percentile	241,818	229,886
Minimum	100,716	101,928
Mean	1,905,336	1,784,705

impose this condition since the depth variable for NASDAQ stocks does not provide a measure of the depth across all dealers. Thus, all quotes studied in this paper reflect a revision in the inside bid and/or inside ask.

Since the market is open between 9:30 A.M. and 4:00 P.M. eastern time, eligible trades must be time-stamped during this interval.[5] Similarly, quotes must be posted during the regular trading hours. We exclude all trades that have condition codes other than a regular sale, and exclude all quotes that are not best bid and offer (BBO)-Eligible.[6] Finally, we eliminate the first trade after the open for NYSE and AMEX stocks, since a call market is used for opening trades, while an auction market is used for all subsequent trades.

---

[5] NYSE/AMEX trades time stamped between 4:00 P.M. and 4:05 P.M. may still represent regular trades since the crowd is permitted to trade until the price is resolved and the clerical reports completed. However, we exclude trades after the close from all exchanges since the duration of regular trades on the NASDAQ after the close is unclear, and we want to align the close of the markets in trading time.

[6] BBO-eligible quotes for NASDAQ stocks represent the actual BBO among all the market makers posting quotes for each security under normal trading conditions. BBO-eligible quotes for exchange-listed stocks indicate the inside spread posted by each exchange. Most BBO-ineligible quotes arise from trading halts or delayed openings.

II. A Comparison of Dollar Spreads for NASDAQ and NYSE/AMEX Stocks

This section establishes the differences in the dollar spreads for similar stocks that trade under different market structures. The data used to document these results consist of all 372,625 inside quotes for the NASDAQ sample and all 544,811 inside quotes for the sample of listed stocks during 1991. The distribution of dollar spreads for the two samples is shown in Figure 1. The figure indicates that the distribution of dollar spreads for NYSE/AMEX stocks is unimodal at $0.25 per share. One-eighth and three-eighths spreads are equally common, while a spread of $0.50 is observed among only 5 percent of all quotes. In contrast, the spreads for NASDAQ stocks are typically multiples of $0.25. Hence NASDAQ spreads of $0.25 and $0.5 are both more common than spreads of $0.375, and spreads of $0.5 and $0.75 are more common than spreads of $0.625. Spreads of $0.125 represent only 10 percent of NASDAQ spreads as compared to 25 percent for listed

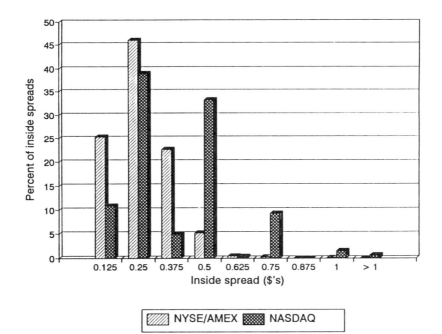

Figure 1. The distribution of inside spreads (in dollars) for 100 NASDAQ and 100 NYSE/AMEX securities of simialr price and end-of-year market capitalization. The distributions are computed using all inside quotes for all stocks in 1991. We exclude quotes where the inside bid and inside ask are unchanged from the previous inside quote within the same trading day. The horizontal axis shows the dollar inside spread. The vertical axis represents the percentage of all inside quote revisions that produce the specified spreads.

stocks. Thus, Figure 1 reveals a fundamental difference in the distribution of dollar spreads for NASDAQ and NYSE/AMEX firms.[7]

While Figure 1 shows that spreads of one-eighth are less common for NASDAQ than listed stocks, it does not convey how rare one-eighth spreads are for some NASDAQ stocks. Figure 2 shows the distribution of the percentage of quotes that produce a one-eighth spread across the 100 NASDAQ and 100 NYSE/AMEX firms, separately. The horizontal axis shows the percentage of all quotes that result in a one-eighth spread, while the height of the bar represents the number of firms with the specific percentage of one-eighth spreads. The figure shows that for most NASDAQ firms, fewer than 4 percent of the quotes result in a one-eighth spread. This pattern is shared by only two listed stocks. In contrast to the NASDAQ sample, between 5 and 40 percent of quote revisions result in a one-eighth spread for most listed stocks.

To provide specific examples of the frequency of one-eighth spreads for NASDAQ stocks, Panel A of Table II reports the percentage of spreads that are $0.125, $0.25, $0.375, and $0.50 for Apple Computer, Lotus Development, and MCI Communication. Although Apple and Lotus are among the most actively traded and highly visible NASDAQ firms, fewer than 1.5 percent of all quoted spreads are $0.125. More striking is that a spread of $0.50 is observed for almost half of the quotes for Apple and Lotus. However, some large and actively traded NASDAQ stocks have spreads that frequently narrow to one-eighth. For example, the distribution of dollar spreads for MCI is heavily concentrated at $0.125 and $0.25.

III. A Comparison of Odd-Eighth Quotes for NASDAQ and NYSE/AMEX Stocks

A. Are NASDAQ and Listed Stocks Quoted Differently?

The pattern of dollar spreads for NASDAQ firms noted in Figure 2 suggests that spreads of $0.25 or multiples thereof are far more common than spreads that require the simultaneous use of odd- and even-eighth quotes. To assess whether the relative frequency of odd-eighth versus even-eighth quotes differs between NASDAQ and the NYSE/AMEX, we compute the percentage of all quotes that lie on each eighth, where the percentage is an average of the frequencies at the bid and the ask. The results are plotted in Figure 3. The figure indicates that the use of odd-eighth quotes is uniformly less frequent than even-eighths for NYSE/AMEX stocks. This finding is consistent with the results reported by Harris (1991). However, it is important to recognize that although the even-eighths appear to be favored relative to the odd-eighths, the percentage of odd-eighth quotes exceeds 10 percent at each odd eighth for NYSE/AMEX stocks. In stark contrast, fewer than 4 percent of the

---

[7] The width of the spread for NYSE/AMEX stocks reflects the quotes that originate from their respective exchange and does not represent the best consolidated quotation. Thus, the contrast between the distribution of spreads for NYSE/AMEX and NASDAQ stocks may be understated.

NASDAQ Market Makers and Avoidance of Odd-Eighth Quotes   1821

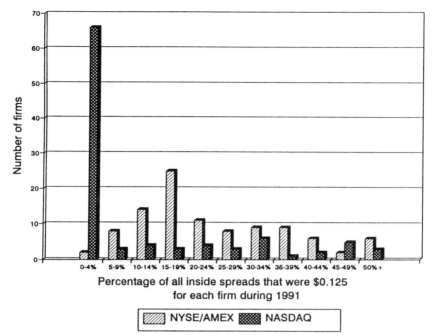

Percentage of all inside spreads that were $0.125
for each firm during 1991

NYSE/AMEX   NASDAQ

Figure 2. The percentage of inside spreads that are $0.125 for 100 NASDAQ and 100 NYSE/AMEX securities of similar price and end-of-year market capitalization. This figure contrasts the frequency of one-eighth spreads for stocks listed on the NYSE/AMEX versus stocks listed on NASDAQ in 1991. For each firm, we compute the percentage of quote revisions that produce a spread of $0.125 using all inside quotes. We exclude quotes where the inside bid and inside ask are unchanged from the previous inside quote within the same trading day. The height of the bar represents the number of firms whose frequency of one-eighth spreads corresponds to the percentages denoted on the horizontal axis. For example, for 66 of the 100 NASDAQ firms in our sample, fewer than 4 percent of all inside spreads are $0.125. In contrast, this small fraction of $0.125 spreads is shared by only 2 NYSE/AMEX stocks.

quotes for NASDAQ stocks fall on each of the odd eighths.[8] Thus, Figure 3 highlights a dramatic difference in the way that stocks are quoted on the NASDAQ relative to the NYSE/AMEX. NASDAQ stocks are, on average, far less likely to be quoted using odd eighths than firms listed on the NYSE or the AMEX.

---

[8] To ensure that our results are not an artifact of ISSM data errors, the analysis was replicated for a small subsample of NASDAQ stocks during a limited period during 1991 by using market maker quotes previously downloaded from the Bridge Quotation System. The frequency of odd-eighth quotes from the Bridge system are essentially identical to those reported in this article.

Table II
The Distribution of Dollar Spreads, Odd-Eighth Bid and Ask Quotes, and the Percentage of Large and Small Trades Executed on Odd Eighths for Selected NASDAQ Stocks

The table provides summary statistics for Apple Computer, Lotus Development, and MCI Communications. The distributions are calculated using all intraday quote updates posted in 1991. In Panel C, the percentages are calculated using all intraday trades executed in 1991 between 9:30 A.M. and 4:00 P.M. Large trades are defined as those trades exceeding 1,000 shares, while small trades are defined as those of 1,000 shares or less.

Panel A: The Proportion of $0.125, $0.250, $0.375, and $0.500 Spreads

Stock	Dollar Spread			
	$0.125 (%)	$0.250 (%)	$0.375 (%)	$0.500 (%)
Apple Computer	1.2	49.3	1.8	47.7
Lotus Development	1.3	49.3	2.0	47.3
MCI Communication	50.3	48.7	1.0	0.0

Panel B: The Percentage of All Bid and Ask Quotes with Odd-Eighth Price Fractions

Stock	Percentage of Bid Quotes at Odd Eighths	Percentage of Ask Quotes at Odd Eighths
Apple Computer	1.4	1.7
Lotus Development	1.7	1.6
MCI Communication	51.0	51.4

Panel C: The Percentage of Large and Small Trades that Are Executed at Odd Eighths

Stock	Small Trades (%)	Large Trades (%)
Apple Computer	9.2	23.6
Lotus Development	9.4	28.0
MCI Communication	47.2	49.3

To determine whether the infrequent use of odd-eighth quotes is shared by all NASDAQ stocks or is common to only a subset of firms, the percentage of odd-eighth quotes is calculated for each firm, where the percentage is an average of the frequencies at the bid and the ask. Figure 4 provides a histogram showing the number of NASDAQ stocks that share a similar percentage of odd-eighth quotes. The figure reveals that the lack of odd-eighth quotes is much more pronounced for some stocks than for others. For the majority of NASDAQ stocks in our sample, less than 2 percent of their quotes appear on all of the odd eighths *combined*. Thus, the lack of one-eighth spreads for some NASDAQ stocks is not surprising in light of the absence of odd-eighth quotes.

A closer examination of Figure 4 indicates that the distribution of odd-eighth quotes is bimodal, as the percentage is close to 0 or 50 percent for a majority of firms. To illustrate, Panel B of Table II reports the distribution of odd-eighth quotes at the bid and at the ask for Apple Computer, Lotus

NASDAQ Market Makers and Avoidance of Odd-Eighth Quotes

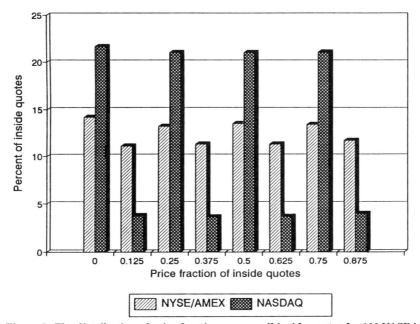

Figure 3. The distribution of price fractions across all inside quotes for 100 NASDAQ and 100 NYSE/AMEX securities of similar price and end-of-year market capitalization. The figure contrasts the percentage of price fractions that fall on each eighth for firms listed on the NYSE/AMEX versus firms listed on NASDAQ. The percentage is an average of the frequencies at the bid and ask, computed using all inside quotes for all stocks throughout 1991. We exclude quotes where the inside bid and inside ask are unchanged from the previous inside quote within the same trading day.

Development, and MCI Communications. Fewer than 2 percent of all bid or ask quotes fall on odd eighths for both Apple and Lotus, while more than half of the bid or ask quotes are on odd eighths for MCI.[9]

The concentration of odd-eighth quote frequencies near 0 and 50 percent suggests that the intermediate percentages between 10 and 40 percent may indicate firms whose market makers ceased or initiated quoting on odd eighths during 1991. To examine whether the pattern of quoting on odd eighths changed during the year for these firms, Figure 5 plots the cumulative monthly percentage of quotes that appear on odd eighths for the five most active of these stocks. As the figure indicates, the percentage of odd-eighth quotes for each stock began the year near 50 percent. However, the percentage of odd-eighth quotes for each stock collapsed to near 0 percent at

---

[9] The absence of odd-eighth quotes for Apple and Lotus is not restricted to the sample period studied in this article. Using data obtained from the Bridge Quotation System, we found that these stocks continued to be quoted solely in even eighths on January 28, 1994.

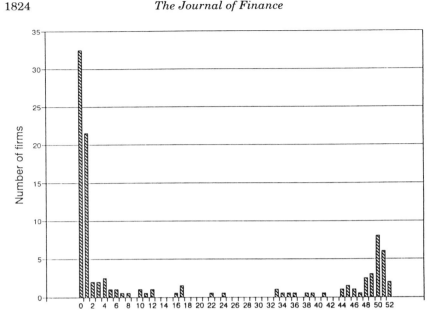

Percentage of inside quotes that contain an odd-eighth
for each firm during 1991

Figure 4. The frequency of odd-eighth quotes across the sample of 100 NASDAQ securities. The frequency of odd-eighth quotes is computed as an average of the frequencies at the bid and the ask, using all inside quotes throughout 1991. We exclude quotes where the inside bid and inside ask are unchanged from the previous inside quote within the same trading day. The horizontal axis represents the percentage of all quotes that result in an odd-eighth quote. The height of the bar represents the number of firms with the specific percentage of odd-eighth quotes in 1991.

different times during 1991, with virtually no odd-eighth quotes present by December. Thus, whatever factors induced market makers to use odd eighths in quoting these stocks early in 1991 vanished during the year.[10]

While Figures 3 and 4 establish the lack of odd-eighth quotes for a majority of NASDAQ firms, the number of odd-eighth quotes may exaggerate their

---

[10] While the five firms studied in Figure 5 cease using odd eighths during 1991, a few of the less active stocks with an intermediate fraction of odd-eighth quotes initiated using odd eighths during the year. We also attempt to identify a common event that could explain why market makers altered the way that they quoted these stocks during 1991. However, an examination of the *Wall Street Journal Index* provides no clues as to the underlying reason why market makers initiated or ceased using odd eighths. We do observe significant average price increases among firms whose market makers ceased using odd eighths, consistent with the hypothesis that higher priced firms would have wider spreads. However, we also note similar price increases for stocks whose dealers began using odd-eighth quotes during 1991. Thus, we are unable to identify a consistent explanation for the decision by market makers to alter their use of odd-eighth quotes.

NASDAQ Market Makers and Avoidance of Odd-Eighth Quotes 1825

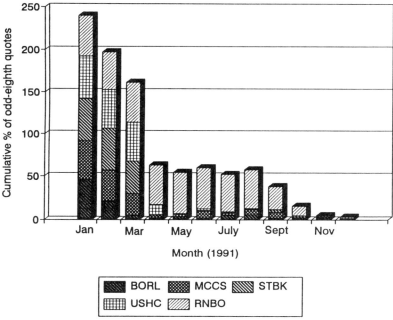

Figure 5. The monthly frequency of odd-eighth quotes for 5 NASDAQ firms whose market makers ceased using odd eighths in 1991. The percentage of odd-eighth quotes represents an average of the frequency of odd-eighth quotes at the inside bid and inside ask. We exclude quotes where the inside bid and inside ask are unchanged from the previous inside quote within the same trading day. The firms used in the figure are: Borland International Inc. (BORL), Medco Containment Services (MCCS), United States Healthcare Inc. (USHC), State Street Boston Corp. (STBK), and Rainbow Technologies Inc. (RNBO). The vertical axis represents the cumulative frequency of odd-eighth quotes summed across the 5 firms. Thus, the cumulative frequency of close to 250 percent in January indicates that odd-eighth quotes represented close to 50 percent of the price fractions for each of these firms at the start of the year. This cumulative frequency collapses to near zero by December 1991.

limited importance if they are effective for shorter time intervals than are even-eighth quotes. To examine this issue, we calculate the average time that odd-eighth quotes (at either the bid or ask) and even-eighth quotes (at both the bid and ask) are in effect. The analysis separately considers the 70 (30) NASDAQ stocks whose market makers rarely (routinely) use odd eighths, where market makers are defined as quoting in odd eighths if at least 25 percent of all the quotes include an odd eighth.

The results are presented in Figure 6. The horizontal axis denotes the mean quote duration (in minutes) for each stock. The height of the bar depicts the number of stocks sharing each average quote duration. Panel A, which presents the results for the 70 issues whose market makers rarely use odd eighths, indicates that for most stocks the average length of time that an odd-eighth quote is effective is less than 2 minutes. In contrast, the mean duration of even-eighth quotes is between 20 and 35 minutes. Thus, the ability to transact at odd-eighth quotes is even rarer than Figures 3 and 4 imply. Panel B, which presents the results for the 30 issues whose market

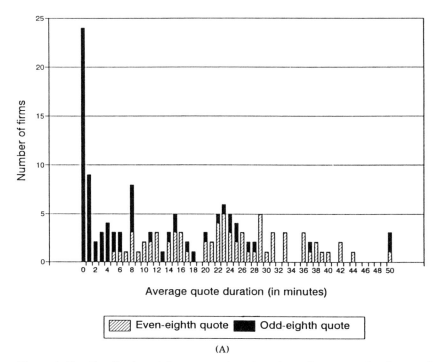

(A)

Figure 6. The distribution of the average duration of standing quotes for the sample of 100 NASDAQ stocks. The figure presents the distribution across firms of the average time (in minutes) that inside quotes remain unchanged for odd-eighth and even-eighth quotes during 1991. We exclude quotes where the inside bid and inside ask are unchanged from the previous inside quote within the same trading day. An even-eighth quote is defined as a quote where both the inside bid and inside ask fall on an even eighth. An odd-eighth quote contains an odd eighth at the inside bid and/or inside ask. The average quote duration for even-eighth and odd-eighth quotes is computed for each stock. Panel A (B) presents the distribution of quote durations across the 70 (30) NASDAQ stocks whose market makers avoid (use) odd eighths. Market makers are designated as avoiding odd eighths if fewer than 25 percent of inside quotes include an odd eighth in 1991. The height of the bar indicates the number of firms whose even-eighth or odd-eighth quote durations correspond to the values indicated on the horizontal axis. For example, the distribution in Panel A indicates that the average quote duration for odd-eighth quotes was less than 3 minutes for 35 of the 70 firms. In comparison, the average quote duration for even-eighth quotes was never less than 3 minutes for any of these 70 stocks.

NASDAQ Market Makers and Avoidance of Odd-Eighth Quotes 1827

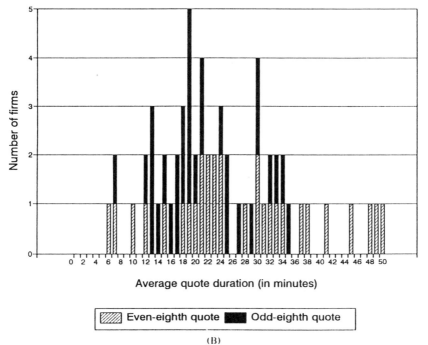

(B)

Figure 6.—Continued.

makers routinely use odd eighths, shows that the mean duration of odd-eighth and even-eighth quotes is quite similar.

Finally, to assess whether the more active stocks (as measured by the total number of trades in 1991) are more likely to be quoted in odd eighths, we calculate the percentage of odd-eighth quotes separately for the 50 most active and the 50 least active stocks in our sample. The results are plotted in Figure 7. The figure shows that trading activity is unable to predict which firms are quoted in odd eighths. Although the fraction of stocks whose market makers use odd eighths for 40 to 50 percent of their quotes is higher for the more active firms, the vast majority of firms in both groups are traded by market makers that avoid odd eighths.

In summary, the differences in spreads, and therefore trading costs, between a majority of NASDAQ and listed securities can be traced to a departure by NASDAQ dealers from using all potential price fractions. In a competitive market with multiple market makers competing for order flow, the almost complete absence of odd-eighth quotes is an enigma. The rest of the article attempts to further understand the nature of this result and pursues possible explanations for its existence.

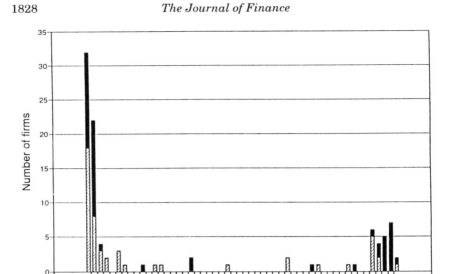

Percentage of inside quotes that contain an odd-eighth

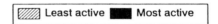

Figure 7. The frequency of odd-eighth quotes for the 50 most active and 50 least active NASDAQ stocks in our sample. The frequency of odd-eighth quotes is computed for each firm using all inside quotes throughout 1991. We exclude quotes where the inside bid and inside ask are unchanged from the previous inside quote within the same trading day. The horizontal axis represents the percentage of all inside quotes that result in an odd-eighth price fraction. The height of the bar represents the number of firms with the specific percentage of odd-eighth quotes. Trading activity is measured by the total number of trades in 1991.

B. The Avoidance of Odd-Eighth Quotes and the Costs of Negotiation

Harris (1991) documents price clustering for NYSE stocks, where prices ending on even dollar amounts are more common than prices ending on halves; halves are more common than odd quarters; and odd quarters are more common than odd eighths. Figure 4 indicates that clustering is present for the NYSE/AMEX quotes in our sample, where odd-eighth quotes constitute between 40 and 50 percent of the total.[11] Harris (1991) suggests that price clustering may serve to lower the costs of negotiation. By using coarse price increments, the time needed to agree on a price and the likelihood of a misunderstanding are minimized. Harris further states that individual deal-

---

[11] Harris notes that clustering is more pronounced for NASDAQ stocks than listed stocks, but when examining NASDAQ stocks he examines the proportion of prices at whole dollars rather than the frequency of odd and even eighths.

ers have an incentive to use coarse price increments to establish "a reputation as low-cost negotiators because they play a repeated game."

This negotiation hypothesis provides testable implications for the relation between trade size and price clustering for NASDAQ stocks. Since this hypothesis requires that trades be negotiated between dealers, the analysis explicitly distinguishes between negotiated and automated executions. Orders of 1,000 shares or less are seldom negotiated but are executed automatically through the Small Order Execution System (SOES). These orders are allocated sequentially among dealers posting inside quotes or preferenced to a market maker who has agreed in advance to execute preferenced trades at the inside market. In contrast, larger orders are directly negotiated between the dealer and the stockbroker acting as agent for the buyer or seller. If quotes are restricted to even eighths to minimize the costs of negotiation, large trades should *not* be transacted on the odd eighths, particularly for firms that are not typically quoted in odd eighths. Alternatively, if the benefits of negotiation for trades that exceed 1,000 shares outweigh the potential costs, market makers may use the full range of possible prices. Under this interpretation, negotiated trades are more likely to involve an odd eighth as market makers attempt to obtain a price that lies inside the posted even-eighth quotes.

Whether the potential benefits outweigh the costs and produce a greater or lesser concentration of odd-eighth trade prices is an empirical issue, which is resolved in Figure 8. Panel A displays the frequency of odd-eighth transaction prices for the 70 stocks whose market makers rarely use odd eighths. The figure indicates that large trades are *far more likely* to occur on odd eighths than are small trades. Indeed, the two distributions of large versus small trades on odd eighths barely overlap. Panel B, which provides the results for the 30 issues whose dealers regularly use odd eighths, shows no discernable difference between the distribution of large and small trades on odd eighths. Thus, when stocks are quoted in even eighths, dealers will execute trades on odd eighths more frequently when the trades are negotiated rather than executed automatically. Therefore, the negotiation hypothesis appears incapable of explaining the lack of odd-eighth quotes for the majority of our sample.

Panel C of Table II provides specific examples of the use of odd-eighth prices for large versus small transactions for three selected NASDAQ firms. For Apple and Lotus approximately 10 percent of small trades are transacted on an odd eighth. In contrast, close to 30 percent of large trades occur on an odd eighth. MCI continues to display characteristics that are similar to listed stocks, with little difference noted in the use of odd eighths for small or large trades.

These results also provide evidence on the costs of transacting from the perspective of trades rather than quotes. The lack of odd-eighth quotes would be unimportant if trades were evenly distributed across all eighths. However, Figure 8 reveals an inordinate number of trades on even rather than odd eighths, especially for trades of 1,000 shares or less. Thus, effective spreads, as well as quoted spreads, are affected by the lack of odd eighths.

C. *Can the Economic Determinants of Spreads Explain the Lack of Odd-Eighth Quotes?*

Cross-sectional differences in the use of odd-eighth quotes across firms may be explained by the underlying economic factors that are thought to determine bid-ask spreads. Spreads may be inversely related to volume if greater volume implies that dealers can unwind risky positions more quickly. Studies by Goldstein (1993), Neal (1992), and Stoll (1978) provide empirical support for this conjecture. Greater volatility implies that dealers face higher inven-

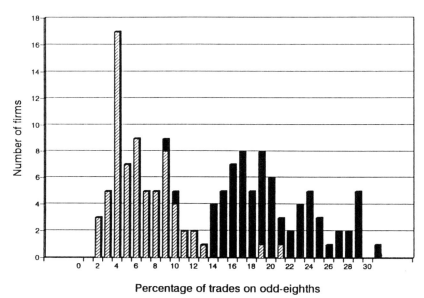

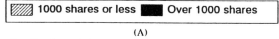

(A)

Figure 8. The distribution of the percentage of large and small trades executed on odd eighths across the sample of 100 NASDAQ stocks. We include all trades that are executed between 9:30 A.M. and 4:00 P.M. for the NASDAQ sample throughout 1991. Small trades are defined as 1,000 shares or fewer, whereas large trades exceed this threshold. The horizontal axis represents the percentage of all trades that were executed on an odd eighth, while the height of the bar represents the number of firms sharing the specific percentage of odd-eighth trades. Panel A (B) presents the evidence for the 70 (30) NASDAQ stocks whose market makers avoid (use) odd eighths. Market makers are designated as avoiding odd eighths if fewer than 25 percent of inside quotes include an odd eighth in 1991.

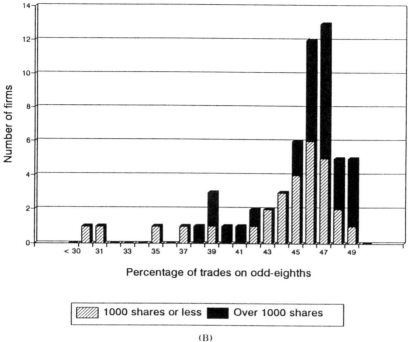

(B)
Figure 8.—Continued.

tory risk and greater losses from trading against informed traders. Benston and Hagerman (1974), Stoll (1978), Neal (1992), and Goldstein (1993) show that wider spreads are also associated with higher standard deviations of returns. Other variables that have been previously shown to affect spread width include market capitalization and, for dollar spreads, the stock price.

To assess whether these variables can help explain the cross-sectional differences in the propensity of market makers to use odd-eighth quotes, we again partition firms based on whether their market makers used or avoided odd eighths. For each stock, we estimate the annual average of the daily closing price, daily size (stock price times shares outstanding), daily trading volume, the daily number of market makers, and the standard deviation of daily returns estimated from the midpoint of the daily closing bid and ask prices.[12] We also include dummy variables to indicate whether trades were

---

[12] Another variable that might be potentially important in predicting the firms whose market makers use odd eighths is the distribution of market concentration. Stocks where the trading volume is concentrated among a small subset of market makers would be more likely to be quoted solely in even eighths. Unfortunately, the distribution of market concentration among dealers could not be identified with our data sources.

executed on a regional exchange and whether listed options were traded in 1991. These latter two factors are predicted to increase the probability that a stock would be quoted in odd eighths, as they imply competition from other sources to trade the stock or securities that are close substitutes for the stock. We then estimate logistic regressions that predict the probability of a firm being quoted using odd eighths. In a separate regression, we include a dummy variable that indicates whether odd-eighth quotes were used in January 1991.

Panel A of Table III reports the maximum likelihood estimates of the coefficients from the logistic regressions, along with their standard errors. The first regression uses the full sample, while the second regression is confined to the period between July and December. Since we estimate the regressions over different periods, the monthly proportion of odd-eighth quotes is averaged separately across months for the two regressions. This averaging classifies 71 of the 100 stocks as not routinely quoted in odd eighths in each period. The results for these two regressions indicate that the coefficients on price and variance are statistically significant at the 5 percent level. Thus, the probability that a stock will be quoted in odd eighths declines with the stock price and return variability. However, the remaining coefficients are insignificantly different from zero in each of the first two regressions.

To demonstrate the logistic model's ability to correctly classify stocks as being quoted or not being quoted in odd eighths, we first partition the sample using the criterion of whether the model predicts a probability of odd-eighths use that is greater or less than 50 percent. We then examine whether this criterion accurately partitions the sample into firms that do or do not use odd eighths. The results are contained in the first two rows of Panel B in Table III. Of the 71 stocks whose market makers rarely use odd eighths, 65 (64) are correctly classified using the probabilities estimated from the first (second) regression. Of the 29 stocks whose market makers routinely used odd eighths, 15 are correctly classified. While the probabilities supplied by the model correctly classify 80 percent of the 100 stocks, a naive prediction that no stocks are quoted in odd eighths correctly classifies 71 percent. These results suggest that the logistic model's ability to predict whether a stock will be quoted in odd eighths is limited, particularly in classifying stocks where odd-eighth quotes are routinely used.[13]

Since the economic fundamentals used in our logistic regressions do not explain the mysterious absence of odd-eighth quotes, the third regression in Panel A in Table III includes a dummy variable, "Past," which equals 1 for

---

[13] The regressions are replicated for a subsample of 96 firms where we can identify the percentage of outstanding shares owned by institutions at the end of 1991, as reported in the *Standard and Poor's Stock Guide*. A higher percentage of ownership among institutions might force market makers to post wider spreads (and avoid the use of odd eighths) if the dealers perceived an increased probability of informed trades. However, the estimated t-statistic for this variable is under 1.0.

Table III
Results of Logistic Regressions that Predict the Probability that Stocks are Quoted Using Odd Eighths

We classify stocks as being quoted in odd eighths if the average monthly proportion of quotes on odd eighths is at least 25 percent. The dependent variable takes a value of 1 for stocks that are quoted in odd eighths. The independent variables used in the logistic regression are as follows. Volume is in 100,000s of shares, daily. Size is measured as the equity capitalization in multiples of $1 million. Variance is measured using daily returns calculated from the midpoint of the closing bid-ask spread. Price is defined as the average of the bid-ask midpoint measured over all quotes. Number of Dealers during 1991 is computed by weighting the number of market makers by the proportion of days that number appeared in 1991. Volume, Size, Variance, Price, and the number of market makers are obtained from the Center for Research in Securities Prices NASDAQ tape. Listed Options is a dummy variable that takes the value of 1 for firms with listed options during 1991. Dual listed is a dummy variable that equals 1 for firms whose shares were traded on the regional exchanges. Past is a dummy variable that takes the value of 1 if the firm had been quoted using odd eighths in January. The regression estimates are presented in Panel A. The logistic regressions estimate a probability that a stock will be quoted in odd eighths. We define stocks as being correctly classified by the model in Panel B if the stock is (is not) quoted in odd eighths and the model assigns a probability of at least 0.5 (less than 0.5) that the stock is quoted in odd eighths. na means not applicable.

Panel A: Coefficient Estimates

Regression Coefficient and Standard Errors (in parentheses)

Regression	Sample Period (1991)	Price	Size ($ millions)	Volume (100,000s)	Variance	Number of Dealers	Listed Options	Dual Listed	Past
1	Full year	−0.157**	−0.00010	−0.00017	−8.573**	0.127	1.326	−0.588	na
		(0.042)	(0.00046)	(0.00159)	(3.370)	(0.073)	(1.040)	(1.048)	
2	July–December	−0.173**	−0.00012	−0.00016	−9.014*	0.117	1.418	−0.462	na
		(0.044)	(0.00042)	(0.00165)	(3.524)	(0.069)	(1.055)	(1.104)	
3	July–December	−0.252*	0.000943	−0.00109	−9.373	−0.014	2.608	0.369	13.138**
		(0.111)	(0.000864)	(0.00262)	(5.811)	(0.164)	(2.171)	(2.377)	(3.686)

Panel B: Classification Accuracy

Regression	Sample Period (1991)	Stocks Not Quoted in Odd Eighths		Stocks Quoted in Odd Eighths	
		Correctly Classified	Incorrectly Classified	Correctly Classified	Incorrectly Classified
1	Full year	65	6	15	14
2	July–December 1991	64	7	15	14
3	July–December 1991	64	7	24	5

* Significantly different from 0 at the 5 percent level.
** Significantly different from 0 at the 1 percent level.

firms where odd eighths had been used in January. The results show that the coefficient for "Past" is 13.14. The standard error of 3.69 indicates that the coefficient is significant at the 1 percent confidence level. The price variable retains its negative coefficient, but is now statistically significant only at the 5 percent level. More importantly, the third row of Panel B shows that classification is much improved with the knowledge of whether odd-eighth quotes had been used in January, particularly for those stocks that are regularly quoted in odd eighths. Specifically, the model now correctly classifies 24 of the 29 firms whose market makers use odd eighths, whereas the regressions that excluded "Past" correctly predicted only 15 of these 29 firms.

To further study the persistence in the avoidance of odd-eighth quotes, we examine the frequency of odd- and even-eighth quotes for NASDAQ stocks that split during 1991. A total of 20 stocks split 3-2, 2-1, or 3-1 from February through November. In the month prior to the split, odd eighths comprised less than 3 percent of the quotes for 16 of the stocks, and more than 42 percent of the quotes for the remaining 4. In the month after the split, there were no significant changes in the proportion of odd-eighth quotes for any of the 20 stocks despite large price declines. These results suggest that if market makers restrict their quotes to quarters, they will continue to do so even when characteristics of the stock change.

D. Tacit Collusion Among Market Makers as an Explanation for the Lack of Odd-Eighth Quotes

Game theory suggests that collusion among NASDAQ market makers may arise despite the large number of dealers in a given market. Market makers interact frequently and over long periods of time with the same population of other market makers. Thus, in setting quotes, NASDAQ dealers are essentially engaged in an infinitely repeated game. Furthermore, current and historical quotes of all market makers are available to all dealers, making it a game of complete and perfect information. The well-known "folk theorem" (see Friedman (1971)) states that under such conditions, and given that the future costs to each player of deserting the equilibrium exceed the immediate gains, collusion is a possible equilibrium. In this context the absence of odd-eighth quotes is not surprising. In situations where agents collude, round numbers can be used as "focal points" to coordinate prices (see Fudenberg and Tirole (1993), pages 19 to 21).

The screen-based trading system used by NASDAQ renders the market sufficiently transparent that dealers who move within the accepted spread are readily observed. Other dealers can easily punish an offender by selecting from a number of alternative sanctions. One sanction is to have brokers divert customer orders away from a violator with the best posted but non-sanctioned price, thereby depriving the violator from receiving the trades.[14]

---

[14] In addition, market makers can elect to execute their retail customers' orders using the inside bid or ask prices. In this case, the orders are never entered into the NASDAQ execution systems, and the offending dealer has no opportunity to receive the trade.

NASDAQ Market Makers and Avoidance of Odd-Eighth Quotes

This is easily accomplished since brokers are allowed to "preference" customer orders to any specific dealer who has agreed in advance to execute trades at the best quoted bid or ask price, independent of their posted quotes. Alternatively, if a violator has agreed to accept preferenced orders, brokers can preference customer orders to the violator on the wrong side of the spread. That is, if the offending dealer has the best quoted ask, sell orders can be directed to that dealer, who is required to execute them at the inside bid. Although the size of the preferenced orders will be 1,000 shares or less per trade, the cumulative effect of forcing a violator to accept these orders from multiple dealers can be significant. A third method for punishing dealers who move within the accepted spread is to direct customer trades to the offending dealer when the trades are perceived to be motivated by information rather than liquidity needs. An important feature of these sanctions is that they do not impose any costs on the brokers who initiate the preferenced orders. Finally, since NASDAQ market makers typically make markets in many stocks, sanctions can be applied in markets for other stocks or by withholding business in other areas (e.g., underwriting).

The presence of tacit collusion among market makers would suggest that odd-eighth quotes that narrow the existing spread would be rare. To examine whether odd-eighth spreads reflect an increase or decrease in the inside spread, Figure 9 plots the proportion of quotes that narrow the spread through the use of an odd eighth for the 70 firms whose dealers routinely avoid them. The analysis is confined to odd-eighth spreads that are $0.375 or wider, since quotes that produce spreads of $0.125 must always narrow the inside spread given the minimum tick size of one eighth for our sample of firms. The implicit collusion hypothesis predicts that the proportion of odd-eighth spreads that are narrower than the previous spread should be relatively low. Consistent with this prediction, Figure 9 indicates that an odd-eighth spread is far more likely to reflect an increasing rather than a narrowing spread.

While this article does not provide conclusive evidence of tacit collusion among market makers, we are unable to offer any other plausible explanation for the lack of odd-eighth quotes. In particular, using an odd eighth to better a spread should result in an instant increase in order flow through SOES to the firm posting the improved quote. Thus, it is difficult to understand why, in the absence of tacit collusion, at least a few of the 50-plus market makers of Apple Computer do not use odd-eighth quotes to attract orders. Furthermore, the increased use of odd eighths for large trades is consistent with a market where dealers agree to maintain wide spreads for smaller customer orders but negotiate larger trades on the odd eighths when trading with a fellow dealer. The exceptionally short duration of odd-eighth quotes arises naturally in the presence of implicit agreements among dealers to rely on the even eighths. Under the hypothesis that our results arise from the presence of an implicit understanding among market makers to not post odd-eighth quotes, our evidence suggests that once tacit agreements are established,

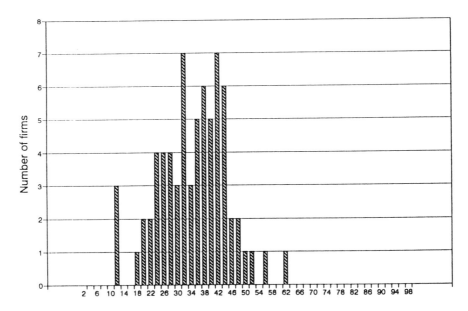

Percentage of odd-eighth spreads that are
narrower than the previous inside spread

Figure 9. The distribution of the percentage of odd-eighth spreads that are narrower than the previous spread across the sample of 70 NASDAQ stocks whose market makers avoid odd-eighth quotes. Market makers are designated as avoiding odd eighths if fewer than 25 percent of inside quotes include an odd eighth. The figure depicts the percentage of odd-eighth spreads of at least $0.375 that are narrower than the previous spread. The frequency of odd-eighth spreads is computed for each firm using all inside quotes throughout 1991. We exclude quotes where the inside bid and inside ask are unchanged from the previous inside quote within the same trading day. The horizontal axis represents the percentage of all quotes that result in an odd-eighth spread of at least $0.375. The height of the bar represents the number of firms with the specific percentage of odd-eighth spreads.

they can be maintained despite changes in market conditions and the number and identity of dealers making markets in these stocks.

It is possible that the higher trading costs imposed on investors through spreads of at least $0.25 may reflect structural characteristics unique to a dealer market that translate into higher costs of market making. Since the total order flow is fragmented across market makers, each dealer observes the order flow directed to that dealer alone. Thus, dealers face increased risks of being "picked off" by informed traders who disperse their trades across numerous dealers. In addition, NASDAQ spreads may be wider than spreads of listed stocks since individual market makers minimize the costs associated with posting locked or crossed quotes.[15] While these explanations suggest that spreads may be wider for NASDAQ stocks than listed stocks on average, they do not explain why one-eighth spreads almost never appear for some of the most active NASDAQ stocks or why some firms are quoted in odd eighths while others are not.

An additional explanation for the persistence of wide spreads among the majority of the NASDAQ sample considers the dynamics of dealer competition in the absence of a time precedence rule (see Harris (1990)). The NASDAQ market does not enforce (and is not designed to enforce) time precedence among its dealers. Spreads may remain wide if dealers who are willing to supply liquidity by posting quotes inside the existing spread are unable to capture the increased order flow from the price improvement. This inability to capture trades exists since other dealers can match their quote or preference orders to dealers who will match the new price. Thus, little incentive exists for individual dealers to improve the spread since such actions would have a very small effect on their ability to attract trades. However, the lack of time precedence also eases the ability of market makers to punish violators, since orders can be easily channeled away from the offending dealer. In addition, the lack of time precedence cannot explain why dealers collectively elected to quote stocks without using odd eighths.

It is important to note that these results do not provide a complete description of the differences between listing on NASDAQ and on the organized exchanges. Hundreds of firms that meet exchange listing requirements elect to remain on the NASDAQ for many years. In equilibrium, additional benefits to listing on the NASDAQ may offset the higher costs that we document for the majority of our sample. Indeed, our results suggest a number of areas for potentially fruitful research. In particular, what determines why certain firms are quoted only in even eighths, and what factors prompt market makers to cease or begin quoting in odd eighths? Further, what are the sources of the additional benefits that accrue to firms that remain listed on the NASDAQ to offset the costs established in this article?

Our results also have implications for the debate concerning the minimum tick size under consideration by the Securities and Exchange Commission, the NASD and the NYSE. For some stocks, the minimum tick size of one-eighth may be larger than necessary, and the movement to a minimum tick size of one-sixteenth may result in narrower spreads and lower trading costs. Harris (1994) presents evidence that suggests the adoption of a one-sixteenth tick size would reduce bid-ask spreads by an average of 38 percent for NYSE stocks, although the depth at these quotes would also decline. Our results strongly suggest that these reductions in spreads would not extend to

---

[15] A related explanation for wider NASDAQ spreads concerns the activity of "SOES Bandits." Since the SOES permits automatic execution of trades for 1,000 shares or less, these traders could exploit cross-sectional discrepancies in dealer quotes to simultaneously buy and sell shares and profit from locked or crossed quotes. Thus, individual dealers need to maintain wider spreads to compensate for losses to the "SOES Bandits." See Stoll (1992) and the December 21, 1993 edition of the *Wall Street Journal* for a more detailed description of these traders.

most stocks listed on NASDAQ. Since the spreads for a large number of NASDAQ stocks in our sample fail to narrow to under $0.25, it seems unlikely that smaller minimum tick sizes would promote narrower spreads.

IV. Summary and Conclusions

While previous studies rely on comparisons of summary measures of bid-ask spreads across markets, we examine the entire distribution of dollar spreads for 100 NASDAQ stocks and compare these results with a sample of 100 NYSE/AMEX firms. Our concern rests not with a direct comparison of trading costs across trading structures, but with how stocks in these different markets are quoted. The volume of data is extensive and includes all trades and quote updates for the entire year of 1991. We find that, unlike NYSE/AMEX stocks, the majority of NASDAQ stocks are virtually never quoted with a spread of $0.125, and that spreads of $0.375 and $0.625 are less common than the surrounding even-eighths spreads. The wider spreads for NASDAQ stocks are directly linked to a pervasive and anomalous distaste for posting bid or ask quotes on odd eighths. We find that when odd-eighth quotes do appear among firms whose market makers rarely use odd eighths, the quotes have the appearance of a mirage since their expected duration is less than 2 minutes, while even-eighth quotes can be expected to last for at least 20 minutes.

The lack of odd-eighth quotes could serve to minimize the costs of negotiation between market makers for executing large trades. However, our results contradict this explanation, since we find that larger trades, which are negotiated, are far more likely to occur on odd eighths than trades of 1,000 shares or less, which are typically executed automatically. Thus, the negotiators appear to gravitate towards odd eighths despite the lack of odd-eighth quotes posted by the same set of dealers. Our logistic regressions indicate that variables previously shown to affect the width of bid-ask spreads have little power in identifying the firms whose market makers avoid or utilize odd eighths. Rather, the variable with the greatest power in classifying firms along this dimension is whether market makers had established a tradition of exclusively using odd-eighth quotes.

In summary, the almost complete absence of odd-eighth quotes for 70 percent of the NASDAQ sample, including such heavily traded stocks as Apple Computer and Lotus Development, imposes obvious and real costs on investors. The results are particularly surprising since they emerge from a dealer market where the inside spread represents the best consolidated quote from as many as 60 market makers. One possible explanation for our results is that we are observing the quote-setting behavior that emerges when individual market makers implicitly agree to maintain spreads of at least $0.25 by not posting quotes on odd eighths. This inference is strengthened by the persistence of this result through time and across stocks and the simultaneous adoption of odd-eighth quotes by NASDAQ market makers when the practice of quoting stocks exclusively in even eighths was made public (see Christie, Harris, and Schultz (1994)).

We are unable to envision any scenario in which 40 to 60 dealers who are competing for order flow would simultaneously and consistently avoid using odd-eighth quotes without an implicit agreement to post quotes only on the even price fractions. However, our data do not provide direct evidence of tacit collusion among NASDAQ market makers. Such inferences would require direct observation of market-maker intervention forcing the withdrawal of nonsanctioned quotes, punishing a dealer who posts nonsanctioned quotes by diverting orders away from that dealer, diverting orders to the offending dealer that would be unwelcome (i.e., information-based trades or trades that would aggravate the violators inventory position), or withholding business in other areas. In light of the absence of odd-eighth quotes and the subsequent inability of spreads to narrow to less than $0.25 for a majority of actively traded NASDAQ stocks, additional research into the source of the apparent lack of competitiveness of the NASDAQ market appears warranted.

REFERENCES

Affleck-Graves, J., S. Hegde, and R. Miller, 1994, Trading mechanisms and the components of the bid-ask spread, *Journal of Finance* 49, 1471–1488.

Benston, G., and R. Hagerman, 1974, Determinants of bid-ask spreads in the over-the-counter market, *Journal of Financial Economics* 1, 353–364.

Brock, W., and A. Kleidon, 1992, Periodic market closure and trading volume: A model of intraday bids and asks, *Journal of Economic Dynamics and Control* 16, 451–489.

Chan, K. C., W. Christie, and P. Schultz, 1995, Market structure and the intraday pattern of bid-ask spreads for NASDAQ securities, *Journal of Business*, Forthcoming.

Chan, K. C., W. Fong, and R. Stulz, 1994, Information, trading and stock returns: Lessons from dually-listed securities, Working paper, Ohio State University.

Christie, W., J. Harris, and P. Schultz, 1994, Why did NASDAQ market makers stop avoiding odd-eighth quotes?, *Journal of Finance* 49, 1841–1860.

Christie, W., and R. Huang, 1994, Market structures and liquidity: A transactions data study of exchange listings, *Journal of Financial Intermediation* 3, 300–326.

Foster, D., and S. Viswanathan, 1993, Variations in trading volume, return volatility, and trading costs: Evidence on recent price formation models, *Journal of Finance* 48, 187–211.

Friedman, J., 1971, A non-cooperative equilibrium for supergames, *Review of Economic Studies* 38, 1–12.

Fudenberg, D., and J. Tirole, 1993, *Game Theory* (MIT Press, Cambridge, Mass.).

Goldstein, M., 1993, Specialist vs. dealer markets: A comparison of displayed bid-ask spreads on NASDAQ and the NYSE, Working paper, University of Pennsylvania.

Harris, L., 1990, *Liquidity, Trading Rules, and Electronic Trading Systems*, Monograph series in finance and economics, New York University.

―――, 1991, Stock price clustering and discreteness, *Review of Financial Studies* 4, 389–415.

―――, 1994, Minimum price variations, discrete bid-ask spreads, and quotation sizes, *Review of Financial Studies* 7, 149–178.

―――, and J. Hasbrouck, 1992, Market vs. Limit orders: The SuperDot evidence on order submission strategy, Working paper, New York University and the University of Southern California.

Kleidon, A., and I. Werner, 1993, Round-the-clock trading: Evidence from U.K. cross-listed securities, Working paper, Stanford University.

McInish, T., and R. Wood, 1992, An analysis of intraday patterns in bid/ask spreads for NYSE stocks, *Journal of Finance* 47, 753–764.

Neal, R., 1992, A comparison of transaction costs between competitive market maker and specialist market structures, *Journal of Business* 65, 317–334.

Schwartz, R., 1991, *Reshaping the Equity Markets: A Guide for the 1990s* (Harper Business, New York).

Stoll, H., 1978, The pricing of dealer security services: An empirical study of NASDAQ stocks, *Journal of Finance* 33, 1153–1172.

———, 1992, Principles of trading market structure, *Journal of Financial Services Research* 6, 75–107.

Vijh, A., 1990, Liquidity of the CBOE equity options, *Journal of Finance* 45, 1157–1179.

C
Competition Across Markets

Market Structures and Liquidity: A Transactions Data Study of Exchange Listings

WILLIAM G. CHRISTIE AND ROGER D. HUANG

Owen Graduate School of Management, Vanderbilt University, 401 21st Avenue South, Nashville, Tennessee 37203

Received April 22, 1993

This paper examines the change in trading costs for firms that choose to move from a dealer market to a specialist system. Using transactions data, our empirical results reveal structurally induced average trading cost reductions of 4.7 (5.2) cents per share for firms that moved from the NASDAQ/NMS to the NYSE (AMEX) in 1990. For NYSE listed stocks, the trading cost reductions are equally divided between quote improvements and the routing of trades to the NYSE. Trading cost improvements vary inversely with trade sizes and positively with dollar spreads. Finally, the greatest liquidity benefits from listing accrue to the less liquid stocks. *Journal of Economic Literature* Classification Numbers: D40, G12, G20. © 1994 Academic Press, Inc.

1. INTRODUCTION

Equity markets with dissimilar trading structures may offer varying levels of market liquidity. Individual and institutional investors prefer liquid markets that can promptly absorb large orders without inducing large price fluctuations. Corporations seek more liquid markets since

---

* The paper has benefitted from the helpful comments and suggestions of Yakov Amihud, Corinne Bronfman, Gene Finn, Richard Goldberg, Sreenivas Kamma, John Lajaunie, Charles Lee, Ron Masulis, Tim McCormick, Tom McInish, Kelly McNamara, Hans Stoll, Bob Wood, workshop participants at the Commodities Futures Trading Commission, George Mason University, Memphis State University, Vanderbilt University, and the 1993 Symposium on Globalization and the Reform of Financial Institutions and Markets at Northwestern University. We are also grateful to Stuart Greenbaum (the editor) and two anonymous referees for their detailed comments. The research was supported by the Dean's Fund for Research and by the Financial Markets Research Center at the Owen Graduate School of Management, Vanderbilt University.

MARKET STRUCTURES AND LIQUIDITY

lower trading costs permit them to obtain lower required rates of return.[1] The decision to switch trading location reflects the outcome of the marriage between the search for liquidity improvements and the provision of liquidity services by markets. Since the decision to relocate exchange listings does not affect a firm's assets or liabilities, the motivation may be linked to the perceived benefits inherent in different trading locations. The purpose of this paper is to test whether structurally-induced reductions in trading costs emerge when firms relocate from a dealer market to a specialist system, and to examine the nature of the hypothesized liquidity improvements.

Our research design draws from two strands of literature. First, the literature on stock listings uses the twin motives of liquidity and reputation to motivate its results.[2] Using event study methodologies and daily return data, this research examines the impact on shareholder wealth from changing trading locations. Since prices would reflect the *expected* benefits of increased liquidity and higher prestige when the intention to switch exchanges becomes public, these studies concentrate their analyses around announcement dates. In contrast, our paper uses transactions data to document the liquidity gains that are *realized* immediately after firms begin trading on their new exchange. Second, there is a growing literature that studies the differences in liquidity across market structures. Most of these studies subscribe to the definition that, in the absence of new information, liquid markets permit prompt low-cost transactions for significant order sizes. Thus, listing studies exploit the arrival of new information while liquidity studies abstract from its presence.

We test for structurally-induced liquidity effects using two relocation pairs: the National Association of Security Dealer Automated Quotation/National Market System (NASDAQ/NMS) to the American Stock Exchange (AMEX), and the NASDAQ/NMS to the New York Stock Exchange (NYSE). The NYSE and the AMEX use an auction/specialist system while the NASDAQ/NMS is a dealer market. The analysis focuses on the costs of trading as captured by both the posted and the realized quotes. The former is represented by dollar and percentage bid-ask spreads. The latter requires calculating "liquidity premiums," or one-

---

[1] Demsetz (1968) argues that illiquid stocks are characterized by wider bid-ask spreads that translate into higher expected returns. Amihud and Mendelson (1986) and Reinganum (1990) provide empirical evidence that highlights the relation between bid-ask spreads and required rates of returns.

[2] This literature has a long history. Ule (1937) provides an early investigation of newly listed stocks. More recent studies include Cowan, *et al.* (1992), Baker and Edelman (1992), and Kadlec and McConnell (1992). Management surveys identify better liquidity and visibility as the main reasons for listing on the AMEX/NYSE (see, for example, Baker and Johnson, 1990). The importance of the reputation motive appears to have declined since the advent of the NASDAQ/NMS in April of 1982 (Sanger and McConnell, 1986).

half the effective bid-ask spreads, measured as the absolute difference between the trade price and the mid-point of the bid-ask quotes.

To attribute the liquidity effects to dissimilar trading structures, we control for several confounding influences. First, we use a portfolio approach that relies on the averaging process across firms to diversify the idiosyncratic effects of new information that may induce quote and price changes unrelated to liquidity. Second, our portfolio approach minimizes the systematic influence of market-wide fluctuations through the dispersion of listing dates in calendar time. Third, we control for firm-specific characteristics across trading locations by following the same firms over a narrow window surrounding the listing date. Thus, our samples are confined to firms that are not just comparable, but identical.

This research design contrasts with previous studies that examine the relation between structural arrangements and market liquidity that have produced conflicting results. For example, Hui and Heubel (1984), Hasbrouck and Schwartz (1986), and Marsh and Rock (1986) find that NYSE/AMEX stocks are more liquid while Cooper et al. (1985) obtain the highest liquidity for NASDAQ/NMS stocks of similar size. Since these comparisons use stocks whose firm-specific characteristics are not perfectly aligned, their results may reflect residual differences in the fundamental values of the assets.[3]

Recent studies place greater emphasis on the careful matching of securities across exchanges. McInish and Wood (1992a) use linear programming techniques to construct comparable portfolios of NASDAQ/NMS and NYSE/AMEX stocks. Since no two stocks are simultaneously listed on both the NASDAQ/NMS and the NYSE/AMEX, the matching of portfolios is only achieved along a limited number of dimensions. An alternative is to study identical firms that are listed on one exchange but are traded on the two systems. Blume and Goldstein (1992), Lee (1992), and Petersen and Fialkowski (1992) study competition in the Third Market, defined as the competition for order flow from the NASDAQ/NMS for securities listed on the AMEX or NYSE, and find that liquidity is generally higher when trades are executed through a specialist.

Our empirical results indicate that large reductions in trading costs are realized when firms move from a dealer market to a specialist system. In light of the magnitude of this reduction, we examine the nature of these liquidity improvements along several dimensions. First, we decompose the liquidity gains into the proportion attributed to quotes that originate from the organized exchanges and to the choice of executing trades on the

---

[3] An exception is the study by Dubofsky and Groth (1984) that follows stocks around their listing date and concludes that NASDAQ/NMS provides higher liquidity than organized exchanges. However, by using daily close-to-close data, their liquidity measures are sampled too infrequently to appropriately capture liquidity effects.

NYSE rather than the Third Market. This distinction is unique to the listing sample as previous studies focused solely on differences in trading costs for trades executed in different trading locations for NYSE-listed stocks. Second, we examine differences in liquidity for different trade sizes and dollar spreads across trading structures. If a specialist system is the more efficient structure for less liquid trades, the largest liquidity gains from listing should emerge for trades with wider spreads and lower sizes. Third, we relate the liquidity improvements to firm-specific characteristics prior to listing. Amihud and Mendelson (1988) argue that the decision to list on organized exchanges involves a trade-off between the cost of listing and the anticipated liquidity improvements. Therefore, smaller firms, for which listing costs are a greater proportion of value, would realize larger reductions in trading costs.

The remainder of the paper is organized as follows. Section 2 outlines the differences in trading systems. Section 3 describes the data and defines our measures of trading costs. Section 4 presents the empirical results that test for differences in liquidity across trading structures, while Section 5 examines the nature of the liquidity improvements. Section 6 concludes the paper.

2. DISSIMILAR MARKET STRUCTURES AND LIQUIDITY

NYSE and AMEX stocks are traded in an auction/specialist setting while NASDAQ/NMS stocks are traded in a multiple dealer market.[4] Under the auction arrangement, stocks are assigned to specialists who post bid-ask quotes to smooth price changes by buying (selling) from their personal accounts when public buy (sell) orders are lacking. The specialist is not without competition since their own orders are superseded by public market orders and limit orders. The structure resembles an auction market since all public orders are exposed to one another on an exchange floor.[5] The execution of trades inside the spread, such as public buy and sell orders that cross with one another, may occur more frequently with this market structure.

The trading structure of the NASDAQ/NMS is fundamentally different from the organized exchanges. NASDAQ/NMS contains the largest and most actively traded firms in the NASDAQ system. It's financial requirements are comparable to those required for listing on the AMEX. Unlike the NYSE that uses floor trading, NASDAQ/NMS uses a screen-based system. NASDAQ/NMS dealers are free to make markets in stocks of

---

[4] Stoll (1992) provides an in-depth discussion of the principles of trading market structure.

[5] However, some of the limit orders may be hidden by the specialists. McInish and Wood (1992b) find that about 50% of limit orders with better quotes are not displayed.

their own choosing and multiple dealers per stock are common. Buyers and sellers interact directly with dealers who take the opposite side of every trade as principals. Similar to trading on the organized exchanges, trading inside the spread may occur, although such price improvement is usually reserved for active investors or for large orders.

Proponents of the two structures have heralded the advantages of their respective trading arrangement. For example, supporters of the NYSE/AMEX argue that their system offers lower trading costs since floor trading is more proficient at uncovering informed trades than the anonymous screen-based system used on the NASDAQ/NMS. Those who favor the NASDAQ/NMS stress the increased competition characterized by a market open to all dealers, not just the specialist. For example, they object to NYSE Rule 390 that prohibits NYSE member trades from being executed on the NASDAQ/NMS.

3. DATA DESCRIPTION AND LIQUIDITY MEASURES

Section A describes the procedures used to select our sample of firms that switch exchanges and provides summary statistics of their size and trading activity. Section B defines the trading cost variables used to compute differences in liquidity across exchanges.

A. Sample Selection and Data Description

The monthly stock master compiled by the Center for Research in Security Prices (CRSP) is used to identify firms that moved between the NASDAQ/NMS, the AMEX, and the NYSE during 1990. The choice of the 1990 calendar year is determined by the availability of trade and quote data compiled by the Institute for the Study of Security Markets (ISSM) for NASDAQ/NMS securities at the time of our study. The exchange code designated by CRSP is used to identify firms that trade on more than one of the three exchanges in 1990. The firm-specific CUSIP numbers are then used to link firms between the CRSP and ISSM data sets. Table I provides a summary of the number of firms moving between exchanges and the elimination criteria used to establish the final sample. The table shows that the procedures fail to match four firms moving from the NASDAQ/NMS to the AMEX, and one firm moving to the NYSE from the NASDAQ/NMS.[6] The ISSM data are then examined to confirm that trades and quotes are present throughout the 60-day interval surrounding

---

[6] To further ensure the integrity of the data set, we match firms across exchanges by manually reconciling the prices from the two data sources with the prices reported in the "Wall Street Journal" on the day the firm began trading on the new location.

MARKET STRUCTURES AND LIQUIDITY

TABLE I
SAMPLE IDENTIFICATION AND ELIMINATION CRITERIA FOR FIRMS MOVING BETWEEN
THE NASDAQ/NMS, THE AMEX, AND THE NYSE DURING 1990

Trading location	Initial sample	Elimination criteria		Final sample
		No match between the CRSP and ISSM CUSIP	Missing ISSM data during the 60 trading days surrounding the new listing	
NASDAQ/NMS to AMEX	33	4	10	19
NASDAQ/NMS to NYSE	33	1	0	32
AMEX to NASDAQ/NMS	4	0	3	1
AMEX to NYSE	15	0	1	14
NYSE to NASDAQ/NMS	1	0	0	1
NYSE to AMEX	1	0	1	0

the listing date on the new exchange, i.e., $[-30, +29]$, where Day 0 signifies the listing date. This procedure identifies 15 firms for which no ISSM data are available.

The restricted sample consists of 19 firms that move from the NASDAQ/NMS to the AMEX, 32 firms that move from the NASDAQ/NMS to the NYSE, and 14 firms that move from the AMEX to the NYSE. We exclude from our analysis the two firms that moved to the NASDAQ/NMS, given the limited sample size. Since our methodology uses a portfolio approach to test for differences in liquidity costs across exchanges, we do not require that firms trade throughout the interval $[-30, +29]$. Thus, some firms will be present for only a portion of the interval when the listing date is close to January or December of 1990. To check whether our calendar year restriction biases our results, we calculated the number of firm-days pre- and post-listing, defined as the sum of the number of trading days that each firm is present within the 60-day window. Our computation uncovered only minor differences in the number of firm-days. The final sample is then subjected to a series of filters. A description of these procedures is summarized in the Appendix.

Table II provides summary statistics for firms that survive the sampling procedures and filter requirements. The table reports the averages and distribution of share prices, number of outstanding shares, market value of equity, and dollar volume per trade for the three samples. The most striking result is the vast difference in both share prices and number of shares outstanding for firms moving from the NASDAQ/NMS to the AMEX relative to firms moving from the NASDAQ/NMS to the NYSE. The average price per share for firms that elect to move to the AMEX is only $6.87, with 25% of the firms trading for under $4.00. In contrast, the NASDAQ/NMS firms that move to the NYSE have an average share price of $19.78, with the 25% quartile reaching a price of $10.125.

TABLE II
DESCRIPTIVE STATISTICS FOR FIRMS THAT CHANGED THEIR TRADING LOCATION IN 1990

	Mean	Quartile 25%	Quartile 50%	Quartile 75%
A. Firms moving from the NASDAQ/NMS to the AMEX in 1990 ($n = 19$)				
Price per share	$6.87	$4.00	$5.75	$9.00
Number of shares (in thousands)	4241	1727	3029	5268
Market value of equity (in thousands)	$27,740	$12,002	$16,651	$38,705
Dollar volume (per trade)	$9436	$1875	$4000	$9500
B. Firms moving from the NASDAQ/NMS to the NYSE in 1990 ($n = 32$)				
Price per share	$19.78	$10.125	$17.375	$25.375
Number of shares (in thousands)	18,538	7677	17,963	23,475
Market value of equity (in thousands)	$396,391	$107,403	$208,238	$503,448
Dollar volume (per trade)	$41,223	$5250	$14,000	$35,525
C. Firms moving from the AMEX to the NYSE in 1990 ($n = 14$)				
Price per share	$14.88	$9.125	$13.00	$18.125
Number of shares (in thousands)	20,420	5221	9972	14,955
Market value of equity (in thousands)	$242,847	$86,050	$136,110	$190,693
Dollar volume (per trade)	$22,570	$2900	$7000	$17,063

Note. The price and share data are measured at the end of the month containing the listing date. Dollar volume includes all trades for the 60 trading days [−30, +29], where Day 0 is the listing date.

Coupling the higher share prices with the larger number of outstanding shares creates a wide disparity in market values between firms listing on the NYSE relative to the AMEX. The 75% quartile of market value for the AMEX-listed firms is only one-third as large as the 25% quartile for firms moving to the NYSE. Thus, firms electing to relocate to the AMEX are small relative to the firms electing to list on the NYSE. This difference in size is also apparent in the average dollar volume of all trades executed during the interval [−30, +29]. The median dollar volume per trade for firms moving to the AMEX from the NASDAQ/NMS is $4000 while the comparable figure for firms moving to the NYSE is $14,000. The median dollar volume for firms moving from the AMEX to the NYSE falls between these values.

B. Variable Definitions

In estimating our trading cost variables, we exclude all quotes that do not reflect a change in either the bid or the ask. Thus, we do not consider quote revisions that reflect changes in the depth alone, where depth is defined as the volume that the dealer/specialist is willing to trade at the posted quotes. We exclude these quote revisions since the depth variables in the ISSM data are uninformative. The variables are defined as follows:

LP. The opportunity to transact at a price inside the bid-ask spread is one measure of liquidity as it provides information on the ability to obtain the "best price." Using the mid-point of the standing bid-ask quotes as a proxy for the "best price," we compare the actual trade price with the best price to calculate the "liquidity premium," defined as:

$$LP = \left| Price - \left(\frac{Ask + Bid}{2}\right) \right|. \quad (1)$$

Price improvements occur when trades are transacted inside the spread since public buyers (sellers) receive a lower (higher) price.

Percentage LP. Since liquidity premiums may vary with the level of stock prices, we also report a standardized measure of the liquidity premium defined as the percentage LP:

$$\%LP = \frac{|Price - (Ask + Bid)/(2)|}{(Ask + Bid)/2}. \quad (2)$$

Dollar spread. Even if all trades are executed at the bid or the ask, a reduction in the width of the spread would lower trading costs. Thus, we also include the traditional liquidity measure, defined as the dollar spread, or the ask quote minus the bid quote.

Percentage spread. Since bid-ask spreads may vary with the level of stock prices, we also report a standardized measure of the dollar spread defined as the percentage spread:

$$\% \, spread = \frac{Ask - Bid}{(Ask + Bid)/2}. \quad (3)$$

4. LIQUIDITY DIFFERENCES ACROSS TRADING STRUCTURES

We organize our empirical tests around the following hypothesis:

For firms that transfer their exchange listing from a dealer market to a specialist system, reductions in trading costs become apparent on the first day of listing and persist thereafter.

This hypothesis specifies that dissimilar trading structures trigger the reduction in liquidity costs. Restricting the emergence of the liquidity effect to the listing date increases our confidence that the differences in market structure produce the results. However, the time period for which the liquidity effects persist is not unlimited. The further removed the trading day is from the listing date, the higher the probability that the fundamental value of the firm has changed. On the other hand, the liquidity effects must not disappear or revert to their pre-listing levels shortly after listing. To judge the persistence of the differences, we use a window of 60 trading days centered on the listing date.

One of the alleged benefits of moving to the organized exchanges is the reputation effect. Since the organized exchanges impose more stringent listing requirements, relocating from the NASDAQ/NMS may serve as a signal of value, resulting in greater visibility and market interest, especially among institutional investors. In an efficient market, the expected liquidity benefits arising from the reputation effect are permanently incorporated in prices when firms announce their intention to list on the organized exchanges. Thus, any differences in liquidity costs on the listing date can be attributed to structural rather than reputation effects. However, to the extent the reputation effect is not reflected in liquidity costs until firms begin trading on the organized exchanges, liquidity differences on the listing date may incorporate both structural and reputation effects.

To further examine the influence of liquidity effects, we include a control sample of firms that move from the AMEX to the NYSE. Since these firms change trading locations but not trading structures, we would not expect the listing date to be associated with a significant change in trading costs. However, firms may not be indifferent between listing on the NYSE and on the AMEX since the NYSE may provide increased visibility and heightened market interest because of its more stringent listing requirements. Specifically, firms listed on the NYSE are more likely to attract the attention of institutional investors. Nonetheless, the listing date should not demarcate the presence of reputation effects if these effects are first impounded on the announcement date.

The testing strategy first compares the liquidity variables using averages measured for the 30 trading days before the listing and for the first 30 days on the new exchange. Having established the pre- and post-listing differences in liquidity, we examine the patterns of the liquidity variables surrounding the listing date to ensure that these differences are structurally induced.

Table III reports the mean values for LP, percentage LP, dollar spreads, and percentage spreads as firms move between exchanges. Table IIIA summarizes the results for the NASDAQ/NMS to AMEX sample, Table IIIB contains the results for the NASDAQ/NMS to NYSE

TABLE III

DIFFERENCES IN TRADING COST VARIABLES FOR FIRMS THAT CHANGED THEIR TRADING LOCATION IN 1990

	Listed on original exchange			Listed on new exchange			t-statistic of differences in means
	Number	Mean	Standard deviation	Number	Mean	Standard deviation	
A. NASDAQ/NMS stocks that move to the AMEX ($n = 19$)							
LP	3815	$0.119	$0.153	3273	$0.067	$0.055	19.38
Percent LP	3815	2.04%	2.06%	3273	1.37%	1.14%	17.09
Dollar spread	1358	$0.52	$0.63	2587	$0.21	$0.10	17.82
Percent spread	1358	8.34%	7.86%	2587	3.84%	1.86%	20.83
B. NASDAQ/NMS stocks that move to the NYSE ($n = 32$)							
LP	75,711	$0.11	$0.091	35,543	0.063	$0.052	115.15
Percent LP	75,711	0.60%	0.58%	35,543	0.43%	0.59%	45.65
Dollar spread	13,040	$0.31	$0.19	15,440	$0.25	$0.10	32.97
Percent spread	13,040	1.63%	1.27%	15,440	1.50%	1.24%	8.73
C. AMEX stocks that move to the NYSE ($n = 14$)							
LP	14,023	$0.067	$0.055	12,334	0.058	$0.051	14.32
Percent LP	14,023	0.48%	0.44%	12,334	0.42%	0.43%	10.87
Dollar spread	5529	$0.22	$0.08	5402	$0.25	$0.12	17.12
Percent spread	5529	1.36%	0.78%	5402	1.68%	0.97%	18.67

Note. LP is computed as the absolute difference between the trade price and the mid-point of the standing bid-ask quotes. Percent LP is computed as the ratio of LP to the average of the bid-ask quotes. The dollar spread is computed as the difference between the ask and bid quotes. Percent spread is the ratio of the dollar spread to the average of the bid-ask quotes.

sample, and Table IIIC presents the results for the AMEX to NYSE sample. Tables IIIA and IIIB reveal striking differences in LP across exchanges. The liquidity premium for firms while listed on the NASDAQ/NMS prior to listing on the AMEX averages 11.9 cents per share. During the first 30 days of trading on the AMEX, the average LP falls by 5.2 cents. Similarly, an average improvement in LPs of 4.7 cents is realized by firms that move to the NYSE. Table III also shows that the percentage LP declines from 2.04% (0.60%) to 1.37% (0.43%) for the NASDAQ/NMS to AMEX (NYSE) sample. Thus, dramatic improvements in LPs are mirrored by the percentage LP that controls for the absolute price level. However, the absolute decline is significantly more important for firms that list on the AMEX.

The differences in average trading costs based on the listing location are also apparent in the decline of the standard deviations for the liquidity measures. Firms that list on the AMEX realize larger declines in both the level and the variability of the trading cost measures than firms that list on the NYSE. This result is due, in large part, to the wider spreads of AMEX-bound firms prior to listing. These wider spreads translate into larger variability given the greater latitude to trade or not trade within the spread.[7]

To test whether these economically meaningful differences are also statistically significant, we estimate the following regression,

$$L_t = \alpha + \beta D_t + \varepsilon_t, \qquad (4)$$

where L_t represents a liquidity variable for trade t and D_t equals 1 for trades executed on the new exchange, and zero otherwise. The t-statistic for β indicates whether the reported differences in liquidity are significant. The last column in Table III confirms that the reduction in LP and percentage LP from transferring to an organized exchange from a dealer market is statistically significant.

Reductions in trading costs are also observed for dollar spreads and percentage spreads. For firms moving from the NASDAQ/NMS to the AMEX, sharp reductions occur in both dollar spreads and percentage spreads, with each declining by over 50% once firms begin trading on the AMEX.[8] However, NASDAQ/NMS to NYSE firms show only modest reductions in the spread, measured in either dollars or percentages.[9]

Table IIIC presents the evidence for firms that change their trading locations but not their trading structure. Despite the continuity in market

---

[7] The differences in standard deviations for the dollar spread of firms that list on the AMEX can be partially attributed to one firm whose dollar spread fell from $4.00 while trading on the NASDAQ/NMS to $1.00 after listing on the AMEX. Removing this firm lowers the NASDAQ/NMS average dollar spread to $0.44 and the standard deviation to $0.31. However, the average LP is virtually unaffected at $0.114 since so few trades were recorded for this security.

[8] To test whether the results are sensitive to extreme observations, the comparisons in Table III were computed using differences in medians on a firm-by-firm basis. The results continue to support the conclusion that significant declines in trading costs are realized by firms that list on the organized exchanges, particularly for firms that list on the AMEX. The statistical inferences using the mean and the median are identical at the 1% level of significance for all but one firm in each of the NASDAQ/NMS–AMEX and NASDAQ/NMS–NYSE samples, where the statistical significance of the medians is computed using a Kruskal–Wallis test statistic.

[9] The average dollar and percentage spreads in Table III correspond closely with those reported in Kadlec and McConnell (1992) despite their larger sample of 273 firms. For example, the average dollar (percentage) spread of $0.25 (1.5%) after listing on the NYSE for our sample compares with $0.27 (1.5%) in their study.

structure, the average LP falls from 6.7 cents on the AMEX to 5.8 cents on the NYSE. However, the sizable gain in liquidity is not shared by our other trading cost variables. Specifically, the size of the average spread widens from $0.22 per share on the AMEX to $0.25 on the NYSE. Similar results are observed when the dollar spread is transformed to percentages: 1.36% on the AMEX versus 1.68% on the NYSE. These results provide conflicting evidence of improvement in liquidity for our control sample. Moreover, the high levels of statistical significance associated with the relatively small changes in liquidity costs for the control sample can be largely attributed to the large number of trades used to compute these statistics.

Figures 1 to 4 provide graphical evidence that identifies whether the reductions in trading costs coincide with the listing date. If the improvements in liquidity are structurally induced, they should first emerge on the listing date and not dissipate shortly thereafter. Figure 1 tracks the average liquidity premiums and confirms that the reduction in LPs is structurally induced. The average value of LP floats between $0.08 and $0.16 for firms that are listed on the NASDAQ/NMS and declines dramatically the day trading begins on the organized exchanges. These lower trading costs persist as the average LP fluctuates between $0.05 and $0.08. Thus, the

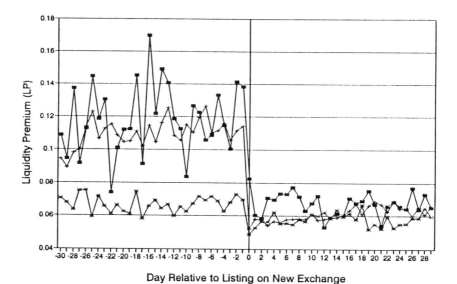

FIG. 1. Liquidity premiums surrounding the listing date.

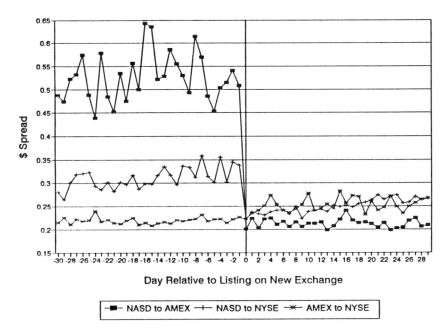

FIG. 2. Dollar spreads surrounding the listing date.

reduction is both immediate and unabating for firms moving to either the AMEX or the NYSE from the NASDAQ/NMS.

For our control sample, the figure illustrates that the reduction in LP corresponds to Day 0. However, the average LP values begin to creep upward almost immediately, violating a requirement of a structurally induced liquidity effect. The evidence is also inconsistent with a reputation effect since a recognition factor should be permanent.

Figure 2 graphs the daily averages for the dollar spreads. Consistent with the evidence in Fig. 1, there is a dramatic and permanent reduction in the dollar spread for firms moving from the NASDAQ/NMS to the AMEX. The reduction for firms moving from the NASDAQ/NMS to the NYSE begins on Day 0, but shows a slight tendency to revert over time. Thus, the NASDAQ/NMS to AMEX sample provides significantly stronger support for our central hypothesis than the NASDAQ/NMS to NYSE sample. For our control sample, dollar spreads exhibit a slight tendency to rise in the post-listing period. However, the listing date does not demarcate the dollar into pre- and post-listing regimes, suggesting that the increase in spreads is not structurally induced. Figures 3 and 4 provide the graphical evidence for LP and dollar spreads transformed into their

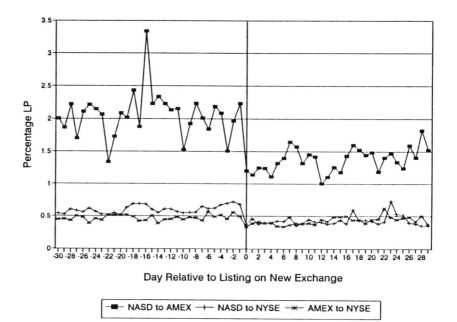

FIG. 3. Percentage liquidity premiums surrounding the listing date.

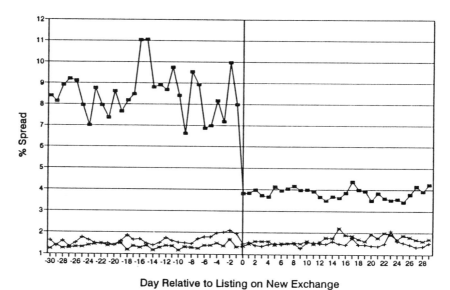

FIG. 4. Percentage spread surrounding the listing date.

proportional values, respectively. The intertemporal patterns reveal that the liquidity improvements on a percentage basis are much more dramatic for firms moving to the AMEX. In contrast, firms that move to the NYSE experience considerably more modest liquidity improvements.

While these results provide strong evidence in support of our central hypothesis, the decline in trading costs may also be induced by differences in trading volume. In particular, the liquidity improvements may arise from greater trading volume after the listing date. However, Table I indicates that the number of trades declines after firms begin trading on the organized exchanges. When trading activity is measured by dollar volume, similar declines are observed.[10] However, these volume figures must be interpreted with caution since trades are counted differently across market structures. For example, the batching procedure used at the open on the organized exchanges may combine a number of trades that would have been observed on the NASDAQ/NMS. The number of reported trades may also differ since a buy order and a sell order involve separate transactions on the NASDAQ/NMS whereas the specialist markets may allow the orders to cross in one trade.

In addition, our trading cost variables capture the costs of liquidity trading rather than informed trading since our portfolio approach controls for information effects and firm-specific characteristics. Admati and Pfleiderer (1988) distinguish between nondiscretionary liquidity traders who trade without regard to the timing of their trades and discretionary traders who do. Discretionary liquidity traders can potentially influence our results since they may postpone trades until the listing date and immediately thereafter. However, given the persistence of the trading cost reductions that we observe, it is unlikely that discretionary liquidity traders postpone trades for over a month.

In summary, the results provide evidence of structurally induced changes in trading costs for firms that elect to move from the dealer market to a specialist system. The direction and the magnitude of the reductions in trading costs contrast with prior studies that report mixed results.[11] Despite the large savings in trading costs, it is inappropriate to judge the superiority of a trading system based on our results. Since firms relocate when the perceived benefits more than offset the costs, the results are potentially biased in favor of finding liquidity improvements for our sample. To examine this possibility, we could study firms that

---

[10] The total dollar volume and the total share volume decline by almost 50% after firms list on the AMEX or the NYSE. In contrast, both dollar and share volumes are virtually unaffected when firms move between different markets within the specialist system.

[11] Examples of evidence in support of lower liquidity costs on the organized exchanges are Hasbrouck and Schwartz (1986) and Marsh and Rock (1986). In contrast, Dubofsky and Groth (1984) and Cooper et al. (1985) are examples of studies that identify the NASDAQ/NMS as providing higher liquidity.

move from the organized exchanges to the NASDAQ/NMS. Unfortunately, only two firms satisfy this requirement in 1990, and were excluded since the liquidity effects would be tainted by idiosyncratic and market-wide influences. Moreover, it is important to recognize that we focus on the trading cost element of liquidity and do not address other components such as speed of execution, broker's commissions, and soft dollar payments.

5. ANALYZING THE NATURE OF THE LIQUIDITY IMPROVEMENTS

In light of the significant decline in trading costs that arise when firms move from a dealer market to the specialist system, Section A separates the observed price improvements into gains attributed to differences in quote setting mechanisms and differences in trading location. Section B explores the characteristics of trading cost reductions across trade size and dollar spreads. Finally, Section C examines whether the characteristics of firms that move to the AMEX differ from those that list on the NYSE.

A. Trades, Quotes, and the Third Market

The market for trading exchange-listed stocks by dealers on the NASDAQ/NMS is referred to as the Third Market. The literature on Third Market competition compares the execution costs of identical stocks under dissimilar market structures. Recent studies of Third Market competition include Blume and Goldstein (1992), Huang and Stoll (1993), Lee (1992), and Petersen and Fialkowski (1992). Lee compares the LP of adjacent trades executed on the NYSE and the NASDAQ/NMS and concludes that trading costs are about 1 cent per share lower for trades routed to the NYSE. Blume and Goldstein find that the lower trading costs for NYSE trades are associated with trades of less than 1000 shares. Petersen and Fialkowski also find that trading costs are lower on the NYSE using proprietary data sets. Huang and Stoll report lower trading costs for the NYSE using various execution cost measures but attribute the lower costs to several factors, including the presence of limit orders that are "picked off" by informed traders and the tendency of trades to occur on the NASDAQ/NMS when NYSE spreads are wide.

Our sample also permits us to address the benefits of trading under different market structures by comparing LPs once firms are listed on the organized exchanges. However, our sample is unique in that it permits us to compare LPs based on NASDAQ/NMS quotes prior to the listing date with LPs for trades that continue to be executed on the NASDAQ/NMS but where quotes originate from the organized exchanges after the listing

TABLE IV
ATTRIBUTING THE IMPROVEMENTS IN LIQUIDITY PREMIUMS TO THE LOCATION OF TRADE EXECUTION AND TO QUOTE ORIGIN

A. NASDAQ/NMS firms that list on the NYSE ($n = 32$)

Listing location:	NASDAQ/NMS		NYSE			
Trading location:	NASDAQ/NMS		NASDAQ/NMS		NYSE	
Number of trades	Average LP		Number of trades	Average LP	Number of trades	Average LP
75,711	$0.110		3675	$0.082[a]	29,065	$0.058[b]

B. AMEX firms that list on the NYSE ($n = 14$)

Listing location: AMEX Trading location: NASDAQ/NMS		NYSE NASDAQ/NMS	
Number of trades	Average LP	Number of trades	Average LP
268	$0.079	406	$0.081[c]

Note. Liquidity premiums (LPs) are computed as the absolute difference between the trade price and the average of the standing bid-ask quotes.

[a] The difference in the average liquidity premiums between trades executed on the NASDAQ/NMS after firms list on the NYSE and trades executed on the NASDAQ/NMS prior to listing are statistically significant (p value = 0.0001).

[b] The difference in the average liquidity premiums between trades executed on the NYSE after firms list on the NYSE and trades executed on the NASDAQ/NMS prior to listing are statistically significant (p value = 0.0001).

[c] The difference in the average liquidity premiums between trades executed on the NASDAQ/NMS after firms list on the NYSE and trades executed on the NASDAQ/NMS prior to listing are statistically insignificant (p value = 0.6091).

date. Therefore, we can estimate the proportion of the liquidity improvement that can be attributed to differences in trading locations and to quote improvements.

Table IV decomposes the reduction in LPs for NASDAQ/NMS firms that move to the NYSE and studies the differences in LPs for Third Market trades for our control sample. We exclude the results for the NASDAQ/NMS to AMEX sample since trading activity on the NASDAQ/NMS virtually evaporates in the post-listing period. Table IVA, which presents the results for firms that move from the NASDAQ/NMS to the NYSE, shows that the average LP declines from 11 cents for trades executed on the NASDAQ/NMS in the pre-listing period to 8.2 cents for trades executed on the Third Market in the post-listing period.[12] Since the

---

[12] The total number of trades on the organized exchanges are lower in Table IV relative to those reported in Table III. The differences are due to our treatment of trades that are executed on the regional exchanges. In testing for liquidity improvements in Table III we do not differentiate transactions by their trading locations. Table IV only considers transactions that are executed on the NYSE or the NASDAQ/NMS.

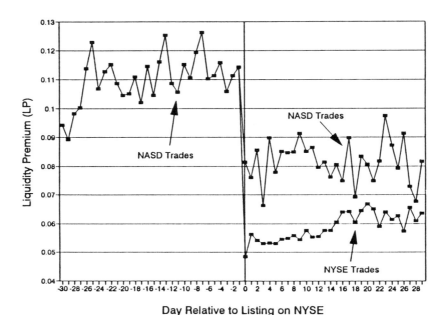

Fig. 5. Decomposing the improvements in liquidity premiums.

trading location is unchanged, this reduction can be attributed to quote improvements from the specialist market.

The average LP for trades executed on the NYSE rather than the Third Market during the post-listing period is 5.8 cents, indicating a further improvement of 2.4 cents due to differences in trading locations. These results are supplemented by Fig. 5, which plots the daily average LP values by exchange listing and by trading location. The decline in LPs on Day 0 is apparent for trades on both the NASDAQ/NMS and the NYSE, as is the difference in LPs between trades executed on the different trading systems. Thus, the differences in quote-setting behavior and the choice of trading location appear to be equally important sources of the liquidity improvements.

Table IVB reports the LP results for trades executed on the NASDAQ/NMS for our control sample of firms that move from the AMEX to the NYSE. Since both the pre- and post-listing quotes are set in the auction/specialist environment, quote-induced liquidity improvements for NASDAQ/NMS trades are predicted to be absent. The evidence in Table IVB supports this prediction since the pre- and post-listing LP values are not significantly different from one another.

TABLE V
TESTS FOR DIFFERENCES IN LIQUIDITY PREMIUMS (LP) ACROSS TRADE SIZE AND DOLLAR SPREAD CATEGORIES

A. Liquidity premiums by trade size

	Trade size (in shares)				
	<500	500–999	1000–1999	2000–4999	≥5000

Average LP values for firms moving from the NASDAQ/NMS to the AMEX

α coefficient	0.1638	0.1295	0.1053	0.0808	0.0789
β_1 coefficient	−0.0962	−0.0592	−0.0377	−0.0161	−0.0201
β_1 t statistic	−14.08	−10.82	−9.67	−4.39	−3.10
$\chi^2(1)$ test of $\beta_3 - \beta_2 - \beta_1 = 0$	na	17.92	10.24	16.32	0.29
p value for $\chi^2(1)$ test	na	0.0000	0.0014	0.0001	0.0591

Average LP values for firms moving from the NASDAQ/NMS to the NYSE

α coefficient	0.1382	0.1149	0.0914	0.0918	0.0978
β_1 coefficient	−0.0750	−0.0547	−0.0328	−0.0350	−0.0424
β_1 t statistic	−98.49	−51.27	−39.84	−30.10	−29.44
$\chi^2(1)$ test of $\beta_3 - \beta_2 - \beta_1 = 0$	na	237.83	266.12	2.45	16.01
p value for $\chi^2(1)$ test	na	0.0000	0.0000	0.1173	0.0001

B. Liquidity premiums by dollar spreads

	Dollar spread		
	$0.125 or under	$0.126 to $0.25	Larger than $0.25

Average LP values for firms moving from the NASDAQ/NMS to the AMEX

α coefficient	0.0458	0.0915	0.2217
β_1 coefficient	0.0184	−0.0246	−0.1001
β_1 t statistic	22.47	−8.06	−6.25
$\chi^2(1)$ test of $\beta_3 - \beta_2 - \beta_1 = 0$	na	145.83	21.48
p value for $\chi^2(1)$ test	na	0.0000	0.0000

Average LP values for firms moving from the NASDAQ/NMS to the NYSE

α coefficient	0.0656	0.1036	0.1819
β_1 coefficient	−0.0023	−0.0502	−0.1056
β_1 t statistic	−9.73	−80.52	−82.42
$\chi^2(1)$ test of $\beta_3 - \beta_2 - \beta_1 = 0$	na	5179.6	1510.1
p value for $\chi^2(1)$ test	na	0.0000	0.0000

Note. LP is defined as the absolute difference between the trade price and the mid-point of the standing bid-ask quotes. Dollar spread is defined as the difference between the ask and bid quotes. To test for differences in liquidity gains between adjacent trade size and dollar spread categories, we estimate the multiple regression

$$L_t = \alpha + \beta_1 D_t^{is} + \beta_2 D_t^{jd} + \beta_3 D_t^{js} + \eta_t, \quad i < j,$$

B. Liquidity Improvements across Trade Sizes and Dollar Spreads

This section tests whether the liquidity improvements reported in Section 4 are universally shared across two important trade characteristics: trade sizes and dollar spreads. If the specialist system can more easily accommodate trades inside the spread as inferred by Lee (1992), Blume and Goldstein (1992), and others, then liquidity gains are expected to show their greatest improvement among trades with wider posted quotes. In addition, Blume and Goldstein (1992) and Huang and Stoll (1993) find that lower liquidity costs for trades routed to the NYSE relative to the NASDAQ/NMS are concentrated in trades of less than 1000 shares. Thus, the reductions in trading costs experienced by firms relocating to the organized exchanges may increase with decreasing trade size and wider quoted spreads.

A prerequisite for measuring the differences in liquidity across market structures is the proper control for firm-specific characteristics. Since we compare liquidity gains within trade size and dollar spread categories, our research design must preserve the composition of both the pre- and the post-listing sample. Thus, we eliminate firms within a specific category when the stipulated trade size or dollar spread is absent on either exchange.

Our results are reported in Table V. Tables VA and VB contain the results for LP as a function of trade size and dollar spread, respectively. Trade sizes (dollar spreads) are partitioned into five (three) categories that contain a similar number of trades. To test for differences in liquidity between adjacent categories, we estimate the regression

$$L_t = \alpha + \beta_1 D_t^{is} + \beta_2 D_t^{jd} + \beta_3 D_t^{js} + \eta_t, \qquad i < j, \qquad (5)$$

where L_t is the liquidity variable for trades in categories i and j, D_t^{is} is the indicator variable that equals 1 for trades in category i that are executed on the specialist system, D_t^{jd} is the indicator variable that equals 1 for trades in category j that are executed on the dealer system, and D_t^{js} is the indicator variable equaling 1 for trades in category j executed on the specialist system. The t-statistic of β_1 tests for liquidity differences within category i. For across-category differences, we specify the null hypothe-

---

where L_t is the liquidity variable for trades in size (spread) categories i and j, D_t^{is} is the indicator variable that equals 1 for trades in size (spread) category i executed on the specialist system, D_t^{jd} is the indicator variable that equals 1 for trades in size (spread) category j executed on the dealer system, and D_t^{js} is the indicator variable that equals 1 for trades in size (spread) category j executed on the specialist system. The t statistic of β_1 tests for liquidity differences within size (spread) category i. The restriction $\beta_3 - \beta_2 - \beta_1 = 0$ tests the null hypothesis that the liquidity gains between adjacent size (spread) categories are insignificantly different from one another. A Wald test of the restriction is distributed as $\chi^2(1)$.

sis that the liquidity gains between adjacent categories are insignificantly different from one another: $\beta_3 - \beta_2 - \beta_1 = 0$. A Wald test of the null is distributed χ^2 with one degree of freedom.

For firms switching to either the AMEX or the NYSE from the NASDAQ/NMS, two common patterns emerge in Table VA. First, a significant reduction in LPs is observed across all trade size categories as indicated by the β_1 coefficients. Second, the reduction in trading costs declines with increasing trade size. For example, an average price improvement of almost 10 cents per share is observed for trades under 500 shares for firms moving to the AMEX. The price improvement for the same data set falls to 2 cents per share for trade sizes exceeding 5000 shares. Additionally, the differences in trading cost reductions between adjacent trade-size categories are generally statistically reliable as indicated by the χ^2 statistics. For the NASDAQ/NMS to NYSE sample, the reduction in LPs is most pronounced for trade sizes of under 500 shares. The reduction in LPs declines with increasing trade size with the exception of the largest trade category.

To confirm that the evidence presented in Table VA is structurally induced, we graph the LPs across trade size categories for the 60 trading days surrounding the listing date. For brevity, we only present the results for the sample of firms moving from the NASDAQ/NMS to the NYSE. This sample also maximizes the number of trades per trade size category. Figure 6 shows that the reduction in LPs coincides with the listing date and persists thereafter, clearly supporting the hypothesis that the reduction in LPs is structurally induced, even when data are categorized by trade size. The width of the relative positions of the LPs pre- and post-listing also illustrate the reduction in LP across trade sizes.

Table VB reports the differences in LPs across dollar spread categories. The results provide strong evidence of significant reductions in LPs with increasing dollar spreads for firms that move to either the AMEX or the NYSE.[13] This evidence is also illustrated in Fig. 7, where the widest pre- and post-listing differentials are reserved for the widest spread categories. More importantly, Fig. 7 shows that the listing date separates the dollar spreads into two regimes, extending the importance of the structurally induced differences in LPs across dissimilar market structures to dollar spread categories. Interestingly, average trading costs increase as firms move from the NASDAQ/NMS to the AMEX for posted spreads of 12.5 cents or less. This increase may arise from the lower minimum tick

---

[13] To the extent that illiquid stocks are characterized by wider posted spreads and smaller trade sizes, our results are consistent with the predictions of Grossman and Miller (1988). Their model predicts that specialist systems (dealer markets) are the preferred choice for illiquid (liquid) stocks.

MARKET STRUCTURES AND LIQUIDITY

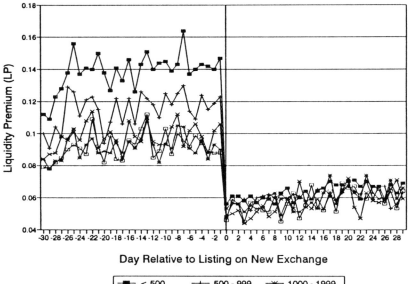

FIG. 6. Liquidity premiums across trade size categories.

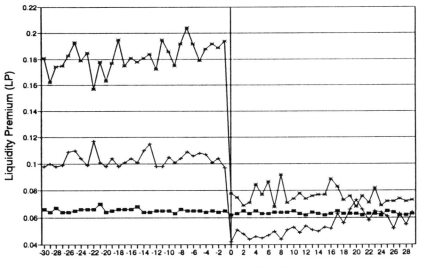

FIG. 7. Liquidity premiums across dollar spread categories.

size (6.25 cents versus 12.5 cents) available for smaller firms trading in a dealer market.[14]

C. Liquidity Improvements and Firm Characteristics

This section attempts to link trading cost improvements to the liquidity of firms prior to listing on the organized exchanges. Amihud and Mendelson (1988) suggest that highly liquid stocks on the NASDAQ/NMS would realize little gain in liquidity from listing on the organized exchanges. In contrast, illiquid firms have higher expected liquidity benefits from listing and will move to the organized exchanges when these benefits exceed the listing costs. Since our results indicate that firms listing on the AMEX realize superior liquidity gains relative to firms listing on the NYSE, we hypothesize that AMEX-bound firms are less liquid. We proxy for liquidity using market value of equity and trading activity measures. Thus, we expect firms that list on the NYSE rather than the AMEX to be larger and more actively traded while they were listed on the NASDAQ/NMS.

The evidence on differences in firm-specific characteristics are contained in Tables II and III. Table II presents the distribution of statistics for price per share, number of shares outstanding, market value of equity, and dollar volume per trade. A comparison of Table IIA and Table IIB shows that these distributions are uniformly lower for firms moving to the AMEX relative to the NYSE. For example, the median market value of firms moving to the AMEX is less than 10% of the median market value of firms listing on the NYSE. Table IIIA and Table IIIB reveal that the number of trades and quote revisions while firms trade on the NASDAQ/NMS are dramatically higher for firms that list on the NYSE. Specifically, the number of trades (quotes) increase by a factor of 20 (10) for firms that move to the NYSE relative to those that move to the AMEX. Thus, based on these firm-specific characteristics, smaller and less active firms move to the AMEX rather than the NYSE, and realize the largest improvements in liquidity from relocating their listing.

6. CONCLUSIONS

Firms often justify a change of trading venue with the expectation of a lower cost of capital that is driven by a reduction in liquidity costs. This paper examines the differences in liquidity for a sample of firms that moves from a dealer market to a specialist system. We find that when the

---

[14] For completeness, we repeated the analysis with the control sample. No systematic reductions in trading costs are observed across trade size or dollar spread categories. This evidence is confirmed by the lack of statistical significance of the χ^2 statistics that test for differences in trading cost improvements between adjacent categories. These results are available from the authors upon request.

trading cost component of liquidity is isolated, the decision to transfer trading location based on anticipated liquidity gains are well founded. The average price improvement for firms that move from the NASDAQ/NMS to the NYSE (AMEX) is 4.7 (5.2) cents per share. While these results are consistent with management making value-maximizing decisions by identifying the lowest-cost trading structure, the magnitudes are unexpectedly large. The results cannot be contested on grounds that they are confounded by a mismatching of firms across exchanges. Attributing the reduction in liquidity costs to structural effects is supported by the coincidence of the reduction in trading costs with the listing date and an absence of a reversal in the immediate post-listing period.

Our analysis also examines the nature of the trading cost reductions along several dimensions. First, by comparing the costs of trading on the NYSE versus the NASDAQ/NMS after firms are listed on the NYSE, our results show an average reduction in trading cost of 2.4 cents per share for trades executed on the NYSE. These savings for firms that elect to relocate are dramatically higher than the savings of about 1 cent per share identified by previous studies that focus on Third Market competition using a broad sample of NYSE securities. Moreover, we identify an additional cost reduction of 2.8 cents per share for trades that continue to be executed on the NASDAQ/NMS after firms list on the NYSE. We show that this added liquidity improvement arises from quotes that originate from the NYSE. Second, we document that the reduction in trading cost varies inversely with trade size and positively with the width of the spread. In addition, we confirm that these liquidity improvements are structurally induced since they coincide with the listing date and tend to persist. Finally, we find that the reduction in trading costs is a much larger proportion of stock price for firms that move to the AMEX as opposed to the NYSE. A comparison of firm characteristics reveals that those listing on the AMEX are significantly smaller, much less actively traded, and generate far fewer quote revisions while they were listed on the NASDAQ/NMS.

In a perfect market, the decision to switch trading location is immaterial since the fundamental determinants of value are unaffected. However, when differences in trading structures are present, the decision to change trading location can be value enhancing when the structural differences translate into varying trading costs. Our results strongly support the importance of microstructure effects and are consistent with firms attempting to minimize their costs of equity with their choice of trading venues.

APPENDIX: DATA FILTERS

This appendix describes the various filters and procedures used to minimize errors in our data set.

A. Suspicious Data

Prior to releasing the data, ISSM uses a filter to flag suspicious trade prices, volumes, and bid-ask quotes. Those prices, volumes, or quotes that are considered to be suspicious are assigned a negative value. Thus, to avoid the use of data that may be incorrect, we eliminate all trades with negative prices or volumes, and all quotes whose bid or ask prices are negative.

Additional efforts to locate potential data errors focus on the intraday range of price differences, bid-ask spreads, and trade sizes (in shares). We check whether unusual price changes are legitimate by comparing them to the nearby quotes. We also sort the trades by share volume to examine whether there are any anomalous trades within the highest trade volumes. This exercise reveals suspicious trades on the AMEX and the NYSE. For example, the largest trade that reappears for different firms is exactly 9,435,000 shares. Elimination of this share size results in the removal of 1 trade for firms moving to the AMEX from the NASDAQ, 13 trades for firms moving from the NASDAQ/NMS to the NYSE, and 4 trades for firms listing on the NYSE after trading on the AMEX. Finally, we eliminate all quotes when the ask price is equal to or less than the bid.

B. Quotes Originating from Regional Exchanges

Once a firm is listed on the AMEX or the NYSE, it becomes eligible for trading on the regional and the NASDAQ/NMS exchanges. We exclude quotes from these exchanges since they tend to be courtesy quotes that are based on the specialists' quotes. The result is that all quotes originate from the AMEX or the NYSE when firms are listed on these exchanges, and from the NASDAQ/NMS when firms are listed on the NASDAQ/NMS.

C. First Trades on the AMEX and the NYSE

The first trade on the AMEX and NYSE executed after the market opens is handled differently than all other trades. Specifically a call market is used for opening trades while an auction market is used for all subsequent trades. Since the initial trade reported on the ISSM system reflects the outcome of the call market, to focus on the structural differences between a continuous auction market and a competitive dealer system, we eliminate the first trade after the open for all stocks trading on the NYSE or AMEX.

D. Timing of Trades and Quotes

The posting of quotes and the execution time of trades are examined to ensure uniformity across exchanges. Since the market is open for trading between 9:30 AM and 4:00 PM, eligible trades must be time-stamped within this trading interval. All trades executed outside the regular trading hours are eliminated. The treatment of quotes is somewhat different across exchanges. For stocks listed on the AMEX or NYSE, we only include quotes posted during normal trading hours. However, since the NASDAQ/NMS operates as a screen-based dealer market, quotes will often be posted before the start of trading at 9:30 AM and are considered legitimate.

In addition, the time stamps associated with the quote and trade records may not accurately reflect their relative position in time. In particular, Lee and Ready (1991) have documented that for a sample of NYSE companies in 1988, the quote record sometimes precedes the related transaction even though the transaction occurs first. They recommend treating quotes that appear up to 5 seconds before the trade as if they occur after it. Application of this rule to our sample is complicated by the presence of different trading systems and the use of 1990 rather than 1988 data. Fortunately, results that are not presented in the paper document that the average elapsed time between trades and the posting of the preceding quote is over 1.5 hours for firms moving to the AMEX and exceeds 20 minutes for firms moving to the NYSE. Given this time differential, the Lee and Ready criterion is unnecessary.

E. *Trades without Preceding Quotes*

We only consider trades and quotes within the day. Thus, trades on Day t must be preceded by a quote on Day t. In those instances where we observe trades for a particular stock without a same-day quote, the trades and quotes for that stock are eliminated for the day in question. This ensures that a trade price can be matched with a prior quote posted during the same trading day.

REFERENCES

ADMATI, A. R., AND PFLEIDERER, P. (1988). A theory of intraday patterns: Volume and price variability, *Rev. Finan. Stud.* **1**, 3–40.

AMIHUD, Y., AND MENDELSON, H. (1986). Asset pricing and the bid-ask spread, *J. Finan. Econ.* **17**, 223–249.

AMIHUD, Y., AND MENDELSON, H. (1988). Liquidity and asset prices: Financial management implications, *Finan. Manage.* **17**, 5–15.

BAKER, H. K., AND EDELMAN, R.B. (1992). AMEX-to-NYSE transfers, market microstructure, and shareholder wealth, *Finan. Manage.* **21**, 60–72.

BAKER, H. K., AND JOHNSON, M. (1990). A survey of management views on exchange listing, *Quart. J. Bus. Econ.* **29**, 3–20.

BLUME, M., AND GOLDSTEIN, M. (1992). "Differences in Execution Prices among the NYSE, the Regionals and the NASD," Working Paper, Wharton School.

COOPER, S. K., GROTH, J. C., AND AVERA, W. E. (1985). Liquidity, exchange listing, and common stock performance, *J. Econ. Bus.* **17**, 19–33.

COWAN, A. R., CARTER, R. B., DARK, F. H., AND SINGH, A. K. (1992). Explaining the NYSE listing choices of NASDAQ firms, *Finan. Manage.* **21**, 73–86.

DEMSETZ, H. (1968). The cost of transacting. *Quart. J. Econ.* **2**, 33–53.

DUBOFSKY, D. A., AND GROTH, J. C. (1984). Exchange listing and stock liquidity, *J. Finan. Res.* **7**, 291–302.

GROSSMAN, S., AND MILLER, M. (1988). Liquidity and market structure, *J. Finance* **43**, 617–633.

HASBROUCK, J., AND SCHWARTZ, R. A. (1986). "The Liquidity of Alternate Market Centers: A Comparison of the New York Stock Exchange, the American Stock Exchange and the NASDAQ National Market System," American Stock Exchange Transactions Data Research Project Report 1.

HUANG, R. D., AND STOLL, H. R. (1993). "Competitive Trading of NYSE Listed Stocks: Trading Costs in the Period 1987–1991," Working Paper, Vanderbilt University.

HUI, B., AND HEUBEL, B. (1984). "Comparative Liquidity Advantages among Major U.S. Stock Markets," Data Resources Inc. Financial Information Group Study Series 84081.

KADLEC, G. B., AND MCCONNELL, J. J. (1992). "The Effect of Market Segmentation and Illiquidity on Asset Prices: Evidence from Exchange Listings," Working Paper, Purdue University.

LEE, C. (1992). "Purchase of Order Flows and Favorable Executions: An Intermarket Comparison," Working Paper, University of Michigan.

LEE, C., AND READY, M. (1991). Inferring trade direction from intraday data, *J. Finance* **46**, 733–746.

MARSH, T., AND ROCK, K. (1986). "Exchange Listing and Liquidity: A Comparison of the American Stock Exchange with the NASDAQ National Market System," American Stock Exchange Transactions Data Research Project Report 2.

MCINISH, T., AND WOOD, R. (1992a). "Volatility of NASD/NMS and Listed Stocks," Working Paper, Memphis State University.

MCINISH, T., AND WOOD, R. (1992b). "Hidden Limit Orders on the NYSE," Working Paper, Memphis State University.

PETERSEN, M. A., AND FIALKOWSKI, D. (1992). "Price Improvement: Stocks on Sale," CRSP Working Paper, University of Chicago.

REINGANUM, M. R., (1990). Market microstructure and asset pricing: An empirical investigation of NYSE and NASDAQ securities, *J. Finan. Econ.* **28**, 127–147.

SANGER, G. C., AND MCCONNELL, J. J. (1986). Stock exchange listing, firm value and security market efficiency: The impact of the NASDAQ, *J. Finan. Quant. Anal.* **21**, 1–25.

STOLL, H. R. (1992). Principles of trading market structure, *J. Finan. Serv. Res.* **6**, 75–107.

ULE, M. G. (1937). Price movements of newly-listed common stocks, *J. Bus.*, 346–369.

Market Integration and Price Execution for NYSE-Listed Securities

CHARLES M. C. LEE*

ABSTRACT

For New York Stock Exchange (NYSE) listed securities, the price execution of seemingly comparable orders differs systematically by location. In general, executions at the Cincinnati, Midwest, and New York stock exchanges are most favorable to trade initiators, while executions at the National Association of Security Dealers (NASD) are least favorable. These intermarket price differences depend on trade size, with the smallest trades exhibiting the biggest per share price difference. Collectively, these results raise questions about the adequacy of the existing intermarket quote system (ITS), the broker's fiduciary responsibility for "best execution," and the propriety of order flow inducements.

IN THE EMERGING GLOBAL economy, the same security is often traded simultaneously at different physical locations. For such securities, market integration—the full and timely communication of intermarket information—is an issue of practical, academic, and regulatory importance.[1] In a fully integrated market, incoming buy (or sell) orders have an opportunity to be matched against the best available sell (or buy) orders across all locations. This intermarket matching process lowers the cost and time delay of trading and enhances the market's price efficiency. Conversely, in a poorly integrated (i.e., "fragmented") market, incoming orders may not be executed at the best available intermarket price. In such markets, the choice of where an order is routed can have a significant effect on the price obtained.

This paper explores the closely related issues of market integration and price execution for a sample of New York Stock Exchange (NYSE) listed securities. Most NYSE-listed securities also trade on at least one of five

---

* School of Business Administration, University of Michigan. I thank Roger Kormendi for directing me to this topic and the Mid America Institute for information and encouragement at the formative stage of the project. My academic colleagues, Vic Bernard, George Foster, Jim Hamilton, Larry Harris, Joel Hasbrouck, Marilyn Johnson, Mark Ready, Paul Seguin, Chester Spatt, Kent Womack, and Robert Wood all provided extremely helpful suggestions. I also benefited from the comments of Gene Finn (NASD), Bill Boye (Webco Securities), Joseph Mahoney (AC Partners), Bernie and Peter Madoff (Madoff Investments), Roger Hendrick (Midwest Stock Exchange), Chuck Black and Lee Korins (Pacific Stock Exchange), George Sofianos and Jim Shapiro (NYSE). Exceptionally detailed suggestions from an anonymous referee on an earlier draft greatly improved the paper. Any remaining errors or omissions are my own.

[1] The term "market integration" is used here to describe the extent that electronic linkages communicate the available trading opportunities at different physical locations. A fully integrated market is one in which all the price-relevant trading information available at each location is communicated quickly to the entire market.

regional exchanges and in the Over-The-Counter (OTC) market. These centers are linked by an electronic system (the Intermarket Trading System, or ITS) that immediately disseminates trades and quote revisions to all locations. In U.S. equity markets, exchange dealers must meet or beat the best ITS quote. Therefore, if the ITS system is fully communicating intermarket trading opportunities, identical market orders should have an equal opportunity for best price execution, regardless of initial routing locations. Conversely, if the ITS system does not fully communicate intermarket trading information, seemingly comparable orders may execute at different prices, depending on where they are routed and how they are handled at each location.[2]

The main proposition of this study is that the location of execution is price relevant for trades in NYSE-listed securities. The issue is timely, pertaining to the current regulatory debate surrounding payments for order flows. Since 1988, members of the National Association of Securities Dealers (NASD) and some regional specialists have paid brokers cash rebates, typically one cent per share, for directing customers orders to their market centers. These cash payments are one of many order flow arrangements between brokers and dealers (collectively called "order flow inducements") that may influence how brokers route their customers' orders.[3] Currently, the Securities and Exchange Commission (SEC) is considering the welfare implications of these inducements. One important issue under deliberation is whether the fiduciary responsibility of brokers to procure "best execution" for customers is compromised by side payments from competing dealers. Evidence of significant intermarket differences in the cost of trade execution would suggest possible conflicts of interest. Conversely, if price execution does not differ by trade location, these dealer-broker arrangements are unlikely to compromise the brokers' primary responsibility to their customers.

Using returns of matched stock portfolios, prior studies have investigated the effect of different market designs on asset prices (e.g., Reinganum (1990)). This study, however, uses Institute for the Study of Security Markets (ISSM) data on individual trades to compare the price execution across different market locations. Three separate tests are conducted using trades and quotes from 1988 and 1989. The first test compares the "liquidity premium" paid on off-Board trades to that paid on adjacent NYSE trades, where the liquidity premium is defined as the absolute difference between the trade price and the midpoint of the bid-ask spread. The second test classifies all trades as buys or sells using the Lee and Ready (1991) algorithm and compares the trade price of off-Board buys (or sells) to adjacent NYSE buys (or sells). The

---

[2] Note that market integration is a necessary, but not sufficient, condition for location indifference. Even in a fully integrated market, dealers may strategically ignore the intermarket information (where laws permit), or traders may gravitate to certain markets for nonpecuniary reasons (see Harris (1992) for a discussion of the economic forces that cause markets to integrate or fragment).

[3] See the report of the Order Flow Committee of NASD (1991), for a review of background information and institutional details. Coffee (1991) provides a good summary of legal issues.

third test examines the relative likelihood of price improvement over the quoted prices by documenting the frequency of inside-the-spread trading across the different exchanges. For all three tests, off-Board trades are matched against NYSE trades of similar size in the same security executed within two minutes. Collectively, these tests provide a framework for comparing execution costs across different markets.

The main result from these tests is that the execution price of similar adjacent trades can differ systematically depending on the location of execution. Even after controlling for the security traded, the trade size, and the time of execution, we still observe significant average execution price differences by location. Most of these differences are attributable to trading inside the best ITS quote, suggesting that the ITS does not fully reflect the available intermarket liquidity.[4] These findings provide empirical evidence about the consequences of market fragmentation. For market practitioners, the intermarket price differences also provide a benchmark for the broader problem of evaluating dealer services.

All three tests document a systematic relation between trade location and execution price. The first test shows liquidity premiums are typically lower at the Cincinnati, Midwest, and New York stock exchanges and higher at the NASD. Similarly, the second test shows investors tend to pay lower prices for buys and obtain higher prices for sells on the NYSE relative to adjacent off-Board trades. On average, the price for non-NYSE trades is 0.7 to 1 cent per share less favorable than that of adjacent NYSE trades. This amount is comparable to the typical cash rebates in payment for order flow agreements suggesting that, during 1988 and 1989, off-Board dealers paying cash inducements were able to recoup these payments in the form of higher effective spreads.[5] In aggregate, estimates of the total additional cost of off-Board executions are $13 to $18 million for 1988 and $36 to $47 million for 1989.

Further, these tests show that the relative price performance of market centers differs by trade size. In the small trades (100 to 400 shares), the NYSE offers the best execution. In the midsize trades (500 to 4900 shares), the Cincinnati and Midwest exchanges significantly outperform the NYSE in both years, while the Pacific exchange outperforms the NYSE for 1988. Relative price performance in the large trade class (5,000 shares or more) is mixed, with the Midwest, Pacific, and Instinet (which caters exclusively to an institutional clientele) all performing well. Only the NASD performs consistently worse than the NYSE in all size categories.

The third test, which is conditional on spread size, shows that price performance is closely related to the frequency of inside-the-spread exe-

---

[4] Harris (1990) defines liquidity in terms of the willingness of some traders (often, but not necessarily, dealers) to allow others to trade on demand. Intermarket liquidity refers to the aggregate liquidity available across all market locations.

[5] This comparison is intended only to help put the intermarket price differences into economic perspective. No causality between the intermarket prices and the existence of dealer-broker arrangements is intended. In fact, many regional dealers did not pay for order flow during this time period.

cutions. The market centers with the most frequent inside-the-spread executions—e.g., the NYSE, Midwest, and Cincinnati—also had the most favorable prices. Conversely, the market center least likely to improve prices over the prevailing ITS quote—the NASD—had the least favorable trade prices. Separate analyses show these results are not attributable to the tighter spreads on NASD trades. In fact, the frequency of price improvement on NASD trades is relatively low for all spread sizes.

Supplemental tests show that these findings are not specific to the choice of the two-minute window used for matching trades, since similar results obtain using one-, five-, or ten-minute windows. These findings are also not attributable to nonsynchronous reporting of trades and quotes on the ISSM tape. When quotes that are five seconds, two minutes, and five minutes ahead of each trade are used, similar intermarket rankings result. Moreover, these findings are not due to cross-sectional differences in firm characteristics, since similar results are obtained when execution costs are aggregated first by firm, then across firms.

Several important caveats should be kept in mind in interpreting these results. First, since the ISSM data present only trade prices, not orders, the identity of the trade initiator is unknown. This study assumes that all trades are initiated by outside public traders, who pay for liquidity. Consequently, the results pertain to execution costs for market orders, not limit or other price-contingent orders (unless these orders are executable upon receipt).[6] Further, trades that are not initiated by public orders (e.g., trades initiated by market makers) are not analyzed separately. Although the exact effect of these trades is difficult to quantify, they represent a relatively small percent of total trades and are not expected to alter significantly the findings reported here.[7]

Second, these tests focus on only one aspect of order execution—the trade price. While the average trade price provides a useful benchmark for price performance, the evaluation of dealer services is a broader problem. Factors such as the speed of execution, the amount of guaranteed depth (shares available at each price), and the reliability of trade settlement are all relevant in assessing execution quality. The brokers' fiduciary responsibility to procure "best execution" for their clients may involve tradeoffs along these different dimensions. Therefore, these results should be viewed as just one element in the evaluation of relative market center performance.

Third, while these results document an association between location and trade price, they do not establish causality. Causality seems to flow from location to price performance, but the reverse could also hold: that is, trades may be sent to particular locations in anticipation of price performance. For

---

[6] See Harris and Hasbrouck (1992) for a discussion of order submission strategies for market versus limit orders.

[7] Trades initiated by market makers are a subset of the intermarket orders sent across the ITS system. Except for the Cincinnati exchange, total trades from ITS orders represent at most 15 percent of the trades at each regional exchange. The related issue of regional trades arising from "limit book protection" is discussed in Section VII.

example, trades may be sent to a regional exchange only when it provides the best price. This possibility is particularly important for locations with relatively low trading volume, such as Instinet or Cincinnati. However, it does not explain the NASD results, since trades seem to be sent to there in spite of inferior price performance. The higher volume of the NASD in recent years may be attributable to payments for order flows, a practice the NASD endorses. However, it could also be explained by better dealer performance on the NASD in other dimensions unrelated to price execution.

Finally, we should not equate lower execution costs with superior market maker performance. In a pure dealer market, such as the NASD, the market maker is the sole supplier of liquidity. However, at the NYSE and most other exchanges, price improvements do not necessarily take place at the specialist's expense. At the NYSE, in particular, where specialist participation is estimated to be 13 to 22 percent of total share volume (Hasbrouck and Sofianos (1992) and Mann and Seijas (1991)), price improvement occurs largely at the expense of public limit orders.[8] The tests in this study measure relative costs of liquidity, but do not evalaute the contribution of specialists to the liquidity supply.

The remainder of the paper is organized as follows. Section I provides background on the order flow debate, Section II discusses why execution costs might differ across market centers, Section III describes the data, Sections IV through VI report the results of the three tests, Section VII addresses other methodological concerns and presents supplemental analyses, and Section VIII concludes.

I. Order Flow Inducements

The market for dealer services is highly competitive. A steady flow of customer orders allows the market maker to make a "dealer's turn"—the profit inherent in purchasing at the bid and selling at the ask.[9] Interestingly, the competition among dealers to attract order flow has focused on brokers,

---

[8] Price improvement can take place on an exchange floor in several ways. First, an incoming order can "cross" with a floor trader with a public order inside the spread (executed against the "crowd"). Alternatively, the specialist may elect to execute the order against his own account inside the quoted spread. Finally, the specialist can "stop" an order, guaranteeing execution at prices at least as favorable as the prevailing quotes. If an offsetting public order arrives in the next few minutes, the two are crossed inside the spread, resulting in price improvement for both sides. If no offsetting order appears, the stopped order is executed at the guaranteed price. In an extreme example, if the specialist only "stops" an incoming market order when the quotes represent public limit orders, then all price improvement from a midpoint cross occurs at a cost to public limit orders.

[9] Dealers also profit from order flows through the division of revenue from the Consolidated Tape Association (CTA). Brokers and other market participants pay CTA for the dissemination of trade information. This revenue is divided among the market centers on the basis of the number of transactions each reports.

rather than directly on investors. Since most investors do not specify a preference for trade location, this decision is typically made by the brokers.

To attract orders, competing market centers offer brokers a myriad of inducements (see NASD (1991)). The most controversial of these inducements involves cash payments. In a typical payment for order flow arrangement, the market maker agrees to pay the broker one cent per share for all directed market orders. The dealer also establishes certain conditions to be met for cash payments. For example, NASD (1991) cites these common stipulations in payment for order flow agreements: trading spreads of at least one eighth, minimum monthly order flow (usually a minimum of 100,000 shares), maximum shares per order (usually 3,000 shares), order source restrictions (no professional or program orders), and no payments for limit orders or orders for low-priced stocks.

Neither brokers nor dealers are required to report the total amount of their payments for order flow.[10] Although estimates of the extent of these activities vary widely (Steptoe (1989), *Securities Week* (1989a, 1989b)), the general consensus is that the practice started in earnest in 1988 and has grown rapidly since. Payment for order flow arrangements are most often associated with the NASD, where the practice first started, with participation from the regional specialists increasing since 1989 (Crawford (1991), NASD (1991)).

One key issue for the SEC is whether customer orders entrusted to a broker should be used as a bargaining chip in contract negotiations. Proponents of payment for order flow inducements argue that investors are not harmed by these arrangements. They note that payment for order flows is in the spirit of fair competition, which in turn lowers execution costs. Moreover, such cash payments are no different from other "soft dollar" arrangements between brokers and dealers, where order flows are exchanged for reciprocal services. Opponents of payments for order flow claim that such payments exacerbate the selective market making of regional dealers (i.e., "cream skimming"). Unlike NYSE specialists, who must make a market for all NYSE-listed stocks, purchasers of order flows can target the more profitable "low end" business, which consists mainly of small trades in more liquid stocks. The NYSE specialist, finding profit margins reduced, may look to recover these losses by increasing the quoted spreads and, thus, the overall liquidity costs.[11]

---

[10] Brokers provide a standard notification to customers indicating that the firm may have received additional remunerations in connection with a customer's order. This notice typically appears on the back of confirmation slips.

[11] Glosten (1991) provides a formal treatment of the economic tradeoff between lower spreads from increased competition and higher spreads due to cream skimming. Empirical tests of the Glosten model using bid-ask spreads are complicated by the possibility that NYSE specialists may widen spreads (and increase inside-the-spread trading on the floor) for strategic reasons, to deter nonprimary exchange traders from free riding on the NYSE price discovery mechanism. This type of gamesmanship is difficult to distinguish from a spread effect due to "cream skimming."

Implicit throughout the regulatory debate is the assumption that the market for NYSE-listed securities is fully integrated, so price execution is the same at all locations. With market integration, the broker's responsibility to procure best execution is unlikely to be compromised by side payments from market makers. Therefore, if an examination reveals that execution costs are not significantly different by location, the debate should focus primarily on the effects of cream skimming versus increased competition. However, if execution costs differ by location, broker-dealer independence (both perceived and substantive) may be of real concern. In particular, if market centers that pay for order flow offer significantly worse price execution, the propriety of order flow inducements may need to be reexamined.

II. Execution Costs and Trade Location

Several reasons lead us to expect a relation between execution costs and trade location. First, and perhaps most important, the ITS quote does not fully reflect available intermarket liquidity. While all the market makers guarantee execution at the best intermarket price, as displayed on the ITS, much of the trading actually takes place inside the ITS spread (e.g., Lee and Ready (1991)). This activity reflects "hidden liquidity" at local markets that is not readily communicated by electronic links such as the ITS. In the case of the NYSE or a regional exchange, this liquidity may be provided by floor traders or the specialist—parties who may not wish to advertise formally their proclivity to trade.[12] The relative performance of individual market centers depends on their ability either to attract this liquidity, or provide it in a dealer capacity (see Harris (1990)). Since each market center has its own procedure for handling customer orders and attracting liquidity suppliers, the average cost of execution can differ by location.

The NYSE has long argued that the most favorable execution occurs on the primary exchange floor, where inside-the-spread executions occur frequently as specialists and floor brokers compete to supply liquidity. In response to this argument, regional specialists and NASD dealers point out that the spread for much of the order flow executed at their centers is only one eighth, leaving little room for price improvement (Stern (1989)). When the spread is wider, regional executions also transact frequently inside the best ITS quote. In fact, most regional exchanges as well as some NASD dealers have developed their own algorithms to improve the likelihood of inside-the-spread executions (see Appendix A for summary). The relative effectiveness of these

---

[12] The NASD operates under a multidealer electronic quote system, without an exchange floor, so floor trading does not explain inside-the-spread trades at the NASD. However, NASD dealers can, and do, improve prices relative to the ITS spread by facilitating execution inside the best ITS quote. This type of liquidity is also "hidden," in the sense that it is not reflected in the ITS system. Mann and Seijas (1991) provide a nontechnical discussion of differences between the NYSE specialist system and the NASD dealer system.

algorithms in reducing execution costs for public market orders is an open empirical issue.

Few prior studies have examined trade execution performance across markets. Reinganum (1990) finds differences in the monthly returns of NYSE and NASD firms matched on size and risk characteristics. He suggests that the multiple dealer market of the NASD may have a liquidity advantage for small firms, but not for large firms. Mayer and Leigh (1991) find that daily extreme prices (highs and lows) are more likely to be off-Board trades. They note that if one assumes the daily highs (or lows) tend to be buys (or sells), this finding is consistent with worse off-Board execution. These studies do not measure the liquidity premium per trade, or control for trade characteristics such as size and time of execution.

Using intraday data and different empirical methods, Blume and Goldstein (1991) provide an analysis much closer to this study. They also compute a liquidity premium per trade based on the absolute difference between the trade price and the quote "midspread." In their study, the average difference in liquidity premiums between NYSE and non-NYSE trades during 1989 is estimated to be 0.79 cents per share. However, Blume and Goldstein do not match regional and NYSE trades by their time of execution, nor do they report results for individual exchanges, or directly compare prices for buys and sells. Instead, their study makes extensive efforts to identify the best intermarket quote and provides detailed comparisons of NYSE and non-NYSE quote prices.

III. Data Description

The data used in this study are obtained from the Institute for the Study of Security Markets (ISSM). The ISSM data contain a record of all trades and quotes for NYSE and AMEX-listed firms. Each trade and quote is time stamped to the nearest second, with the originating exchange identified. The study period covers all 505 trading days in 1988 and 1989, except October 25, 1989. The quotes for this date are missing in the version of the ISSM tape used for this study, so all trades from this day are excluded. Opening batch trades on the NYSE (the first trade of each day not preceded by an opening quote) are excluded because they do not have a regional exchange counterpart. In addition, all late trades, trades reported out of sequence, or trades with special settlement conditions are excluded since their prices are not comparable to adjacent trades.

The sample of firms used is the first 500 NYSE common stocks on the 1988 and 1989 tape that were listed for the full year and had a CUSIP number. The firms are sorted by ticker symbol on the ISSM tape. Since it is unlikely that symbol order is related to execution costs, this sample should represent the total population of NYSE-listed securities. Table I reports the distribution of trades for the 500 sample firms in each year. Just over 7.3 million trades were transacted for these firms during 1988, of which 1.9 million (26 percent)

Table I
Distribution of Total Trades by Size and Exchange

Table values represent the number of trades (in thousands) in each exchange and size category for the 500 sample NYSE firms during 1988 and 1989.

	Trade Size (in Shares)						
	100–400	500–900	1000–1900	2000–4900	5000–9900	10,000 +	All
Panel A: 1988							
NYSE	2409.1	977.8	896.2	653.8	288.6	229.1	5454.6
Boston	81.3	25.1	19.5	8.5	2.9	2.4	139.8
Cincinnati	6.7	9.1	10.1	6.2	1.2	1.2	34.6
Midwest	461.0	124.4	89.0	33.5	10.7	11.9	730.5
Pacific	363.5	135.1	81.7	24.0	4.4	2.4	611.0
Philadelphia	147.3	35.3	19.1	6.4	2.3	2.8	213.2
NASD	106.2	23.3	19.0	6.7	2.0	3.5	160.6
Instinet	0.3	0.3	0.5	0.6	0.4	0.5	2.5
Total	3575.4	1330.3	1135.1	739.6	312.3	253.9	7346.7
Non-NYSE	1165.7	352.5	238.9	85.8	23.7	24.8	1892.1
(%)	(32.9)	(26.5)	(21.0)	(11.6)	(7.6)	(9.8)	(25.8)
Panel B: 1989							
NYSE	2694.4	1056.9	986.6	742.2	336.0	275.0	6091.1
Boston	157.2	41.4	30.7	11.9	4.4	3.1	248.7
Cincinnati	6.6	14.9	15.9	7.5	0.6	1.2	46.8
Midwest	594.6	156.4	116.9	46.4	12.4	13.0	939.6
Pacific	397.4	137.2	82.9	26.6	4.8	2.7	651.6
Philadelphia	185.7	38.6	20.9	7.5	2.9	3.5	259.0
NASD	260.2	49.1	36.6	12.1	2.7	4.5	365.3
Instinet	0.2	0.3	0.5	0.7	0.4	0.6	2.7
Total	4296.4	1494.8	1291.0	854.9	364.2	303.6	8604.9
Non-NYSE	1602.0	437.9	304.4	112.7	28.2	28.6	2513.8
(%)	(37.3)	(29.3)	(23.6)	(13.2)	(7.7)	(9.4)	(29.2)

were executed away from the NYSE. Similarly, 8.6 million trades were transacted in 1989, of which 2.5 million (29 percent) were executed off-Board. The proportion of regional trades for this sample is similar to that reported for the total population of NYSE-listed securities during this period. The overall movement of volume away from the NYSE, with the NASD as the main beneficiary, is also consistent with the aggregate statistics reported in the NYSE *Fact Book* (1991).

With the exception of the Cincinnati exchange and Instinet, the regional exchanges tend to execute smaller trades. For example, in 1988 trades of 900 shares or less (a rough proxy for individual investor trades) represent over 75 percent of all transactions in NYSE-listed securities on the Boston, Midwest, Pacific, and Philadelphia exchanges, as well as the NASD. On the NYSE, only 62 percent of the total trades are 900 shares or less. These differences may be due, in part, to the maximum order size stipulation of many order flow arrangements.

IV. Liquidity Premium Tests

A. Full Sample

In the first set of tests, the liquidity premium for each trade is computed as the absolute difference between the actual trade price and the "midspread" (average of bid and ask prices) of the prevailing quote at the time of the trade. Assuming that, on average, the specialist's spread is set symmetrically around the equilibrium price, the liquidity premium provides an estimate of the effective "half-spread" for each trade.[13] The liquidity premium paid on off-Board trades is compared to the liquidity premium paid on NYSE trades. All quotes eligible for the Best-Bid-Or-Offer (BBO) calculation, except regional exchange "autoquotes," are used.[14]

Case 1 of Figure 1 illustrates the liquidity premium test. Regional trades T4 and T6 have liquidity premiums of 12.5 cents and 0 cents per share, respectively. Assuming the NYSE trades T3 and T5 are matched to T4, then the excess cost of the T4 execution is computed as 6.25 cents per share in favor of the NYSE. Similarly, the excess cost for T6 is -6.25 cents per share, favoring the regional exchange.

Table II provides a profile of the average liquidity premium paid for the trades in each size and exchange category, expressed in cents per share. For 1988, the average liquidity premium on NYSE trades is 9.6 cents per share, which is slightly lower than the average liquidity premium on off-Board trades. However, intermarket comparisons based on these numbers may be misleading for two reasons. First, if regional dealers "skim the cream" by making markets only in more liquid stocks, regional trades should have a lower average liquidity premium than NYSE trades. Thus, lower execution costs may, in fact, be a product of the stock selection procedure followed by regional dealers. Second, quoted and effective spreads are known to display pronounced intraday patterns (e.g., Lee, Mucklow and Ready (1993)). The exact reasons for these patterns are not known, but their existence suggests it may not be appropriate to match trades from different times of the day. To

---

[13] Following the recommendation in Lee and Ready (1991), any quote in the five seconds preceding the trade is ignored in favor of the previous quote. This mitigates against situations where a quote triggered by a trade is recorded on the ISSM tape with the same time stamp as, or just ahead of, the triggering trade.

[14] The current version of the ISSM tape does not contain noncompetitive regional quotes (defined as regional quotes which are worse than NYSE quotes). Most of the excluded quotes are electronically generated "autoquotes" of 100 shares each. Such quotes automatically adjust as NYSE quotes change to avoid becoming the best available quote. In theory, the best ITS bid or offer cannot be identified without a full set of regional quotes, because a regional quote that is noncompetitive when issue may become competitive when the prevailing quote changes. However, as discussed later, the qualitative results remain the same when only NYSE quotes are used.

Market Integration and Price Execution

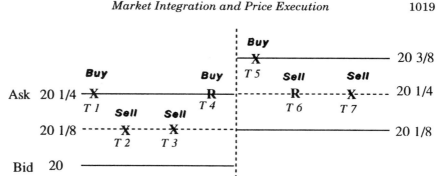

Quote Revision

Figure 1. Liquidity premium and directional price tests. NYSE trade (X). Regional or NASD trade (R).

Case 1: Liquidity Premium Test

The liquidity premium (LPrem) for each trade is defined as the distance between the trade price and the midspread of the best ITS quote at the time of the trade. The Liquidity Premium Test compares the LPrem for each regional trade to the LPrem for adjacent NYSE trades.

Regional Trade	Liquidity Premium on Regional Trade (LPremReg)	Matching NYSE Trade(s)	Liquidity Premium on NYSE trade(s) (LPRemNYSE)	Excess Cost of Regional Execution (LPRemReg − LPremNYSE)
T4	12.5 ¢/share	T3, T5	$(0 + 12.5)/2$ = 6.25 ¢/share	6.25 ¢/share (favors NYSE)
T6	0 ¢/share	T5, T7	$(12.5 + 0)/2$ = 6.25 ¢/share	−6.25 ¢/share (favors regional)

Case 2: Direction Price Test

Each trade is classified as a buy or sell, using the best ITS quote at the time of the trade and the price of adjacent trades. The price of regional buys (or sells) is then compared to the price of adjacent NYSE buy (or sells).

Regional Trade	Direction of Trade	Regional Trade Price (PrReg)	Matching NYSE Buy of Sell	NYSE Trade Price (PrNYSE)	Excess Cost of Regional Trade (PrReg − PrNYSE)
T4	Buy	20 1/4	T5	20 3/8	−12.5 ¢/share (favors regional)
T6	Sell	20 1/4	T7	20 1/4	0

Table II
Average Liquidity Premium by Size and Exchange

Table values represent the average liquidity premium paid for the trades in each size and exchange category, expressed in cents per share. The liquidity premium is computed as the absolute difference between the trade price and the midspread of the best ITS quote at the time of the execution. The midspread is the average of the bid price and ask price.

	Trade Size (in Shares)						
	100–400	500–900	1000–1900	2000–4900	5000–9900	10,000 +	All
Panel A: 1988							
NYSE	9.2	9.6	9.8	10.0	10.0	10.5	9.6
Boston	11.1	11.7	11.1	11.2	11.3	11.2	11.2
Cincinnati	13.1	12.0	9.7	12.1	9.9	9.5	11.4
Midwest	10.1	9.6	9.0	8.6	9.1	9.1	9.8
Pacific	10.4	10.1	9.1	7.9	7.3	8.5	10.0
Philadelphia	10.4	10.6	9.6	9.5	10.4	9.9	10.4
NASD	9.7	9.6	9.4	9.8	9.9	10.6	9.7
Instinet	11.1	9.7	9.6	9.9	9.2	9.1	9.7
All	9.5	9.8	9.7	9.9	9.9	10.4	9.7
Panel B: 1989							
NYSE	8.5	8.7	8.7	8.7	8.8	15.6	9.2
Boston	9.6	9.6	9.4	9.6	9.8	10.2	9.6
Cincinnati	13.6	11.9	9.0	11.0	9.3	8.5	10.9
Midwest	9.2	8.6	8.2	8.1	8.1	8.4	8.9
Pacific	9.4	9.2	8.5	7.5	7.1	8.2	9.1
Philadelphia	10.7	9.8	9.4	9.0	9.1	9.4	10.3
NASD	9.5	9.0	8.8	8.7	9.1	9.3	9.3
Instinet	10.3	9.1	8.6	8.9	8.0	7.5	8.6
All	8.9	8.8	8.7	8.7	8.8	15.4	9.2

control for this potential selection bias, this study uses a time-matched design in all the following tests.[15]

B. Time-Matched Sample

Tables III and IV control for the potential selection bias created by cream skimming. Table III shows the distribution of regional trades that have at

---

[15] The findings in Table II provide only weak evidence for the prediction that larger trades involve higher liquidity premiums (e.g., Easley and O'Hara (1987)). This may be due to the pooling of different firms in the analysis, since firms with greater frequency of large trades are likely to have lower average liquidity premiums. Alternatively, the larger trades tend to be brokered nonanonymously, thus reducing the adverse selection costs. The large average liquidity premium for 1989 NYSE trades over 10,000 shares is due to outliers that do not affect the time-matched sample, since they do not have matching regional trades.

Market Integration and Price Execution

Table III
Distribution of Off-Board Trades in Matched Sample

Table values represent the number of regional or OTC trades (in thousands) with at least one adjacent trade of similar size on the NYSE. NYSE trades are considered adjacent if they are in the same size class and occur in the same security, on the same day, and within two minutes of the regional or OTC trade.

	Trade Size (in Shares)						
	100-400	500-900	1000-1900	2000-4900	5000-9900	10,000 +	All
Panel A: 1988							
Boston	32.6	6.1	5.3	2.3	0.6	0.4	47.3
Cincinnati	3.2	3.2	4.2	3.0	0.3	0.2	14.2
Midwest	184.3	30.1	24.5	9.1	1.7	1.7	251.5
Pacific	148.6	32.1	21.7	5.8	0.7	0.4	209.3
Philadelphia	59.7	8.3	4.9	1.5	0.3	0.4	75.0
NASD	54.3	6.7	6.0	1.8	0.3	0.4	69.4
Instinet	0.1	0.1	0.1	0.1	0.0	0.0	0.5
Total	482.6	86.6	66.6	23.7	3.9	3.5	667.2
Panel B: 1989							
Boston	69.2	10.9	8.9	3.5	0.9	0.6	94.1
Cincinnati	3.3	5.4	6.4	3.6	0.1	0.2	19.2
Midwest	237.9	39.1	33.5	13.4	2.4	2.3	328.6
Pacific	174.0	34.3	22.9	6.8	0.8	0.5	239.3
Philadelphia	80.9	10.1	6.2	2.0	0.5	0.6	100.3
NASD	136.8	15.1	11.9	3.3	0.4	0.5	167.9
Instinet	0.1	0.1	0.1	0.2	0.1	0.1	0.6
Total	702.2	115.0	90.1	32.8	5.2	4.7	950.0

least one matching trade on the NYSE. A NYSE trade is considered a match if it is for the same security, in the same size class, and occurs on the same day within two minutes of the regional trade. A later test examines results using matching windows of one, five, and ten minutes. Using a two-minute window, approximately 667,000 (35 percent) of the off-Board trades in 1988 have at least one adjacent trade of similar size on the NYSE. Similarly, in 1989, approximately 950,000 (38 percent) off-Board trades have a matched observation on the NYSE. If more than one matching NYSE trade is found, the liquidity premium for the control group is the average of all qualifying NYSE trades. All regional trades executed between 9:40 A.M. and 3:50 P.M. are eligible for inclusion in this sample.[16] A total of 64 paired observations (5 in

---

[16] The exclusion of regional trades in the first and last ten minutes of trading ensures the distribution of matching NYSE trades has an equal chance of occurring in any of the ten minutes on either side of a regional trade. It also mitigates against the strong market trends at the opening of trading reported by Wood, McInish, and Ord (1985). However, none of the main results are changed if regional trades in the first and last ten minutes are included.

Table IV
Average Excess Liquidity Premium Paid for Off-Board Trades in Matched Sample

Table values represent the average excess liquidity premium paid for off-Board trades, expressed in cents per share (negative values represent savings relative to the NYSE execution). The liquidity premiums on off-Board trades are compared to the liquidity premiums for adjacent NYSE trades of similar size. NYSE trades are considered adjacent if they occur within two minutes of the regional or NASD trade. The average by trades is the excess liquidity premium paid for the average trade at that exchange; the average by shares is the excess liquidity premium paid for the average share traded at that exchange (each trade is weighted by the number of shares transacted).

	Trade Size (in Shares)						Average by Trades	Average by Shares
	100–400	500–900	1000–1900	2000–4900	5000–9900	10,000+		
Panel A: 1988								
Boston	1.4*	0.71	0.67*	−0.03	2.11*	1.83*	1.23*	1.20
Cincinnati	1.36*	−1.21**	−1.36**	−0.02	0.73	1.54	−0.34**	0.43
Midwest	0.68*	−0.70**	−0.95**	−0.90**	−0.28**	−0.69**	0.28*	−0.20
Pacific	1.10*	−0.23**	−0.18**	−0.50**	−0.71**	−1.47**	0.71*	0.01
Philadelphia	1.56*	0.50*	−0.50	−0.41	0.32	−0.51	1.26*	0.35
NASD	1.51*	0.76*	0.59*	0.21*	2.61*	0.31*	1.32*	1.10
Instinet	2.21	0.67	−0.46	−0.52	0.48	−3.93	0.05*	−4.02
All	1.07*	−0.22**	−0.42**	−0.49**	0.31	−0.28	0.69*	0.20
Panel B: 1989								
Boston	1.04*	0.55*	0.33	0.35	0.88*	1.61*	0.89*	0.91
Cincinnati	2.65*	0.44	−0.44**	1.49*	1.32	1.57	0.74	1.62
Midwest	0.87*	−0.03**	−0.27**	−0.32**	−0.06	−0.25	0.58*	−0.01
Pacific	1.19*	0.38	0.23	−0.02**	0.42	0.58	0.94*	0.48
Philadelphia	1.82*	1.21*	0.89*	0.46	1.26	1.17*	1.66*	1.28
NASD	1.58*	1.23*	0.89*	1.13*	2.26*	1.00*	1.49*	1.29
Instinet	1.72	1.42	1.81*	1.35	0.77	0.07	1.33*	0.81
All	1.22*	0.45*	0.14	0.22**	0.51	0.46	0.98*	0.59

* Favors the NYSE and is significantly different from zero at 0.01 level (two-tailed) using the Fisher sign test.
** Favors the regional exchange and is significantly different from zero at 0.01 level (two-tailed) using the Fisher sign test.

1988, 59 in 1989) are removed as a result of outlier tests. The main filter is the requirement that the absolute difference in liquidity premium between adjacent NYSE and regional trades be less than $2.00 per share.

Table IV reports the excess liquidity premium paid on the regional exchange relative to the liquidity premium for the control group of matched NYSE trades. Table values represent the liquidity premium for the regional trade minus the liquidity premium for the paired NYSE trade(s), averaged across all pairs and expressed in cents per share. Positive (or negative) values reflect higher (or lower) execution costs on the regionals. To average across trade sizes, two calculations are made for each exchange:

1. Average by trades

$$\text{Average Excess Liquidity Premium} = \frac{\sum_{i=1}^{n}(\text{LPremReg}_i - \text{LPremNYSE}_i)}{n}$$

2. Average by shares

$$\text{Average Excess Liquidity Premium} = \frac{\sum_{i=1}^{n}(\text{LPremReg}_i - \text{LPremNYSE}_i) \times \text{Shr}_i}{\sum_{i=1}^{n}\text{Shr}_i}$$

where:

n = the number of matched observations for this exchange.
LPremReg_i = the liquidity premium paid on the regional trade in the ith matched sample for this exchange
LPremNYSE_i = the liquidity premium paid on the NYSE trade(s) in the ith matched sample for this exchange
Shr_i = the number of shares traded for the regional trade in the ith matched sample for this exchange.

The first measure reflects the additional liquidity premium paid on the average trade executed at the given exchange. The second measure places greater weight on the larger trades and captures the additional liquidity premium paid on the average share executed at the given exchange.

The number of positive values in both panels of Table IV shows the liquidity premium is generally lower for NYSE trades. The NYSE advantage is most pronounced in the 100 to 400 shares class. The regional markets receive a disproportionately large share of these trades, yet appear to provide poorer price execution. For small trades, a Fisher sign test of statistical significance readily rejects the null hypothesis that the execution cost of off-Board trades is the same as the execution cost of adjacent NYSE trades. Given the large number of observations, this result is not surprising. Perhaps more important, however, is the economic magnitude of the estimated differences. The average excess liquidity premium per trade (the next to last column of Table IV) shows that off-Board trades generally involve higher execution costs in the order of 0.5 to 1.5 cents per share. The equally weighted average excess liquidity premium per non-NYSE trade is 0.69 cents per share in 1988 and 0.98 cents per share for 1989. Interestingly, this is approximately the magnitude of the payments in many order flow agreements. The evidence suggests that the higher effective spreads in the off-Board trades is sufficient to cover the cost of these payments.

The last column shows the volume-weighted difference by exchange. Here the difference between NYSE and non-NYSE performance is less pronounced, reflecting the better performance of the regional exchanges in the larger trade classes. In 1988, the Midwest exchange and Instinet had better volume-weighted performance than the NYSE. In 1989, only the Midwest performed better.

Although price execution is generally more favorable at the NYSE, results vary significantly by trade size and location. For example, the Cincinnati, Midwest, and Pacific exchanges tend to perform better than the NYSE in the midsized (500 to 5,000 share) trades. The NASD trades, however, display consistent higher liquidity premiums than their matching NYSE trades. This result holds in each size category in both years. Instinet, an electronic display system that allows large financial institutions to trade directly with each other, tends to perform better than the NYSE in the larger trade sizes.

C. Explaining the NASD Results

One of the most consistent results in Table IV is the performance of the NASD. In most trade sizes and across both years, NASD executions seem the least favorable to investors. These results may reflect the greater reliance of NASD dealers on intermarket quotes. Section VI examines this possibility by evaluating the frequency of inside-the-spread trades. The NASD result may also reflect the method of measuring liquidity premium. An important feature of the liquidity premium test is its reliance on the quote midspread at the time of the trade. This computation does not include any price "slippage" due to a movement in the quoted spread between the time of the order issuance and trade execution.[17] For example, if the midspread moves higher by one eighth between the time a buy order is issued and when it is executed, the additional one-eighth cost will not be included in the liquidity premium computed above. In short, this approach measures only the execution cost relative to an existing spread, when an investor may, in fact, face a significant additional risk due to slippage. The potential effect of price slippage is examined next.

V. Tests Based on Buy and Sell Prices

A. Directional Price Tests

Some argue that best price execution is more than simply execution inside the bid-ask spread (e.g., NASD (1991)). During 1988 and 1989, NASD dealers

---

[17] Price slippage is a natural consequence of adverse selection costs as market makers adjust prices to reflect the information revealed in incoming trades. See Glosten and Milgrom (1985) or Easley and O'Hara (1987) for formal treatments. Empirically, Hasbrouck (1988), Lee and Ready (1991), and Petersen and Umlauf (1991) show that buys (or sells) tend to be followed by upward (or downward) revisions in the specialist's quote. Also see Perold (1988) for an alternative way to measure slippage costs. Perold's "implementation shortfall" approach compares the actual profit from a real portfolio to a paper portfolio. It cannot be used here since no information is available about an order's time of origination.

typically executed at the best ITS bid-ask quote without attempting further price improvement.[18] Although this strategy reduces the chance of an inside-the-spread trade, it does provide faster execution. Since the benefit of an inside-the-spread execution may be outweighed by the cost of price slippage, NASD dealers may provide superior price execution that the liquidity premium test fails to capture. The tests in this section directly compare the trade price for buys (or sells) on regional exchanges to the trade price for adjacent buys (or sells) on the NYSE. If the price advantage from faster executions is greater than the price advantage of inside-the-spread executions, the NASD performance should improve under these tests.

Lee and Ready (1991) propose an algorithm that classifies each trade as buyer or seller initiated. This algorithm (summarized in Appendix B) relies on the prevailing bid and ask prices as well as the prior price changes ("tick tests") in classifying trades. In this study, the algorithm provides a direct way of comparing the price of buys (or sells) executed in a regional exchange to the price of adjacent buys (or sells) on the NYSE. The market that provides better execution should have lower average trade prices on market buys and higher average trade prices on market sells. The same algorithm is applied to trades from all exchanges, so even though trade misclassifications may introduce noise, they should not bias the results in favor of a particular exchange.

Case 2 of Figure 1 illustrates the directional trade test. The key trade in this sequence is T4. Under the liquidity premium test, this trade is compared to T3 and T5, and the regional execution is less favorable by 6.25 cents. However, the quote revision between T4 and T5 (i.e., price slippage) shows that the initiator of T4 actually bought at a cheaper price than the initiator of T5. The directional price test recognizes the better price obtained on the T4 trade and credits the regional exchange for a more favorable execution.[19]

Table V reports the average difference between the price of buyer-initiated regional trades and the price of matching buyer-initiated trades on the NYSE, expressed in cents per share. Positive table values indicate a higher price paid for buys on the regional exchanges. Negative values indicate savings from the NYSE. The number of positive values in Table V suggests that the price obtained for similar buys is generally higher for regional executions. These findings are consistent with the results of the liquidity premium tests in Table IV. Once again, the NYSE advantage is most evident

---

[18] More recently, some regional and OTC market makers have established methods to improve price execution by exposing an investor's order inside the quoted spread for a limited period of time. A primary example of this is Madoff Investment's MISSION system, implemented in the latter part of 1990. These price improvement algorithms may improve NASD and regional test results for future studies using post-1989 data.

[19] T4 is classified as a buy in the Lee and Ready (1991) algorithm because it is executed at the ask price. Note that it is also a buy using the "tick test" (based on the direction of the previous price change). It would be classified as a sell using the "reverse tick test" (based on the direction of the next price change), but Lee and Ready (1991) show the reverse tick test is generally inferior to the tick test.

Table V
Average Additional Cost for Off-Board Buys

Table values represent the average additional cost of buying for off-Board trades, expressed in cents per share (negative values represent savings relative to the NYSE execution). The Lee and Ready (1991) algorithm is used to infer buy-sell directions. The price of each off-Board buy is compared to the price for two adjacent NYSE buys of similar size. NYSE buys are considered adjacent if they occur within two minutes of the off-Board trade. The additional cost of buying is the difference between the off-Board trade price and the NYSE trade price (PrReg − PrNYSE). Sample size is 207,818 matched buy executions for 1988 and 332,121 matched buy executions for 1989.

	Trade Size (in Shares)						Average by Trades	Average by Shares
	100–400	500–900	1000–1900	2000–4900	5000–9900	10,000+		
Panel A: 1988								
Boston	1.14*	0.35	0.07	−0.02	0.15	2.74	0.84*	0.70
Cincinnati	0.60*	−0.71**	−0.82**	0.01	0.95*	0.51	−0.29**	−0.17
Midwest	0.25°	−0.69**	−0.56**	−0.93**	−0.12	−0.69**	−0.04	−0.39
Pacific	0.79*	−0.69**	−0.42**	−0.57**	−0.91**	−0.06	0.36*	−0.21
Philadelphia	1.41*	0.41*	−0.27**	0.10	0.17	0.56	1.12*	0.46
NASD	1.58*	1.23*	0.85*	0.41	0.21*	1.25	1.44*	0.65
Instinet	−2.84	0.00	1.07	0.33	1.41	−0.83	−0.03	0.01
All	0.78*	−0.38**	−0.35**	−0.46**	−0.07	0.13	0.43*	−0.04
Panel B: 1989								
Boston	0.65*	0.13	0.15	−0.01	0.61	0.65	0.52*	0.30
Cincinnati	0.32	−0.71**	−0.49**	0.58*	0.30	0.90	−0.18**	0.26
Midwest	0.66*	−0.32**	−0.41**	−0.43**	−0.19	−0.34	0.35*	−0.18
Pacific	0.80*	−0.55**	−0.36**	−0.21**	0.04	0.51	0.45*	0.25
Philadelphia	1.64*	0.49*	0.29	0.41	1.10	1.26*	1.40*	0.97
NASD	1.59*	1.15*	1.01*	1.02*	2.85*	0.74	1.50*	0.77
Instinet	−1.32	0.31	2.89	1.06	1.73	0.00	1.03*	1.03
All	0.99*	−0.12**	−0.12**	−0.02**	0.29	0.21	0.70*	0.23

* Favors the NYSE and is significantly different from zero at 0.01 level (two-tailed) using the Fisher sign test.
** Favors the regional exchange and is significantly different from zero at 0.01 level (two-tailed) using the Fisher sign test.

in the small trades, with the Cincinnati, Midwest, and Pacific exchanges doing well in the midsize trades. The results for seller-initiated trades are symmetrical and also favor the NYSE; prices for NYSE sells are generally higher than prices for regional sells. The magnitudes of the price differences for seller-initiated trades (not reported) are similar to those reported in Table IV for buyer-initiated trades.

These results show that price slippage is not a significant factor in explaining the NASD performance. For example, the average excess cost per trade for 1988 using the directional price test is 0.63 cents per share (0.43 for buys and −0.84 for sells), which is only slightly lower than the 0.69 cents per share reported in Table IV. Under the directional price test, the average excess cost for NASD actually increases from 1.10 cents per share to 1.45 cents per share. For the NASD trades in this sample, faster execution does not translate into lower execution costs.

B. An Estimate of Aggregate Costs

Table VI presents an estimate of the aggregate additional costs borne by investors whose orders are executed away from the NYSE. The per share execution costs are based on the time-matched sample, which includes over one third of the total off-Board trades. In Table VI, the volume-weighted per share cost is applied to the total share volume in each exchange to obtain an estimate of the total additional cost of regional trades. Panel A provides an estimate based on the excess liquidity premium method used to produce Table IV. Panel B provides an estimate based on the average additional cost using the directional price tests. These costs are obtained by averaging additional regional costs on all matched observations of buys and sells.

For 1988, the estimated additional cost of execution borne by investors is $13 million using the liquidity premium approach and $18 million using direct buy-sell prices. These totals increase to $47 million and $36 million respectively in 1989. The increase from 1988 to 1989 is due not only to a volume shift away from the NYSE, but also to an increase in the additional cost of off-Board execution. Thus, trade volume is moving away from the NYSE even as the performance gap between the NYSE and non-NYSE trade is widening. Despite its superior price performance, volume on the Cincinnati exchange actually decreases between 1988 and 1989. Meanwhile, the fastest volume increase is at the NASD, the market with the least favorable execution costs.[20]

VI. Price Improvement Tests

Panel A of Table VII reports the results of price improvement tests, based on the percentage of trades inside the best ITS spread for each exchange. The NYSE trades in the match sample are executed inside the spread 39 percent of the time in 1988 and 37 percent in 1989. By comparison, the Cincinnati trades are inside the spread 48 and 49 percent of the time in 1988 and 1989, respectively. NASD trades are inside the spread only 30 and 27 percent of the time in 1988 and 1989. As expected, the price improvement observed in the earlier tests is related to the frequency of inside-the-spread trading at each location.

Since much of the order flow targeted for purchase is executed when the spread is one eighth, these trades provide little opportunity for price improve-

---

[20] The flow of trading volume is not a comment about investor rationality. Investors may be fully rational, but not informed with respect to this aspect of their execution costs. Alternatively, investors may be attracted to the regional markets by factors other than price execution.

Table VI
Estimated Additional Cost of Off-Board Executions

This table presents the estimated total additional execution costs incurred by investors who had their trades executed at regional exchanges and OTC markets during 1988 and 1989. The Panel A results are based on the excess liquidity premium paid relative to adjacent NYSE trades of similar size. The Panel B results are based on the average additional cost of buying-selling relative to adjacent NYSE buys-sells of similar size. NYSE trades are deemed adjacent if they occur within two minutes of the regional or OTC trade.

Panel A: Based on the Excess Liquidity Premium Test

	1988			1989		
	Average Excess Liquidity Premium (¢/Share) from Table IV	Volume During Year (Millions of Shares)	Additional Cost (Millions of Dollars)	Average Excess Liquidity Premium (¢/Share) from Table IV	Volume During Year (Millions of Shares)	Additional Cost (Millions of Dollars)
Boston	1.20	593.1	7.09	0.91	799.6	7.08
Cincinnati	0.43	251.9	1.08	1.62	228.6	3.71
Midwest	-0.20	2632.8	-5.20	-0.01	2784.4	-0.22
Pacific	0.01	1329.8	0.08	0.48	1536.9	7.43
Philadelphia	0.35	631.7	2.22	1.28	910.2	11.69
NASD	1.10	1034.1	11.43	1.29	1594.5	20.64
Instinet	-4.02	67.3	-2.71	0.81	67.5	0.55
All	0.20	6540.7	12.97	0.59	7901.7	46.96

Continued Overleaf

Table VI—Continued

Panel B: Based on the Directional Price Test

	1988			1989		
	Average Additional Cost to Buy and Sell (¢/Share)*	Volume During Year (Millions of Shares)	Additional Cost (Millions of Dollars)	Average Additional Cost to Buy and Sell (¢/Share)*	Volume During Year (Millions of Shares)	Additional Cost (Millions of Dollars)
Boston	0.93	593.1	5.52	0.84	779.6	6.54
Cincinnati	0.44	251.9	1.11	0.21	228.6	0.47
Midwest	−0.09	2632.8	−2.34	0.07	2784.4	1.93
Pacific	−0.02	1329.8	−0.23	0.27	1536.9	4.12
Philadelphia	0.61	631.7	3.82	0.92	910.2	8.41
NASD	1.35	1034.1	13.96	1.23	1594.5	19.65
Instinet	0.13	67.3	0.09	1.18	67.5	0.80
All	0.28	6540.7	17.99	0.46	7901.7	36.32

*Computed as the average additional cost to buy and sell.

Table VII
Relative Performance by Frequency of Inside-the-Spread Trading

Panel A presents the frequency of inside-the-spread trades as a percentage of all trades in the matched sample for that exchange. Panel B table values represent the percentage of trades at a given spread size executed inside the spread. As such, Panel B table values capture the probability that an execution will be inside the spread, conditional on location and spread size. In both panels, the spread is computed using the best available ITS quote at the time of the trade execution.

	Spread Size (1988)				Spread Size (1989)			
	1/4	3/8	1/2 or More	All	1/4	3/8	1/2 or More	All
Panel A: Percentage of Trades Inside the Spread By Exchange and Size of Spread								
NYSE	19.2	10.9	9.4	39.5	20.0	9.6	7.7	37.3
Boston	15.4	10.6	11.0	37.0	16.1	9.7	8.5	34.3
Cincinnati	21.1	14.4	12.1	47.6	22.8	14.1	11.8	48.8
Midwest	16.9	10.8	9.9	37.6	17.7	10.2	8.4	36.3
Pacific	16.7	10.6	9.8	37.1	17.4	9.9	8.5	35.8
Philadelphia	13.3	9.9	8.6	31.9	13.5	8.4	7.3	29.2
NASD	13.3	9.2	7.7	30.1	13.4	7.3	6.6	27.4
Instinet	17.9	10.9	11.9	40.7	16.1	12.5	9.5	39.1
Panel B: Inside-the-Spread Trades as a Percentage of Total Trades at Each Spread Size								
NYSE	61.6	66.9	62.7		64.7	68.6	65.4	
Boston	44.2	64.3	62.5		45.6	66.9	62.0	
Cincinnati	61.6	59.9	49.5		62.4	61.9	48.9	
Midwest	47.2	66.2	65.7		49.3	68.4	66.4	
Pacific	47.8	65.0	63.1		48.8	67.8	64.8	
Philadelphia	37.7	59.3	60.7		38.1	59.0	59.2	
NASD	38.0	60.8	64.8		39.0	59.4	62.2	
Instinet	44.9	65.9	77.3		47.5	67.2	69.3	

ment (Stern (1989)). For example, if relatively more NASD trades are executed when the NYSE spread is only one eighth, the results in Panel A might simply reflect fewer opportunities for price improvement at the NASD. To address this possibility, Panel B reports the inside-the-spread trades as a percentage of the total number of trades at each spread size. Thus, Panel B measures the likelihood of price improvement at each location, conditional on the spread size.

Two results are striking. First, when the best ITS quote is greater than one eighth, a substantial proportion of the trading takes place inside the spread. At a one-quarter spread, a full 62 percent (or 38 percent) of the NYSE (or NASD) trades execute between the best bid and ask prices. This finding shows the best ITS quote is not capturing all the liquidity available in the market. Second, the relative ranking across exchanges is the same as in the first two tests. The market centers that are most likely to improve on quoted prices (NYSE, Cincinnati, Midwest, and Pacific) are the locations with the best price execution. The NASD is least likely to improve prices relative to the ITS quote, even when price improvement is possible.

VII. Supplemental Analyses

A. Size of the Match Window

All the reported results are for trades matched on the basis of a two-minute window. A wider window provides larger sample sizes, but less assurance that market conditions are similar for NYSE and off-Board trades. To examine the sensitivity of the results to this parameter, I recompute the excess liquidity premiums using one-, two-, five-, and ten-minute windows. Since the results do not vary significantly by window size, they are not reported separately. In general, as the window size decreases, the NYSE performance tends to improve against the performance of other markets. However, intermarket rankings are largely unchanged.

B. Timing Issues

A potential concern with the research design is the mismatching of trades due to intermarket differences in the timeliness of reporting. If matching NYSE trades are systematically recorded ahead of the corresponding regional trades (for example, if NYSE traders tend to respond faster on both upward and downward price moves), the earlier results could be biased in favor of the NYSE. The two-minute match window, while mitigating the problem, may not fully alleviate it. To examine this possibility, Figure 2 shows the distribution of adjacent NYSE trades for the ten minutes around a regional trade. The slight increase in the NYSE volume in the same minute as the regional trades suggests the arrival time of orders across the exchanges is correlated. However, matched NYSE trades do not appear to be executed earlier than their regional counterparts. In fact, the regional trades have a slight speed advantage over their NYSE control sample.

Another timing issue is the problem of identifying the appropriate quote for each trade. Lee and Ready (1991) show trades that trigger quote revisions may be recorded on the ISSM tape after the quote revision. This is because the NYSE quote revision is typically entered electronically, while many trades are still recorded using the slower card readers. Since the new quote tends to bracket the trade that triggered it, the triggering trade will have the appearance of price improvement. If NYSE trades are more likely to trigger quote revisions, the reported results might reflect this bias. The five-second quote delay can mitigate this problem, but not resolve it.

Ideally, this problem should be addressed by identifying the prevailing quote at the time each order is submitted. Since this is impossible with the ISSM data, an alternative test is performed. Specifically, the liquidity pre-

1988

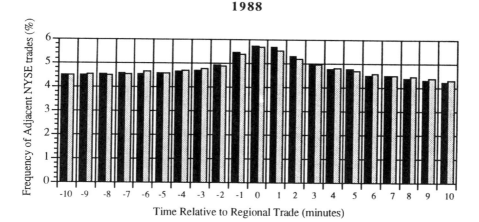

1989

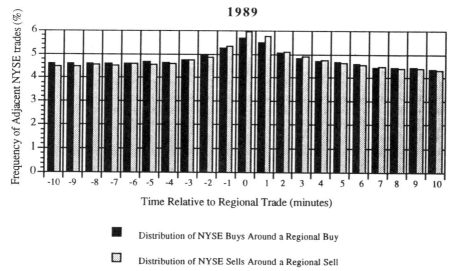

■ Distribution of NYSE Buys Around a Regional Buy

▒ Distribution of NYSE Sells Around a Regional Sell

Figure 2. The distribution of adjacent NYSE trades of similar size and direction around a regional trade.

mium test is repeated twice, using the prevailing best ITS quote at least two minutes and at least five minutes before each trade. Some of these quotes are superseded by newer quotes, so this approach will introduce noise into the calculation. However, it provides less risk of a bias toward a particular exchange. The results (not reported) remain similar, with no change in the intermarket rankings.

C. Regional Trades Due to "Limit Book Protection"

The regional exchanges and the NYSE handle public limit orders differently in one important respect. On the NYSE, public limit orders have the opportunity to be exposed to a large volume of incoming market orders. To ensure that public limit orders at the regionals receive comparable execution, regional market makers typically guarantee execution of these orders when the limit order price is penetrated by a transaction in another market center. To implement this limit book protection, the regional market maker initiates a "shadow" trade at his own exchange for the same price as the triggering trade. This trade triggers the regional limit order, thus ensuring it receives as good an execution as the limit orders on other exchanges.

Since these shadow trades are not initiated by public market orders, the argument could be made that they should be excluded from the analysis. This exclusion is not possible with ISSM data, nor is the extent of this activity easily quantified. However, the likely effect of including these trades is to understate reported intermarket differences. Since regional shadow trades are typically triggered by a NYSE trade at the same price, paired observations caused by limit book protection should show identical execution costs. Therefore, the inclusion of these observations in the sample reduces the average price difference between NYSE and non-NYSE executions.

D. Accounting for Cross-Sectional Firm Characteristics

We should note that these tests do not control for cross-sectional differences across the sample firms. The unit of analysis is individual trades, so that securities with greater volume receive greater proportional weight. This approach is reasonable given the research focus on price execution per trade. However, since the extent of off-Board trading varies widely across securities, the results may be due to a small proportion of the sample firms. To examine this possibility, the liquidity premium tests are recomputed so that the excess cost per trade is first averaged for each firm, then aggregated across firms. Statistical significance is measured by the proportion of firms in which the NYSE (or the regional exchange) demonstrates superior price performance. Once again, since the findings for these tests confirm the earlier results, they are not separately reported.

E. Other Potential Matching Problems

Finally, since no two orders are identical in all respects, other matching problems could remain between NYSE and non-NYSE trades. For example, larger market orders are sometimes broken up in execution as they march through the limit book. Since the NYSE tends to receive large orders, a large trade sent to the NYSE may appear as a series of smaller trades, all poorly executed relative to the prevailing quote. In this case, the price performance of the NYSE would appear worse. In other situations, regional price performance could be slighted. Short of a controlled laboratory experiment, such differences are difficult to eliminate. Therefore, this study should be regarded as a first step in the continuing process of understanding market integration and intermarket price performance.

VIII. Summary

This paper presents three simple ways to measure the execution and price performance of different market centers. The results show that for NYSE-listed securities the price obtained on similar adjacent trades can differ by location of execution. In particular, the results for 1988 and 1989 suggest that Cincinnati, Midwest, and NYSE executions are generally more favorable to the initiator of the trade than executions on the other exchanges. The average price difference between the NYSE and matched off-Board trades is 0.7 to 1 cent per share. These results are statistically significant at any reasonable level of confidence. In total dollars, the aggregate excess cost for off-Board trades is estimated at $13 to $18 million for 1988 and $36 to $47 million for 1989.

Several implications derive from these results. First, the existing intermarket structure for NYSE securities is much less integrated than many had previously assumed. These findings suggest that order routing may warrant consideration by investors and regulators. Brokers currently rely on the ITS quote to fulfill "best execution" obligations. This strategy may be inappropriate given the effects of market fragmentation documented here. Many investors currently delegate the responsibility of choosing the best market center to their broker. These results suggest individual investors may wish to consider other arrangements, discussed below, to ensure the benefits of order inducements flow directly to them.

These results also suggest that full integration may be difficult to attain under the current ITS system. Under ITS, liquidity providers at the primary exchange may not be motivated to reveal their presence to off-Board traders. Thus, the current system encourages gamesmanship between exchanges, as each probes the other for "hidden liquidity" not revealed in the intermarket quote. The price improvement algorithm recently implemented by a prominent NASD member firm, Madoff Investments, is a prime example of this type of intermarket price exploration (see Appendix A). A long-term solution to the market integration problem may involve more fundamental changes to the intermarket quote system. One possibility is a consolidated electronic limit book with strict price and time priority. This appears to be a promising area for future research.

The order flow debate involves factors not considered in this study. However, these results do raise several interesting issues pertinent to the debate. First the magnitude of the price differences is comparable to order flow cash inducements. In light of these price differences, the broker's primary responsibility could potentially be compromised by order flow inducements. Second, the performance gap between NYSE and off-Board executions is most evident in the small trades. This finding is disturbing, since small trades are the primary target of order flow inducements and small traders may be least aware of the dealer-broker arrangements. Finally, some (limited) evidence suggests that trading volume is not flowing in the direction of better price execution. Prices obtained on the NASD are typically least favorable, yet the trading volume on this exchange has increased most dramatically in recent years. In contrast, the better performing centers, such as Cincinnati and the NYSE, actually experienced a decline in market share between 1988 and 1989. Investors may be moving to the NASD for nonpecuniary reasons, but the volume shift may also reflect broker response to cash inducements. The finding is at least suggestive that order flow patterns may be responsive to cash inducements, rather than price execution.[21]

While investors appear to pay more for off-Board executions, brokers who receive order flow inducements might indirectly pass on these savings through lower commission fees. Given competition among brokers, investors may be partially compensated for the additional costs through lower broker commissions. However, investors whose orders are diverted are unlikely to be fully compensated for two reasons. First, unless enough traders exercise their right to direct orders, brokers are not compelled to pass on all the inducement benefits to investors. Second, even if all the inducement benefits are reflected in the commission structure, these savings are spread out across all investors, so investors who have their orders diverted still subsidize those who do not.

More importantly, investors should recognize that dealer and broker services are fundamentally separable. Traders that engage a broker do not legally commit themselves to a particular dealer. Since investors can shop for both the lowest broker commission and the lowest dealer (execution) cost, these costs are not fungible. Currently, many investors delegate the choice of a dealer to their broker, presumably because the choice appears inconsequential. The evidence here suggests some investors—e.g., small traders—may be better off not delegating this decision. An investor could either direct an order to a particular location or "sell" this right by choosing a low-priced broker who does not allow location choices. In either case, the benefit of order flow inducements passes directly to the ultimate consumer. These arrangements reflect the fact that order flows belong to investors, not brokers.

Finally, the existence of intermarket price differences suggests brokers should be called to higher level of accountability for their trade execution performance. A simple first step is to require brokers to report the location where the order is executed. Another step is to make available periodic measures of comparative execution costs by location, and perhaps even by brokerage house. Given information on the comparative costs of alternative executions, informed investors can decide for themselves whether to take further action. As the consuming public focuses on these measures of perfor-

---

[21] Two years of data cannot provide strong conclusions. Future studies should be able to provide more evidence on this issue.

mance, the various parties competing for their business should modify their actions to provide the most favorable execution possible.

Appendix A: Electronic Systems at Regional Exchanges and the NASD

Most regional and OTC markets have their own price improvement procedures. These typically involve guaranteeing the best ITS price and further exposing an incoming order to either the floor of the local exchange or the ITS system for a period of time (i.e., "stopping" a trade). While incoming orders may be manually "stopped" at any time, electronic systems at many exchanges automatically "stop" certain types of orders. These automated systems are briefly summarized below.

Boston, Pacific, and Midwest

These three exchanges have similar systems. The BEACON (Boston), Scorex (Pacific), and MAX (Midwest) systems all display orders of up to 1,099 shares for 15 seconds to the local floor for possible improvement. If a better price is not obtained in 15 seconds, the order is executed against the best intermarket quote at the time of receipt.

In addition, during 1990, the Midwest exchange introduced a new price improvement algorithm that offers a one-eighth improvement on all trades if its execution at the intermarket quote generates a double down or double up tick (i.e., two successive negative or positive price changes).

Cincinnati

Cincinnati has no exchange floor and operates solely on a quote display system. The NSTS system at Cincinnati automatically executes orders of up to 2,099 shares at the best intermarket quote.

Philadelphia

The PACE system of Philadelphia automatically executes at the best intermarket quote for up to 599 shares.

NASD

Most NASD market makers during this study period automatically executed orders at the best intermarket quote. However, during the latter part of 1990, Madoff Investment (a prominent member of NASD), instituted an automated execution system dubbed MISSION. For orders of 300 shares or greater, in stocks trading at one-fourth or more spread, MISSION adjusts the Madoff ITS bid or ask to reflect the customer's order for one minute. If this quote is taken within the one minute, the entire order is cleared at the improved price.

Appendix B: Inferring Trade Direction

The direction of individual trades is inferred by the following algorithm developed in Lee and Ready (1991). The only modification is that Lee and Ready use only NYSE quotes, while this study uses all BBO-eligible quotes on the ISSM tape (a quote is BBO-eligible if it qualifies for the NASD Best-Bid-Or-Offer calculation):

1. Current Quote Match—If the trade price is at the bid or ask, and the current quote was not revised within the last 5 seconds, then the direction of the trade is determined by the current quote (i.e. a buy if it is at the ask and a sell if it is at the bid).
2. Delayed Quote Match—If the current quote is less than 5-seconds old, it is ignored and the trade price is compared to the bid and ask prices of the previous quote.
3. Outside the Spread—If the trade price, when compared to the quote in either 1 or 2, is greater than the ask (or less than the bid), then the transaction is deemed a buy (or sell).
4. Tick Test—If the trade is at the midpoint of the spread, or if a BBO-eligible quote is not available, the tick test is used to determine trade direction. A BBO-eligible quote is deemed to be unavailable if the last NYSE-quote issued has a nontradable condition code. Using the tick test, if the last price change was positive (or negative), then the current trade is deemed a buy (or sell). All out-of-sequence trades are ignored in updating price changes.
5. Proximity to Bid-Ask—If a trade is between the spread but not at the midpoint, then the trade is classified according to its proximity to the bid or ask price. Trades at prices above the midpoint are classified as buys and trades at prices below the midpoint are classified as sells.
6. Indeterminable—This classification is assigned to a trade when none of the above conditions apply. Specifically, it applies to the first trade of the year for each firm and any trade which is reported out of sequence.

REFERENCES

Blume, Marshall E., and Michael A. Goldstein, 1991, Differences in execution prices among the NYSE, the regionals and the NASD, Working paper, University of Pennsylvania.

Coffee, John C., Jr., 1991, Brokers and bribery, *New York Law Journal*, September 27, 5.

Crawford, William B., Jr., 1991, Brokerage fees stir debate on exchange floors, *Chicago Tribune*, August 26.

Easley, David, and Maureen O'Hara, 1987, Price, trade size, and information in securities markets, *Journal of Financial Economics* 19, 69–90.

Glosten, Lawrence R., 1991, Asymmetric information, the third market and investor welfare, Working paper, Columbia University.

——— and Paul Milgrom, 1985, Bid, ask and transaction prices in a specialist market with heterogeneously informed traders, *Journal of Financial Economics* 14, 71–100.

Harris, Lawrence E., 1990, *Liquidity, Trading Rules, and Electronic Trading Systems*, New York University Monograph Series in Finance and Economics, No. 1990-4.

———, 1992, Consolidation, fragmentation, segmentation and regulation, Working paper, University of Southern California.

——— and Joel Hasbrouck, 1992, Market vs. limit orders: The SuperDOT evidence on order submission strategy, Working paper, University of Southern California and New York University.

Hasbrouck, Joel, 1988, Trades, quotes, inventories and information, *Journal of Financial Economics* 22, 229–252.

——— and George Sofianos, 1992, The trades of market-makers: An analysis of NYSE specialists, Working paper, New York University and New York Stock Exchange.

Lee, Charles M. C., Belinda Mucklow, and Mark J. Ready, 1993, Spreads, depths and the impact of earnings information: An intraday analysis, *Review of Financial Studies* 6, Forthcoming.

Lee, Charles M. C., and Mark J. Ready, 1991, Inferring trade direction from intraday data, *Journal of Finance* 46, 733–746.

Mann, Steven V., and Robert W. Seijas, 1991, Bid-ask spreads, NYSE specialists, and NASD dealers, *Journal of Portfolio Management*, 17, 54–58.

Mayer, Marcia Kramer, and Bradford Leigh, 1991, Does off-board trading compromise execution quality? The evidence from high and down low, Working paper, American Stock Exchange Research Department.

National Association of Securities Dealers, 1991, *Inducement For Order Flow, A Report of the Order Flow Committee to the Board of Governors* (National Association of Securities Dealers, Inc., Washington, D.C.).

Perold, Andre F., 1988, The implementation shortfall: Paper versus reality, *Journal of Portfolio Management* 14, 4–9.

Petersen, Mitchell, and Steve Umlauf, 1991, An empirical examination of intraday quote revisions on the New York Stock Exchange, Working paper, University of Chicago.

Reinganum, Marc R., 1990, Market microstructure and asset pricing, *Journal of Financial Economics* 28, 127–147.

Securities Week, 1989a, NASD continues studying payment for order flow study, asks for more time, May 8.

———, 1989b, Industry ponders question of exchanges paying for order flow, March 6.

Steptoe, Sonja, 1989, Debate over order flow payments grows hotter as competition increases, *Wall Street Journal*, February 21.

Stern, Richard, 1989, Living off the spread, *Forbes*, July 10, 66–67.

Wood, Robert A., Thomas H. McInish, and J. Keith Ord, 1985, An investigation of transactions data for NYSE stocks, *Journal of Finance* 40, 723–739.

Part IV
Other Markets

A
Options Markets

Liquidity of the CBOE Equity Options

ANAND M. VIJH*

ABSTRACT

We examine the CBOE option market depth and bid-ask spreads. Absence of price effects surrounding large option trades suggests excellent market depth. However, bid-ask spreads for the CBOE options and the NYSE stocks are nearly equal, even though an average option is equivalent to less than half a stock plus borrowing. We explain this tradeoff between market depth and bid-ask spreads on the CBOE and the NYSE by differences in market mechanisms. We also show that the adverse-selection component of the option spread, which measures the extent of information-related trading on the CBOE, is very small.

THIS STUDY EXAMINES EMPIRICALLY the liquidity of the options market. In particular, we examine the tradeoff between market depth and market spread arising from differences in market mechanisms of the Chicago Board Options Exchange (CBOE) and the New York Stock Exchange (NYSE). Market depth is the ability of a market to absorb sudden increases in trading volume and is measured by the extent of a large trade's impact on the security's price. Market spread is the difference between the lowest ask and the highest bid prices at which dealers stand ready to trade a minimum-size order.

The basic theory motivating our analysis has been developed by a number of researchers, but perhaps most effectively by Ho and Macris (1985). They argue that increasing the number of dealers in a given security leads to greater market depth at the cost of wider bid-ask spreads. Their basic reasoning is as follows. Consider first the situation facing a specialist who is the only designated dealer in a particular security. The specialist uses the bid-ask spread to recover the cost of market-making and uses the position of the spread (i.e., the location of the spread midpoint) to control his or her costs arising from carrying an inventory of securities. For example, if the specialist has a large negative inventory, he or she raises both the bid and the ask prices, which encourages potential sellers and discourages potential buyers. Now compare a multiple dealer market, such as the CBOE, to the NYSE, where a single dealer (the specialist) makes the market in each stock. In a multiple dealer market, the collective ability of dealers to carry inventory to absorb imbalances in buying and selling activity is much higher. Also, the ability of any one dealer to move bid-ask prices is limited because he or she faces competition from other dealers who may have small inventories.

---

* Assistant Professor, University of Southern California, Los Angeles. This paper is based on the fourth essay of my dissertation completed at the University of California, Berkeley. I am obliged to Mukesh Bajaj, Tim Campbell, Gregory Connor, Larry Harris, Terry Marsh, and Mark Rubinstein (dissertation advisor) for helpful comments. I am especially obliged to the referee and the editor for many helpful suggestions which improved this paper considerably.

Thus, increasing the number of dealers results in higher market depth; that is, the market can absorb large orders with little change in the price. However, this improvement in market depth occurs at a cost. All of the dealers together pay higher inventory costs for carrying more inventory; furthermore, fixed costs, such as the opportunity cost of dealers' time, increase in direct proportion to the number of dealers. Higher fixed and inventory costs lead to wider bid-ask spreads as the number of dealers increases.

There is a long history of empirical studies of both depth and bid-ask spreads in equity markets dating back to at least the Institutional Investor Study (1971). Important contributions on the topic of the NYSE market depth include studies by Kraus and Stoll (1972), Dann, Mayers, and Raab (1977), and Holthausen, Leftwich, and Mayers (1987). In addition, Branch and Freed (1977) and Glosten and Harris (1988) provide estimates of the NYSE bid-ask spreads. However, perhaps due to the more recent history of option trading on organized exchanges, the evidence on liquidity of the options markets is comparatively scarce. Many exchanges trade equity options today, but the CBOE has remained the leading options market since it began trading options in 1973. We focus on the NYSE stocks and the CBOE options in this study for two reasons: first, the market mechanisms on these two exchanges differ in ways most pertinent for the tradeoff between market depth and bid-ask spreads, and second, these exchanges are the leading markets for equities and equity options.

Besides the number of dealers allowed to compete for a given security, a market's liquidity is also influenced by the extent of information-related trading in that market. Since the first study of this issue by Bagehot (1971), many theoretical models have suggested that information trading increases transaction costs because dealers must recover from uninformed traders what they lose (on average) to informed traders. This incremental cost, commonly termed the adverse-selection component of bid-ask spread, may have an effect on bid-ask spreads quite apart from effects related to market mechanisms discussed above. Therefore, any attempt to study the relative liquidity of different markets with a view to understanding the effectiveness of different market mechanisms must take into account differences in liquidity due to information-related trading.

While the extent of information trading in the NYSE stocks has been the subject of intense scrutiny, comparatively little evidence exists for the CBOE options. Glosten and Harris (1988) and Stoll (1989) provide estimates of the adverse-selection component of the transaction costs on the NYSE, but there are no direct estimates of transaction costs arising from adverse selection on the CBOE.[1] It is sometimes argued that the leverage implicit in options is particularly attractive to informed traders. However, and for precisely the same reason,

---

[1] This topic, however, has been investigated in a different context. Manaster and Rendleman (1982) show that the CBOE closing prices (sometimes) predict the subsequent changes in stock prices. Vijh (1988) shows that their results may be explained by a selection bias. Bhattacharya (1987) also shows that Manaster and Rendleman's results almost disappear when transaction data are used. Neither Manaster and Rendleman nor Bhattacharya investigate how often stock prices lead option prices, so one cannot infer the relative information content of stock and option trades from their studies. In a recent paper, however, Stephan and Whaley (1989) examine both lead and lag relations between stock and option prices and show that stock prices lead option prices by fifteen to twenty minutes.

options are also attractive to noise traders—those traders who think they have superior information but actually have only a different opinion. Depending on their investment horizons, liquidity traders may or may not find options an alternative to stocks. The compositions of the investor populations on the two exchanges, in terms of information traders, noise traders, and liquidity traders, are difficult to ascertain. The relative influence of information trading on the two exchanges must therefore be empirically determined. This paper provides specific estimates of the impact of information trading on the liquidity of the CBOE options and compares these estimates with corresponding estimates for the NYSE stocks obtained by previous researchers.

The organization of the paper and the principal results are as follows. Section I estimates the depth of the CBOE options market. Both stock and option prices surrounding large option trades are surprisingly unaffected. Neither the bid-ask spread nor the location of the spread midpoint changes with a large option trade. Section II shows that the depth of the CBOE options market occurs at the cost of wider bid-ask spreads. Specifically, although an average option is equivalent to less than half a stock (an option can be replicated by "delta" stock plus bond, and the average option delta is less than 0.50), stock and option bid-ask spreads are nearly equal. Section III investigates the extent and nature of information trading on the CBOE. The asymmetry in information among option traders, as evidenced by the adverse-selection component of bid-ask spread, is found to be small in comparison with similar estimates for the NYSE stocks from Glosten and Harris (1988) and cannot explain why option spreads are so large. It is also shown that the information content of option trades is uncorrelated with trade size. Section IV summarizes the findings and implications of the paper.

Overall, we show that the CBOE options market offers greater depth but wider bid-ask spreads than the NYSE equities market. These differences apparently arise from the different market mechanisms on the CBOE and the NYSE. Contrary to popular belief, however, information effects in option trades are very small and do not have a substantial influence on option liquidity.

I. The CBOE Option Market Depth

Below, we ascertain the magnitude and duration of the price effects of large option trades on the CBOE. Whereas many studies show that block trades on the NYSE cause both temporary and permanent price effects, we show that the multiple-dealer market on the CBOE can absorb large trades without any effect on price.

Our data base contains a complete time-stamped history of bid-ask quotes in addition to trade prices and quantities for stocks and options during March and April 1985. Only options on NYSE-listed stocks are included.[2] The bid-ask prices enable us to identify trades as buyer- or seller-initiated, and the record of

---

[2] The options data were obtained from the Berkeley Options Database tapes, and the stock transaction data were obtained from the AMEX. Both stock and option prices were electronically recorded from the tape and show a high degree of synchrony. Options on 141 NYSE-listed stocks were traded on the CBOE during the period of this study.

simultaneous stock prices enables us to distinguish between information-related and inventory-related price effects.

To be included in this study, an option trade has to be equivalent to at least 250 round lots of stock. Since an option can be replicated by delta (hedge ratio) stock plus bonds, equivalent round lots of stock are obtained by multiplying the option trade size by the option delta. Only two other criteria are used in sample selection. First, because an option pricing function cannot be estimated reliably for very short-maturity or deep-in or out-of-the-money options, the selected large trades must have a time to maturity of greater than a week and the option delta must lie between 0.15 and 0.85. Second, straddles and combinations are excluded because they combine two or more options and limit the risk borne by the dealers. Imposition of these criteria produced a sample of 188 call and 11 put trades. The average large trade is equivalent to $1.9 million worth of stock and represents two-thirds of the daily volume for all options on that stock.[3] We classify trades into three categories: (i) trades occurring in the upper half of the spread, presumed to be buyer-initiated, (ii) trades exactly at the middle, and (iii) trades in the lower half, presumed to be seller-initiated. There are 51, 53, and 95 trades in these three categories.

Our methodology is based on the following observations. First, if large option trades are motivated by superior information about future stock prices, they should be accompanied by a permanent change in both stock and option prices. Second, if dealers perceive that the inventory risk of large option trades requires an additional premium or discount, there should also be a temporary divergence between the stock and option prices. Measuring the latter price effect requires estimating a pricing function which gives option prices implied by the contemporaneous stock prices while ignoring effects of the large trade. This study uses the Black and Scholes (1973) formula with dividend correction to estimate the option pricing function from the previous day's data.

We first estimate the information-related permanent price effects of large option trades by examining the surrounding stock prices. Because the time it takes the stock price to reflect the information may vary across the sample (and because sometimes the market may learn about a large trade before it occurs), we examine stock prices from ten minutes before to thirty minutes after the large option trades. Let S_{tj} represent the stock price (midpoint of last quoted stock spread) t minutes after the jth large option trade. To test whether large trades are motivated by superior information concerning future stock prices, define

$$s_t = \sum_{j=1}^{n} S_{tj}/nS_{0j}.$$

Thus, the statistic s_t measures the average stock price at time t relative to S_{0j}, which is the stock price prevalent at $t = 0$, *just before* the large trade occurs. Ignoring the small expected return over thirty minutes (less than 0.0001), s_t should equal 1.0 for all t if there is no information in large trades. However, if large option trades are motivated by superior information, then s_t should increase with time for trades that would benefit from an increase in the stock price

---

[3] Alternatively, the average large trade represents the right to buy 72,300 shares, worth $3.6 million. If the option is considered to be equivalent to delta stock, the average trade size is $1.9 million.

(buyer-initiated calls and seller-initiated puts) and decrease for trades that would benefit from a decrease in the stock price (the converse).[4]

The results in Table I (also Figure 1) show that stock prices are unaffected by large option trades. Even after a lapse of thirty minutes, s_t equals 0.9992 or 1.0000 for trades that would benefit from an increase or a decrease in the stock price. For the average stock, these s_t values represent a deviation of −4 cents and 0 cents from the stock price prevailing before the large trade and are statistically insignificant. There is no evidence to suggest that large option trades are motivated by superior information about future stock prices.

Since the surrounding stock prices are unaffected, we next examine whether the inventory-related price effects of large option trades cause a deviation between the stock and option prices. We look at the five trades preceding and the five trades following large option trades. In the following discussion, the subscript j refers to one of these large trades, or *events*; $j = 1, 2, \cdots, n$, where n is the number of large trades. The subscript i denotes the event *transaction* time; e.g., $i = 0$ refers to the large trade (the event), and $i = -1$ refers to the immediately preceding trade in the same option. The *trade* price of the ith option trade surrounding the jth event is denoted by W_{ij}^t. For example, W_{0j}^t represents the trade price of the jth large trade, while W_{-1j}^t represents the immediately preceding trade price. Finally, W_{ij}^b and W_{ij}^a represent the option *bid* and *ask* prices effective at the time of the ith trade.

The following tests require three kinds of prices (trade, bid, and ask) observed for two related securities (stocks and options). To summarize notation, W and S denote the option and stock prices; the superscripts t, b, and a denote that the price is the trade, the bid, or the ask price; and the subscripts j and i denote the particular event (large trade) under consideration and the time relative to that event.

The null hypothesis states that large option trades cause no price effects that result in a deviation between the stock and option prices. In other words, option prices depend only on the contemporaneous stock prices. Assuming that the stock spread midpoint is an unbiased estimator of the "true" stock price, we use an option pricing function fitted from the previous day's data to calculate $W_{ij}^*(S_{ij})$, the "true" option prices implied by the contemporaneous "true" stock prices.[5] If large trades do not cause a deviation between the stock and option prices, then the observed option spread midpoint, $0.5 \times [W_{ij}^b + W_{ij}^a]$, should equal the implied true option price, W_{ij}^*. So we use the following test statistic to measure the price effects:

effect on spread midpoint ("q"): $\quad T_i^q = \dfrac{100}{n} \sum\limits_{j=1}^{n} \dfrac{1}{S_{ij}} [0.5 \times (W_{ij}^a + W_{ij}^b) - W_{ij}^*]$,

---

[4] (i) Because the time taken for stock prices to reflect the information (next quote after the stock market learns of the event) will vary across the sample, s_t will increase or decrease *gradually*, even though individual S_{ij}'s will jump. (ii) Strictly speaking, $E(s_t) > 1$ for $t < 0$ under the null hypothesis. Note that $E(s_t) = E[S_{ij}E(1/S_0 | S_{ij})] > E[S_{ij}/E(S_{0j}|S_{ij})] = 1$ for $t < 0$. However, for a small time interval, $E(s_t) = 1.00 + \text{var}(\xi_{ij})$, $t < 0$, where $S_{ij} = S_{0j}(1 + \xi_{ij})$. Over ten minutes, $\text{var}(\xi_{ij}) = 0.000007$ for the typical stock which has an annual volatility of 25 percent. Therefore, $E(s_t) \approx 1$.

[5] Note that $S_{ij} = 0.5 \times (S_{ij}^b + S_{ij}^a)$. As in microstructure models, we assume that the trade price equals a "true" price, the dealer's best estimate of security value, plus half of the bid-ask spread.

Table I

Stock Prices Surrounding Large Option Trades

This table examines whether large option trades are perceived to be motivated by superior beliefs about the stock price. Our sample includes all option trades on the CBOE during March and April 1985 which are equivalent to at least 25,000 shares of the underlying stock (one option is considered to be equivalent to delta stock) and which also satisfy the following criteria: 1) trade must not be part of a straddle or a combination, and 2) the option delta must lie between 0.15 and 0.85 and the time to maturity must exceed a week. Trades in the upper half of the spread are considered to be buyer-initiated, and trades in the lower half of the spread are considered to be seller-initiated. Thus, the 48 buyer-initiated call and six seller-initiated put trades will result in a profit for the initiator of the trade if the stock price rises, and the 89 seller-initiated call and three buyer-initiated put trades will result in a profit for the initiator of the trade if the stock price falls. Fifty-one call and two put trades otherwise satisfying the preceding criteria but occurring at the spread midpoint are not reported in this table. The stock price reaction is measured by s_t, which is the average value of stock price at time t (in minutes) relative to stock price at time $t = 0$ (just before the large option trade). Specifically, $s_t = \sum_{j=1}^{n} S_{tj}/nS_{0j}$, where S_{tj} is the stock price at t.

Variable	48 Call and 6 Put Trades That Will Benefit from an Increase in the Stock Price		89 Call and 3 Put Trades That Will Benefit from a Decrease in the Stock Price	
	Estimate	Std-error	Estimate	Std-error
s_{-10}	1.0002	0.0005	0.9989	0.0004
s_{-8}	1.0002	0.0004	0.9990	0.0004
s_{-6}	1.0002	0.0004	0.9992	0.0004
s_{-4}	1.0001	0.0004	0.9993	0.0003
s_{-2}	1.0001	0.0002	0.9996	0.0002
s_0	1.0000	0.0000	1.0000	0.0000
s_2	1.0000	0.0002	1.0000	0.0002
s_4	0.9999	0.0003	1.0001	0.0003
s_6	1.0001	0.0004	1.0003	0.0003
s_8	0.9998	0.0004	1.0004	0.0004
s_{10}	0.9998	0.0004	1.0004	0.0004
s_{12}	0.9994	0.0005	1.0003	0.0004
s_{14}	0.9996	0.0005	1.0001	0.0004
s_{16}	0.9995	0.0006	1.0002	0.0004
s_{18}	0.9996	0.0006	1.0004	0.0005
s_{20}	0.9995	0.0006	1.0000	0.0004
s_{22}	0.9993	0.0006	1.0001	0.0004
s_{24}	0.9993	0.0006	1.0002	0.0005
s_{26}	0.9992	0.0006	1.0002	0.0005
s_{28}	0.9991	0.0006	1.0001	0.0005
s_{30}	0.9992	0.0007	1.0000	0.0006

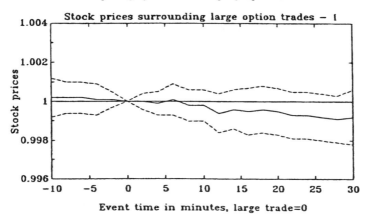

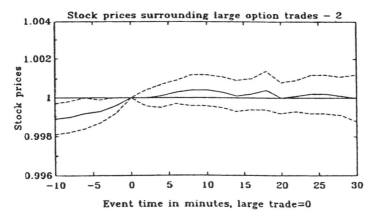

Figure 1. Stock price behavior around large option trades. This figure includes CBOE option trades during March and April 1985 which are equivalent to at least 25,000 shares, are not part of a straddle or a combination, and have an option delta between 0.15 and 0.85. The stock price reaction is measured by $s_t = 1/n \sum_{j=1}^{n} S_{tj}/S_{0j}$, where S_{tj} is the stock price at time t (in minutes), and S_{0j} is the stock price at $t = 0$, just before the large option trade occurred. The solid line represents s_t, and the broken line represents the two-sigma band around s_t. The top panel includes 48 buyer-initiated call and six seller-initiated put trades that will benefit from an increase in the stock price. The bottom panel includes 89 seller-initiated call and three buyer-initiated put trades that will benefit from a decrease in the stock price. Data points used in this figure are from Table I.

where n is the number of trades in the particular category. Note that T_i^q (and many other statistics to follow) are normalized by the stock price. Because option prices are so variable, and often close to zero, they are unsuitable for normalizing.

Under the null hypothesis of no price effects, T_i^q will equal zero for all i. The alternate hypothesis states that dealers incur significant costs in carrying a large negative inventory as the result of a large buy order. To control inventory costs, dealers raise both the bid and the ask prices, thus encouraging potential sellers and discouraging potential buyers. Under the alternate hypothesis, T_i^q will be positive for large buy orders and (using a similar argument) negative for large sell orders.

The first rows of Panels 1, 2, and 3 in Table II (also Figure 2) show the T_i^q values for $i = -5$ to $+5$, for each of the three trade categories, based on whether the trade was in the upper half of the spread, at the middle, or in the lower half. The slight but steady downward trend in T_i^q values across all categories simply reflects the loss in time value of the options. The typical standard error of T_i^q is 0.05, or 2.5 cents. Most T_i^q values lie within two standard errors around 0.00. The largest deviation from the two-standard-error band is 0.0240, or 1.2 cents. We conclude that the option middle prices surrounding large option trades are indistinguishable from what they would be in absence of the large trades.

Since both the stock prices and the option middle prices are unchanged, the only possible price effect of large option trades can be a higher bid-ask spread. We find some evidence that the quoted option spread (defined simply as the difference between quoted bid and ask prices) surrounding the large trades is somewhat higher than normal. The bid-ask spread preceding the large trade is higher than the median bid-ask spread for the same option series during the previous day in 76 cases, the same in 81 cases, and lower in 42 cases. Equality between the two is rejected by a nonparametric z-statistic of 3.13. In addition, we use the following parametric statistic to estimate the increase in quoted spread:

effect on quoted spread ("qs"): $\quad T_i^{qs} = \dfrac{100}{n} \sum\limits_{j=1}^{n} \dfrac{1}{S_{ij}} [(W_{ij}^a - W_{ij}^b) - QTSP_j],$

where $QTSP_j$ is the average of all quoted bid-ask spreads from the previous day. The third rows of Panels 1, 2, and 3 in Table II show that T_0^{qs} is greater than zero across all three trade categories, but it is significantly greater only for trades occurring at the quote midpoint. Perhaps the trade occurred at the midpoint because the quoted spread was too wide and could be negotiated to a lower value. We therefore examine *effective* spreads paid for large trades versus smaller trades.

Many trades on both stock and option markets occur inside the bid-ask quote. Hasbrouck (1988) points out that inside-the-spread trades are usually the result of bargaining, which leads to better prices. Therefore, if a trade occurs below (above) the quote midpoint, we assume that the trade price is the effective bid (ask) price. We then compute the effective spread paid for that trade as the difference between the effective bid (ask) and the quoted ask (bid) prices, which equals $\max[W_{ij}^t - W_{ij}^b, W_{ij}^a - W_{ij}^t]$. The increase in effective spread surrounding large option trades is measured by T_i^{es} as follows:

change in effective spread ("es"):

$$T_i^{es} = \dfrac{100}{199} \sum\limits_{j=1}^{199} \dfrac{1}{S_{ij}} [\max(W_{ij}^t - W_{ij}^b, W_{ij}^a - W_{ij}^t) - EFSP_j],$$

Table II
Option Prices Surrounding Large Option Trades

This table examines the effect of a large option trade on the surrounding option prices. The sample includes all option trades on the CBOE during March and April 1985 which are equivalent to at least 25,000 shares of the underlying stock (one option is considered to be equivalent to delta stock) and which also satisfy the following criteria: 1) trade must not be part of a straddle or a combination, and 2) the option delta must lie between 0.15 and 0.85 and the time to maturity must exceed a week. To understand the many statistics reported here, let i denote event time. Thus, $i = 0$ is the large option trade and $i = -1$ refers to the preceding trade. Let W_{ij}^a, W_{ij}^b, and W_{ij}^t represent the ask, the bid, and the trade prices of the ith trade surrounding the jth observation of a large option trade. Let also W_{ij}^* represent the option price implied by the last quoted stock middle price and the option pricing information from the previous day. Then the first line of each panel reports the difference between the spread midpoint and the implied option price, measured by $T_i^s = (100/n) \sum_{j=1}^{n} [0.5 \times (W_{ij}^a + W_{ij}^b) - W_{ij}^*]/S_{ij}$. The second line reports the difference between the trade price and the implied price, measured by $T_i^t = (100/n) \sum_{j=1}^{n} (W_{ij}^t - W_{ij}^*)/S_{ij}$. The third line reports the effect on quoted spread, measured by $T_i^s = (100/n) \sum_{j=1}^{n} [(W_{ij}^a - W_{ij}^b) - QTSP_j]/S_{ij}$, where $QTSP_j$ is the average quoted spread from the previous day. Panel 4 reports change in the "effective" spread, measured by $T_i^e = (100/199) \sum_{j=1}^{199} [\max(W_{ij}^t - W_{ij}^b, W_{ij}^a - W_{ij}^t) - EFSP_j]/S_{ij}$, where $EFSP_j$ is the average effective spread from the previous day. If large option trades cause no price effects, then T_i^s, T_i^t, T_i^s, and T_i^e should equal zero for all i. Also, T_i^s should equal 0.5 and -0.5 times the effective spread for $i = 0$ in Panels 1 and 3, and zero otherwise. All figures are expressed in percents and 0.01 equals roughly one-half cent.

Statistic and Std-error†		Trade Relative to Large Option Trade										
		−5	−4	−3	−2	−1	0	1	2	3	4	5
Panel 1. 48 call and 3 put trades in upper half of the spread (buyer-initiated), previous day's effective spread = 0.3												
T_i^s	0.06	0.0017	0.0044	0.0006	−0.0114	−0.0177	−0.0892	−0.0520	−0.0619	−0.0272	−0.0553	−0.0598
T_i^t	0.06	0.0184	0.0206	0.0330	−0.0087	0.0604	0.0972	0.0483	−0.0288	−0.0004	0.0155	0.0310
T_i^s	0.05	0.0104	0.0307	0.0399	0.0190	0.0351	0.0528	0.0557	−0.0194	0.0147	−0.0115	−0.0118
Panel 2. 51 call and 2 put trades at the spread midpoint (initiator uncertain), previous day's effective spread = 0.4												
T_i^s	0.05	0.0875	0.0942	0.1038	0.0800	0.0350	−0.0734	−0.0747	−0.1051	−0.0879	−0.1167	−0.1054
T_i^t	0.05	0.0524	0.0935	0.1144	0.0930	0.0612	−0.0734	−0.0587	−0.0368	−0.0267	−0.0383	0.0020
T_i^s	0.04	0.0093	−0.0180	−0.0252	−0.0066	0.0384	0.1320	0.0534	0.0138	0.0208	−0.0173	−0.0208
Panel 3. 89 call and 6 put trades in lower half of the spread (seller-initiated), previous day's effective spread = 0.53												
T_i^s	0.04	0.0461	0.0393	0.0411	0.0612	−0.0055	−0.0634	−0.0825	−0.0904	−0.0999	−0.0937	−0.1040
T_i^t	0.04	0.0554	0.0657	0.0005	−0.0010	−0.0860	−0.3080	−0.1527	−0.1208	−0.1170	−0.1399	−0.1114
T_i^s	0.03	0.0334	0.0438	0.0455	0.0322	0.0547	0.0448	0.0452	0.0202	−0.0067	−0.0195	−0.0552
Panel 4. 199 trades in all three categories above												
T_i^e	0.02	−0.0520	−0.0724	−0.0684	−0.0691	−0.0708	−0.0386	−0.0732	−0.0989	−0.0947	−0.1139	−0.1367

† The t-statistics can be obtained by dividing figures by the corresponding standard errors, except for T_0^s (see above).

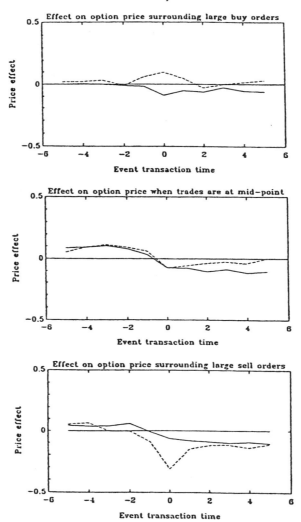

Figure 2. Price effects in the CBOE option market surrounding large option trades. This figure includes option trades during March and April 1985 which are equivalent to at least 25,000 shares, are not part of a straddle or a combination, and have an option delta between 0.15 and 0.85. The samples used in the three panels include 48 call and three put trades initiated by buyers, 51 call and two put trades occurring at the spread midpoint which may have been initiated by buyer or seller, and 89 call and six put trades initiated by sellers. The solid line in each panel shows the position of the spread midpoint for the five trades preceding and following the large option trade. The position of the spread midpoint is measured by $T_i^* = \sum_{j=1}^{n} [0.5 \times (W_{ij}^a + W_{ij}^b) - W_{ij}^*]/nS_{ij}$. The broken line shows the position of the trade price, measured by $T_i = \sum_{j=1}^{n} (W_{ij} - W_{ij}^*)/nS_{ij}$. Both T_i^* and T_i are expressed as percents. Data points used in this figure are from Table II.

where $EFSP_j$ is the average effective spread similarly estimated from all trades on the previous day.[6] The last row of Table II gives the T_i^{ep} values. Surprisingly, the effective spread for trades surrounding the large trade is lower than on the previous day. There is no obvious explanation for the higher quoted but lower effective spreads around large option trades. The effective spread paid for a large trade is higher than the effective spread paid for the surrounding trades but lower than on the previous day, although by only 0.0386, or 1.9 cents. It may be that in some cases the large trade occurred because the dealers were then accepting lower spreads.

Our investigation shows that large option trades on the CBOE do not cause any price effects or command any premium specific to the large trade. Figure 2 shows that, in fact, large buy (sell) orders occur in the middle of buying (selling) activity yet have no price impact. This inference is based on the following statistics:

trade price minus *implied* spread midpoint $= T_i^t = \dfrac{100}{n} \sum_{j=1}^{n} \dfrac{1}{S_{ij}} [W_{ij}^t - W_{ij}^*]$;

trade price minus *observed* spread midpoint

$$= \dfrac{100}{n} \sum_{j=1}^{n} \dfrac{1}{S_{ij}} [W_{ij}^t - 0.5 \times (W_{ij}^b + W_{ij}^a)]$$

$$= T_i^t - T_i^q.$$

During periods when buy orders outnumber sell orders, $T_i^t - T_i^q$ will be positive, and vice versa. Note that $T_i^t - T_i^q$ is positive around large buy orders and negative around large sell orders.

Although we expected price effects on the CBOE to be small, given the multiple-dealer structure, the complete absence of price effects surrounding large option trades is surprising. One may argue that their absence can be explained by a selection bias.[7] If large orders are taken up by one dealer when inventory and information effects are perceived to be insignificant, and broken up among two or more dealers when these effects are significant, then price effects will occur only when there is a sequence of two or more large trades. Because existing databases do not identify when a large order has been broken up, a rigorous test of this proposition is difficult. Regardless of the selection criteria used to detect related trades, both type I error (not detecting a sequence of trades resulting from breaking up a large order) and type II error (showing trades as related when they are not) will be substantial. Keeping these limitations in mind, we repeated our tests using a set of 108 observations, each consisting of two or more large trades (at least 100 option contracts) reported within an interval of five minutes. The results (not reported) show that even a sequence of two or more large trades on the CBOE does not cause price effects.

Our tests indicate that the CBOE options market has great depth. Unlike studies of NYSE stocks by Kraus and Stoll (1972), Dann, Mayers, and Raab

---

[6] If effective spreads were computed separately for the three categories, one would find that figures for categories 1 and 3 are overstated because trades at the middle have been excluded.

[7] I am obliged to the referee for pointing out this and several other necessary cross-checks.

(1977), and Holthausen, Leftwich, and Mayers (1987), our study finds no evidence of temporary or permanent price effects surrounding large option trades on the CBOE. The absence of inventory-related price effects can be explained by the multiplicity of dealers. Ho and Macris (1985) show that, when transaction prices are determined by order-processing and inventory carrying costs, increasing the number of dealers leads to greater market depth at the cost of wider bid-ask spreads. Because of competition among dealers, prices do not change simply because one dealer has a large positive or negative inventory. However, there is no obvious explanation for the lack of superior information motivating large option trades.

II. The Stock and Option Bid-Ask Spreads

We have shown that the CBOE options market has great depth. If this depth results from allowing many dealers to compete for the order flow in a security, then the option bid-ask spreads would be expected to be large relative to stock spreads. Below, we show that this is indeed the case.

To compare bid-ask spreads across active stocks and active options, we choose a subset of data consisting of every constant stock-price interval (time over which both the stock bid and ask prices remain unchanged) during which there is at least one stock trade and one option quote followed by a trade. Thus, stock and option bid-ask spreads too wide to attract a trade are excluded. There are 94,704 such constant stock price intervals over March and April 1985. Many of these constant stock price intervals, however, include two or more different options which have a quote followed by a trade, in which case a quote for each option is included. Our sample used for comparing stock and option bid-ask spreads includes 94,704 stock and 161,589 option quotes and 434,262 stock and 593,165 option trades.

Table III gives the frequency distribution of the size of stock and option bid-ask spreads that were followed by at least one trade. Averaged across the sample, the quoted stock spread is 23.7 cents. In comparison, the average quoted option spread is ten percent lower, at 21.3 cents.[8] The option spread is also more variable than the stock spread.[9]

---

[8] Sometimes two or more quotes for the same option may occur during a constant stock price interval (CSPI). It may be argued that in such cases combining bid and ask prices from different dealers can yield spreads that are tighter than the spreads from either dealer. Vijh (1987) shows that combining the minimum ask and maximum bid prices from different quotes over a CSPI gives an average quoted option spread of 15.11 cents as compared with 21.3 cents if averaged over separate quotes. Vijh (1987) also shows that the minimum-ask-maximum-bid considerably underestimates the option spread; it is negative or zero once out of six times (implausible), and one out of four option trades lies outside this estimator of spread. Because a quote is valid only for the moment after it is spoken, and only 2.5 percent quotes are followed by a different quote within 15 seconds, last quoted bid-ask prices are the best estimate of dealers' guaranteed prices. Furthermore, to make sure that options are not over-represented in comparison with stocks, which have exactly one quote per CSPI, we also choose only one quote randomly when there are multiple quotes for the same option during a CSPI.

[9] With a view to estimating liquidity, this paper provides only aggregate estimates of bid-ask spread. Vijh (1987) shows that the variation in option spreads can be explained in terms of a few option parameters.

Table III
Quoted Stock and Option Bid-Ask Spreads

This table compares the quoted bid-ask spread across the CBOE options and the NYSE stocks during March and April 1985. To compare bid-ask spreads across only active stocks and active options, we choose a subset of data consisting of every constant stock-price interval (time over which both the stock bid and ask prices remain unchanged) during which there is at least one stock trade and one option quote followed by a trade. We find 94,704 distinct constant stock price intervals. Our procedure excludes stock and option bid-ask quotes too wide to attract a trade. Many of these constant stock price intervals, however, include two or more different options which have a quote followed by a trade, in which case a quote for each option is included. Our sample used for comparing stock and option bid-ask spreads includes 94,704 stock and 161,589 option quotes. Stock prices are quoted as multiples of an eighth of a dollar. However, option prices may be quoted as multiples of a sixteenth of a dollar if the quoted price is less than three dollars.

Quoted Bid-Ask Spread in Dollars	Frequency Stocks	Frequency Options
1/16	—	19.7
2/16	35.2	32.1
3/16	—	5.0
4/16	48.0	22.6
5/16	—	0.5
6/16	11.2	8.4
8/16	4.8	10.5
>8/16	0.8	1.2
Total	100.0	100.0

The quoted spreads measure the difference between the best prices at which dealers *guarantee* to buy or sell the minimum trading unit, which is 100 shares (a round lot) or the option to buy or sell 100 shares (an option contract). However, traders can sometimes obtain better prices by bargaining, in which case the actual or effective spreads are lower than the quoted spreads. Also, sometimes buy and sell orders from different traders reach the floor simultaneously, in which case the orders are crossed without dealer participation, and the effective spread is zero.

Hasbrouck (1988) investigates several inside-the-quote trades on the NYSE and finds that these trades are usually the result of the trader being able to bargain for better prices and are only rarely the result of crossing orders from the floor. This finding is also confirmed by his discussions with the NYSE specialists. We expect crossing orders to be even less frequent on the CBOE, given the greater heterogeneity of options. In the following discussion, we assume that all inside-the-quote trades on the CBOE and the NYSE result from bargaining between traders and dealers. This assumption results in the *measured* effective spreads being larger than the *actual* effective spreads, but more so for stocks than options because more trades occur inside the stock spread (shown below) and because crossing orders on the NYSE are more likely than on the CBOE.

Table IV shows how stock and option trades are distributed relative to the last quoted bid-ask prices. Only 25.40 percent of option trades occur inside the option spread, whereas 35.14 of the stock trades occur inside the stock spread. It appears that option dealers generally quote the best prices they can offer, possibly in order to preclude competition. The difference between the effective and the quoted bid-ask spreads will therefore be smaller for options than for stocks.

We estimate the effective spreads as follows. If a dealer buys (sells) at a certain price, by definition that price is the effective bid (ask) price. If a trade occurs below (above) the quote midpoint, we assume that it was the dealer's purchase (sale), and therefore the trade price is the effective bid (ask) price. Then it follows that

$$\text{effective spread} = \max[\text{trade price} - \text{quoted bid}, \text{quoted ask} - \text{trade price}].$$

Table IV

Distribution of Stock and Option Trade Prices over the Bid-Ask Spread

This table examines the frequency of inside-the-quote trades during March and April 1985 for evidence on effective spreads for the CBOE options and the NYSE stocks. The sample used is the same as in Table III. We choose a subset of data consisting of every constant stock-price interval (time over which both the stock bid and ask prices remain unchanged) during which there is at least one stock trade and one option quote followed by a trade. We find 94,704 distinct constant stock price intervals. Our procedure excludes stock and option bid-ask quotes too wide to attract a trade. Many of these constant stock price intervals, however, include two or more different options which have a quote followed by a trade, in which case a quote for each option is included. Our sample includes 434,262 stock and 593,165 option trades. Every trade price is compared with the immediately preceding bid-ask spread to obtain the frequencies reported in this table.

Description	Percentage of Trades	
	Stocks	Options
Trade price is ...		
1. Higher than the ask price	0.29	2.51
2. Equal to the ask price	32.86	40.94
3. Between the ask price and the spread midpoint	3.30	4.46
4. Equal to the spread midpoint	28.63	17.11
5. Between the spread midpoint and the bid price	3.21	3.83
6. Equal to the bid price	31.29	29.21
7. Lower than the bid price	0.42	1.94

Given the distribution of stock and option trades with respect to the last quoted bid-ask prices from Table IV, the effective option spread equals 0.916 times the quoted spread, or 19.5 cents. In comparison, the effective stock spread is 20.0 cents. Although the average option is equivalent to a levered position in less than half of a stock and costs one-tenth as much as the stock, the effective stock and option spreads are nearly equal. Alternatively stated, a trader pays twice the bid-ask spread for options as for an equivalent position in stock.

In Section I we showed that the options market can absorb large trades without any premium or price effects. Now we find that options dealers do charge higher bid-ask spreads to recover costs of market-making. We argue that a tradeoff between these two major components of liquidity should be expected. Multiple-dealer markets have higher fixed costs, such as the opportunity cost of dealers' time. The greater market depth resulting from the market's ability to carry higher overall inventory increases the variable inventory costs. The heterogeneity of options compounds these costs because it forces dealers to monitor the prices and inventories of several related yet different options on a stock. Furthermore, the sources of revenue to option dealers are restricted to the bid-ask spread. Stoll (1985) shows that the NYSE specialists derive a substantial part of their revenues from brokering for limit orders. In comparison, the limit order book on the CBOE is separately handled by an employee of the exchange, thus depriving the dealers of a source of both revenue and information.

Given these substantial costs and limited sources of revenue, it would be surprising if the CBOE options outperformed the NYSE stocks on both major dimensions of market liquidity. In that case, either options as a security would dominate stocks on both dimensions of liquidity, or the CBOE's market structure would be strictly preferable to the NYSE's market structure, or both. Given the continued popularity of both stocks and options and the existence of both kinds of market mechanism, our finding of a tradeoff between market depth and bid-ask spreads when choosing between the CBOE options and the NYSE stocks is not surprising.

III. Information Trading on the CBOE

We have shown that the bid-ask spread is the major transaction cost facing option traders on the CBOE. We have argued that the CBOE's market mechanism and the heterogeneity of options can explain these higher option spreads. However, large option spreads could also be the result of active information trading on the CBOE. Microstructure models show that the bid-ask spread consists of two components: a transitory component and an adverse-selection component. The transitory component represents the dealer's compensation for costs incurred in processing orders and carrying an inventory. The adverse-selection component arises because of the presence of information traders and represents the dealer's compensation for losses to informed traders.

Below, we investigate whether adverse selection is a major factor behind large option spreads. The absence of price effects surrounding large option trades provides evidence against active information trading. However, one must recognize that ours was a *biased* sample, a set of only 199 of the largest trades. The very largest trades may be motivated by factors other than superior information, such as an institution wanting to earn premium income by selling call options protected by its stock holdings. Therefore, the following tests of the information content of option trades employ a comprehensive data set consisting of every transaction, regardless of trade size, for twenty of the most active options on the CBOE during March and April 1985. The relation between asymmetric information and trade size is specifically examined.

We start with how stock and option prices are related in perfect capital markets and then modify the relation to include the effects of information in option trades. The Black and Scholes no-arbitrage condition states that, in perfect capital markets,

$$dW = \Delta dS + r(W - \Delta S)dt, \qquad (1)$$

where W and S represent the *true* option and stock prices and Δ is the option delta. Now suppose there are $i = 1, 2, \cdots, M$ bid-ask quotes for the option under consideration. Let t_i denote the time when the ith option quote occurs. Thus, (t_{i-1}, t_i) represents the time interval between the $(i-1)$th and the ith quotes. Let W_{t_i} represent the midpoint of the ith bid-ask quote. Then, assuming that bid-ask prices are symmetric around the true price, $W_{t_i} - W_{t_{i-1}}$ equals the change in true option price over (t_{i-1}, t_i). Using equation (1), price changes over the time period (t_{i-1}, t_i) are related as follows:

$$W_{t_i} - W_{t_{i-1}} = \Delta_{t_{i-1}} (S_{t_i} - S_{t_{i-1}}) + r(W_{t_{i-1}} - \Delta_{t_{i-1}} S_{t_{i-1}})(t_i - t_{i-1}). \qquad (2)$$

Equation (2) is now modified to include the effect of information in option trades. Based on Glosten and Milgrom (1985), if the information contained in option trades over the time interval (t_{i-1}, t_i) revises market makers' estimates of the true option price by I_{t_i}, then, assuming that the stock price does not reflect this information immediately, the change in option price is given by

$$W_{t_i} - W_{t_{i-1}} = \Delta_{t_{i-1}} (S_{t_i} - S_{t_{i-1}}) + r(W_{t_{i-1}} - \Delta_{t_{i-1}} S_{t_{i-1}})(t_i - t_{i-1}) + I_{t_i}. \qquad (3)$$

Equation (3) assumes that S_{t_i}, the last quoted stock price (a few minutes) before t_i, does not include the information in option trades over the time interval (t_{i-1}, t_i). Whereas the stock prices eventually must contain the information in option trades, it is reasonable to assume that the process involves a small delay. We analyze only the most active options to ensure that the effect of information in option trades is not mitigated by the simultaneous presence of S_{t_i} in equation (3). Table V lists twenty stocks underlying the most active options during March and April 1985. The average time between successive quotes for the most active option on each of these stocks each day is given in the second column of Table V.[10] The typical time interval is five minutes, which will later be shown to be less than the time it takes for stock prices to reflect the impact of option floor activity.

---

[10] Thus, for ALS (Allied Stores), $W_{t_i} - W_{t_{i-1}}$ was measured as the change in price between successive quotes for ALS/6/55 (call with June expiration and exercise price of $55) on March 21, which happened to be the most active option for the day. On March 22, ALS/6/60 prices were used since it was now the most active option, etc.

Over small intervals, the second term in equation (3),

$$r(W_{t_{i-1}} - \Delta_{t_{i-1}} S_{t_{i-1}})(t_i - t_{i-1}),$$

is much smaller than the other terms and can be dropped.[11] Next, we decompose the information in option trading activity over the interval (t_{i-1}, t_i) as follows:

$$I_{t_i} = I_{t_i}^+ - I_{t_i}^-, \tag{4}$$

where $I_{t_i}^+$ and $I_{t_i}^-$ are the total information in option trades over (t_{i-1}, t_i) that would benefit from an increase and a decrease in the stock price, respectively. Because an option trader possessing positive information about the stock price buys calls or sells puts, I_{t_i} is aggregated over all related (i.e., any of the multiple options written on the same stock) buyer-initiated call and seller-initiated put trades. We denote the number of such trades over the time interval (t_{i-1}, t_i) by $N_{t_i}^+$. Similarly, $I_{t_i}^-$ is aggregated over the $N_{t_i}^-$ trades which all benefit from a decrease in the stock price (namely, all related buyer-initiated put and seller-initiated call trades). Trades in the upper half of the last quoted spread are treated as buyer-initiated and those in the lower half as seller-initiated. Finally, to allow for the possibility of information being a function of the trade size, we specify the information content of the jth option trade as $\beta_1 + \beta_2 v_j$ (a log specification is tried later), where v_j is the trade size and β_1 and β_2 are constants. Then,

$$I_{t_i}^+ = \sum_{j=1}^{N_{t_i}^+} (\beta_1 + \beta_2 v_j) = \beta_1 N_{t_i}^+ + \beta_2 V_{t_i}^+,$$

and

$$I_{t_i}^- = \sum_{j=1}^{N_{t_i}^+} (\beta_1 + \beta_2 v_j) = \beta_1 N_{t_i}^- + \beta_2 V_{t_i}^-. \tag{5}$$

Because information is measured by aggregating trades in several related but different options on the stock and because every trade may be going to a different dealer, the specification in equation (5) will also abstract from inventory-related price changes. Equation (3) can now be modified to

$$[W_{t_i} - W_{t_{i-1}}] - \Delta_{t_{i-1}}(S_{t_i} - S_{t_{i-1}}) = \beta_0 + \beta_1(N_{t_i}^+ - N_{t_i}^-) + \beta_2(V_{t_i}^+ - V_{t_i}^-) + \epsilon_{t_i}. \tag{6}$$

Let

$$y_{t_i} = (W_{t_i} - W_{t_{i-1}}) - \Delta_{t_{i-1}}(S_{t_i} - S_{t_{i-1}}), \quad N_{t_i} = N_{t_i}^+ - N_{t_i}^-, \quad \text{and} \quad V_{t_i} = V_{t_i}^+ - V_{t_i}^-.$$

Then,

$$y_{t_i} = \beta_0 + \beta_1 N_{t_i} + \beta_2 V_{t_i} + \epsilon_{t_i}. \tag{7}$$

---

[11] In the Black and Scholes framework, the stock price follows a geometric diffusion process described by $dS = \mu S\, dt + \sigma S \xi \sqrt{dt}$, where S is the stock price, μ and σ are diffusion parameters, and ξ is a normal random variable. As $dt \to 0$, the second term on the right-hand side becomes much larger than the first one. Therefore, over small periods, dS and dW are the order of $\sigma S \sqrt{dt}$. It can also be shown that $r(W - \Delta S)dt$ (continuous-time version of the second term in equation (3)) equals $rKe^{-rt}N(d_2)dt$, which is of a lower order than dS or dW over small intervals (i.e., as $dt \to 0$).

Table V
Adverse Selection in Option Trades

This table estimates the adverse information conveyed by an option trade on the CBOE. The dataset consists of twenty of the most active CBOE stocks during March and April 1985. Suppose that a bid-ask quote for the option in question is recorded at time t_{i-1} and the next quote is recorded at t_i. The change in option price after accounting for the change in stock price is given by $y_{t_i} = (W_{t_i} - W_{t_{i-1}}) - \Delta_{t_i}(S_{t_i} - S_{t_{i-1}})$, where W, S, and Δ represent the option price, the stock price, and the option delta. N_{t_i} (V_{t_i}) represents the number of option trades (option contracts) over (t_{i-1}, t_i) that would benefit from an increase in the stock price minus trades (contracts) that would benefit from a decrease in the stock price. Assuming that adverse information increases linearly with the option trade size, the first regression in Panel A tests the following model:

$$y_{t_i} = \beta_0 + \beta_1 N_{t_i} + \beta_2 V_{t_i} + \epsilon_{t_i}.$$

Finding β_2 to be insignificant, the second regression in Panel B tests

$$y_{t_i} = b_0 + b_1 N_{t_i} + e_{t_i}.$$

The third regression in Panel C tests the same specification as the second regression, but only over the period from three days before to one day after an earnings announcement. Coefficients are estimated using the OLS technique, but the t-statistics are calculated using Hansen's (1982) correction. Intvl gives the average length of the period (t_{i-1}, t_i) in minutes.

Stock		Panel A				Panel B			Panel C		
STK	Intvl	β_0	β_1	β_2	R^2	b_0	b_1	R^2	b_0	b_1	R^2
ALS	8.00	−0.0022	0.0028	0.000009	0.0057	−0.0023	0.0029	0.0056			
		−1.30	2.84*	0.95		−1.33	3.00*				
ARC	9.11	−0.0002	−0.0002	0.000081	0.0091	0.0022	0.0014	0.0020			
		−1.61	−0.16	1.69		1.24	1.44				
BMY	8.48	0.0018	0.0017	−0.000042	0.0047	0.006	0.0014	0.0036			
		0.49	3.03*	−1.94		0.61	2.52*				
C	4.08	0.0128	0.0018	−0.000045	0.0232	0.0123	0.0019	0.0320	−0.0010	0.0038	0.0699
		6.45	3.62*	−2.68*		6.61	4.09*		−0.74	5.27*	
CBS	1.86	−0.0007	−0.0002	0.000131	0.0037	−0.0009	0.0014	0.0011			
		−0.82	−0.17	2.34*		−1.05	2.00*				
EK	4.73	−0.0007	0.0010	−0.000014	0.0031	−0.0007	0.0009	0.0029			
		−1.42	2.26*	−0.75		−1.31	2.13*				
F	3.84	−0.0013	0.0010	−0.000003	0.0042	−0.0014	0.0010	0.0042	−0.0007	0.0014	0.0039
		−2.67	2.83*	−0.19		−2.88*	3.34*		−0.74	1.50	

Table V—Continued

Stock		Panel A				Panel B			Panel C		
STK	Intvl	β_0	β_1	β_2	R^2	b_0	b_1	R^2	b_0	b_1	R^2
GD	9.37	0.0004	0.0013	0.000117	0.0041	0.0005	0.0021	0.0023			
		0.20	1.15	1.64		0.30	2.01*				
GM	3.32	0.0006	0.0040	-0.000012	0.0777	0.0015	0.0033	0.0664	-0.0000	0.0005	0.0016
		0.85	5.60*	-0.50		1.91	4.92*		-0.00	0.89	
GW	9.31	0.0114	0.0016	0.000006	0.0015	0.0011	0.0017	0.0015			
		3.88	0.85	0.09		3.87*	1.02				
HON	5.76	0.0016	0.0006	0.000144	0.0053	0.0014	0.0019	0.0021	-0.0025	0.0035	0.0050
		1.70	0.50	2.29*		1.52	1.65		-1.12	1.25	
HWP	5.24	0.0001	0.0007	0.000020	0.0025	0.0001	0.0008	0.0022			
		0.15	1.57	1.00		0.10	2.03*				
IBM	2.15	-0.0026	0.0019	0.000001	0.0282	-0.0025	0.0019	0.0252	-0.0005	0.0002	0.0003
		-3.60	8.11*	0.09		-3.49*	8.74*		-0.35	0.44	
ITT	4.71	-0.0004	0.0003	0.000029	0.0048	-0.0005	0.0007	0.0020	-0.0005	0.0002	0.0004
		-0.68	0.72	2.61*		-0.86	1.83		-0.46	0.36	
PEP	8.67	-0.0008	-0.0001	0.000092	0.0022	-0.0011	0.0005	0.0006	-0.0000	-0.0015	0.0069
		-0.47	-0.12	1.88		-0.69	1.08		-0.00	-2.19*	
RCA	5.35	-0.0009	0.0010	0.000027	0.0036	-0.0010	0.0012	0.0023			
		-1.18	2.00*	1.90		-1.28	2.40*				
REV	8.24	0.0016	0.0008	0.000030	0.0061	0.0014	0.0011	0.0044			
		1.60	1.69	1.79		1.46	2.52*				
ROK	8.34	0.0047	0.0011	0.000084	0.0023	0.0045	0.0016	0.0018	-0.0020	0.0046	0.0141
		2.34	0.79	0.74		2.28*	1.27		-0.13	2.01*	
SY	3.11	-0.0008	0.0012	-0.000001	0.0035	-0.0007	0.0013	0.0013			
		-1.00	2.35*	-0.57		-1.00	2.72*				
XRX	10.46	0.0007	0.0002	0.000015	0.0003	0.0005	0.0003	0.0002	0.0019	0.0001	0.0001
		0.78	0.29	0.37		0.56	0.55		1.01	0.07	

* Significant at the 5 percent level.

We estimated equation (7) using the ordinary-least-squares (OLS) technique. Because future values of regressors N_{t_i} and V_{t_i} may be correlated with current residuals, we obtained the unbiased t-statistics using Hansen's (1982) correction. Detailed estimates of equation (7) are presented in Panel A of Table V, but the $\hat{\beta}_1$ and $\hat{\beta}_2$ values are summarized below:

	$\hat{\beta}_1$ values	$\hat{\beta}_2$ values
Positive and significant at 5%	9	3
Positive but insignificant	8	11
Negative but insignificant	3	5
Negative and significant at 5%	0	1

The null hypothesis, $\beta_1 = 0$, can be rejected, but $\beta_2 = 0$ cannot be rejected. $\hat{\beta}_2$ is generally insignificant, although positive more often than negative, which can be explained by the positive correlation between V_{t_i} and N_{t_i}. An alternative specification of the information content of option trades as $[\beta_1 + \beta_2 \log v_j]$ leads to even less significant β_2 values (not reported). Combined with evidence from Section I, the null hypothesis of no correlation between trade size and adverse selection for CBOE options cannot be rejected.

Because β_2 is not significantly different from zero, V_{t_i} is dropped from equation (7). The following model results:

$$y_{t_i} = b_0 + b_1 N_{t_i} + e_{t_i}. \qquad (8)$$

Panel B of Table V presents OLS estimates of equation (8). All values of $\hat{b}_1$ are now positive, and 13 out of 20 t-statistics are larger than 2.00. The average $\hat{b}_1$ value is \$0.0015, implying that 85 net trades, which are all bullish (bearish) on the stock, would increase (decrease) the option price by an eighth of a dollar. Because the change in option price equals delta times the change in stock price, nearly 40 trades would be required to change the underlying stock price by an eighth of a dollar. Forty average-sized option trades represent the right to buy or sell 320 round lots of stock. In comparison, Glosten and Harris (1988) found that the asymmetric information is proportional to trade size for NYSE stocks and that roughly 120 round lots of stock are required to create the price effect of an eighth. The asymmetric information in option trades appears to be quite small.

If stock prices respond very quickly to options activity, then b_1 understates the information in option trades. We infer the likely downward bias in b_1 as follows. First, we re-estimate equation (8) using alternate quotes instead of successive quotes, thereby doubling the time interval to an average of ten minutes. In 15 out of 20 cases, b_1 declines, suggesting that, over a period of ten minutes, some of the information in option trades does become a part of the stock price. Next, we estimate the same equation over the period from three days before to one day after an earnings announcement, when the information in trades is likely to be higher and, because of increased activity, the time interval between quotes is likely to be shorter. Panel C of Table V shows the results for the nine stocks which had an earnings announcement during this period. These results suggest that there is no further increase in b_1 values. The comparison was extended to another eleven stocks with similar results.

As b_1 does not increase with further shortening of the time interval, the downward bias in b_1 values estimated using successive option quotes should be small. Other important contingent claims, such as the S&P 500 futures contract, tend to be in disequilibrium with their underlying securities over longer periods of time, offering opportunities for program-trading activity.[12] Stock prices are unlikely to reflect information conveyed by option trades so fast that stocks and options are in equilibrium at all times.

The above results suggest that the CBOE options market is not dominated by information traders. Although the asymmetric information in option trades is statistically significant, it is small and uncorrelated with trade size. The adverse-selection half-spread averages 0.15 cents for twenty of the most active options. For this sample, the effective spread (transitory plus adverse-selection) was 14 cents. Apparently, asymmetric information cannot explain the large magnitude of option spreads. That asymmetric information is also independent of trade size is surprising, although it confirms our earlier finding that large trades are not motivated by superior information. Theoretical models by Kyle (1985) and Glosten (1987) suggest that informed investors will trade large blocks of securities before their information becomes public. At present, there is no satisfactory explanation for the observed independence of trade size and information.[13]

IV. Summary

This paper provides estimates of the CBOE options market liquidity. Comparing the liquidity of the CBOE options and the NYSE stocks shows that a tradeoff exists between the two major dimensions of liquidity: market depth and bid-ask spreads. On one hand, the CBOE options market is highly liquid, in the sense that large trades can be absorbed without a change in the prevailing prices. On the other hand, stock and option bid-ask spreads are nearly equal, even though an average option is equivalent to a levered position in less than half of a stock and costs one-tenth as much as the stock. This tradeoff between the two major dimensions of liquidity is explained by the CBOE's market mechanism. Multiplicity of dealers on the CBOE leads to greater market depth because prices do not change unless all dealers have skewed inventories. However, substantial costs are incurred by the CBOE dealers because multiplicity of dealers also leads to higher fixed costs (opportunity cost of dealers' time) and higher variable costs

---

[12] See Harris (1989) and Stoll and Whaley (1988) for evidence on relative pricing of the S&P 500 futures contract and the underlying stocks.

[13] However, a recent theoretical model of competitive market-making under asymmetric information by Chang (1989) may offer an explanation. Chang shows that the difference in informational impact of large and small trades decreases as the number of dealers increases. He points out that the dealers are required to post firm bid and ask quotations for minimum-size orders, but they usually negotiate the prices for large orders. The informed traders in his model want to trade large quantities but find it advantageous to first trade small quantities with dealers at their posted prices. Since the informed traders' ability to trade small orders at favorable prices increases with the number of dealers, the dealers correctly perceive that many small orders are motivated by the same quality of information as large orders.

(reduced ability to balance inventory). The heterogeneity of options compounds these costs. Furthermore, institutional arrangements on the CBOE prevent dealers from handling limit orders, which are a substantial source of revenue to the NYSE specialist. The large option bid-ask spreads reflect both the substantial costs of market-making on the CBOE and the limited sources of dealer revenue.

If only market depth and market spread were considered, the CBOE would appear to be better equipped than the NYSE to handle large trades. Since bid-ask spread is the major transaction cost facing small traders, they would appear to be better off under the NYSE specialist system. Other factors, such as the preferred investment horizon and the desired leverage, may of course affect the choice.

This paper also shows that information trading has only a small influence on the liquidity of the CBOE options and that the information content of option trades does not increase with trade size. That option dealers charge only a small premium to recover losses inflicted by informed traders suggests that the options market is not dominated by informed traders. What many option traders consider to be superior information may be just a different opinion.

REFERENCES

Bagehot, Walter (Jack Treynor), 1971, The only game in town, *Financial Analysts Journal* 22, 12–14.

Bhattacharya, Mihir, 1987, Price changes of related securities: The case of call options and stocks, *Journal of Financial and Quantitative Analysis* 22, 1–15.

Black, Fisher and Myron S. Scholes, 1973, The pricing of options and corporate liabilities, *Journal of Political Economy* 81, 637–659.

Branch, Ben and Walter Freed, 1977, Bid-asked spreads on the AMEX and the big board, *Journal of Finance* 32, 159–163.

Chang, Chun, 1989, A model of competitive market making and the costs of immediacy, Working Paper, Carlson School of Management, University of Minnesota.

Dann, Larry Y., David Mayers, and Robert J. Raab, 1977, Trading rules, large blocks and the speed of price adjustment, *Journal of Financial Economics* 4, 3–22.

Glosten, Lawrence R., 1987, Components of the bid-ask spread and the statistical properties of transaction prices, *Journal of Finance* 42, 1293–1308.

—— and Lawrence E. Harris, 1988, Estimating the components of the bid-ask spread, *Journal of Financial Economics* 21, 123–142.

—— and Paul R. Milgrom, 1985, Bid, ask, and transactions prices in a specialist market with heterogeneously informed traders, *Journal of Financial Economics* 14, 71–100.

Hansen, Lars P., 1982, Large sample properties of generalized method of moments estimators, *Econometrica* 50, 1269–1286.

Harris, Lawrence E., 1989, The October 1987 S&P 500 stock-futures basis, *Journal of Finance* 44, 77–99.

Hasbrouck, Joel, 1988, Trades, quotes, inventories, and information, *Journal of Financial Economics* 22, 229–252.

Ho, Thomas S. Y. and Richard G. Macris, 1985, Dealer market structure and performance, in Y. Amihud, S. Y. Ho, and R. A. Schwartz, eds.: *Market Making and the Changing Structure of the Securities Industries* (Lexington Books).

Holthausen, Robert W., Richard W. Leftwich, and David Mayers, 1987, The effect of large block transactions on security prices, *Journal of Financial Economics* 19, 237–267.

Institutional Investor Study Report, 1971, U.S. Securities and Exchanges Commission.

Kraus, Alan and Hans R. Stoll, 1972, Price impacts of block trading on the New York Stock Exchange, *Journal of Finance* 27, 569–588.

Kyle, Albert S., 1985, Continuous auctions and insider trading, *Econometrica* 53, 1315–1335.
Manaster, Steven and Richard J. Rendleman, Jr., 1982, Option prices as predictors of equilibrium stock prices, *Journal of Finance* 37, 1943–1057.
Stephan, Jens A. and Robert E. Whaley, 1989, Intraday price change and trading volume relations in the stock and stock option markets, *Journal of Finance* 45, 191–220.
Stoll, Hans R., 1985, The stock exchange specialist system: An economic analysis, *Monograph Series in Finance and Economics* (New York University, New York).
———, 1989, Inferring the components of the bid-ask spread: Theory and empirical tests, *Journal of Finance* 44, 115–134.
——— and Robert E. Whaley, 1988, The dynamics of stock index and stock index futures returns, Working Paper 88-101, The Fuqua School of Business, Duke University.
Vijh, Anand M., 1987, Liquidity of equity options on the CBOE: Analysis of the bid-ask spread, and the price and information effects of trading volume, Dissertation Paper, Graduate School of Business Administration, University of California, Berkeley.
———, 1988, Potential biases from using only trade prices of related securities on different exchanges: A comment, *Journal of Finance* 43, 1049–1055.

B
Futures Markets

[15]
Organized Futures Markets: Costs and Benefits

Lester G. Telser and
Harlow N. Higinbotham
University of Chicago

A futures contract is to a forward contract as payment in currency is to payment by check. An organized market facilitates trade among strangers. Such a market trades a standardized contract under appropriate rules. The equilibrium distribution of market clearing prices is asymptotically normal with a standard deviation that varies inversely with the volume of trade, given underlying supply and demand conditions. Empirical relations giving the commission and margin per contract as a function of the volume of trade and outstanding commitments for 23 commodities support the theory. Also, comparisons of pertinent aspects of 51 commodities divided into active, less active, and dormant groups are consistent with the theory.

I. Introduction

Of all of the hundreds of thousands of commodities in the economy only a few have ever been traded on an organized futures market. This is a puzzle. The basic idea we use to give an answer to this puzzle draws on the theory of money. An organized futures market creates a medium of exchange, a futures contract, with many of the attributes of money. A futures contract facilitates trade in the commodity in the same way that the use of money in exchange has advantages over trade by barter under normal conditions. Nor is this all. A futures contract is a temporary abode

We gratefully acknowledge the financial support of the National Science Foundation. Members of the Industrial Organization Workshop and of the Seminar in Applied Price Theory of the University of Chicago gave helpful comments on earlier drafts. Charles Cox, Edward Lazear, George Stigler, and an anonymous referee deserve our thanks. All remaining errors and defects are our sole responsibility.

of purchasing power in terms of the commodity. It is these aspects of a futures contract and not the more common view that futures contracts enable hedgers to avoid risks that explain the benefits of an organized futures market.

A transaction in a physical commodity in the real world has many unique characteristics stemming partly from the identities of the parties to the transaction, their reliability, credit worthiness, promptness, honesty, and flexibility; the qualities of the good; and the circumstances of the trade. These particulars make a transaction in the physical commodity resemble a barter trade. The two parties in a mutually acceptable trade have costs like those that arise in the double coincidence of trade by barter. The introduction of a standard futures contract by an organized futures market creates a financial instrument that can be traded without knowing the actual identity of the two parties in the transaction. The seller of the futures contract incurs a liability to the organized futures market, and the buyer acquires an asset from this market. Neither need have concern about the integrity of the other in the same sense that one who accepts a $10 banknote in payment for something need not worry about the credit rating of the buyer. This argument implies that any commodity not made to order can benefit from the introduction of an organized futures market. The latter has a cost. Therefore, the use of this commercial invention, the futures contract, appears only for those commodities where the benefits outweigh the costs.

The development of a formal theory of these costs and benefits begins with a stochastic model of market clearing prices which has its roots in the economics of information and search. This model shows that the distribution of market clearing prices is asymptotically normal. The standard deviation of the limiting normal distribution depends on certain properties of the underlying schedules of bids and offers. Also, the realized market clearing price approaches the asymptotic market clearing price in probability as the number of traders increases. This theory is a marriage of economics and probability.

The standard deviation of the distribution of market clearing prices measures the liquidity of the market. There is a cost of lowering the standard deviation and there are benefits. The optimal amount of liquidity takes both the costs and benefits into account and results in some positive value of the standard deviation.

Although the standard deviation is an important element in our theory and seems to be a roundabout way of introducing risk, our emphasis is different and leads to different implications than a theory of futures markets based on the concept of reducing risk. An organized futures market is not necessary in order to obtain the advantages of hedging. These can result from a system of long-term contracts. However, an organized futures market can reduce the costs of moral hazards by the introduction of a standard contract. A long-term contract between two parties depends on their integrity. In a situation with many participants, a standard contract with the backing of the organized market has less moral hazard. Ours is not a theory of why there may be advantages in long-term contracts; it is a theory of the net benefit of an organized exchange. There is some common ground since a long-term contract and a futures contract both refer to dates in the future. Hence an organized futures market is more likely to occur in commodities where the timing of transactions is more important. This only gives a set of necessary conditions, and it does not furnish sufficient conditions for the emergence of an organized futures market.

More generally, this theory asserts that a necessary feature of an organized market is a standard contract traded in that market. This standard contract need not be a futures contract. It may be a certificate that allows the bearer to obtain on demand a specified quantity of a good. Certain forms of certified warehouse receipts, gold and silver certificates, and similar financial instruments, such as shares of stock, have these properties. If the standard contract represents a physical good, then some legal entity is liable for fulfilling the terms of the contract on demand. This person would hold sufficient reserves to maintain the probability of default at an optimal level. Reserves equal to a fraction of the outstanding commitments of the standard contracts may suffice. These standard contracts may circulate among the traders at market determined prices, and the participants may never wish to convert their standard contracts into the physical good. This is plain in the case of shares of stock since rarely do the shareholders wish to liquidate the corporation.

This argument implies that the number and identity of the participants in a potential organized market is important. If this number is small, if the potential participants know each other, and if there is little turnover of these participants, then they may not need a standard contract to deal with each other. If there is a large number of potential participants and a rapid turnover of these traders, then this raises the benefit of a standard contract as well as the benefit of having an organized exchange. The members of the exchange meet certain requirements so that those who deal with them can rely on their integrity. The members of the organized exchange also face the problem that their clients may lack integrity. That is, as the number of potential participants in an organized market increases, the cost of having them all trade on their own account in the organized market may rise more than proportionally. This is not only because of the increasing congestion this would cause but also because there may be increasing costs of having one organization certify all of the potential traders.

Even without an organized market in a standard contract the traders may have confidence in each other if each is a legal representative of well-known principals. This is an important consideration when the trade is in financial instruments that represent actual goods or assets instead of trade in the physical goods or assets themselves. The latter does occur in, say, a flea market. Even if the buyer is a good judge of the commodity before him in the flea market, there is still the problem that he must know that the seller is the legal owner of the good or is the agent of the legal owner. These are important problems in the real world that are often overlooked in some formal theories of market exchange.

The theory herein owes a debt to some important contributions by others. Most notable is Holbrook Working, who always put the emphasis on the functions of a futures market aside from its advantages to hedgers. In some of his work he came close to regarding a futures contract as a temporary abode of purchasing power in the physical commodity (1953, 1967). H. S. Houthakker also points out the similarities between money and futures contracts in his 1959 article. In contrast, most of the economists who have written on the subject, beginning with Marshall's *Industry and Trade* (1920), follow the convention of focusing their attention on hedging and speculation, which loses sight of the more fundamental properties of an organized exchange.

There is another important aspect of the subject that is peripheral to our main interest, and we do not discuss it. This refers to the actual rules of the exchange and the operation of the market. This topic deserves the close attention of economists because it deals with the practical problem of creating a set of conditions that can make a real market function according to the theoretical model of a perfectly competitive market. Informed observers of actual futures markets know that this is a difficult task. An organized futures market cannot survive unless it does approximate a perfectly competitive market.

II. Properties of an Organized Exchange

Before presenting a theory of the costs and benefits of an organized futures market, it is helpful to describe some of its important properties. Trade occurs in one physical place, the floor of the exchange, during specified hours, called the trading session. The traders cry out bids and offers, making a bilateral auction market. Only members of the exchange may trade on the floor, and no member of the exchange may make transactions off the floor of the exchange. Members of the exchange either trade for themselves or under the instructions of their clients who are typically not members of the exchange. Many organized exchanges are responsible for ensuring that the terms of a transaction are fulfilled. The two parties in a transaction agree on price and quantity of the given futures contract. All other terms of the contract are specified by the rules of the exchange.

The exchange determines the number of members who may trade on the floor. A membership is often called a seat on the exchange. A member may sell his seat to a nonmember. However, this is subject to some control by the exchange. The exchange investigates the character of potential members, and it may refuse permission to a potential buyer of a seat. The price of the seat is mutually agreed upon by the seller and buyer and is not subject to control by the exchange.

The exchange can discipline its members by imposing fines, suspending their trading privileges, or by expelling them. The oldest organized futures exchanges, such as the Chicago Board of Trade, have evolved elaborate rules as a result of their long experience. These rules intend to give those who trade on the exchange confidence in the reliability of the transaction executed on the exchange. Members of the exchange must execute the orders of the public, that is, nonmembers, before they execute their own trades. Exchange members who make fictitious trades are subject to penalties. Such fictitious trades intend to record prices that will mislead others. The exchange defines the terms of a contract such that all contracts of a given class are perfect substitutes and such that the validity of a transaction in that contract does not depend on the identity of the principals. Thus, a standard contract for the delivery of 5,000 bushels of wheat in July 1976 executed on the floor of the Chicago Board of Trade in January 1976 at a price mutually agreeable to the parties is as well defined as currency. A futures contract is to a forward contract as currency is to a check drawn against a demand deposit in a commercial bank. The validity of a genuine $10 bill, one printed in the U.S. Bureau of Engraving, does not depend on who offers it in payment, while the validity of a $10 check depends on the identity of the person who writes or presents it and on the identity of the bank. Similarly, the validity of a July futures contract on the Chicago Board of Trade is as good as the faith and credit of the Chicago Board of Trade, while the validity of a forward contract for July delivery depends on the integrity of the buyer and seller in the transaction.

A forward contract shares with a futures contract the important property that the buyer and the seller agree in the present on the terms of a transaction that will be completed at a specified time in the future. The important distinction between the two kinds of contracts lies in this. In a forward contract the actual identity of the buyer and seller is important. Neither has recourse in case of dispute to a third party other than a court of law. The validity of the forward contract depends on the good faith of the two parties themselves. A futures contract has a third party, the organized exchange or its designated representative, that guarantees the validity of the contract and will enforce the terms. When A sells forward to B, the consummation of the transaction depends on their honesty. When A sells a futures contract to B, A incurs a liability to the organized exchange and B acquires an asset from the organized exchange. The exchange, or its clearinghouse, enters the transaction as a third party. It records the sale by A as an asset on its books and the purchase by B as a liability on its books. The outstanding commitments in a futures contract constitute the open interest in that contract and correspond to the stock of money. This analogy with money is important.

It follows from these arguments that the introduction of an organized futures market has consequences resembling those that occur when money is introduced into an economy to facilitate trade. Before the introduction of money we may assume there is trade by barter with all of the disadvantages of trade by barter. Money provides a means of making trades at a lower cost and it is a temporary abode of purchasing power. Similarly, a futures contract facilitates trade in the commodity and it is a temporary abode of purchasing power in that commodity. A futures contract in wheat is to actual wheat as a $10 banknote is to a market basket of $10 worth of actual commodities.

Price quotations on an organized exchange convey reliable information about mutually agreed upon terms of genuine transactions. Some individuals may contrive to gain from deception by violations of the rules or by exploiting defects in their wording, thereby violating the spirit of the rules. The result of long experience leads the exchange to make more elaborate rules in order to reduce the expected return to potential violations. In an organized market with bona fide transactions among honest men, the transaction prices convey such information as would approximate the equilibrium of a competitive market. Departures from a competitive equilibrium, called corners, cannot occur unless there is a violation of the rules of exchange. It appears that a necessary condition for a corner is the ability of one or more traders to deceive others by having the record show false transactions and false prices.

The conditions for the emergence and survival of an organized exchange are costly to bring about. Without these costs every commodity would have an organized market since surely such markets are beneficial. Therefore, to explain the presence or the absence of an organized futures market in a commodity requires a theory of the costs and benefits of such a market.

III. The Distribution of Market Clearing Prices

A futures contract enables trade to occur in the present with reference to dates in the future. It is equivalent in its effects to a means of classifying different grades or qualities of a commodity. It sorts trades with respect to time. Without futures trading a given set of spot transactions would be more heterogeneous with respect to the preferred timing of the traders. The set includes trades that may have taken place earlier or would take place later and which do occur now because the traders lack the alternative of trading in futures contracts. The use of futures contracts sorts the transactions with respect to time so that transactions in contracts of a given maturity date are more nearly alike with respect to those attributes that are correlated with time.

This sorting out of transactions with respect to time that results from the possibility of trading futures contracts has several effects. It can lower the dispersion of the distribution of market clearing prices without necessarily changing the mean price of this distribution. Therefore, a given number of transactions can occur at more nearly equal prices. Also, the traders incur less delay in making their transactions at mutually acceptable prices. For these reasons futures trading increases the liquidity of the market.

An organized market has another important property. It tends to attract trade from a wide geographical territory. Since characteristics and qualities of a commodity are correlated with their location in space for reasons similar to those giving a correlation between timing and relevant aspects of the good, the pooling of trades from many locations into a central market increases the heterogeneity of the potential transactions in the market. This in turn increases the dispersion of the distribution of market clearing prices. An offsetting force is the larger volume of trade attracted to the central market that reduces the dispersion of the distribution of market clearing prices.

Underlying these arguments is a basic theory about market clearing prices. The traders present in a market at a given moment can be regarded as if they were a random sample from the underlying population of traders. The latter has a distribution of minimal acceptable prices for offers and maximal acceptable prices for bids. The distribution of offers is given as follows:

$$U(p) = \int_0^p u(r) \, dr \tag{1}$$

where $U(p)$ is the cumulative distribution of the offers that would accept a price not less than p. Similarly, the pertinent distribution of bids is

$$1 - V(p) = \int_p^\infty v(r) \, dr, \tag{2}$$

giving the cumulative proportion of the bids willing to pay a price equal to or greater than p. Observe that in this theory the asymptotic supply curve has a slope given by $dU(p)/dp = u(p) \geq 0$, and the asymptotic demand curve has a slope given by $(d/dp)[1 - V(p)] = -v(p) \leq 0$. The equilibrium price in the population, p_e, is the solution of the equation

$$U(p) = 1 - V(p). \tag{3}$$

As the number of traders in the market increases indefinitely, the market clearing price approaches the solution given by (3).

Under mild assumptions about the cumulative densities, $U(\cdot)$ and $V(\cdot)$, this theory implies that the distribution of the market clearing prices is asymptotically normal. This result also holds even if individual traders each make bids or offers for more than one unit of the good, provided each trader has a negatively sloping excess demand and is small, in an appropriate sense, relative to the whole market. Since the details are available elsewhere (Telser, forthcoming), the proof here is brief. The population quantile of offers that can expect acceptance at the asymptotic market clearing price p_e is $U(p_e)$. Given a random sample of m offers, calculate the sample fractile, which is some price, corresponding to the population fractile $U(p_e)$. If (3) has a unique solution and if $U(p)$ has a derivative in a neighborhood of p_e and at p_e, then the random variable $\sqrt{m}(p_m - p_e)$ converges in distribution to normality with mean zero and standard deviation $\sigma(p_m)$, where

$$\sigma(p_m) = \{1/u(p_e)\}\{\sqrt{[U(p_e)(1 - U(p_e))/m]}\}. \quad (4)$$

Similarly, for a random sample of n bids, the random variable $\sqrt{n}(p_n - p_e)$ converges in distribution to normality with mean zero and standard deviation $\sigma(p_n)$ where the expression for $\sigma(p_n)$ is the same as for $\sigma(p_m)$, after making the appropriate substitutions, $1 - V$ for U, V for $1 - U$, v for u, and n for m. By hypothesis, the samples of bids and offers are independent. Therefore, the distribution of market clearing prices is also asymptotically normal with mean zero and standard deviation $\sigma(p_{m,n})$, where

$$\sigma^2(p_{m,n}) = \sigma^2(p_m) + \sigma^2(p_n). \quad (5)$$

Several important propositions follow from this analysis. First, the standard deviation of the distribution of market clearing prices is a decreasing function of the square root of the number of transactions. Second, the standard deviations are lower the larger the slopes of the cumulative densities. The slopes measure the homogeneity of the offers or bids in the population. If all offers were the same in the population then $dU(p_e)/dp = \infty$, which corresponds to an infinitely elastic supply. Consequently, (4) asserts, $\sigma(p_m) = 0$. If all offers in the population were different so that dU/dp approaches zero, then $U(p)$ would approach an improper uniform distribution on the halfline $[0, \infty]$ and $\sigma(p_m)$ would increase indefinitely. Therefore, the homogeneity of offers varies inversely with dU/dp. Third, the standard deviation has a maximum if $V(p_e) = U(p_e) = \frac{1}{2}$.[1]

---

[1] The effect of heterogeneity on the standard deviation is given as follows. Assume there are n normal distributions, denoted by N_i, $i = 1, \ldots, n$. Let α_i be the probability of a random drawing from N_i. Let μ_i denote the mean of N_i and σ_i the standard deviation of

According to this theory the standard deviation of the distribution of market clearing prices approaches zero as the number of potential transactions per unit time increases. A given batch of transactions has one market clearing price at which mutually acceptable trades can occur. It is the size of this batch that determines $\sigma(p_{m,n})$. The cost is an increasing function of m and n and there is also a benefit. The optimal volume of trade depends on both. The analysis of costs and benefits in the next section determines the optimal value of σ and shows that it is positive. In this way we obtain a theory of the equilibrium price distribution with both the mean and σ explained by the theory.

IV. A Theory of the Net Benefit of an Organized Futures Market

The preceding section shows that the distribution of market clearing prices is asymptotically normal with a standard deviation, σ, given by

$$\sigma = \alpha K x^{-1/2}, \qquad (6)$$

where x is the volume of trade corresponding to m and n in the preceding section, K a parameter that depends on the underlying supply and demand for the commodity, and α represents certain exogenous factors that we consider in more detail below. For present purposes it is convenient to write (6) in a more general form:

$$\sigma = g(x, \alpha), \qquad (7)$$

N_i. Let X denote a random variable. Then

$$\mu = EX = \sum_i E(X:N_i) \Pr(N_i) = \sum \alpha_i \mu_i. \qquad (i)$$

Also,

$$EX^2 = \sum_i E(X^2:N_i) \Pr(N_i) = \sum \alpha_i(\sigma_i^2 + \mu_i^2), \qquad (ii)$$

$E(X^2:N_i) = \sigma_i^2 + \mu_i^2$. Since var $X = EX^2 - (EX)^2$, it follows that

$$\text{var } X = \sum \alpha_i(\sigma_i^2 + \mu_i^2) - (\sum \alpha_i \mu_i)^2. \qquad (iii)$$

However, $\sum \alpha_i(\mu_i - \mu)^2 = \sum \alpha_i \mu_i^2 - \mu^2$, so that (iii) becomes

$$\text{var } X = \sum \alpha_i \sigma_i^2 + \sum \alpha_i(\mu_i - \mu)^2. \qquad (iv)$$

If $\sigma_i^2 = \sigma^2$ for all i then (iv) reduces to

$$\text{var } X = \sigma^2 + \sum \alpha_i(\mu_i - \mu)^2. \qquad (v)$$

Therefore,

$$\text{var } X - \text{var } X_i = \sum \alpha_i(\mu_i - \mu)^2 \geq 0, \qquad (vi)$$

with equality if and only if $\mu_i = \mu$ for all i. This shows that heterogeneity raises the standard deviation of the distribution of the random variable X. For the application to the distribution of market clearing prices,

$$\sigma_i^2 = F_i(1 - F_i)/[m_i(\partial F_i/\partial p)^2], \qquad (vii)$$

where m_i denotes the size of the random sample from N_i. Let p_e^i denote the asymptotic market clearing price in market i. If $F_i(p_e^i) \neq F_j(p_e^j) \ i \neq j$, then there are differences both with respect to μ_i and with respect to σ_i.

and, in conformity with (6), $g_x < 0$, $g_\alpha > 0$, and $g_{\alpha x} < 0$. We assume that the same function $g(\cdot)$ applies to all commodities and that differences among commodities express themselves via different values of α.

The total cost function of having and operating an organized market is

$$c = h(x, X, \sigma), \tag{8}$$

where X is the size of the outstanding commitment of futures contracts, called the open interest. The presence of x, the volume of trade, as an argument of this total cost function needs no discussion. Assume $h_x > 0$. The open commitment, X, enters for two reasons. First, there is a cost of record keeping. A buyer and seller in the market agree on the price and quantity. This transaction creates a financial instrument on the balance sheet of the futures market, or, more exactly, its clearinghouse. The seller of a futures contract has a liability to the clearinghouse and the buyer has an asset of the clearinghouse. The clearinghouse must keep track of the identity of its debtors, called the shorts, and its creditors, the longs. This imposes a cost that is an increasing function of X. Some of the trade on an organized market comes from outsiders who are not members of the exchange. These trades go through the exchange members who carry out the orders of their customers. Hence the exchange members incur costs as a result of the actions they take on behalf of their customers. These costs depend on x, X, and σ and are included in the function $h(\cdot)$. Accordingly, $h_X > 0$.

The total cost also depends on both X and σ because an exchange member is liable to the clearinghouse for the commitments of his customers. The commodity price may change adversely to the customer of the exchange member. This can impose a loss on the exchange member although he can liquidate the customer's commitment in order to limit the loss. The exchange member normally requires a security deposit, called the margin, from his customer in order to protect himself against loss. This gives a cost per futures contract to the customer that is proportional to the margin per contract. If the only traders on the floor of the exchange were principals then it would not be necessary to have margins and this component of the total cost could be avoided. The higher is σ, the larger is the margin per unit of X and the higher is the total cost. Therefore, $h_X > 0$, $h_\sigma > 0$, and $h_{X\sigma} > 0$.

The net marginal cost with respect to volume is dh/dx given as follows:

$$dh/dx = h_x + h_\sigma g_x. \tag{9}$$

Since the theory stipulates $h_x > 0$, $h_\sigma > 0$, and $g_x < 0$, the net marginal cost can be negative. If the net marginal cost is positive, then, since $g_x < 0$, dh/dx can be a U-shaped function of x. It is more convenient to return to the analysis of this function in conjunction with the discussion of the equilibrium conditions given below.

The total benefit, denoted by b, is an increasing function of x and X. Since σ is the standard deviation of the distribution of market clearing prices, if it enters the benefit function at all, it should do so as a "bad." That is, an increase in σ lowers the total benefit. There would be little point in making σ an argument in the benefit function because this would simply complicate the algebra without yielding new results. The theory does assume that the total cost is an increasing function of σ. Consequently, as it stands, the net benefit, which is the total benefit minus the total cost, is a decreasing function of σ. This means that σ now enters the net benefit function as a bad.

There is another separate issue related to price variability. One reason often given for having an organized futures market is to enable hedging by dealers in the actual commodity. Someone who has a commitment in the actual good, according to this argument, can take an offsetting position in commodity futures contracts and thereby reduce the effects of a change in the price of the commodity. The price risk per unit of the commodity is an increasing function of the unpredictable price variability, denoted by β. Therefore, the benefit of an organized futures market is an increasing function of β. Write the benefit function as follows:

$$b = f(x, X, N, \beta). \tag{10}$$

Assume that f_x, f_X, and f_β are all positive. Now if β represents the unpredictable price variability, it should also affect σ, which is the standard deviation of the distribution of market clearing prices. Hence we modify (7) and write

$$\sigma = g(x, \alpha, \beta), \quad g_\alpha > 0 \text{ and } g_\beta > 0. \tag{7'}$$

This formulation distinguishes between those factors as given by the parameter α that affect σ and those which affect price variability over longer periods of time as represented by β. For instance, seasonal variation can raise σ and does not necessarily affect β (see n. 1). This formulation shows that the effect of a rise of β on the net benefit is indeterminate because both the cost and the benefit are increasing functions of β.

The parameter N in the benefit function represents the number of traders who can benefit from the organized market. Recall that we regard a futures contract as analogous to a form of money that facilitates trade in the commodity. A futures contract corresponds to trade with a common medium of exchange. Since a common medium of exchange is more useful the larger the number of participants, the total benefit increases with N, $f_N > 0$. Also, let $f_{xN} > 0$ and $f_{XN} > 0$.

Assume that the equilibrium values of x and X give the maximal net benefit

$$J(x, X) = b - c, \tag{11}$$

and assume that the observed values of x and X are the equilibrium values. A sufficient condition for the existence of an equilibrium is that the net benefit function, $J(x, X)$, is strongly concave in x and X. Hence the equilibrium is given by the necessary conditions for a maximum of the net benefit subject to the nonnegativity constraints, x and $X \geq 0$. We obtain

$$df/dx - dh/dx \leq 0 \quad \text{and} \quad df/dX - dh/dX \leq 0. \quad (12)$$

The terms df/dx and df/dX giving the marginal benefit with respect to the volume of trade and open interest correspond to the demand for the services of an organized exchange. The terms dh/dx and dh/dX giving the marginal cost with respect to the volume of trade and open commitments correspond to the supply of services of an organized exchange. If the equilibrium values of x and X are positive, there is equality in both equilibrium conditions of (12). The two conditions are independent although one refers to x and the other to X, and under suitable conditions x is the rate of change of X. One can have $X = 0$ and $x > 0$, giving the implication of an upward jump of X. One may have $X > 0$ and $x = 0$ so that although there are positive outstanding commitments, there happens to be no trade. Finally, if the equilibrium values of x and X are both zero there is no organized market in the good. This theory states the absence of an organized market as a corner solution of the equilibrium conditions.

There is the complication that the net marginal cost, dh/dx, is not necessarily monotonic. Under the hypothesis that the net benefit function is strongly concave and that the benefit function $f(x, X, N, \beta)$ is concave in the first two arguments, there are definite restrictions on the properties of dh/dx. Thus, dh/dx must be increasing wherever it is negative. If dh/dx is positive and decreasing, then it must decrease less rapidly than df/dx at corresponding values of x.

Let t denote the commission per transaction. The theory asserts that in equilibrium with $x > 0$ the commission per transaction satisfies the equation

$$t = dh/dx = df/dx. \quad (13)$$

In practice the situation is more complicated. First, the members of the exchange determine the smallest unit that may be traded and the minimum allowable price change per contract. For example, a wheat futures contract is 5,000 bushels and the minimum allowable price change per contract is $12.50 on the Chicago Board of Trade. There are floor traders on the exchange who do not carry an open position overnight and who make many trades during a trading session. Their activities may increase x and lower σ. The return to these traders depends on their cost and is a function of the minimum quantities that may be traded and the minimum allowable price change. The marginal cost also depends on the rate of arrival of information, the level of trading activity, and the distribution of the sizes of the transactions.

There is another important aspect of an organized market. There are traders and brokers who specialize in the commodity and who furnish an inventory of their services during a trading session almost independently of the volume of trade during the session. The number of these specialists in the long run varies directly with the expected volume of trade. For an inactive commodity the commission per unit transaction may include a fixed component that remunerates the specialists for the services they provide by their continued presence on the floor even when trade is light. As the expected volume of trade rises relative to the stock of outstanding contracts, this phenomenon diminishes in importance.

Let m denote the margin per contract. Assume that the cost of the margin is proportional to m. In equilibrium with $X > 0$, the margin per contract, up to the factor of proportionality to represent the cost, satisfies the equation

$$m = df/dX = dh/dX. \tag{14}$$

In practice the size of the margin depends on the nature of the commitment, whether it is speculative, a straddle, a spread, or a hedge. It also depends on the exchange rule that determines the maximum allowable change in the price per contract during a single trading session. Trade during a session cannot continue unless price changes remain within prescribed limits. As a result there is a relation between the margin per contract and the maximum allowable price change per contract. Recall that the members of the exchange often act on the instructions of their customers and that many of the principals do not directly participate in the trade on the floor of the exchange. This relation between the margin per contract and the maximum allowable price change per contract gives all of the brokers time to consult their customers to determine whether the customers wish to continue their commitments in the face of adverse price change by furnishing additional margin. Otherwise, a broker would close out the commitment of his customer. The larger is the maximal allowable price change during a trading session the larger is the margin that the broker demands from his customer. The margin is between one and two times the daily maximal allowable price change per contract.[2]

---

[2] For the 17 commodities in the sample of actively traded goods, the simple correlation between the maximal allowable daily price change per contract and the margin per contract is 0.812. The margin increases by $1.972 per contract for each $1 increase in the maximal allowable daily price change per contract. For the 23-commodity sample, the simple correlation is 0.796 and the slope is different. For each $1.00 increase in the maximal daily allowable price change per contract, the margin rises by $1.744. The 23-commodity sample includes six less actively traded ones. These results show that the increment in margin per dollar increment in daily price limit is lower for the less actively traded commodities.

This argument implies that in those organized markets where the principals trade directly it would be unnecessary to stop trading so that there would be no maximum allowable price change. In such markets margins would also not be needed.

We study the properties of this theory in two different ways. First, we see how changes in the values of the exogenous parameters, α, β, and N affect the equilibrium values of x and X. Second, we study how the margin and the commission depend on these exogenous parameters. We maintain the hypothesis that the functional forms of the benefit and cost functions are the same for all commodities and that differences among the commodities express themselves via the values of the exogenous parameters.

Assume positive values of the initial equilibrium of x and X so that the equilibrium conditions given by (12) are equalities. Write the first-order conditions of the maximum of $J = b - c$ in the form $J_x = J_X = 0$. Use the symbol z to denote one of the exogenous variables, α, β, or N. Differentiate the equilibrium conditions with respect to z and obtain the equations as follows:

$$\begin{bmatrix} J_{xx} & J_{xX} \\ J_{Xx} & J_{XX} \end{bmatrix} \begin{bmatrix} dx/dz \\ dX/dz \end{bmatrix} + \begin{bmatrix} J_{zx} \\ J_{zX} \end{bmatrix} = 0. \qquad (15)$$

Call the matrix on the left-hand side of (15) M. The hypothesis that J is strongly concave implies that M is a negative definite matrix. Hence multiplication of the expression in (15) on the left by the row vector $[dx/dz \; dX/dz]$ gives

$$(dx/dz)J_{zx} + (dX/dz)J_{zX} > 0. \qquad (16)$$

If $z = \beta$, then $J_{zx} = J_{\beta x}$ and $J_{zX} = J_{\beta X}$. Consequently,

$$\begin{cases} J_{\beta x} = f_{x\beta} - h_{x\sigma}g_\beta - h_\sigma g_{\beta x} - h_{\sigma\sigma}g_\beta g_x, \\ J_{\beta X} = f_{X\beta} - h_{X\sigma}g_\beta. \end{cases} \qquad (17)$$

Both of these expressions are of an indeterminate sign. Therefore, (16) does not fix the signs of $dx/d\beta$ and $dX/d\beta$. This is an important result because it means that a rise in exogenous price variability represented by the parameter β has an effect on x and X that depends on the actual numerical values of the terms in (15) and that knowledge of the signs of the components is not sufficient to predict the effects. The same conclusion applies to α since

$$J_{\alpha x} = -h_{x\sigma}g_\alpha - h_{\sigma\sigma}g_\alpha g_x, \qquad (18)$$

$$J_{\alpha X} = -h_{X\sigma}g_\alpha < 0. \qquad (19)$$

The indeterminacy of the sign of $J_{\alpha x}$ is due to the negative value of g_x. As we shall see from the empirical results, the figures give strong support to the view that $g_x < 0$.

Take $z = N$. Then

$$J_{Nx} = f_{xN} > 0 \quad \text{and} \quad J_{NX} = f_{XN} > 0. \tag{20}$$

It is now convenient to write out the solution of (15) for $z = N$. We obtain

$$dx/dN = (-J_{XX}f_{xN} + J_{Xx}f_{XN})/\det M, \tag{21}$$

$$dX/dN = (J_{Xx}f_{xN} - J_{xx}f_{XN})/\det M. \tag{22}$$

The only terms with an open sign in (21) and (22) involve J_{Xx}. If J_{Xx} is positive, then both dx/dN and dX/dN must be positive. If so, the larger the number of potential participants in the market the larger is the equilibrium volume of trade and equilibrium open interest:

$$J_{Xx} = f_{Xx} - h_{Xx} - h_{\sigma X}g_x. \tag{23}$$

Assume X and x are complements in the benefit function so that $f_{Xx} > 0$. By the preceding argument, $h_{\sigma X} > 0$ and $g_x < 0$. Hence two of the three terms in J_{Xx} would be positive. Even if $J_{Xx} > 0$, one may have h_{xx} of either sign. To settle some of these questions we now consider the additional evidence that commissions and margins can furnish.

Equations (13) and (14) give the equilibrium relating the commission t to the marginal benefit and marginal cost and the margin m to the marginal benefit and marginal cost. That is,

$$t = f_x = h_x + g_x h_\sigma \quad \text{and} \quad m = f_X = h_X. \tag{24}$$

Hence t and m are functions of α, β, and N. If one can identify the cost or the benefit function using econometric techniques, then this would contribute to our knowledge of the relevant parameters and it would remove some of the indeterminacies above. To this end, we proceed as follows:

$$t_x = f_{xx} = h_{xx} + g_x(2h_{\sigma x} + g_x h_{\sigma\sigma}) + h_\sigma g_{xx}, \tag{25}$$

$$t_X = f_{Xx} = h_{Xx} + g_x h_{\sigma X}, \tag{26}$$

$$t_\alpha = (h_{x\sigma} + h_{\sigma\sigma}g_x)g_\alpha + h_\sigma g_{x\alpha},$$
$$\text{(recalling that } \alpha \text{ does not appear in } f), \tag{27}$$

$$t_\beta = f_{x\beta} = (h_{x\sigma} + h_{\sigma\sigma}g_x)g_\beta + h_\sigma g_{x\beta}, \tag{28}$$

$$t_N = f_{xN}$$
(recalling that N does not appear in h or g by hypothesis). (29)

Now one may write

$$dt = t_x\,dx + t_X\,dX + t_\alpha\,d\alpha + t_\beta\,d\beta + t_N\,dN \tag{30}$$

in two different ways by using either the partials from the cost side or the partials from the demand side. Taking a convex combination of the partials from the cost and the demand side gives a continuum of possible ways of writing dt in terms of the underlying structure. That is,

$$dt = [\theta(\delta h/\delta x) + (1 - \theta) f_{xx}] dx + [\theta(\delta h/\delta X) + (1 - \theta) f_{Xx}] dX$$
$$+ [\theta(\delta h/\delta \alpha) + (1 - \theta) 0] d\alpha + [\theta(\delta h/\delta \beta) + (1 - \theta) f_{x\beta}] d\beta \quad (31)$$
$$+ [0 + (1 - \theta) f_{xN}] dN,$$

where $0 \leq \theta \leq 1$, and $\delta h/\delta x$, $\delta h/\delta X$, $\delta h/\delta \alpha$, $\delta h/\delta \beta$, and $\delta h/\delta n$ denote the right-hand sides of (25)–(29) where this is applicable. Since the cost function excludes N while the benefit function includes N, a regression of t on the variables on the right-hand side of (31) that excludes dN requires $\theta = 1$, so that the cost function is identifiable.

A similar argument applies to the margin. We have

$$m_x = f_{Xx} = h_{Xx} + h_{X\sigma} g_x, \quad (32)$$

$$m_X = f_{XX} = h_{XX}, \quad (33)$$

$$m_\alpha = h_{X\sigma} g_\alpha \quad (\text{cf. [27]}), \quad (34)$$

$$m_\beta = f_{X\beta} = h_{X\sigma} g_\beta, \quad (35)$$

$$m_N = f_{XN} \quad (\text{cf. [29]}). \quad (36)$$

Therefore, a regression of m on the explanatory variables excluding dN would identify the pertinent parameters of the cost function.

This theory determines the equilibrium values of σ together with the equilibrium values of x and X. Given x and X, the distribution of market clearing prices is asymptotically normal with a standard deviation depending on x. The values of x and X give the maximum net benefit. Hence the theory determines the optimal value of σ which takes into account the marginal benefit and the marginal cost of trade on an organized exchange. Consequently, σ is an endogenous variable in this theory.

Section VI continues this analysis empirically.

V. The Sources of Price Variability

Since the empirical evidence refers to physical commodities, not financial instruments such as foreign exchange or bonds which sometimes also have organized futures markets, we parcel out the sources of price variability among the explanatory variables regarded as random variables in the following function:

$$\log p_{it} = a_{0i} + a_{1i} \log q_{it} + a_{2i} \log y_t + u_{it}, \quad (37)$$

where

p_{it} = U.S. price of commodity i in year t during the month of peak stocks divided by the U.S. wholesale price index,[3]

q_{it} = stocks of commodity i in year t during the month of peak stocks in the United States or the world, depending on which is more suitable,

y_t = U.S. gross national income divided by the U.S. consumer price index,

u_{it} = residual.

The coefficient a_{1i} gives the elasticity of the price with respect to the stock, called EPQ; the coefficient a_{2i} gives the elasticity of the price with respect to deflated national income, called EPY; VPAV is the coefficient of variation of the annual average price of the commodity; STDERR is the standard deviation of the residual. We also measure the variability of monthly prices in terms of a parameter called VPM2 (see the Appendix for the details). All of these measures are in percentage terms and are dimensionless numbers comparable across commodities.[4]

In terms of the theory in the preceding section, these statistics are among the determinants of β which enter the benefit function. They are also among the determinants of α which affect σ in (7′). We claim that α and β are increasing functions of EPQ, EPY, VPAV, STDERR, and VPM2.

We take the explanatory variables in (37) as exogenous. First, the more elastic the underlying supply and demand curves for the commodity the closer a_{1i} is to zero. Hence annual variability of stocks has less effect

---

[3] Under a system of market-determined foreign exchange rates, the nominal price in U.S. dollars of internationally traded goods, the goods in our sample for the most part, would depend on the factors that determine the U.S. aggregate price level. Under fixed exchange rates this is no longer true. The prices in U.S. dollars of internationally traded goods respond to the forces determining the U.S. aggregate price level only insofar as these forces also influence the world market for these goods. The U.S. economy is a substantial fraction of the world economy. Therefore, even with fixed foreign exchange rates, the prices of internationally traded goods denominated in U.S. dollars depends on the factors influencing the aggregate price level in the U.S. Our analysis treats the U.S. relative price as an endogenous variable. It is, therefore, consistent with floating exchange rates determined by free market forces or with fixed exchange rates and the U.S. economy as a substantial fraction of the world economy. To the extent that the U.S. dollar was a reserve currency during the time of fixed exchange rates, the case for treating the U.S. price level as a function of U.S. monetary and fiscal policy is even stronger. Our empirical experiments with various alternatives led us to the formulation we use.

[4] Even if the R^2 in (37) were 1 for one or even for all commodities, this would not affect the logic of the decomposition of the sources of price variability in terms of the explanatory variables of (37). One may regard (37) as giving an analysis of variance of the price in terms of the variability of the explanatory variables, log q_{it} and log y_t, regarded as random variables. To the extent that log y_t and log q_{it} are predictable 1 or more years in advance it would be desirable to represent this in the analysis of variance. For present purposes this is outside the scope of our analysis.

on annual price variability as a_{1i} approaches zero. For example, the better the substitutes for a given commodity in either demand or supply the closer a_{1i} is to zero. Second, price is less responsive to income as a_{2i} approaches zero. The level of income affects the demand for the commodity. As a result, a_{2i} is the compound effect of the size of the income elasticity of demand and the size of the elasticity of supply. The larger is the income elasticity of demand, the larger is a_{2i}. The smaller is the elasticity of supply, the larger is a_{2i}. Therefore, a high income elasticity of demand and a low elasticity of supply combine to give a large value of a_{2i}. The standard deviation of the residuals measures the effects of exogenous factors on price variability that are uncorrelated with the variables explicitly included. Since VPM2 gives the mean value of the standard deviation of prices around the monthly means, it measures the effects of short-term price variability in contrast to the preceding statistics, which give measures of different aspects of annual price variability.

The sample has 51 commodities for the period 1959–71 (an appendix, available to the reader on request, describes the sources). We divide the sample into three subsamples of equal size such that the first has 17 actively traded goods, the second has 17 less actively traded goods, and the third has 17 with little or no trade as far as we know. Each commodity in a subsample has two companions, one in each of the other two subsamples, with roughly similar gross characteristics—metal, meat, fowl, wood, etc. We use three criteria to place a commodity into a subsample—the size of the open interest, the volume of trade, and the duration and timing of trading activity. Each subsample has commodities difficult to place. For example, we put plywood and broilers in the active group and wool and oats in the inactive group, although the latter two have a larger open interest than the former two. We took as decisive the fact that plywood and broilers have a larger volume of trade. If trade in a commodity came to a halt at some point in the sample period and did not revive during the remainder of the sample period, we put that commodity into the inactive group. This explains our placement of cottonseed meal, coffee, and zinc. A few commodities in the inactive group are actively traded in London, such as tin and zinc. Cocoa is active in both London and New York. We put cocoa in the active group. Copper, in the active group, is more active in London than in New York. There have been attempts to start futures markets for some commodities in the dormant group that so far have failed. These commodities are nickel, apples, hams, and rice. We have been unable to discover any attempts to organize futures trading for some commodities in the dormant group, including newsprint, lamb, veal, and frozen strawberries. Except for platinum, our active group includes every commodity actively traded on an organized futures market in the United States during the sample period.

In some cases the absence of an organized futures market probably results from highly stable prices due to governmental policies or actions of private concerns. Foreign exchange, though not in our sample, best illustrates this point. Market determined foreign exchange rates began in 1971. Before the United States closed its gold window the fiscal authorities of various nations had a coordinated price-support program for foreign exchange that maintained a web of fixed exchange rates. Prior to 1971 futures markets in foreign exchange were unimportant. Similarly, the U.S. government price-support program in peanuts and tobacco stifles interest in futures trading in these commodities. Trading in cotton, a commodity with an organized spot market in New York since the eighteenth century, virtually expired when government stocks were large and growing. Trading did not revive until after the disappearance of the government inventory. Published prices of petroleum crude oil and newsprint are very stable. This seems to have the same effect as a price-support program, but we know of no government policy as the explanation. Perhaps the Texas Railroad Commission is to blame for stable crude-oil prices. The end of our sample period precedes the Arabian oil embargo to the United States by 2 years.

Accepting this classification of the commodities into the three groups, we now examine the pertinent evidence. Table 1 gives the means and standard deviations of the variables related to price variability.

According to table 1, VPAV is highest for the active group, next highest for the inactive group, and lowest for the dormant group. This pattern could occur by chance with a probability of 1 percent. Both VPM2 and STDERR show the same pattern. Therefore, prices are most variable for the actively traded group, next most variable for the inactive group, and least variable for the dormant group.

Consider now the pattern with respect to the sources of price variability. The EPQ approaches zero as we move from the active to the dormant group. This is clearer if, instead of calculating the percentage price change with respect to a 1 percent change in stocks, we compute the percentage price change with respect to a 1 percent change of the coefficient of variation of stocks, a parameter denoted QRSK (quantity risk). The inverse relation between trading activity and QRSK is significant at the 99 percent level. Also, EPY decreases with trading activity but the pattern has a low level of significance, 83 percent. Finally, observe that the R^2 (RSQ) and DW statistics do not differ significantly among the three subsamples.

Table 1 shows two other aspects of the difference among commodities that are relevant for our argument. First, the seasonal index of prices is positively correlated with the marginal cost of storage and with the holding of stocks. Observe that the price seasonal varies inversely with trading activity. That is, the actively traded commodities show a more

TABLE 1

MEANS AND STANDARD DEVIATIONS OF SELECTED CHARACTERISTICS RELATED TO PRICE VARIABILITY OF 17 ACTIVE, 17 INACTIVE, AND 17 DORMANT COMMODITIES

Parameter	Active 1–17	Inactive 18–34	Dormant 35–51	Total 1–51	Significance Level*
VPAV	16.4610 (6.6498)	12.7476 (4.7874)	11.5544 (6.0370)	13.5877 (6.1319)	.010
VPM2	5.5363 (3.0607)	4.7726 (3.9698)	2.9326 (2.3594)	4.4139 (3.3277)	.016†
EPQ	−0.6007 (0.8914)	−0.3628 (0.9100)	−0.2322 (0.4596)	−0.3986 (0.7814)	.071
QRSK	11.6102 (8.9936)	8.2079 (7.1992)	4.8470 (3.5411)	8.2217 (7.3660)	.006
EPY	0.1557 (0.9810)	0.1118 (0.4470)	0.06297 (0.5439)	0.1102 (0.6841)	.170
RSQ	0.5264 (0.2706)	0.4962 (0.2660)	0.4863 (0.2628)	0.5029 (0.2617)	.176
STDERR	11.3271 (4.6238)	8.7645 (4.3014)	6.6858 (4.0692)	8.9258 (4.6622)	.004
DW	1.6900 (0.4803)	1.6929 (0.4734)	1.6412 (0.6224)	1.6747 (0.5197)	.199
Seasonal of prices	29.4229 (35.1045)	22.6903 (19.33)	14.2013 (12.3177)	21.4421 (24.71)	.018†
Seasonal of stocks	49.1009 (33.5402)	50.2590 (30.5552)	60.1442 (33.6604)	52.8282 (31.9250)	.090

* The numbers in parentheses are the estimated standard deviations of the population. The statistic as follows

$$[(m_1 - m_2)/\sqrt{(n_1 s_1^2 + n_2 s_2^2)}]\sqrt{[n_1 n_2(n_1 + n_2 - 2)/(n_1 + n_2)]}$$

has a t-distribution where m_i denotes the sample mean and s_i^2 the sample variance. Let $i = 1$ denote the active, $i = 2$ the inactive, and $i = 3$ the dormant. The theory predicts the signs of $m_2 - m_1$ and $m_3 - m_2$. The significance level gives the probability of observing the two independent t-statistics on the hypothesis that the true differences are zero (Cramèr 1946, sec. 31.2.1).
† There is a slight complication because we lack monthly price series for two commodities, tomato paste, which is in the inactive group, and strawberries, which is in the dormant group. Therefore, we cannot calculate VPM2 and the price seasonal for these two commodities. Consequently, with respect to these two parameters, the sample size is 16 for both the inactive and the dormant group. The significance levels take this into account.

pronounced seasonal price pattern than do the less actively traded ones. The pattern is significant at the 98 percent level. It is also true that there is a more highly seasonal pattern of stocks for the actively traded goods than for the others but with a significance level of only 91 percent. (The stock seasonal is the trough stock level divided by the peak level, where the peak and trough refer to an appropriate 12-month period.) Nevertheless, consistent with our theory that the introduction of futures trading permits a sorting of transactions over time, we find more seasonality for the actively traded goods, which implies a greater benefit from organized futures trading in these goods.

VI. Effects of Price Variability on the Open Interest and the Volume of Trade

The preceding material shows the presence of an inverse association between trading activity and price variability across the three subsamples. According to the theory of the costs and benefits of futures trading given above, the relation between the volume of trade, open interest, and various measures of price variability does not necessarily imply that more price variability raises the volume of trade and open interest. Although greater price variability implies a greater benefit from organized futures trade, it also implies a greater cost. The greater cost is from two sources. First, the higher the price variability, the higher is the cost of holding a given open commitment. Second, the higher the price variability, the larger is the dispersion of the distribution of market clearing prices for a given volume of trade, which is a cost-increasing phenomenon. Therefore, estimates of how the volume of trade and open interest depend on various measures of price variability can give useful information about the nature of the costs and benefits. The purpose of this section is to furnish some empirical evidence in order to narrow the range of theoretical alternatives.

We now use a sample of 25 commodities, which adds data for eight commodities in the inactive sample to the 17 actively traded commodities.[5] The eight additional observations include all commodities in the less active group for which there was some nonnegligible volume of trade and open interest during the sample period. Table 2 lists the commodities and the pertinent data. The velocity of the open interest, the average annual volume of trade divided by the average end-of-quarter open interest, ranges from a low of 14 for coffee to a high of 86 for pork bellies. These are large numbers by comparison with, say, the velocity of the money supply. Soybean future contracts have a daily average volume of trade of $110 millions, and for pork bellies this figure is $66 millions! Table 3 gives the simple correlations, means, and standard deviations of the variables in the regression analysis. Observe that the simple correlations between the log of open interest and price variability are all small, and the same is true of the corresponding correlations for the log of volume of trade. However, since the various measures of price variability are dimensionless pure numbers, while the volume of trade and open interest are in dollars and depend on the size of the demand for the commodities, the two sets of variables are not comparable. Also, the theory implies the presence of a scale variable as a separate factor to explain the size of the open interest and volume of trading in the commodity. The level of stocks suggests itself as one way of measuring scale. This has the

---

[5] The 25 commodities in this sample are as follows: 1–18, 20, 21, 25, 27, 28, 29, and 30 (see table 2 for the names of these commodities).

TABLE 2

DATA BY COMMODITY

No. and Commodity	Volume of Trade (10^9 \$)	Open Interest (10^6 \$)	Stocks (10^6 \$)	Seasonal of Stocks	VPAV (%)	STDERR (%)	VPM2 (%)
1. Cotton	1.116	52.6	1374	32.559	16.928	11.82	2.85
2. Soybeans	27.510	552.8	1453	14.127	10.661	5.53	4.42
3. Wheat	9.173	195.8	1418	48.441	15.824	8.10	4.15
4. Cocoa	2.096	124.0	82	20.987	26.902	7.58	7.90
5. Sugar	2.646	110.5	264	42.614	10.875	6.57	5.21
6. Copper	1.073	31.1	244	100.0	23.794	7.72	2.14
7. Silver	5.935	376.3	450	100.0	27.701	11.81	3.88
8. Corn	7.522	216.8	3045	30.354	8.149	5.67	3.49
9. Soymeal	1.808	94.1	497	14.127	12.509	9.58	5.34
10. Soy oil	3.705	95.5	351	14.127	15.304	13.22	6.31
11. Plywood	0.835	16.9	503	96.053	8.614	14.95	6.96
12. Broilers	0.508	10.0	299	75.868	8.348	19.75	2.71
13. Cattle	4.984	170.6	5951	79.178	14.227	6.68	3.28
14. Eggs	1.649	23.8	982	92.738	12.967	19.70	8.24
15. Frozen orange juice	0.715	24.6	181	32.478	25.687	14.21	4.79
16. Pork bellies	16.573	192.5	620	15.448	21.582	14.44	7.54
17. Potatoes	0.659	19.3	416	25.619	19.766	15.24	14.90
18. Wool	0.231	22.1	205	41.190	17.823	16.82	3.38
19. Cottonseed meal	0.002	0.1	149	7.470	11.884	10.85	5.02
20. Rye	0.610	14.2	25	40.079	6.681	3.97	3.37
21. Coffee	0.246	17.8	173	87.735	15.107	13.05	3.63
22. Propane	0.018	3.2	318	48.859	7.390	4.04	1.23
23. Tin	0.003	0.4	72	88.279	20.070	7.19	4.05
24. Zinc	0.011	1.5	45	94.934	11.201	5.17	1.74
25. Oats	0.457	17.2	539	34.598	4.672	4.49	3.06
26. Milo	0.023	2.4	445	41.020	8.184	7.22	3.56
27. Cottonseed oil	0.475	16.0	170	32.426	16.078	8.29	5.95
28. Lumber	0.390	10.1	625	96.053	15.303	8.47	4.07
29. Turkeys	0.162	4.6	384	27.326	9.160	5.88	3.98
30. Hogs	0.374	8.2	1947	83.226	17.770	10.50	5.94
31. Butter	0.056	0.0	114	48.426	6.908	3.10	1.88
32. Tomato paste	0.0	0.0	102	12.114	17.149	10.27	4.77
33. Lard	0.051	71.7	10	65.426	16.321	16.76	6.41
34. Onions	0.0	0.0	14	5.242	15.008	12.91	19.10
35. Tobacco	0.0	0.0	2755	65.026	9.345	3.36	0.83
36. Peanuts	0.0	0.0	282	15.705	9.088	4.82	2.79
37. Rice	0.0	0.0	389	12.629	4.446	4.90	1.74
38. Tea	0.0	0.0	34	60.000	7.549	4.33	1.59
39. Coal	0.0	0.0	394	86.170	25.416	13.42	1.77
40. Aluminum	0.0	0.1	728	100.00	7.620	3.39	1.23
41. Nickel	0.0	0.0	129	100.00	22.544	8.27	2.54
42. Barley	0.0	0.0	412	34.088	8.243	6.58	3.28
43. Petroleum crude oil	0.0	0.0	779	93.637	4.901	1.25	0.66
44. Peanut oil	0.0	0.0	14	15.705	12.173	13.55	4.36
45. Newsprint	0.0	0.0	88	100.00	5.459	1.35	0.56
46. Lamb	0.0	0.0	249	75.00	13.363	8.32	3.86
47. Veal	0.0	0.0	278	79.178	12.571	6.39	5.34
48. Cheese	0.0	0.0	158	74.445	19.852	4.27	1.93
49. Strawberries	0.0	0.0	19	41.806	11.850	10.10	2.93
50. Hams	0.0	0.0	1057	67.833	8.701	5.22	4.08
51. Apples	0.0	0.0	197	1.230	13.304	14.13	10.35

NOTE.—A detailed description of the sources and of the methods for estimating these figures is available to readers on request.

TABLE 3

SIMPLE CORRELATIONS BETWEEN LOG VOLUME, LOG OPEN, AND SELECTED MEASURES OF PRICE VARIABILITY, MEANS, AND STANDARD DEVIATIONS FOR 25 COMMODITIES

	SIMPLE CORRELATIONS						
VARIABLES	Log Open	Log Volume	VPM2	STDERR	VPAV	MEAN	SD
Log open	1	.93267	−.02780	−.21903	.25128	3.75921	1.29777
Log volume	...	1	.05703	−.17166	.13909	0.31176	1.36342
VPM2..........	...	...	1	.35044	.24315	5.09960	2.60072
STDERR.......	...	...	...	1	.24568	10.56160	4.51223
VPAV..........	...	...	...	...	1	15.29728	6.22404

disadvantage of introducing serious measurement errors for some commodities. As an alternative, one can use the volume of trade as a scale variable to explain the open interest and the open interest as a scale variable to explain the volume of trade. In effect this treats the system of equations (15) as candidates for direct estimation by least squares.

Substitute β for z in (15) and write out the result as follows:

$$J_{xx}(dx/d\beta) + J_{Xx}(dX/d\beta) = -J_{x\beta}, \tag{38}$$

$$J_{Xx}(dx/d\beta) + J_{XX}(dX/d\beta) = -J_{X\beta}. \tag{39}$$

Take $dx/d\beta$ as the dependent variable in the first and $dX/d\beta$ as the dependent variable in the second to give the following representation:

$$dx = -(J_{Xx}/J_{xx}) \, dX - (J_{x\beta}/J_{xx}) \, d\beta, \tag{40}$$

$$dX = -(J_{Xx}/J_{XX}) \, dx - (J_{X\beta}/J_{XX}) \, d\beta. \tag{41}$$

Take a linear approximation to these equations and use the three measures of price variability for β. We estimate by least squares the following equations:

$$\log x = a_0 + a_1 \log X + a_2(\text{VPM2}) + a_3(\text{STDERR}) \\ + a_4(\text{VPAV}) + \varepsilon, \tag{42}$$

$$\log X = c_0 + c_1 \log x + c_2(\text{VPM2}) + c_3(\text{STDERR}) \\ + c_4(\text{VPAV}) + \zeta. \tag{43}$$

There is the complication that x and X are endogenous variables. It seems plausible that the random disturbances are more likely to shift the benefit functions than the cost functions, because changes in weather affect production of agricultural goods and cyclical factors affect the demand for all goods, which shifts the hedging demand and, therefore,

TABLE 4

SELECTED STATISTICS FROM REGRESSIONS RELATING FUTURES TRADING ACTIVITY TO PRICE VARIABILITY FOR A SAMPLE OF 25 COMMODITY FUTURES

EXPLANATORY VARIABLES	DEPENDENT VARIABLES			
	Log Open Interest		Log Volume of Trade	
	Elasticity	t-Ratio of Coefficient	Elasticity	t-Ratio of Coefficient
Log volume	0.8591	12.412	. . .	. . .
Log open	. . .	. . .	1.0302	12.412
VPM2	−0.2406	−1.240	0.2793	1.321
STDERR	−0.2182	−0.920	0.1329	0.504
VPAV	0.1769	2.235	−0.4790	−1.773
R^2	.9020	. . .	.8953	. . .

the benefit function. Therefore, ε will be positively correlated with log X and ζ will be positively correlated with log x. Hence least-squares estimates of the coefficients, a_1 and c_1, are both upward biased. We deal directly with one aspect of this problem below by studying how commissions and margins depend on the pertinent variables as given in (24).

Table 4 gives the estimates of the elasticities derived from (42) and (43) together with the t-ratios of the coefficients. The coefficient of log X in (42) corresponds to $-(J_{Xx}/J_{xx})$ in (40) while the coefficient of log x in (43) corresponds to $-(J_{Xx}/J_{XX})$ in (41). The other coefficients in (42) and (43) relate similarly to their counterparts in (40) and (41). Consider the regression with the log of the open interest as the dependent variable. Of the three measures of price variability, the only one that enters with a large t-ratio is VPAV, the coefficient of variation of annual prices. It has a t-ratio of 2.2 and an elasticity of 0.18. The other two measures of price variability enter with t-ratios around 1 and have negative elasticities. Also observe that in the regression equation with log x as the dependent variable each coefficient of price variability enters with a sign opposite to that which it has in the regression with log X as the dependent variable. One is immediately tempted to conclude from these results that a rise in some aspect of price variability tends to move the open interest and the volume of trade in opposite directions. This may be true, but the high correlation between log x and log X is consistent with an alternative and a simpler explanation of these results. The simple correlation between log X and log x is 0.933 according to table 3. Also, the multiple R^2 in the log open regression in table 4 is .902 ($R = .95$). One may then say that these regressions are nearly identities and it would follow by simple arithmetic that the coefficients of price variability in one equation are nearly perfectly predictable by the coefficients in the other. For instance, solve for log x in the regression equation with log X

TABLE 5

Selected Statistics from Regressions to Explain Log of Open Interest and Log of Volume of Trade for 25 Commodity Futures

EXPLANATORY VARIABLES	DEPENDENT VARIABLES			
	Log Open Interest		Log Volume	
	Elasticity	t-Ratio of Coefficient	Elasticity	t-Ratio of Coefficient
Log stock	0.4451	2.13	0.5594	2.47
VPM2	0.0167	0.03	0.3010	0.55
STDERR	−0.9155	−1.49	−0.8122	−1.24
VPAV	1.2109	1.93	0.8031	1.20
R^2	.3048	...	.2893	...

as the dependent variable and you will come close to the estimated regression with log x as the dependent variable.

For these reasons it is of some interest to try an alternative to these equations which uses the log of stocks as a scale variable. These results appear in table 5. Here we see that each measure of price variability has a coefficient of the same sign in the regressions with log X and log x as the dependent variables. This is hardly surprising given the high positive correlation between log X and log x. Nevertheless it is worth noting that an increase in stocks of 1 percent will lead to a larger percentage increase in the volume of trade than in the open interest.[6]

We now study how the commission per transaction and the margin per contract depends on the pertinent variables according to the theory

---

[6] It has not escaped our attention that one may use the regression equations in table 5 to predict the log of the open interest and the log of the volume of trade for the 26 (= 51 − 25) commodities which now lack an active organized futures market. In our earlier work we did precisely this. We have doubts about the reliability of these results for several reasons. The most important caveat is with respect to the measure of stocks to represent the scale of potential interest in the commodity. Empirically, it turns out to be a very important variable for explaining lack of interest in a commodity. That is, commodities with a small potential market are bad candidates for an organized futures market. In some cases there are large government holdings of the commodity (e.g., peanuts and tobacco), and it is difficult to determine how to measure the relevant stocks. (For empirical work on this problem, see Telser 1958.) There may also be a price-stabilizing effect of organized futures trading so that the relevant measure of price variability between traded and untraded goods is larger than would appear from the observed differences in price variability. (For a theoretical analysis of the stabilizing effects on prices of profitable speculation, see Telser [1959].) A third important factor, the tax incentive for trading in futures contracts in the United States, does not appear in our theoretical or empirical analysis. Such trading may allow a shift of capital gains and losses from various speculations between years and thereby lowers the income tax of the speculator, who can take advantage of the lower tax rate on capital gains. The trade believes this is important. (For a careful analysis of portfolio aspects of futures trading, see Dusak [1973].)

in Section IV.[7] We assume that the cost and benefit functions are of the same form for all commodities and that differences among commodities express themselves via different values of the exogenous variables, α, β, and N. In equilibrium the commission, t, and the margin, m, satisfy (24). The argument in Section IV shows that the cost functions are identified in a regression that excludes the scale variable N and includes the other exogenous variables related to α and β. We have two regressions that we estimate by ordinary least squares. In the first the commission is the dependent variable and in the second the margin is the dependent variable. In addition to the proxies for α and β, we include among the explanatory variables, log x, log X, and the average price per futures contract over the sample period, a variable we label CONPR (contract price). The relevance of CONPR as a determinant of m hardly needs discussion. Plainly, the potential cost to a broker of a customer default is an increasing function of the size of the customer's commitment or open interest. Hence m should be an increasing function of CONPR. It is not equally plain why CONPR should affect the commission. Empirically, one can hardly doubt that t is an increasing function of CONPR. This result is consistent with the belief that it is more costly to arrange a mutually satisfactory trade for a contract of larger value, such as coffee, than for one of lesser value, such as potatoes, even holding the volume of trade constant. That is, a broker's execution according to his instructions is more costly for a contract of a larger value. It may not be superfluous to add that this argument would be consistent with the theory of optimal search.

If a good measure of scale were available, this would enable the application of simultaneous-equations techniques in an attempt to estimate the structural relations of the model. The only candidate is an estimate of stocks by commodity, and this is subject to considerable measurement error. Therefore, we focus our attention on the cost side which is identifiable and we accept a possible simultaneous equations bias in so far as log x and log X are both positively correlated with the variable we omit, the scale factor. This gives an upward bias to the coefficients of both log x and log X if t is positively related to N and m is positively related to N, where N denotes the scale factor.

---

[7] We use a sample of 23 commodities. The two missing commodities are cottonseed oil and turkeys. Both have been inactive since 1965. We lack data giving the commissions and margins for these two, and this explains their absence from our sample. The commission per transaction and the margin per contract were obtained from brokerage firms and refer to the first half of 1976. The sample period gives averages of the explanatory variables for an earlier period. This should cause no problem. One may argue that the commissions and margins do in fact depend on long-term averages. In any case, since these variables appear as the dependent variables in the regression equations, the presence of measurement error does not bias the estimates of the regression coefficients. However, it does lower the R^2 and increase the standard errors of the estimated regression coefficients.

TABLE 6
Selected Statistics from Regressions to Explain Commissions and Margins for a Sample of 23 Commodity Futures

	DEPENDENT VARIABLES			
	Commission		Margin	
EXPLANATORY VARIABLES	Elasticity	t-Ratio of Coefficient	Elasticity	t-Ratio of Coefficient
Log volume	−0.218	−2.72	−0.419	−2.80
Log open interest	0.141	1.58	0.449	2.69
CONPR.............	0.536	4.62	0.729	3.36
STDERR............	−0.189	−1.75	−0.425	−2.10
VPAV	0.076	0.72	−0.265	−1.33
VPM2	0.130	1.48	0.415	2.53
Constant............	−0.1997	−0.01	−1,227.00	−1.59
R^2	.688	...	.662	...
SE..................	8.678	...	397.1	...

We claim that the regressions given in table 6 using the data in table 7 furnish estimates of the slopes of the commission and margin with respect to the various variables for the cost equation. Thus, the slope of t with respect to x in table 6 gives an estimate of t_x on the cost side, which is the right-hand side of (25), and so on. Similarly, the slope of m with respect to x gives an estimate of $h_{Xx} + h_{X\sigma}g_x$ according to the right-hand side of (32), and so on. With the theoretical interpretations in hand as given by (25)–(29) and (32)–(35), consider the evidence in table 6.

Both the commission and the margin regressions display a similar pattern of results.[8] With only one exception all of the explanatory variables have coefficients of the same sign in both regression equations. The higher is the volume of trade the lower is the commission and the margin. The higher is the open interest, the higher is the commission and the margin. The higher is the average price per contract, the higher is the commission and margin. Although the t-ratios indicate a high level of significance by the usual standards, one should regard this with some skepticism because, for one thing, simultaneous-equations bias is present due to the omission of a scale variable that may be positively correlated with $\log x$ and $\log X$. The coefficients of $\log x$ and $\log X$ both give strong support to the belief that $g_x < 0$ (cf. [25] and [32]). The negative coefficient of $\log x$ in the margin regression is also consistent with the view that a rise in the volume of trade for a given open interest lowers the marginal cost with respect to the open interest ($h_{Xx} < 0$).

Now consider the regression coefficients of the various measures of price variability in table 6. In the commission regressions these coefficients

---

[8] The simple correlation between m and t is 0.643. This seems too low to explain the similarity in the pattern of results.

TABLE 7

AVERAGE CONTRACT PRICE (CONPR), COMMISSION (COMM), AND MARGIN (MARG) FOR 23 COMMODITY FUTURES CONTRACTS IN DOLLARS PER CONTRACT

Commodity	CONPR	COMM	MARG
Cotton	14,368	70	1,300
Soybeans	13,715	50	2,500
Wheat	8,858	45	1,250
Cocoa	8,511	70	2,400
Sugar	8,034	75	2,000
Copper	9,949	50	750
Silver	7,926	50	1,200
Corn	6,100	40	1,000
Soy meal	7,527	40	1,500
Soy oil	6,005	40	1,000
Plywood	5,947	40	700
Broilers	6,250	35	500
Cattle	10,925	50	900
Eggs	8,071	40	700
Frozen orange juice conc.	6,712	45	450
Pork bellies	14,425	60	1,500
Potatoes	1,892	35	750
Wool	6,947	50	1,500
Rye	5,941	40	1,500
Coffee	12,764	80	2,000
Oats	3,357	35	750
Lumber	4,198	55	700
Hogs	4,087	40	900

refer to t_α or t_β in (27) and (28). If $h_{x\sigma} + h_{\sigma\sigma} g_x$ is negative because g_x is negative, then the coefficient of the measure of price variability can also be negative. Nor is this all. Given the hypothesis about the signs of the various partials in (27) and (28), a negative value of g_x is *necessary* but is not sufficient for an observed negative value of the coefficient of a price variability parameter; STDERR does have a negative coefficient in the commission regression. Both VPAV and VPM2 have positive coefficients in the commission regression.

Next consider the margin regression. Equations (34) and (35) predict positive coefficients of the variables that are positively related to price variability if $h_{x\sigma}$ is positive and if X is not an argument in $g(\cdot)$. According to table 6, VPM2 does have a positive coefficient with an elasticity of 0.415 and a t-ratio of 2.5. Recall that VPM2 measures the coefficient of variation around the monthly price seasonal so that it reflects shorter term sources of price variability than either VPAV or STDERR. Both STDERR and VPAV have negative coefficients. The elasticities are -0.425 and -0.265, and the t-ratios are -2.1 and -1.3. These results are not consistent with the present model. There are two possible explanations of this discrepancy of which the first is econometric and the second is economic. The regression equation omits the scale variable, N. According to the theory N is positively related to x and X and is also positively related to m (and to t) as is shown in (36) (and [29]). This imparts a positive bias to the estimates of the coefficients of log x and log X. It is also possible that N is correlated with the exogenous variables α and β. If N is negatively related to α and β, then this would impart a downward bias to the estimates of the coefficients of price variability. We do have a weak proxy for the scale variable given by the log of stocks, a variable which we regard with suspicion because of measurement error for some commodities. Nevertheless, we do find negative, albeit small, correlations between the three measures of price variability and the log of stocks. The simple correlations, denoted by $R(\cdot)$, are as follows:

$$R(\log \text{stock}, \text{VPAV}) = -.149, \quad R(\log \text{stock}, \text{STDERR}) = -.064,$$

$$R(\log \text{stock}, \text{VPM2}) = -.045.$$

Observe that it is the variable with the correlation closest to zero that has a positive effect on the margin.

This econometric argument agrees with an economic argument. The size of the elasticity of the excess demand function increases with the stock of outstanding commitments. According to (4), this tends to lower σ. We believe that a closer investigation of the function $\sigma = g(x, \alpha, \beta)$ is desirable since these arguments suggest that the variable X should enter this function. Such research would directly study the determinants of liquidity in the market.

VII. Summary and Conclusions

In an organized market the participants trade a standardized contract such that each unit of the contract is a perfect substitute for any other unit. The identities of the parties in any mutually agreeable transaction do not affect the terms of exchange. The organized market itself or some other institution deliberately creates a homogeneous good that can be traded anonymously by the participants or their agents.

Although the discussion centers on organized futures markets, the basic theory applies equally well to any organized market. The benefit of an organized market is an increasing function of the number of potential participants. It is also an increasing function of the turnover of the potential participants in that market. It would not be necessary for a small group of traders who know each other well and who have had and will continue to have contacts with each other to bear the expense of organizing a formal market. In such markets the terms of sale often do depend on the identity of the parties in addition to the characteristics of the goods. An organized market deals in a highly fungible good that is readily traded among strangers. In an organized market the transactions prices alone convey a considerable amount of useful information to those who are not currently trading in the market. In those markets where heterogeneous goods are traded and where the identity of the buyer and seller affects the terms of trade, the transaction price alone conveys only partial information to outsiders.

In addition to scale, price variability affects the benefit of having an organized market. It also affects the cost. There is more price variability for those goods that have an organized futures market than for the goods that lack such markets. It does not follow that futures trading causes greater price variability. The organization of a futures market is the response to an increase of price variability. For example, when the government allows the price of a good to fluctuate and abandons its attempt to control the price, this may create an incentive to organize a futures market if the potential scale of operation is large enough, as witness the creation of organized futures markets in some foreign exchange.

We find that the volume of trade increases relative to the open interest, the higher is the level of the open interest. As the open interest in a commodity declines, the volume of trade declines even more rapidly. According to the empirical results relating commissions to $\log x$ and $\log X$, commissions are higher, the less active the trade in the commodity. Let price variability be the driving force as represented by the parameter β. Let the price of some good become more stable. The open interest declines and the volume of trade falls relative to the open interest. This raises the commission and the margin. A sequence of events now begins that may well end in a corner equilibrium with no trade and no open interest in the commodity. In this way the theory predicts the disappearance of an organized market. Similarly, a rise in price variability may lead to the appearance of an organized market.

The best concise summary of the theory is as follows: An organized market facilitates trade among strangers.

Appendix

Description of Cross-Section Data and Sources

I. Trading activity and market structure variables

Seasonal of stocks. Average ratio of trough-month stocks to peak-month stocks, 1959–71, expressed as a percentage.

Open. Average number of open contracts, end-of-quarter, 1959–71 or subperiod of active futures trading. *Journal of Commerce and Commercial.*

Opnint. Open × average dollar value of one contract, 1959–71 or subperiod of active futures trading, in millions of nominal dollars.

Stocks. Value of average privately held stocks in millions of nominal dollars, 1959–71 or subperiod of active futures trading. Computations are described in appendix II, Average U.S. Stocks. Conceptually, stocks are computed as pipeline stocks plus average intraseasonal inventories. They give the peak holdings during the year.

Volume. Average annual volume of futures transactions on all U.S. contract markets, 1959–71 or subperiod of active futures trading, × average dollar value of one contract, expressed in billions of nominal dollars. Association of Commodity Exchange Firms, Inc.

II. Variables derived from monthly price series P_{im}

VPAV. Coefficient of variation across years of $\sum_{m=1}^{12} P_{im}$, 1959–71. When weighted average yearly prices are available (i.e., weighted by quantities sold), such data are used.

VPM2. Let P_{im}^{*} equal P_{im} deflated by a 12-month moving average, centered at the sixth month. For each month m, let σ_m equal 100 × standard deviation of P_{im}^{*}; VPM2 equals the mean of σ_m across months.

Seasonal of prices. Maximum own rate of interest, at annual rate, displayed by averages across years of P_{im} (one for each month), 1959–71. Example: if $P \cdot {}_{\text{DEC}}$ and $P \cdot {}_{\text{SEP}}$ represent average December and September prices, and if $P \cdot {}_{\text{DEC}} > P \cdot {}_{\text{NOV}} > P \cdot {}_{\text{OCT}} > P \cdot {}_{\text{SEP}}$, then season equals $400 \log (P \cdot {}_{\text{DEC}}/P \cdot {}_{\text{SEP}})$, if $P \cdot {}_{\text{DEC}}$ and $P \cdot {}_{\text{SEP}}$ are the maximizing pair. Months are indicated in table 1.

III. Variables from regressions of price on stocks and income

For each commodity, regress via ordinary least squares:

$$\log \left(\frac{\text{PSK}}{\text{WPI}}\right)_t = a_0 + a_1 \log (\text{QSK})_t + a_2 \log \left(\frac{\text{GNI}}{\text{CPI}}\right)_t + u_t, \ 1959\text{–}71,$$

where

$\quad$ QSK = peak-month stocks
$\quad$ PSK = U.S. nominal spot (monthly) price
$\quad$ GNI = U.S. gross national income. *Statistical Abstract*
$\quad$ WPI = U.S. wholesale price index. *Statistical Abstract*
$\quad$ CPI = U.S. consumer price index. *Statistical Abstract*.

DW. Durbin-Watson coefficient.
EPQ. $\hat{a}_1$.
EPY. $\hat{a}_2$.
ERR. Standard error of regression × 100 (i.e., expressed as a percentage coefficient of variation).
QRSK. $|\hat{a}_1|$ × coefficient of variation across years of QSK.
RSQ. Coefficient of determination (R^2).
STDERR.[9] ERR × $[\text{DW}(1 - 0.25\text{DW})]^{1/2}$.

---

[9] The indicated adjustment is given as follows:

Let

$$u_t = v_t + \rho u_{t-1}, \ Eu_t v_\tau = 0, \ t \neq \tau, \ Ev_t^2 = \sigma^2.$$

Then

$$\text{var } u_t = E(v_t^2 + 2\rho v_t u_{t-1} + \rho^2 u_{t-1}^2) - \rho^2 (Eu_{t-1})^2,$$

$$\text{var } u_t = \sigma^2/(1 - \rho^2). \tag{A1}$$

Since

$$\text{DW} \equiv \sum (u_{t+1} - u_t)^2 / \sum u_t^2,$$

$$E(\text{DW}) = 2[1 - E(\sum u_{t+1} u_t / \sum u_t^2)].$$

Hence

$$E(\text{DW}) = 2(1 - \rho). \tag{A2}$$

Substitution of (A2) into (A1) implies the indicated formula.

References

Arrow, Kenneth J. *Essays in the Theory of Risk Bearing.* Chicago: Markham, 1971.
———. "Vertical Integration and Communication." *Bell J. Econ.* 6 (Spring 1975): 173–83.
Bresciani-Turroni, C. "L'Influence de la speculation sur les fluctuations des prix du coton." *L'Egypte contemporaine* 22 (March 1931): 308–42.
Cramèr, Harald. *Mathematical Methods of Statistics.* Princeton, N.J.: Princeton Univ. Press, 1946.
Demsetz, Harold. "The Cost of Transacting." *Q.J.E.* 82 (February 1968): 33–53.
Dusak, Katherine. "Futures Trading and Investor Returns: An Investigation of Commodity Market Risk Premiums." *J.P.E.* 81, no. 6 (November/December 1973): 1387–1406.
Higinbotham, Harlow N. "The Demand for Hedging in Grain Futures Markets." Ph.D. dissertation, Univ. Chicago, 1976.
Houthakker, H. S. "The Scope and Limits of Futures Trading." In *The Allocation of Economic Resources*, edited by Moses Abromovitz et al. Stanford, Calif.: Stanford Univ. Press, 1959.
Marshall, Alfred. *Industry and Trade.* 3d ed. London: Macmillan, 1920.
Telser, Lester G. "Safety First and Hedging." *Rev. Econ. Studies* 23 (December 1955): 1–16.
———. "Futures Trading and the Storage of Cotton and Wheat." *J.P.E.* 66, no. 3 (June 1958): 233–55.
———. "A Theory of Speculation Relating Profitability and Stability." *Rev. Econ. and Statis.* 41 (August 1959): 295–301.
———. "The Supply of Speculative Services in Wheat, Corn, and Soybeans." *Food Res. Inst. Studies* 7, suppl. (1967): 131–76.
———. *Economic Theory and the Core.* Chicago: Univ. Chicago Press, forthcoming.
Working, Holbrook. "Theory of the Inverse Carrying Charge in Futures Markets." *J. Farm Econ.* 30 (February 1948): 1–28.
———. "Futures Trading and Hedging." *A.E.R.* 43 (June 1953): 314–43.
———. "New Concepts concerning Futures Markets and Prices." *A.E.R.* 52 (June 1962): 431–59.
———. "Toward a Theory concerning Floor Trading on Commodity Exchanges." *Food Res. Inst. Studies* 7, suppl. (1967): 5–48.

[16]

Life in the Pits: Competitive Market Making and Inventory Control

Steven Manaster
University of Utah

Steven C. Mann
Texas Christian University

We use futures transaction data to investigate cross-sectional relationships between market-maker inventory positions and trade activity. The investigation documents strongly that traders control inventory throughout the trading day. Despite this evidence of inventory management, typical inventory control models are contradicted by our data. These inventory models predict that market-maker reservation prices are negatively influenced by inventory. Surprisingly, our evidence shows, as a strong and consistent empirical regularity, that correlations between inventory and reservation prices are positive. We interpret the evidence as consistent with active position taking by futures market floor traders.

We thank Chester Spatt (the editor), two anonymous referees, Jeff Coles, Avner Kalay, Ron Lease, Peter Locke, Uri Loewenstein, Fallaw Sowell, Elizabeth Tashjian, Jaime Zender, and participants at the 1993 Western Finance Association meetings, the 1994 UCLA/USC/NYSE Microstructure Conference, the 1994 Chicago Board of Trade Fall Research Seminar, the 1995 SWFA meetings, and seminar participants at the University of Utah, Texas Christian University, Indiana, Virginia Tech, and New Hampshire for helpful discussions and comments. We thank Zhiming Zhang for adding to our understanding of the Brownian bridge process. Appropriately, the authors retain sole responsibility for any errors. We thank Ron Hobson, Jonathan Smith, Hans Dutt, and Jay Huhman of the Commodity Futures Trading Commission for assistance in the provision of the data, and the Utah Supercomputing Institute (particularly Rich Reynolds) for technical support. Steven C. Mann acknowledges financial support from the Marriner S. Eccles Foundation and the Charles Tandy American Enterprise Center. Address correspondence to Steven C. Mann, M. J. Neeley School of Business, Texas Christian University, P.O. Box 32868, Fort Worth, TX 76129.

Two ideas dominate the theoretical market microstructure literature: inventory control[1] and adverse selection.[2] Inventory control models assume that market makers face exogenous demands to buy and sell. These market makers earn profits by selling at the ask price and buying at the bid price. The risk associated with this profitable trading is inventory risk. The models predict that market makers will manage risk and control inventory levels by adjusting bid and ask prices. When inventory is greater (less) than desired, prices are reduced (increased) to motivate sales (purchases). Adverse selection models analyze trading environments populated by agents with differential information. The models typically assume that market-maker inventory has no impact on prices in order to facilitate analysis of issues such as the information revealed by order flow.

This article uses detailed futures audit trail transaction data to provide evidence on cross-sectional inventory behavior and relationships between inventory and prices. The evidence shows that neither the adverse selection models nor the inventory control models provide an accurate description of market-maker behavior.

With respect to the inventory control literature, we find that market makers manage the levels of their inventories, but the predictions regarding price and inventory together are strongly contradicted in our data. For example, we find that when dealers hold positive inventory, they tend to become net sellers, consistent with inventory control theory. However, they tend to sell at higher prices, not lower prices, in direct contradiction of traditional inventory control theories.

With respect to adverse selection, its principal conclusion that price responds to the information content of order flow is verified empirically in our data. However, some simplifying assumptions employed to develop that conclusion are contradicted in our experiments. Our observation that market makers attempt to control their inventory levels contradicts the assumption of *inventory neutrality* implicit in most adverse selection models.[3] We use the term inventory neutrality to describe market-maker behavior that is impervious to inventory levels [as in Admati and Pfleiderer (1988) and Kyle (1985)]. Inventory neutrality is a strong assumption, requiring risk-neutral utility for the market

---

[1] Inventory control articles include Amihud and Mendelson (1980), Biais (1993), Demsetz (1968), Garman (1976), Stoll (1976), Ho and Macris (1985), Ho and Stoll (1980, 1981, 1983), Laux (1995), Mildenstein and Schleef (1983), O'Hara and Oldfield (1986), and Zabel (1981).

[2] Some examples of adverse selection models include Copeland and Galai (1983), Kyle (1985), Glosten and Milgrom (1985), Admati and Pfleiderer (1988, 1989), Foster and Viswanathan (1990), and Benveniste, Marcus, and Wilhelm (1992).

[3] Work such as Subrahmanyam (1991) suggests that the primary insights of the adverse selection literature may not require inventory neutrality.

makers, zero inventory carrying costs, and either no constraints on wealth or zero costs for default.

Interestingly, empirical attempts to contradict the assumption of inventory neutrality through examination of the time-series behavior of prices or of market-maker inventories are likely to be inconclusive. Some inventory neutral models, such as Kyle (1985), suggest time series for inventory and prices that are similar to predictions of inventory control models.[4] Fortunately, cross-sectional tests are available to resolve the ambiguity, and our examination of the cross-sectional relationship between inventory positions and trade activity provides convincing evidence of inventory management. At a typical point in time, traders with long positions are the most active sellers, while traders with short positions are the most active buyers.

Additional price evidence contradicts the inventory neutral paradigm. We find that the price change in response to customer order flow (market depth) varies, conditioned on market-maker inventory levels. Inventory neutrality is inconsistent with market depth that varies with inventory.

Our empirical findings suggest avenues for future modeling design. From our investigation we infer that market makers have informational advantages that enable them to adjust inventory in anticipation of favorable price movements. Thus, this article's evidence provides support for the recent articles by Madhavan and Smidt (1993) and Spiegel and Subrahmanyam (1995), in which market makers have more information than "noise" or liquidity traders, but face adverse selection from traders with access to finer information partitions.

The rest of the article is organized as follows. Section 1 describes the data. Section 2 provides analysis of the time-series and cross-sectional behavior of trader inventory. Our investigation of the relationship between individual trader inventory and prices is presented in Section 3. Section 4 examines relationships between characteristics of aggregate pit inventory and market liquidity. Section 5 provides a concluding comment.

---

[4] Kyle's dealer inventory can be shown to conform to the nonstandard Brownian bridge process

$$dI(t) = -\left[\frac{v - p_0}{(1-t)\lambda} + \frac{I(t)}{1-t}\right]dt - dU(t),$$

where net "noise" trades $dU(t) \sim N(0, \sigma_t^2)$; $\lambda > 0$ is the price response per unit net order flow; $I(t)$ is dealer inventory at the start of instant t ($0 < t < 1$); and $\tilde{v}$, the ex post liquidation value of the asset, is normally distributed with mean p_0. The informed trader observes v, the realization of $\tilde{v}$. For $v = p_0$ inventory follows a standard Brownian bridge process, where if $I(0) = 0$, then $I(1) = 0$ with probability one. Although Kyle's model is inventory neutral the time series for inventory is in some cases indistinguishable from the predictions of inventory control models.

1. Data

The CFTC provided audit trail transaction records for all Chicago Mercantile Exchange (CME) futures trades for the first half of 1992. This data set consists of more than 12 million records that detail complete trade history for more than 2,000 individual floor traders in 16 different commodity pits. To protect trader privacy, the CFTC mapped each trader's audit trail identification (exchange badge numbers) to a randomly selected number unique to each trader. Therefore, the data provides a 6-month history of trade activity for each trader, but codes each trader's badge number.[5] Besides the audit trail data, we also use Time and Sales data that records all price changes for the contracts and period represented in the sample.

The audit data records each trade twice, once for each party to each trade. The trade is timed to the nearest minute. Traders report time in 15-minute brackets. An exchange algorithm known as computerized trade reconstruction (CTR) uses each trader's independently reported sequence of trades in conjunction with the time and sales data to time each trade to a specific minute of the bracket. While some timing errors are likely, the timing of the trade is a critical element in the use of the audit trail data in internal (exchange) and external (CFTC enforcement) investigations of legal trading practices.

In addition to trade time, the audit trail record details price, quantity, the contract, and the traders' identification. Unique to this data, the record also specifies the trade direction (whether the trade was a buy or a sell) and a classification of the customer types for both sides of the trade. There are four customer type indicators (CTI), labeled 1 through 4. The CTI 1 trades are market-making trades for personal accounts, and account for 46.6% of total CME volume for the period. CTI 2 trades (6.8% of volume) are trades executed for the account of the trader's clearing member. CTI 3 trades (6.2% of volume) are trades executed for the account of any other exchange member.[6] CTI 4 trades are the trades of outside customers, and account for 40.4% of volume. For example, if a commercial clearing member's floor trader executes a trade for the firm, it will be a CTI 2 trade, but trades for any other member's account will be CTI 3 trades. The most frequent CTI combination is a customer order (CTI 4) filled by a market maker (CTI 1), or local.[7]

---

[5] Fishman and Longstaff (1992) use a smaller sample of audit trail data (15 days for one pit at the Chicago Board of Trade) in their investigation of dual trading.

[6] Only a subset of exchange members are also members of the exchange clearinghouse. Floor traders that are not clearing members must maintain margin accounts with their clearing member in order to clear trades.

[7] The term "local" is futures market jargon for "professional market maker." While overall local

Competitive Market Making and Inventory Control

2. Inventory Management

2.1 Tracking inventory changes

The audit data times trades to the nearest minute. We therefore track each local's (CTI 1) inventory changes minute by minute. For each commodity, we define each trader's change in inventory as the difference between the number of contracts of all delivery months bought and sold during the minute. This definition treats all contract delivery months as essentially the same security, as price movements on different delivery months are strongly correlated.

Tracking intraday inventory changes is straightforward. However, tracking inventory over longer periods is problematic. About 6.2% of total CME volume for the period is listed as CTI 3 trade, or trades executed on behalf of other members other than the trader's clearing member. The data does not identify the other member, so that if some proportion of CTI 3 volume is executed on behalf of the account of market makers, observed inventory changes may not provide a complete history.[8] The CME's mutual offset system with SIMEX (Singapore) also poses potential problems, as traders can unwind positions on SIMEX overnight. SIMEX trades are not included in the audit trail data. Due to CTI 3 trades, SIMEX, and potential data errors, trader inventory positions that we calculate at the end of that day may not precisely correspond to actual opening positions for the next trading day. If traders pervasively carry inventory overnight, then the audit data is not well suited for tracking inventory changes over periods longer than a day. For the empirical analysis we assume that each trader begins each day with zero inventory.

There is strong anecdotal support for the conjecture that traders rarely take positions home with them, preferring to end the day with zero inventory, or a "sleeping position."[9] We provide evidence regarding the propensity of traders to close out positions by the end of the day by examining daily net inventory changes. Figure 1 shows the

---

volume is higher than customer volume, locals are more likely to trade with customers than each other. Concurrently, customers are much more likely to trade with a local than another customer. Overall, 48.7% of total volume in our sample represents customers trading against locals.

[8] Our conversations with floor traders lead us to believe that delta hedging by futures options traders accounts for a large part of CTI 3 volume. The conversations indicated that the CTI 3 order flow is unidirectional, as the futures floor traders do not use the futures options to hedge.

[9] Kolb (1991) categorizes floor traders as either scalpers, day traders, or position traders. Kolb (p. 158) writes, "The overwhelming majority of speculators are either scalpers or day traders, which indicates just how risky it can be to take a position home overnight." Trader studies by Silber (1984) and Working (1967) confirm this "market lore." Working provides empirical evidence on the distribution of floor trader inventory positions, and reports that 44% carried no overnight inventory, another 23% carry less than 10% of their daily volume home for either night, and of the remaining 33%, a "substantial" number carried no more than 1 contract home on either night. Trader reluctance to carry positions overnight is influenced by margin funding costs.

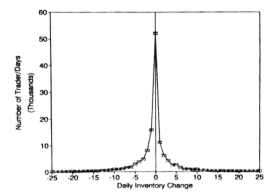

Figure 1
Trader daily inventory changes
Inventory changes are standardized across pits by dividing the ending number of contracts by the pit median trade size. The figure represents 135,015 trades/day, except for 1,528 (1.13%) inventory changes less than −25 and 1,456 (1.07%) inventory changes greater than 25.

frequency distribution of the calculated daily inventory changes. To facilitate comparison across pits, changes are scaled by the median trade size for each pit.[10] Well over half the 135,015 daily trader inventory changes are less than or equal in size to one median trade. For raw (nonscaled) inventory changes, more than 50% of daily changes were no more than two contracts.

The evidence shows that daily inventory changes are concentrated about zero. If traders are starting the day flat, they are generally ending the day flat. Of the observed nonzero daily inventory changes, many are likely due to CTI 3 trades, errors, and/or pending SIMEX offsets. Based on the foregoing observations we believe that our procedure of assuming that all traders begin the day with a zero inventory position provides the most accurate estimate of market-maker inventory that is attainable with the available data.

2.2 Inventory management over time

Consider a simple model of minute-by-minute inventory time-series behavior consistent with inventory control models:

$$\Delta I_t = \alpha + (\rho - 1)I_t + \epsilon_t. \tag{1}$$

---

[10] In our sample, the median trade is one contract for the S&P 500 index, hogs, pork bellies, lumber, and feeder cattle. The median trade is two contracts for the live cattle, Swiss franc, pound, S&P Midcap 400, and the Canadian and Australian dollar. Three contracts is the median trade for the duetschemark, yen, and the Nikkei index. Interest rate contracts trade in higher quantity, as median trades are four contracts for T-bills, 10 contracts for LIBOR, and 15 contracts for Eurodollars.

Competitive Market Making and Inventory Control

We define I_t as inventory at the start of minute t, and define ΔI_t as the net inventory change during the minute t. Inventory control implies that market makers adjust inventory toward a desired level, inducing mean reversion. A method of testing for inventory control is to examine whether a given inventory series follows a random walk. If $\rho = 1$, then inventory is a random walk; mean reversion predicts that $\rho < 1$.

A random walk inventory hypothesis seems to be an easy target. Stoll (1976) presents evidence of NASDAQ net daily inventory changes consistent with mean reverting inventory. However, other than Stoll's groundbreaking article, random walk inventory has been a remarkably stalwart "straw man." Hasbrouck (1988), proxying inventory with estimated order flow, finds evidence of inventory mean reversion for only the lowest decile NYSE stocks. Madhavan and Smidt (1993) formally test specialist inventory for a unit root, but reject the random walk for less than half the 16 stocks in their sample. Hasbrouck and Sofianos (1993) examine inventory autocorrelations for a sample of 144 NYSE stocks and estimate that inventory adjustment takes place at a "very slow rate."

We directly estimate Equation (1) for daily inventory time-series of individual traders. Table 1 reports summary statistics on the estimates of $\hat{\rho}$ for all daily individual inventory series for which a trader traded at least 20 times. In marked contrast to evidence from equity markets, floor trader inventory exhibits strong mean reversion over a short time horizon. Hasbrouck and Sofianos (1993) and Madhavan and Smidt (1993) report that it takes a typical equity specialist a matter of weeks to reduce an inventory imbalance by 50%. Table 1 shows that the median S&P 500 index trader reduces inventory by almost 50% in the next trade![11] Table 1 also reports the percentage of daily series that Phillips–Perron [Perron (1988)] tests reject the null hypothesis that $\rho = 1$.[12] For the S&P 500 index pit, 79.6% of the Phillips-Perron statistics reject the random walk hypothesis at the 5% level. Floor trader inventory does not follow a random walk, but instead exhibits very rapid mean reversion.

---

[11] Our construction of inventory, assuming that traders start flat with zero inventory, has potential impact on the results reported in Table 1. If any traders begin trade with nonzero inventory, then our measured inventory deviates from true inventory by a constant for each day of trading. However, as each regression summarized in Table 1 represents one day of trading, the effect is that of adding a constant to inventory, which has no impact on the slope coefficient. The impact will be reflected in the regression intercept. It may be more precise to state that for the median S&P 500 trader, the deviation of absolute inventory from desired inventory is reduced by 50% in one trade.

[12] The Phillips–Perron test reported ($Z(t_\alpha^*)$), is used in conjunction with the Newey and West (1987) adjustment procedure with three lags.

Table 1
Floor trader inventory time-series: estimates of the model $\Delta I_t = \alpha + (\rho - 1)I_t + \epsilon_t$

Pit	Number of series	Median number of trades	Median $\hat{\rho}$	Percentage of tests rejecting $\rho = 1$
S&P 500 index	20,490	49	0.51	79.5
Eurodollars	10,518	32	0.55	62.5
Deutschemark	7,681	48	0.43	85.5
Swiss franc	4,945	47	0.54	75.9
Yen	3,656	46	0.48	83.8
Live cattle	3,402	41	0.70	50.6
Pound sterling	2,869	49	0.51	79.9
Live hogs	2,126	40	0.70	43.6
Pork bellies	2,060	38	0.60	58.8
Canadian dollar	972	37	0.64	55.1
Feeder cattle	914	36	0.75	31.6
T-bills	584	26	0.63	41.1
Lumber	455	31	0.74	27.7
Nikkei index	179	27	0.55	53.1
LIBOR	147	23	0.70	17.7
S&P Midcap 400	22	23	0.51	54.5
Australian dollar	14	24	0.78	14.3

The table summarizes the results of estimating the model $\Delta I_t = \alpha + (\rho - 1)I_t + \epsilon_t$ (where I_t is trader inventory at the start of minute t and ΔI_t is the inventory change during minute t), for all trader daily inventory series with at least 20 trade/minutes (minutes with at least one trade). The last column reports the percentage of Phillips–Perron [Perron (1988)] unit root tests ($Z(\hat{\rho})$) that reject the null that $\rho = 1$ at the 5% level. The Phillips–Perron tests incorporate the Newey and West (1987) modification procedure with three lags.

2.3 Inventory management in the cross section

Competitive dealer models [e.g., Biais (1993), Ho and Macris (1985), Ho and Stoll (1983), and Laux (1995)] make strong predictions about the cross-sectional relationship between relative inventory positions of market makers and contemporaneous trade activity. In competitive dealer models, the trader with the longest inventory position is the most likely to sell, and the shortest trader is the most likely to buy. This prediction has been untested due to lack of cross-sectional trader inventory data. The futures audit data provides a unique opportunity to investigate cross-sectional inventory behavior.

Table 2 examines the contemporaneous relation between trades and inventory for all 1-minute periods with reasonable activity. We report Spearman rank correlations between trader inventory (I_{it}) rank (at the start of the minute) and subsequent inventory change (ΔI_{it}) rank for all minutes in which at least 10 locals traded for personal account (five locals for the lower volume pits).[13] Table 2 reports the number of valid minutes for each pit (e.g., 41,734 for the S&P 500), the median rank correlation, and the percent of negative correlations. For example, 85.6% of the correlations between start-of-minute inventory

---

[13] We report the nonparametric Spearman rank correlation rather than the more familiar Pearson statistic due to the Spearman statistics' superior small sample properties with potentially nonnormal data.

Competitive Market Making and Inventory Control

Table 2
Cross-sectional inventory management: Spearman rank correlations (r_s)

Pit	Number of minutes	Percent of $r_s < 0$	Median r_s	Median number of observations	% negative with p-value < 0.25	% positive with p-value < .025
Panel A: Spearman rank correlation statistics calculated for all minutes that at least 10 locals traded for personal account						
S&P 500 index	41,734	85.6	−0.26	25	30.4	0.3
Eurodollars	19,508	83.5	−0.26	19	27.7	0.5
Deutschemark	19,421	84.5	−0.32	15	27.4	0.4
Swiss franc	10,709	82.0	−0.31	13	23.1	0.4
Live cattle	7,884	71.8	−0.18	13	12.9	0.9
Yen	5,948	83.1	−0.33	12	25.4	0.5
Pound sterling	3,069	79.8	−0.31	11	24.2	0.8
Pork bellies	2,466	76.5	−0.22	12	18.8	0.9
Live hogs	2,359	67.1	−0.15	12	14.3	1.5
Panel B: Due to lower trading volume, we report statistics for the following pits based on all minutes that at least 5 locals traded for personal account						
Feeder cattle	2,275	59.6	−0.13	6	11.6	2.4
Canadian dollar	2,187	69.3	−0.30	5	13.9	1.2
T-bills	1,785	59.0	−0.11	6	15.9	3.2
Lumber	1,510	63.5	−0.21	6	15.8	2.0
LIBOR	280	59.4	−0.06	6	18.2	2.0
Nikkei index	209	74.6	−0.39	5	25.4	1.7
S&P Midcap 400	43	70.5	−0.34	5	13.6	2.3

The Spearman correlations (r_s) are cross-sectional correlations of trader inventory (I_{it}) ranks at the start of each minute and subsequent trader inventory change (during the minute) (ΔI_{it}) ranks. P-values come from treating the statistic calculated as $r_s\sqrt{n-2}/\sqrt{1-(r_s)^2}$ as coming from a t-distribution with $n-2$ degrees of freedom.

and subsequent trade are negative for the S&P 500 pit, and the median correlation is −0.26. For the CME as a whole, generally 70–80% of active trading minutes have negative correlations.

The last two columns of Table 2 report the proportion of negative and positive rank correlation estimates (transformed into t-statistics) that are classically significant at the two-sided 5% level. For the S&P 500 pit, 30.4% of the estimated correlations are negative and significant, while 0.3% are positive and significant.

The evidence reported in Table 2 provides much support for competitive dealer models. As the models predict, the most active sellers are traders with long positions, and the most active buyers are the traders with shorter inventory positions.

3. Individual Inventory and Relative Trade Prices

Inventory control models suggest that trades increasing the absolute level of excess dealer inventory are made on terms that are favorable to the dealer. Favorable terms compensate dealers for the increased cost and/or risk exposure associated with increases in absolute inventory. Conversely, the models suggest that trades reducing dealer inventory are made on terms that are unfavorable to dealers.

Evidence presented in Section 2 shows that futures floor traders manage their inventory continually throughout each trading day. Does the desire to manage inventory impact trade performance? If bid and ask prices never changed, traders accumulating positive inventory due to buying at the bid would be able to wait until they could sell at the ask, thus earning the bid-ask spread while managing inventory costlessly. But prices do change. Consider a trader buying at the bid one moment and attempting to sell at the ask the next moment. Frequently the market ask has changed between the moment of purchase and the moment of attempted sale. Indeed, as adverse selection models show, the price change is likely to be correlated with the direction of customer order flow and therefore have a negative expected impact on the trader's inventory. However, even if order flow has no information content, pure uncertainty about the income from this market-making round trip is "costly" to a risk-averse market maker.

In fact, most futures markets exhibit considerable short-term volatility, and market makers buy at varying prices in brief intervals. The existence of stable bid and ask prices seems unlikely given rapid price movement in a competitive pit trading environment. Indeed, as Stoll (1992, p. 76) writes, "In pit trading, as on futures markets, many bilateral negotiations occur simultaneously, and slightly different prices may be agreed upon at the same time."

Table 3 provides evidence on short-term variation in market-maker purchase prices for each pit's most active daily contract (usually the nearby). The table reports distributional percentiles for the number of different buy prices for CTI 1 (personal account) trades during 1-, 5-, and 15-minute intervals. For example, Table 3 shows that market makers buy the most active S&P 500 contract at eight different prices in the median 5-minute interval. As the tick is $25 for the S&P 500 contract, the price range of market-maker purchases is at least $175 during the median 5-minute period.[14]

Traders have the opportunity to transact at a variety of prices during short time frames. In a typical period, some floor traders buy contracts at relatively low prices and some buy at relatively high prices. Given a decision to buy, executing the trade at the lowest price available is clearly desirable. We introduce trade execution skill as a measure designed to indicate an ability to transact at "desirable prices."

---

[14] While $175 is the minimum price range for eight different prices with a $25 minimum price variation (tick), larger price ranges are possible if some ticks are skipped. Market-maker sell-price variability, not reported, is virtually identical to buy-price variability.

Competitive Market Making and Inventory Control

Table 3
Price variability: number of different prices for local (CTI 1) buy trades (purchases)

Pit	1-minute intervals			5-minute intervals			15-minute intervals		
	Med	Q3	P90	Q1	Med	Q3	Q1	Med	Q3
S&P 500 index	1	2	3	6	8	10	10	14	18
Eurodollars	1	1	2	1	2	2	2	2	3
Deutschemark	1	2	3	3	5	6	6	8	11
Swiss franc	1	2	3	3	5	7	6	9	13
Yen	1	2	2	2	4	5	4	6	10
Pound	1	2	2	3	4	6	6	8	12
Live cattle	1	1	2	2	3	4	4	6	8
Hogs	1	1	2	2	2	3	3	5	6
Canadian dollar	1	1	2	1	2	2	2	3	4
Pork bellies	1	1	2	2	3	4	4	6	8
Feeder cattle	1	1	2	1	1	2	2	3	4
90-day T-bills	1	1	1	1	1	1	1	1	2
Lumber	1	1	1	1	2	2	2	3	5
LIBOR	1	1	1	1	1	1	1	1	1
S&P 400 Midcap	1	1	1	1	1	1	1	1	2
Australian dollar	1	1	1	1	1	1	1	1	2

The number of different prices for local buy trades per period for the daily most active contract, Chicago Mercantile Exchange, 1/1/92–6/30/92.
Q1 = lower quartile, Q3 = upper quartile, Med = median.
For 1-minute intervals the lower quartile is not reported and is replaced by the 90th percentile.
Price variability for local sell trades is virtually identical.

We define execution skill for buy trades (purchases) as

$$\pi_{ti}^b = \bar{p}_\tau^b - p_{ti}^b, \qquad (2)$$

where $\bar{p}_\tau^b$ is the volume-weighted mean buy price for all floor trader personal account trades during interval τ, and p_{ti}^b is trader i's buy price paid during minute t where $t \in \tau$.[15] We define execution skill for sales as

$$\pi_{ti}^s = p_{ti}^s - \bar{p}_\tau^s. \qquad (3)$$

Therefore, trading skill is measured for each minute of buying and each minute of selling by comparing the trader's price with the benchmark buy or sell price. Benchmark prices are computed for 5-minute intervals, so that a 15-minute bracket has three 5-minute local buy-price benchmarks and three local sell-price benchmarks.

Execution skill associates good trades with positive execution. Positive selling execution shows that a trader sells at a higher price than the average CTI 1 (market maker) sales price, and positive buy execution represents a purchase at a lower price than the average CTI 1 purchase.

---

[15] If a trader buys the same contract more than once during a minute, the trader's volume-weighted mean price for the minute is used. We report results using 5-minute intervals. Mann (1994) provides evidence using both 1- and 5-minute intervals for the above specification of trading skill as well as alternative skill measures.

Inventory control models imply that relative trade execution will be affected by relative inventory. Models such as Biais (1993), Ho and Macris (1985), Ho and Stoll (1983), and Laux (1995), assuming homogeneous information and homogeneous risk aversion, predict that reservation prices of traders are negatively correlated with inventory. In theory, traders offer prices that discourage inventory increasing trades and encourage trades that reduce inventory exposure. Inventory's predicted impact on trade execution depends on the trade direction. Inventory models suggest that traders with relatively long positions will have good buy execution (charging a premium to increase inventory), but poor sell execution (making a concession to reduce inventory). Conversely, traders with relatively short positions are predicted to have good sell execution, but poor buy execution. We label this predicted trader behavior "price concessions."

Relative inventory is determined by subtracting the average inventory position of the traders in the pit ($\bar{I}_{t,pit}$) from each trader's inventory position ($I_{t,i}$) for the beginning of each minute.[16] As inventory's predicted effects on trade execution depend on the trade direction, we define orthogonal vectors for each trader's relative inventory, I^B (for buys) and I^S (for sells), specified as

$$I^B_{ti} = I_{ti} - \bar{I}_{t,pit} \quad \text{for buy trades of trader } i \text{ at time } t,$$
$$= 0 \quad \text{for sell trades of trader } i \text{ at time } t, \quad (4)$$

and similarly,

$$I^S_{ti} = I_{ti} - \bar{I}_{t,pit} \quad \text{for sell trades of trader } i \text{ at time } t,$$
$$= 0 \quad \text{for buy trades of trader } i \text{ at time } t, \quad (5)$$

so that the elements of each vector are either relative inventory or zero. To test for inventory effects on trade execution, the following model is estimated once for each trader for the entire sample period:

$$\pi_{ti} = \alpha + \beta(I^B_{ti} - I^S_{ti}) + \epsilon_t, \quad (6)$$

where π_{ti} is execution skill (either buy or sell), α is a constant, and ϵ_t is an error term. The term β measures the effect of relative inventory on subsequent relative trade prices. If traders make price concessions, then we expect β to be positive. Table 4 reports summaries for each

---

[16] The average inventory position for traders in the pit for a minute is defined as the aggregate pit inventory (the summed current inventory of all traders) divided by the number of traders that have inventory positions. A trader is defined as having an inventory position for a minute if the trader executes personal account trades in the pit prior to or inclusive of each minute. If the pit is net long 400 contracts, and 100 traders have positions, then the average position is four contracts. A trader short three contracts at that time has defined relative inventory of negative seven contracts (short seven contracts).

Competitive Market Making and Inventory Control

pit of regression estimates of Equation (6) for each trader with at least 126 trades over the 6-month (126 day) sample period.

Table 4 provides little evidence that traders make price concessions. Roughly 30% of the regressions have an estimated $\hat{\beta}$ that is positive, as suggested by inventory models. Overall, only 2% or 3% of the estimates are positive and significant by classical standards (two-sided 5% level). On the other hand, about two-thirds of the β estimates are negative, and overall, about 20% of the estimates are negative and significant.

Although individual $\hat{\beta}$s range widely, taken as a whole, inventory's impact on execution skill appears to be contrary to the implications of inventory models. There is little evidence that traders make price concessions for trades reducing absolute inventory, or extract better prices for trades that increase inventory exposure. In fact, most traders appear to obtain better prices for trades that decrease absolute inventory. Thus, while long traders are the most active sellers, the selling activity is not due to price concessions, as they seem to sell at higher, not lower, prices.

We directly compare contemporaneous trade prices of short and long traders in Table 5, classifying traders as either short or long based on existing inventory at the start of each trade minute. We define buy price differences for 5-minute intervals as the mean purchase price secured by buying long traders ($\bar{p}_L^b$) less the mean purchase price secured by buying short traders ($\bar{p}_S^b$). Selling price differences are also calculated for each interval by subtracting the mean sell price obtained by short traders from the mean sell price obtained by long traders. Inventory control models, predicting negative correlations between reservation prices and inventory, imply that $\bar{p}_L - \bar{p}_S < 0$, both for buying and selling price differences.[17]

Table 5 summarizes price differences by pit.[18] The table reports the median of buy- and sell-price differences for each pit ($\bar{p}_L - \bar{p}_S$), a t-statistic testing a mean zero null hypothesis, and the percent positive and negative (some price differences are zero). For example, the median price difference for the S&P 500 pit is $3.25, the mean is reliably positive ($t = 28.7$), and 60.2% of the calculated price differences are positive. For all 12 pits with valid observations, the median price difference is positive. The mean price difference is significantly positive

---

[17] To conserve space we combine buying and selling price differences in Table 5. The distributions of buying and selling price differences are very similar. See Mann (1994).

[18] Only 5-minute intervals with at least five short traders and five long traders buying for personal account are included. Intervals with no local personal account price variation (e.g., all locals buy at the same price for the entire period) are dropped. Analogous criteria are used to report sell-price differences.

Table 4
Inventory and trade execution: distribution of the inventory coefficient $\hat{\beta}$

Pit	Number of traders	Percent of $\hat{\beta} \geq 0$	Percent of $t(\hat{\beta}) \geq 1.96$	Percent of $t(\hat{\beta}) \leq -1.96$	Median number of observations for each regression	t-statistic for the mean of all regression t-statistics
S&P 500 index	370	30	2	20	3,272	-10.20
Eurodollars	329	34	3	14	1,609	-7.82
Deutschemark	145	36	3	17	2,929	-4.65
Live cattle	116	30	2	20	924	-5.01
Swiss franc	100	32	3	25	1,969	-6.02
Yen	71	27	0	27	2,816	-4.57
Live hogs	65	31	3	23	755	-3.36
Pound	52	27	4	12	3,336	-2.65
Pork bellies	52	23	6	27	1,641	-4.45
Lumber	25	36	4	4	810	-1.62
T-bills	22	55	4	14	1,610	-0.38
Canadian dollar	21	33	0	57	2,493	-3.91
Feeder cattle	23	43	0	13	1,115	-1.08
LIBOR	13	69	8	0	1,001	1.23
Australian dollar	2	0	0	0	1,286	-1.15
S&P Midcap 400	8	75	0	0	402	1.51

The table summarizes for each pit the results from estimating the following regression model for each trader with at least 126 trades over the sample period: $\pi_{it} = \alpha + \beta(I_{it}^B - I_{it}^S) + \epsilon_{it}$, where π_{it} is the execution skill for trader I for trade at time t, and the orthogonal vectors I^B and I^S represent trader I's relative inventory at time t; I_{it}^B is trader I's start-of-minute inventory less average pit start-of-minute inventory if the trade is a buy; $I_{it}^B = 0$ if the trade is a sell; I_{it}^S is the trader's start-of-minute inventory less average pit start-of-minute inventory if the trade is a sale; $I_{it}^S = 0$ if the trade is a buy.

The statistic $t(\hat{\beta})$ for each regression is the t-statistic associated with testing whether the parameter estimate $\hat{\beta}$ is significantly different from zero.

Competitive Market Making and Inventory Control

Table 5
Price differences for long versus short traders ($\bar{p}_L - \bar{p}_S$)

Pit	Number of intervals	Median price difference $\bar{p}_L - \bar{p}_S$	t-statistic for difference	Percent negative	Percent positive	Mean customer execution spread
S&P 500 index	19,479	$ 3.25	28.7	39.7	60.2	$ 4.33
Eurodollars	9,122	0.73	10.7	43.0	54.3	1.55
Deutschemark	12,558	0.93	10.5	44.3	55.4	3.30
Swiss franc	8,545	1.91	12.1	42.5	57.3	5.30
Yen	5,436	1.82	10.6	41.6	57.9	3.56
Live cattle	3,536	1.00	6.6	42.6	56.6	1.75
Pound sterling	3,629	1.83	3.2	44.6	55.1	4.44
Pork bellies	947	2.26	3.3	42.0	56.6	7.71
Live hogs	564	0.83	3.0	45.9	52.8	3.97
Canadian dollar	100	1.67	1.8	43.0	56.0	3.06
Feeder cattle	16	4.90	0.6	31.3	68.8	6.58
T-bills	8	5.68	0.7	37.5	62.5	3.62

Comparisons of contemporaneous (5-minute brackets) buy or sell prices obtained by traders with long (positive) or short (negative) inventory positions. Every minute, each active trader's mean buy and/or sell price is calculated. Price differences ($\bar{p}_L - \bar{p}_S$) for buy trades and sell trades for each interval are defined as the mean price secured by long traders ($\bar{p}_L$) less the mean price secured by short traders ($\bar{p}_S$). Each price difference compares either long trader buy prices to short trader buy prices or long trader sell prices to short trader sell prices. If traders with long positions trade at prices less than traders with short positions, the differences would be negative. Intervals without at least five long and five short traders with transactions are dropped. Each 5-minute interval may have two price differences, one for buys and one for sells, given enough trades by both long and short traders. Four pits had no intervals that satisfied the criteria.

for 9 of the 12 pits. Consistent with the results of Table 4, long traders are trading at higher prices than short traders. To provide a benchmark for the economic significance of the price difference, mean 5-minute customer execution spreads for the most active contract are also reported in Table 5. The customer execution spread is defined as the mean customer buy price less the mean customer sell price, and is a pure measure of the realized bid-ask spread.[19] Comparing the S&P 500 pit's mean execution spread ($4.33) to the median price difference ($3.25), it appears that long traders are trading at economically as well as statistically higher prices than short traders. Evidently, long traders obtain higher selling prices than contemporaneous traders with short positions, but they also pay more to purchase contracts.

Tables 4 and 5 show that long traders, while active sellers, buy and sell at high relative prices. Over time (Table 4), long traders have good skill at selling (selling higher than other traders) and poor skill at buying (paying a higher price to buy). At a particular point in time (Table 5), long traders sell and buy at higher prices than other traders. Conversely, short traders, while active buyers, buy and sell at low relative prices. These results are inconsistent with received inven-

---

[19] The execution spread is used by the CFTC (1989) and Chang and Locke (1993).

tory models. However, extant competitive dealer models assume both homogenous information and homogenous risk aversion. These assumptions probably do not hold in the trading pits. Development of a formal model incorporating heterogeneous risk aversion and information is beyond our scope. However, the results from Tables 4 and 5 do provide empirical guidance for future modeling efforts. To be consistent with our evidence future models must incorporate heterogeneous information among market makers. Differences in risk aversion alone might produce differences in reservation prices conditional on inventory, but differences in risk aversion alone will never cause market makers with long positions to have reservation prices greater than market makers with short positions. We conjecture that this empirical regularity can only be supported by a model that contains differential information among market makers.

4. Market Liquidity and Aggregate Pit Inventory

In this section we examine predicted relationships between characteristics of aggregate pit inventory and market liquidity characteristics, specifically spreads and depth.

4.1 Inventory dispersion and customer spreads

Biais (1993), Ho and Macris (1985), Ho and Stoll (1980, 1983), and Laux (1995) argue that competitive dealer inventory positions will not diverge substantially, as dealer price concessions act as an equilibrating mechanism for inventory. If inventory does diverge, the models imply that the market bid-ask spread will be reduced. According to the theory, the spread is squeezed as long traders reduce ask prices and short traders increase bids.

Besides potential inventory effects, trade volume and volatility may also affect the spread. Brock and Kleidon (1992) argue that spreads increase as volume (demand for liquidity) increases. Models of the spread from both the inventory control and asymmetric information literature imply that increased price volatility widens the spread. Measuring volume is straightforward. However, a wider spread will affect most price volatility estimates. Therefore, we employ the detail of the audit trail data to calculate a volatility measure that eliminates bid-ask bounce. For each 5-minute period, we compute one quantity weighted standard deviation for customer buy trade prices and one for customer sell trade prices. We define the volatility measure as the maximum of the customer buy-price or sell-price standard deviation. The maximum is used to avoid potential problems such as no customer trade on the buy side despite considerable activity on the sell side. This one-sided volatility measure eliminates bid-ask bounce by exclusively using either buy or sell prices for each 5-minute interval.

We examine the impact of inventory dispersion on the spread by estimating the following regression model:

$$Spread_t = \alpha + \beta_1 \sigma_t + \beta_2\, Volume_t + \beta_3\, Range(I^*)_t + \epsilon_t, \qquad (7)$$

where the dependent variable is the 5-minute customer execution spread (recall that the execution spread is the mean customer buy price less the mean customer sell price), *volume* is measured as contemporaneous total two-sided (buys and sells) customer volume, and σ_t is the bid-ask bounce-free measure of contemporaneous price volatility. To measure inventory dispersion, we define $Range(I^*)_t$ as an interfractile inventory range of trader inventory positions at the start of a 5-minute period. We calculate the range by ranking trader inventory positions at the start of each minute for all traders active in the commodity that day, before or inclusive of the minute. The inventory range is calculated as an interfractile range of the inventory positions at the start of the first minute of each 5-minute period, where the fractiles are varied depending upon the number of traders. For less than 20 traders, we use the interquintile range (80th less 20th percentile). For at least 20 but less than 100 traders, we use the interdecile range, and for 100 or more traders, we use the intervigintile range (95th less 5th percentile).

Table 6 reports estimates of Equation (7) for each pit. As predicted by all models, volatility is associated with wider spreads. Of 16 estimated coefficients on volatility, all are positive, and only one (Swiss franc) is not classically significant at the 1% level. Contemporaneous volume has a more ambiguous impact; loose interpretation suggests that increased volume is associated with wider spreads for high-volume pits, but reduced spreads in lower volume pits.

The evidence regarding the relationship between inventory ranges and realized spreads is difficult to interpret. The coefficients for inventory range should be negative if, as available theories predict, inventory dispersion narrows the spread. However, only three pits (Eurodollars, yen, and the S&P Midcap 400) have estimated inventory range coefficients that are negative and significant at a classical 5% level. The estimated inventory range coefficient is negative for only 8 of 16 regressions. Our interpretation is that inventory range does not appear to affect the spread in a manner consistent with available theory. However, based on the evidence we report, there is room for other interpretations. For example, if market-maker inventory is held in anticipation of favorable price movements [as described in Ho and Stoll (1981, Section 8)], then at a point in time locals may be content with their divergent inventories and have no incentives to narrow the

Table 6
Inventory dispersion and the spread

Pit	Number of observations	Intercept	Standard deviation of one-sided customer prices	Customer volume	Interfractile inventory range
S&P 500 index	10,325	−0.38	0.017	0.004	0.083
		(−0.5)	(4.8)	(6.3)	(2.2)
Eurodollars	8,034	1.40	0.023	0.000	−0.005
		(5.1)	(11.1)	(0.7)	(−3.1)
Deutschemark	9,946	0.98	0.050	0.001	−0.010
		(4.2)	(15.8)	(2.9)	(−1.5)
Live cattle	5,776	0.30	0.059	0.001	0.012
		(1.0)	(7.38)	(1.13)	(1.2)
Swiss franc	9,744	3.41	0.005	0.009	0.007
		(8.1)	(1.3)	(10.2)	(0.3)
Yen	9,460	2.62	0.041	0.000	−0.036
		(8.9)	(10.0)	(0.6)	(−2.5)
Live hogs	5,092	3.13	0.084	−0.003	−0.010
		(8.8)	(7.3)	(−2.4)	(−0.9)
Pound	9,226	1.94	0.075	−0.002	−0.036
		(4.9)	(17.5)	(−1.9)	(−1.5)
Pork bellies	4,854	4.79	0.089	0.010	0.030
		(7.6)	(6.6)	(2.4)	(0.8)
Lumber	2,466	9.86	0.224	−0.081	0.073
		(7.9)	(10.9)	(−2.7)	(0.6)
T-bills	2,213	2.81	0.145	−0.011	0.001
		(7.9)	(13.0)	(−3.9)	(0.1)
Canadian dollar	6,093	2.78	0.064	−0.009	0.013
		(14.2)	(8.2)	(−9.7)	(1.0)
Feeder cattle	2,983	3.77	0.213	−0.036	0.050
		(7.3)	(12.3)	(−4.4)	(1.7)
LIBOR	901	0.94	0.052	−0.003	−0.007
		(3.2)	(7.7)	(−2.1)	(−1.0)
Australian dollar	375	3.91	0.305	−0.093	−0.020
		(3.1)	(6.8)	(−2.9)	(−0.4)
S&P Midcap 400	908	7.63	0.098	−0.098	−0.322
		(5.0)	(3.7)	(−2.6)	(−2.9)

The table reports estimates of the model $S_t = \alpha + \beta_1 \hat{\sigma}_t + \beta_2 Volume_t + \beta_3 Range(I^*)_t + \epsilon_t$, where S_t is a 5-minute customer execution spread (mean customer buy price less mean customer sell price) for each day's most active contract, σ_t is contemporaneous one-sided customer price standard deviation, volume is aggregate (buy plus sell) customer volume, and $Range(I^*)_t$ is an interfractile range of trader inventory positions at the start of each 5-minute period (t-statistics in parentheses).

spread.

4.2 Pit inventory and market depth

Inventory-neutral models that focus on price discovery assume that market-maker inventory has no impact on the price response to order flow (market depth). In contrast, models that incorporate both price discovery and inventory control, such as Chordia and Subrahmanyam (1992), Diamond and Verrecchia (1991), Laux (1993), and Madhavan and Smidt (1991, 1993), predict that market-maker inventory does affect the price response to order flow.

Our empirical analysis of the relationship between the price response to order flow and aggregate pit inventory is based on a generic

Competitive Market Making and Inventory Control

implied relationship between the price response to order flow and inventory:

$$p_{t+1} - p_t = f(\omega_t, I_{pit,t}), \qquad (8)$$

where ω_t is net customer order flow (positive for net customer buys) during minute t, p_{t+1} is the price at the end of minute t, and $I_{pit,t}$ is total pit inventory at the beginning of minute t. The common prediction of all models is that $\partial p/\partial \omega > 0$.

The models diverge regarding the effect of inventory, as inventory-neutral models imply that $f(\omega, I) = g(\omega)$ [for example, in Kyle (1985), $g(\omega) = \lambda \omega$]. In contrast, models incorporating price discovery and inventory control imply that market-maker inventory does affect market depth, or that $\partial f(\omega, I)/\partial I \neq 0$. In these models, inventory has an effect because dealers use price to manage inventory. In essence, the models predict that market depth is greater (lesser price response) for order flow that moves dealer inventory to a preferred position, and that order flow that increases market-maker inventory exposure is associated with larger price impacts.

To examine inventory's impact on market depth, we estimate the following regression:

$$p_{t+1} - p_t = \alpha + \beta_1 \omega_t + \beta_2 \delta_t \omega_t + \epsilon_t \qquad (9)$$

for 1-minute price changes, net customer (CTI 4) order flow, and a dummy variable δ_t set equal to one if order flow increases absolute aggregate pit inventory, and zero otherwise.[20] All microstructure models predict that the coefficient on order flow will be positive. The inventory management models suggest that the coefficient on the dummied order flow will also be positive. Intuition for the prediction can be developed by considering the case of a market maker with long inventory. Customer sales (negative order flow) to the market maker lead to inference that "true" price is lower [as in Kyle (1985)], and this is captured in the term $\beta_1 \omega_t$. However, selling to a long market maker also increases the market maker's inventory exposure, which, according to the theory, further lowers the price at which the market maker is willing to make a purchase.

---

[20] The 1-minute price change is taken from the time and sales data records, which record all price changes to the nearest second. We define the last price for the contract prior to the start of minute t as p_t. If any price changes are recorded for minute t then the last price for the minute is defined as p_{t+1}. If no price changes are recorded, price change is designated as zero. Net customer order flow is calculated as the summed quantity of customer buys of the contract less the total sells for the minute. Price changes and order flow are for the most active contract for each day (usually the nearby, or closest to maturity, contract).

Table 7
Inventory and the price impact of order flow

Pit	Number of observations	Intercept	Contract order flow	Inventory dummy times order flow
S&P 500 index	50,816	0.18	0.200	−0.030
		(0.6)	(14.6)	(−1.5)
Eurodollars	33,956	0.13	0.005	−0.007
		(1.4)	(6.9)	(−6.7)
Deutschemark	47,618	0.08	0.048	−0.004
		(0.5)	(14.4)	(−1.0)
Live cattle	25,024	0.13	0.061	−0.028
		(1.5)	(10.9)	(−3.7)
Swiss franc	45,258	0.08	0.101	−0.007
		(0.5)	(13.6)	(−0.7)
Yen	42,404	0.03	0.056	0.008
		(0.2)	(12.0)	(1.3)
Live hogs	20,239	0.08	0.129	−0.043
		(0.7)	(13.7)	(−3.2)
Pound	41,388	0.10	0.100	0.010
		(0.5)	(8.7)	(0.7)
Pork bellies	19,798	0.13	0.573	−0.144
		(0.7)	(19.2)	(−3.3)
Lumber	9,498	0.29	1.920	−1.620
		(0.5)	(13.0)	(−7.3)
T-bills	9,922	−0.06	0.069	−0.029
		(−0.4)	(8.9)	(−2.7)
Canadian dollar	24,474	−0.12	0.087	−0.009
		(−1.4)	(10.5)	(−0.8)
Feeder cattle	11,449	0.20	0.359	−0.031
		(0.9)	(10.2)	(−0.6)
LIBOR	3,362	0.30	0.063	−0.053
		(0.9)	(5.5)	(−3.44)
Australian dollar	2,178	0.13	1.613	−1.339
		(0.1)	(5.8)	(−4.4)
S&P Midcap 400	4,451	−1.30	0.285	−0.104
		(−1.2)	(1.5)	(−0.4)

Model: $p_{t+1} - p_t = \alpha + \beta_1 \omega_t + \beta_2 \delta_t \omega_t + \epsilon_t$. Price ($p_{t+1}$) is end-of-minute t-price for the most active contract, ω_c is net customer (CTI 4) order flow (most active contract), and δ_t is a dummy variable equal to one if customer order flow increases absolute pit inventory, and equal to zero if customer order flow reduces pit absolute inventory. Pit inventory is aggregate pit trader inventory at the start of minute t (t-statistics in parentheses).

Table 7 reports estimates of Equation (9) for daily most active contracts for each pit. As predicted, order flow moves price. The coefficient for net customer order flow is positive for all 16 pits, and significant at the 1% level for 15 of the 16. However, inventory's predicted impact is not evidenced in the data. Only 2 of the 16 pits (pound and yen) have a positive estimated coefficient on inventory-increasing order flow (neither is significant). In fact, of the 14 negative estimated coefficients for inventory-increasing order flow, 8 are significantly negative at the classical 1% level. As with results for individual trader inventory, the results for aggregate pit inventory seem opposite to the predictions of inventory models.

5. Conclusion

The empirical investigations reported in the previous sections reveal several strong and consistent empirical regularities for the CME futures trading activities. Two principal conclusions deserve emphasis.

First, we conclude that CME locals aggressively manage their inventories. This conclusion is based on the observation that individual market-maker inventories are rapidly mean reverting (Table 1), and that trade direction is negatively correlated with inventory (Table 2). Simply put, long market makers are more likely to sell, short market makers are more likely to buy.[21] Compared with other studies, which are based on stock trading data, our empirical results show that the speed of inventory adjustment for futures markets is much greater than for equity markets. We do not regard any of these results as surprising.

Second, despite the strong evidence that market makers attempt to control their inventory risk exposure, the influence of inventory on price is contrary to the predictions of inventory control theory. Overall, we find that locals make inventory-reducing trades on more favorable terms (to the local) than inventory-increasing trades (Table 4), we find that price changes are less responsive to order flow that increases (absolute) pit inventory (Table 7), and we find no conclusive evidence that inventory dispersion reduces customer execution spreads (Table 6). These are surprising results. Furthermore, our experiments show that these results are not attributable to differential levels of risk aversion among market makers (Table 5). From this we infer that market makers are not merely passive order fillers, as depicted in some microstructure models, but are active profit-seeking individuals with heterogeneous levels of information and/or trading skill.

Heterogeneous market-maker information and the management of market-maker inventory are important issues. These issues, however, are not simultaneously included in the most widely cited theoretical models of market microstructure. We hope that the evidence we have presented will motivate model building that will abandon the implicit assumption of inventory neutrality and integrate the joint influences of inventory management and asymmetric information on individual and market behavior more precisely.

References

Admati, A. R., and P. Pfleiderer, 1988, "A Theory of Intraday Patterns: Volume and Price Variability,"

---

[21] Additional evidence from logit regressions (not reported) shows that the probability that a market maker's next trade will be a sell (buy) increases the longer (shorter) his/her inventory. See Mann (1994).

Review of Financial Studies, 1, 3–40.

Admati, A. R., and P. Pfleiderer, 1989, "Divide and Conquer: A Theory of Intraday and Day-of-the-Week Mean Effects," *Review of Financial Studies*, 2, 189–223.

Amihud, Y., and H. Mendelson, 1980, "Dealership Market: Market-Making With Inventory," *Journal of Financial Economics*, 8, 31–53.

Benveniste, L. M., A. J. Marcus, and W. J. Wilhelm, 1992, "What's Special About the Specialist?," *Journal of Financial Economics*, 32, 61–86.

Biais, B., 1993, "Price Formation and Equilibrium Liquidity in Fragmented and Centralized Markets," *Journal of Finance*, 48, 157–185.

Brock, W. A., and A. W. Kleidon, 1992, "Periodic Market Closure and Trading Volume," *Journal of Economic Dynamics and Control*, 16, 451–489.

CFTC (U.S. Commodity Futures Trading Commission), 1989, "Economic Analysis of Dual Trading on Commodity Exchanges," Report prepared by the Division of Economic Analysis.

Chordia, T., and A. Subrahmanyam, 1992, "Off-Floor Market Making, Payment-for-Order-Flow, and the Tick Size," working paper, University of California, Los Angeles.

Chang, E. C., and P. R. Locke, 1993, "The Performance and Market Impact of Dual Trading: CME Rule 552," working paper, Commodity Futures Trading Commission.

Copeland, T., and D. Galai, 1983, "Information Effects and the Bid-Ask Spread," *Journal of Finance*, 38, 1457–1469.

Demsetz, H., 1968, "The Cost of Transacting," *Quarterly Journal of Economics*, 82, 33–53.

Diamond, D., and R. Verrecchia, 1991, "Disclosure, Liquidity, and the Cost of Capital," *Journal of Finance*, 46, 1325–1359.

Fishman, M., and F. Longstaff, 1992, "Dual Trading in Futures Markets," *Journal of Finance*, 47, 643–671.

Foster, F. D., and S. Viswanathan, 1990, "A Theory of the Interday Variations in Volume, Variance, and Trading Costs in Securities Markets," *Review of Financial Studies*, 3, 593–624.

Garman, M., 1976, "Market Microstructure," *Journal of Financial Economics*, 3, 257–275.

Glosten, L., and P. Milgrom, 1985, "Bid, Ask and Transaction Prices in a Specialist Market With Heterogeneously Informed Traders," *Journal of Financial Economics*, 14, 71–100.

Hasbrouck, J., 1988, "Trades, Quotes, Inventories, and Information," *Journal of Financial Economics*, 22, 229–252.

Hasbrouck, J., and G. Sofianos, 1993, "The Trades of Market-Makers: An Analysis of NYSE Specialists," *Journal of Finance*, 48, 1565–1593.

Ho, T. S. Y., and R. G. Macris, 1985, "Dealer Market Structure and Performance," in Y. Amihud, T. S. Y. Ho, and R. Schwartz (eds.), *Market Making and the Changing Structure of the Securities Industry*, Lexington Books, Lexington, Massachusetts.

Ho, T. S. Y., and H. R. Stoll, 1980, "On Dealer Markets Under Competition," *Journal of Finance*, 35, 259–267.

Ho, T. S. Y., and H. R. Stoll, 1981, "Optimal Dealer Pricing Under Transactions and Return Uncertainty," *Journal of Financial Economics*, 9, 47–73.

Competitive Market Making and Inventory Control

Ho, T. S. Y., and H. R. Stoll, 1983, "The Dynamics of Dealer Markets Under Competition," *Journal of Finance*, 38, 1053–1074.

Kolb, R. W., 1991, *Understanding Futures Markets*, Kolb Publishing, Miami.

Kyle, A. S., 1985, "Continuous Auctions and Insider Trading," *Econometrica*, 53, 1315–1336.

Laux, P. A., 1993, "Intraday Price Formation in the Stock Index Futures Market," working paper, University of Texas at Austin.

Laux, P., 1995, "Dealer Market Structure, Outside Competition, and the Bid-Ask Spread," *Journal of Economic Dynamics and Control*, 19, 683–710.

Madhavan, A., and S. Smidt, 1991, "A Bayesian Model of Intraday Specialist Pricing," *Journal of Financial Economics*, 30, 99–134.

Madhavan, A., and S. Smidt, 1993, "An Analysis of Changes in Specialist Inventories and Quotations," *Journal of Finance*, 48, 1585–1628.

Mann, S. C., 1994, "Competitive Marketmaking on Futures Exchanges," Ph.D. dissertation, David Eccles School of Business, University of Utah.

Mildenstein, E., and H. Schleef, 1983, "The Optimal Pricing Policy of a Monopolistic Marketmaker in the Equity Market," *Journal of Finance*, 38, 218–231.

Newey, W., and K. West, 1987, "A Simple Positive Definite, Heteroscedasticity and Autocorrelation Consistent Covariance Matrix," *Econometrica*, 55, 703–715.

O'Hara, M., and G. Oldfield, 1986, "The Microeconomics of Market Making," *Journal of Financial and Quantitative Analysis*, 21, 361–376.

Perron, P., 1988, "Trends and Random Walks in Macroeconomic Time Series," *Journal of Economic Dynamics and Control*, 12, 297–332.

Silber, W., 1984, "Marketmaker Behavior in an Auction Market: An Analysis of Scalpers in Futures Markets," *Journal of Finance*, 39, 937–953.

Spiegel, M., and A. Subrahmanyam, 1995, "On Intraday Risk Premia," *Journal of Finance*, 50, 319–339.

Stoll, H. R., 1976, "Dealer Inventory Behavior: An Empirical Investigation of NASDAQ/NMS Stocks," *Journal of Financial and Quantitative Analysis*, 11, 359–380.

Stoll, H. R., 1992, "Principles of Trading Market Structure," *Journal of Financial Services Research*, 6, 75–106.

Subrahmanyam, A., 1991, "Risk Aversion, Market Liquidity, and Price Efficiency," *Review of Financial Studies*, 4, 417–441.

Working, H., 1967, "Tests of a Theory Concerning Floor Trading on Commodity Exchanges," *Food Research Institute Studies: Supplement*.

Zabel, E., 1981, "Competitive Price Adjustment Without Market Clearing," *Econometrica*, 49, 1201–1221.

C
Currency Markets

Tests of microstructural hypotheses in the foreign exchange market

Richard K. Lyons

Haas School of Business, University of California at Berkeley, Berkeley, CA 94720, USA
National Bureau of Economic Research, Cambridge, MA 02138, USA

(Received August 1993; final version received March 1995)

Abstract

Data in this paper support both the inventory-control and asymmetric-information approaches to microstructure theory. Strong evidence of an inventory-control effect on price is new. The transactions dataset chronicles a trading week of a spot foreign exchange dealer whose daily volume averages over $1 billion. In addition to controlling inventory with his own price, the dealer also lays off inventory at other dealers' prices and through brokers. These results highlight the importance of inventory-control theory in understanding trading in this market.

Key words: Foreign exchange; Microstructure; Inventory; Information
JEL classification: G15; F31

1. Introduction

Empirical work on microstructures focuses primarily on the NYSE and its specialist structure. At least two reasons account for this focus on the specialist: Theory is better developed in this area, and the concentration of the market provides more readily available data. Current interest, however, is shifting towards various nonspecialist markets. This paper exemplifies that shift. It examines the spot deutschemark/dollar (DM/$) market, which has a decentralized

---

I thank the following for helpful comments: two anonymous referees, Charles Engel, Richard Levich, James McCarthy, Eric Noyes, Carol Osler, Linda Tesar, Sabine Toulson, Jianxin Wang, and seminar participants at Columbia, Harvard, Rochester, Berkeley, Santa Cruz, the NBER Summer Institute, and the ASSA Meetings. I also thank Euysung Kim and Eric Noyes for valuable research assistance and Merrill Lynch and Lasser Marshall for access to dealers and brokers while trading. Financial assistance from the National Science Foundation and the Berkeley Program in Finance is gratefully acknowledged. Any errors are my own.

0304-405X/95/$09.50 © 1995 Elsevier Science S.A. All rights reserved
SSDI 0304405X9500832 Y

dealership structure. The objective is to test models of price determination using a dataset appropriate for this market.

Microstructure theory emphasizes two channels through which order flow affects price. First, an inventory-control channel emerges when dealers adjust price to control inventory fluctuation due to order flow (e.g., Amihud and Mendelson, 1980; Ho and Stoll, 1983; O'Hara and Oldfield, 1986; among others). Second, an information channel emerges when dealers adjust price in response to order flow that may reflect private information (e.g., Kyle, 1985; Glosten and Milgrom, 1985; Admati and Pfleiderer, 1988; among others). Note that both channels imply that buyer-initiated trades push price up, while seller-initiated trades push it down. In empirical work, disentangling them is the central objective.

I find that both channels are significant in the foreign exchange (FX) market, providing support for both modeling approaches. Specifically, information asymmetry induces dealers to decrease price about one pip – or DM 0.0001/$ – for every incoming sell order of $10 million (conversely for buy orders); inventory control induces dealers to decrease price about three-quarters of a pip per $10 million of undesired inventory. Though information effects on price have been found elsewhere (e.g., Madhavan and Smidt, 1991; Hasbrouck, 1988, 1991; among others), strong evidence of an inventory effect on price is new (see Madhavan and Smidt, 1991; Manaster and Mann, 1992; Laux, 1993; among others). The previous evidence supporting inventory control is indirect, relying wholly on the time-series properties of inventory (e.g., Hasbrouck and Sofianos, 1993; Madhavan and Smidt, 1993).

Why is the direct effect on price so strong in FX when it leaves little trace in equity and futures markets? The following facts provide some prima facie evidence. Most FX dealers – including the one I track – begin and end each trading day with a zero net position. This, coupled with per-dealer volumes over $1 billion per day, implies substantial inventory control. Still, it is not clear why this should show up so clearly in price. (For example, FX dealers have other methods for controlling inventory, such as laying it off on another dealer's price or through a broker.) I offer two additional thoughts. First, dealers in FX quote bilaterally, so shading the quote provides a signal of inventory to one person only, not to the whole market. Second, the dataset available is remarkably powerful. It distinguishes between incoming orders (counterparty initiated), outgoing orders, and brokered orders. Specialist datasets, in contrast, provide no such taxonomy. These different categories provide extra power for disentangling inventory effects from information effects.[1]

---

[1] Another reason inventory effects may be relatively sharp here involves hedging. Dealers in the major currencies trade only one currency. Specialists, in contrast, typically trade several stocks and hedge their overall risk, rather than focusing on any one stock, which may mute the price effects of inventory. Similarly, futures traders sometimes cross-hedge in neighboring pits.

My dataset has significant advantages over FX data used previously. In particular, it chronicles the trading activity of a spot DM/$ dealer over a five-day trading week. The time-stamps on the quotes and trades are assigned by computer, without lags. Previous work on intraday spot trading has relied on a series of indicative quotes called FXFX, which is provided by Reuters (see Goodhart and Figliuoli, 1991; Goodhart et al., 1994). There are two key shortcomings of the FXFX data: These 'quotes' are not firm prices at which dealers can transact; and there is no measure of order flow or transaction prices. Clearly, the FXFX data are not sufficient for addressing the issues considered here.

The paper is organized as follows: Section 2 develops the model; Section 3 describes the dataset and provides some relevant institutional detail; Section 4 presents the model's results; and Section 5 concludes.

2. A Bayesian model of pricing behavior

This model extends the Madhavan and Smidt (1991) model in two ways. First, on the information side, it introduces a role for marketwide order flow. This is an important dimension of dealing in a decentralized multiple-dealer setting (see Lyons, 1994). Second, on the inventory-control side, it incorporates the fact that FX dealers use tools not available to a specialist (e.g., laying off inventory at another dealer's price).

Consider a pure exchange economy with two assets, one riskless (the numeraire) and one with a stochastic liquidation value, representing FX. The FX market is organized as a decentralized dealership market with n dealers. Here, I focus on the pricing decision of a representative dealer, denoted dealer i; accordingly, a period is defined by an incoming order at dealer i's quote, where incoming means initiated by dealer i's counterparty, denoted dealer j. Periods run from $t = 1, 2, \ldots, T$.

To accommodate the model's information asymmetry, I assume that transactions are *ex post* regret-free for the quoting dealer, in the sense of Glosten and Milgrom (1985). This means, for example, that when dealer i quotes an offer for quantity ten, built into the quote is an answer to the question: How would my expectation of value change if dealer j bought ten, given that he may have private information? Similarly, the bid side rationally incorporates any updating a sale of ten would engender. To accommodate all possible order sizes, the dealer quotes a schedule assigning a price to each quantity, buy or sell. This schedule therefore internalizes the proper inference for any potential order, and ensures the quoting dealer will not regret the quote *ex post*.

The rest of the model's specification is presented in three blocks: First the information environment, then the formation of expectations conditional on the information environment, and finally the determination of bid/offer quotes as a function of expectations and current inventory.

2.1. The information environment

The full information price of FX at time T is denoted by $\tilde{V}$, which is composed of a series of increments – e.g., interest differentials – so that $\tilde{V} = \sum_{i=0}^{T} \tilde{r}_i$, where r_0 is a known constant. The increments are i.i.d. mean zero. Each increment r_t is realized immediately after trading in period t. Realizations of the increments represent the flow of public information over time. The value of FX at t is thus defined as $V_t = \sum_{i=0}^{t} r_i$. At the time of quoting and trading in period t, i.e. before $\tilde{r}_t$ is realized, V_t is a random variable. Given this structure, without transaction costs or further information, the quoted price of FX at time t would equal V_{t-1}, which is the expected value of the asset conditional on public information at t.

The following three signals define each period's information environment prior to dealer i's quote to dealer j. The first two are received simultaneously, prior to the third:

$$\tilde{S}_t = V_t + \tilde{\eta}_t,\qquad(1)$$

$$\tilde{C}_{jt} = V_t + \tilde{\omega}_{jt},\qquad(2)$$

$$\tilde{Q}_t = V_t + \tilde{\xi}_t.\qquad(3)$$

The noise terms η_t, ω_{jt}, and ξ_t are normally distributed about zero, are independent of one another and across periods, and have variances σ_η^2, σ_ω^2, and σ_ξ^2, respectively. At the outset of each period t, all dealers receive a public signal S_t of the full-information value V_t. Also at the outset of each period t, dealer j receives a private signal C_{jt} of V_t. One potential source of private signals at the FX dealer level is order flow from nondealer customers. Each dealer has sole knowledge of his own-customer order flow; to the extent this flow conveys information it is private information, and can be exploited in interdealer trading (Lyons, 1994).

The third signal, Q_t, is an additional public signal introduced here to reflect the institutions of the FX market. It is distinct from S_t in that it is measurable by the econometrician. In particular, Q_t represents a signal of marketwide order flow. As indicated above, there is one source of information on marketwide order flow that provides transparency in an otherwise opaque FX trading process. This signal is provided verbally by interdealer brokers via intercoms at the dealers' desks. Specifically, when a brokered trade clears either the bid or offer at that broker, this is communicated to dealers marketwide. Though the precise quantity is not announced, dealers can infer a quantity on the basis of their knowledge of typical sizes; since the direction of the aggressor is established by whether the bid or offer was cleared, the quantity can be signed. To put this statistic in perspective, note that (i) about half of interdealer trading is arranged through brokers, (ii) typically 50% or more of brokered transactions clear the best bid or offer, and (iii) this is the only source of marketwide order flow available to dealers. The next section provides some additional institutional background regarding brokers and the precise information they convey. The important point for this model is that in the FX market, dealers do receive information regarding other dealers' orders, and proxies for this information are available to the econometrician.

The last conditioning variable dealer i uses to determine his quote schedule is the quantity dealer j might trade in period t, denoted Q_{jt}. That is, consistent with the regret-free property discussed above, dealer i quotes a schedule of prices that protects him from adverse selection. Of course, the realized quantity Q_{jt} still provides a signal of the $\tilde{C}_{jt}$ received by dealer j. Under the usual assumptions (exponential utility defined over end-of-period wealth), the quantity dealer j chooses to trade is linearly related to the deviation between dealer j's expectation and the transaction price, plus a quantity representing liquidity demand X_{jt} that is uncorrelated with V_t (e.g., inventory-adjustment trading):

$$Q_{jt} = \theta(\mu_{jt} - P_{it}) + X_{jt}, \tag{4}$$

where μ_{jt} is the expectation of V_t conditional on information available to dealer j at t, and the value of X_{jt} is known only to dealer j. Note that Q_{jt} can take either sign.

Fig. 1 summarizes the timing of the model in each period.

2.2. The formation of expectations

Dealer i's quote schedule is a function of the expectation of V_t at the time of quoting, which is denoted μ_{it}. This expectation, in turn, is conditioned on the

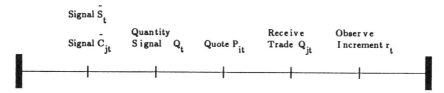

Fig. 1. Timing within each period, where a period is defined over each incoming order at dealer i's quote.

Definitions: $\tilde{S}_t$ is a public signal of the full information value V_t; $\tilde{C}_{jt}$ is dealer j's private signal of V_t, where j denotes the dealer requesting the quote from dealer i; Q_t is a public signal of interdealer trading not involving dealer i; P_{it} is dealer i's bilateral quote to dealer j, a schedule matching each transaction quantity with a particular price; Q_{jt} is the signed incoming order, positive for dealer j purchases, negative for sales; and r_t is the period t increment to V_t.

signals described above: S_t, Q_t, and Q_{jt} (the fourth variable described above, $\tilde{C}_{jt}$, is the signal embedded in Q_{jt}).

Dealer i's prior belief regarding V_t is summarized by the first public signal S_t. After observing the second public signal Q_t, dealer i's posterior belief, denoted μ_t, can be expressed as a weighted average of S_t and Q_t:

$$\mu_t \equiv \rho S_t + (1 - \rho) Q_t, \tag{5}$$

where $\rho \equiv \sigma_\xi^2/(\sigma_\xi^2 + \sigma_\eta^2)$. These posterior beliefs μ_t are normally distributed with mean V_t and variance $\sigma_\mu^2 \equiv \rho^2 \sigma_\eta^2 + (1 - \rho)^2 \sigma_\xi^2$.

After observing Q_t, dealer i then conditions on various possible Q_{jt}'s (and the schedule he quotes internalizes this inference). In particular, dealer i can form the statistic Z_{jt} (see Appendix):

$$Z_{jt} \equiv \frac{Q_{jt}/\theta + P_{it} - \lambda \mu_t}{1 - \lambda} = V_t + \tilde{\omega}_{jt} + [1/\theta(1 - \lambda)] \tilde{X}_{jt}, \tag{6}$$

where $\lambda \equiv \sigma_\omega^2/(\sigma_\mu^2 + \sigma_\omega^2)$. This statistic is also normally distributed, with mean V_t and variance equal to the variance of the last two terms, both of which are orthogonal to V_t. Let σ_{Zj}^2 denote this variance. Note that Z_{jt} is statistically independent of μ_t, since Z_{jt} is orthogonal to both S_t and Q_t. Thus, dealer i's posterior μ_{it}, expressed as a function of any Q_{jt}, takes the form of a weighted average of μ_t and Z_{jt}:

$$\mu_{it} = \kappa \mu_t + (1 - \kappa) Z_{jt}, \tag{7}$$

where $\kappa \equiv \sigma_{Zj}^2/(\sigma_{Zj}^2 + \sigma_\mu^2)$. This expectation plays a central role in determining dealer i's quote, to which I now turn.

2.3. The determination of bid/offer quotes

Consider the following prototypical inventory model: Here, price P_{it} is linearly related to the dealer's current inventory, which is optimal in a number of inventory-control models:

$$P_{it} = \mu_{it} - \alpha(I_{it} - I_i^*) + \gamma D_t, \tag{8}$$

where μ_{it} is the expectation of V_t conditional on information available to dealer i at t, I_{it} is dealer i's current inventory position, and I_i^* is i's desired position. The inventory-control effect, governed by α, will in general be a function of relative interest rates, firm capital, and carrying costs.

The term γD_t picks up bid–offer bounce in the model. D_t is a direction-indicator variable that equals one when the transaction price P_{it} is the offer and minus one when P_{it} is the bid. For a given expectation μ_{it}, γD_t thus picks up half of the spread. (Of course, to protect against adverse selection, the quoted spread widens with quantity due to effects on μ_{it}; γD_t should therefore be viewed as half the spread for quantities close to zero.) This term can be interpreted as compensation resulting from execution costs, price discreteness, or rents.

Consistent with the regret-free property of quotes, I substitute dealer i's expectation μ_{it} in Eq. (7) into Eq. (8), yielding

$$P_{it} = \kappa \mu_t + (1 - \kappa) Z_{jt} - \alpha(I_{it} - I_i^*) + \gamma D_t, \tag{9}$$

which is equivalent to (see Appendix)

$$P_{it} = (1 - \rho) Q_t + \rho S_t + \left[\frac{1 - \phi}{\phi \theta}\right] Q_{jt} - \left[\frac{\alpha}{\phi}\right](I_{it} - I_i^*) + \left[\frac{\gamma}{\phi}\right] D_t, \tag{10}$$

where the parameter $\phi \equiv (\kappa - \lambda)/(1 - \lambda)$ and $0 < \phi < 1$ since $0 < \kappa < 1$, $0 < \lambda < 1$, and $\kappa < \lambda$.

2.4. An estimable equation

Eq. (10) is not directly estimable for two reasons: First, the signal of marketwide order flow Q_t must be proxied in estimation (and I have to take into account that the proxy does not have the simple stochastic properties of the signal Q_t). Second, S_t is not observable to the econometrician.

I address first the impact of the proxy for Q_t. In estimation, I use data on marketwide order flow at a particular broker as a proxy for Q_t. This brokered order flow does not involve dealer i, but provides a signal observed by dealer i. I specify the signal of brokered order flow, B_t, in the following way:

$$B_t = \sum_{k=1}^{m} Q_{kt} + \psi_t. \tag{11}$$

The sum represents the net order flow of m brokered trades not involving dealer i. The noise ψ_t is independently distributed normal, with mean zero and variance σ_ψ^2. I assume that the information content of these m trades has the same structure as the trade of dealer j; that is, using the definition of Q_{jt} in Eq. (4), I have

$$\sum_{k=1}^{m} Q_{kt} = \sum_{k=1}^{m} [\theta(\mu_{kt} - \mu_t) + \tilde{X}_{kt}], \tag{12}$$

where μ_{kt} is the expectation of V_t conditional on information available to dealer k at t, and X_{kt} is a liquidity component of each trade, the value of which is known only to the aggressor. The individual expectations μ_{kt} are a function of private signals C_{kt}, where

$$\tilde{C}_{kt} = V_t + \tilde{\omega}_{kt}, \tag{13}$$

which parallels Eq. (2) describing the private signal available to dealer j, the dealer trading on i's prices. The ω_{kt}'s are distributed i.i.d. normal with mean zero and variance σ_ω^2. With this specification, the relationship between the observable B_t and a canonical signal Q_t is (see Appendix)

$$Q_t = \left[\frac{1}{m\theta(1-\lambda)\rho}\right] B_t + S_t. \tag{14}$$

Substituting this relationship into Eq. (10) yields

$$P_{it} = S_t + \left[\frac{1-\phi}{\phi\theta}\right] Q_{jt} - \left[\frac{\alpha}{\phi}\right](I_{it} - I_i^*) + \left[\frac{\gamma}{\phi}\right] D_t + \left[\frac{1-\rho}{m\theta(1-\lambda)\rho}\right] B_t. \tag{15}$$

I turn now to the unobservability of S_t. The assumptions about the signals available and the evolution of V_t allow me to express the period t prior as equal to the period $t-1$ posterior from Eq. (8) lagged one period, plus an expectational error term ε_{it}:

$$S_t = \mu_{it-1} + \varepsilon_{it} = P_{it-1} + \alpha(I_{it-1} - I_i^*) - \gamma D_{t-1} + \varepsilon_{it}. \tag{16}$$

Substituting this expression for S_t into Eq. (15) yields

$$P_{it} = [P_{it-1} + \alpha(I_{it-1} - I_i^*) - \gamma D_{t-1} + \varepsilon_{it}] + \left[\frac{1-\phi}{\phi\theta}\right] Q_{jt}$$

$$- \left[\frac{\alpha}{\phi}\right](I_{it} - I_i^*) + \left[\frac{\gamma}{\phi}\right] D_t + \left[\frac{1-\rho}{m\theta(1-\lambda)\rho}\right] B_t.$$

Therefore,

$$\Delta P_{it} = \left[\frac{\alpha}{\phi} - \alpha\right] I_i^* + \left[\frac{1-\phi}{\phi\theta}\right] Q_{jt} - \left[\frac{\alpha}{\phi}\right] I_{it} + \alpha I_{it-1} + \left[\frac{\gamma}{\phi}\right] D_t - \gamma D_{t-1}$$

$$+ \left[\frac{1-\rho}{m\theta(1-\lambda)\rho}\right] B_t + \varepsilon_{it}. \tag{17}$$

This corresponds to a reduced-form estimating equation of

$$\Delta P_{it} = \beta_0 + \beta_1 Q_{jt} + \beta_2 I_{it} + \beta_3 I_{it-1} + \beta_4 D_t + \beta_5 D_{t-1} + \beta_6 B_t + \varepsilon_{it}. \tag{18}$$

The model thus predicts that $\{\beta_1, \beta_3, \beta_4, \beta_6\} > 0$, $\{\beta_2, \beta_5\} < 0$, $|\beta_2| > \beta_3$, and $\beta_4 > |\beta_5|$, where the latter inequalities derive from the fact that $0 < \phi < 1$.

2.5. The error structure

As in Madhavan and Smidt (1991), this model implies a particular structure for the error term ε_{it} in Eq. (18). To see this, note that Eq. (16) allows me to write: $\varepsilon_{it} = S_t - \mu_{it-1}$. The two components on the right-hand side reduce to

$$S_t = V_t + \eta_t, \tag{16a}$$

$$\mu_{it-1} = \kappa \mu_{t-1} + (1-\kappa) Z_{jt-1}, \tag{16b}$$

using Eqs. (1) and (7), respectively. The latter expression for μ_{it-1}, after substitutions from Eqs. (5), (6), and (A.1), can be expressed as

$$\mu_{it-1} = V_{t-1} + \kappa \rho \eta_{t-1} + \kappa(1-\rho)\left[m^{-1} \sum_{k \neq j}^{m} \tilde{\omega}_{kt-1} + [m\theta(1-\lambda)]^{-1} \sum_{k \neq j}^{m} \tilde{X}_{kt-1} \right.$$

$$\left. + [m\theta(1-\lambda)]^{-1} \tilde{\psi}_{t-1} \right] + (1-\kappa)[\tilde{\omega}_{jt-1} + [1/\theta(1-\lambda)] \tilde{X}_{jt-1}]. \tag{16c}$$

Now, to determine $E[\varepsilon_{it} \varepsilon_{it-1}]$, recall that $\tilde{\psi}$ and the increments to V are independent across time, and that ω, $\tilde{X}$, and $\tilde{\psi}$ are independent across dealers and time. Accordingly, $E[\varepsilon_{it} \varepsilon_{it-1}] = E[-\kappa \rho \eta_{t-1} \eta_{t-1}] = -\kappa \rho \sigma_\eta^2$, where the first η_{t-1} comes from the μ_{it-1} component of ε_{it} and the second comes from the S_{t-1} component of ε_{it-1}. Thus, the model predicts the error term ε_{it} should conform to an MA(1):

$$\varepsilon_{it} = \beta_7 v_{it-1} + v_{it}, \tag{19}$$

with $\beta_7 < 0$. Henceforth, I include this substitution in Eq. (18).

2.6. Additional tools for controlling inventory

I can extend the model further by incorporating the fact that FX dealers control inventory in ways not available to a specialist. Specifically, a dealer can sell inventory at another dealer's price (i.e., an outgoing trade), or a dealer can sell inventory through a broker. To capture this, I decompose dealer i's inventory at time t:

$$I_{it} = I_{it-1} + Q_{i,it}^o + Q_{i,it}^b - Q_{jt}, \tag{20}$$

or equivalently,

$$\Delta I_{it} = Q_{i,it}^o + Q_{i,it}^b - Q_{jt}. \tag{21}$$

Here, Q^o_{iAt} denotes dealer i's outgoing trades (net) occurring between $t-1$ and t (recall that periods are defined by incoming trades), Q^b_{iAt} denotes dealer i's brokered trades (net) occurring between $t-1$ and t, and ΔI_{it} denotes dealer i's inventory change from $t-1$ to t, which includes the incoming order Q_{jt}.[2]

To provide perspective on this decomposition, note that disentangling information effects from inventory-control effects requires breaking the perfect collinearity in a pure specialist market between incoming trades Q_{jt} and inventory changes ΔI_{it}. In this model, perfect collinearity is broken in two ways: (i) In addition to incoming trades Q_{jt}, ΔI_{it} includes outgoing trades and brokered trades; and (ii) brokered trades not involving dealer i provide signed volume information, but have no effect on I_{it} (proxied here by B_t). The first of these is made explicit by the decomposition.

Bringing this back to the reduced form in Eq. (18), I can write

$$\Delta P_{it} = \beta_0 + \beta_1 Q_{jt} + \beta_2 \Delta I_{it} + (\beta_2 + \beta_3) I_{it-1} + \beta_4 D_t + \beta_5 D_{t-1}$$
$$+ \beta_6 B_t + \beta_7 v_{it-1} + v_{it}. \tag{22}$$

Clearly, collinearity prevents estimation of separate coefficients for each of the three components of ΔI_{it} in Eq. (21). The data do, however, provide enough discriminating power to estimate an equation of the form:

$$\Delta P_{it} = \beta_0 + \beta_1 Q_{jt} + \beta_2 Q^o_{iAt} + \beta'_2 (Q^b_{iAt-1} - Q_{jt}) + (\beta_2 + \beta_3) I_{it-1}$$
$$+ \beta_4 D_t + \beta_5 D_{t-1} + \beta_6 B_t + \beta_7 v_{it-1} + v_{it}. \tag{23}$$

Here, Q^o_{iAt} is included as a separate inventory-control variable. The model then predicts that the inventory-control effects β_2 and β'_2 should be equal. Note, too, that $\beta_2 + \beta_3 = \alpha(1 - \phi^{-1})$, which approaches zero from below as the structural parameter $\phi \in (0, 1)$ approaches one (a larger ϕ implies that private information is imprecise relative to public information). Finally, I can test whether the presence of outgoing trades or brokered trades affects the other estimated coefficients in the model.

2.7. Two final comments on the model

The empirical implementation of the model warrants two further comments. First, note that with a slight reinterpretation, the model can accommodate variability in desired inventories, that is, an I^*_i that varies through time. Consider the following model: $I^*_{it} = \bar{I}_i + \delta(\mu_{it} - \mu_t)$, which is consistent with the

---

[2] In addition to incoming and outgoing orders and brokered trades (all of which are interdealer), FX dealers also trade with nondealer customers. Over this sample, the dealer did virtually no customer trading. For the FX market as a whole, interdealer trading accounts for about 90% of volume, and customer–dealer trading accounts for about 10%.

linear demands arising from negative exponential utility, where μ_t represents the market price away from dealer i. Since Q_{jt} is the only information available to dealer i that is not reflected in μ_t, it can be shown under the assumptions of this model that $(\mu_{it} - \mu_t)$ is proportional to Q_{jt}. Accordingly, I write $(\mu_{it} - \mu_t) = \pi Q_{jt}$, and can therefore express the desired inventory as follows: $I_{it}^* = \bar{I}_i + \delta \pi Q_{jt}$. In estimation, $\bar{I}_i$ will be absorbed in the constant. The estimate of β_1 now represents $[(1 - \phi)/\phi\theta] + [(\alpha/\phi) - \alpha]\delta\pi$, whose significance still evinces an information effect, though I have to be more careful in interpreting its magnitude.

A second issue relevant to empirical implementation is simultaneity. To see that simultaneity is not a problem here, recall that though quoting precedes trading, a quote is a schedule from which dealer j, by selecting Q_{jt}, determines the transaction price P_{it}. By design, there is no intrinsic-value information available to dealer i that is not available to dealer j. Hence, under the null there is no feedback here from P_{it} to the information content of Q_{jt}, which is what the coefficient β_1 measures. To think of it a different way, suppose a public announcement occurs during this period that raises the expectation of V_t conditional on public information. Though P_{it} will be higher, this does not help predict dealer j's trade this period since j's trade reflects only the orthogonal component of his beliefs relative to P_{it}, i.e., his C_{jt}.[3]

3. Data

The dataset introduced in this paper is qualitatively different from any yet employed in the exchange rate literature. The main difference is that it contains transaction prices and quantities. The existing alternative is constructed from what are called 'indicative' quotes, which are input to Reuters by trading banks (see Goodhart and Figliuoli, 1991; Bollerslev and Domowitz, 1993; Bessembinder, 1994). Some of the shortcomings of the indicative quotes include the following: First, they are not transactable prices. Second, while it is true that the indicated spreads usually bracket actual quoted spreads in the interbank market, they are typically two to three times as wide (documented below). Third, the indications are less likely to bracket true spreads when volatility is highest since there are limits to how frequently the indications can change. And finally, my experience, sitting next to dealers at major banks, indicates that they pay no attention whatsoever to the current indication; rather, dealers garner most of their high-frequency market information from signals

---

[3] The argument that the correlation between S_t and ε_{it} from Eq. (16) implies that Q_{jt} and ε_{it} are correlated is flawed: Both S_t and ε_{it} are known by dealer i at the time of quoting; correlation between Q_{jt} and ε_{it} is thus inconsistent with regret-free quoting.

transmitted via intercoms connected to interdealer brokers (see Lyons, 1994). In reality, the main purpose of the indicative quotes is to provide nondealer participants with a gauge of where the interdealer market is trading.

The dataset employed here consists of three interlinked components, covering the five trading days of the week August 3–7, 1992 from the informal start of trading at 8:30 a.m. Eastern Standard Time to roughly 1:30 p.m. Eastern Standard Time. The first component includes the time-stamped quotes, prices, and quantities for all the direct interdealer transactions of a single DM/$ dealer at a major New York bank. The second component comprises the same dealer's position cards, which include all indirect (brokered) trades. The third component includes the time-stamped prices and quantities for transactions mediated by one of the major New York brokers in the same market. These trades do not involve 'our' dealer.

3.1. Dealer data: Direct quotes and trades

The first component of the dataset includes the dealer's quotes, prices, and quantities for all direct transactions. The availability of this component is due to a recent change in technology in this market, the Reuters Dealing 2000-1 system. This system – very different from the system that produces the Reuters indications – allows dealers to communicate bilateral quotes and trades via computer rather than verbally over the telephone. Dealers can request multiple quotes simultaneously, and the computerized documentation reduces paperwork. The use of this technology differs by dealer and is growing rapidly. For example, our dealer uses Dealing 2000-1 for nearly all of his direct interdealer trades: Less than 0.4% of all transactions were done over the phone during the sample week, as indicated on the position cards.

Each record for the data covering the dealer's direct trades includes the following seven variables:

(1) the time the communication is initiated (to the minute, with no lag),
(2) whether the quote request is incoming or outgoing,
(3) the quote quantity,
(4) the bid quote,
(5) the offer quote,
(6) the transaction quantity (providing Q_{jt} if trade is incoming),
(7) the transaction price (providing P_{it} if trade is incoming).

This part of the dataset includes 952 transactions amounting to $4.1 billion. Fig. 2 provides an example of a dealer communication as recorded by the Dealing 2000-1 printout (see Reuters, 1990, for more details). Note especially

```
From CODE    FULL NAME HERE   * 1250GMT  030892 */1080
Our Terminal : CODE   Our user   : DMK
   SP DMK 10
#  8891
   BUY

#  10 MIO AGREED
#  VAL 6AUG92
#  MY DMK TO FULL NAME HERE
#  TO CONFIRM AT 1.5891 I SELL 10 MIO USD
#
   TO CONFIRM AT 1.5891 I SELL 10 MIO USD
   VAL 6AUG92
   MY USD TO FULL NAME HERE  AC 0-00-00000
   THKS N BIFN
#
#  #END LOCAL#
#
^  ## WRAP UP BY DMK DMK 1250GMT 3AUG92

^  #END#

( 265 CHARS)
```

Fig. 2. Example of a Reuters Dealing 2000-1 communication.

'From' establishes this as an incoming call; the caller's four-digit code and institution name follow; 'GMT' denotes Greenwich Mean Time; the date follows, with the day listed first; 'SP DMK 10' identifies this as request for a spot DM/$ quote for $10 million; '8891' denotes a bid of 88 and an offer of 91 (only the last two digits are quoted); the confirmation provides the complete transaction price of DM 1.5891/$, and verifies the transaction quantity.

that all Dealing 2000-1 transactions in the dataset takes place at the quoted bid or the quoted offer; the interdealer FX market is not one in which transaction prices are negotiated within the spread.

3.2. Dealer data: Position cards

The second component of the dataset is composed of the dealer's position cards over the same five days covered by the direct-transaction data, August 3–7, 1992. To track their inventories, dealers in the spot market record all their transactions on handwritten position cards as they go along. An average day consists of approximately twenty cards, each with about fifteen transaction entries.

There are two key benefits to this part of the dataset. First, it provides a clean measure of the dealer's inventory I_t at any time since it includes both direct trades and any brokered trades. Second, it provides a means of error-checking the first part of the dataset.

Each card includes the following information for every trade:

(1) the quantity traded (which determines I_t),
(2) the transaction price,
(3) the counterparty, including whether brokered.

Note that the bid/offer quotes at the time of the transaction are not included, so this component of the dataset is not sufficient for estimating the model. Note also that each entry is not time-stamped; at the top of every card, and often within the card too, the dealer records the time to the minute. Hence, the exact timing of some of the brokered transactions is not pinned down, since these trades are not confirmed via a Dealing 2000-1 record. Nevertheless, this is not a drawback for the purposes of this paper: The observations for the empirical model are the direct transactions initiated at our dealer's quoted prices; since the timing of these is pinned down by the Dealing 2000-1 records, and since these transactions appear sequentially in both components, any intervening changes in inventory due to brokered trades can be determined exactly.

3.3. Broker data

The data covering the New York broker's activities include time-stamped transaction prices and quantities over the same week covered by the other two components of the dataset. These data are transcribed from transaction tickets, which are filled out by the brokers themselves in their dealing room. The tickets are collected in small batches by an attendant and time-stamped. This component of the dataset includes 1172 transactions amounting to roughly $6.7 billion.

The data on the broker's transactions do not include the bid and offer at the time of each transaction, so I infer the trade direction from the transaction prices. I use the method recommended by Lee and Ready (1991), which codes price upticks as buyer-initiated, price downticks as seller-initiated, and no change in price as initiated by the same side as the previous transaction.

The resulting series provides a measure of B_t for the model. To insure that information in B_t is prior to the transaction Q_{jt}, I construct B_t by summing the signed trades from the two minutes prior to the minute in which Q_{jt} is effected, where two minutes corresponds to the median intertransaction time.

To put these data in perspective, remember that dealers in the major currencies trade while listening to so-called 'broker boxes', the intercoms over which interdealer brokers provide information on dealer prices and, when transactions occur, signed quantities. For each of the major currencies, there are typically four or five brokers who account for nearly all of the brokered trading. Hence, by listening to these brokers, dealers receive a common signal of signed volume and transaction prices. This statistic is the core of the dealer's high-frequency information set.

In spot FX, there is no source other than broker intercoms for marketwide order-flow information. While it is true that dealers have other motivations for using brokers, the fact that brokered trading defines the degree of transparency is undeniable. To determine the overall degree of order-flow transparency, consider first the share of spot trading that is brokered: 39% on average in 1989 across the seven countries with the highest turnover whose statistics are comparable, with a high of 44% and a low of 35% (Bank for International Settlements, 1990). (The remaining shares of total volume not brokered are about 50% from direct interdealer trades and about 10% customer–dealer trades.) Of the $\approx$ 40% of total trading that is brokered, only a portion of these trades generates a signal of signed volume. This is because a sale or purchase is announced only when it clears the bid or offer at the given broker. Though the likelihood of this depends on the currency, two dealers that trade different currencies for different firms estimated for me that this occurs for 50% to 75% of brokered trades. For example, if a broker is advertising underlying dealer prices of DM1.6045–DM1.6050 per dollar, and a buyer of dollars clears the offer, the broker will announce '50 paid', which indicates that the aggressor was a buyer. Though the exact size is not known, the median brokered quantity is about $5 million.

In light of this institutional background, three concerns regarding the broker data deserve attention. First, the data cover the trading activity of only one of the four for five main DM/$ brokers. Hence, just as dealer data reflect but a piece of the whole market, the broker data reflect only a piece of the brokered trading activity. Second, there is no way to determine on the basis of broker data available whether the bid or offer was cleared by any given transaction. Hence, some of the trades in this component of the dataset did not provide a signal to our dealer. Third, while the Dealing 2000-1 records include a precise, to-the-minute time stamp, the time stamps on the brokered transactions have a slight lag that corresponds to the time it takes the attendant to collect the tickets and stamp them. Due to these data shortcomings, I present estimates both with and without the signed brokered order flow B_t.

3.4. Descriptive statistics

Tables 1–3 present descriptive statistics. Because the dataset is new, the statistics are more detailed than usual. To convey a sense of the typical day's activity, Table 1 presents the data in the form of daily averages. This masks some daily variation in the sample: The heaviest day (8/7/92) is nearly twice as active as the lightest day (8/5/92). Note that this dealer averages well over $1 billion of interdealer trading daily (brokered trades are necessarily interdealer). With respect to quoting, because our dealer is among the larger players in this market, he has $10 million 'relationships' with many other dealers; that is, quote requests from other high-volume dealers that do not specify a quantity are

Table 1
Overview statistics, August 3–7, 1992

Data for the dealer's direct (not brokered) interdealer transactions are from the Reuters Dealing 2000-1 communications; these statistics include all direct transactions executed using Dealing 2000-1, regardless of which party is the aggressor. Incoming refers to communications initiated by another dealer; outgoing refers to communications initiated by our dealer. Data for the dealer's brokered transactions are from the dealer's position sheets; it is not possible to identify the aggressor from these data. Data from the broker are transcribed from transaction tickets; it is not possible to identify the aggressor from these data. The trades in the two dealer columns reflect more than 95% of this dealer's trading; the trades that make up the remainder are executed either (i) over the phone, (ii) with a nondealer customer, or (iii) in the futures market (IMM). The dealer's average trading day begins at 8:30 a.m. and ends around 1:30 p.m. EST.

	Dealer		Broker
	Direct	Brokered	
(1) Ave. # transactions daily	190	77	234
(A) incoming	170		
(B) outgoing	20		
(2) Ave. value transactions daily	$0.8 B	$0.4 B	$1.3 B
(A) incoming	$0.65 B		
(B) outgoing	$0.15 B		
(3) Median transaction size	$3 M	$4 M	$5 M
(A) incoming	$3 M		
(B) outgoing	$5 M		
(4) Median spread	DM 0.0003		
(A) incoming	DM 0.0003		
(B) outgoing	DM 0.0003		

understood to be good for $10 million. Note the tightness of the median spread. For comparison, the median spread in the Reuters indications dataset constructed by Goodhart is DM 0.001, more than three times as large. A bid/offer spread of three pips corresponds to less than 0.02% of the spot price.

Tables 2 and 3 present sample moments and a sample correlation matrix for the relevant variables used in estimation plus the intertransaction times. The first column of Table 3 bodes well for the model; these regressors all have the predicted correlation with the dependent variable ΔP_{it}. Note also that the intertransaction times are uncorrelated with the model variables (all are insignificant).

Figs. 3 and 4 present two plots. The first is the transaction price over the full sample, Monday, August 3 to Friday, August 7, 1992. The second plot provides the position (inventory) variability over the week; the maximum long dollar position was $56.8 million, the maximum short dollar position $42.7 million.

Table 2
Descriptive statistics: Sample moments

SD denotes standard deviation. 25% and 75% denote the 25th and 75th percentile values, respectively. ΔP_{it} is the change in the incoming transaction price (DM/$) from $t-1$ to t, expressed in pips, or DM 0.0001. All quantity variables are in $ millions. Q_{jt} is the quantity transacted directly at dealer i's quoted prices, positive for purchases (i.e., effected at the offer) and negative for sales (at the bid). I_t is i's position at the end of period t. B_t is the net quantity of third-party brokered trading over the previous two minutes, positive for buyer-initiated trades and negative for seller-initiated trades. Δt denotes the intertransaction time, in minutes. Sample: August 3–7, 1992, 839 observations.

	Mean	SD	25%	75%
ΔP_{it}	−0.2	4.7	−3.0	2.0
$\|\Delta P_{it}\|$	3.2	3.4	1.0	4.0
Q_{jt}	−0.4	5.2	−3.0	2.0
$\|Q_{jt}\|$	3.8	3.6	1.0	5.0
I_{it}	2.2	15.4	−6.7	9.3
$\|I_{it}\|$	11.3	10.7	3.4	16.0
B_t	−0.1	4.5	0.0	0.0
$\|B_t\|$	1.3	4.3	0.0	0.0
Δt	1.8	2.7	0.0	2.0

Table 3
Descriptive statistics: Sample correlation matrix

ΔP_{it} is the change in the incoming transaction price (DM/$) from $t-1$ to t, expressed in pips, or DM 0.0001. All quantity variables are in $ millions. Q_{jt} is the quantity transacted directly at dealer i's quoted prices, positive for purchases (i.e., effected at the offer) and negative for sales (at the bid). I_t is i's position at the end of period t. ΔI_t is $I_t - I_{t-1}$. D_t is an indicator variable with value 1 if the incoming order is a purchase and value −1 if a sale. B_t is the net quantity of third-party brokered trading over the previous two minutes, positive for buyer-initiated trades and negative for seller-initiated trades. Δt denotes the intertransaction time, in minutes. Sample: August 3–7, 1992, 839 observations.

	ΔP_{it}	Q_{jt}	I_{it}	ΔI_{it}	D_t	B_t	Δt
ΔP_{it}	1.00						
Q_{jt}	0.38	1.00					
I_{it}	−0.14	−0.28	1.00				
ΔI_{it}	−0.32	−0.58	0.22	1.00			
D_t	0.38	0.73	−0.12	−0.44	1.00		
B_t	0.08	−0.02	0.00	0.02	0.03	1.00	
Δt	0.00	−0.01	−0.02	−0.01	−0.01	0.02	1.00

A natural concern is whether our dealer is representative of the interbank spot market. While I cannot answer this definitively, I can offer a few relevant facts. First, he has been trading in this market for many years and is well known among the other major dealers. Second, in terms of trading volume, he is

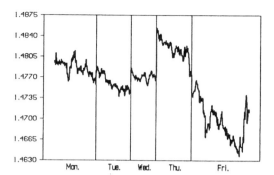

Fig. 3. Plot of the transaction price (DM/$) for all incoming orders in the sample, Monday, August 3 to Friday, August 7, 1992.

These 843 price observations are recorded by Reuters Dealing 2000-1. Their first differences correspond to the dependent variable in the model, ΔP_{it}. The vertical lines designate the four overnight periods through which the dealer did not trade. The discrete jumps at the vertical lines reflect price movements during these inactive periods.

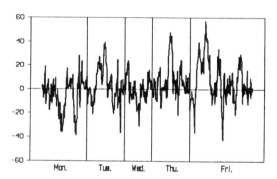

Fig. 4. Plot of dealer's dollar inventory I_{it} (in millions) at the time of each incoming order in the sample, Monday, August 3 to Friday, August 7, 1992.

These 843 inventory observations are constructed from the dealer's position sheets. Short dollar positions correspond to long DM positions, and vice versa. The vertical lines designate the four overnight periods through which the dealer did not trade.

without doubt one of the key players, trading well over $1 billion per day and maintaining $10 million quote relationships with a number of other dealers. Though this would probably not put him in the top five in terms of volume, he is not far back, possibly in the sixth to fifteenth range. He is certainly representative, at least with respect to the issues addressed here. There is no doubt, however, that different trading styles exist.

3.5. Relevant institutional background

Here, I highlight two institutional factors relevant to this analysis, trading limits imposed on dealers, and trading on the IMM futures market.

There is an important distinction between intraday trading limits and overnight limits. At our dealer's bank, which is typical of major banks, there is no explicit intraday limit on senior dealers, though dealers are expected to communicate particularly large trades to their immediate supervisor (about $50 million and above for many banks in the current DM/$ market). In contrast, most banks impose overnight limits on their dealers. Currently, a common overnight limit on a single dealer's open position is about $75 million, considerably larger than the largest open position in the sample. Most dealers, however, close their day with a zero net position; carrying an open position means monitoring it through the evening, an unattractive prospect after a full day of trading. Our dealer ends his day with a zero net position each of the five days in the sample. Finally, though broader risk-management programs are in place at the bank for which our dealer trades, it is rare in FX that a dealer's position is hedged because it aggregates unfavorably with others. When this does occur, it is typically without the participation of the individual dealer.

Trading on the IMM futures market while dealing spot differs by dealer. Our dealer's position cards show that he trades less than $1 million daily over the sample period, which is negligible relative to his daily spot volume. Like other spot dealers, he listens to an intercom that communicates futures prices. [Unlike equity markets, the spot FX market is many times larger than the futures market: In 1992, the average daily volume in New York in spot DM/$ was roughly $50 billion (New York Federal Reserve Bank, 1992). In the same year, the average daily volume on all IMM DM/$ contracts was less than $5 billion.]

4. Model estimation

4.1. The baseline model

Table 4 presents estimation results over the full five-day period. The sample size is determined by the number of incoming direct transactions, for a total of 839 observations. I have excluded the four overnight price changes, since the model is intended to explain intraday quoting dynamics, not price changes over periods through which the dealer is not active. The first row presents estimates of the full reduced form, i.e., including the information effects of third-party brokered order flow. The second row excludes the brokered-order-flow variable. It is therefore more directly comparable to results from work on the stock market, for example, Glosten and Harris (1988), Foster and Viswanathan (1990), and

Table 4
Baseline model estimates

$$\Delta P_{it} = \beta_0 + \beta_1 Q_{jt} + \beta_2 I_{it} + \beta_3 I_{it-1} + \beta_4 D_t + \beta_5 D_{t-1} + \beta_6 B_t + \beta_7 v_{it-1} + v_{it}$$

T-statistics in parentheses. The last row indicates the signs predicted by the model. ΔP_{it} is the change in the incoming transaction price (DM/$) from $t-1$ to t. Q_{jt} is the incoming order transacted at dealer i's quoted prices, positive for purchases (i.e., effected at the offer) and negative for sales (at the bid). I_t is dealer i's inventory at the end of period t. D_t is an indicator variable with value 1 if the incoming order is a purchase and value -1 if a sale. B_t is the net quantity of third-party brokered trading over the previous two minutes, positive for buyer-initiated trades and negative for seller-initiated trades. All quantity variables are in $ millions. All coefficients are multiplied by 10^5. Sample: August 3–7, 1992, 839 observations. I use the Hildreth–Lu procedure to estimate β_7.

β_0	β_1	β_2	β_3	β_4	β_5	β_6	β_7	R^2
−1.30	1.44	−0.98	0.79	10.15	−8.93	0.69	−0.09	0.23
(−0.96)	(3.10)	(−3.59)	(3.00)	(4.73)	(−6.12)	(2.21)	(−2.55)	
−1.34	1.40	−0.97	0.78	10.43	−9.16		−0.09	0.22
(−0.99)	(3.03)	(−3.56)	(2.95)	(4.86)	(−6.28)		(−2.61)	
	>0	<0	>0	>0	<0	>0	<0	

Madhavan and Smidt (1991). Row three indicates the predicted signs of the coefficients under the null that both information and inventory-control effects are present.

The main results from Table 4 are the very significant and properly signed coefficients on the information (order-flow) variables Q_{jt} and B_t and the inventory variables I_{it} and I_{it-1}. The size of β_1 implies that our dealer widens his spread about 2.8 pips per $10 million (1.4 doubled) to protect against adverse selection. The size of the inventory-control coefficient β_3 [which equals α in Eq. (8)] implies that our dealer motivates inventory decumulation by shading his DM price of dollars by 0.8 pips for every $10 million of net open position.

The coefficients on the indicator variables D_t and D_{t-1}, which measure the effective spread for Q_{jt} close to zero, are very significant, and have the predicted relative size as well, $\beta_4 > |\beta_5|$. (Recall that there is a one-to-one correspondence between D_t and the sign of Q_{jt}, so D_t controls perfectly for whether Q_{jt} is at the bid or the offer.) The coefficient β_4 suggests that once I control for the information and inventory effects, the baseline spread for this dealer is about two pips (2 times β_4 divided by 10^5). Note too that the moving average coefficient β_7 is significant and properly signed, providing further support for the model. Finally, the levels of the R^2's reflect the fact that Q_{jt} and B_t together are a small fraction of the trading activity in the wider market.

One possible way to control for the wider market would be to include ΔP from the broker data in the regression. Given the broker data available, however, there are three problems: First, the ΔP_{it}'s that make up the dependent variable come from the dealer data, which are strictly ordered and time stamped to the minute (no lag). With a mean intertransaction time less than two minutes, in many cases P_{it-1} and P_{it} have the same time stamp. Even if the broker data were time stamped immediately, there would be no way to determine whether a brokered transaction carrying the same time stamp as two dealer transactions actually occurred between the two transactions. Second, a short lag is present in the time stamping of the brokered transactions, as described in the data section. Finally, ΔP's from the broker data would incorporate bid–ask bounce that could not be netted as the dealer data can. These arguments notwithstanding, I experimented by including brokered price changes in the regression with various lags, and even leads up to five minutes to account for the time stamp lags; these proxies proved too crude to generate any significance.

4.2. Other methods of inventory control

Section 2.6 outlines two methods of inventory control available to the dealer that are not reflected in the baseline model: Trading directly on another dealer's price (outgoing trades) and trading indirectly via a broker. First, I determine whether our dealer uses these methods. Then, I determine whether use of these additional methods biases the baseline estimates of inventory control via own price. Finally, I present estimates that show exactly how these other methods of inventory control enter the baseline model.

To determine if the dealer manages inventory by trading directly on other dealers' prices or trading through brokers, I perform the following simple test: My null hypothesis is that outgoing direct trades and brokered trades are unrelated to inventory control, and are therefore equally likely to result in inventory accumulation as decumulation. Under the alternative that these trades are used for inventory control, I expect that significantly more than half of these trades result in decumulation. Table 5 presents the results.

The results are unambiguous: The incidence of decumulating trades in these two categories is far too high to explain under the null of equal likelihood. Note, too, that the test is conservative, in the sense that nonzero desired inventories can result in trades that accumulate inventory in an absolute sense, even though they are decumulating undesired inventory.

In light of the strong results in Table 5, I examine whether these two additional methods of inventory control affect the baseline estimates of inventory control via own price. That is, these three methods may be substitutes, and their relative appeal may vary over time with the value of immediacy, anonymity, and other factors. I test this in the following way: At any given time, a dealer reveals his preference for these two other methods of inventory control by using

Table 5
Null hypothesis: Outgoing direct trades and brokered trades are as likely to be inventory decumulating as accumulating

The test statistic corresponds to a test of the null that trades of the specified type – outgoing direct or brokered – are inventory decumulating with probability 1/2 (normal approximation of binomial). Sample: August 3–7, 1992.

	Outgoing direct trades	Brokered trades
Total observations	96	383
Decumulating trades	76	297
Accumulating trades	20	86
Test statistic: Standard deviations	5.7	10.8

them. Accordingly, I construct a dummy variable that equals one if either of these two methods is used between the realization of transaction prices P_{it} and P_{it-1} (which determine the dependent variable ΔP_{it} in the model), and equals zero otherwise. Of 839 observations of ΔP_{it} there are 270 for which there is at least one intervening outgoing or brokered trade. I then re-estimate the baseline model with two additional variables, the dummy multiplied by I_{it} and this product's lagged value. Under the null hypothesis, the coefficients on the inventory-control variables should not vary with my proxy for the attractiveness of the other methods; that is, the coefficients on the additional regressors should not be significantly different from zero. The alternative hypothesis is that inventory control via own prices is affected by the attractiveness of these other methods. The result: I could not reject the null that both of these additional variables have zero coefficients (p-value = 59%). In summary, though there is strong evidence that all three inventory-control methods are used, I found no evidence that this biases the baseline model estimates.

Below are estimates that show how these other methods of inventory control enter the baseline model. The way they enter follows from the decomposition of ΔI_{it} in Eq. (21) and the reformulation of the baseline model that isolates ΔI_{it} in Eq. (22). Indeed, it is precisely the systematic effect that changes in inventory have on changes in price that allows me to disentangle inventory control in the data. Substituting Eq. (21) into Eq. (22) yields

$$\Delta P_{it} = \beta_0 + \beta_1 Q_{jt} + \beta_2(Q^o_{iAt} + Q^b_{iAt} - Q_{jt}) + (\beta_2 + \beta_3)I_{it-1} + \beta_4 D_t$$
$$+ \beta_5 D_{t-1} + \beta_6 B_t + \beta_7 v_{it-1} + v_{it}, \qquad (24)$$

where Q^o_{iAt} denotes dealer i's outgoing trades (net) occurring between $t-1$ and t, Q^b_{iAt} denote dealer i's brokered trades (net) occurring between $t-1$ and t, and $Q^o_{iAt} + Q^b_{iAt} - Q_{jt} = \Delta I_{it}$. Table 6 presents estimates of Eq. (24).

Table 6
Inventory change specification

$$\Delta P_{it} = \beta_0 + \beta_1 Q_{jt} + \beta_2(Q^o_{i,tt} + Q^b_{i,tt} - Q_{jt}) + (\beta_2 + \beta_3)I_{it-1} + \beta_4 D_t + \beta_5 D_{t-1} + \beta_6 B_t + \beta_7 v_{it-1} + v_{it}$$

T-statistics in parentheses. The last row indicates predicted signs. ΔP_{it} is the change in the incoming transaction price (DM/$) from $t-1$ to t. Q_{jt} is the incoming order transacted at dealer i's quoted prices, positive for purchases (i.e., effected at the offer) and negative for sales (at the bid). $Q^o_{i,tt}$ is the net quantity of dealer i's outgoing trades in the interval $t-1$ to t. $Q^b_{i,tt}$ is the net quantity of dealer i's brokered trades in the interval $t-1$ to t. I_t is dealer i's inventory at the end of period t. D_t is an indicator variable with value 1 if the incoming order is a purchase and value -1 if a sale. B_t is the net quantity of third-party brokered trading over the previous two minutes, positive for buyer-initiated trades and negative for seller-initiated trades. All quantity variables are in $ millions. All coefficients are multiplied by 10^5. Sample: August 3–7, 1992, 839 observations. I use the Hildreth–Lu procedure to estimate β_7.

β_0	β_1	β_2	$\beta_2 + \beta_3$	β_4	β_5	β_6	β_7	R^2
-1.30	1.44	-0.98	-0.19	10.15	-8.93	0.69	-0.09	0.23
(-0.96)	(3.10)	(-3.59)	(-2.09)	(4.73)	(-6.12)	(2.21)	(-2.55)	
	> 0	< 0	< 0	> 0	< 0	> 0	< 0	

This formulation of the model shows more clearly the role of $Q^o_{i,tt} + Q^b_{i,tt}$ in disentangling information effects from inventory control. The coefficient β_2 here picks up the strong control effect. (Recall that $\beta_2 + \beta_3$ approaches zero from below as the relative precision of private to public information goes to zero.) Finally, though collinearity prevents estimation of separate coefficients for each of the three components of ΔI_{it}, I can test the Eq. (23) prediction that separate coefficients for $Q^o_{i,tt}$ and $(Q^b_{i,tt} - Q_{jt})$ should be equal [coefficients β_2 and β'_2 in Eq. (23)]. This null hypothesis is not rejected (p-value $= 27\%$).

4.3. Nonlinearities and time-of-day effects

This subsection addresses two additional questions. First, are there (simple) nonlinearities in the information and inventory-control effects of trading activity? And second, are there important time-of-day effects in the data, such as increased inventory control near the end of the trading day?

First, I test for nonlinearities in the information effect of received trades by introducing a piecewise linear specification. I create a dummy variable L_t that equals one when the absolute value of Q_{jt} is above its median absolute value ($2.5 million), and zero otherwise. I then re-estimate the baseline model in Table 4 with the additional explanatory variable $L_t Q_{jt}$, and test whether its coefficient is significant. The p-value of the test is 49%. Defining L_t with the 10th, 25th, 75th, and 90th percentiles produced similar results. Hence, I find no evidence for a piecewise linear specification of the impact of Q_{jt}. Note the significance of this in light of the incentive to break up larger trades that is implicit in the estimated coefficient on Q_{jt}. Comments from dealers on this point typically emphasize the offsetting cost of the additional time required to execute multiple orders in such a rapidly traded market.

Next I consider nonlinearities in the inventory-control effect. In a market like FX, inventory-control effects must exhibit a nonlinearity at some level: Arbitrage is possible if the quoting dealer's offer falls below another's bid, or if the bid rises above another's offer. Recall that the inventory-control effect corresponds to the size of α in Eq. (17), and is estimated as the coefficient on I_{t-1}: $\beta_3 \approx 0.79$ pips per $10 million net open position. Thus, a $40 million open position translates into prices that are adjusted about three pips to induce decumulation. To examine more formally the incremental inventory-control effects at high inventory levels, I perform the following test: I distinguish between inventory up to some threshold level, and increments beyond that threshold. Specifically, in lieu of the series I_t in the baseline model, I use I_t^T and I_t^+, where (i) I_t^T is defined equal to I_t if $|I_t|$ is less than the threshold $\bar{I}$, and $\bar{I}R$ otherwise, with R an indicator variable equal to one when $I_t > 0$ and minus one when $I_t < 0$, and (ii) I_t^+ is defined equal to zero if $|I_t| < \bar{I}$, and equal to the increment $I_t - \bar{I}R$ otherwise. Accordingly, I test whether the coefficient on $I_{t-1}^+ = 0$, i.e., that the α for these incremental positions is zero, and find that incremental effects are significant up to the $40 million level. Beyond that level, however, the coefficient is no longer significant. This is consistent with avoidance of arbitrage. From the dealer's position sheets it is clear that at higher inventory levels, it is preferable to reduce inventory via outgoing or brokered trades. Fig. 4 provides prima facie evidence that open positions above $40 million are reduced rapidly.

Concerning time-of-day effects, it is well known that FX dealers typically zero out their positions by the end of the trading day, and this is the case for each of the five days in this sample (see Fig. 4). This temporal structure may influence the inventory-control parameters, among others. Accordingly, I perform chow tests to determine whether coefficients are stable through the day. For each day, I cut the sample into an early and late period, three different ways: (i) at the median transaction time, (ii) at the time when 25% of the transactions remain, and (iii) at the time when 10% of the transactions remain. I find no evidence at conventional significance levels for instabilities in any of the coefficients at any of the breaks except the inventory-control coefficients. Table 7 presents the results in that case.

In the case of the final 10%, the coefficients β_2 and β_3 are muted at the end of the day, rather than amplified. When I asked the dealer about this result, he responded: 'Of course. Remember, all of us listen to broker prices, so when I shade my price it gives the caller a sense of my position. At the end of my trading day it is important to keep my position to myself, since other dealers are also getting rid of positions in order to go home flat'. This dealer clearly prefers the other methods of inventory control late in the day.

Table 7
Null hypothesis: Inventory-control coefficients β_2 and β_3 are constant through the day

$$\Delta P_{it} = \beta_0 + \beta_1 Q_{jt} + \beta_2 I_{it} + \beta_3 I_{it-1} + \beta_4 D_t + \beta_5 D_{t-1} + \beta_6 B_t + \psi_{it} + \beta_7 \psi_{it-1}$$

P-values correspond to the marginal significance level of the Chow test that both β_2 and β_3 in the baseline model are the same value late in the day as early, where 'late in the day' is defined as either the final 50%, 25%, or 10% of the trades each day. ΔP_{it} is the change in the incoming transaction price (DM/$) from $t-1$ to t. Q_{jt} is the incoming order transacted at dealer i's quoted prices, positive for purchases (i.e., effected at the offer) and negative for sales (at the bid). I_t is dealer i's inventory at the end of period t. D_t is an indicator variable with value 1 if the incoming order is a purchase and value -1 if a sale. B_t is the net quantity of third-party brokered trading over the previous two minutes, positive for buyer-initiated trades and negative for seller-initiated trades. Sample: August 3–7, 1992, 839 observations.

	Final 50%	Final 25%	Final 10%
P-value	79.7%	10.8%	3.8%

4.4. Transaction time versus real time

The last dimension of my analysis addresses the use of transaction time as the empirical basis. Though intertransaction times are tightly distributed and uncorrelated with the model's variables (Tables 2 and 3), the coefficient β_1 on Q_{jt} will be affected if the flow of information from the various sources is not proportional to real time. To see this, note that the structural interpretation of β_1 is $(1-\phi)/\phi\theta$ [see Eq. (17)]. The key here is ϕ, defined equal to $(\kappa - \lambda)/(1 - \lambda)$. κ and λ, in turn, are signal extraction coefficients that are time-invariant if the relative precision of the various signals in the model does not change. The question, then, is whether intertransaction time is related to relative precision, in which case the information content of order flow is related to intertransaction time. In the context of this model, it is not clear a priori why intertransaction time should be related to relative signal precision.

Other modeling approaches do imply a relation between intertransaction time (or 'trading intensity') and the information content of order flow. For example, in the Admati and Pfleiderer (1988) model, order flow is less informative when trading intensity is high, due to bunching of discretionary liquidity traders. In contrast, order flow in the Easley and O'Hara (1992) model is more informative when trading intensity is high, because intense trading signals that uncertain information events have occurred. Of course, the trading mechanisms of these models differ substantially from the FX market, so caution should be used in applying their insights here.

To determine in the context of FX whether intertransaction time is related to the informativeness of order flow, I perform the following test: I introduce two dummy variables, s_t and l_t. The dummy variable s_t equals one if the time since

Table 8
Is order-flow less informative when intertransaction time is short?

$$\Delta P_{it} = \beta_0 + \beta_1 s_t Q_{jt} + \beta'_1 l_t Q_{jt} + \beta_2 I_{it} + \beta_3 I_{it-1} + \beta_4 D_t + \beta_5 D_{t-1} + \beta_6 B_t + \beta_7 v_{it-1} + v_{it}$$

T-statistics in parentheses. The coefficient β_1 measures the information effect of incoming orders for which the time since the previous incoming order is short ($s_t = 1$ and $l_t = 0$ in the equation in the heading), where short is defined as having the same time stamp (stamps are precise to the minute); 262 of 839 observations conform to this definition of a short intertransaction time. The coefficient β'_1 measures the information effect of incoming orders for which the time since the previous incoming order is long ($s_t = 0$, $l_t = 1$), where long is defined as 'not short'. ΔP_{it} is the change in the incoming transaction price (DM/$) from $t-1$ to t. Q_{jt} is the incoming order transacted at dealer i's quoted prices, positive for purchases (i.e., effected at the offer) and negative for sales (at the bid). I_t is dealer i's inventory at the end of period t. D_t is an indicator variable with value 1 if the incoming order is a purchase and value -1 if a sale. B_t is the net quantity of third-party brokered trading over the previous two minutes, positive for buyer-initiated trades and negative for seller-initiated trades. All quantity variables are in $ millions. All coefficients are multiplied by 10^5. Sample: August 3–7, 1992, 839 observations. I use the Hildreth–Lu procedure to estimate β_7.

β_0	β_1	β'_1	β_2	β_3	β_4	β_5	β_6	β_7
−0.97	0.07	2.33	−0.88	0.67	9.82	−8.94	0.69	−0.09
(−0.72)	(0.12)	(4.55)	(−3.25)	(2.57)	(4.62)	(−6.18)	(2.24)	(−2.71)

β_1: short, β'_1: long.

the previous incoming order is short, and zero if long, where short is defined as having the same time stamp (262/839 observations). The dummy variable l_t equals one if intertransaction time is long, zero if short. These dummies allow me to partition the information content of the incoming-order-flow variable Q_{jt} by including $s_t Q_{jt}$ and $l_t Q_{jt}$ in the baseline specification in lieu of Q_{jt}. Table 8 presents the results.

The coefficients on $s_t Q_{jt}$ and $l_t Q_{jt}$ imply that incoming trades occurring when trading is less intense are more informative. A test of the restriction that these two coefficients are equal is rejected at the 1% level.

I view this result as an early step in the empirics of the endogeneity of time in trading models. Earlier work (e.g., Hausman, Lo, and MacKinlay, 1992) rejects the assumption of exogenous intertransaction times, but makes little progress in establishing empirical regularities. Whether these effects are specific to the FX market remains to be determined.

5. Conclusion

I find that order flow affects prices through both an information channel and an inventory-control channel, providing support for both branches of microstructure theory. Of the two channels, the evidence for inventory control is the more novel. I estimate that inventory control induces price shading of about three-quarters of a pip for every $10 million of net open position. The strong inventory-control effect on price contrasts with previous work on the NYSE and futures markets. Further, this applies even though FX dealers have tools for controlling inventory that a specialist does not. In fact, there is strong evidence that our dealer uses these other tools: He systematically lays off inventory at other dealers' prices, trading both directly and through brokers. These results highlight the importance of inventory-control theory for understanding trading in this market.

For the information channel, the coefficient on incoming order flow implies a price response of about one pip for every $10 million. Since inside information in the usual sense is less relevant in FX, this finding calls for a broader view of what constitutes private information at the dealer level. One possibility, for example, is that the information in incoming order flow also pertains to inventories, though in an aggregate sense. Aggregate inventories may be price-relevant due to transitory liquidity effects or – at the other extreme – they may be communicating more fundamental information, because they are themselves caused by informative trades. Either way, the traditional distinction between information and inventory effects is less clear. Put differently, under this view the key distinction is aggregate versus idiosyncratic inventories. This role for aggregate dealer inventories is given further credence by the fact that price discovery relies on signals at the interdealer level; customer–dealer trades in spot FX are not publicly observed. Unfortunately, the multiple-dealer data required to test this interpretation of the information effect are not currently available.

This points to an important difficulty in focusing on a dealership market like FX. Empirical work on the specialist structure has the luxury of describing the behavior of a lone dealer. It is much more difficult to argue that by documenting the behavior of a single dealer in the FX market, I have similarly captured the FX market. Nevertheless, the dealer tracked here is without a doubt one of the key players in this market, trading well over $1 billion per day and maintaining $10 million quote relationships with a number of other dealers. Is he representative of dealers in the core of the wholesale spot market? Probably yes, at least with respect to the issues addressed here.

Appendix

A.1. Derivation of the statistic Z_{jt} in Eq. (6)

Beginning with

$$Q_{jt} = \theta(\mu_{jt} - P_{it}) + X_{jt}, \tag{4}$$

$$\Rightarrow$$

$$Q_{jt}/\theta + P_{it} = \mu_{jt} + X_{jt}/\theta,$$

and since $\mu_{jt} = \lambda \mu_t + (1 - \lambda) C_{jt}$, where $\lambda \equiv \sigma_\omega^2/(\sigma_\mu^2 + \sigma_\omega^2)$, I have

$$Q_{jt}/\theta + P_{it} - \lambda \mu_t = (1 - \lambda)(V_t + \tilde{\omega}_{jt}) + \tilde{X}_{jt}/\theta \quad \text{since} \quad C_{jt} = V_t + \tilde{\omega}_{jt},$$

$\Rightarrow$

$$Z_{jt} \equiv \frac{Q_{jt}/\theta + P_{it} - \lambda \mu_t}{1 - \lambda} = V_t + \tilde{\omega}_{jt} + [1/\theta(1 - \lambda)] \tilde{X}_{jt}. \tag{6}$$

A.2. Derivation of the price representation in Eq. (10)

Beginning with

$$P_{it} = \mu_{it} - \alpha(I_{it} - I_i^*) + \gamma D_t, \tag{8}$$

I can write:

$$\mu_{it} = \kappa \mu_t + (1 - \kappa) Z_{jt} \quad \text{where} \quad \kappa \equiv \sigma_{Zj}^2/(\sigma_{Zj}^2 + \sigma_\mu^2)$$

$$= \kappa \mu_t + \left[\frac{1 - \kappa}{1 - \lambda}\right][Q_{jt}/\theta + P_{it} - \lambda \mu_t]$$

$$= \kappa \mu_t - \left[\frac{\lambda(1 - \kappa)}{1 - \lambda}\right]\mu_t + \left[\frac{1 - \kappa}{1 - \lambda}\right][Q_{jt}/\theta + P_{it}]$$

$$= \left[\kappa - \frac{\lambda(1 - \kappa)}{1 - \lambda}\right]\mu_t + \left[\frac{1 - \kappa}{1 - \lambda}\right][Q_{jt}/\theta + P_{it}]$$

$$\equiv \phi \mu_t + (1 - \phi)[Q_{jt}/\theta + P_{it}] \quad \text{since} \quad \left[\kappa - \frac{\lambda(1 - \kappa)}{1 - \lambda}\right] + \left[\frac{1 - \kappa}{1 - \lambda}\right] = 1.$$

Note also that $0 < \phi < 1$ since $0 < \kappa < 1, 0 < \lambda < 1$, and $\kappa > \lambda$ – each of which follows from the definitions of κ and λ, above, and the fact that $\sigma_{Zj}^2 = \sigma_\omega^2 + [\theta(1 - \lambda)]^{-2} \sigma_X^2$.

Substituting this expression for μ_{it} into Eq. (8) yields

$$P_{it} = \phi \mu_t + (1 - \phi)[Q_{jt}/\theta + P_{it}] - \alpha(I_{it} - I_i^*) + \gamma D_t,$$

$\Rightarrow$

$$P_{it} = \mu_t + \left[\frac{1 - \phi}{\phi \theta}\right]Q_{jt} - \left[\frac{\alpha}{\phi}\right](I_{it} - I_i^*) + \left[\frac{\gamma}{\phi}\right]D_t,$$

but from Eq. (5) μ_t can be written as

$$\mu_t = \rho S_t + (1-\rho)Q_t \quad \text{where} \quad \rho \equiv \sigma_\xi^2/(\sigma_\xi^2 + \sigma_\eta^2).$$

Hence, I can write:

$$P_{it} = (1-\rho)Q_t + \rho S_t + \left[\frac{1-\phi}{\phi\theta}\right]Q_{jt} - \left[\frac{\alpha}{\phi}\right](I_{it} - I_i^*) + \left[\frac{\gamma}{\phi}\right]D_t.$$

A.3. Derivation of the relation between B_t and Q_t in Eq. (14)

The approach is as follows: I begin with the definition of the observable order-flow signal, B_t. I then determine a Q_t from B_t with the properties set out in Section 1, i.e., such that $Q_t = V_t + \xi_t$, where ξ_t is distributed normally and independently of the noise in S_t and C_{jt}. The resulting relation between Q_t and B_t establishes the structural interpretation of the coefficient β_6 in Eq. (18).

Beginning with Eq. (11):

$$B_t = \sum_{k=1}^{m} Q_{kt} + \tilde{\psi}_t = \sum_{k=1}^{m} [\theta(\mu_{kt} - \mu_t) + \tilde{X}_{kt}] + \tilde{\psi}_t. \tag{11}$$

But:

$$\mu_{kt} = (1-\lambda)C_{kt} + \lambda\mu_t = (1-\lambda)C_{kt} + \lambda[\rho S_t + (1-\rho)Q_t].$$

Substituting this value for μ_{kt} into Eq. (11) yields

$$B_t = \theta(1-\lambda)\sum_{k=1}^{m} C_{kt} + m\theta(\lambda-1)[\rho S_t + (1-\rho)Q_t] + \sum_{k=1}^{m} \tilde{X}_{kt} + \tilde{\psi}_t,$$

$$\Rightarrow$$

$$B_t + m\theta(1-\lambda)[\rho S_t + (1-\rho)Q_t] = \theta(1-\lambda)\sum_{k=1}^{m}[V_t + \tilde{\omega}_{kt}] + \sum_{k=1}^{m}\tilde{X}_{kt} + \tilde{\psi}_t,$$

$$\Rightarrow$$

$$[B_t + m\theta(1-\lambda)[\rho S_t + (1-\rho)Q_t]][m\theta(1-\lambda)]^{-1}$$

$$= V_t + m^{-1}\sum_{k=1}^{m}\tilde{\omega}_{kt} + [m\theta(1-\lambda)]^{-1}\sum_{k=1}^{m}\tilde{X}_{kt} + [m\theta(1-\lambda)]^{-1}\tilde{\psi}_t$$

$$\equiv V_t + \xi_t,$$

where ξ_t is composed of the independent sources of noise $\tilde{\omega}_{kt}$, $\tilde{X}_{kt}$, and $\tilde{\psi}_t$. I now define implicitly a statistic Q_t, such that:

$$Q_t \equiv [B_t + m\theta(1-\lambda)[\rho S_t + (1-\rho)Q_t]][m\theta(1-\lambda)]^{-1} = V_t + \xi_t, \quad (A.1)$$

$$\Rightarrow$$

$$Q_t = [B_t + m\theta(1-\lambda)\rho S_t][m\theta(1-\lambda)]^{-1}$$
$$+ [m\theta(1-\lambda)(1-\rho)][m\theta(1-\lambda)]^{-1}Q_t,$$

$$\Rightarrow$$

$$Q_t[1-(1-\rho)] = [B_t + m\theta(1-\lambda)\rho S_t][m\theta(1-\lambda)]^{-1},$$

$$\Rightarrow$$

$$Q_t = \left[\frac{1}{m\theta(1-\lambda)\rho}\right]B_t + S_t. \quad (14)$$

References

Admati, A. and P. Pfleiderer, 1988, A theory of intraday patterns: Volume and price variability, Review of Financial Studies 1, 3–40.

Amihud, Y. and H. Mendelson, 1980, Dealership market: Market making with inventory, Journal of Financial Economics 8, 31–53.

Bank for International Settlements, 1990, BIS survey of foreign exchange market activity, Feb. (Monetary and Economic Department, BIS, Basel).

Bessembinder, H., 1994, Bid-ask spreads in the interbank foreign exchange markets, Journal of Financial Economics 35, 317–348.

Bollerslev, T. and I. Domowitz, 1993, Trading patterns and prices in the interbank foreign exchange market, Journal of Finance 48, 1421–1444.

Easley, D. and M. O'Hara, 1987, Price, quantity, and information in securities markets, Journal of Financial Economics 19, 60–90.

Easley, D. and M. O'Hara, 1992, Time and the process of security price adjustment, Journal of Finance 47, 577–605.

Flood, M., 1994, Market structure and inefficiency in the foreign exchange market, Journal of International Money and Finance 13, 131–158.

Foster, D. and S. Viswanathan, 1990, Variations in volumes, variances, and trading costs, Working paper no. 88-108 (Duke University, Durhan, NC).

Garman, M., 1976, Market microstructure, Journal of Financial Economics 3, 257–275.

Glosten, L. and L. Harris, 1988, Estimating the components of the bid–ask spread, Journal of Financial Economics 21, 123–142.

Glosten, L. and P. Milgrom, 1985, Bid, ask, and transaction prices in a specialist market with heterogeneously informed agents, Journal of Financial Economics 14, 71–100.

Goodhart, C. and L. Figliuoli, 1991, Every minute counts in financial markets, Journal of International Money and Finance 10, 23–52.

Goodhart, C., T. Ito, and R. Payne, 1994, One day in June 1993: A study of the working of Reuters' dealing 2000-2 electronic foreign exchange trading system, in: J. Frankel, ed., The microstructure of the foreign exchange market (University of Chicago Press, Chicago, IL) forthcoming.

Hasbrouck, J., 1988, Trades, quotes, inventories, and information, Journal of Financial Economics 22, 229–252.

Hasbrouck, J., 1991, Measuring the information content of stock trades, Journal of Finance 46, 179–208.

Hasbrouck, J. and G. Sofianos, 1993, The trades of market makers: An empirical analysis of NYSE specialists, Journal of Finance 48, 1565–1593.

Hausman, J., A. Lo, and C. MacKinlay, 1992, An ordered probit analysis of transaction stock prices, Journal of Financial Economics 31, 319–379.

Ho, T. and H. Stoll, 1983, The dynamics of dealer markets under competition, Journal of Finance 38, 1053–1074.

Kyle, A., 1985, Continuous auctions and insider trading, Econometrica 53, 1315–1335.

Kyle, A., 1989, Informed speculation with imperfect competition, Review of Economic Studies 56, 317–356.

Laux, P., 1993, Intraday price formation in the stock index futures market, Working paper (University of Texas, Austin, TX).

Lee, C. and M. Ready, 1991, Inferring trade direction from intradaily data, Journal of Finance 46, 733–746.

Lyons, R., 1994, Information externalities in the microstructure of the foreign exchange market, Manuscript, Oct., (Berkeley Business School, Berkeley, CA).

Madhavan, A. and S. Smidt, 1991, A Bayesian model of intraday specialist pricing, Journal of Financial Economics 30, 99–134.

Madhavan, A. and S. Smidt, 1993, An analysis of changes in specialist inventories and quotations, Journal of Finance 48, 1595–1628.

Manaster, S. and S. Mann, 1992, Life in the pits: competitive market making and inventory control, Working paper (University of Utah, Salt Lake City, UT).

New York Federal Reserve Bank, 1992, Summary of results of the U.S. foreign exchange market turnover survey conducted in April 1992, Mimeo. (Federal Reserve Bank, New York, NY).

O'Hara, M. and G. Oldfield, 1986, The microeconomics of market making, Journal of Financial and Quantitative Analysis 21, 361–376.

Reuters Ltd., 1990, The Reuters dealing 2000-1 service: User guide, Version 3 (Reuters Ltd., London).

Stoll, H., 1989, Inferring the components of the bid–ask spread: Theory and empirical tests, Journal of Finance 44, 115–134.

D
Treasury Auction

Treasury Auction Bids and the Salomon Squeeze

NARASIMHAN JEGADEESH*

ABSTRACT

Recent press accounts claim that collusion is common practice in Treasury auctions and that as a result the auction profits are excessive. But, this paper finds that the auction prices are on average marginally higher than the secondary market bid prices. The auction profits, however, are systematically related to the total fraction of winning bids tendered by banks and dealers. The postauction prices of the two-year notes in which Salomon Brothers had a 94 percent holding are also examined. The secondary market prices of these notes were significantly higher than the estimated competitive prices in the four-week postissue period.

THE MARKET FOR U.S. Treasury notes and bonds is widely considered as one of the most active and liquid markets in the world. The recent revelation that Salomon Brothers accumulated a large position in the two-year notes issued in the May 1991 auction and allegedly manipulated the price of this issue has led many investors to question the price efficiency in this market. For instance, one of the lead articles in the *Wall Street Journal* dated August 19, 1991 (p. A1) reports that "Collusion and price fixing in the $2.3 trillion Treasury securities market have been routine for more than a decade, according to traders and top Wall Street executives."

Such assertions have led to calls for changes in the auction rules and tighter regulation of the market for Treasury securities and evidently, such measures are being contemplated by the Treasury. For instance, the same issue of the *Wall Street Journal* (p. A5) reports that the "Treasury is considering significant changes in how it sells government debt," and the *Wall Street Journal* dated August 26, 1991 (p. A1) quotes the Fed Vice Chairman David Mullins as saying "We need to examine mechanisms to improve the efficiency of the market, (and) reduce the cost of Treasury finance..." While it is possible that technicalities such as position limits were violated in Treasury auctions, models of rational economic behavior predict that collusion cannot be sustained in a market with as many participants as in the Treasury auctions. It is therefore important to investigate

---

*University of California, Los Angeles and University of Illinois at Urbana-Champaign. I would like to thank Jim Brandon, Michael Brennan, Brad Cornell, Darrell Duffie, Francis Longstaff, Jill Ousley, Jerome Powell, Gary Rasmussen, René Stulz, Suresh Sundaresan, Sheridan Titman, Bruce Tuckman, and an anonymous referee for helpful comments and/or discussions. Phong Chan, Karen Gess, and Ravi Jain provided excellent research assistance. This research was partially supported by a UCLA Faculty Career Development Award and a research grant from the UCLA Academic Senate. I am solely responsible for any error in this paper.

whether or not these theory-based predictions are borne out in practice in order to evaluate the need for new, potentially costly, government regulations.

The regulators, naturally, attempt to continuously monitor whether bids in Treasury auctions are fixed as a result of collusion among the primary dealers or other participants. For instance, an ongoing Securities and Exchange Commission probe seeks to investigate whether bids in any of the auctions were "collusive, prearranged or concerted."[1] Establishing whether there were collusive, prearranged, or concerted bids in any given auction is an elaborate legal endeavor and is clearly beyond the scope of this paper. This paper pursues a more general objective and measures the profits of the winning bidders in Treasury auctions and investigates whether these profits are systematically related to the proportion of winning bids tendered by commercial banks and nonbank primary dealers (hereafter "banks and dealers")[2] in order to evaluate whether there is prima facie evidence of pervasive price fixing.

The expected economic profits to winning the auctions are estimated as the average change in the differences between the prices of newly issued bonds and matched seasoned bonds on the auction dates and on selected dates following the auctions.[3] The evidence indicates that on average the primary dealers buy bonds in the auctions at prices marginally higher than the prices that they are willing to pay in the secondary markets after the auctions.

The next test examines whether the postauction price changes are systematically related to the percentage of new issues won by banks and dealers. If they routinely collude then it is likely that when they collectively bid less aggressively, or when the percentage of winning bids tendered by this group is low, the profits to the winning bids will be high. Interestingly, it is found that the allocation to banks and dealers are negatively related to auction profits. This result is consistent with the collusion hypothesis and suggests that further analysis using data on bids by individual dealers is warranted.

Finally, the validity of claims that the secondary market prices of the two-year Treasury notes issued in the May 1991 auction were manipulated is investigated. Salomon Brothers admitted to having controlled 94 percent of

---

[1] See the *Wall Street Journal*, August 27, 1991, page C6.

[2] Ideally, I would have liked to examine the relation between auction profits and allocations to primary dealers while banks and dealers includes nonprimary dealer commercial banks. The allocations to primary dealers, however, are not publicly available and the Treasury Department indicated that this is proprietary information. The average proportion of winning bids from commercial banks is 14.60 percent while that from nonbank primary dealers is 58.78 percent (see Table IV). These statistics suggest that the allocation to nonprimary dealer commercial banks, which is a fraction of the total allocation to commercial banks, is small relative to the allocation to primary dealers. Therefore, I expect that any association that may exist between auction profits and primary dealer allocations will likely be evident when allocation to banks and dealers is used as a proxy, although there may be a loss of power due to the inclusion of allocations to nonprimary dealer commercial banks in this proxy.

[3] The auction data are obtained from the *Treasury Bulletin* and the secondary market bond prices are collected from the *Wall Street Journal*.

the two-year notes issued in this auction in violation of the Treasury regulation that no bidder may bid for more than 35 percent of the issues in any single auction. Although the holding of Salomon Brothers appears large, the analysis in Kyle (1984) suggests that any position less than 100 percent will not result in a market squeeze. Contrary to this prediction, however, it is found that the prices of the two-year notes issued in May 1991 were significantly higher than the estimated competitive prices in the four-week postissue period.

The rest of the paper is organized as follows. Section I describes the institutional aspects of the Treasury note and Treasury bond auctions. Section II presents estimates of the profits to winning allocations in Treasury auctions. Section III examines the relation between auction profits and allocations to banks and dealers. Section IV examines the secondary market prices of the two-year notes issued in May 1991 and Section V concludes.

I. The Process of Treasury Auctions

Treasury notes and bonds of various maturities are issued periodically through discriminatory price auctions. The Treasury announces the quantities of notes and bonds of different maturities that will be sold in upcoming auctions and accepts competitive and noncompetitive tenders until 1:00 P.M. eastern standard time on the auction date. The competitive bidders, mainly designated primary dealers[4] and commercial banks, submit bids for yield-quantity pairs. The noncompetitive bidders submit tenders for quantities that they are willing to purchase at the quantity-weighted price of the accepted competitive bids. Bidders other than the primary dealers and commercial banks are required to deposit 2 percent of the amount bid along with their tenders. These deposits do not earn interest and may be held for up to two weeks. Therefore, the deposit requirement makes it costly for many investors to bid directly and provides incentives for them to bid through the primary dealers. In addition to these bidders, the Fed also places a noncompetitive bid for a quantity announced prior to the auction.

The Fed collects the bids and nets out the noncompetitive bids and allocates the balance to the highest bidders among the competitive bidders. The coupon rate is set at the highest bid below the quantity-weighted average yield in the auction, rounded off to the nearest one-eighth. The winning bidders make the payments for their allocations on the issue date, which is typically a week from the auction date.

Table I presents the summary statistics for Treasury notes and bonds issued during the January 1986 to June 1991 sample period. The Treasury

---

[4] The primary dealers are members of the Primary Dealer Association whose membership is conferred by the Federal Reserve Bank of New York. The primary dealers have the responsibility to bid in all Treasury auctions and to actively make secondary markets in the Treasury securities, among other things. See Bollenbacher (1988), for example, for further details on the role of primary dealers.

Table I
Issues of Treasury Notes and Treasury Bonds—January 1986 to June 1991

This table presents summary information on Treasury notes and bonds of different maturities issued through public offerings. Subscription is the average of the ratio of total bids in an auction to the amount issued, Price and Yield Ranges are the differences between the maximum and minimum accepted bid prices (dollars) and yields to maturity (percentages) respectively.

Years to Maturity	Number of Issues	Amount ($ Millions)	Subscription	Range Price	Range Yield
2	66	771960	2.63	0.0497	−0.028
3	22	289976	2.52	0.0657	−0.026
4	20	168958	3.08	0.0554	−0.017
5	26	221910	2.87	0.0902	−0.022
7	22	165411	2.67	0.1752	−0.035
10	23	275409	2.16	0.2378	−0.037
20	1	4753	2.72	0.8950	−0.100
30	21	199385	2.27	0.3134	−0.030
All	201	2097767	2.61	0.1243	−0.028

raised about $2.1 trillion through these issues. The two-year notes were issued monthly and the other securities were generally issued quarterly during this sample period. There was, however, only one issue of twenty-year bonds in this sample period.

The amounts of bids tendered are on average 2.61 times the amounts of bonds issued. The yield range of accepted bids is typically about three basis points for all maturities. The price range, however, is generally higher for longer term bonds and it ranges from 4.97 cents for the two-year notes to 31.34 cents for the thirty-year bonds. The yield and price ranges for the single issue of the twenty-year bonds, however, are substantially higher.

II. Profits to Winning Bids

This section first examines the average ex post profits to winning bids in Treasury auctions. The sample used in this section comprises all two-, five-, seven-, and ten-year notes issued in the January 1986 to June 1991 period.[5] This sample contains 67.7 percent of the issues and 68.3 percent of the value of the bonds issued in this period.

The ex post profit to winning a bid in an auction and holding the newly issued bond till time t, denoted as π_t, is:

$$\pi_t = P_t - (P_A + \text{Holding cost}_t), \qquad (1)$$

---

[5] The Treasury offered one issue of foreign-targeted ten-year notes in February 1986, within my sample period. This issue is excluded from the sample.

where P_A is the value-weighted average of the prices paid by the winning bidders for the newly issued bonds in the auction, as reported in the *Treasury Bulletin*. P_t is the average of the bid and ask prices of these bonds quoted at the close of date t plus accrued coupon; $t = 0$ denotes the issue date, $t = 1$ denotes one week from the date of issue and so on. These price quotations, which are for payment two business days after the quote date, are obtained from various issues of the *Wall Street Journal*. Holding cost is the cost of financing the investment in the bond from the date of issue to two business days after t.[6] The auction date interest rate on the Treasury bill that matures in about a week after that date is used as the rate at which the bidder can finance his investment in the bond.[7] The Treasury bill interest rates (r_A) are also obtained from the *Wall Street Journal*. π_t is computed as:

$$\pi_t = P_t - P_A(1 + r_A)^{n/365}, \tag{2}$$

where n is the number of calendar days from the issue date to two business days after date t.

Table II presents the average profit to purchasing a bond at the auction and holding it till the issue date and also for holding periods of one to four weeks from the issue date. Table II also presents the average changes in the yields-to-maturity from the auction date to date t. The average profits for the two-year notes over these holding periods range from 13.93 cents to 21.30 cents per $100 face value and they are significantly positive. For the five-, seven-, and ten-year Treasury notes, however, the average profits are not reliably different from zero.

These average ex post profits, however, need not measure the economic profits to bidding since they potentially include compensation for bearing interest rate risk from the auction date until date t. Moreover, interest rates generally declined over this sample period which was probably not anticipated. For example, the yield to maturities of the two-year notes issued in January 1986 and June 1991 were 8.17 and 7.06 percent respectively. Consequently, the ex post profits measured here may overstate the expected holding period profits at the time of bidding.

Therefore, the expected economic profits to the winning bids are estimated as the average change in the differences between the prices of newly issued bonds and matched seasoned bonds on the auction dates and on selected dates following the auctions. The method used for measuring the prices of matched seasoned bonds is as follows. In the first step, for each newly issued bond the market price of a comparable seasoned bond, denoted as P^c, is estimated using the secondary market prices of maturity matched bonds. The matched bonds are two seasoned bonds with maturity dates closest to that of the newly issued bond. The maturity dates of the matched seasoned bonds

---

[6] Recall that the payment for the purchase of bonds in Treasury auctions has to be made on the issue date.

[7] The time to maturities of the Treasury bills used in the empirical analysis varied from seven to ten days from the date of the auction.

Table II
Ex Post Profits to Winning Bids in Treasury Note Auctions

This table presents average ex post profits to purchasing two-, five-, seven-, and ten-year notes in Treasury auctions in the January 1986 to June 1991 period. π_t denotes the average profit to purchasing notes at the auctions and holding them up to t; $t = 0$ denotes the issue date, $t = 1$ denotes one week from the date of issue and so on. The ex post profit in an auction is computed as follows:

$$\pi_t = P_t - (P_A + \text{Holding cost}_t),$$

where P_t and P_A are the bond price including accrued coupon at time t and the auction prices respectively. Holding cost$_t$ is the cost of holding a bond from the auction date to date t, computed at the Treasury bill rate. π_t is expressed as dollars per $100 face value. The average differences between the yields to maturity (expressed in percentages) on the auction date (Y_A) and on date t (Y_t) are also presented. N is the number of observations for which price data on date t were available in the *Wall Street Journal*. The t-statistics are reported in parentheses.

Years to Maturity		Week				
		0	1	2	3	4
2	π_t	0.1393	0.1732	0.2130	0.1904	0.2010
		(3.95)	(3.46)	(3.04)	(2.49)	(2.30)
	$Y_t - Y_A$	-0.0732	-0.0782	-0.0851	-0.0557	-0.0456
		(-3.64)	(-2.69)	(-2.09)	(-1.25)	(-0.89)
	N	52	64	66	66	66
5	π_t	0.1296	0.2453	0.3422	0.1963	0.3469
		(0.90)	(1.05)	(1.48)	(0.83)	(1.20)
	$Y_t - Y_A$	-0.0284	-0.0471	-0.0614	-0.0146	-0.0423
		(-0.79)	(-0.81)	(-1.06)	(-0.24)	(-0.59)
	N	25	26	26	26	26
7	π_t	-0.0099	0.4212	0.6653	0.4007	0.3829
		(-0.04)	(1.50)	(1.57)	(0.87)	(0.77)
	$Y_t - Y_A$	0.0074	-0.0777	-0.1191	-0.0615	-0.0491
		(0.13)	(-1.39)	(-1.43)	(-0.68)	(-0.50)
	N	17	20	22	22	22
10	π_t	0.2675	0.2836	0.3237	0.5246	0.4742
		(0.87)	(0.74)	(0.66)	(0.85)	(0.77)
	$Y_t - Y_A$	-0.0394	-0.0334	-0.0324	-0.0573	-0.0430
		(-0.81)	(-0.55)	(-0.42)	(-0.59)	(-0.44)
	N	20	22	22	22	22
All	π_t	0.1374	0.2434	0.3288	0.2796	0.3025
		(1.84)	(2.66)	(2.80)	(2.06)	(2.11)
	$Y_t - Y_A$	-0.0454	-0.0645	-0.0775	-0.0490	-0.0451
		(-2.70)	(-2.90)	(-2.68)	(-1.52)	(-1.26)
	N	114	132	136	136	136

Treasury Auction Bids and the Salomon Squeeze

are also constrained to straddle the maturity date of the newly issued bond. The comparable bond yield is then obtained by linearly interpolating between the yields of the matched bonds. Specifically, let N_1, N_2, and N_n be the number of days to maturity of the two seasoned bonds and the newly issued bond respectively and let Y_1 and Y_2 be the yield to maturities of the seasoned bonds. The comparable bond yield Y^c is computed as:

$$Y^c = \frac{N_2 - N_n}{N_2 - N_1} Y_1 + \frac{N_n - N_1}{N_2 - N_1} Y_2. \quad (3)$$

P^c is the price at which the yield to maturity of the comparable bond equals Y^c. P^c provides an estimate of the price at which a seasoned bond with the same maturity as the newly issued bond will trade. Let ΔP_t be the difference between the prices of the newly issued bond and the comparable seasoned bond on date t, i.e., $\Delta P_t \equiv P_t - P_t^c$ and let ΔP_A denote this difference on the auction date.

Newly issued bonds usually command a "liquidity premium" relative to comparable seasoned bonds because they are more actively traded.[8] The components of ΔP_t can therefore be written as:

$$\Delta P_t = \lambda_t + e_t, \quad (4)$$

where λ_t is the liquidity premium at time t and e_t is the error in using P^c as an estimate of the equivalent seasoned bond price. The error term e_t has two components. The first component is the measurement error in quoted bond prices due to factors such as nonsynchronous trading of the matched seasoned bonds and the newly issued bond. The measurement error component of e_t is assumed to be zero on average. In addition, e_t also potentially contains a model misspecification error. Specifically, since bonds need not be priced so that yields are linear functions of time to maturity, expression (3) may be a biased estimator of comparable seasoned bond yields. The potential magnitude of this misspecification error is assessed in the Appendix and it is fairly small.

Consider the components of ΔP_A.

$$\Delta P_A = -\gamma + \lambda_A + e_A, \quad (5)$$

where γ is the expected profit to a winning bid in the auction. From expressions (5) and (4),

$$\delta_t \equiv \Delta P_t - \Delta P_A = \gamma + (\lambda_t - \lambda_A) + (e_t - e_A). \quad (6)$$

I assume that $E(e_t - e_A) = 0$. If the misspecification error at the auction date is systematically different from that at time t then this assumption will not be valid. The experiment described in the Appendix, however, indicates that

---

[8] For instance, Amihud and Mendelson (1991) document that the prices of newly issued Treasury bills are generally higher than the prices of seasoned bonds with the same maturity and attribute this price difference to the liquidity of the Treasury bills.

the magnitude of misspecification error is likely to be small and the misspecification error on the auction date is virtually the same as that four weeks after the auction.

Therefore, $E(\delta_t)$ equals the expected auction profits less the expected change in the liquidity premium from the auction date to date t. When t is close to the auction date the change in liquidity premium will likely be small. The volume of trade for a given bond issue generally declines over time as more and more of that issue are used in dedicated portfolios and taken out of circulation. Therefore, as the time between the auction date and t increases the expected holding period profit will likely decrease.

Table III presents the estimates of expected profits to winning bids in the two-, five-, seven-, and ten-year note auctions. The average profit to winning bids is 4.17 cents per $100 face value when the bonds are held till the issue date.[9] The winning bids for ten-year notes earn the highest profit of 12 cents (t-statistic = 2.35) while the winning bids for seven-year notes lose 4.27 cents (t-statistic = -0.60). The profits to winning bids dissipate entirely if the bonds are held for four weeks after the issue, probably because of the declining liquidity premia in the prices.[10]

To put the magnitude of the auction profits in perspective the quoted bid-ask spreads for these Treasury notes are examined. The total spread was on average 9.35 cents per $100 face value. The average auction profit is therefore less than half the bid-ask spread. In other words, on average the primary dealers purchase bonds in the auctions at prices that are marginally higher than the prices that they are willing to pay for the same bonds in the secondary markets soon after the auctions. Therefore, using the postauction secondary market prices as benchmarks, the auction prices on average do not seem to be particularly low.[11]

III. Auction Profits and Allocations to Banks and Dealers

Press accounts claim that primary dealers exploit their preferential status and collude in the bidding process. If these investors collude then it can be expected that when they collectively tender lower bids the profits for the winning bids will be higher. Of course, it is not possible for an outsider to

---

[9] When the May 1991 issue of the two-year note is excluded the average profit is 3.96 cents per $100 face value.

[10] In addition to estimating P_c using maturity matched bonds, the comparable seasoned bond prices were also computed using Macaulay duration-matched bonds. These matched bonds were selected so that their durations straddled that of the newly issued bonds. The results using duration-matched bonds were similar to those reported here with maturity-matched bonds and are therefore not reported. The time series standard errors of $\Delta P_t - \Delta P_A$, however, were larger using duration-matched bonds than when using maturity-matched bonds.

[11] One may argue that the primary dealers make markets in the Treasury bonds and hence sell their auction purchases at the ask prices and hence this price is the appropriate benchmark. However, the profits due to buying at the bid and selling at the ask are returns to market making and not profits as a result of winning auction bids.

Table III
Expected Profits to Winning Bids in Treasury Note Auctions

This table presents estimates of average expected profits to purchasing two-, five-, seven-, and ten-year notes in Treasury auctions in the January 1986 to June 1991 period. The expected profit to purchasing a note at the auction and holding it up to time t, denoted as δ_t, is estimated as follows. Let P_t denote the price of a newly issued bond at time t, and P_t^c the price of a comparable seasoned bond. Subscript $t = A$ denotes the auction date, $t = 0$ denotes the issue date, $t = 1$ denotes one week from the date of issue and so on. Let $\Delta P_t \equiv P_t - P_t^c$.

$$\delta_t = \Delta P_t - \Delta P_A.$$

δ_t is expressed in dollars per $100 face value.

The average changes in the yield differences (expressed in percentages) between the newly issued bond and a comparable seasoned bond on the auction date (ΔY_A) and on date t (ΔY_t) are also presented for reference. N is the number of observations for which matched and newly issued bond prices on the auction date and on date t were available in the Wall Street Journal. The t-statistics are reported in parentheses.

Years to Maturity		Week				
		0	1	2	3	4
2	δ_t	0.0502	0.0392	0.0104	0.0061	−0.0022
		(4.66)	(3.17)	(0.95)	(0.57)	(−0.17)
	$\Delta Y_t - \Delta Y_A$	−0.0286	−0.0227	−0.0063	−0.0040	0.0007
		(−4.68)	(−3.18)	(−1.01)	(−0.65)	(0.10)
	N	51	64	66	66	66
5	δ_t	0.0181	0.0026	0.0049	−0.0337	−0.0267
		(0.50)	(0.06)	(0.13)	(−0.77)	(−0.58)
	$\Delta Y_t - \Delta Y_A$	−0.0053	−0.0014	−0.0022	0.0072	0.0053
		(−0.60)	(−0.15)	(−0.23)	(0.67)	(0.47)
	N	24	25	26	26	26
7	δ_t	−0.0427	0.0313	0.0345	−0.0064	−0.0097
		(−0.60)	(0.51)	(0.57)	(−0.12)	(−0.16)
	$\Delta Y_t - \Delta Y_A$	0.0087	−0.0062	−0.0062	0.0009	0.0015
		(0.60)	(−0.50)	(−0.51)	(0.08)	(0.13)
	N	17	20	22	22	22
10	δ_t	0.1200	0.1454	0.0931	0.1708	0.1069
		(2.35)	(2.91)	(1.52)	(2.66)	(1.27)
	$\Delta Y_t - \Delta Y_A$	−0.0184	−0.0224	−0.0146	−0.0264	−0.0167
		(−2.29)	(−2.85)	(−1.51)	(−2.65)	(−1.26)
	N	20	22	22	22	22
All	δ_t	0.0417	0.0488	0.0266	0.0231	0.0096
		(2.43)	(3.02)	(1.61)	(1.32)	(0.48)
	$\Delta Y_t - \Delta Y_A$	−0.0161	−0.0161	−0.0068	−0.0047	−0.0011
		(−3.66)	(−3.51)	(−1.59)	(−1.07)	(−0.22)
	N	112	131	136	136	136

observe whether or not the primary dealers tender low collusive bids. However, if they collectively bid less aggressively in certain auctions then the allocations that they are likely to receive in those auctions will be less than that in the other auctions. Therefore, the collusion hypothesis implies that the auction profits will be negatively related to the proportion of winning bids tendered by the primary dealers and this hypothesis is tested in this section.

Table IV presents the average percentage of winning bids tendered by various groups of investors in the two-, five-, seven-, and ten-year Treasury note auctions. The commercial banks and nonbank primary dealers tendered 14.60 and 58.78 percent of the winning bids on average in these auctions.[12] The combined average percentage of the winning bids submitted by banks and dealers ranged from a low of 68.16 percent in the two-year note auctions to 81.13 percent in the ten-year note auctions.

Tests to examine whether the expected auction profit δ is systematically related to the proportion of winning bids tendered by banks and dealers are carried out next.[13] These tests control for differences in the level of competition in the auctions and differences in the extent of dispersion of opinion among the bidders regarding the bond value. Auction models of Reece (1978), Milgrom and Weber (1982), and Bikhchandani and Huang (1989) predict that the auction profits will be related to these variables.[14] These predictions are fairly intuitive. When there are a finite number of bidders who can each bid for finite quantities then each bidder optimally bids below the expected bond value conditional on his information set and on his bid winning the auction.

Table IV
Treasury Note Allocations

This table presents the average percentage of the newly issued two-, five-, seven-, and ten-year Treasury notes that were issued to different investor classes in the January 1986 to June 1991 period. The column headings denote the investor classes. N is the number of observations for which the investor class breakdown was available in the *Treasury Bulletin*.

Years to Maturity	N	Fed	Individuals	Corporations	Commercial Banks	Nonbank Primary Dealers	Others
2	64	8.04	7.28	5.60	16.74	51.42	10.92
5	25	0.58	4.86	11.71	11.60	62.53	8.72
7	22	1.60	4.74	7.74	14.25	66.31	5.35
10	20	3.31	3.37	8.29	11.75	69.38	3.90
All	131	4.82	5.80	7.54	14.60	58.78	8.46

[12] These data are obtained from various issues of the *Treasury Bulletin*. Although the *Treasury Bulletin* groups the allocations to brokers with nonbank dealers, in private communication the Treasury Department indicated that virtually all the allocation in this group is to primary dealers.

[13] See footnote 2.

[14] See Cammack (1991) for a discussion of the predictions of auction theory in the context of Treasury bill auctions, which are conducted in a manner similar to the Treasury note auctions examined here.

Treasury Auction Bids and the Salomon Squeeze

Since a bidder's marginal probability of losing an auction by lowering his bid increases with the level of competition the equilibrium bids on average increase, and the expected profits decrease, as the number of bidders increases. When there is an increase in the dispersion of opinion about the value of the bond, however, the marginal probability of losing an auction by lowering the bid decreases. Therefore, the bids will on average be lower and the expected profits to winning bids will be higher when there is larger dispersion of opinion than otherwise.

The ratio of the amount of bids tendered in an auction to the total value of bonds offered (denoted as SUBS below) is used as the proxy for the level of competition. The price range of accepted bids (RANGE-P) is used as the proxy for dispersion of opinion. The following regression is fitted to examine whether there is any systematic relation between the expected auction profits δ and the percentage of winning bids tendered by the banks and dealers after controlling for the other variables discussed above:

$$\delta_t^i = a_{1t} \text{ SUBS}^i + a_{2t} \text{ RANGE-P}^i + a_{3t} \text{ FRAC}^i + \sum_{j=1}^{4} d_j D^i + e_t^i \qquad (7)$$

where the superscript i denotes the ith auction, FRAC is the fraction of winning bids tendered by banks and dealers and the dummy variables D_1, D_2, D_3, and D_4 equal 1 if the time to maturity of the bond offered in auction i is two, five, seven, and ten years respectively and zero otherwise. Regression (7) is fitted using the weighted least squares procedure. The standard deviations of δ_t for bonds of a given maturity are estimated and the inverse of these standard deviations are used to weight the respective observations.

Table V presents the regression estimates. The slope coefficients on SUBS in regression (7) are reliably positive, contrary to theoretical predictions. Since this variable includes both the expected and the unexpected levels of participation in an auction, it is possible that its positive relation with auction profits may be due to the ex post information that the unexpected component conveys. The sign of the slope coefficient on RANGE-P is positive as predicted but it is not reliably different from zero except for $t = 1$.

The estimate (t-statistic) of the slope coefficient on FRAC using issue date profits is -0.2336 (-2.32) which indicates a reliable negative relation between the proportion of winning bids tendered by banks and dealers. In order to assess the economic significance of this result, the sample of bonds of each maturity is partitioned into three roughly equal groups (labelled "Low," "Medium," and "High") based on the proportion of winning bids tendered by banks and dealers. Table VI presents the average profits to winning the auction and holding the bond till the issue date for each group. The average profits for the Low groups are larger than that for the High groups for two-, seven-, and ten-year notes. The differences in profits, however, are not reliably different from zero when five-, seven-, and ten-year notes are considered separately. For the entire sample, the average profit for the Low group is 8.14 cents per $100 which is more than that for the High group by 4.57 cents

Table V
Association between Auction Profits, Bids Tendered, Price Range, and Allocations to Banks and Dealers

This table presents the estimates of the following regression:

$$\delta_t^i = a_{1t} \text{SUBS}^i + a_{2t} \text{RANGE-P}^i + a_{3t} \text{FRAC}^i + \sum_{j=1}^{4} d_j D^i + e_t^i$$

where δ_t^i is the profit to purchasing a Treasury note in auction i and holding it until time t. (See Table III for details on the computation of δ_t^i.) $t = 0$ denotes the issue date, $t = 1$ denotes one week from the date of issue and so on. SUBS is the ratio of the total amount of bids to the amount issued; RANGE-P is the difference between the prices of the maximum and minimum accepted bids; and FRAC is the ratio of the winning bids tendered by banks and dealers to the amount issued. D_1, D_2, D_3, and D_4 are dummy variables that equal 1 if the year to maturity of the bond is two, five, seven, and ten years respectively and zero otherwise. The sample consists of all two-, five-, seven-, and ten-year Treasury notes issued in the January 1986 to June 1991 period. N is the number of observations. The t-statistics are reported in parentheses.

t	SUBS	RANGE-P	FRAC	N
0	0.0713	0.1771	-0.2336	108
	(2.89)	(0.83)	(-2.32)	
1	0.0475	0.5301	-0.2764	126
	(1.74)	(2.18)	(-2.43)	
2	0.0581	0.1546	-0.0630	131
	(2.20)	(0.63)	(-0.57)	
3	0.0606	0.2418	-0.1398	131
	(2.30)	(1.02)	(-1.26)	
4	0.0739	0.1544	-0.2192	131
	(2.48)	(0.56)	(-1.73)	

Table VI
Auction Profits and Allocations to Banks and Dealers

This table presents the average auction profits (δ) to purchasing a Treasury note in an auction and holding it until issue date within three groups sorted based on the ratio of winning bids tendered by banks and dealers (FRAC) to the amount issued.

Years to Maturity		Allocation to Banks and Dealers		
		Low	Medium	High
2	δ	0.0825	0.0473	0.0253
	FRAC	56.43%	69.02%	76.60%
5	δ	0.0701	-0.1164	0.1094
	FRAC	61.36%	75.20%	85.00%
7	δ	-0.0135	-0.0464	-0.0632
	FRAC	71.73%	79.09%	85.18%
10	δ	0.1709	0.1719	0.0629
	FRAC	73.14%	81.79%	87.88%
All	δ	0.0814	0.0210	0.0357
	FRAC	62.65%	74.26%	81.78%

per $100. While there does not seem to be a natural benchmark that can be used to evaluate the economic significance of this difference, the fact that it is roughly the same as the average profits in Treasury auctions suggests that it is nontrivial.

The evidence presented in this section is consistent with the implications of the collusion hypothesis. However, it is also possible that the association between FRAC and auction profits is due to banks and dealers *legitimately* sharing information, such as their forecasts of macroeconomic variables that may not be available to other bidders. It is not possible to determine conclusively which of these explanations is more appropriate based on analysis of publicly available data. These results, however, suggest that a more detailed analysis to resolve these issues is warranted.

IV. Secondary Market Prices of Two-Year Notes Issued in May 1991

The total amount of the two-year notes auctioned in May 1991 was $12.25 billion. Salomon Brothers admitted to having controlling interest over 94 percent of this issue, well in excess of the 35 percent statutory ceiling.[15] The claims by the other investors that Salomon Brothers manipulated the secondary market prices of this issue led to widespread calls for overhauling the auction rules.[16]

Kyle (1984) examines theoretically how a large investor can potentially corner a market by taking large positions in the spot and forward (or when-issued) markets and squeeze the short investors. In his model, the dominant investor can manipulate the market prices and effect a short squeeze only if he controls more than 100 percent of the asset supply. In Kyle's model investors other than the dominant player act competitively. Therefore, when the net holding of the small investors is positive, the short sellers can all close out their positions by purchasing assets from the competitive investors at fair market prices and avoid a short squeeze. In this setting the 94 percent position held by Salomon Brothers in the May 1991 issue is not sufficient to manipulate the market prices. This section examines the secondary market prices of the May 1991 issue in order to test whether the allegations of price manipulations are true or whether the market prices are competitively set as in Kyle's model.

---

[15] The controlling interest held by Salomon Brothers included a $590 million dollar long position in the when-issued market, $4.2 billion purchased in its own account in the auction, and $500 million transferred from a customer account due to unauthorized bids. Salomon purchased an additional $5.92 billion of this issue in the auction on behalf of different customers (the source is U.S. Department of Treasury, *Joint Report* (1992)) which also seems to have been considered as a part of Salomon's controlling interest.

[16] While there have been widespread allegations that the price of this note was manipulated by Salomon Brothers, none of the published accounts that I am aware of, including the *Joint Report* (1992), document evidence that the market price during the postauction period was abnormally high.

Table VII, Panel A, presents the average estimates of ΔP_t, the differences between the prices of newly issued bonds and comparable seasoned bonds, for all two-year note issues in the 1986 to 1991 sample period except the May 1991 issue. The auction prices are on average 2.55 cents per $100 higher than the matched bond prices. The matched price differences range from 6.82 cents on the issue date to 1.74 cents four weeks from the issue date and the yields to maturity of the newly issued bonds are on average 1.09 to 3.94 basis points below that of comparable seasoned bonds over this period.

Table VII, Panel B, presents the price and yield comparisons for the May 1991 two-year notes. The auction price is 4.98 cents higher than the comparable seasoned bond price, which is not statistically different from the corresponding price difference in Panel A. The postauction matched price differences, however, are significantly higher than the corresponding price differences in Panel A. The average matched price difference for this two-year note from the date of issue to four weeks after the issue is 31.36 cents per $100 face value and this difference is significantly larger than the average difference of 4.23 cents for the other two-year notes. In addition, the matched price difference of 31.36 cents is the largest average matched price difference for the two-year notes in the sample. Therefore, contrary to

Table VII
Relative Prices of Two-Year Notes

This table presents a comparison of the prices and the yields of newly issued two-year Treasury notes issued in the January 1986 to June 1991 period with that of comparable seasoned bonds. Panel A presents the comparison for all two-year notes except the May 1991 issue and Panel B presents the comparison for the two-year note issued in the May 1991 auction. ΔP_t and ΔY_t are the differences between prices (expressed in dollars per $100 face value) and yields (expressed in percentages) of the newly issued bonds and that of matched seasoned bonds on date t. $t = Auction$ denotes the auction date, $t = 0$ denotes the issue date, $t = 1$ denotes one week from the date of issue and so on.

	Auction	0	1	2	3	4
	Panel A. All Two-year Notes Other than May 1991 Issue					
ΔP_t	0.0255	0.0682	0.0642	0.0331	0.0285	0.0174
	(2.48)[a]	(5.74)	(5.42)	(3.33)	(3.39)	(2.11)
ΔY_t	−0.0150	−0.0394	−0.0374	−0.0198	−0.0173	−0.0109
	(−2.57)	(−5.83)	(−5.49)	(−3.44)	(−3.51)	(−2.23)
	Panel B. Two-year Note Issued in May 1991					
ΔP_t	0.0498	0.3277	0.3163	0.2387	0.2561	0.4294
	(0.29)[b]	(3.09)	(2.68)	(2.56)	(3.35)	(6.17)
ΔY_t	−0.0286	−0.1853	−0.1819	−0.1386	−0.1497	−0.2519
	(−0.29)	(−3.06)	(−2.67)	(−2.57)	(−3.34)	(−6.11)

[a] The t-statistics under the hypothesis that mean ΔP_t and ΔY_t are different from zero are presented in Panel A.

[b] The t-statistics in Panel B indicate the number of standard deviations away from the sample mean reported in Panel A.

the implications of Kyle's model, the evidence indicates that the market prices were reliably higher than the estimated competitive prices although Salomon Brothers held less than 100 percent of the outstanding two-year notes.

V. Concluding Remarks

Recent press accounts claim that collusion in Treasury auctions is common practice and that the bidders profit at the expense of the Treasury. Such assertions have instigated the Treasury into considering new auction regulations. This paper examined the profits of the winning bids in Treasury auctions and investigated whether these profits are systematically related to the proportion of winning bids tendered by banks and dealers in order to evaluate whether there was prima facie evidence of price fixing.

The average profit to winning bids in the two-, five-, seven-, and ten-year Treasury note auctions is 4.17 cents per $100 face value. This profit is less than half the average bid-ask spread in the secondary markets and it indicates that on average the primary dealers purchase bonds at marginally higher prices in the auctions than in the secondary markets. It was found, however, that the auction profits are negatively related to the proportion of winning bids tendered by commercial banks and nonbank dealers. While this result is consistent with the collusion hypothesis, further analysis using finer data is required in order to draw more conclusive inferences.

This paper also examined the secondary market prices of the two-year notes issued in the May 1991 auction in which Salomon Brothers admitted to having violated auction regulations. The evidence here indicates that the prices of these notes were reliably higher than the estimated competitive prices in the four-week period after issue. This finding indicates that the concerns of bond market participants about potential squeezes are justified.[17] The possibility of price manipulation could potentially have an adverse effect on bond market liquidity. For example, if a squeeze were a real possibility, it may not be possible to purchase large amounts of bonds in the market without moving the prices away from the competitive levels. Since the evidence indicates that liquidity is priced in the bond market,[18] reduced liquidity will adversely affect market prices. Therefore, steps to curb potential price manipulations will likely be beneficial.

To alleviate this problem the Treasury has announced that it will reopen an issue in the event of "an acute, protracted squeeze." The practicality of this policy was tested when the *Wall Street Journal* (dated August 20, 1992)

---

[17] The *Wall Street Journal* also reported that there was a squeeze in the April 1992 two-year note issue. The profit from the auction date to the issue date for this note was 22.87 cents per $100 which, among all two-year notes, was second only to the May 1991 issue.

[18] The five-, seven- and ten-year newly issued notes were on average priced 46, 41, and 39 cents per $100 face value higher than comparable seasoned bonds on the issue date.

reported that there was a squeeze in the 5½ percent July 1997 Treasury note. Although the New York Fed launched an investigation in response to these allegations, the Treasury declined to reopen this issue. This episode illustrates one of the problems with this policy of selectively reopening issues when the criteria for judging whether or not there is a squeeze are not clear cut.

The Treasury may want to consider other market-based approaches to deter potential squeezes, such as standardizing the bond issues. One way to standardize bonds would be to issue all bonds of a given year to maturity with the same coupon and maturity date. For example, all two-year notes issued in, say 1993, may be issued with the same coupon and with December 1995 maturity. Alternatively, all bonds may be issued as pure discount bonds that mature at the end of selected months, say June and December, over a twenty- or thirty-year period.[19,20] Standardization of bond issues will periodically bring to the market a new supply of bonds of any given maturity and hence will make it more difficult for any investor to corner the market. There are likely to be other benefits to standardization as well. For instance, increasing the supply of the standardized bonds will increase the liquidity of these issues and hence possibly increase the prices that investors are willing to pay for them. In addition, auction theory indicates that a decrease in uncertainty about the value of bonds sold in the auctions will likely increase auction revenues. If bonds identical to that sold in the auctions are publicly traded at the time of the auctions then the extent of differences of opinion about their values will likely be less than otherwise, which in turn will potentially increase auction revenues.

Appendix

This appendix evaluates the potential magnitude of the misspecification error due to pricing comparable seasoned bonds using yields interpolated between the yields to maturity of matched bonds.

The prices of discount bonds with maturities ranging from one to eleven years are generated using the Cox, Ingersoll, and Ross (1985) (CIR) single factor model. Under the CIR model, the short interest rate is generated by the following diffusion process:

$$dr_t = \kappa(\mu - r_t)\,dt + \sigma\sqrt{r_t}\,dz,$$

---

[19] The first approach may pose a problem if a particular bond trades at a discount at the time of scheduled reissue. Then, under the current tax treatment of original issue discounts, the reissued bond will not be a substitute for a bond with the same maturity and coupon issued earlier at par or at a premium. I would like to thank Jerome Powell of the Treasury for pointing this out. This problem also applies to the reopening policy currently used by the Treasury. This tax issue, however, does not arise in the case of the second alternative suggested above since under the current regulations that apply to STRIPS, whenever the pure discount bonds are purchased they are treated as newly issued discount securities.

[20] Currently, certain designated issues are stripped by primary dealers and the principal and coupons are traded separately as discount bonds. This practice, however, is not intended to and does not serve the purpose of standardization.

where r_t is the instantaneous interest rate at time t, μ is the mean rate, κ is the speed of adjustment parameter and $\sigma^2 r_t$ is the instantaneous variance of the changes in the short rate. The parameter values used in the experiment are $\kappa = 0.8$, $\mu = 0.08$ and $\sigma = 0.06$. The experiment was conducted with two values for the short rate, one above μ with $r_t = 0.1$, and one below μ with $r = 0.06$. The local expectations hypothesis is assumed.

Bonds with maturities of $T - 1/4$ years and $T + 1/4$ years were used as the maturity-matched bonds to compute the comparable yields of bonds with maturities of two, five, and seven years and bonds with maturities of $T - 1$ years and $T + 1$ years were used as the maturity-matched bonds to compute the comparable yields of bonds with maturities of ten years.[21] The maximum difference between the model and the interpolated yields of less than 1 basis point was observed for the two-year discount bonds and the maximum difference between the model prices and the respective prices based on interpolated yields was less than 1 cent per $100. These results indicate that the magnitude of the misspecification errors are likely to be small. Moreover, the differences in these yields at the time of the auction and four weeks after the bond issue ($t = 4$) (the differences between the misspecification errors) were virtually zero for bonds of all maturities.

[21] For the two-, five-, and seven-year notes the maximum differences between the maturities of the newly issued bonds and matched bonds were 42, 60, and 126 days respectively, and for the ten-year notes the maximum differences on the short and long sides of maturity were 126 and 1838 days respectively. Using longer matched bond maturity differences for the ten-year bonds did not make much difference since the term structure under the CIR model was fairly flat at long horizons.

REFERENCES

Amihud, Yakov, and Haim Mendelson, 1991, Liquidity, maturity, and the yields on Treasury securities, *Journal of Finance* 46, 1411–1426.

Bikhchandani, Sushil, and Chi-Fu Huang, 1989, Auctions with resale markets: An exploratory model of Treasury bill markets, *Review of Financial Studies* 2, 311–340.

Bollenbacher, George M., 1988, *The Professional's Guide to the U.S. Government Securities Markets* (New York Institute of Finance, New York).

Cammack, Elizabeth B., 1991, Evidence on bidding strategies and the information in Treasury bill auctions, *Journal of Political Economy* 99, 100–130.

Cox, John, C., Jonathan E. Ingersoll, and Stephen A. Ross, 1985, An intertemporal general equilibrium model of asset prices, *Econometrica* 53, 385–408.

Kyle, Albert, 1984, A theory of futures market manipulations, in R. Anderson, ed.: *The Industrial Organization of Futures Markets* (Lexington Books, Lexington, Mass.).

Milgrom, Paul R., and Robert J. Weber, 1982, A theory of auctions and competitive bidding, *Econometrica* 50, 1089–1122.

Reece, Douglas K., 1978, Competitive bidding for offshore petroleum leases, *Bell Journal of Economics* 9, 369–384.

U.S. Department of Treasury, Securities and Exchange Commission, and Board of Governors of the Federal Reserve System, 1992, *Joint Report on the Government Securities Market* (U.S. Government Printing Office, Washington, D.C.).

Part V
Market Microstructure and Asset Pricing

ASSET PRICING AND THE BID–ASK SPREAD*

Yakov AMIHUD

Tel Aviv University, Tel Aviv, Israel
New York University, New York, NY 10006, USA

Haim MENDELSON

University of Rochester, Rochester, NY 14627, USA

Received August 1985, final version received April 1986

This paper studies the effect of the bid–ask spread on asset pricing. We analyze a model in which investors with different expected holding periods trade assets with different relative spreads. The resulting testable hypothesis is that market-observed expected return is an increasing and concave function of the spread. We test this hypothesis, and the empirical results are consistent with the predictions of the model.

1. Introduction

Liquidity, marketability or trading costs are among the primary attributes of many investment plans and financial instruments. In the securities industry, portfolio managers and investment consultants tailor portfolios to fit their clients' investment horizons and liquidity objectives. But despite its evident importance in practice, the role of liquidity in capital markets is hardly reflected in academic research. This paper attempts to narrow this gap by examining the effects of illiquidity on asset pricing.

Illiquidity can be measured by the cost of immediate execution. An investor willing to transact faces a tradeoff: He may either wait to transact at a favorable price or insist on immediate execution at the current bid or ask price. The quoted ask (offer) price includes a premium for immediate buying, and the bid price similarly reflects a concession required for immediate sale. Thus, a natural measure of illiquidity is the spread between the bid and ask

---

*We wish to thank Hans Stoll and Robert Whaley for furnishing the spread data, and Manny Pai for excellent programming assistance. We acknowledge helpful comments by the Editor, Clifford W. Smith, by an anonymous referee, by Harry DeAngelo, Linda DeAngelo, Michael C. Jensen, Krishna Ramaswamy and Jerry Zimmerman, and especially by John Long and G. William Schwert. Partial financial support by the Managerial Economics Research Center of the University of Rochester, the Salomon Brothers Center for the Study of Financial Markets, and the Israel Institute for Business Research is acknowledged.

0304-405X/86/$3.50©1986, Elsevier Science Publishers B.V. (North-Holland)

prices, which is the sum of the buying premium and the selling concession.[1] Indeed, the relative spread on stocks has been found to be negatively correlated with liquidity characteristics such as the trading volume, the number of shareholders, the number of market makers trading the stock and the stock price continuity.[2]

This paper suggests that expected asset returns are increasing in the (relative) bid–ask spread. We first model the effects of the spread on asset returns. Our model predicts that higher-spread assets yield higher expected returns, and that there is a clientele effect whereby investors with longer holding periods select assets with higher spreads. The resulting testable hypothesis is that asset returns are an increasing and concave function of the spread. The model also predicts that expected returns net of trading costs increase with the holding period, and consequently higher-spread assets yield higher net returns to their holders. Hence, an investor expecting a long holding period can gain by holding high-spread assets.

We test the predicted spread–return relation using data for the period 1961–1980, and find that our hypotheses are consistent with the evidence: Average portfolio risk-adjusted returns increase with their bid–ask spread, and the slope of the return–spread relationship decreases with the spread. Finally, we verify that the spread effect persists when firm size is added as an explanatory variable in the regression equations. We emphasize that the spread effect is by no means an anomaly or an indication of market inefficiency; rather, it represents a rational response by an efficient market to the existence of the spread.

This study highlights the importance of securities market microstructure in determining asset returns, and provides a link between this area and mainstream research on capital markets. Our results suggest that liquidity-increasing financial policies can reduce the firm's opportunity cost of capital, and provide measures for the value of improvements in the trading and exchange process.[3] In the area of portfolio selection, our findings may guide investors in balancing expected trading costs against expected returns. In sum, we demonstrate the importance of market-microstructure factors as determinants of stock returns.

In the following section we present a model of the return–spread relation and form the hypotheses for our empirical tests. In section 3 we test the

---

[1] Demsetz (1968) first related the spread to the cost of transacting. See also Amihud and Mendelson (1980, 1982), Phillips and Smith (1982), Ho and Stoll (1981, 1983), Copeland and Galai (1983), and West and Tinic (1971). For an analysis of transaction costs in the context of a fixed investment horizon, see Chen, Kim and Kon (1975), Levy (1978), Milne and Smith (1980), and Treynor (1980).

[2] See, e.g., Garbade (1982) and Stoll (1985).

[3] See, e.g., Mendelson (1982, 1985, 1986, 1987), Amihud and Mendelson (1985, 1986) for the interaction between market characteristics, trading organization and liquidity.

predicted relationship, and in section 4 we relate our findings to the firm size anomaly. Our concluding remarks are offered in section 5.

2. A model of the return–spread relation

In this section we model the role of the bid–ask spread in determining asset returns. We consider M investor types numbered by $i = 1, 2, \ldots, M$, and $N + 1$ capital assets indexed by $j = 0, 1, 2, \ldots, N$. Each asset j generates a perpetual cash flow of $\$d_j$ per unit time ($d_j > 0$) and has a relative spread of S_j, reflecting its trading costs. Asset 0 is a zero-spread asset ($S_0 = 0$) having unlimited supply. Assets are perfectly divisible, and one unit of each positive-spread asset j ($j = 1, 2, \ldots, N$) is available.

Trading is performed via competitive market makers who quote assets' bid and ask prices and stand ready to trade at these prices. The market makers bridge the time gaps between the arrivals of buyers and sellers to the market, absorb transitory excess demand or supply in their inventory positions, and are compensated by the spread, which is competitively set. Thus, they quote for each asset j an ask price V_j and a bid price $V_j(1 - S_j)$, giving rise to two price vectors: an ask price vector $(V_0, V_1, \ldots, V_N)$ and a bid price vector $(V_0, V_1(1 - S_1), \ldots, V_N(1 - S_N))$.[4]

A type-i investor enters the market with wealth W_i used to purchase capital assets (at the quoted ask prices). He holds these assets for a random, exponentially distributed time T_i with mean $E[T_i] = 1/\mu_i$, liquidates his portfolio by selling it to the market makers at the bid prices, and leaves the market. We number investor types by increasing expected holding periods, $\mu_1^{-1} \leq \mu_2^{-1} \leq \cdots \leq \mu_M^{-1}$, and assets by increasing relative spreads, $0 = S_0 \leq S_1 \leq \cdots \leq S_N < 1$. Finally, we assume that the arrivals of type-i investors to the market follow a Poisson process with rate λ_i, with the interarrival times and holding periods being stochastically independent.

In statistical equilibrium, the number of type-i investors with portfolio holdings in the market has a Poisson distribution with mean $m_i = \lambda_i/\mu_i$ [cf. Ross (1970, ch. 2)]. The market makers' inventories fluctuate over time to accommodate transitory excess demand or supply disturbances, but their *expected* inventory positions are zero, i.e., market makers are 'seeking out the market price that equilibrates buying and selling pressures' [Bagehot (1971, p. 14); see also Garman (1976)]. This implies that the expected sum of investors' holdings in each positive-spread asset is equal to its available supply of one unit.

Consider now the portfolio decision of a type-i investor facing a given set of bid and ask prices, whose objective is to maximize the expected discounted net

---

[4] Competition among market makers drives the spread to the level S_j of trading costs. In a different scenario, V_j may be viewed as the sum of the market price and the buying transaction cost, and $V_j(1 - S_j)$ as the price net of the cost of a sell transaction.

cash flows received over his planning horizon. The discount rate ρ is the spread-free, risk-adjusted rate of return on the zero-spread asset. Let x_{ij} be the quantity of asset j acquired by the type-i investor. We call the vector $\{x_{ij}, j = 0, 1, 2, \ldots, N\}$ 'portfolio i'. The expected present value of holding portfolio i is the sum of the expected discounted value of the continuous cash stream received over its holding period and the expected discounted liquidation revenue. This sum is given by

$$E_{T_i}\left\{\int_0^{T_i} e^{-\rho y}\left[\sum_{j=0}^{N} x_{ij}d_j\right]dy\right\} + E_{T_i}\left\{e^{-\rho T_i}\sum_{j=0}^{N} x_{ij}V_j(1-S_j)\right\}$$

$$= (\mu_i + \rho)^{-1}\sum_{j=0}^{N} x_{ij}\left[d_j + \mu_i V_j(1-S_j)\right].$$

Thus, for *given* vectors of bid and ask prices, a type-i investor solves the problem

$$\max \sum_{j=0}^{N} x_{ij}\left[d_j + \mu_i V_j(1-S_j)\right], \qquad (1)$$

subject to

$$\sum_{j=0}^{N} x_{ij}V_j \leq W_i \quad \text{and} \quad x_{ij} \geq 0 \quad \text{for all} \quad j = 0, 1, 2, \ldots, N, \qquad (2)$$

where condition (2) expresses the wealth constraint and the exclusion of investors' short positions.[5] Under our specification, the usual market clearing conditions read

$$\sum_{i=1}^{M} m_i x_{ij} = 1, \qquad j = 1, 2, \ldots, N \qquad (3)$$

(recall that m_i is the expected number of type-i investors in the market).

When an $M \times (N+1)$ matrix X^* and an $(N+1)$-dimensional vector V^* solve the M optimization problems (1)–(2) such that (3) is satisfied, we call X^* an equilibrium allocation matrix and V^* – an equilibrium ask price vector [the corresponding bid price vector is $(V_0^*, V_1^*(1-S_1), \ldots, V_N^*(1-S_N))$]. The

---

[5] In our context, the use of short sales cannot eliminate the spread effect, since short sales by themselves entail additional transaction costs. Note that a constraint on short positions is necessary in models of tax clienteles [cf. Miller (1977), Litzenberger and Ramaswamy (1980)]. Clearly, market makers are allowed to have transitory long or short positions, but are constrained to have zero expected inventory positions [cf. Garman (1976)].

above model may be viewed as a special case of the linear exchange model [cf. Gale (1960)], which is known to have an equilibrium allocation and a unique equilibrium price vector. Our model enables us to derive and interpret the resulting equilibrium in a straightforward and intuitive way as follows.

We define the expected *spread-adjusted return* of asset j to investor-type i as the difference between the gross market return on asset j and its expected liquidation cost per unit time:

$$r_{ij} = d_j/V_j - \mu_i S_j, \tag{4}$$

where d_j/V_j is the gross return on security j, and $\mu_i S_j$ is the *spread-adjustment*, or expected liquidation cost (per unit time), equal to the product of the liquidation probability per unit time by the percentage spread. Note that the spread-adjusted return depends on *both* the asset j and the investor-type i (through the expected holding period).

For a given price vector V, investor i selects for his portfolio the assets j which provide him the highest spread-adjusted return, given by

$$r_i^* = \max_{j=0,1,2,\ldots,N} r_{ij}, \tag{5}$$

with $r_1^* \leq r_2^* \leq r_3^* \leq \cdots \leq r_M^*$, since, by (4), r_{ij} is a non-decreasing function of i for all j. These inequalities state that the spread-adjusted return on a portfolio increases with the expected holding period. That is, investors with longer expected holding periods will earn higher returns *net* of transaction costs.[6]

The *gross* return required by investor i on asset j is given by $r_i^* + \mu_i S_j$, which reflects both the required spread-adjusted return r_i^* and the expected liquidation cost $\mu_i S_j$. The equilibrium gross (market-observed) return on asset j is determined by its highest-valued use, which is in the portfolio i with the minimal required return, implying that

$$d_j/V_j^* = \min_{i=1,2,\ldots,M} \{r_i^* + \mu_i S_j\}. \tag{6}$$

Eq. (6) can also be written in the form

$$V_j^* = \max_{i=1,2,\ldots,M} \{d_j/(r_i^* + \mu_i S_j)\}, \tag{7}$$

---

[6] This is consistent with the suggestions that while the illiquidity of investments such as real estate [Fogler (1984)] coins [Kane (1984)] and stamps [Taylor (1983)] excludes them from short-term investment portfolios, they are expected to provide superior performance when held over a long investment horizon (the same may apply to stock-exchange seats) [Schwert (1977)]. See also Day, Stoll and Whaley (1985) on the clientele of small firms, and Elton and Gruber (1978) on tax clienteles.

implying that the equilibrium value of asset j, V_j^*, is equal to the present value of its perpetual cash flow, discounted at the gross return $(r_i^* + \mu_i S_j)$. Alternatively, V_j^* can be written as the difference between (i) the present value of the perpetual cash stream d_j and (ii) the present value of the expected trading costs for all the present and future holders of asset j, where both are discounted at the spread-adjusted return of the holding investor. To see this, assume that the available quantity of asset j is held by type-i investors; then (7) can be written as

$$V_j^* = d_j/r_i^* - \mu_i V_j^* S_j/r_i^*,$$

where the first term is, obviously, (i). As for the second, the expected quantity of asset j sold per unit time by type-i investors is μ_i, and each sale incurs a transaction cost of $V_j^* S_j$; thus, $\mu_i V_j^* S_j/r_i^*$ is the expected present value (discounted at r_i^*) of the transaction-cost cash flow.

The implications of the above equilibrium on the relation between returns, spreads and holding periods are summarized by the following propositions.

Proposition 1 (clientele effect). Assets with higher spreads are allocated in equilibrium to portfolios with (the same or) longer expected holding periods.

Proof. Consider two assets, j and k, such that in equilibrium asset j is in portfolio i and asset k is in portfolio $i+1$ (recall that $\mu_i \geq \mu_{i+1}$). Applying (5), we obtain $r_{ij} \geq r_{ik}$ and $r_{i+1,k} \geq r_{i+1,j}$; thus, substituting from (4), $d_j/V_j^* - \mu_i S_j \geq d_k/V_k^* - \mu_i S_k$ and $d_k/V_k^* - \mu_{i+1} S_k \geq d_j/V_j^* - \mu_{i+1} S_j$, implying that $(\mu_i - \mu_{i+1})(S_k - S_j) \geq 0$. It follows that if $\mu_i > \mu_{i+1}$, we must have $S_k \geq S_j$. The case of non-consecutive portfolios immediately follows. Q.E.D.

Proposition 2 (spread–return relationship). In equilibrium, the observed market (gross) return is an increasing and concave piecewise-linear function of the (relative) spread.

Proof. Let $f_i(S) = r_i^* + \mu_i S$. By (6), the market return on an asset with relative spread S is given by $f(S) \equiv \min_{i=1,2,\ldots,M} f_i(S)$. Now, the proposition follows from the fact that monotonicity and concavity are preserved by the minimum operator, and that the minimum of a finite collection of linear functions is piecewise-linear. Q.E.D.

Proposition 2 is the main testable implication of our model. Intuitively, the positive association between return and spread reflects the compensation required by investors for their trading costs, and its concavity results from the clientele effect (Proposition 1). To see this, recall that transaction costs are amortized over the investor's holding period. The longer this period, the

Y. Amihud and H. Mendelson, Asset pricing and the bid-ask spread

Table 1

An example of the equilibrium relation between asset bid-ask spreads, returns and values (see section 2). There are 10 assets (j), each generating $1 per period, with relative bid-ask spreads S_j (= dollar spread divided by asset value) ranging from 0 to 0.045 (column 2), and 4 investor types (i) with expected holding periods, μ_i^{-1}, of 1/12, 1/2, 1 and 5 periods.[a] The return on the zero-spread asset is ρ; all returns are measured in excess of ρ. A type-i investor chooses the assets j which maximize his spread-adjusted return, r_{ij}, given by the difference between the gross market return on asset j and its expected liquidation cost per unit time. The equilibrium solution gives the excess spread-adjusted returns, $r_{ij} - \rho$, in columns 3–6, where the boxes highlight the assets with the highest excess spread-adjusted return for each investor-type. The equilibrium portfolio for each investor-type is composed of the boxed assets. Column 7 shows the assets' equilibrium excess gross returns observed in the market, which include the expected liquidation cost to their holders. Column 8 shows the resulting asset values, obtained by discounting the perpetuity by the respective equilibrium market return, as a fraction of the value of the zero-spread asset.

Asset, j	Relative bid-ask spread, S_j	Investor type, i				Market return in excess of ρ, the return on the zero-spread asset	Value of asset j relative to that of the zero-spread asset, V_j/V_0
		1	2	3	4		
		Length of holding period, μ_i^{-1}					
		1/12	1/2	1	5		
		Excess spread-adjusted return, $r_{ij} - \rho$					
(1)	(2)	(3)	(4)	(5)	(6)	(7)	(8)
0	0	0	0	0	0	0	1
1	0.005	0	0.05	0.055	0.059	0.06	0.943
2	0.01	0	0.10	0.11	0.118	0.12	0.893
3	0.015	−0.05	0.10	0.115	0.127	0.13	0.885
4	0.02	−0.10	0.10	0.12	0.136	0.14	0.877
5	0.025	−0.155	0.095	0.12	0.140	0.145	0.873
6	0.03	−0.21	0.09	0.12	0.144	0.15	0.870
7	0.035	−0.265	0.085	0.12	0.148	0.155	0.866
8	0.04	−0.324	0.076	0.116	0.148	0.156	0.865
9	0.045	−0.383	0.067	0.112	0.148	0.157	0.864

[a] Investors have the same wealth, and the expected number of investors of each type is 1.

smaller the compensation required for a given increase in the spread. Since in equilibrium higher-spread securities are acquired by investors with longer horizons, the added return required for a given increase in spread gets smaller. In terms of our model, longer-holding-period portfolios contain higher-spread assets and have a lower slope μ_i for the return-spread relation.

A simple numerical example can illustrate the spread–return relation. Assume $N = 9$ positive-spread assets and $M = 4$ investor types whose expected holding periods are $1/\mu_1 = 1/12$, $1/\mu_2 = 1/2$, $1/\mu_3 = 1$, and $1/\mu_4 = 5$. For simplicity we set $\lambda_i = \mu_i$, implying that the expected number of investors of each type i is $m_i = 1$. Assets yield $d_j = \$1$ per period, and all investors have equal wealth. The relative spread of asset j is $S_j = 0.005j$, $j = 0, 1, 2, \ldots, 9$; thus, asset percentage spreads range from zero to 4.5%.

Using this data, we solve (1)–(3) and obtain the results in table 1 and figs. 1 and 2. Note that the additional excess return per unit of spread goes down

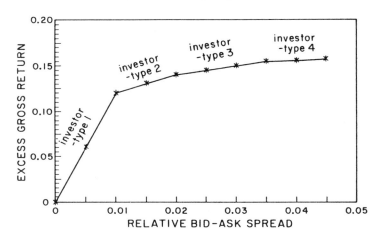

Fig. 1. An illustration of the relation between observed market return in excess of the return on the zero-spread asset (the excess gross return) and the relative bid–ask spread (see the numerical example of section 2 and table 1, column 7). There are 10 assets, each generating $1 per period, with relative bid–ask spreads (= dollar spread divided by asset value) ranging from 0 to 0.045, and 4 investor types with expected holding periods ranging from 1/12 to 5 periods. Investors have equal wealth, and the expected number of investors of each type is 1.

The relation between asset returns and bid–ask spreads is piecewise-linear, increasing and concave, with each linear section corresponding to the portfolio of a different investor type.

from $\mu_1 = 12$ in portfolio 1 to $\mu_2 = 2$ for portfolio 2, then to $\mu_3 = 1$ in portfolio 3, and finally to $\mu_4 = 0.2$ in portfolio 4. The behavior of the excess market return as a function of the spread is shown in fig. 1, which demonstrates both the positive compensation for higher spread and the clientele effect which moderates the excess returns, especially for the high-spread assets. This figure summarizes the main testable implications of our model: The observed market return should be an increasing and concave function of the relative spread. The piecewise-linear functional form suggested by our model provides a specific and detailed set of hypotheses tested in the next section. The effect of the spread on asset values (or prices) is demonstrated in fig 2: the equilibrium values are decreasing and convex in the spread.

While the above model provides a lucid demonstration of the spread–return (or spread–price) relation, our main results do not hinge on its specific form, and hold as well under different specifications. Consider $(N + 1)$ assets, each generating the same stochastic (gross) cash flow given by the process $\{X(t), t \geq 0\}$. Assume that each transaction in asset j entails a cost of $\$c_j$, with $0 = c_0 < c_1 < c_2 < \cdots < c_N$ (asset 0 having zero spread). There are M investor types numbered by $i = 1, 2, \ldots, M$, and the transaction epochs of type-i investors follow a renewal process with given parameters (depending on i).[7]

---

[7]An investor could be viewed as owning a number of portfolios with different liquidation horizons, without changing the results.

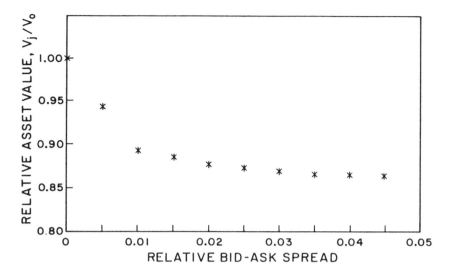

Fig. 2. The relation between asset values and bid-ask spreads for the numerical example of section 2 (see table 1, column 8, and fig. 1). The figure depicts the value of each asset j relative to the value of the zero-spread asset, V_j/V_0, as a function of the bid-ask spread relative to the asset's value. Asset values are a decreasing function of the spread.

Denote the highest price a type-i investor will pay for asset j by V_{ij}. When the price of each asset j is determined by its highest-valued use, we have $V_j = \max_{i=1,2,\ldots,M} V_{ij}$ with $V_{ij} = V_{i0} - c_j \theta_i$, where θ_i is the value (for investor-type i) of $1 at each transaction epoch. Letting $f_i(c) = V_{i0} - c\theta_i$, and following the arguments of Proposition 2, we obtain that the price [given by $\max_{i=1,2,\ldots,M} f_i(c)$] is decreasing and convex in c. Further, it can be shown that the price is a decreasing and convex function of the relative transaction cost, thus demonstrating the robustness of our results. Qualitatively, similar results will hold as long as a longer investment horizon mitigates the burden of transaction costs by enabling their amortization over a longer holding period.

The next section presents empirical tests of our main testable hypotheses (Proposition 2).

3. Empirical tests

This section presents an empirical examination of the relation between expected returns and bid-ask spreads of NYSE stocks, focusing on the particular functional relationship predicted by our model. Specifically, our hypothesis is that expected return is an increasing and concave function of the spread.

3.1. The data and the derivation of the variables

Our data consist of monthly securities returns provided by the Center for Research in Security Prices and relative bid–ask spreads collected for NYSE stocks from *Fitch's Stock Quotations on the NYSE*. The relative spread is the dollar spread divided by the average of the bid and ask prices at year end. The actual spread variable used, S, is the average of the beginning and end-of-year relative spreads for each of the years 1960–1979 [the data is the same as in Stoll and Whaley (1983)].

The relationship between stock returns, relative risk[8] (β) and spread[9] is tested over the period 1961–1980. Following the methodology developed by Black, Jensen and Scholes (1972), Fama and MacBeth (1973) and Black and Scholes (1974), we first formed portfolios by grouping stocks according to their spread and relative risk, and then tested our hypotheses by examining the cross-sectional relation between average excess return, spread and relative risk over time. We divided the data into twenty overlapping periods of eleven years each, consisting of a five-year β estimation period E_n, a five-year portfolio formation period F_n, and a one-year cross-section test period T_n ($n = 1, 2, \ldots, 20$).[10] The three subperiods of each eleven-year period are now considered in detail:

(i) *The beta estimation period* E_n was used to estimate the β coefficients from the market model regressions

$$R^e_{jt} = \alpha_j + \beta_j R^e_{mt} + \varepsilon_{jt}, \qquad t = 1, \ldots, 60,$$

where R^e_{jt} and R^e_{mt} are the month-t excess returns (over the 90-day T-bill rates) on stock j and on the market,[11] respectively, and β_j is the estimate of the relative risk[12] of stock j.

(ii) *The portfolio formation period* F_n was used to form the test portfolios and estimate their β and spread parameters. All stocks traded through the

---

[8] By the CAPM, the β risk is the major determinant of asset returns. Our analysis in section 2 dealt with certainty-equivalent rates of return.

[9] The cost of transacting also includes brokerage commissions. In Stoll and Whaley (1983), the correlation between portfolio spreads and brokerage fees was 0.996, hence we omitted the latter.

[10] To illustrate, $E_1 = 1951$–1955, $F_1 = 1956$–1960, $T_1 = 1961$; $E_2 = 1952$–1956, $F_2 = 1957$–1961, $T_2 = 1962$; ... $E_{20} = 1970$–1974, $F_{20} = 1975$–1979, $T_{20} = 1980$.

[11] Throughout this study, R_m and the test portfolios are equally weighted. See Black, Jensen and Scholes (1972), Fama and MacBeth (1973) and Stoll and Whaley (1983, p. 71).

[12] Jensen (1968) has shown that the measure of relative risk, β_j, may be used for a holding period of any length (p. 189).

entire eleven-year period n and for which the spread was available for the last year of F_n were ranked by that spread and divided into seven equal groups. Within each of the seven spread groups, stocks were ranked by their β coefficients, obtained from E_n, and divided into seven equal subgroups. This yields 49 (7×7) equal-sized portfolios,[13] with significant variability of the spreads as well as the betas within the spread groups. Then, we estimated β for each portfolio from the market model regression over the months of F_n,

$$R^e_{pt} = \alpha_p + \beta_p R^e_{mt} + \varepsilon_{pt}, \qquad t = 1, \ldots, 60, \quad p = 1, \ldots, 49,$$

where R^e_{pt} is the average[14] excess return of the securities included in portfolio p in month t. Finally, we calculated the portfolio spread S_{pn} by averaging the spreads (of the last year of F_n) across the stocks in portfolio p. Each portfolio p in period n is thus characterized by the pair (β_{pn}, S_{pn}) ($p = 1, 2, \ldots, 49$, $n = 1, 2, \ldots, 20$). Altogether, we have 980 ($= 49 \times 20$) portfolios.

(iii) *The cross-section test period* T_n was used to test the relation between R^e_{pn}, β_{pn} and S_{pn} across portfolios, where R^e_{pn} is the average monthly excess return on the stocks in portfolio p in T_n, the last year of period n.[15]

Table 2 presents summary statistics for the 49 portfolio groups, classified by spread and β. Note that both β and the excess return increase with the spread. The correlation coefficients between the portfolio excess returns R^e_p, the portfolio betas β_p and the spreads S_p, presented in table 3, show that both β_p and S_p are positively correlated with excess returns; the correlation between R^e_p and the spread over the twenty-year period is about twice as high as that between R^e_p and β. Also, note the high positive correlation between β and the spread.

3.2. Test methodology

We now turn to test the major hypothesis of model, namely, that expected return is an increasing and concave function of the relative spread. This is a classical case of covariance analysis and pooling of cross-section and time-series data [see Kmenta (1971, ch. 12-2), Maddala (1977, ch. 14), Judge et al. (1980, ch. 8)], where the estimation model has to allow for differences over cross-sec-

---

[13] The long trading-period requirement might have eliminated from our sample the riskier and higher-spread stocks, thus reducing the variability of the data. Throughout, 'equal' portfolios may differ from one another by one security due to indivisibility.

[14] Throughout, averaging means arithmetic averaging.

[15] Note that our test is predictive in nature, using estimates of risk and spread which are available at the beginning of the test period. See Fama (1976, 349–351).

Table 2

Average relative bid-ask spread, monthly excess return, relative risk (β) and firm size for the 49 portfolios for the 20 test-period years 1961–1980. Portfolios are indexed by the spread group i ($i = 1$ for the smallest spread) and by the beta group j ($j = 1$ for the smallest beta). Portfolio composition changes every year and the sample size ranges between 619 and 900 stocks.

The relative bid-ask spread of a stock is its dollar spread divided by the average of the bid and ask prices at year end. The portfolio spread is the average relative spread of stocks in the portfolio.

The portfolio (monthly) excess return is the 12-month arithmetic average of the monthly average returns on the stocks in the portfolio in excess of that month's Treasury-Bill rate.

The portfolio beta is the average relative risk (β) coefficient for the stocks in the portfolio, estimated over the 5 years preceding the test period. Size is the market value of the firm's equity in millions of dollars at the end of the year preceding the test period, averaged over the firms included in the portfolio.

Spread group, i		1	2	3	Beta group, j 4	5	6	7	Mean
1	Spread	0.004765	0.004850	0.004860	0.004789	0.004878	0.004891	0.004980	0.00486
	Excess return	0.002706	0.001306	0.003380	0.004409	0.003427	0.005416	0.003781	0.00349
	Beta	0.54001	0.67797	0.75890	0.77867	0.83231	0.91651	1.08973	0.799
	Size	4089.8	3245.5	3231.9	2317.3	1430.0	1418.8	595.7	2333
2	Spread	0.007435	0.007445	0.007463	0.007414	0.007508	0.007412	0.007452	0.00745
	Excess return	0.003174	0.003543	0.003549	0.004995	0.003050	0.006424	0.011061	0.00511
	Beta	0.55369	0.71874	0.81652	0.84596	0.90668	1.02999	1.21992	0.870
	Size	780.2	880.3	741.5	707.6	656.1	605.9	282.7	665
3	Spread	0.009392	0.009386	0.009400	0.009375	0.009339	0.009350	0.009425	0.00939
	Excess return	0.001838	0.003165	0.006707	0.002619	0.004473	0.006133	0.005063	0.00429
	Beta	0.56069	0.67271	0.79543	0.89866	1.00357	1.04518	1.20940	0.884
	Size	476.2	502.1	695.9	370.1	363.9	293.3	227.1	418

		1	2	3	4	5	6	7
4	Spread	0.011470	0.011473	0.011411	0.011464	0.011449	0.011487	0.011411	0.01145
	Excess return	0.003217	0.002447	0.005296	0.004521	0.008505	0.008033	0.009178	0.00589
	Beta	0.58821	0.69158	0.84828	0.92208	0.99515	1.07535	1.26739	0.913
	Size	331.9	362.7	370.6	248.4	250.5	192.4	174.5	276
5	Spread	0.014015	0.013913	0.013955	0.013998	0.013883	0.013969	0.013988	0.01396
	Excess return	0.002583	0.004340	0.003318	0.006763	0.008076	0.011460	0.010266	0.00669
	Beta	0.60153	0.71197	0.82031	0.92906	1.04923	1.12224	1.28927	0.932
	Size	243.1	257.3	213.6	166.3	149.2	146.2	111.3	184
6	Spread	0.017662	0.017513	0.017699	0.017759	0.017789	0.017763	0.017967	0.01774
	Excess return	0.003637	0.006937	0.007209	0.007415	0.011254	0.010877	0.012516	0.00855
	Beta	0.65522	0.73861	0.87193	0.94479	1.07714	1.16769	1.33498	0.970
	Size	135.6	131.1	127.1	113.1	91.2	89.9	72.8	109
7	Spread	0.032890	0.029385	0.031614	0.031472	0.031647	0.033169	0.034385	0.03208
	Excess return	0.006683	0.008876	0.008044	0.007405	0.012335	0.013384	0.014929	0.01024
	Beta	0.76132	0.88340	0.99811	1.12656	1.23899	1.33249	1.46259	1.115
	Size	75.2	67.8	57.5	54.7	44.0	47.8	37.3	55
Mean	Spread	0.013947	0.013424	0.013772	0.013753	0.013792	0.014006	0.014230	0.01385
	Excess return	0.003405	0.004373	0.005357	0.005447	0.007303	0.008818	0.009542	0.00632
	Beta	0.60867	0.72785	0.84421	0.92083	1.01472	1.09849	1.26761	0.926
	Size	876	778	777	568	426	399	214	577

Table 3

Correlation coefficients between the annual average portfolio spread S_p, excess return R_p^e and beta β_p for the entire sample period 1961–1980 and for its two 10-year subperiods, 1961–1970 and 1971–1980. Portfolio spread is the average bid–ask spread as a fraction of the year-end average of the bid and ask prices for all securities in the portfolio. Excess returns are the average monthly returns in excess of the monthly T-Bill rate.

Period	Correlation coefficient between			Number of observations
	R_p^e and S_p	R_p^e and β_p	β_p and S_p	
1961–80	0.239	0.123	0.361	980
1961–70	0.179	0.132	0.163	490
1971–80	0.285	0.118	0.540	490

tional units (portfolios) and over time. This is done by employing two sets of dummy variables: The first set consists of 48 portfolio dummy variables, defined by $DP_{ij} = 1$ if the portfolio is in group (i, j) and zero otherwise; $i = 1, 2, \ldots, 7$ is the spread-group index and $j = 1, 2, \ldots, 7$ is the β-group index, with $DP_{7,7} \equiv 0$. By construction, the spread increases in i, and β increases in j. A second set of dummy variables, defined by $DY_n = 1$ in year n ($n = 1, 2, \ldots, 19$) and zero otherwise, accounts for differences in returns between years.

An important implication of our model is that the slope of the return–spread relation declines as we move to higher-spread groups. To allow for different slope coefficients across spread groups, we decomposed the spread variable S_{pn} into seven variables S_{pn}^i ($i = 1, 2, \ldots, 7$) defined by $S_{pn}^i = S_{pn}$ if in spread group i ($i = 1, 2, \ldots, 7$) and zero otherwise. Due to the high correlation between S_{pn}^i and $\sum_{j=1}^{7} DP_{ij}$, we constructed the mean-adjusted spread variables, $\hat{S}_{pn}^i = S_{pn}^i - \bar{S}^i$ if portfolio (p, n) is in group i and zero otherwise, where $\bar{S}^i$ is the mean spread for the ith spread group. The means of $\hat{S}_{pn}^i$ are zero and their correlations with $\sum_{j=1}^{7} DP_{ij}$ are zero. Replacing S_{pn}^i by the mean-adjusted variables thus leads to a separation between the level effects among groups (captured by DP_{ij}) and the slope effects within spread groups (captured by $\hat{S}_{pn}^i$).

Using the above variables, we carried out the pooled cross-section and time-series estimation of our model:

$$R_{pn}^e = a_0 + a_1 \beta_{pn} + \sum_{i=1}^{7} b_i \hat{S}_{pn}^i + \sum_{i=1}^{7} \sum_{j=1}^{7} c_{ij} DP_{ij} + \sum_{n=1}^{19} d_n DY_n + \varepsilon_{pn}, \quad (8)$$

where a_0, a_1, b_i, c_{ij} and d_n are coefficients and the ε_{pn} are the residuals. The slope coefficients b_i measure the response of stock returns to increasing the spread *within* spread group i, and the dummy coefficients c_{ij} measure the difference between the mean return on portfolio (i, j) and that of portfolio $(7, 7)$ which corresponds to the highest spread and β group.

The sums $\sum_{i=1}^{7} c_{ij}$ measure the differences in mean returns between β groups j, while $\sum_{j=1}^{7} c_{ij}$ measure the differences in mean returns between spread groups i. Thus, for any given β, model (8) represents a piecewise-linear functional form of the return–spread relation. This follows the Malinvaud (1970, pp. 317–318) and Kmenta (1971, pp. 468–469) methodology for estimating non-linear relationships, which groups the data based on the values of the explanatory variable, and fits a piecewise linear curve using two sets of variables: group dummies to capture differences between group means, and products of the explanatory variable by the group dummies to allow for the different slopes.

Estimation of the pooled model (8) using OLS is problematic due to the possibility of cross-sectional heteroskedasticity and cross-sectional correlations among residuals across portfolio groups. While the estimated OLS coefficients are unbiased and consistent, their estimated variances are not, leading to biased test statistics. This calls for a generalized least squares (GLS) estimation procedure. Given that the variance–covariance matrix of the residuals in (8) is $\sigma^2 V$, where σ^2 is a scalar and V is a symmetric positive-definite matrix, the GLS procedure uses a matrix Q satisfying $Q'Q = V^{-1}$ to transform all the regression variables by pre-multiplication. The variance–covariance matrix V was assumed to be block diagonal (reflecting independence between years), where the diagonal blocks consist of twenty identical 49×49 positive definite matrices U. Then, $V = I \otimes U$, where I is the 20×20 identity matrix and $\otimes$ denotes the Kronecker product. To obtain the 49×49 matrix U, we first estimated model (8) by OLS and then used the data month by month to obtain the residuals $\hat{\varepsilon}_{pm}$ ($p = 1, 2, \ldots, 49$) for each month m ($m = 1, 2, \ldots, 240$). Then, we estimated U by averaging the resulting 240 monthly variance–covariance matrices – the resulting estimate of the variance–covariance matrix V is known to be consistent [cf. Kmenta (1971, ch. 12)]. The transformation matrix Q was calculated using the Choleski decomposition method. The variables of model (8) were then pre-multiplied by the transformation matrix Q, and the transformed version of model (8) was estimated to provide the GLS results.

3.3. The results

We first ran a simple OLS regression of the excess returns on β, the spread and the nineteen-year dummy variables:

$$R^e_{pn} = 0.0040 + 0.00947\beta_{pn} + \sum_{n=1}^{19} d_n DY_n + e_{pn},$$
$$(9.17)$$

and

$$R^e_{pn} = 0.0036 + 0.00672\beta_{pn} + 0.211 S_{pn} + \sum_{n=1}^{19} d_n DY_n + e_{pn}.$$
$$\qquad\qquad\quad (6.18)\qquad\;\;(6.83)$$

(t-statistics are in parentheses.) The results show that excess returns are increasing in both β and the spread. The coefficient of S_{pn} implies that a 1% increase in the spread is associated with a 0.211% increase in the monthly risk-adjusted excess return. The coefficient of β declines when the spread variable is added to the equation, indicating that part of the effect which could be attributed to β may, in fact, be due to the spread.[16] The coefficient of β is 0.00672, very close to 0.00671, which is the average monthly excess return on common stocks for this period.

Next, we estimated the detailed model (8) using both OLS and GLS. The slope coefficients of the spread variables are presented in table 4, and the coefficients of DP_{ij} are given in table 5. To estimate the pattern of the dummy coefficients, we employed the model

$$c_{ij} = \alpha + \sum_{i=1}^{6} \gamma_i DS_i + \sum_{j=1}^{6} \delta_j DB_j + e_{ij}, \qquad (9)$$

where the spread dummy DS_i ($i = 1,\ldots,6$) is one if the portfolio is in spread group i and zero otherwise, and the β dummy DB_j ($j = 1,\ldots,6$) is one if the portfolio is in β group j and zero otherwise. Thus, the coefficients γ_i in (9) measure the difference between the average return of spread group i and that of the seventh (highest) spread group, and the coefficients δ_j measure the corresponding differences between β groups.

The estimates of (8)–(9) presented in tables 4 and 6 support our two hypotheses:

(i) The coefficients γ_i of DS_i in model (9) are negative and generally increasing in i, implying that risk-adjusted excess returns increase with the spread. The difference in the monthly mean excess return between the two extreme spread groups is 0.857% when estimated by OLS and 0.681% when estimated by GLS.

(ii) The slope coefficients of the spreads, b_i, are positive and generally decreasing as we move to higher spread groups. This is consistent with the hypothesized concavity of the return–spread relation, reflecting the lower sensitivity of long-term portfolios to the spread.

---

[16] Given the strong positive correlation between S_{pn} and β_{pn}, the omission of S_{pn} from the regression equation which tests the CAPM results in an upward bias in the estimated coefficient of β; see Kmenta (1971, p. 392).

Table 4

Estimated regressions of the portfolio monthly excess returns, R^e, on the mean-adjusted spread variables $\hat{S}^i$ and relative risk, β, for the years 1961–1980, using ordinary least squares and generalized least squares estimation methods. The regression model (8)[a] applies pooled cross-section and time-series estimation.
The coefficient of $\hat{S}^i$ reflects the response of stock returns to an increase in the bid–ask spread within spread group i, where $i = 1$ corresponds to the lowest-spread group.
(t-values are in parentheses).

Independent variable	Ordinary least squares coefficients	Generalized least squares coefficients		
	Entire period 1961–1980	Entire period 1961–1980	Subperiod 1961–1970	Subperiod 1971–1980
$\hat{S}_1$	3.641 (2.76)	1.310 (1.16)	0.080 (0.05)	2.303 (1.27)
$\hat{S}_2$	3.242 (3.50)	1.747 (2.56)	0.975 (0.91)	2.505 (2.41)
$\hat{S}_3$	2.854 (3.93)	1.660 (3.01)	0.934 (1.10)	2.27 (2.80)
$\hat{S}_4$	1.657 (3.06)	0.482 (1.16)	−0.149 (0.21)	0.983 (1.69)
$\hat{S}_5$	2.224 (5.69)	1.206 (3.84)	0.922 (1.67)	1.500 (3.47)
$\hat{S}_6$	1.365 (5.28)	0.650 (2.96)	0.838 (2.21)	0.475 (1.50)
$\hat{S}_7$	0.605 (5.28)	0.256 (2.56)	0.176 (1.49)	0.489 (2.49)
β	−0.0058 (2.53)	−0.000 (0.10)	−0.002 (0.47)	−0.003 (0.72)

[a] The regression model is

$$R^e_{pn} = a_0 + a_1 \beta_{pn} + \sum_{i=1}^{7} b_i \hat{S}^i_{pn} + \sum_{i=1}^{7}\sum_{j=1}^{7} c_{ij} DP_{ij} + \sum_{n=1}^{19} d_n DY_n + \varepsilon_{pn}, \qquad (8)$$

where R^e_{pn} is the average excess return for portfolio p in year n, β_{pn} is the average portfolio relative risk, $\hat{S}^i_{pn}$ is the mean-adjusted spread within spread group i (= the deviation of the spread of portfolio p in year n from the mean spread of its spread group, i), DP_{ij} are the portfolio-group dummy variables (= 1 in portfolio group (i, j), zero otherwise), DY_n are the year dummy variables (= 1 in year n, 0 otherwise), and ε_{pn} are the residuals. The GLS estimated coefficients of the portfolio-group dummies DP_{ij} are reported in table 5.

The effect of the relative risk is measured in model (8) by both β and the dummy variables and is further summarized by the DB_j coefficients of model (9). The emerging pattern is that (spread-adjusted) excess returns increase with β as depicted by the significant negative and increasing coefficients δ_j. The effect of β is captured mainly through the dummies rather than the coefficient a_1, which is highly insignificant in the GLS estimation. Finally, we estimated

Table 5

Generalized least squares estimates of the difference between the mean monthly excess return of the portfolio with the highest spread and beta – portfolio (7,7), the 49th portfolio – and the mean monthly excess returns of each of the other 48 portfolios. These are the estimated coefficients of the 48 portfolio dummy variables DP_{ij} in the pooled cross-section and time-series regression model (8), using GLS, over the entire period 1961–1980.
t-statistics for all unmarked table entries are greater than 1.96, implying that the estimated coefficient is significant at better than the 2.5% level (one-tail test).

Spread group, i	Beta group, j							Mean
	1 (low)	2	3	4	5	6	7 (high)	
1 (low)	−0.0117	−0.0132	−0.0111	−0.0100	−0.0111	−0.0091	−0.0108	−0.0110
2	−0.0113	−0.0109	−0.0109	−0.0094	−0.0115	−0.0079	−0.0033[b]	−0.0093
3	−0.0127	−0.0113	−0.0078[a]	−0.0118	−0.0100	−0.0082	−0.0094	−0.0102
4	−0.0113	−0.0120	−0.0091	−0.0099	−0.0059[a]	−0.0064	−0.0052[b]	−0.0085
5	−0.0120	−0.0101	−0.0111	−0.0077	−0.0062[a]	−0.0030[b]	−0.0041[b]	−0.0077
6	−0.0108	−0.0074[a]	−0.0072	−0.0070	−0.0032[b]	−0.0035[b]	−0.0020[b]	−0.0059
7 (high)	−0.0080	−0.0049[b]	−0.0063	−0.0068	−0.0019[b]	−0.0013[b]	0.0000	−0.0042
Mean	−0.0111	−0.0100	−0.0091	−0.0089	−0.0071	−0.0056	−0.0050	

[a] $1.645 < t < 1.96$, implying significance at better than the 5% level (one-tail test).
[b] $t < 1.645$, insignificant at the 5% level (one-tail test).

models (8)–(9) for the two ten-year subperiods, with generally the same pattern of results.

Detailed tests of our main hypotheses are presented in table 7. In 7(B), we test the significance of the spread effect by omitting all spread-related variables and examine the resulting increase in the unexplained variance. In 7(C) we test whether the mean excess returns of all spread groups are equal by eliminating all spread-related dummy variables. The significance of the non-linearities was tested in two ways: First we replaced all the spread-related variables (eliminating the $\hat{S}^i_{pn}$ and replacing the DP_{ij} with six β dummies) by the original spread variable S_{pn} [see 7(D)]. Then we tested the equality of the slope coefficients across spread groups by re-estimating model (8), replacing the variables $\hat{S}^1$ through $\hat{S}^7$ by their sum [see 7(E)]. In all four cases, the F-tests for the changes in the sum of squared residuals reject the null hypotheses at better than the 0.01 level. Thus, our hypotheses are fully supported by the data.

4. Firm size, spread and return

The well-known negative relationship between spread and firm size suggests that our findings may bear on the 'small-firm anomaly': Banz (1981) and Reinganum (1981a, b) found a negative relation between risk-adjusted mean

Table 6

Regression estimates of the difference between the mean return of the spread and beta groups and the mean return of the highest-spread and highest-beta portfolio. The estimation model is

$$c_{ij} = \alpha + \sum_{i=1}^{6} \gamma_i DS_i + \sum_{j=1}^{6} \delta_j DB_j + e_{ij}, \qquad (9)$$

where c_{ij} are the dummy coefficients estimated from model (8) (table 5); $DS_i = 1$ for the ith spread group and zero otherwise; and $DB_j = 1$ for the jth beta group and zero otherwise. Spreads are increasing in i, and betas are increasing in j.
(t-statistics are in parentheses).

	Estimated regression coefficients			
	Entire 1961–1980 period		Subperiods	
Independent variable	From OLS regression	From GLS regression	1961–1970 GLS	1971–1980 GLS
DS_1	−0.00857 (9.05)	−0.00681 (7.74)	−0.00730 (7.46)	−0.00397 (3.33)
DS_2	−0.00654 (6.90)	−0.00517 (5.88)	−0.00578 (5.91)	−0.00267 (2.24)
DS_3	−0.00729 (7.70)	−0.00599 (6.82)	−0.00556 (5.69)	−0.00483 (4.05)
DS_4	−0.00552 (5.83)	−0.00439 (4.99)	−0.00446 (4.56)	−0.00301 (2.53)
DS_5	−0.00461 (4.86)	−0.00359 (4.08)	−0.00335 (3.42)	−0.00272 (2.28)
DS_6	−0.00252 (2.66)	−0.00172 (1.95)	−0.00246 (2.52)	0.00051 (0.42)
DB_1	−0.00964 (10.18)	−0.00614 (6.98)	−0.00669 (6.84)	−0.00454 (3.81)
DB_2	−0.00767 (8.10)	−0.00500 (5.68)	−0.00495 (5.06)	−0.00421 (3.53)
DB_3	−0.00626 (6.61)	−0.00411 (4.67)	−0.00325 (3.32)	−0.00434 (3.64)
DB_4	−0.00568 (6.00)	−0.00398 (4.53)	−0.00260 (2.66)	−0.00485 (4.07)
DB_5	−0.00336 (3.55)	−0.00214 (2.43)	−0.00098 (1.00)	−0.00293 (2.46)
DB_6	−0.00147 (1.56)	−0.00065 (0.74)	0.00017 (0.18)	−0.00121 (1.01)

returns on stocks and their market value, indicating either a misspecification of the CAPM or evidence of market inefficiency [see Schwert (1983) for a comprehensive review]. Thus, it is instructive to estimate the effects of a firm-size variable and to test its significance vis-a-vis our variables.

We re-estimated our models adding a new explanatory variable – *SIZE*, the market value of the firm's equity in millions of dollars at the end of the year

Table 7

Tests of hypotheses on the return-spread relation. All regressions are estimated by GLS.

Model[a]	Degrees of freedom of the model	SSR, sum of squared residuals	Difference from model (A)[b]			F-statistic
			DF	SSR	MS	
(A)	75	76.7877	–	–	–	–
(B)	26	85.5489	49	8.7612	0.1788	2.10
(C)	33	83.3506	42	6.5629	0.1563	1.84
(D)	27	84.7339	48	7.9462	0.1655	1.95
(E)	69	78.4249	6	1.6372	0.2729	3.21

[a]The regression models are as follows.

Model (A) – the full model:

$$R^c_{pn} = a_0 + a_1 \beta_{pn} + \sum_{i=1}^{7} b_i \hat{S}^i_{pn} + \sum_{i=1}^{7}\sum_{j=1}^{7} c_{ij} DP_{ij} + \sum_{n=1}^{19} d_n DY_n + \varepsilon_{pn}, \qquad (8)$$

where $p = 1, 2, \ldots, 49$, $n = 1, 2, \ldots, 20$, and $DP_{77} = 0$.

Model (B) – a restricted model for testing the existence of any spread effect:

$$R^c_{pn} = a_0 + a_1 \beta_{pn} + \sum_{j=1}^{6} \gamma_j DB_j + \sum_{n=1}^{19} d_n DY_n + \varepsilon_{pn}.$$

Model (C) – a restricted model for testing the equality of mean excess returns across spread groups:

$$R^c_{pn} = a_0 + a_1 \beta_{pn} + \sum_{i=1}^{7} b_i \hat{S}^i_{pn} + \sum_{j=1}^{6} \gamma_j DB_j + \sum_{n=1}^{19} d_n DY_n + \varepsilon_{pn}.$$

Model (D) – a restricted model for testing the non-linearity of the return-spread relation:

$$R^c_{pn} = a_0 + a_1 \beta_{pn} + a_2 S_{pn} + \sum_{j=1}^{6} \gamma_j DB_j + \sum_{n=1}^{19} d_n DY_n + \varepsilon_{pn}.$$

Model (E) – a restricted model testing the equality of the slope coefficients across spread groups:

$$R^c_{pn} = a_0 + a_1 \beta_{pn} + a_2 \left(\sum_{i=1}^{7} \hat{S}^i_{pn} \right) + \sum_{i=1}^{7}\sum_{j=1}^{7} c_{ij} DP_{ij} + \sum_{n=1}^{19} d_n DY_n + \varepsilon_{pn}.$$

The regression variables are:

R^c_{pn} = average portfolio excess return (the dependent variable) for portfolio p in year n,
β_{pn} = average portfolio relative (β) risk,
S_{pn} = average portfolio relative spread,
$\hat{S}^i_{pn}$ = mean-adjusted spread (the deviation of the spread S_{pn} of portfolio p in year n from the mean spread of its spread group, i),
DP_{ij} = portfolio group dummy; one in portfolio group (i, j), zero otherwise,
DY_n = year dummy; one in year n, zero otherwise,
DB_j = β group dummy; one in β group j, zero otherwise. $DB_j = \sum_{i=1}^{7} DP_{ij}$ ($j = 1, 2, \ldots, 6$).

[b]Data for the F-test on each of the restricted models:

DF = difference in the number of degrees of freedom between the full and restricted model,
SSR = difference in the sum of squares between the full and restricted model,
MS = SSR/DF, the mean square.

just preceding the test period. As seen in table 2, there is a negative relationship between *SIZE* and both spread and β. The effect of firm size on stock returns was tested by incorporating *SIZE* in all our models, but its estimated effect was negligible and highly insignificant.

To allow for a possible non-linear effect (as other studies do), we replaced *SIZE* by its natural logarithm and examined the impact of adding log(*SIZE*) to our regression equations. First, we estimated the simple linear model

$$R^e_{pn} = 0.0082 + 0.0060\beta_{pn} + 0.158 S_{pn} + 0.0006 \log(SIZE)_{pn}$$
$$\phantom{R^e_{pn} = 0.0082 +}(5.05)\phantom{\beta_{pn} +}(3.44)\phantom{S_{pn} +}(1.56)$$

$$+ \sum_{n=1}^{19} d_n DY_n + e_{pn}.$$

The results indicate that the risk and spread effects prevail, whereas the size effect is insignificant. We then re-estimated our detailed model (8) with the added variable log(*SIZE*) using GLS over the entire sample period and its two ten-year subperiods. The results in table 8(B) suggest that the size effect is insignificant, and it remains insignificant when the only spread variable appearing in the regression equation is S_{pn} [see 8(C)]. The coefficient of log(*SIZE*) becomes significant only when all the spread-related variables are altogether omitted [table 8(D)]. Finally, we performed an *F*-test for the significance of our set of spread variables given log(*SIZE*). The test produced $F = 2.02$, significant at better than the 0.01 level. Thus, while our spread variables render the size effect insignificant, they remain highly significant even with log(*SIZE*) in the regression equation. In sum, our results on the return–spread relation cannot be explained by a 'size effect' even if the latter exists. In fact, any 'size effect' may be a consequence of a spread effect, with firm size serving as a proxy for liquidity. And, rather than suggesting an 'anomaly' or an indication of market inefficiency, our return–spread relation represents a rational response by an efficient market to the existence of the spread.

A number of studies have attempted to explain the size effect in terms of the bid–ask spread. Stoll and Whaley (1983) suggested that investors' valuations are based on returns net of transaction costs, and observed that the costs of transacting in small-firm stocks are relatively higher. They thus subtracted these costs from the measured returns and tested for a small-firm effect. Using an interesting empirical procedure based on arbitrage portfolios, they found that if round-trip transactions occurred every three months, the size effect was eliminated. They thus concluded that the CAPM, applied to after-transaction-cost returns over an appropriately chosen holding period, cannot be rejected.

Table 8

Effects of firm size on portfolio returns, controlling for the effects of the bid-ask spread, over the period 1961–1980 and its two 10-year subperiods.

Model[a]	Sample period	Definition of size variable	Estimates for the size variable		Spread variables included in the regression equation
			Coefficient	t-value	
(A)	1961–80	$SIZE$	-0.23×10^{-6}	0.74	all[b]
(B)	1961–80	$\log(SIZE)$	-0.000650	1.52	all[b]
(B)	1961–70	$\log(SIZE)$	-0.000916	1.46	all[b]
(B)	1971–80	$\log(SIZE)$	-0.000216	0.34	all[b]
(C)	1961–80	$\log(SIZE)$	-0.00032	1.08	S ($a_2 = 0.153$, $t = 2.51$)
(D)	1961–80	$\log(SIZE)$	-0.00057	2.0	none

[a]The models used are as follows.

Model (A) is obtained by adding $SIZE$ to (8), i.e.,

$$R^e_{pn} = a_0 + a_1 \beta_{pn} + \sum_{i=1}^{7} b_i \hat{S}^i_{pn} + \sum_{i=1}^{7} \sum_{j=1}^{7} c_{ij} DP_{ij} + \psi \cdot SIZE_{pn} + \sum_{n=1}^{19} d_n DY_n + \varepsilon_{pn}.$$

Model (B) is obtained by adding $\log(SIZE)$ to (8), i.e., replacing $SIZE_{pn}$ in (A) by $\log(SIZE_{pn})$.

Model (C) includes $\log(SIZE)$ and the spread variable S_{pn}:

$$R^e_{pn} = a_0 + a_1 \beta_{pn} + a_2 S_{pn} + \sum_{j=1}^{6} \gamma_j DB_j + \eta \cdot \log(SIZE_{pn}) + \sum_{j=1}^{19} d_n DY_n + \varepsilon_{pn}.$$

Model (D) is obtained by omitting S_{pn} from model (C).

The regression variables are:

R^e_{pn} = average excess return for portfolio p in year n (the dependent variable),
β_{pn} = average portfolio relative (β) risk,
S_{pn} = average portfolio relative spread,
$\hat{S}^i_{pn}$ = mean-adjusted spread (the deviation of the spread S_{pn} of portfolio p in year n from the mean spread of its spread group, i),
DP_{ij} = portfolio group dummy; one in portfolio group (i, j), zero otherwise,
DB_j = β-group dummy; one in β-group j, zero otherwise. $DB_j = \sum_{i=1}^{7} DP_{ij}$ ($j = 1, 2, \ldots, 6$).
DY_n = year dummy; one in year n, zero otherwise,
$SIZE_{pn}$ = average market value of the equity of firms in portfolio p in the year just preceding n, in millions of dollars.

[b]Results obtained by adding the size variable to the full model (8).

This conclusion was challenged by Schultz (1983), who claimed that transaction costs do not completely explain the size effect. Extending Stoll and Whaley's sample to smaller AMEX firms, Schultz found that small firms earn positive excess returns after transaction costs for holding periods of one year. He thus concluded that transaction costs cannot explain the violations of the CAPM. This criticism, however, hardly settles the issue, and in fact highlights a basic problem. Given the higher returns and higher spreads of small firms' stocks, it is always possible to find an investment horizon which nullifies the abnormal return after transaction costs. But then, finding that a horizon of one year does not eliminate the size effect is insufficient to determine whether or not transaction costs are the proper explanation.

Our examination of the relation between stock returns and bid–ask spreads is based on a theory which produces well-specified hypotheses. In the context of our model, the after-transaction-cost return, as defined in the above studies, is not meaningful. Stoll–Whaley and Schultz consider this key variable to be a property of the security, and calculate it by subtracting the transaction cost from the gross return, implicitly assuming the same holding period for all stocks. By our model, the spread-adjusted return depends not only on the stock's return and spread, but also on the holding horizon of its specific clientele [see (4)]. Thus, their method is inapplicable to test our hypotheses on the return–spread relation.

The different objective guiding our empirical study has shaped its different methodology and structure. Stoll–Whaley and Schultz aim at explaining the 'small firm' anomaly through the bid–ask spread, hence their portfolio construction and test procedure are governed by firm size.[17] We start from a theoretical specification of the return–spread relation, and the objective of our empirical study is to test the explicit functional form predicted by our model. Thus, our empirical results are disciplined by the theory and in fact the test procedure is called for by the theory.

A second issue raised by Schultz (1983) is the seasonal behavior of the size effect, which is particularly pronounced in the month of January.[18] In the context of our study, there is a question whether liquidity has a seasonal. A test of this hypothesis requires data on monthly bid–ask spreads which was unavailable to us. Given our data of a single spread observation per year, we are unable to carry out a powerful test incorporating seasonality, a topic which is worthy of further research.

An empirical issue in the computation of returns on small firms is the possible upward bias due to the bid–ask spread, suggested by Blume and Stambaugh (1983), Roll (1983) and Fisher and Weaver (1985). Blume and Stambaugh estimate the bias to be $\frac{1}{4}S^2$, where S is the relative spread. Given the magnitudes of the spreads and the excess returns, this difference is negligible. Indeed, we re-estimated models (8)–(9), applying the Blume–

---

[17]Stoll–Whaley and Schultz subordinate their study of the bid–ask effect to the small-firm classification, a procedure which is natural for studying the small-firm anomaly. Our portfolio-construction method is motivated by the prediction that stock returns are a function of the bid–ask spread and β, and is designed specifically to test this hypothesis.

[18]Lakonishok and Smidt (1984) found that the small-firm effect prevails at the turn-of-the-year when returns are measured net of transaction costs, using the high and low prices as proxies for the ask and bid prices.

5. Conclusion

This paper studies the effect of securities' bid–ask spreads on their returns. We model a market where rational traders differ in their expected holding periods and assets have different spreads. The ensuing equilibrium has the following characteristics: (i) market-observed average returns are an increasing function of the spread; (ii) asset returns to their holders, net of trading costs, increase with the spread;[20] (iii) there is a clientele effect, whereby stocks with higher spreads are held by investors with longer holding periods; and (iv) due to the clientele effect, returns on higher-spread stocks are less spread-sensitive, giving rise to a concave return–spread relation. We design a detailed test on the behavior of observed returns, and our results support the theory. The robustness and statistical significance of our results are very encouraging, especially when compared to the Fama–MacBeth (1973) benchmark. These results do not point at an anomaly or market inefficiency; rather, they reflect a rational response by investors in an efficient market when faced with trading friction and transaction costs.

The higher yields required on higher-spread stocks give firms an incentive to increase the liquidity of their securities, thus reducing their opportunity cost of capital. Consequently, liquidity-increasing financial policies may increase the value of the firm. This was demonstrated for our numerical example in fig. 2, which depicts the relation between asset values and their bid–ask spreads. Applying our empirical results, consider an asset which yields $1 per month, has a bid–ask spread of 3.2% (as in our high-spread portfolio group) and its proper opportunity cost of capital is 2% per month, yielding a value of $50. If the spread is reduced to 0.486% (as in our low-spread portfolio group), our estimates imply that the value of the asset would increase to $75.8, about a 50% increase, suggesting a strong incentive for the firm to invest in increasing the liquidity of the claims it issues. In particular, phenomena such as 'going public' (compared to private placement), standardization of the contractual forms of securities, limited liability, exchange listing and information disclosures may be construed as investments in increased liquidity. It is of interest to examine to what extent observed corporate financial policies can be explained by the liquidity-increasing motive. Such an investigation could

---

[19] To illustrate, the coefficient of DS_1 in model (9), which reflects the difference in returns between the highest and lowest spread groups, was -0.00765 ($t = 8.15$) by the OLS method and -0.00587 ($t = 6.73$) by GLS.

[20] Recall that, in the context of our model, net returns cannot be defined as stock characteristics, since they depend on both the stock and the owning investor. Our result is that despite their higher spread, the net return on high-spread stocks to their holders is higher.

create a link between securities market microstructure and corporate financial policies, and constitutes a natural avenue for further research.

This also suggests that a more comprehensive model of the return–spread relation could consider supply response by firms. Rather than set the spread exogenously, as in our model, firms may engage in a supply adjustment, increasing the liquidity of their securities at a cost. In equilibrium, the marginal increase in value due to improved liquidity will equal the marginal cost of such an improvement. Then, differences in firms' ability to affect liquidity will be reflected in differences in bid–ask spreads and risk-adjusted returns across securities.[21]

We believe that this paper makes a strong case for studying the role of liquidity in asset pricing in a broader context. The generality of our analysis is limited in that we do not consider the difference between marginal liquidity and total liquidity, and the associated relation between liquidation uncertainty and holding period uncertainty. This issue deserves further attention. In our model, all assets are liquidated at the end of the investor's holding period. Thus, there is no distinction between the liquidity of an asset when considered by itself and its liquidity in a portfolio context, nor is it necessary to consider the dispersion of possible holding periods for each asset in the portfolio. In a more general model, each investor may be faced with a sequence of stochastic cash demands occurring at random points in time. The investor would then have to determine the quantities of each security to be liquidated at each point in time. In such a setting, an investor's portfolio is likely to include an array of assets with both low and high spreads, whose proportions will reflect both the distribution of the amounts to be liquidated and the dispersion of his liquidation times. Then, there would be a distinction between the liquidity of an asset and its marginal contribution to the liquidity of an investor's portfolio. A study along these lines should focus on the interrelationship between total and marginal liquidity and its effect on asset pricing.

Further research could also be carried out on the interplay between liquidity and risk, and on the relation between asset returns and a more comprehensive set of liquidity characteristics. And finally, it is of interest to pursue the link between corporate financial theory and the theory of exchange, possibly leading to a unified framework which will enhance our understanding of organizations and markets.

References

Amihud, Yakov and Haim Mendelson, 1980, Dealership market: Market-making with inventory, Journal of Financial Economics 8, 31–53.

Amihud, Yakov and Haim Mendelson, 1982, Asset price behavior in a dealership market, Financial Analysts Journal 29, 50–59.

---

[21] Even if some firms could issue an unlimited supply of zero-spread securities, our results show that there will still be differentials in investors' net yields.

Amihud, Yakov and Haim Mendelson, 1985, An integrated computerized trading system, in: Y. Amihud, T.S. Ho and R.A. Schwartz, eds., Market making and the changing structure of the securities industry (Lexington Heath, Lexington, MA) 217–235.

Amihud, Yakov and Haim Mendelson, 1986a, Liquidity and stock returns, Financial Analysts Journal 42, 43–48.

Amihud, Yakov and Haim Mendelson, 1986b, Trading mechanisms and stock returns: An empirical investigation, Working paper.

Bagehot, Walter, 1971, The only game in town, Financial Analysts Journal 27, 12–14.

Banz, Rolf W., 1981, The relationship between return and market value of common stocks, Journal of Financial Economics 9, 3–18.

Benston, George and Robert Hagerman, 1974, Determinants of bid–ask spreads in the over-the-counter market, Journal of Financial Economics 1, 353–364.

Black, Fischer, Michael C. Jensen and Myron Scholes, 1972, The capital asset pricing model: Some empirical tests, in: Michael C. Jensen, ed., Studies in the theory of capital markets (Praeger, New York) 79–121.

Black, Fischer and Myron Scholes, 1974, The effects of dividend yield and dividend policy on common stock prices and returns, Journal of Financial Economics 1, 1–22.

Blume, Marshall E. and Robert F. Stambaugh, 1983, Biases in computing returns: An application to the size effect, Journal of Financial Economics 12, 387–404.

Chen, Andrew H., E. Han Kim and Stanley J. Kon, 1975, Cash demand, liquidation costs and capital market equilibrium under uncertainty, Journal of Financial Economics 2, 293–308.

Day, Theodore, E., Hans R. Stoll and Robert E. Whaley, 1985, Taxes, financial policy and small business (Lexington Heath, Lexington, MA) forthcoming.

Demsetz, Harold, 1968, The cost of transacting, Quarterly Journal of Economics 82, 35–53.

Elton, Edwin J. and Martin J. Gruber, 1978, Taxes and portfolio composition, Journal of Financial Economics 6, 399–410.

Fama, Eugene F., 1976, Foundations of finance (Basic Books, New York).

Fama, Eugene F. and James MacBeth, 1973, Risk, return and equilibrium: Empirical tests, Journal of Political Economy 81, 607–636.

Fisher, Lawrence and Daniel G. Weaver, 1985, Improving the measurement of returns of stocks, portfolios, and equally-weighted indexes: Avoiding or compensating for 'biases' due to bid–ask spread and other transient errors in price, Mimeo.

Fogler, H. Russel, 1984, 20% in real estate: Can theory justify it?, Journal of Portfolio Management 10, 6–13.

Gale, David, 1960, The theory of linear economic models (McGraw-Hill, New York).

Garbade, Kenneth, 1982, Securities markets (McGraw-Hill, New York).

Garman, Mark B., 1976, Market microstructure, Journal of Financial Economics 3, 257–275.

Ho, Thomas and Hans Stoll, 1981, Optimal dealer pricing under transactions and return uncertainty, Journal of Financial Economics 9, 47–73.

Ho, Thomas and Hans Stoll, 1983, The dynamics of dealer markets under competition, Journal of Finance 38, 1053–1074.

Jensen, Michael C., 1968, Risk, the pricing of capital assets, and the evaluation of investment portfolios, Journal of Business 42, 167–247.

Judge, George G., William E. Griffiths, R. Carter Hill and Tsoung-Chao Lee, 1980, The theory and practice of econometrics (Wiley, New York).

Kane, Alex, 1984, Coins: Anatomy of a fad asset, Journal of Portfolio Management 10, 44–51.

Kmenta, Jan, 1971, Elements of econometrics (Macmillan, New York).

Lakonishok, Josef and Seymour Smidt, 1984, Volume, price and rate of return for active and inactive stocks with applications to turn-of-the-year behavior, Journal of Financial Economics 13, 435–455.

Levy, Haim, 1978, Equilibrium in an imperfect market: A constraint on the number of securities in a portfolio, American Economic Review 68, 643–658.

Litzenberger, Robert H. and Krishna Ramaswamy, 1980, Dividends, short selling restrictions, tax-induced investor clienteles and market equilibrium, Journal of Finance 35, 469–482.

Maddala, G.S., 1977, Econometrics (McGraw-Hill, New York).

Malinvaud, E., 1970, Statistical methods of econometrics (Elsevier, New York).

Mendelson, Haim, 1982, Market behavior in a clearing house, Econometrica 50, 1505–1524.

Mendelson, Haim, 1985, Random competitive exchange: Price distributions and gains from trade, Journal of Economic Theory 37, 254–280.
Mendelson, Haim, 1986, Exchange with random quantities and discrete feasible prices, Working paper (Graduate School of Management, University of Rochester, Rochester, NY).
Mendelson, Haim, 1987, Consolidation, fragmentation and market performance, Journal of Financial and Quantitative Analysis, forthcoming.
Miller, Merton H., 1977, Debt and taxes, Journal of Finance 32, 261–275.
Milne, Frank and Clifford W. Smith, Jr., 1980, Capital asset pricing with proportional transaction costs, Journal of Financial and Quantitative Analysis 15, 253–265.
Phillips, Susan M. and Clifford W. Smith, Jr., 1980, Trading costs for listed options: The implications for market efficiency, Journal of Financial Economics 8, 179–201.
Reinganum, Marc R., 1981a, Misspecification of capital asset pricing: Empirical anomalies based on earnings yields and market values, Journal of Financial Economics 9, 19–46.
Reinganum, Marc R., 1981b, The arbitrage pricing theory: Some empirical evidence, Journal of Finance 36, 313–320.
Roll, Richard, 1983, On computing mean return and the small firm premium, Journal of Financial Economics 12, 371–386.
Ross, S.M., 1970, Applied probability models with optimization applications (Holden-Day, San Francisco, CA).
Schwert, G. William, 1977, Stock exchange seats as capital assets, Journal of Financial Economics 6, 51–78.
Schwert, G. William, 1983, Size and stock returns, and other empirical regularities, Journal of Financial Economics 12, 3–12.
Schultz, Paul, 1983, Transaction costs and the small firm effect: A comment, Journal of Financial Economics 12, 81–88.
Stoll, Hans R. and Robert E. Whaley, 1983, Transaction costs and the small firm effect, Journal of Financial Economics 12, 57–79.
Stoll, Hans, 1985, Alternative views of market making, in: Y. Amihud, T. Ho and R. Schartz, eds., Market making and the changing structure of the securities industry (Lexington Heath, Lexington, MA) 67–92.
Treynor, Jack, 1980, Liquidity, interest rates and inflation, Unpublished manuscript.
West, Richard R. and Seha M. Tinic, 1971, The economics of the stock market (Praeger, New York).

[20]

Market microstructure and asset pricing: On the compensation for illiquidity in stock returns

Michael J. Brennan[*,a,b], Avanidhar Subrahmanyam[a]

[a] *Anderson Graduate School of Management, University of California at Los Angeles, Los Angeles, CA 90095, USA*
[b] *London School of Economics, Sussex Place, London NW1 4SA, UK*

(Received November 1994; final version received December 1995)

Abstract

Models of price formation in securities markets suggest that privately informed investors create significant illiquidity costs for uninformed investors, implying that the required rates of return should be higher for securities that are relatively illiquid. We investigate the empirical relation between monthly stock returns and measures of illiquidity obtained from intraday data. We find a significant relation between required rates of return and these measures after adjusting for the Fama and French risk factors, and also after accounting for the effects of the stock price level.

Key words: Asset pricing; Market microstructure
JEL classification: G12; G14

1. Introduction

At least since Bagehot (1971), it has been recognized that a primary cause of illiquidity in financial markets is the adverse selection which arises from the presence of privately informed traders. The theoretical implications of the

---

*Corresponding author.

We are particularly grateful to Kenneth French (the referee) and John Long (the editor) for insightful and constructive comments on earlier drafts. We also thank Yakov Amihud, Eugene Fama, Larry Harris, Ananth Madhavan, Maureen O'Hara, Richard Roll, Eduardo Schwartz, Walter Torous, and seminar participants at Cornell University, Boston College, UCLA, University of Washington, London Business School, Hong Kong University of Science and Technology, and the University of California at Irvine for helpful comments, and Jim Brandon for his advice and assistance.

0304-405X/96/$15.00 © 1996 Elsevier Science S.A. All rights reserved
SSDI 0304-405X(95)00870-K

adverse selection paradigm for financial market equilibrium have been analyzed extensively, and considerable effort has been expended on developing empirical techniques to measure adverse selection costs. In view of the considerable effort directed to the adverse selection paradigm, it is important to ask whether illiquidity due to information asymmetry significantly affects a firm's required rate of return.

Previous research on the return–illiquidity relation has focused on the quoted bid–ask spread as a measure of illiquidity. Thus, Amihud and Mendelson (1986) find evidence that asset returns include a significant premium for the quoted spread, while Eleswarapu and Reinganum (1993) question this result by showing that the return premium associated with the spread is primarily a seasonal phenomenon. However, the quoted bid–ask spread is a noisy measure of illiquidity because many large trades occur outside the spread and many small trades occur within the spread (see, e.g., Lee, 1993). Further, the theoretical models of Glosten (1989), Kyle (1985), and Easley and O'Hara (1987) and the empirical analysis of Glosten and Harris (1988) suggest that the liquidity effects of asymmetric information are most likely to be captured in the price impact of a trade, or the variable component of trading costs.

In this paper, we bring together diverse empirical techniques from asset pricing and market microstructure research to examine the return–illiquidity relation. Specifically, we estimate measures of illiquidity from intraday transactions data and use the Fama and French (1993) factors to adjust for risk. The use of transactions data enables us to estimate both the variable (trade-size-dependent) and the fixed costs of transacting. By empirically examining the effects of both variable and fixed components of illiquidity on asset returns we are able to shed light on the importance of the empirical measures of adverse selection in influencing asset returns. Moreover, since there is evidence that the activities of brokerage house analysts increase liquidity (Brennan and Subrahmanyam, 1995a), our findings have implications for the social value of security analysis.

We use intraday data from the Institute for the Study of Securities Markets for the years 1984 and 1988 and the methods of Glosten and Harris (1988) and Hasbrouck (1991) to decompose estimated trading costs into variable and fixed components. The basic data consist of the monthly returns on portfolios sorted by the estimated Kyle (inverse) measure of market depth, 'λ' (estimated using the Glosten–Harris method), and firm size for the period 1984–1991. As mentioned earlier, unlike Amihud and Mendelson (1986) and Eleswarapu and Reinganum (1993), who use the simple capital asset pricing model to adjust returns for risk, we take as our null hypothesis the three-factor model developed by Fama and French (1993). These factors are the excess market return, the return on a portfolio which is long in small stocks and short in large stocks, and the return on a portfolio which is long in high book-to-market stocks and short in low book-to-market stocks.

We first estimate the intercepts from the time-series regressions of the excess returns on our λ-sorted portfolios on the Fama–French factors. We are able to reject the null hypothesis that these intercepts are jointly zero. Our next step is to investigate directly the relation between the portfolio returns and our measures of market illiquidity. To accomplish this, we pool the time-series and cross-sectional data and perform generalized least squares (GLS) regressions of the portfolio returns simultaneously on measures of trading costs and the three Fama–French risk factors. This allows us to jointly estimate the factor coefficients and the coefficients of the illiquidity variables. We thus avoid the errors-in-variables problems associated with more traditional two-step Fama and MacBeth (1973) procedures.

We first perform regressions using indicator variables that correspond to the λ groups of the portfolios, in addition to the Fama–French risk factors, as our independent variables. We find that the coefficients on the indicators increase monotonically as we move from low-λ to high-λ portfolios. In subsequent regressions, we find that estimates of both the variable and the fixed components of the proportional cost of transacting are also significantly positively related to excess returns. The coefficient of the proportional spread, however, is negative, both when it is the only trading cost variable in the regression and when it is included along with our transaction cost variables. The sign of the spread coefficient is inconsistent with the role of this variable as a measure of the cost of transacting. We hypothesize that the spread is proxying for a risk variable associated with price level or firm size that is not captured by the Fama–French three-factor model. Our findings indicate that the explanatory power of the bid–ask spread appears largely to be due to the effect of (the reciprocal of) the price level. Indeed, the coefficient of the spread is not significant in the presence of the price level variable and our cost of illiquidity variables.

We also address the issue of seasonality raised by Eleswarapu and Reinganum (1993). A likelihood ratio test of seasonality leads us to conclude that there are no significant monthly seasonal components in the compensation for our transaction cost measures, the bid–ask spread, or the inverse price level variable, after allowing for the effect of the Fama–French risk factors.

The paper is organized as follows. Section 2 describes the estimation of the market illiquidity parameters and the portfolio formation procedure. Sections 3 and 4 report results obtained from performing Fama–French and GLS regressions, respectively, while Section 5 concludes.

2. Estimation of the market illiquidity parameters

We refer to a trading cost that is a constant proportion of the value of the transaction as a fixed (proportional) cost; if the cost varies with the value of the transaction, it is referred to as a variable (proportional) cost. We estimate the parameters associated with fixed and variable proportional trading costs, denoted by ψ and λ, respectively, using Institute for the Study of Security

Markets (ISSM) data for the calendar years 1984 and 1988. This data set consists of all bid-ask quotations and time-stamped transaction prices and quantities for each NYSE/AMEX stock. We use two different empirical models of price formation, which we label the *Glosten–Harris (GH)* and *Hasbrouck–Foster–Viswanathan (HFV)* models and describe below.

2.1. The Glosten–Harris model

Let m_t denote the expected value of the security, conditional on the information set at time t, of a market maker who observes only the order flow, q_t, and a public information signal, y_t. Models of price formation such as Kyle (1985) and Admati and Pfleiderer (1988) imply that m_t will evolve according to

$$m_t = m_{t-1} + \lambda q_t + y_t, \tag{1}$$

where λ is the (inverse) market depth parameter. While theorists have attributed the costs of transacting in securities markets to adverse selection, inventory holding costs, and fixed costs, empirical studies have found that inventory holding costs appear to be small in an intraday setting (see, for example, Stoll, 1989; George, Kaul, and Nimalendran, 1991; Madhavan and Smidt, 1991). In order to allow for a fixed cost component of the price response to a transaction, we proceed as follows.

Let D_t denote the sign of the incoming order at time t (+ 1 for a buyer-initiated trade and − 1 for a seller-initiated trade). Since not all trades occur at the bid or ask quotes, we follow the convention of Lee and Ready (1991) and Madhavan and Smidt (1991) to assign values to D_t, i.e., to classify trades as buyer- or seller-initiated trades: if a transaction occurs above the prevailing quote mid-point, it is regarded as a purchase and vice versa. If a transaction occurs exactly at the quote mid-point, it is signed using the previous transaction price according to the tick test (i.e., a purchase if the sign of the last nonzero price change is positive and vice versa).

Given the order sign D_t, denoting the fixed cost component by ψ, and assuming competitive risk-neutral market makers, the transaction price, p_t, can be written as

$$p_t = m_t + \psi D_t. \tag{2}$$

Substituting out m_t using (1), we have

$$p_t = m_{t-1} + \lambda q_t + \psi D_t + y_t. \tag{3}$$

However, since $p_{t-1} = m_{t-1} + \psi D_{t-1}$, the price change, Δp_t, is given by

$$\Delta p_t = \lambda q_t + \psi [D_t - D_{t-1}] + y_t, \tag{4}$$

where y_t is the unobservable error term. Eq. (4) is used to estimate the Glosten–Harris λ as described below.

2.2. The Hasbrouck–Foster–Viswanathan model

Our second model closely parallels the framework used by Foster and Viswanathan (1993, pp. 202–206) to analyze intraday and interday variations in trade informativeness. Their framework, in turn, is based on Hasbrouck (1991). The advantage of using this approach is that it is valid for a relatively broad range of theoretical specifications. The model focuses on the price response to *unexpected* volume as the measure of the adverse selection component of the price change. The rationale is that if trades are autocorrelated or predictable from past price changes, then part of the contemporaneous order flow is predictable and should not be included in measuring the information content of a trade. In contrast to Hasbrouck (1991), and following Foster and Viswanathan (1993), we apply the model to transaction prices, rather than to bid–ask quotes.

Let Δp_t be the transaction price change for transaction t, let q_t be the signed trade quantity corresponding to the price change, and let D_t be the indicator corresponding to the direction of a trade, assigned a value following the procedure described in the previous subsection. The following model with five lags is considered for estimation:

$$q_t = \alpha_q + \sum_{j=1}^{5} \beta_j \Delta p_{t-j} + \sum_{j=1}^{5} \gamma_j q_{t-j} + \tau_t, \tag{5}$$

$$\Delta p_t = \alpha_p + \psi[D_t - D_{t-1}] + \lambda \tau_t + \nu_t. \tag{6}$$

The informativeness of trades in Eq. (6) is measured by the coefficient of τ_t, the residual from the regression in (5). Thus, it is the response to the unexpected portion of the order flow in Eq. (5) (measured by τ_t) that measures trade informativeness. The coefficient on $D_t - D_{t-1}$, as before, measures the fixed cost component of the trading cost.

2.3. Empirical procedure

The estimation of the GH and HFV liquidity parameters proceeds as follows. First, we discard quotations and transactions which were reported out of sequence. Second, we omit the overnight price change in order to avoid contamination of the price change series by dividends, overnight news arrival, and special features associated with the opening procedure. Thus, the Hasbrouck–Foster–Viswanathan specification, which involves lagged values of price changes, uses missing values for the lags that involve the overnight price change. Third, to correct for reporting errors in the sequence of trades and quotations, we follow the convention employed in Madhavan and Smidt (1991) (and elsewhere) of delaying all quotations by five seconds. Finally, we use an error filter to screen out typographical errors. The error filter discards a trade if the trade price is too far outside the price range defined as the minimum range that includes both the preceding bid and ask quotations and the immediately following trade price or bid and ask quotations. If the price falls outside this range by more than four times the width of the range, the trade is discarded. This filter is conservative and discards fewer than one in 40,000 observations in the sample considered.

Noting that ISSM identifies firms by their ticker symbols, we first identify the NYSE-listed firms on the 1984 (1988) ISSM tape whose ticker symbols were listed as active at any time in 1984 (1988) in the 1992 Center for Research in Security Prices (CRSP) name matrix (our study is restricted to common stock). There were 1,629 and 1,784 such firms in 1984 and 1988, respectively. The Glosten–Harris model represented by Eqs. (4) and the two-equation model of Foster–Viswanathan represented by Eqs. (5) and (6) are then estimated by ordinary least squares (OLS) for each of the 1,629 (1,784) firms separately for 1984 (1988), retaining the resulting estimates of λ and ψ. These estimates are used to form portfolios and to compute the cost of illiquidity measures described below.

Note that our estimation procedure ignores the discreteness of the price quotes. While Glosten and Harris (1988) find that this does not have a material effect on the estimated value of the market depth parameter, λ, they also conclude that the estimates of the fixed cost parameter, ψ, 'are quite sensitive to whether or not discreteness is modeled in the estimation process' (Glosten and Harris, 1988, p. 135). Glosten and Harris model discreteness for only 20 stocks, finding the econometric modeling of discreteness to be too costly for their full sample of 250 stocks. This exercise is prohibitive for our much larger sample of stocks. Therefore, our results concerning the influence of fixed costs of transacting must be interpreted with this limitation in mind.

In a Kyle-type model, the cost of trading x shares is λx^2, so that, given the share price P, the marginal cost per dollar transacted when x shares are traded is $2\lambda x/P$ and varies with the trade size. Thus, to take account of the variable proportional cost of transacting in different securities it is necessary to make an assumption about the sizes of the transactions in the securities. A natural approach is to use the average measured trade size. Thus, our first measure of the variable proportional cost of transacting is $C_q \equiv \lambda q/P$, where q is the average size of a transaction in the security. Since the marginal cost of transacting is linear in trade size, this procedure yields the average of the marginal costs realized by all transactors. This is the measure used by Glosten and Harris (1988) in their cross-sectional analysis of the λ's.

A limitation of this measure of the variable proportional cost of transacting is that it takes no account of the distortionary effect of trading costs on the average transaction size.[1] Thus, if transaction sizes in extremely illiquid securities were

---
[1] Both Glosten and Harris (1988) and Brennan and Subrahmanyam (1995b) find a significant negative effect of λ on average transaction size.

sufficiently small, this approach might yield a *lower* estimated variable cost for illiquid securities than for the relatively liquid ones. Thus, a second way to proxy for x is to assume that, in the absence of differential liquidity, the average transaction would be proportional to the total number of shares of a firm's stock outstanding. The relevant measure of the variable cost then becomes $C_n \equiv \lambda n/P$, where n is the number of shares outstanding. We recognize that both C_q and C_n are imperfect proxies for the variable cost. Therefore, in our empirical analysis, we use indicator variables based on λ, as well as transformations of C_q and C_n.

2.4. Portfolio formation procedure

The portfolio formation proceeds as follows. First, all NYSE-listed securities on the CRSP tape at the beginning of each year from 1984 to 1987 are assigned to one of 30 portfolios according to their size and λ estimate based on 1984 transaction data. Thus, the securities are divided first into size quintiles according to the market value of the equity at the end of the previous year and then, within each size quintile, they are assigned to one of five portfolios with equal numbers of securities, based on their estimated GH λ. Securities for which no estimate of λ is available (for lack of transactions data on the ISSM tape) are assigned to a sixth portfolio for each size quintile. To facilitate usage of log-linear specifications involving λ (see Table 5 to be discussed later), we omit firms with negative estimates of λ from our portfolios. However, this procedure leads to the omission of no more than one firm per portfolio per year. The same portfolio formation procedure is repeated for CRSP data from 1988 to 1991 using estimates of λ derived from 1988 transaction data. This procedure yields a total of 30 portfolios, for five of which there is no estimate of λ.

Equally weighted monthly excess returns are calculated for each of the 30 portfolios from January 1984 to December 1991, using the one-month risk-free rate from the CRSP bond files. The values of λ and ψ for each portfolio are taken to be the equally weighted average λ and ψ, which are based on the 1984 estimates for the years 1984 to 1987 and on the 1988 estimates for the years 1988 to 1991. The fixed proportional cost component, ψ/P, is calculated by first dividing the estimated ψ by the average closing price in 1984 (1988) for each stock and then taking an equally weighted average across stocks within a portfolio. The *proportional spread* for each security in 1984 and 1988 is computed by averaging the proportional quoted spread (i.e., the quoted spread divided by the average of the bid and ask prices) across all quotations during the year. The proportional spread for each portfolio, SP, is the equally weighted average of the security spreads using the 1984 calculation for 1984-1987 and the 1988 calculation for 1988-1991.

For each calendar year, the equally weighted average size of the firms in each portfolio is calculated using the logarithm of the market value of equity outstanding at the end of the previous year as the measure of size. (A firm is eliminated from the sample if the relevant market value of equity is missing from the CRSP tape.) Finally, for each portfolio the equally weighted values of our variable cost of transacting variables, $C_q = \lambda q/P$ and $C_n = \lambda n/P$, are calculated for each year; for portfolios formed in 1984 through 1987 (1988 through 1991) λ is the value estimated from the 1984 (1988) transactions data, q is the average transaction size in 1984 (1988), n is the (monthly) average number of shares outstanding in 1984 (1988), and P is the (monthly) average price of the relevant stock in 1984 (1988). For certain firms and certain months, data on the number of shares outstanding and/or the price level in the relevant year are missing from the CRSP tape. We use a firm in our portfolio formation procedure if there is data on both these variables for at least one month, otherwise the firm is eliminated from the sample. We do not update n and P each year since we expect λ to be affected by changes in n and P and, due to lack of data availability, we are unable to update the λ or q component of the cost. Our procedure amounts to assuming that for a given security $\lambda q/P$ and $\lambda n/P$ are intertemporal constants. To the extent that this assumption is not valid, the power of our tests will be reduced. The time-series mean values of the monthly returns, sizes, illiquidity, and cost of illiquidity measures (based on the GH λ), and proportional spreads for each of the 30 portfolios are presented in Table 1. Panel A of Table 1 shows that for a given size group the average return tends to increase with λ, and for a given λ group the average return tends to increase with firm size. As can be seen from panel B, λ and the fixed and variable cost of transacting measures show considerable variation within each size group and are positively related. Also, the average proportional fixed cost component ψ/P is smaller than the average proportional spread, reflecting the notion that a large proportion of transactions take place within the quoted bid-ask spread.

Table 2 reports the correlations between the variables. Average return is positively correlated with size and negatively correlated with both the spread and the proportional fixed cost, ψ/P. The proportional spread and ψ/P have a correlation of 0.78, which is to be expected since they are both measures of the fixed proportional component of trading costs. The two measures of the variable proportional cost of transacting, C_n and C_q, have a correlation of 0.93, but their correlations with the spread are only 0.16 and 0.38, respectively. An interesting feature of the data is that while λ has only a low correlation with the spread and ψ/P in the overall sample (Table 2), within each size group λ is almost perfectly negatively correlated with these variables (panel B of Table 1).[2] Thus, within a size group the estimated fixed proportional cost of transacting is negatively related to the variable cost. We are not aware of any model of market making that would predict such a relation. The pattern may be related to market

---

[2] We are grateful to the referee for bringing this point to our attention.

Table 1
Summary statistics: Average values of monthly return, size, and liquidity variables for 30 portfolios of NYSE stocks sorted by size and the Glosten–Harris measure of illiquidity, λ, for the period 1984–1991

λ estimates the derivative of transaction price ($/share) with respect to signed trade size (shares, positive for trades initiated by buyers). Portfolios are formed annually from all NYSE firms active at the beginning of the year. Within each calendar year, size is measured as market value of equity at the end of the preceding year. C_q equals λ times the average trade size divided by the monthly average closing price, C_n equals λ times the monthly average number of shares outstanding divided by monthly average closing price, and ψ/P denotes the fixed component of trading costs as a proportion of the monthly average closing price. The proportional spread is calculated by averaging the proportional quoted spread (i.e., the quoted spread divided by the average of the bid and ask prices) across all quotations during the year. For the 1984–1987 period, λ and all other liquidity variables are estimated using 1984 data. For the 1988–1991 period, they are estimated from 1988 data. The portfolio labeled 0 in the λ group column denotes the portfolio for which data on the above liquidity variables are not available. The variable and fixed components of liquidity, λ and ψ, respectively, are estimated using the Glosten–Harris (1988) method.

(A) Average monthly returns (percentages) and firm size (millions of dollars)

Size group	λ group					
	0	1	2	3	4	5
Average return						
1	−0.87	−1.35	−0.42	−0.40	−0.40	0.34
2	0.18	0.77	0.93	1.19	1.42	1.62
3	0.54	1.20	1.13	1.41	1.52	1.68
4	1.30	1.43	1.39	1.35	1.74	1.87
5	1.30	1.69	1.78	1.82	1.86	2.03
Average firm size						
1	38.40	46.18	48.66	49.97	49.99	49.32
2	134.58	166.71	166.46	158.10	159.94	149.42
3	341.75	464.21	470.75	457.30	461.83	434.58
4	2,525.33	1,234.82	1,270.71	1,265.69	1,227.04	1,146.93
5	5,107.72	7,107.38	7,546.87	8,535.76	4,837.67	5,164.03

(B) Liquidity variables

Size group	λ group				
	1	2	3	4	5
$\lambda*100$					
1	0.0074	0.0244	0.0472	0.0899	0.2784
2	0.0058	0.0175	0.0334	0.0640	0.2347
3	0.0035	0.0106	0.0201	0.0347	0.1304
4	0.0027	0.0079	0.0136	0.0227	0.0559
5	0.0019	0.0058	0.0102	0.0151	0.0395

Table 1 (continued)

Size group	λ group				
	1	2	3	4	5
Proportional spread					
1	0.0262	0.0179	0.0142	0.0131	0.0124
2	0.0131	0.0100	0.0095	0.0088	0.0075
3	0.0114	0.0086	0.0076	0.0068	0.0062
4	0.0079	0.0081	0.0065	0.0059	0.0054
5	0.0053	0.0049	0.0049	0.0044	0.0040
$C_q * 100$					
1	0.0262	0.0418	0.0536	0.0834	0.1267
2	0.0080	0.0166	0.0234	0.0318	0.0566
3	0.0043	0.0098	0.0132	0.0168	0.0285
4	0.0026	0.0062	0.0089	0.0121	0.0192
5	0.0016	0.0037	0.0052	0.0069	0.0089
C_n					
1	2.42	3.54	3.67	6.84	8.49
2	1.02	1.60	2.15	3.02	6.08
3	0.92	1.67	1.70	2.15	4.09
4	0.82	1.36	1.73	2.19	3.28
5	1.08	2.15	2.74	2.51	3.27
ψ/P					
1	0.0173	0.0094	0.0073	0.0070	0.0050
2	0.0061	0.0044	0.0041	0.0037	0.0032
3	0.0051	0.0034	0.0030	0.0028	0.0024
4	0.0036	0.0026	0.0022	0.0022	0.0021
5	0.0023	0.0018	0.0015	0.0015	0.0014

makers' tradeoffs between the fixed and variable components across stocks that differ in trading volume and transaction frequency.

3. Fama–French intercepts

Fama and French (1993) propose a three-factor model of common stock returns. These factors are the market excess return, a size factor, and a book-to-market factor. The size factor is the return on a portfolio that is long in small stocks and short in large stocks. Similarly, the book-to-market factor is the

Table 2
Cross-sectional correlation matrix: Matrix provides correlations between monthly return, size, and liquidity variables for 25 portfolios of NYSE stocks sorted by size and the Glosten–Harris measure of illiquidity, λ, for the period 1984–1991

Five portfolios for which data on λ are not available are omitted from the sample. λ estimates the derivative of transaction price ($/share) with respect to signed trade size (shares, positive for trades initiated by buyers). Portfolios are formed annually from all NYSE firms active at the beginning of the year. Within each calendar year, size is measured as market value of equity at the end of the preceding year. C_q equals λ times the average trade size divided by the monthly average closing price, C_n equals λ times the monthly average number of shares outstanding divided by monthly average closing price, and ψ/P denotes the fixed component of trading costs as a proportion of the monthly average closing price. The proportional spread is calculated by averaging the proportional quoted spread (i.e., the quoted spread divided by the average of the bid and ask prices) across all quotations during the year. For the 1984–1987 period, λ and all other liquidity variables are estimated using 1984 data. For the 1988–1991 period, they are estimated from 1988 data. The variable and fixed components of liquidity. λ and ψ, respectively, are estimated using the Glosten–Harris (1988) method.

	Average return	Average size	λ	Prop. spread	C_q	C_n	ψ/P
Avg. return	1.00	0.49	−0.08	−0.95	−0.52	−0.30	−0.92
Avg. size	0.49	1.00	−0.29	−0.52	−0.41	−0.21	−0.44
λ	−0.08	−0.29	1.00	0.03	0.82	0.88	−0.03
Prop. spread	−0.95	−0.52	0.03	1.00	0.38	0.16	0.78
C_q	−0.52	−0.41	0.83	0.38	1.00	0.93	0.31
C_n	−0.30	−0.21	0.88	0.16	0.93	1.00	0.13
ψ/P	−0.92	−0.44	−0.03	0.78	0.31	0.13	1.00

return on a portfolio that is long in stocks with high book-to-market ratios and short in stocks with low book-to-market ratios. We take the Fama–French model as our null hypothesis and test whether variables related to the cost of transacting have additional explanatory power for the cross-section of returns. First, following Fama and French (1993), we perform OLS time-series regressions of the excess returns on our 30 portfolios on the factors:[3]

$$R_{it} = \alpha_i + \beta_i R_{mt} + \delta_i SML_t + \kappa_i HML_t + e_{it}, \qquad (7)$$

where R_{mt} is the excess return on the market portfolio in month t, SMB_t and HML_t are the returns in month t on the Fama–French size and book-to-market factors, respectively, and R_{it} is the excess return on portfolio i. Under the null hypothesis that the costs of transacting have no effect on expected returns the intercepts in these regressions are equal to zero. Following Fama and French,

---
[3] We thank Gene Fama and Ken French for making the returns on their factor portfolios available to us.

we test the null hypothesis using the Gibbons, Ross, and Shanken (1989) statistic, which can be defined as follows. Let there be N time-series observations, L portfolios, and $K - 1$ explanatory variables (excluding the intercept). Further, let X denote the matrix of regressors. Then, the test statistic is given by

$$(A' \Sigma^{-1} A) \frac{N - K - L + 1}{L*(N - K)*\omega_{1,1}},$$

where A is the column vector of the regression intercepts, Σ is the variance-covariance matrix of the residuals from the regressions, and $\omega_{1,1}$ is the diagonal element of $(X'X)^{-1}$ corresponding to the intercept. Under the null hypothesis this statistic has an F-distribution with L and $N - K - L + 1$ degrees of freedom. The estimated coefficients of Eq. (7) for each of the 30 portfolios are reported in Table 3. The F-test strongly rejects at the 5% and 1% levels the null hypothesis that the intercepts are jointly equal to zero, both when the intercepts for the missing-λ portfolios are included and when they are excluded from the test. This suggests that the size and book-to-market effects documented by Fama and French do not proxy for transaction cost effects. However, the three-factor model, by accounting for variation in returns that is unrelated to trading costs, makes the relationship between trading costs and returns more transparent. There also appears to be a pattern associated with firm size (unrelated to λ) in the intercepts, in that they generally increase as one moves from the smallest to largest firm quintiles. To account for this finding, we include firm size in addition to the illiquidity variables in the GLS regressions whose results appear in the next section.

4. GLS regressions

In this section, we report the results of pooled cross-section time-series regressions of the portfolio returns on various trading cost measures and the three Fama–French risk factors. By estimating simultaneously the factor coefficients and the coefficients of the trading cost variables, we avoid the errors-in-variables problems associated with more traditional Fama and MacBeth (1973) procedures. Throughout the analysis, we restrict our attention to the 25 portfolios for which estimates of λ are available. The estimation proceeds as follows. Define R as the $(25T \times 1)$ vector of portfolio excess returns, where T is the total number of time-series observations, and the vector is ordered by month so that the first 25 observations correspond to the portfolio returns in month 1. Define X as the partitioned matrix

$$X = [WZ], \tag{8}$$

Table 3
Intercepts from Fama–French OLS regressions for 30 portfolios of NYSE stocks sorted by size and the Glosten–Harris measure of illiquidity, λ, for the period 1984–1991

λ estimates the derivative transaction price (\$/share) with respect to signed trade size (shares, positive for trades initiated by buyers). Portfolios are formed annually from all NYSE firms active at the beginning of the year. Within each calendar year, size is measured as market value of equity at the end of the preceding year. For the 1984–1987 period, λ and all other liquidity variables are estimated using 1984 data. For the 1988–1991 period, they are estimated from 1988 data. The portfolio labeled 0 in the λ group column denotes the portfolio for which data on λ are not available. The table presents intercepts from the following time-series regressions:

$$R_{it} = \alpha_i + \beta_i MKT_t + \delta_i SMB_t + \kappa_i HML_t + u_{it},$$

where R_{it} is the excess return on portfolio i in month t, and MKT_t, SMB_t, and HML_t denote the returns on the Fama and French (1993) factors related to the market, firm size, and the book-to-market ratio in month t. The bottom of the table presents the Gibbons, Ross, and Shanken (1989) test of the hypothesis that the intercepts jointly equal zero. Intercepts are reported in percentage terms (t-statistics are in parentheses).

	λ group					
Size group	0	1	2	3	4	5
1	−1.21	−2.14	−1.51	−1.34	−1.25	−0.45
	(−2.50)	(−3.62)	(−3.17)	(−3.34)	(−3.78)	(−1.76)
2	−0.39	−0.42	−0.19	0.13	0.37	0.80
	(−1.18)	(−1.76)	(−0.99)	(0.72)	(1.99)	(4.63)
3	0.03	0.02	−0.17	0.26	0.41	0.66
	(0.11)	(0.09)	(−1.04)	(1.39)	(2.57)	(4.55)
4	0.86	0.27	0.07	−0.07	0.41	0.63
	(2.24)	(1.54)	(0.51)	(−0.47)	(2.42)	(4.16)
5	0.71	0.29	0.33	0.38	0.38	0.60
	(1.47)	(2.05)	(3.03)	(3.96)	(3.11)	(4.74)

(1) F-value for the Gibbons, Ross, and Shanken test that the intercepts jointly equal zero is 4.77 (p-value $= 9.08*10^{-8}$). (2) F-value for the Gibbons, Ross, and Shanken test that the intercepts equal zero (excluding portfolios with missing liquidity parameters) is 5.70 (p-value $= 5.50*10^{-9}$).

where Z is a $(25T \times 75)$ matrix of the Fama–French factors. The first 25 columns of Z consist of T stacked (25×25) diagonal matrices with identical elements R_{mt}, the excess return on the market in month t, $t = 1, \ldots, T$; the second 25 columns consist similarly of the size factor, SML_t, and the last 25 columns contain the book-to-market factor, HML_t. W is a $(25T \times (k + 1))$ matrix, whose first column is a vector of units and whose remaining k columns are the vectors of the k portfolio attributes (trading cost measures) whose influence on returns we wish to assess.

We first perform the OLS pooled cross-section time-series regression

$$R = X\beta + \varepsilon, \tag{9}$$

where β is a $k + 76$ vector of coefficients, the first element of which is the constant term of the regression, the next k elements of which are the coefficients of the k trading cost measures included in the regression, and the last 75 elements of which are the coefficients of the three Fama–French factors for the 25 portfolios ordered by portfolio. ε is a $25T \times 1$ vector of errors. In our application the sample consists of monthly returns from January 1984 to December 1991 so that $T = 96$. In order to obtain the GLS estimator of β, Ω, the variance–covariance matrix of errors in (9), is estimated assuming that the portfolio return errors are serially independent, but allowing for cross-sectional dependence. Then Ω is a $(25T \times 25T)$ block-diagonal matrix, whose typical element is the 25×25 covariance matrix of portfolio return errors: it is estimated using the residuals from (9). The GLS estimate of β is given by

$$\hat{\beta} = (X'\hat{\Omega}^{-1}X)^{-1}X'\hat{\Omega}^{-1}Y,$$

where $\hat{\Omega}$ is the estimate of Ω from the first-stage regressions.

4.1. GLS regressions using indicator variables for the λ groups

Our first set of regressions uses dummy variables for the λ quintiles, treating the smallest λ group as the base case. Then $k = 4$ and the last four columns of W contain the dummy variables for group membership. The GLS estimates of the constant term and the dummy variable coefficients are presented in Table 4 along with the average characteristics of the five portfolios within each λ quintile. (The coefficients of the Fama–French factors are omitted to save space.) The dummy variable coefficients increase monotonically as we move from low to high λ quintiles, and the coefficients are statistically significant for all the four nonbase λ quintiles. Note that the variation in average firm size across the quintiles is not monotonic, while the average value of λ increases monotonically across the quintiles. This suggests that the pattern in the indicator variable coefficients is unrelated to firm size.[4]

4.2. The functional form of the cost of illiquidity

While our results thus far confirm the hypothesis that portfolios with a higher λ have a higher risk-adjusted return, they do not distinguish between the influence of the λ variable and the transaction cost variables C_q and C_n. To explore this issue, as well as to analyze the influence of the proportional fixed

---

[4] Using the actual λ values for the portfolios in the GLS regression, as opposed to indicator variables, leads to essentially similar results. Further, including firm size as an independent variable in the regression does not materially alter the coefficients of the indicator variables. For brevity, these results are not reported.

Table 4
Dummy variable GLS regressions, using the Fama-French factors, for the 25 portfolios of NYSE stocks sorted by size and the Glosten-Harris measure of illiquidity, λ, for the period 1984-1991

Five portfolios for which data on λ are not available are omitted from the sample. λ estimates the derivative of transaction price ($/share) with respect to signed trade size (shares, positive for trades initiated by buyers). Portfolios are formed annually from all NYSE firms active at the beginning of the year. Within each calendar year, size is measured as market value of equity at the end of the preceding year. For the 1984-1987 period, λ and all other liquidity variables are estimated using 1984 data. For the 1988-1991 period, they are estimated from 1988 data. Variables L2 through L5 denote indicators corresponding to the second through fifth λ groups, arranged in increasing order of λ. The group with the smallest λ forms the base case. The regression equation is

$$R_{it} = \alpha_i + \sum_{k=2}^{5} \gamma_k L_{ik} + \beta_i MKT_t + \delta_i SMB_t + \kappa_i HML_t + \varepsilon_{it},$$

where R_{it} denotes the excess return on portfolio i in month t, the L's denote the dummy variables, and MKT, SMB, and HML denote the Fama-French factors related to the market, firm size, and the book-to-market ratio, respectively. The second through fourth columns report the average values of firm size, λ, C_q, which equals λ times the average trade size divided by monthly average closing price, and C_n, which equals λ times the number of shares outstanding divided by monthly average closing price for each of the five λ groups (t-statistics are in parentheses).

	Estimate$*10^3$ (t-statistic)	Average size ($ millions)	$\lambda*100$	C_q*10^3	C_n
Constant	0.01 (0.01)				
L1	Base case	1,735.79	0.0042	0.085	1.25
L2	1.63 (2.05)	1,773.08	0.0132	0.156	2.06
L3	2.82 (2.88)	1,955.04	0.0249	0.208	2.40
L4	4.37 (3.86)	1,298.49	0.0452	0.302	3.34
L5	5.52 (5.26)	1,324.33	0.1478	0.479	5.04

component ψ/P, we repeat the generalized least squares regressions of the type (9), with different regressors for the last k columns of the matrix W. We use, in turn, both the GH and the HFV measures of λ and ψ to compute C_q, C_n, and ψ/P.

First, for direct comparability with Amihud and Mendelson (1986), we perform the GLS regression including the time-series average of the bid-ask spread as a regressor; the results appear in the first column of panel A in Table 5. (Again, we omit the estimated portfolio factor loadings which are close to those reported in Table 3.) The spread enters the regression with a strongly significant

Table 5
Pooled time-series cross-sectional GLS regressions using the cost of illiquidity variables for 25 portfolios of NYSE stocks sorted by size and the Glosten–Harris measure of illiquidity, λ, for the period 1984–1991

Five portfolios for which data on λ are not available are omitted from the sample. λ estimates the derivative of transaction price ($/share) with respect to signed trade size (shares, positive for trades initiated by buyers). Portfolios are formed annually from all NYSE firms active at the beginning of the year. Within each calendar year, size is measured as market value of equity at the end of the preceding year. C_q equals λ times the average trade size divided by the monthly average closing price, C_n equals λ times the monthly average number of shares outstanding divided by monthly average closing price, and ψ/P denotes the fixed component of trading costs as a proportion of the monthly average closing price. The proportional spread is calculated by averaging the proportional quoted spread (i.e., the quoted spread divided by the average of the bid and ask prices) across all quotations during the year. $\log(C_q)$ and C_q^2 are defined as the average of the logarithm of C_q and the average of the squared value of C_q for the relevant portfolio respectively, and C_n, C_n^2, and $(\psi/P)^2$ are defined similarly. For the 1984–1987 period, λ and all other liquidity variables are estimated using 1984 data. For the 1988–1991 period, they are estimated from 1988 data. $(1/P)$ is the mean of the inverse monthly average closing price for each portfolio. The regression equation is

$$R_{it} = \alpha + \sum_{k=1}^{N} \gamma_k L_{ik} + \beta_i MKT_t + \delta_i SMB_t + \kappa_i HML_t + \varepsilon_{it},$$

where R_{it} denotes the excess return on portfolio i in month t, the L's denote the illiquidity variables, and the inverse price variable (if included), and MKT, SMB, and HML denote the Fama–French factors related to the market, firm size, and the book-to-market ratio, respectively. N is the total number of illiquidity variables plus one if the inverse price level variable is included in the regression (t-statistics are in parentheses).

(A) C_q as measure of the cost of illiquidity

	(1)	(2)	(3)	(4)	(5)
Constant * 1000	9.04	10.78	27.41	9.02	− 26.90
	(8.42)	(8.94)	(1.99)	(7.06)	(− 0.94)
		10.41	25.59	9.10	− 31.54
		(8.54)	(1.91)	(7.15)	(− 1.16)
C_q		3.21		1.55	2.18
		(2.03)		(4.90)	(3.24)
		3.48		1.37	2.23
		(2.07)		(4.27)	(3.28)
ψ/P		1.52		0.82	7.64
		(2.45)		(0.86)	(2.85)
		1.38		0.79	9.32
		(2.20)		(0.84)	(3.41)
$\log(C_q)/1000$			1.08		
			(3.14)		
			1.13		
			(3.18)		

Table 5 (continued)

	(1)	(2)	(3)	(4)	(5)
$\log(\psi/P)/1000$			0.96		
			(0.49)		
			0.67		
			(0.35)		
$C_q^2 * 1000$				− 6.44	− 8.19
				(− 4.39)	(− 3.76)
				− 5.22	**− 7.75**
				(− 3.65)	**(− 3.63)**
$(\psi/P)^2 * 100$				0.31	0.79
				(0.36)	(3.53)
				0.38	**0.95**
				(0.46)	**(4.37)**
$(1/P)$					− 0.45
					(− 3.26)
					− 0.57
					(− 3.99)
Prop. spread	− 0.93	− 1.88	− 1.21	− 1.48	− 0.57
	(− 6.00)	(− 4.89)	(− 3.94)	(− 3.04)	(− 0.99)
		− 1.75	**− 1.12**	**− 1.45**	**− 0.37**
		(− 4.49)	**(− 3.73)**	**(− 3.01)**	**(− 0.66)**
Avg. log (size)/10^3					1.43
					(1.22)
					1.60
					(1.44)

(B) C_n as measure of market illiquidity

	(1)	(2)	(3)	(4)	(5)
Constant * 1000	9.04	8.94	26.86	8.22	− 3.02
	(8.42)	(7.36)	(1.95)	(6.62)	(− 0.15)
		8.28	**24.95**	**7.65**	**− 6.52**
		(6.65)	**(1.87)**	**(6.01)**	**(− 0.35)**
$C_n/1000$		0.64		1.01	1.18
		(3.24)		(4.30)	(3.19)
		0.70		**0.98**	**1.25**
		(3.30)		**(4.01)**	**(3.40)**
(ψ/P)		1.56		2.52	11.23
		(2.65)		(2.54)	(4.42)
		1.41		**2.06**	**12.04**
		(2.39)		**(2.09)**	**(4.75)**

Table 5 (continued)

	(1)	(2)	(3)	(4)	(5)
$\log(C_n)/100$			0.15		
			(2.90)		
			0.16		
			(2.90)		
$\log(\psi/P)/100$			0.27		
			(1.40)		
			0.25		
			(1.33)		
$C_n^2/1000$				−0.01	−0.02
				(−2.74)	(−4.81)
				−0.01	**−0.02**
				(−2.15)	**(−4.67)**
$(\psi/P)^2 * 100$				−0.88	1.06
				(−0.98)	(4.42)
				−0.61	**1.14**
				(−0.70)	**(4.92)**
$(1/P)$					−0.63
					(−4.56)
					−0.70
					(−5.05)
Prop. spread	−0.93	−1.79	−1.18	−2.14	−1.19
	(−6.00)	(−5.14)	(−3.83)	(−4.56)	(−2.25)
		−1.65	**−1.09**	**−1.88**	**−0.85**
		(−4.65)	**(−3.59)**	**(−3.99)**	**(−1.61)**
Avg. log (size)/10^3					0.36
					(0.45)
					0.46
					(0.62)

but negative sign. This finding is contrary to the hypothesized role of the spread as a proxy for market illiquidity, but is consistent with the results in Eleswarapu and Reinganum (1993) for the 1981–90 period (see panel B of their Table 4).

In order to investigate whether the negative sign on the spread can be explained by the inclusion of our transaction cost variables, we include the time-series averages of C_q and ψ/P in the GLS regression. The coefficients are reported in the second column of panel A in Table 5.[5] The coefficients of the

---

[5] Note that there is time-series variation in C_q only on account of changing portfolio membership and the switch from the 1984 to 1988 estimates of C.

variable cost measure C_q and the fixed cost measure ψ/P are both positive and significant for both the GH and HFV measures of λ, but the coefficient of the spread remains negative and strongly significant.

Amihud and Mendelson (1986) suggest that investors with long horizons will require a smaller premium for illiquidity and, in equilibrium, will tend to hold the relatively illiquid stocks. This clientele effect will give rise to a concave relation between returns and the costs of transacting. However, the consideration of both the fixed and variable components of transaction costs gives rise to the possibility of a second clientele, this time in trade sizes. Thus, investors who trade small orders will be at a comparative advantage relative to large traders in trading high λ/P stocks. We should therefore expect the stocks with high values of λ/P to be held by investors who have long horizons *and* small trade sizes. Stocks with high values of the proportional fixed component ψ/P, however, would be held by investors with long horizons, *regardless* of the investors' preferred trade sizes. This suggests that the variable element of the proportional cost admits two clientele effects (associated with both trade size and horizon), while the fixed element admits only one (associated only with horizon). We would therefore expect the concavity between the relation between returns and the proportional cost of transacting to be greater for the variable component than for the fixed component.

To take account of potential nonlinearities in the relation between return and the cost of illiquidity, we replace C_q and ψ/P with the time-series average of the portfolio value of the logarithms of C_q and ψ/P. The results are reported in the third column of panel A in Table 5. With this modified specification, the variable cost of transacting variable becomes more strongly significant for both measures of λ, consistent with the trade size clientele effect discussed above. However, the fixed cost of transacting variable, ψ/P, is now less significant, suggesting that the horizon clientele effects discussed by Amihud and Mendelson may not be so important.

As an alternative empirical specification, we also include quadratic functions of C_q and ψ/P in the GLS regression, with squared terms computed by taking the time-series average of the average values of the squared measures within each portfolio. The relevant coefficients are reported in the fourth column of the table. For both measures of λ, the coefficient of the linear term C_q is positive, and that of the squared term C_q^2 is negative, confirming the concave nature of the relation; both coefficients are strongly significant. This finding supports the notion that clientele effects cause the effect of our illiquidity measures on returns to be overstated for portfolios with large values of these measures. Note, however, that the coefficients of the linear and squared terms involving ψ/P, the fixed cost component, are not significant, though they are both positive.

The negative and significant coefficient on the bid–ask spread in all the regressions discussed above is puzzling and points to some misspecification in our regressions. One possibility is that the spread proxies for risk variables related to firm size and the price level (see Miller and Scholes, 1982, pp. 1132–1133) that are omitted from the Fama–French model. To test this hypothesis, we include the average of the inverse price level and the average of the portfolio value of (the logarithm of) firm size in the regression represented by column (5) of panel A in Table 5. (The inverse price level for each security is computed as the inverse of the closing price at the end of the previous month.) The price variable is strongly significant, while in the presence of this variable, the spread variable becomes insignificant; the logarithm of firm size is not significant either. This suggests that the spread effect observed in the first four regressions is due to the spread proxying for a risk variable that is associated with (the reciprocal of) the price variable. This would explain why Amihud and Mendelson find a positive premium associated with the spread in one sample period while Eleswarapu and Reinganum find a negative premium in a different sample period. The coefficients of both ψ/P and $(\psi/P)^2$ are now positive and strongly significant, while there is not much alteration in the magnitude or significance of the coefficients associated with C_q for either measure of λ.

Thus the results of the extended regression are consistent with a risk model in which the Fama–French risk factors are complemented with a price factor. Further, there are premiums associated with both the fixed and variable proportional costs of trading. The relation between the premium and the variable element is increasing and concave, consistent with a clientele effect in trade sizes. The relation between the premium and the fixed element is increasing but convex which is inconsistent with a clientele effect in horizons of the type suggested by Amihud and Mendelson (1986). One possible reason for this convex relation is that (as we noted earlier) the techniques used by Glosten and Harris (1988), Hasbrouck (1991), and Foster and Viswanathan (1993) (and thus, by us) ignore discreteness on the grounds that it is prohibitively expensive to address. This may cause the fixed component to be underestimated when it is large. A second possibility is that even with the inclusion of the inverse price variable we have been unable to capture completely the structure of risk premiums.

Panel B of Table 5 repeats the same regressions as those in panel A using C_n as the variable component of illiquidity. The results are qualitatively very similar, and indeed somewhat stronger, using this measure of illiquidity. In particular, the coefficients of the linear terms of both the variable and fixed components of transacting are now significant in the quadratic specification. Further, the results using (log) firm size and the inverse of the price level mimic those reported in panel A.

The results reported in this section are consistent with our fixed and variable transaction cost variables having a significant positive effect on equilibrium rates of return, particularly when the C_n measure of variable trading costs is used.

4.3. Seasonality in the compensation for market illiquidity

Eleswarapu and Reinganum (1993) report that the association between the bid–ask spread and returns is seasonal, and is mainly confined to the month of January. In the context of the results in Table 5, it is of interest to examine two issues. First, is there a seasonal component to the compensation for our transaction cost measures? Second, does the seasonal component in the coefficient of the bid–ask spread found by Eleswarapu and Reinganum survive in the expanded Fama–French model setting?

We assess the presence of seasonal effects using a likelihood ratio test. Thus, we estimate regressions of the form of Eq. (9) by GLS, allowing for seasonal effects. First, the regression is estimated including the Fama–French factors and allowing for seasonal effects in the coefficients of all the six variables in column (5) of Table 5, i.e., the inverse price level and the five illiquidity variables (C_q, C_q^2, ψ/P, $[\psi/P]^2$, and the proportional bid–ask spread). We do this by expanding the column corresponding to a given variable in (9) to a 12-column matrix whose columns consist of the variable interacted with 12 monthly dummy variables. Let the estimated variance–covariance matrix from this unconstrained regression be denoted by $\hat{\Omega}_u$ and the vector of regression residuals by ε_u.

Consider a test of whether the coefficients of a subset consisting of $N \leq 6$ variable(s) X_i, $i = 1, \ldots, N$, have seasonal components associated with them. For this, we perform a constrained GLS regression, which includes all of the five illiquidity variables and the price level, but in which the variables $X_1, \ldots, X_N$ are constrained to have the same coefficient each month. Let ε_c denote the vector of residuals from this constrained regression. Then, under the null hypothesis of no seasonals associated with the coefficients of $X_1, \ldots, X_N$,

$$\varepsilon_c' \hat{\Omega}_u^{-1} \varepsilon_c - \varepsilon_u' \hat{\Omega}_u^{-1} \varepsilon_u$$

is asymptotically distributed χ^2 with degrees of freedom equal to the number of constraints, which, in turn, is equal to $11 \times N$.

Our first test is of the null hypothesis of no seasonal in the coefficients of the linear and quadratic measures of the fixed and variable elements of the proportional cost of trading, C_q, C_q^2, ψ/P, and $(\psi/P)^2$. As shown in the first panel of Table 6, we cannot reject the null of no seasonal in the premium associated with these transaction cost measures. Nor can we reject the null of no seasonal in the risk premium associated with the inverse price variable. Finally, unlike Eleswarapu and Reinganum, we are also unable to reject the null of no seasonal in the coefficient associated with the bid–ask spread. Thus we find no evidence of seasonality in the premium associated with transaction costs.

It is natural to ask why the seasonal in the spread premium documented by Eleswarapu and Reinganum disappears in our regressions. We are unable to provide a definitive answer because our analysis uses a different sample period. However, a second major difference between our analysis and that of

Table 6
Seasonality in the compensation for illiquidity: This table presents the results of testing for seasonality in the coefficients of the various cost of illiquidity variables, using pooled time-series cross-sectional GLS regressions for 25 portfolios of NYSE stocks sorted by size and the Glosten Harris measure of illiquidity, λ, for the period of 1984–1991

Five portfolios for which data on λ are not available are omitted from the sample. λ estimates the derivative of transaction price ($/share) with respect to signed trade size (shares, positive for trades initiated by buyers). Portfolios are formed annually from all NYSE firms active at the beginning of the year. Within each calendar year, size is measured as market value of equity at the end of the preceding year. C_q equals λ times the average trade size divided by the monthly average closing price, C_n equals λ times the monthly average number of shares outstanding divided by monthly average closing price, and ψ/P denotes the fixed component of trading costs as a proportion of the monthly average closing price. The proportional spread is calculated by averaging the proportional quoted spread (i.e., the quoted spread divided by the average of the bid and ask prices) across all quotations during the year. C_q^2 is defined as the average of the squared value of C_q for the relevant portfolio; $(\psi/P)^2$ is defined similarly. For the 1984–1987 period, λ and all other liquidity variables are estimated using 1984 data. For the 1988–1991 period, they are estimated from 1988 data. $(1/P)$ is the mean of the inverse monthly average closing price for each portfolio.

The quantity $-2\ln(LLR)$ denotes twice the natural logarithm of the likelihood ratio; $-2\ln(LLR)$ is calculated as $\varepsilon_c' \hat{\Omega}_u^{-1} \varepsilon_c - \varepsilon_u' \hat{\Omega}_u^{-1} \varepsilon_u$, where ε_c is the vector of residuals from a constrained GLS regression in which some variable(s) is(are) constrained to have the same coefficient each month, ε_u is the vector of residuals from the unconstrained regression, and $\hat{\Omega}_u$ is the estimated residual variance–covariance matrix from the unconstrained regression in which the coefficients of all the variables are allowed to differ across months. Each of the constrained and unconstrained GLS regressions contains the Fama and French factors, the five illiquidity variables, i.e., C_q, C_q^2, ψ/P, $(\psi/P)^2$, and the proportional spread, together with the inverse price level variable $1/P$.

Under the null hypothesis, $-2\ln(LLR)$ is distributed χ^2 with degrees of freedom equal to the number of constraints, which in turn, is equal to 11 times the number of variables whose coefficients are constrained to be the same each month.

Null hypothesis	No. of constraints (k)	$-2\ln(LLR)$	p-value
No seasonal in the coefficient of C_q, C_q^2, ψ/P, $(\psi/P)^2$	44	19.07	0.9996
No seasonal in the coefficient of (1/price)	11	1.77	0.9991
No seasonal in the coefficient of the proportional spread	11	9.23	0.6011

Eleswarapu and Reinganum is the use of the Fama–French risk factor model which absorbs any seasonality associated with firm size or book-to-market ratio. Further, the January coefficient of the spread is *negative* and **significant** (and indeed is the only significant coefficient among the 12) in the unconstrained GLS regression. This appears to support the notion that the spread proxies for some omitted risk factor, rather than for illiquidity, in our sample period.

5. Conclusion

In this paper, we unify recent techniques from the asset pricing and market microstructure literatures to examine the association between average risk-adjusted rates of return and both the variable and the fixed components of the cost of transacting. As the variable component is derived from models that take account of the adverse selection caused by privately informed traders, we are able to shed light on the significance of the empirical measures of adverse selection costs in determining required rates of return on equity. This exercise takes on particular significance given the voluminous work, both theoretical and empirical, on the adverse selection paradigm in recent years.

Our main findings are that there is a significant return premium associated with both the fixed and variable elements of the cost of transacting. The relation between the premium and the variable cost is concave, which is consistent with clientele effects caused by small traders concentrating in the less liquid stocks. However, the relation between the premium and the estimated fixed cost component is convex. This is inconsistent with the horizon clientele effect proposed by Amihud and Mendelson (1986), and may be the result of our inability to estimate this parameter accurately on account of price discreteness. Alternatively, it may be due to incomplete risk adjustment by the three-factor Fama–French model we use. We also find that even after risk adjustment using this model there is an additional risk premium associated with an inverse price factor. There is no evidence of seasonality in the premiums associated with our cost of transacting variables. Finally, an interesting byproduct of our analysis is the finding that controlling for firm size, there appears to be a negative relation between the variable and fixed costs of transacting. Theoretical and empirical understanding of this phenomenon appears to be a fruitful area for future research.

References

Admati, Anat and Paul Pfleiderer, 1988, A theory of intraday patterns: Volume and price variability, Review of Financial Studies 1, 3–40.

Amihud, Yakov and Haim Mendelson, 1986, Asset pricing and the bid-ask spread, Journal of Financial Economics 17, 223–249.

Bagehot, Walter, 1971, The only game in town, Financial Analysts Journal 27, 12–14.

Brennan, Michael and Avanidhar Subrahmanyam, 1995a, Investment analysis and price formation in securities markets, Journal of Financial Economics 38, 361–381.

Brennan, Michael and Avanidhar Subrahmanyam, 1995b, The determinants of average trade size, Working paper (University of California, Los Angeles, CA).

Easley, David and Maureen O'Hara, 1987, Price, trade size and information in securities markets, Journal of Financial Economics 19, 69–90.

Eleswarapu, Venkat and Marc Reinganum, 1993, The seasonal behavior of the liquidity premium in asset pricing, Journal of Financial Economics 34, 281–305.

Fama, Eugene and Kenneth French, 1993, Common risk factors in the returns on stocks and bonds, Journal of Financial Economics 33, 3–56.

Fama, Eugene and James Macbeth, 1973, Risk, return, and equilibrium: Empirical tests, Journal of Political Economy 71, 607–636.

Foster, F. Douglas and S. Viswanathan, 1993, Variations in trading volume, return volatility, and trading costs: Evidence on recent price formation models, Journal of Finance 48, 187–211.

George, Thomas, Gautam Kaul, and M. Nimalendran, 1991, Estimating the components of the bid–ask spread: A new approach, Review of Financial Studies 4, 623–656.

Gibbons, Michael, Stephen Ross, and Jay Shanken, 1989, A test of the efficiency of a given portfolio, Econometrica 57, 1121–1152.

Glosten, Lawrence, 1989, Insider trading, liquidity, and the role of the monopolist specialist, Journal of Business 62, 211–235.

Glosten, Lawrence and Lawrence Harris, 1988, Estimating the components of the bid–ask spread, Journal of Financial Economics 21, 123–142.

Hasbrouck, Joel, 1991, Measuring the information content of stock trades, Journal of Finance 46, 179–207.

Kyle, Albert, 1985, Continuous auctions and insider trading, Econometrica 53, 1315–1335.

Lee, Charles, 1993, Market fragmentation and price-execution in NYSE-listed securities, Journal of Finance 48, 1009–1038.

Lee, Charles and Mark Ready, 1991, Inferring trade direction from intradaily data, Journal of Finance 46, 733–746.

Madhavan, Ananth and Seymour Smidt, 1991, A Bayesian model of intraday specialist pricing, Journal of Financial Economics 30, 99–134.

Miller, Merton and Myron Scholes, 1982, Dividends and taxes: Some empirical evidence, Journal of Political Economy 90, 1118–1141.

Stoll, Hans, 1989, Inferring the components of the bid–ask spread: Theory and empirical tests, Journal of Finance 44, 115–134.

Name Index

Admati, A.R. 177, 277, 384, 410, 433, 493
Affleck-Graves, J. 234
Amihud, Y. 77, 95, 135, 191, 194, 198, 266, 285, 410, 449, 491, 504, 508–9, 511
Athans, M. 68, 73

Bagehot, W. 326, 465, 490
Banz, R.W. 480
Beebower, G.L. 27, 41, 43
Beja, A. 77, 198
Benston, G.J. 77, 95, 251
Beneviste, L.M. 177
Berkowitz, S. 41
Bessembinder, H. 419
Bhattacharya, M. 326
Biais, B. 390, 394, 398
Bikhchandani, S. 452
Black, F. 153, 165, 174, 192, 194, 196, 209, 328, 472
Blume, M.E. 36, 208, 265, 278, 282, 297, 485–6
Bollerslev, T. 419
Branch, B. 77, 326
Brennan, M. 491, 495
Brinson, G.L. 41
Brock, W. 235, 398

Calahan, E.A. 62
Chan, K.C. 235
Chan, L.K.C. 29, 34, 40, 41, 54
Chang, C. 345
Chordia, T. 400
Christie, W. 234–5, 259
Cohen, K.J. 77, 95, 111, 176, 194
Cooper, S.K. 265
Copeland, T. 95, 112
Cox, J.C. 458
Crawford, W.B. 318

Dann, L.Y. 326, 335
De Long, J.B. 39
DeGroot, M.H. 138
Demsetz, H. 77, 95, 218, 464
Diamond, D. 400
Domowitz, I. 419
Dubofsky, D.A. 265

Easley, D. 44, 128, 153, 433, 491
Eiteman, D. 60
Eiteman, W. 60
Eleswarapu, V. 491–2, 507, 509–11

Fama, E.F. 40, 201–2, 472, 486, 491–2, 499–501
Farrar 77
Fialkowski, D. 265, 278
Figliuoli, L. 411, 419
Finney, L. 41
Fisher, L. 485–6
Fishman, M. 386
Fogler, H.R. 467
Fong, N. 235
Foster, D. 129, 235, 427, 494, 509
Freed, W. 77, 326
French, K. 195, 203, 491–2, 499–501
Friedman, J. 254
Fudenberg, D. 254

Galai, G. 95, 112
Gale, D. 467
Gale, I. 153
Garbade, K.D. 96, 192, 198
Garman, M.B. 77, 95, 465
George, T. 493
Gibbons, M. 501–2
Goldman, B.M. 195
Goldstein, M. 234, 250–51, 265, 278, 282, 297
Golsten, L. 122–3, 128–9, 135, 150, 153, 161, 169, 171, 174–5, 183, 295, 326–7, 340, 344–5, 410–11, 427, 491, 495, 498, 500, 509
Goodhart, C. 411, 419, 424
Gottlieb, G. 194
Grossman, S. 283
Groth, J.C. 265
Grubel, H.G. 231

Hagerman, R.L. 77, 95, 251
Haitovsky, Y. 222
Hakansson, N.H. 77
Hamilton, J.L. 77
Hansen, L.P. 344
Harris, J. 259, 292, 296
Harris, L. 129, 135, 235, 240, 248, 257, 326–7, 344, 427, 491, 495, 498, 500, 509

Hasbrouck, J. 203–4, 235, 265, 294, 305, 332, 337, 389, 410, 491, 494, 509
Hausman, J. 29, 434
Hawawini, G. 111
Hedge, S. 234
Hellwig, M. 158
Heubel, B. 265
Ho, T. 77, 95, 99, 102, 107, 128, 191–2, 194, 204, 325, 336, 390, 394, 398, 410
Holthausen, R.W. 29, 40, 44, 54, 326, 336
Hood, R. 41
Hotchkiss, H. 62
Houthakker, H.S. 354
Huang, C.F. 452
Huang, R. 234, 278, 282
Hui, B. 265

Jarecki, H.G. 63, 193
Jensen, M.C. 472
Judge, G.G. 473

Kalay, A. 194
Kane, A. 467
Kaul, G. 493
Keim, D. 29, 31, 40, 54
Kladec, G.B. 273
Kleidon, A. 235, 398
Kmenta, J. 473, 477
Kolb, R.W. 387
Kraus, A. 29, 39, 40, 44, 54, 326, 335
Kyle, A.S. 44, 124, 126, 153, 158, 345, 384–5, 401, 410, 445, 455, 491, 493

Lakonishok, J. 29, 32, 34, 40–41, 44, 54, 485
Laux, P. 390, 394, 398, 400, 410
Lee, C. 31, 265, 278, 282, 288, 291, 296, 299, 305–6, 312, 318, 422, 493
Leftwich, R. 29, 40, 44, 54, 326, 336
Leigh, B. 297
Levy, H. 231
Lo, A. 29, 434
Logue, D. 41
Longstaff, F. 386
Lyons, R. 412, 420

MacBeth, J. 472, 486, 492, 501
MacKinlay, C. 29, 434
Macris, R.G. 325, 336, 390, 394, 398
Maddala, G.S. 473
Madhavan, A. 29, 31, 40, 54, 129, 385, 389, 400, 410–11, 417, 428, 493–4
Maier, S.F. 77, 95, 111, 176, 194
Malinvaud, E. 477
Manaster, S. 326, 410

Mann, S.C. 398, 410
Mann, S.V. 294
Marsh, T. 265
Marshall, A. 354
Mayer, M.K. 297
Mayers, D. 29, 40, 44, 54, 326, 335–6
McConnell, J.J. 273
McInish, T. 128, 235, 265–6, 302
Meeker, J.E. 62
Mehra, R. 69
Melsa, J. 68, 73
Mendelson, H. 77, 135, 191–4, 198–9, 201, 266, 285, 410, 449, 491, 504, 508–9, 511
Merton, R.C. 81
Mildenstein, E. 77, 95
Milgrom, P. 123, 128, 153, 175, 340, 410–11, 452
Miller, M. 283, 509
Miller, R. 234
Mucklow, B. 299
Mullins, D. 443
Murgia, M. 135

Neal, R. 250–51
Newey, W. 389–90
Newton, W. 77, 113
Nimalendran, M. 493

O'Hara, M. 44, 128, 153, 410, 433, 491
Ohlson, J. 209
Oldfield, G. 410
Ord, J.K. 302

Peake, J.W. 177
Penman, S.H. 209
Perold, A. 32, 305
Perron, P. 389–90
Petersen, M. 29, 265, 278, 305
Pfleiderer, P. 177, 277, 384, 410, 433, 493
Priest, W. 27, 43

Quandt, R.E. 77, 113

Raab, R.J. 326, 335
Ready, M. 31, 288, 291, 296, 299, 305–6, 312, 318, 422, 491, 493
Reece, D.K. 452
Reinganum, M.R. 291, 297, 480, 491–2, 507, 509–11
Rendelman, R.J. 326
Rock, K. 153, 265
Roll, R. 195, 203, 205, 208, 485
Ross, S. 501–2
Ross, S.A. 458

Ross, S.M. 465

Sage, A. 68, 73
Sarnat, M. 231
Scharfstein, D.S. 39
Schleef, H.J. 77, 95
Scholes, M.S. 17, 20, 328, 472, 509
Schultz, P. 235, 259, 484–5
Schwartz, R.A. 77, 95, 111, 176, 191–2, 194, 203, 236, 265
Schwert, G.W. 467, 481
Seijas, R.W. 294
Shanken, J. 501–2
Shleifer, A. 32, 40, 41, 44
Silber, W.L. 60, 96, 192, 198, 387
Sirri, E. 32
Smidt, S. 40, 77, 95, 129, 204, 385, 389, 410–11, 417, 428, 485, 493–4
Smith, V.L. 194
Sobel, R. 61–2
Sofianos, G. 294, 389, 410
Spiegel, M. 385
Stambaugh, R.F. 36, 208, 485
Stein, J.C. 39
Steptoe, S. 295
Stern, R. 296, 311
Stigler, G.J. 77
Stoll, H.R. 29, 39, 40, 43–4, 54, 77, 95, 99, 102, 107, 128, 135, 192, 208, 250–51, 278, 282, 326, 335, 339, 389–90, 392, 394, 398, 410, 472, 483, 485, 493
Subrahmanyam, A. 385, 400, 491, 495
Surz, R.J. 27

Telser, L.G. 358
Tinic, S.M. 77, 95, 218, 223
Tirole, J. 254
Treynor, J.K. 27

Umlauf, S. 29, 305

Verrecchia, R. 400
Vijh, A.M. 234, 326, 336
Vishny, R. 32, 40, 41, 44
Vishwanathan, S. 129, 235, 427, 494, 509

Weaver, D.G. 485–6
Weber, R.J. 452
Werner, I. 235
West, K. 389–90
West, R.R. 77, 95, 218, 223
Whaley, R.E. 135, 208, 326, 472, 483
Whitcomb, D.K. 77, 95, 111, 176, 191–2, 194
Wilhelm, W.J. 177
Wood, R. 128, 235, 265–6, 302
Working, H. 122, 354, 387